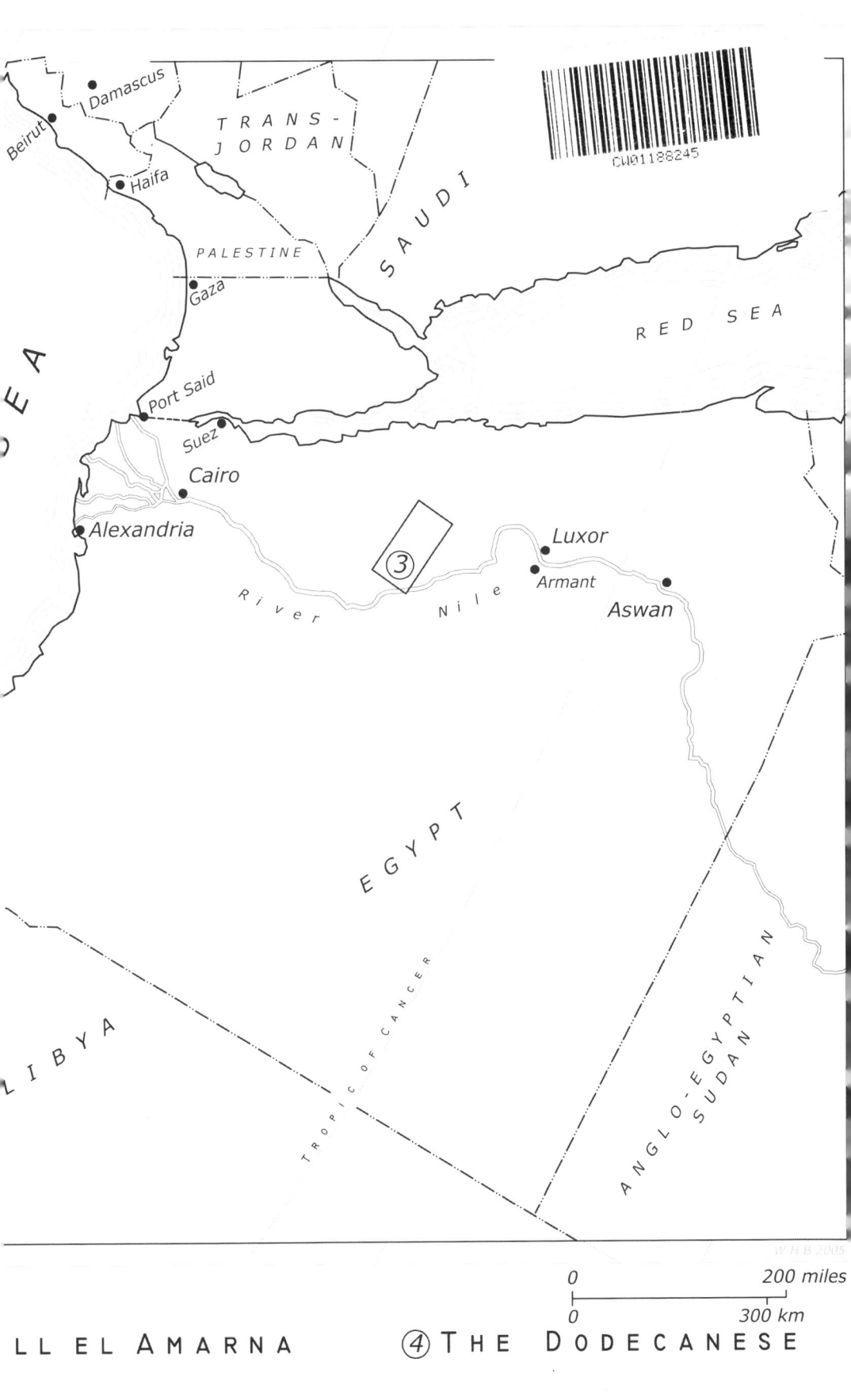

Damascus
Beirut
Haifa
TRANS-JORDAN
PALESTINE
SAUDI
Gaza
Port Said
Suez
RED SEA
Cairo
Alexandria
③
Luxor
Armant
River Nile
Aswan
EGYPT
LIBYA
TROPIC OF CANCER
ANGLO-EGYPTIAN SUDAN

W.H.B 2005

0 200 miles
0 300 km

LL EL AMARNA ④ THE DODECANESE

THE RASH ADVENTURER

A LIFE OF JOHN PENDLEBURY

THE RASH ADVENTURER

A LIFE OF JOHN PENDLEBURY

By Imogen Grundon

With a Foreword by Patrick Leigh Fermor

LIBRI

Published by Libri Publications Ltd in 2007

© Imogen Grundon, 2007
Foreword © Patrick Leigh Fermor, 2007

The right of Imogen Grundon to be identified as the author of this Work has been asserted by her in accordance with the Copyright, Designs and Patents Act 1988

To my mother and father, Jacqueline and John Grundon, without whose support this book would never have happened.

ISBN 1 901965 066

All rights reserved. No part of this publication may be reproduced, stored in a retrieval system, or transmitted, in any form or by any means, electronic, mechanical, photocopying or otherwise, without the prior written permission of the copyright owners

Cover: John Pendlebury in Amarna, wearing an ancient Egyptian necklace, c. 1929

Libri Publications Limited
Suite 296, 14 Tottenham Court Road
London, W1T 1JY

Contents

List of illustrations	vi
List of maps	viii
Acknowledgements	ix
Foreword	xi
Prologue	xv
The Rash Adventurer	1
Notes	334
Bibliography	353
Dramatis Personae	359
Chronology	364
Index	366

List of Illustrations

Between pages 104 and 105
1. John Pendlebury aged nine, 1913
2. John, aged five, with his father, Herbert
3. John and Hilda's children, David and Joan Pendlebury, at Cromer in Norfolk
4. John, the athlete, Pembroke College, Cambridge, 1923–4
5. John competing in the Oxford v. Cambridge hurdle relays, 1925 (with Cleckley of Oxford beside him)
6. Bob Dixon, Hilda White and John Pendlebury on the boat to Chalkis, Greece, 1927
7. John and Hilda Pendlebury on their wedding day, September 15th 1928
8. John and Hilda at Broughshare, Caldy, on their way off to their wedding night at Claridges in London
9. Hilda at Olympia, Greece 1928
10. One of many visits to the Imperial Airways yacht, *SS Imperia*, stationed at Spina Longa, Crete 1932. Left to right: Rosaleen Angas, unknown, Skipper Poole, Seton Lloyd, John Pendlebury and Mary Chubb
11. The 3300-year-old North Dig House, North City, Tell el-Amarna, 1931
12. The Villa Ariadne, Knossos
13. Sir Arthur Evans, c.1930
14. Mr Elliadi, the British Vice-Consul
15. Reconstructing the Throne Room, Knossos, 1930
16. John fencing on the front terrace of the Villa Ariadne, Knossos, 1931
17. John arriving at Mallawi Railway station, 1931–2 Amarna season
18. Rosaleen Angas and Hilda Pendlebury on the Great Wall in the North City at Amarna, 1931–2
19. Work at Amarna in progress, with children in the background emptying the baskets of spoil, 1931–2
20. Mary Chubb giving first aid to one of the basket girls, Tell el-Amarna 1931–2
21. The Taverna, Knossos, after renovation by Ralph Lavers
22. John on horseback at Khafaje, Iraq, 1933
23. Rachel Jacobsen, Jettie Frankfort and John at Khafaje, Iraq, 1933

Between pages 234 and 235
24. John Pendlebury on top of Aphendis with local Lasithiots looking out across the Lasithi Plain
25. John walking through a village in Crete
26. John, Stephen Sherman and Hilary Waddington outside the Royal Tomb, Tell el-Amarna 1936
27. Hilda and Mercy Money-Coutts with R.W. Hutchison, the 'Squire', with their local guide on the summit of Mt Ida, Crete 1936
28. Martin and Molly Hammond with Hilda on the summit of Aphendis, Crete 1936

29. Agiou Giorgiou Papoura – Armos site 1937
30. The Spanakis family, major Tzermiado landowners around Karphi
31. Karphi at the end of the excavations, looking south towards the dig hut and Mikre Koprana
32. Dance (or *glendi*) at the end of the Karphi excavations, July 8th 1939
33. Kronis Bardakis (the 'Old Krone'), David Bowe of Field Security and Manolis Akoumianos (Manolaki - 'the Old Wolf'), Heraklion, November 1940–March 1941.
34. Kapetan Antonis Grigorakis, known as 'Satanas', probably during the Venizelist rebellion of 1935
35. Kapetan Petrakogiorgis, one of the most steadfast of Cretan resistance leaders
36. Kapetan Manolis Bandouvas, who was brave but reckless and indiscreet
37. Unloading bombs for the RAF at the harbour, Heraklion 1940. John acted as Liaison Officer between the British forces and the Cretans
38. John at target practice with his .38 revolver, under the guidance of Lt Col Stephen Rose of 50 Middle East Commando, November 1940–March 1941
39. Bill Burton (Company commander), McFie with back to camera, Symons, Nicholl ('Nick the NOIC'), the Capt of the *Derby* (with his bull terrier) and Ken Hermon (DLI Company Command) on the mole at Heraklion harbour
40. Fusilier George Williams, bodyguard and batman to Lt Col Stephen Rose, 50 ME Cdo with an unexploded sea mine containing about 500lbs of explosive. It was rolling around dangerously on the beach at Matala. The gun cotton charge Williams is holding was to blow it up
41. 50 ME Cdo training with requisitioned landing craft in Sitia Bay before the attempted landings on the Dodecanese island of Kasos in January 1941
42. Decanting red wine from the barrel for 50 ME Cdo's Christmas dinner, Heraklion December 1940.
43. December 1940. Procession to Heraklion Cathedral for a Thanksgiving Service after the first major Greek victory against the Italians at Argyrocastro during the Albanian campaign. Here, John and Lt. Col. Stephen Rose parade past the 50 Middle East Commando standing to attention, with RW Hutchinson, 'the Squire', behind John on the left
44. *The Dolphin*, the armed caique crewed by Mike Cumberlege, Nick Hammond et al. John became an honorary member of the crew
45. German parachute regiments being dropped by Junker 52s into Crete at the start of the Battle of Crete, May 1941
46. A street in Heraklion showing the devastation of the German bombing
47. Heraklion mole and harbour after severe German bombing, looking towards the quarter where John's HQ was situated
48. Official ceremony at John's grave 1947. Hilda is just to the left of the cross

Maps and Plans

Front endpaper	The Eastern Mediterranean
Back endpaper	Crete
Page 39	Greece
Page 53	The route of Pendlebury's 1928 walk
Page 90	Tell el Amarna: the Main City
Page 93	Tell el Amarna: the North Suburb
Page 108	The route of Pendlebury's 1929 walk
Page 121	Survey of the Estate of Knossos
Page 138	Tell el Amarna: the North City
Page 166	The route of Pendlebury's 1933 walk
Page 170	Tell el Amarna: the Central and South City
Page 176	Pendlebury's sketch map of his 1934 walk
Page 190	Pendlebury's sketch map of his Spring 1935 walk
Page 192	Pendlebury's sketch map of his Late Spring 1935 walk
Page 196	Perspective sketch of Tell el Amarna, part of the Central City, by Ralph Lavers (Courtesy of the Egypt Exploration Society)
Page 202	Sketch map of the Plain of Lasithi
Page 263	The Dodecanese Islands

Illustration credits: The Ashmolean Museum, 13; David Baillieu, 4; The Bodleian Library, 26; Rose Mary Braithwaite, 1; The British School at Athens, 3, 6, 7, 8, 9, 10, 12, 15, 16, 21, 22, 23, 24, 25, 27, 28, 29, 30, 31, 32; Mary Chubb, 17, 18, 19, 20; Alan Deller, 44; Manolis Doulgerakis, 34, 35, 36, 45, 46, 47; David Pendlebury, 5, 48; Stephen Rose, 37, 38, 39, 40, 41, 42, 43; Maxwell Tasker Brown, 14, 33; Hilary Waddington 11; Dorothea Ward Clarke, 2.

Acknowledgements

There are many people whom I would like to thank for their help over the years it has taken to produce this book, in the very different areas of research that were involved. I apologise if I have left anybody out. There is also a deep sense of regret that many on the list that follows died before this book reached publication.

Principally, I would like to thank my parents, John and Jacqueline Grundon, for their endless support, patience and enthusiasm, and my father for his invaluable help researching and translating in the German archives. I would also like to thank my two sisters Tessa Grundon and Pippa Duncan. All of them suffered with me and this book feels to me like a family achievement.

I am greatly indebted to the Committee and staff of the British School at Athens since 1986 for giving me permission to use their Pendlebury archive, and to my fellow students at the School who made periods of research there such a pleasure. I would also like to thank the Committee and Staff of the Egypt Exploration Society since 1986, who bent over backwards to help me wade through the then uncatalogued archive. I would like to thank the members and staff of the Special Forces Club for their considerable support and enthusiasm, and the Ashmolean Museum for its help towards one of the research trips to the German archives.

On John Pendlebury's family background, I would like to thank Rose Mary Braithwaite for her anecdotes and friendly pressure to finish this book about her childhood friend; David Pendlebury, for a wonderful correspondence and much help; Penelope Uden, mother of four of John's grandchildren, for her insight into Hilda ; Olga Pendlebury, mother of John's two other grandchildren; Dorothea (née Devitt) and Jenny Ward-Clarke, for sharing their knowledge of the Devitt and Pendlebury families; John Devitt, to whom I can only apologise.

For their help on Winchester, I particularly thank Gerry Dicker, with whom I had many happy conversations about Winchester; Roger Custance for looking in the Winchester College archives; Christopher Hawkes, Estelle Morgan, Lord Sherfield.

For their help on the Cambridge years, I am deeply grateful to the following: Anthony Abrahams, Patrick D. .Ainslie, David Baillieu (then London chapter), David Baillieu (Sydney chapter), H. Roland Bourne, Sir Patrick Browne, Niels Ronald Bugge, Sir Thomas G. Devitt, Piers Dixon, Sandy Duncan, H. Lionel Elvin, C. Gilbraith, Elizabeth Rowe Harding, His Honour Rowe Harding, W.S. Hutton, Pamela Judd, Lady Victoria Leatham (née Cecil, daughter of Lord Burghley), Lord Luke, Alan Malcolm, Sir Arthur Marshall, Jane O'Rorke (née Harding, daughter of Rowe Harding), Lord (Arthur) Porritt, John Pumphrey, Jayne Ringrose, J.R.P. Soper, Dr Christopher Thorne, Sir Roger Tomkys, Paul Willcox, Rex Woods (Mk 2).

On the research on and in Greece and Crete, I would especially like to thank the following: Micky Akoumianakis, Antony Beevor, Gerald Cadogan, Douglas Dodds-Parker, Nicholas Hammond, Sir Patrick Leigh Fermor, Charles Messenger, Dilys Powell, Sir Brooks Richards, Stephen Rose, Guy Sanders, Mercy Seiradaki (née Money-Coutts), Sophia Seiradaki, Ralph Stockbridge, Maxwell Tasker-Brown. Also:

Dr Peter Burr, Tom Burr, Jill Carrington-Smith, Evangelos Christou, May Clarke, Edith Clay, Richard Clogg, Reg Close, Nicholas Coldstream, Artemis Cooper, Gervase Cowell, Geoffrey Cox, Alan Deller, Doreen Dunbabin, Hagen Fleischer, M.R.D. Foot, Elizabeth French, Charalambos Giannadakis, Kostas Giannadakis, Ronald Gurrey, Robin Hammond, Vaughan Harries, Colin Haycraft, John May, A.H.S. (Peter) Megaw, Robert D. Mitchell, M. Timothy Myres, Darren Nolan, Kostas Phanourakis, Manolis Platys, Martin Robertson, Marion Sarafis (née Pascoe), Theocharis Saridakis, Patrick Savage, Gerhard Schirmer, Shan and Roxanni Sedgwick, Jack Smith-Hughes, Sir Michael Stewart, Frank Stubbings, Hans Teske, Peter Thwaites, Constantinos Tzinis, Sir Edward Warner, Lady Helen Waterhouse (née Thomas), Tony Weir, Sarah Westcott, Peter Wilkinson, Christopher (Monty) Woodhouse, Tim Mitford.

For her help on Tell el-Amarna and Egypt I would like to thank especially Mary Chubb, with whom I spent many happy hours discussing Amarna and many other subjects. Also, for their help with Egypt and Amarna: Barry Kemp, who gave me the chance to work at Amarna; Kate Spence, who kindly vetted the text from the Egyptological point of view; Pat Spencer, who guided me through the EES archive; Hilary Waddington, for his mischievous sense of humour, and his wife, Olive, for her help in tracking down her husband's Amarna documents after his death. For their support or help in filling in the gaps, I also thank John Cook, Martin Davies, Margaret (Peggy) Hackforth-Jones (nee Drower), Vronwy Hankey (née Fisher), T.G.H. James, Rosalind Janssen, Seton Lloyd, Geoffrey Martin, Jacke Phillips, Günter Rudnitzky, Julia Samson (née Lazarus), Peter Shore.

For their help in the German archives, I would like to thank Dr Detlef Vogel, for his help at the Bundesarchiv-Militärarchiv and his hospitality in Freiburg; Theodor Gehling, for his help at the Archiv des Auswärtigen Amts in Bonn, and for his infectious enthusiasm for his beloved archive, some extraordinary items from which he proudly shared with me and my father.

On a more general note, I would like to thank Bill Blake for the maps and plans; Neil Brodie, Moraig Brown, Andy Goodwin, John Moore for their support in good and bad times; Anna Lethbridge, my publisher, for her often tried patience; Rachel Calder, my agent; Jeremy Lewis, for his helpful suggestions on the manuscript; Jonathon and Rosemary Musgrave, for giving me support and ideas right at the start of the research in 1986; Anne Sacket, for her invaluable work cataloguing the Pendlebury letters of the British School; Mervyn Popham, for arranging a grant from the British School and the Ashmolean to go to Germany to search for Pendlebury's missing Cretan dig diaries; Terry Message and Douglas Dodds-Parker of the Special Forces Club for their help and support; Laura Preston and Professor Peter Warren, for compiling the chronology; Dora Kemp and Jenny Doole, for compiling the index; Kristina Rassidaki, for so often giving me a place to stay when in Athens; Peter Warren, the first to know that I planned this book; Liz Waywell, for being the longest-standing supporter of this book; and Penny Wilson-Zarganis, for endless help in the British School archives and library.

Foreword

In Crete, in late May 1941, I was among the British troops lining up on the waterfront of Heraklion, waiting to be evacuated by the Royal Navy to Egypt, leaving behind us Greek allies and friends who had been fighting beside us against the German invaders. It had been a fierce battle lasting eight days and the battered city we were leaving reeked of smoke and death. Our military fortunes were at a low ebb. The Cretan Division had been left behind on the mainland, retreating from Albania, where they had fought with great spirit. The half-armed civilian response to the German attack on Crete was one of the inspiring aspects of this grim stretch of the war.

As junior Intelligence dogsbody and interpreter to Brigadier Chappel, it fell to me to translate when an elderly Cretan mountaineer, obviously a leader, approached the Brigadier. The Brigadier was a tall man, tanned by a lifetime's soldiering in India, and an excellent commander. The Cretan was a short and resolute figure, a distinguished kapetan, with a clear and cheerful glance, a white beard clipped under the chin and the butt of his ancient rifle was embossed with wrought-silver plaques. He lifted his hand to the Brigadier's shoulder and said, "My child" – 'paidi mou' in Greek – "we know you are leaving tonight; but you will soon be back. We will carry on the fight till you return. But we have very few guns. Leave us all you can spare". The Brigadier was deeply moved. Orders were given and a Black Watch lieutenant led away the kapetan and his retinue. As we made our farewells, he said, in a kind but serious voice, "May God go with you, come back soon."

This man was Antonis Grigorakis – nicknamed 'Satanas' after his youthful recklessness. He had fought in both Balkan wars, the Great War and the Asia Minor Campaign against the Bulgarians and the Turks. He was one of the mountain leaders John Pendlebury thought of most highly for the coming fight against the Germans, and he was with him when the German parachute landings began. Satanas and his followers did in fact face the German onslaught with great resolution.

I had met John Pendlebury just over a week before, a long week of bitter fighting across northern Crete. He had come to see the Brigadier to find out where he and his men could be of most use. I was enormously impressed by that splendid figure, with a slung rifle, instead of an ordinary officers' service revolver, and the swordstick he carried. Our Brigade HQ, between Heraklion and the aerodrome, was a deep cave supported by a pillar in the middle; I remember him stooping to come down the stairs that led into it. He had a Cretan guerilla fighter with him, festooned with bandoliers, and

John Pendlebury himself made a wonderfully buccaneer and rakish impression, perhaps partly due to his glass eye. Anyway, our dismal cave was suddenly full of noise and laughter... He was famous for his knowledge of Crete and the Cretans, for his incredible stamina on the steepest mountains and his capacity for drinking strong Cretan wine without turning a hair and then striding across another mountain range. He was an astonishing mixture of scholar and man of action. His presence filled everyone with life and optimism and a feeling of fun, and this spirit seemed to hang in the air long after his death.

In the days following the British evacuation, the German SS got to know of Pendlebury. They called him 'der kretische Lawrence' – the Cretan Lawrence – and rumours spread amongst Pendlebury's hillmen that Hitler could not rest until he had Pendlebury's glass eye on his desk in Berlin.

When a handful of SOE officers, including me, were landed, one by one, by submarine or caique into enemy-occupied Crete, it took a while to pick up the pieces of Pendlebury's network. But the main regional kapetans presented themselves to the British officers, helping us from the start because we could say we were friends of Pendlebury. We could not have recovered the organisation so quickly without the respect and goodwill that the Cretans felt towards Pendlebury.

John Pendlebury had spent twelve years in Crete. In this time he had become a mythical figure on the island, famous for his energy and enthusiasm, his dedication and his toughness. There was no part of the often harsh Cretan landscape that he would not or could not tackle; he covered over 1000 miles of the island's wild and steep terrain in a single archaeological season, discovering unknown ancient sites all the way. He built up friendships throughout the island, becoming known and trusted by those who worked with him as well as by the shepherds and mountain villagers whose home was in the wild peaks he knew and loved. He knew their dialects and all their names and his strength and humour were a real bond with these indestructible men.

As soon as war threatened, Pendlebury volunteered his services, typically seeking out the challenge. His intimate knowledge of the island's topography and its people put him in a unique position to help organise resistance should the island ever be taken. He understood the passion for freedom that had shaped the whole of Cretan history.

It will be clear to the reader of this biography how strongly even those who met its protagonist as briefly as I did were struck by the encounter. Many people who knew John Pendlebury have felt drawn to write about him, but their accounts only deal with certain aspects of his life. I can't think of anyone better equipped, with her knowledge of Crete and Greece and her archaeological experience, than Imogen Grundon, and her book is the first to try to answer the question posed about John Pendlebury by the German SS: 'Wer war dieser Engländer?' – 'Who was this Englishman?'

Patrick Leigh Fermor

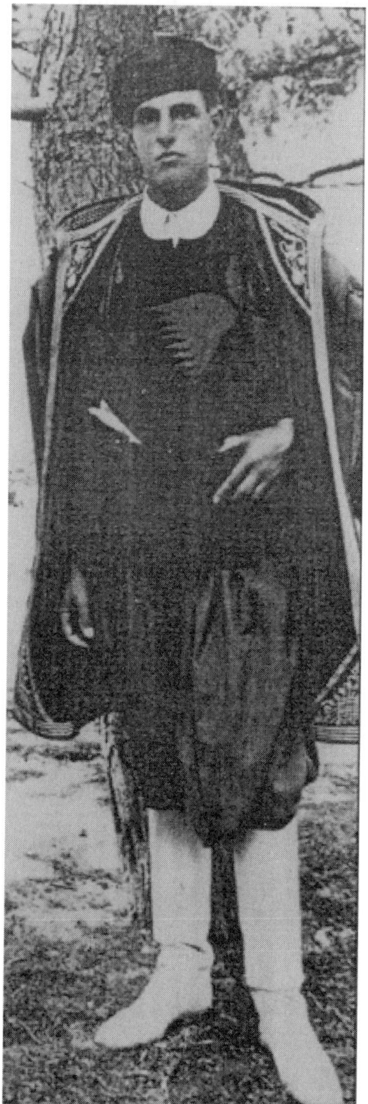

Prologue

ON JUNE 4th 1941, Baron Eberhard von Künsberg, an officer of the SS, walked into the British Vice-Consulate in Heraklion, Crete. Von Künsberg headed a Sonderkommando, or special unit, of the Auswärtiges Amt, the German Foreign Office. The unit had arrived in Crete a few days after the German invasion of the island to search the enemy consulates and embassies. On the wall of the office he saw the usual pictures of King George VI and Queen Elizabeth; but there was another photograph between them.

'It shows a man of about thirty-five, with unmistakably English features, in Cretan national dress: high boots, wide breeches like a skirt, a close-fitting black waistcoat, heavily embroidered cape and a black cap. This picture gave us our first acquaintance with Mr John Pendlebury. Who was this Englishman?'

1

1904–1923

ONE AFTERNOON IN 1915, a cold wind was sweeping across the leaden grey of the English Channel as a small group of schoolboys played on the Kent shore, chasing each other between soldiers' trenches. Their school, St George's, Broadstairs, was nearby, facing out to sea – a window onto the war on and across the Channel. Although the children were woken by air raid alarms almost every night, they were full of the excitement of near danger.

Until the spring of 1915, the closest that civilians in Britain had come to the Great War was the distant boom of guns pounding the trenches. The drone of the Zeppelins and the bombs they dropped had come as a shock, accompanied by a weird sort of fascination. Within a few months they were joined by the aeroplanes, Taubes leading the way. The war had taken to the sky. The east coast, being closest to the Front, was the worst and soonest affected. The enemy planes were given an increasingly rigorous reception by the newly-formed Royal Flying Corps and, when abandoning their missions, the Zeppelin crews often jettisoned their bomb loads on Kent before flying home.

London also suffered from occasional raids. Nonetheless, it was an unusual decision on the part of Herbert and Lily Pendlebury of 44 Brook Street, Mayfair, to send their only son away in September 1915 to the small school on the North Foreland, directly under the flight path from the Continent. For John Pendlebury, just about to turn eleven, their choice was pure heaven.

John was a fair child, though his hair would turn darker brown as he grew older. His high brow was framed by lightly waved hair that swept sharply across to the right. A lively, active child with a passion for practical jokes and silly pranks, he had unexpectedly acquired the source of many of these as a young boy. When he was about two years old, Lily and Herbert went away for a couple of days, leaving John with friends. Some said that he picked up a pen and accidentally stabbed his left eye with it, others that he walked into a thorn bush. By the time Lily and Herbert returned, John's eye was beyond saving; from that time on he always wore a glass one. It became so natural to him that it often passed unnoticed. As a consequence of his left eye not being used, his right eyebrow lifted, giving him a slightly amused and rather engaging look.

John devoured adventure stories from the pages of the children's magazine

Chums, and he read and re-read the novels of Rider Haggard with relish. These alone were enough to fire his imagination, but he now found himself closer to real action than most children in Britain could ever hope to be. He and his school friends were in their element.

With telescopes and torches, aeroplanes and tanks made from whatever came to hand, the boys equipped themselves to watch every manoeuvre that took place off the coast and in the air, and re-enacted them in the wars they waged between dormitories. They drew silhouettes of the ships that passed the Foreland, learning to distinguish surfacing submarines from destroyers and monitors, and spotting the Orient boats that passed on more peaceful journeys. Like all British schoolboys, they were fed on the glories of fighting for King, Country and Empire. Even lantern slide lectures showing the devastation of Louvain and Termonde could not convey the fierce reality of war in the trenches.

John's father, Herbert Pendlebury, knew it only too well. As an officer in the Royal Army Medical Corps of the Territorial Army since 1908, with the outbreak of war he was transferred to the 4th London General Hospital. He was a Lancashire man, a Wiganer, and proud of it. John's grandfather, John Pendlebury senior, had made his fortune running a silk mercers and general drapers store in Wigan. The son of a farmer in Standish, north of the town, he had risen from apprentice to owner of the store that eventually bore his name. He married his cousin and together they had four children, of whom Herbert, born in 1870, was the eldest.

John's grandfather was a typical Victorian northern philanthropist. He used his money and position to improve the education of the poor in Wigan, where he co-founded the voluntary schools and the two St George's schools. But he had little of the severity that often accompanied such devout reformers. When he died in 1898, the streets were lined with people as his cortège passed through the town.

He passed on to his eldest son his love of learning. Educated at Grimsargh College near Preston, then at Pembroke College, Cambridge, where he took a first in the Natural Sciences Tripos, Herbert had interests far beyond his chosen profession. By the time of his father's death he had become house surgeon and house physician at St George's Hospital, Hyde Park Corner. He practised as a surgeon and taught surgery and anatomy at St George's Medical School.[1]

John's mother Lilian, or Lily, was the daughter of Sir Thomas Lane Devitt, Bt., Chairman of Lloyd's Register of Shipping and President of the Chamber of Shipping of the United Kingdom. Lily, one of seven children, was an attractive woman, kind, gentle and humorous, but not very strong. She married Herbert in 1903, when they were both thirty-two, and John was born almost a year later on October 12th 1904. He was their only child, though it was said that others were born prematurely and did not survive.[2]

Herbert had established a private practice alongside his work at St George's. This he ran, along with another doctor and a dentist, from the ground floor of his elegant new house in Brook Street. This large house, with stables in Davies Mews, was where John grew up, spending holidays with cousins, often accompanied by his nanny, Mrs Comber. Until he was ten, John went to a small school nearby – Mr Egerton's in Somerset Place, off Portman Square.

When he moved to the school in Broadstairs, he grew if anything closer to his parents. He wrote mostly to Lily and there was little formality between them. His letters – smudged and messy, with large rounded writing and atrocious spelling – show an appealing openness, and are bursting with affection. In his passion for the war, John enrolled in an organisation called the 'Navy League', which aimed to thwart the decline of investment in the Navy; Lily nicknamed him her 'Imperial Kitten'. Before long, he wrote that her Imperial Kitten had turned into a cat and had learnt to scratch. Herbert, though a warm and humorous man, had inherited his own father's insistence on discipline and punctuality. John was more relaxed than his father; he always maintained that without Herbert's influence he would have been rather lazy, but he applied himself with humour and lightheartedness. His manner towards both parents was cheerfully irreverent; his letters to Lily begin with 'Wotcher Mum!', and he asks her 'to give Daddy a thick ear for me'. It was always to Herbert that he wrote about work, and he would start with, 'Nah ven 'Erb', and close with 'Yours till death, from your very most affectionate son with a lot of filial love etc. John'.

John described everything he got up to at school, and, though brief, his letters conjure up the busy life on the Foreland. 'We are having a pretence war so please send me 3 pistols. 2 cardboard tomahawks. 2 knives. 2 shields. Don't buy anything and make me two Indian hats. Send everything as quick as you can as we want to raid the other dormitory. Please excuse the writing and spelling as I am afraid some of the other side may crib or chis it. PS Please make the shield plain. I am sending it in an envelope in case it frightens some alert postman!'[3] There is a breathless urgency and spontaneity about his requests for supplies: 'Please send me a bad egg to throw at Mr Martin's white waistcoat'.[4] Although these requests may make John appear a demanding boy, he was involving Lily in his life away from home in a way that few children did in those days.

The next year, 1916, brought no sign of an end to the war. Every week ships went down, a hospital ship and a P&O liner joining the toll of destroyers, monitors and submarines, with many lives lost. But the news was not always bad. 'Have you heard about the German smack with twenty Germans on board being captured just off here and taken into Ramsgate harbour? It has escaped from Spain where it had been interned and had just passed the Straits of Dover safely but was caught here.' When one of the boys was sent a telescope, the others borrowed it in turns. 'The other day an aeroplane came down on the sea and a lot of patrol-boats, which had been at anchor just off the Foreland, steamed up to it, but it was apparently quite all right and soon sailed away but it could not rise and had to go along the water.'[5]

As labour was short, the boys were sometimes called on to help on the land instead of doing normal school sports, and in the autumn they picked hops or dug trenches in the sands when the weather was too bad for football. As a treat they were taken to see a secret dug-out by the lighthouse where valuable papers were kept. 'It's not half as good as ours', John wrote to Lily, innocently adding a plan of it for her.[6]

Herbert and Lily came to visit far more frequently than other parents, and would take John to tea or to see the aeroplanes at Westgate. But even though they always brought things that John could share, John had to ask them not to come down so often: 'Some of the boys will be jealous.'[7]

Towards the end of November 1916, south-east England experienced its first attack from the sea when six German destroyers opened fire on the north end of the Downs. Little damage was done, but John was fascinated. 'On Thursday night there was a small naval engagement opposite our window and the bangs and flashes were beautiful. It was 20 to 11. Have you heard of the Bremen being captured? Did you see that destroyer with a searchlight as you were going to the station?'[8]

With episodes like these to relay, it is hardly surprising that John scarcely mentioned schoolwork to his mother. But the elegantly written reports of his headmaster, Mr Ashley Bickersteth, show that John was often top of the class in every subject by a wide margin. He started to learn ancient Greek, as well as Latin, and to work in earnest for a scholarship to Winchester College.

At the end of January 1917, Germany declared that she would no longer recognise any 'non-combatant' vessel within the war zone. This included all neutral shipping, which contradicted an undertaking that Germany had given to the United States. This hastened the deterioration of relations between the two countries, which ended in the Americans joining the war against Germany. Britain was now effectively cut off from her allies and countries friendly to her; the most immediate result was a food shortage.

At the beginning of March 1917, more German destroyers turned their guns towards the shore, this time on Broadstairs and Margate, and bombarded the towns for a full ten minutes. John's school was moved further inland, but Lily and Herbert decided that it was time to take their son away. He was devastated at having to leave and sobbed bitterly. By May Herbert and Lily had managed to get John into Beaudesert Park, a small school in Henley-in-Arden, Warwickshire.

The small medieval market town with its castle mound was a quiet place with several similar schools, and a lot more to eat. The food shortage had reached crisis point, so meals became something to write home about, although John's request for a rifle must have raised a few eyebrows. 'Altogether we have shot nine rooks which leaves about fifty more to be shot before we can have a pie. I hit one but only knocked a few feathers off.'[9] When he wrote, 'Goodman and I are making "fly-pie" from the flies we shoot with our garters in the dormitory. This place makes you very hungry', Lily must have wondered whether the school was feeding him at all.[10]

As the war receded for John, his play began to reflect new interests. He was thrown into searching for blackbird eggs and butterflies instead of battleships and Zeppelins. He and his friends made temples, sacred pools and groves in the school garden, and collected stamps of Egyptian kings and queens as well as cigarette cards ('I wonder if you could ask Daddy to try and get some cigarette cards from the men at the hospitals?').[11] Now thirteen, John was having a wonderful time: 'We had chariot races in the playroom on roller skates. Muir was my horse and we nearly killed some of the others by the pace we bowled along at, round and round, up and down until we were all so puffed we could not go any further. All the time we were shooting at each other with catapults and bits of elastic and slings.'[12]

In March 1918, he sat for his Winchester entrance exams and was accepted, 'rather above the average place for a Commoner'. Pupils were divided into Commoners and Scholars, the latter being those of exceptional ability. John was delighted. Scholars and Commoners led very different lives, the former living in College and dining off wooden platters in a medieval hall, the Commoners lodging in houses on the edge of the town. John was to enter Culver House, the housemaster of which was Mr F. P. David.

Herbert wrote to Mr David to ask if Lily might meet the house matron, as she was worried about the boys' reaction to John's glass eye. Mr David replied that of course she could, but his wife had most of the responsibility for the boys. 'The matron – by the way – is a perfect jewel, a very old family retainer, though still in the prime of life, and a good deal younger than that sometimes implies.'[13] Mrs David's description of her is rather more revealing of the attitudes of the time: 'She is a particularly nice, capable woman – not a lady and not hospital trained, but very full of common sense and kindness'.[14]

Winchester College, set on the edge of the quiet cathedral town, is one of the oldest of the great public schools. It was founded in 1382 by William of Wykeham, and many of the original buildings are still in use. When John arrived for the winter term of 1918, he found that not only were most of the buildings medieval, but so too was the language of the masters and pupils, who used words and expressions long since obsolete elsewhere.[15] They played crocket instead of cricket, taking wockets rather than wickets. Wykehamical Notions, as the language was called, also included abbreviations, so that exercise became 'ekker', athletics 'athla', and examination 'examina'. So, not only was the standard of work expected considerably higher than John was used to, but also, in the first term, much time was spent learning Notions, on which they were regularly tested.

Arriving in 1918 as a new 'man', John was assigned a 'tégé', to show him the ropes. He wrote to his parents that there had been no 'brocking' ('badgering') about his glass eye, but it took some time for him to be as extrovert as he had been. He came across to Mr David as 'quiet and undemonstrative – all to the good, that; and I have only succeeded in raising one smile out of him so far; but the Matron says he is very jolly with her.'[16]

John kept up his growing interest in wildlife by nursing a baby snipe with a broken leg which he had found in his first week. The college had a Natural History Society, which had talks on an odd variety of subjects from bees and butterflies to matrimony among the lower orders. On free afternoons, John and his friends would take off on bicycles to look for plants or butterflies; Lily was still the source of all equipment. 'The butterfly box is beautiful, I spent one and a half hours chasing a small tortoiseshell and it got away.' She probably wished that her involvement stopped there: 'About that moth, keep him in the sun until his wings are out, then suffocate him with ammonia or squeeze his neck. Then just put a pin through his body not wings and put him in a tin box with a layer of wet blotting paper under him and bring him with you, and so for all the others.'[17]

The war was dragging through its last months, but there were more reminders of it at Winchester than at Beaudesert Park. Many of the boys were members of the Officer Training Corps (OTC), some of the older ones going on to fight for real ('Daddy must come in uniform so as the OTC men can salute him'), and there were Canadian and American soldiers stationed in tents on the College land.

At first John's academic progress was slow – for the first time he faced real competition – and, although the masters felt that he had 'ability and taste' and would soon make his mark, there had been a particularly good field that year. John became a little cagey about his work, which was very average, and did not yet feel comfortable with his housemaster. 'He is curiously brusque and almost unfriendly in his manner', Mr David wrote to Herbert. 'I am not worrying much about that, but it makes me think that he is very likely rather slapdash and superficial in his methods of work.'[18] By the end of the first term, however, things were much better. 'He seems to have come quite into the first flight in the second half of term, and I gather that his work is much more consistent and effective.'[19] John's confidence grew with the improvement in his work, and he became again the friendly and responsive child he had been before.

The College had a close relationship with the Cathedral, and the boys were regularly invited to tea with one or other of the canons – an arduous duty for which they were required to wear top hats and make conversation. John went through this several times a term and was delighted when, on one occasion, 'There was a tremendous thunderstorm and as I was watching a thunderbolt hit a shed and smashed it, and in the middle of tea water suddenly poured down on us from the ceiling and we had to get pails and buckets and flower pots to stop it. My top hat was totally drenched.'[20]

In the summer holidays of 1919, many of the older boys went off to agricultural camps on Dartmoor or Anglesea, as part of the drive to stave off the food shortage. The late start to the summer holidays and late return to school meant that many pupils were free to answer the government's appeal for 'thousands of boys for the potato-harvest in Lincolnshire'. John, however, spent the holidays with cousins in north Devon. His Uncle Herbert had just bought a wagonette, which was a huge success with the children. They drove to Lynton and Lynmouth and, on his cousin Grace's birthday, took a picnic to the Valley of the Rocks. John swam in the sea, somersaulting in the huge waves, and delighting in tormenting his nanny, Mrs Comber, who was convinced that his glass eye would wash away; John took it out under water and returned to the surface, pretending that it had been lost.

John worked hard at the subjects he enjoyed – Greek, Latin and History – and a keen interest in other ancient civilizations, especially that of Egypt, began to appear in his essays. His initial fascination with the land of the pharaohs became a passion for Egyptology, encouraged by Herbert who, since he had been invalided out of the war in early 1918, had time to share more fully in John's interests. John wrote illustrated stories about the pharaohs, sometimes in the style of ancient fragmentary papyri, and would sign his letters in mock hieroglyphs and Assyrian cuneiform, as well as in Latin, Greek and French.

Where he was not so keen, he bothered less. Christopher Hawkes, a contemporary of John's at Winchester, who went on to become a well-known archaeologist, remembered the boys being asked to learn a poem each week to recite to the class. He recalled that John had a slight stammer at the time and that he hammed it up dreadfully when announcing that he had chosen 'The Rime of the Ancient Mariner'. He recited the first three stanzas with extreme difficulty and slowness, until finally stopped by the teacher and told to sit down. Hawkes was convinced that it was a deliberate ploy to avoid having to learn the entire poem.[21]

The last evening of the autumn term was always celebrated with 'Illumina'. The boys would set candles in tiny niches in the medieval walls of the College grounds until the whole place was lit up by hundreds of flickering flames. Ancient traditions such as this, and John's passion for romantic adventure, would inspire a lifelong love of heraldry, chivalry and all things medieval.[22]

Lily often came down to Winchester and took John to a café called the 'God-Begot' from its origins as a medieval sanctuary, but her visits became fewer as her health declined. John was always bitterly disappointed when his mother had to cancel a visit, even if Herbert managed to come alone. He still wrote weekly, and would tell her of his growing interest in athletics. For a competition in which they had to enter at least three events, John had chosen the long and high jumps and the hurdles, more or less at random. Even with snow thick on the ground he did very well in the last two, and his house won the Taylor Cup.

He was inspired by this early success to work harder at the high jump ('I have a beautiful picture of myself jumping 5ft'), so that he could win the junior contest and qualify to enter the senior. The sepia photograph is faded and tattered and shows John in mid-air as he clears the bar – the cat's gallows as they called it – a wonderful shot.

John had entirely 'found himself', Mr David wrote to Herbert, in his work, in his athletics and in his interests. He praised John's excellent competitive spirit and staying power, 'among many other good qualities'.[23] His diligence and competitiveness carried him easily through the school until he was a year and three months younger than the average boy in his division.

When Lily was well enough to get out and about again she came down to Winchester to spend some time with John. 'My dear Pendlebury', Mr David wrote, 'I am very glad Mrs Pendlebury's visit has been fixed up all right. John will be able to see a good deal of her, really, without missing any of his daily round. Leave out to meals, perhaps, had better be limited to Sundays, in accordance with the usual practice here; but of course he can often look in on weekdays, and there is no reason why he shouldn't spend a half rem [half day off] there, if he happens to be unemployed... Meanwhile I am very well satisfied with all I see and hear of John... He is also enjoying life very much, to judge from his face and spirits.'[24]

When John was fifteen, undeterred by his glass eye, he joined the College Rifle Corps, founded so that young men would never be as unready as the Great War had found them. 'My uniform came on Wednesday eventually, it is quite nice but the collar of the tunic is rather, well greasy from the neck of the man who had it before me!'[25]

In 1920 John sat the exams for his School Certificate and passed the standard required by the Little-go, the entrance examination for Cambridge, intending to follow his father to Pembroke College. As Mr David observed, John was pursuing his own way with remarkable independence and concentration. 'Opinion seems divided whether he really has "scholarship" in the Cambridge sense of the word; but there can be no question that his mind is very quick and sure, and that he will some day go far – though on what particular line it is too soon to say.'[26]

John's grasp of history, particularly ancient history, was much firmer than his knowledge of ancient languages; yet he found that in the classical Greek plays the two dovetailed. At the time, Late Bronze Age discoveries were being made at Mycenae in the Greek Argolid, the legendary capital of Agamemnon, leader of the Greeks in the Trojan War. John was fascinated by their set Greek text, Sophocles' *Electra*, which was set in Mycenae some time after Agamemnon was killed by his wife, Clytaemnestra, on his return from the Trojan War. In March 1921 one of John's teachers, Mr Robinson, known as the Bince, put on a production of Aeschylus' *Agamemnon*, the story of his murder, and John described it to Herbert in detail. 'The Bince had painted the scenery, a Mycenaean Gateway with steps leading up, and on either side curtains with great shields on them. It was all very correct except the Bince said he hadn't the courage to put the pillars upside down.'[27] John's descriptions of the scenery and costumes show his grasp of the styles which were being revealed at Mycenae, as well as by Sir Arthur Evans at Knossos in Crete.

However, it was Egypt that was John's overriding passion. In 1922 he joined the Egypt Exploration Society (EES) to follow the results of their fieldwork and meet those working in the field. In November that year, Howard Carter discovered the tomb of Tutankhamen. The exquisite beauty, craftsmanship and charm of the objects left in the tomb of the young king inspired many, like John, to a life in Egyptology, and ancient Egyptian motifs found new life in the art and architecture of the time. John, however, could already distinguish between Egyptology and archaeology. Egyptologists concentrated on tombs, temples and other grand architecture that would provide them with inscriptions. Archaeologists such as Flinders Petrie, on the other hand, excavated sites scientifically in order to establish a physical sequence for dating artefacts which would act as a check on the information provided by the inscriptions. John had already decided that he wanted to be a field archaeologist working in Egypt rather than a conventional Egyptologist. Cambridge at that time, however, had no department of Egyptology; so John was advised to sit for the Classical Tripos – seen as a sound basis for any career.

Just as John had secured a place at Cambridge and was finding the path he wanted to follow, tragedy struck the Pendlebury family. Lily was staying at Folkestone when, on September 8th 1921, she died of heart failure. She was only fifty, and John nearly seventeen. There is no further mention of Lily in any of John's surviving correspondence with his father, but there is no doubt that her loss hit John and Herbert very hard. John returned to Winchester, as a prefect now, and threw himself into his work. His housemaster, Mr David, wrote of him, two months after Lily's death, 'I believe he has begun to look at things in a new way, and will make sensible use of his position and responsibilities'.[28]

A year and a half later, during the Easter holiday of 1923, when John was reaching the end of his final year at Winchester, Herbert arranged for him to spend a month in Greece. Accompanying him would be James Cullen, a young Classics master with a keen interest in Aegean archaeology. John, now eighteen, and certain that he wanted to become an archaeologist, longed to see the places he had learnt so much about and to meet some of the archaeologists who had excavated them.

At the beginning of April 1923, John sailed with James Cullen from Dover to Calais, and then travelled through Paris, Lausanne, Milan, past the lakes of Northern Italy to Venice. From there the train took them into Yugoslavia, only recently forged from the ruins of an annihilated Serbia and other smaller Slav regions. Passing through Belgrade, they stopped at Skopje. 'It is a purely Serbian town', he wrote, 'entirely populated, built and governed by Turks, Bulgarians and Spanish Jews. It is very picturesque and very Eastern with camels and things all over the place and beautiful costumes, for in S.Serbia the costumes seem to improve immensely and are really splendid.' They crossed into Greece from the north, through Macedonia, which Greece had won from Turkey in the Balkan Wars and fought hard to keep from the Bulgarians in the Great War. Passing Mount Olympos, the train took them down through the idyllic Vale of Tempe, of which John wrote to his father, 'If I'd been the Greeks in the Persian War, I'd have hung on like hell!'[29]

They reached Athens in the middle of the night. There was only one cab and they haggled for ages before persuading the driver to take them to the Hotel Majestic on Panepistimiou Street, near the University. Next morning, after a night in the dining room after confusion over their rooms, they turned up rather bleary-eyed at the British School of Archaeology at Athens.

Arthur Woodward, the recently-appointed Director, was away in the Peloponnese, but much to John's delight they met Alan Wace, his predecessor, who had been running the excavations at Mycenae. Wace recognized not only John's enthusiasm for Bronze Age archaeology, but also his astonishing grasp of the subject. Wace later recalled that 'he much impressed me by his anxiety to see things for himself, so as to be able to form a fresh, independent, first-hand idea of them'.[30]

Basing themselves in Athens for a few days, they toured the main classical sites within reach. James Cullen was the ideal companion, for he too had a passion for archaeology and the ancient and modern Greek world. He would later give up teaching Classics to work in the Antiquities Department of Cyprus. He was also a splendid walker, and did not flinch from expeditions that began at dawn and ended at nightfall or later. For John, this was an initiation into one of the most intoxicating aspects of archaeology. Their long walks along the coast and over Mount Hymettos were punctuated by simple meals of bread, cheese and Retsina ('ruinous native wine'), and there is little doubt that Cullen set the pattern – and the pace – which John would later follow. It was far more than a study tour; John was captivated by the countryside, the people and the language. They had begun to work a spell on him which would hold him for the rest of his life.

But it was the exquisite Bronze Age finds that John saw in the National Museum in Athens which were the greatest inspiration. The objects from Mycenae, Tiryns, Orchomenos, Thorikos and other Mycenaean sites were familiar to him from books and journals, but no photograph could do justice to the beauty and intricacy of the worked metal, ivory and stone. From Crete came bronze swords and daggers decorated with gold, silver and niello, depicting scenes of captivating movement and life: men with spears and figure-of-eight shields as tall as themselves attacking three lions, while one of the hunters succumbs to the enraged king of the pride; a cat pouncing on panic-stricken ducks and geese in the marshes. The complex action scenes loved by the Cretan Minoans contrasted with the more reserved, though elegant, geometric or repetitive designs of the Mycenaeans of mainland Greece. Sealstones created from tiny precious and semi-precious stones, and carved stone vases, revealed the skill of the stoneworkers, while delicate figurines and fine relief plaques for inlaying in wood, were fashioned from ivory.

Before the Museum shut for lunch, John and Cullen went to look for Wace in his 'playroom', where he was reconstructing a Mycenaean altar and some vases. John began by questioning the interpretation on which some of the reconstructions depended. Then Wace showed him a Hittite seal, 'well worn, discovered last year at Mycenae'. On being told that one of the great figures of Aegean Bronze Age archaeology, D.G. Hogarth, had dated it to no later than 1300 BC, John replied, 'I should put it later, personally, but it seems to fit.' Wace was unlikely to forget the young John Pendlebury.

John and Cullen then went north-west from Athens to Boeotia, visiting Thebes, the legendary home of Oedipus, and the classical battle sites of Delium, Tanagra and Haliartos, where they fell in with a party of shepherds. 'Drank retsinata with them and took these photographs. Ended up terrific pals. Curious custom of pouring a libation after drinking one's health. We did the last five miles in an hour, under the influence of *retsinata* and the guidance of two shepherds.' In the photographs, John appears in an old tweed jacket and an open-necked white shirt, his hands usually thrust deep into his misshapen pockets. His now more grown-up face wears a wide grin, though he also had a tendency to pull a daft expression for the benefit of the camera. James Cullen appears as casual as John, but rather more elegant, in his dark jacket and trousers, white open-necked shirt and trilby hat. John blends in better with the shepherds and urchins surrounding him.

Ending up at the monastery of Osios Loukas (Holy Luke) at Stiris, they were generously entertained and put up for the night. Rising at 5.30 they set out on foot, with a parcel of eggs, cheese and bread provided by the abbot. Near Delphi they passed Schiste, where the roads from Delphi, Thebes and Daulis crossed, and where Oedipus, having been abandoned at birth, had met and killed his real father, before going on to Thebes unknowingly to marry his newly widowed mother. Here they 'bathed in the fountain where he must have washed the blood off his hands'.

John had already acquired a healthy appetite for drinking with everyone they met on their walks. So they were understandably rather tired by the time they reached Arachova, where they stopped for a short while (for a drink) before walking the last two hours to Delphi. After a walk of about nine hours they then proceeded to climb around the steep site of the sanctuary of Apollo and home of the Delphic Oracle, which may, along with the effects of alcohol, have contributed to John's perception of Delphi as 'a wonderful place but dead'.

They descended to the port of Itea and sailed south across the Gulf of Corinth to the Peloponnese and thence overland to Olympia, birthplace of the Olympic Games. From Olympia they went down to Kalamata, walking through the impressive Langada Pass towards Sparta, ancient enemy of Athens during the Peloponnesian War, passing by the ruins of the Byzantine city of Mistra. Here had been crowned the last Byzantine Emperor, Constantine, who died attempting to defend Constantinople from the Turks in 1453.

At last they came to Mycenae. The citadel was one of the great Bronze Age sites excavated by the German archaeologist Heinrich Schliemann in pursuit of the history behind the Homeric accounts of the Trojan War. Here legend placed the palace of Agamemnon, son of Pelops and commander of the Greeks against Troy. Here Agamemnon's perfidious wife, Clytaemnestra, had waited for his return from the war unloosed by the elopement of her sister, Helen, and had murdered him in the hour of his triumphant homecoming. The finds Schliemann made in 1876, particularly those in the royal shaft graves, were spectacular. The excavation of the site was conceded to the British School by the Greek archaeologist Christos Tsountas and excavation had continued under Wace's direction between 1920 and 1923.

At the inn of the 'Belle Hélène', which had been used by Schliemann while he excavated the nearby citadel, they met Wace with a party of guests. The attractive but simple two-storied inn, though sparsely furnished, offered the warmest of welcomes. Since Schliemann's time, particularly throughout the 1920s and '30s, it had become one of *the* places to visit in Greece. Its visitors books contain the witty, sometimes illustrated, comments and signatures of archaeologists, artists, writers and politicians of many nationalities – including some, such as Heinrich Himmler, who would one day be high up in the Nazi regime, drawn by the fame of the German Schliemann. The inn was run by an elderly couple, Dimitri and Ioanna Dassis, and their five adult children, Helen, Constantine, Agamemnon, Spiro and Orestes.

'We had a most excellent dinner and afterwards strolled up to one or two of the tombs in one of which Wace had excavated last year.' The large stone-lined chamber tomb, the finest of its kind at Mycenae, was impenetrably black inside, even in daylight. A long passage or 'dromos', open to the sky, led to the tall stone doorway into the side of the hill, surmounted by massive lintel stones. Shaped like an old-fashioned beehive, its corbelled interior rose to a point high above. Impressive by day, it inspired awe at night, not least because 'Wace insisted on telling a ghost story.'

John was very impressed by the 'wonderful' Wace, who seemed to know 'absolutely everything about everything', and had been a Fellow of Pembroke

College, Cambridge, John's chosen college. Wace, in turn, took to John and from this time on acted very much as his mentor. Wace was a charming man who delighted in telling stories, especially ghost stories, some of which were later published by his daughter.[31] Compton Mackenzie, who had known Wace as Director of the British School during the Great War, saw in him a 'delightful combination of great scholarship and humour, a worldly humour too and not in the least pedagogic. He was a tall slim man full of nervous energy, with a fresh complexion and an extraordinarily merry pair of light blue eyes.'[32]

At the end of the month John and Cullen boarded a Lloyd Triestino ship and sailed through the Corinth Canal, past Odysseus' island home of Ithaca, to Corfu. Here they briefly disembarked to see the medieval ruins before continuing to Brindisi, the train to Milan and so back to England.

For Herbert, John's travels were to remain a largely vicarious pleasure, for he very rarely intruded into John's world. Though repeatedly invited, there is evidence that he went to Greece with John only once, in October 1926. In his letters, John had the ability to draw people into his world and had already begun to develop the succinct, humorous snapshots of his travels and the people he encountered that are so characteristic of his later writing. His letters were never long or very descriptive, but they were immediate and vivid. The original letters from the trip of Easter 1923 do not survive, but Herbert transcribed them into a journal of the journey. It was an extraordinary thing for him to do: he built up an itinerary of John's travels, writing out the relevant excerpts from his correspondence in his own hand and updating the journal as each new letter dropped through the letterbox. The left-hand page he left blank for the two-inch square photographs that John had taken, to be pasted in and annotated when he got back.

John took to the idea of keeping a journal. It set a pattern for his future travels, which were recorded in bulging notebooks crammed full of photographs and notes. He traced maps of walks and plans of sites that he had visited or planned to visit, keeping a thorough record of his movements and the time it took to complete each journey. He refined this over the years, boiling his notes down to times, distances and prices, names of people, hotels and muleteers. It was a habit he never lost and it nearly caused considerable trouble when in 1941 his last notebook fell into the hands of the German SS.

2

1923–27

IN THE EARLY 1920s, Pembroke College Cambridge was described in the college rag, *The Pem*, as a peaceful place. Nothing could be heard in the evenings but the murmuring of a kettle on a primus, the slow footfall of 'ruminating Dons', and the 'drowsy twittering' of Blues.[1] This atmosphere of tranquillity, however, was probably because undergraduates and dons had been up most of the previous night. Cambridge at the time was overflowing with the exuberant, perhaps a little desperate, energy of those who had been through the Great War and survived, together with the unscarred high spirits of the normal intake of schoolboys. This produced problems of discipline for the University. For, as the newly-appointed Dean of Jesus College pointed out, 'You could not tell a Brigadier or an Air Commodore that he must be in by ten o'clock or pay a fine of tuppence'.[2] Nonetheless, the traditions of the college survived, and Herbert Pendlebury, who had gone up to Pembroke in 1890, would have recognised several faces, for in those days it was not unusual for the college servants to start work as children and continue until retirement or death. The Porter's Lodge opened onto First Court, dominated by the 19th-century Hall, which separated First Court from Ivy Court. On the south side of these was the 17th-century block in which John, an Exhibitioner, had his rooms, facing towards the Library.

It was not just undergraduates who had experienced the war first hand. Many of the Pembroke dons had left the comfort and security of college life to volunteer. The College Tutor was the Classics don Jock Lawson, who lived in the famously haunted Abbey House, on the site of Barnwell Priory off the Newmarket Road. As a student he had travelled widely in Greece researching modern folklore and ancient religion. Much to the amusement of most, he claimed that he had seen a Dryad or wood nymph there, and had steadfastly believed in fairy folk ever since, writing stories about them for the children of his dead brother. He, like John in a later war, was determined to use his knowledge of modern Greek and his experience of the Aegean in the Great War. Taking a commission in the RNVR, he was posted to the Naval Intelligence Branch and sent out to Crete. Later he was sent to Athens as a member of the British Naval Mission to Greece. His work in Greece earned him the OBE, the Greek Order of the Redeemer and the Medal for Military Merit.

Two resident dons were at the centre of life at the college, Henry Comber and Aubrey Attwater. Comber was a Modern Language don known affectionately as the 'Old Man'. It was as an undergraduate at Pembroke that Comber had first met Herbert Pendlebury, known to his friends as Pen. Both were sportsmen and had gained Blues as hockey players for Cambridge. Comber had been Provost Marshal at Boulogne towards the end of the war, and returned to Pembroke with the DSO. As one of Herbert Pendlebury's closest friends, the Old Man had known John all his life. 'I know what he means to you', Comber wrote to Herbert, 'for he stands not only as the loved son but as the link with the loved one who is no longer with you.'[3] Following now for the first time in Herbert's footsteps, John had a lot to live up to at Pembroke, for, as well as his sporting achievements, Herbert had gained a first class degree in Natural Sciences.

Aubrey Attwater was a young English don and College Librarian in his early thirties, who had been a keen rower. He became an officer in the Royal Welch Fusiliers in 1914 instead of finishing his final year at Pembroke, and was so badly wounded a year later while on patrol that he never fully recovered. Unable to become a lawyer as he had hoped, he was invited back to teach the new English Tripos at his old college. He veiled the constant pain he was in with light-hearted humour. He and Comber delighted in good company, conversation and storytelling, and would hold court in one or other of their rooms after dinner in Hall. It paid to turn up early at Attwater's rooms, as those who had him as a tutor knew only too well. His sitting room was a minefield of books hazardously piled all over the floor. Any latecomer would be unlikely to find anywhere to perch, if they could enter the room at all, for not only did Attwater smoke like a chimney, but so also did many of the undergraduates, John among them. The atmosphere of the room would become so thick with smoke that late arrivals usually beat a hasty retreat. As well as their academic interests, Attwater and Comber shared a love of sport, and many of those who frequented these companionable evenings were the Blues and scholars of the college. These regular guests became known as the Old Man's family, and met for an annual dinner on his birthday. John, who had proved himself a passable athlete at Winchester, was introduced by Comber into this crowd early on, and equally early was recruited into the Pembroke College Athletics Club.

Consequently, most of the friends John made in his first year were Pembroke men and athletes, and they were for the most part friendships that endured all his life. One of the scholarly non-athletes among these men was the red-haired Pierson ('Bob') Dixon, a Classics scholar with a fine brain and a sharp wit, whose conversation was both amusing and stimulating. 'The enduring impression of my first meeting with Pendlebury in his rooms at Pembroke in

1923, is the neatness and orderliness of the man, and an indefinable air of restrained power.'[4]

At Cambridge the Classical Tripos concentrated on the classical Greek and Roman worlds, with only minor forays into earlier periods and cultures. Bob and John shared a passion for the ancient world and its languages, both boasting that they could express themselves better in ancient Greek than in English. Less of a classical scholar than Bob, John nonetheless had the greater self-assurance of one who had already found what he wanted to do in life. John was a good classicist, but although he had the capacities and instincts of a 'good and careful' scholar, Bob noted that 'he did not show or admit too much enthusiasm for the Greece or Rome of the Golden Age, any more than for textual criticism or Greek Iambics'. Scholarship for John was a means to an end, not an end in itself; archaeology was his vocation. 'Even before he left Winchester', Bob observed, 'his mind was firmly set on following down the paths which Schliemann and Evans had blazed through the Heroic Age.'[5] This certainty and the confidence born from it were unusual in an undergraduate, and a great draw to his friends, as though they felt that some of John's self-assurance might rub off on them. More than one of John's contemporaries at Cambridge followed John's career after Cambridge, and saw that on the surface at least he never

Some of John's drawings from a letter to Rose Mary Braithwaite

veered from his chivalric ideal. Fellow athlete Arthur Willis wrote of him years later, 'There is something thrilling in a sense of vocation so unusual, yet so strong and clearly defined, and so faithfully followed'.[6]

His enthusiasm was deeply contagious, whether it was for the ideals of medieval chivalry, the heroes of Greek legends and Homeric epics or tales of the Egyptian pharaohs. 'Nothing he touched but sprang to vivid life', Bob wrote.[7] Less than a fortnight after arriving at Pembroke, John wrote a charming letter to Rose Mary Braithwaite, the nine-year-old niece of his mother's friend, Violet Mitchell.[8] John's imagination spills out from the letter, which he illustrated with pen-and-ink drawings of his favourite historical and fictional characters. Among other Egyptian figures, he drew Ankhsenamen, wife of Tutankhamen, whose tomb had been found only eleven months earlier. Sharing the page were Richard Coeur de Lion, hero of John's favourite book, *The Life and Death of Richard Yea and Nay* by Maurice Hewlett, first published in 1900, and two other knights. Alongside them was Masrur, Haroun ar-Rashid's executioner from Flecker's play *Hassan*, the premiere of which John had seen in London less than a month earlier. Like *Richard Yea and Nay*, this play made a lasting impression on John, appealing to his vividly romantic ideal of life. Alongside these Egyptian and medieval characters was a proud Achilles, hero of the Trojan War, depicted alongside a Zulu prince. For years afterwards his doodles would continue to be of knights in armour and Haroun ar-Rashid, Caliph of Baghdad.

John drew on the heroic notions he found in these stories to develop a peculiar code of his own, combining physical stamina and speed with an acute, academically rigorous and imaginative mind. To John, imagination was as important as scholarly detail. As Bob noticed, John had an enthusiasm that those around him could not help but share. Many who knew him at Cambridge had a sense that he was preparing himself for some future trial of which he was acutely aware but could not define. However, he wore with tremendous ease the gravity which his friends detected, leavening it with a wicked sense of humour and a broad repertoire of bawdy music hall songs, and he never lost his boyhood enthusiasm for practical jokes. Valuing highly good company in his friends, he was intolerant of fools, and if he disliked someone or found him stupid then his comments were damning, verging on the vitriolic. As another contemporary, Rowe Harding, later wrote, John had a contempt 'for what was vile and mean'.[9] He rarely expressed himself in half measures, a trait which showed itself increasingly as he grew older, and was often too quick to see only the best or only the worst in people. Some of this was the arrogance of youth and was rooted in a profound sense of honour. He was an unusual person, but he was valued highly by his friends and contributed greatly to their happiest memories of Pembroke.

Although archaeology was a very minor part of the Tripos, John made up for this through his own study. Where Egypt was concerned, it was the site of Tell el-Amarna, on the banks of the Nile in Middle Egypt, which fired his imagination. Founded on virgin soil by the 'heretic' pharaoh Akhenaten and his queen Nefertiti as a centre for the new worship of the sun disc, the Aten, the city was, for a short while, the capital of a vast Egyptian Empire. In 1891–2, Flinders Petrie had carried out the first excavation of the ruins. He published his results in 1894 and John later wrote to Petrie, 'I should like to thank you for the inspiration to archaeology your books gave me when I was still at school'.[10] Tell el-Amarna became a passion, appealing as much to John's imagination as to his intellect. He avidly followed the Egypt Exploration Society's work there in *The Daily Telegraph*, *The Illustrated London News*, and published academic reports. What drew John to Tell el-Amarna was the large quantity of Mycenaean pottery that Petrie found on the site, suggesting that there had been considerable contact between Egypt and the Greek mainland and Aegean islands, particularly Rhodes, during the lifetime of the city. The Aegean trade connection intrigued John. One of the primary trading partners of the Egyptian empire up until the time of Akhenaten's father was the Minoan world that Sir Arthur Evans and others had been bringing to light in Crete. Evans published the first volume of his massive work on the Minoan civilisation at Knossos, *The Palace of Minos*, in 1921, and John was often to be found absorbed in its pages. 'He did not work', Bob wrote later of him, 'like the ordinary run of undergraduate, in a litter of texts, lexicons, papers and notebooks; and he was always manifestly in training. My portrait of John at nineteen is of a friendly athlete sitting in a hard chair with one book open. It might be *The Iliad* or the latest volume of *The Palace of Minos* or it might be Maurice Hewlett's *Forest Lovers*.'[11]

The 'friendly athlete' was also coming into his own. John met many of the college sportsmen at Comber's gatherings, including the man the American press had already dubbed 'indisputably the fastest half-miler on the face of the earth and the second best in history'. Douglas Lowe, the handsome President of the Pembroke College Athletic Club (PCAC), hearing of John's athletic achievements at Winchester, wasted no time in recruiting him to try out for the Freshmen's sports in the first term.

John made friends easily with the college athletes, among them Darren Baillieu, a tall and powerfully built Australian student, who had been roped in to the PCAC because his build alone made him a good weight-putter. Baillieu's jovial and clownish outlook was similar to John's, but he was not interested in taking athletics further than college level. John, on the other hand, decided to go as far as he could. He began training in the high jump, hurdles and relays with Alec Nelson, the coach of the Cambridge University Athletics Club (CUAC). Nelson had been a runner in his youth but was also a particularly good trainer in the field events. John ignored, as he always had, the disadvantage of having sight in only one eye. His high-jumping improved steadily, though it demanded very keen body and eye co-ordination, especially in the days when scissor jumps were still the norm, before the days of the backwards Fosbury flop.

John's first appearance was in the very public arena of the Freshmen's Sports at Fenner's, the athletics and cricket ground in east Cambridge, keenly watched by a large crowd. Several papers covered the University sports in detail, the *Sporting Life* among them. On the morning of the contest the weather was appalling, with thick snow followed by heavy rain. John's take-off on the high jump was bad, but he managed to clear 5'7", enough to win the event. With growing confidence he took his place on the starting line for the hurdles. John started well but was closely followed by another unknown freshman athlete, Lord Burghley of Magdalene College. Burghley kept close to John right to the finish, but John won by inches. Lord Burghley, the hurdling Lord Lindsay of the film *Chariots of Fire*, was to become, also under the tutelage of Alec Nelson, one of the finest hurdlers of his generation, but this time John just bettered him. The next day's report in the *Sporting Life* came under the heading 'JDS Pendlebury's Fine Double', concluding that without any doubt he had come away with the chief honours of the day.[12]

After this early, though modest, triumph, John was hooked. He knew he had a long way to go to compete with Cambridge's best, but he was determined to work at it, for at that time Cambridge's best were among the finest in the world. Fenner's was a remarkable place to be in the early 1920s, and not a little daunting to a freshman athlete like John. Harold Abrahams, also celebrated in *Chariots of Fire*, was President of the CUAC, and he and others, such as Douglas Lowe, were already known, nationally and internationally, in the build up to the 1924 Olympics, which would take place in Paris at the end of John's first year.

John soon learned how hard athletics at this level were in the next contest, the Seniors v. Freshmen Sports. He did not stand a chance in the high jump, encountering for the first time the elegant Singhalese high-jumper Carl van Geyzel, who seemed to glide nonchalantly over the bar. In the hurdles, it was Lord Burghley who this time took the laurels, though John scraped in as a reserve for the University Relays against Oxford.

The athletic year was largely dictated by the weather, as well as the availability of the ground at Fenner's, which doubled as the University cricket club. The main field and track competitions took place in the Lent term; the highlights of the year were the Cambridge University Sports at Fenner's, and the Inter-Varsity Sports at Queen's Club in London at the end of the Lent term.

In spite of the hours of training required and the frequent trials or contests, John was as disciplined in his studies as in his athletics, and at the end of his first year he was awarded the Schoolbred Scholarship for Classics.

John, however, loved beer and company far too much to spend all his time studying or training. One of the attractions of Fenner's was its pavilion clubhouse, which was a lively venue and a breeding ground for risqué stories and tales. These appealed enormously to his sense of humour and he would gather the best of them to retell at Pembroke after dinner.

By now John was a confident public speaker; he and Bob Dixon joined the Pembroke College Debating Society (whose President was the young RAB Butler) and the Martlets Society, named after the apparently legless birds that appeared in the college arms, which met to hear papers on an outlandish variety of subjects. The Debating Society was a light-hearted affair, the minutes written up in whatever style suited the prevailing mood. On one occasion, they were scripted in the form of a light opera, with interjections to the tunes of 'Yes, we have no bananas', 'What'll I do when you are far from me?', and the 'Song of the Vulgar Boatmen', a noisy rendition of which was performed at the next meeting.[13]

By the end of his first year John had been elected a member of the Achilles Club, which encouraged Oxford and Cambridge to produce athletes capable of competing internationally. In June 1924, with the CUAC at its peak, one of the most important competitions of the year, the Amateur Athletic Association (AAA) Championship, was held at Stamford Bridge in London. In the 1920s, the AAA Championship was second only to the Olympic Games internationally; it was where athletes could qualify for a place in the Olympic team going to Paris the following month. For John the timing of the Paris Olympiad was unfortunate as he had not quite reached a high enough standard to qualify. He took part in the high jump, but was beaten by a jump of 5' 11", a height he would easily surpass a few months later. Arthur Willis, ten years John's senior and a veteran of the Great War, who would become one of John's keenest high jumping rivals, did qualify, and the Achilles Club performed extremely well at the Olympics. Lord Burghley, by now a good friend of John's, also managed to qualify, thus competing for Britain before even being considered for the Cambridge team.

*

1924's crop of freshmen contained some very fine athletes, with a liking for beer and good company almost equal to John's. Pembroke acquired Tom

Livingstone-Learmonth, another Wykehamist and a fine hurdler, and Rowe Harding, a Welsh sprint champion and rugby international. New at Clare College was John Rinkel, another sprinter and long jumper, to challenge another of John's Fenner's friends, the long jumper Villiers ('Pip') Powell, of Caius.

The athletics year began with the relay races, both the Inter-Collegiate Competition and the trials for the main event of the Michaelmas Term, the Inter-Varsity Relay Matches. John was hurdling particularly well and, with the help of Tom Livingstone-Learmonth, they won the event, and Pembroke won the First Division Cup from Jesus College. John was chosen to compete against Oxford in the relays, so gaining his half colours. The draw of several Olympic runners on both the Oxford and the Cambridge sides made the event a sell-out at what was said to be one of the largest and most enthusiastic gatherings ever seen at Fenner's. Oxford and Cambridge were neck and neck with two events each; the contest would be decided by the hurdles.

The *Cambridge Review* called it the finest exhibition of hurdling seen at Fenner's for years, and concluded that 'Cambridge won the meeting because every single man ran up to and above form, and every event included four men of almost equal merit, whereas Oxford had usually one man not quite so good as the rest.'[14] It was the correspondent of *The Times Sporting News*, though, who gave the most picturesque account of the 'Great Race'. 'Up and down the ten flights ran the couples with never a yard between them. It seemed almost as if they were mechanical figures, joined by an unseen thread, moving backwards and forwards according as the board beneath them was tilted by an unseen hand.'[15]

The University Sports showed that the Cambridge team was strong all round. The competition was close and records were broken. In the high jump John tied in second place at 5'9" with the Blue, Arthur Willis, but van Geyzel was not to be beaten, setting a new Fenner's record of 6'3". John failed by a very narrow margin to get selected for the team against Oxford so to his great disappointment was still not eligible for a full Blue.

*

John's third year began auspiciously. On October 12th 1925, he turned twenty-one and, with an inheritance from his mother, became a man of independent means. He celebrated with family and friends in style at Claridge's, near his childhood home. His grandfather, Sir Thomas Lane Devitt, had left his fortune to John's cousin, Tom Devitt, who was two years older and also a prominent athlete at Cambridge. But the amount John inherited was, by the time of his own death, worth more than £66,000, and he did his best at Cambridge to enjoy it.[16] Twenty years or more later, when the country was in the grip of rationing, Rowe Harding remembered that, 'For several terms John, Tom

Livingston-Learmonth and I always breakfasted together, now in Tom's room, now in John's and now in mine. And they were such breakfasts as now we can only dream about – flakes in cream, scrambled eggs and bacon, and all the other breakfast delicacies of those special days.'[17]

John was becoming increasingly flamboyant and had taken to wearing a monocle over his glass eye whenever he jumped, gaining the sobriquet in the sports press of the 'monocled high-jumper'. For parties and balls he wore a patch, which gave him a distinctly piratical look. Though it seemed merely quirky affectation, it successfully disguised his glass eye. Many of even his closest friends realised only years later that it was, in fact, false.

That Michaelmas term of 1925 John founded Ye Joyouse Companie of Seynt Pol, a secret drinking club. The Companie combined his passion for chivalry and romance with his delight in storytelling – preferably risqué – and his love of beer and good company. The club was named after Marie St Pol de Valence, the Countess of Pembroke, who had founded the college in 1347. The name was also a reference to Jehane St Pol, the heroine of his favourite book, *The Life and Death of Richard Yea-and-Nay*.[18] The Joyouse Companie had three objects, as set out in the statutes, composed by John in bogus Middle English: 'firstlie ye Glorificatioun of Ye Lady Founderesse; secondlie ye Consoumptioun of Goode Englishe Ale; thirdlie ye Discouragemente of Cannibalisme'.[19]

There were ten members. John (Le Sieur Jehan Pendleburie) was the Companie's first 'Grande Seneschale', with Messire Darren de Baillieu as his Constable. Bob Dixon, Granville Streatfeild, William MacGregor, Tom Learmonth, Rowe Harding and Malcolm MacGougan, their names all rewritten in a suitably Norman French manner, became the first six 'Gentilmenne Armigers' of Pembroke College. Pip Powell (Villiers de Powelle), by now President of the CUAC, became the single Gentilmanne Armiger allowed from another college. The guest of honour was, unbeknown to him, the Master of Pembroke.

They were to meet once a term in one or other of their rooms, drink draught beer (bottled was absolutely forbidden), and each one would have to come up with an amusing story. The Grande Seneschale would tell a story on behalf of the absent Master, preferably of a kind that would have horrified the Master. Then, 'On a secrete vote, ye fairest and most wittie tayle be acclaimed and ye teller bee named ye Constable for ye nexte meeting, for thenne shall ye Constable ascende and bee Grande Seneschale for a space.' The Grande Seneschale and Constable elect would then drink one pint of good draught ale, 'and no heel taps'. Any member who did not comply with the rules would 'cause to falle upon himself a curse – to witte a plague of boiles', and any who missed a meeting, 'a plague of emerods'.[20]

Each founder member would have his own tankard with his name and position in the company engraved on it, along with a coat of arms which they were each to make up according to the rules of heraldry. When they went down from Cambridge, their tankard and colours would be passed on to the new man they had proposed, who would create his own device in the same colours.

John was the first Grande Seneschale, and when he passed his mantle on to his successor the following year, he wrote some notes of guidance for future Grande Seneschales, 'Written in liquor 5th June 1926', insisting that the chivalric courtesies be observed. 'Be regular in calling down the curses and plagues. Insist upon the courtesy title of 'Messire', and don't for God's sake let the show become a mere bawdy rag. Allow no talking during the stories, let each one, however bad, have a fair hearing and (this in your ear), if the one voted the worst proceeds from a man who you are afraid would take it frightfully to heart – why – lie like a Trojan! and let some hearty chap who doesn't care a damn be condemned.'[21]

John and his friends also founded 'Ye Ordre of Ye Sevene Gai Tippelers', which contained some but not all of the members of the Joyous Company. The club was founded on August 5th 'in ye yere of Redemcioun nineteen hondrede and twentie six'. It was simply a drinking club, the seven members of which vowed to spend thirty-five days over the following five years seeking out the taverns and hostels of London, never visiting the same one twice. At the end of the five years, they ordained that 'ye Order mete ate som gud Taverne and yere festeie. And who hath cum into ye moest Tavernes shall have hys soper ate our aller cost'.[22]

*

At long last, in October 1925, John cleared 6'1/4" at Fenner's and won the high jump in the Seniors' Sports. 'JDS Pendlebury thoroughly deserves the many and hearty congratulations he has received,' wrote the *Cambridge Review*.[23]

'There were great men at Fenner's in those days,' Rowe Harding recalled. 'Lord Burghley, Douglas Lowe, GC Weightman-Smith and many more, but I think nothing stands out more vividly in my mind than John leaping six foot at Fenner's. There was a Singalese, van Geyzel, who was a very graceful and accomplished jumper, but he did not give me the thrill that John did when he ran straight at the bar, and cleared it like a bird in flight, with that queer mixture of recklessness and nonchalance which was so characteristic of him.'[24]

Another Pembroke man who followed the athletics keenly was S.C. Roberts, head of the Cambridge University Press (which would later publish John's first book) and eventually Master of Pembroke. He wrote, 'To see John at Fenner's waiting for his turn in the high jump was to realise the alert perfection of physical training. Stepping delicately on his toes in preparation for the actual contest, he seemed to embody all the springy tautness, all the controlled power of the thoroughbred and one appreciates more clearly one of the elements of his kinship with the Cretans.'[25]

*

On November 24th 1925, not long after John had started his third year, he travelled to Great Malvern for a wedding. Some time earlier, Herbert Pendlebury had met a widow called Mabel Dickinson (née Webb), who had consulted him at his Brook Street practice. Dickie or Dicky, as she was known, was a New Zealander by birth who had spent a great deal of her earlier married life in Kenya, where her brother, Will Webb, still farmed coffee and sisal. At forty-one she was thirteen years younger than Herbert. Four years after Lily's death, they married. Dickie lived with her son, Robin, at a large house called Winstanley in Malvern, near the Priory Church where she and Herbert were married. Robin was still at Malvern College, so Herbert wound up his practice in Brook Street and retired to Winstanley.

John's relationship with Dickie and Robin thrived on mutual banter. His letters to Herbert usually finished with asides to Dickie casting aspersions on her drinking or other faults and to Robin with comments such as 'tell him that I was about to write to him but my gorge rose.' The step-brothers were very different, and while John was at Cambridge and Robin at school, they spent little time together. Robin was eight years John's junior, and rather lazy and slapdash, except when it came to his future vocation – journalism (he was already bringing out a weekly magazine at school). While he was more of a rebel than John, he eventually followed him to Pembroke, where his ruthless journalistic bent raised many eyebrows.

Both John and Herbert, who was known to all as 'Uncle Pen', fitted well into Malvern life. 'John was an intensely amusing young man', recalled Rosalind Bayfield, niece of Dickie and Herbert's neighbour. 'In fact, when I, at the age of sixteen, had my appendix out, I had to beg him not to make me laugh when he and his father came to see me in the nursing home, as I was frightened of bursting my stitches... He had the most perfect manners, was kind, very charming to older people as well as young; my mother loved him, and we all admired and respected him.' Winstanley had become in all senses the family home, and John's Cambridge friends often came to stay for the weekend, to the delight of Rosalind and her sister Vera. 'John's friends in the Achilles Club used to come down sometimes for dances at Winstanley... I remember Lord Burghley very well, and also Douglas Lowe, tall and good looking.'[26]

It was not only Herbert who had found love. John too had fallen in love, although the identity of the woman is not known. A photograph of the 1926 Pembroke Ball shows John, in white tie and black eye-patch, flanked by two young women; whether one was his mystery girlfriend remains unknown.[27] But it seems that she had no desire to share the life of archaeology that he wished to pursue. Years later a contemporary at Pembroke, John Soper, remembered John's concern about 'whether it would be best to marry a girl with the same interests, or should one follow the dictates of one's heart'.[28] This suggests that the relationship was serious enough for John to consider giving up his own dreams to marry her. Judging by some of the comments in the 1927 edition of the satirical college rag magazine, *The Pem,* ('Does Mr Pendlebury prefer breakfasting in sin to dining in liquor?'), they did have an affair, and John later admitted to a friend that he had wanted to marry her.[29] That very term he proposed the motion at the Pembroke College Debating Society, 'It is better to have loved and lost, than never to have loved at all'.[30]

In Maurice Hewlett's novel *The Life and Death of Richard Yea-and-Nay,* Richard the Lionheart puts his duty as king before his own longing for the woman he loves. It is a tragic story of tortured love and loyalty and there is little doubt that for John it was a reflection of his own romantic turmoil. The novel had a lasting effect on John. His high jump opponent from Emmanuel, Arthur Willis, was struck by 'the naïve, almost personal friendships that could exist between him and a book, especially, I remember, the historical romances of Maurice Hewlett.'[31] When Darren Baillieu had to return to Australia at the end of the 1926 Lent term, following the sudden death of his older brother, he went to John's rooms to say goodbye. 'I was surprised, but secretly flattered', he recalled later, 'to find him rather sentimental about our parting. He had not realised I would be returning so soon to Australia, and wanted to give me something as a farewell present. He looked around for a token...and then pounced on his *Richard, Yea and Nay,* by Maurice Hewlett, which he gave me with instructions to think of him when I read it. This was a much bigger gesture than it appeared, for this grubby little book was, to John, a symbol of heroism and romance.'[32]

*

John's athletic form was improving all the time. He competed in the University Sports in early March 1926, and tied for first place with his old friend Arthur Willis, the 1924 Olympic high-jumper, rather surprising given the fact that John had added a white flannel cloak to his jumping outfit. According to *The Cambridge Review,* 'Each one was too much of a gentleman to jump 6 ft in case his friend could not do it. At Queen's, however, there is little doubt that they will take their gloves off'.[33]

The afternoon of March 19th saw John's first participation in the Inter-Varsity sports at Queen's Club, London. Dr Adolphe Abrahams, brother of Harold, noted that little interest was taken in the high jump. 'Willis and Pendlebury had shown such equality at Cambridge that they were left to fight out the issue at Queen's, and unless both were simultaneously off-colour, a Cambridge success was inevitable.' Both jumped 5'9½in, another tie which earned them the name 'The Heavenly Twins' in the sports press. They were declared joint winners and were both awarded full Blues, 'which,' wrote Harold Abrahams, 'they thoroughly deserve'. So, as a Blue, John became a member of the Hawks Club. But the barrier of six feet remained, as yet never cleared at Queen's by either Oxford or Cambridge.

*

During the last days of April 1926, a political crisis was brewing. What had started as a dispute over pay and working hours between the miners, the mine-owners and the government of Stanley Baldwin, suddenly erupted into a General Strike. The Trades Union Congress called for a complete withdrawal from work, in sympathy with the miners, to start at one minute to midnight on May 3rd 1926. The country was brought to a standstill.

On May 5th, Jock Lawson, as College Tutor at Pembroke, received a notice from the Cambridge Civil Commissioner. He announced that he was 'of the opinion that the time has come when no obstacle should be put in the way of the undergraduates wishing to drop academic work for service of national importance, except in the cases where an undergraduate has a chance of a first class honours degree in a tripos to be taken this term.'[34]

More than 200 Pembroke students took up the call with the greatest enthusiasm. John's gang of volunteers was sent to be Special Constables in Brentwood, Essex. In the college logbook John wrote down that he had also been a 'sapper'. Bob Dixon went to London with Rowe Harding and Darren Baillieu, while Tom Livingstone-Learmonth volunteered as a Goods Porter and Special Constable in Paddington.

On May 12th, the General Strike was called off, and the country tried to return to normal – a process made easier by the maintenance of essential services by volunteers, such as the students.

*

The Lent term of 1927 brought Part II of the tripos a lot closer for John. He had done less well than he would have wanted in his Part I in 1925, getting a good second, owing to illness that term, including a spell in hospital for an ear operation. But he soon made up lost ground, and stuck with his ambition to become an archaeologist.

John had gone to Greece with his father in the summer of 1926, and was by now getting to know many of the archaeologists working there, such as the German, Georg Karo, who was to become a good friend. In England, he and Bob Dixon were meeting academics in related fields, such as Professor Richard Dawkins of Emmanuel College, Cambridge, a former Director of the British School in Athens and a specialist in Modern Greek language, dialect and folklore. Charles Seltman was another. A Fellow of Queen's College, Cambridge and University Lecturer in Classics, Seltman was a collector of antiquities who had been involved the year before in the Fitzwilliam Museum's acquisition of a Minoan ivory statuette that turned out to be a fake.[35]

At the time Oxford dominated the world of Aegean prehistoric archaeology, and particularly the committee of the British School in Athens. John's earlier acquaintance with Professor Wace proved useful. Wace had personal experience of dealing with the Oxford committee men, such as John Myres and Arthur Evans, and was a good example of how divisions of this sort could affect a career. Evans and Myres had made acerbic criticisms, both professional and personal, of the conclusions Wace had, in 1924, drawn from his work at Mycenae. Wace and others were certain that Mycenae had not originated under Minoan rule and that what they were finding there was not Cretan in origin. The Minoan contingent thought this ignorant madness and were instrumental in Wace not being re-appointed as Director of the School. Wace was disgusted and did not work in Greece again for ten years, falling back on his hobby – textiles – to become Deputy Keeper of Textiles at the Victoria and Albert Museum.

*

At about this time, John was involved in perpetrating a hoax on the Pembroke College Classical Society. It hinged on the supposed discovery of a papyrus from Tell el-Amarna, which appeared to record the story of 'Hybrias the Cretan', a brother of the great King Minos. Hybrias had apparently fled Crete on the death of his hated brother to live in the Egyptian capital. John provided the Egyptological and Minoan background and the illustrations, but the paper was delivered by a friend. It was a great success. 'The whole Society was completely taken in.'[36] John would later use it as the basis of a short story when he had worked both at Tell el-Amarna and in Crete.

John also took part in amateur theatricals at Cambridge, which satisfied his love of dressing up. His most memorable performance was in W.W. Jacobs' play *In the Library* in February 1927 for the college's Mission in East London. 'There are two fights and a murder in it. I am a burglar and shall have a critical audience probably mostly composed of professionals! Thank goodness it is a tiny part consisting only of an occasional My Gawd! and a fight.'[37] The part seemed to grow on him. 'The play was a great success, and as we hadn't time to change into ordinary clothes before catching the 10.12 to Cambridge, Liverpool Street was the scene of my arrival in those Bill Sykes clothes, handcuffed and held by Edwards Jones as an enormous policeman. I shook him off and ran away up the platform. A howling mob pursued me over most of the station, I've never heard such pandemonium. I was eventually caught by a man I know quite well who never recognized me and really thought he had captured a desperate murderer or something. I was then escorted back to our carriage where I made an impassioned speech to an interested multitude on the sins of the police. The train then went out.'[38]

*

With his finals looming, John used his time in London to visit the British Museum and memorise the more famous collections for the 'spots' (identification and interpretation of objects from an image) in his examinations, followed by some practice jumping with another high jumper at Queen's Club. 'We both cleared 5'10"'.

The Inter-Varsity sports at Queen's Club in March 1927 marked the zenith of John's athletic career. Each ground had its idiosyncrasies to which some athletes adapted better than others. For nearly fifty years the Inter-Varsity sports had been held at Queen's, after they left the ground at Lilley Bridge where M. J. Brooks had achieved the Inter-Varsity record of 6'2½" in 1876. But, however strong the competition, no one from either Oxford or Cambridge had ever managed to clear six feet at Queen's. The ground appeared to lack the firmness needed for a good take-off and deadened the spring. Every Oxford and Cambridge high jumper was driven by the ambition to be the first to break the six foot barrier, and John was no exception. To jump six feet elsewhere was almost commonplace, but at Queen's it would be stupendous. When Saturday March 26th dawned, the weather in London was bad, with a strong wind and plenty of rain. One after another, the events went to Cambridge. The Oxford team was barely noticed in the hurdles, which was dominated by Weightman-Smith and Burghley. Pip Powell took the long jump for Cambridge, and 'Bonzo' Howland the weight putting. Then came the high jump.

'JDS Pendlebury had the best style of the four competitors', according to a newspaper review. 'He approaches from the front, and uses good leg leverage to get well up, and then to thrust both legs over in a clean jump.' John eliminated the opposition to win the event at 5'10½", but he was still determined to go for the record and clear 6'. On his first try he just brought the bar down. He tried again, and again failed. John had only one chance left, and this time he succeeded. 'For the first time in the history of Queen's Club', wrote Harold

Abrahams, 'six feet was accomplished'.[39] John gained his second Blue and an Inter-Varsity record for Queen's Club.

*

As exams approached, the atmosphere at Cambridge was tense. 'RAB' — probably R. A. 'RAB' Butler — writing in *The Bystander*, made great fun of the tension. 'Cambridge just now is rather a place to be avoided, for this poor old university is now having a three week's season as a seat of learning. "Too much work" has become a fashionable and even a plausible, excuse for refusing an invitation. Real live undergraduates can be seen actually at work on the seats outside John's New Court, and it is computed that quite a number of undergraduate rooms are being used for the same purpose.'[40]

Looking ahead to his postgraduate research, John applied for the Studentship to the British School of Archaeology at Athens, and for both the Craven and Warr scholarships. He was recommended to the selectors by Charles Seltman and Arthur Cook, his lecturers in classical archaeology, art and architecture. There were two possible subjects that he wanted to pursue: Creto-Egyptian relations or Greek athletics from the point of view of the athlete. He chose the former as it had greater possibilities when it came to a career in archaeology and would give him the chance to gain experience in both areas. 'Cook told me I had quite a flair for archaeology but that practically no notice is taken of it in the Trip. — or as little as the examiners can. Though of course it counts all right for appointments at the School etc.'[41]

Averaging by now six hours revision a day, John spent a lot of time arguing through certain subjects with Bob Dixon until they were both sure of their facts. 'Mr Bicknell [who was revising them in archaeology] is a wild and savage cove. There are only four up to him and I seem to be the only one who disputes his statements on principle. Hence he varies between high regard and deep loathing for me! I can't think what the real standard for archaeology is since the three who go to the wild man Bicknell all seem to be completely held in eggbound ignorance! ... Bicknell seems to think my archaeology is well up to standard and unless I break down badly or have very bad luck I have no cause for worry.' John was beginning to feel fairly confident in his favourite subject. 'As to the rest — it is after all, as I have always realized, mostly an act of God but I have taken steps to reduce the necessary divine interference to its minimum, I hope.'[42]

His father was more involved than ever, writing frequently to John on subjects ranging from 'the odd note on Architecture in S. Italy' to 'a small precis of Warren's arguments against wooden origin for the Doric'. Eventually the time for revision ran out. 'Well, tomorrow, Moriturus te saluto! The litterature

[sic] I think I ought to be able to do reasonably – the history also if the gods are kind. Philosophy as you know is largely a matter for divine providence but I think I ought to be able to acquit myself reasonably... I am panicking really properly at the moment!'[43]

The 'spotting' work at the British Museum paid off well. 'The coins etc was a gem. I only got one definite mistake in which I assigned one of the casts to the wrong mint at Olympia, however as I got the date and everything [else] right that wasn't so bad. In the question on Duris I found myself remembering about fifty vases of his!' He positively enjoyed the archaeological paper. 'I of course wrote for the most on Egypt. Sculpture, architecture, painting – also the Hittites, Assyria (ivories at Ephesos and Layard at Nineveh) and Phoenicia. I suddenly thought of a new theory viz. that Greece owed nothing to Crete since the Dorians had sacked it and it was all Egypt. I might have written more, but I finished about a quarter to twelve and I knew it wasn't worth while adding things at the end and spoiling the symmetry.'[44]

A week after the Tripos was over John had his viva. 'I was asked: 1. A fragment of a steatite Minoan vase - which I knew. 2. A coin of Samos (which I dated to end of 5th instead of beginning of 4th) and a coin of Naxos. 3. An Early 'Classical' cylix which I dated and described all right after beginning badly, but finding out my mistake in time. 4. A fragment of the Parthenon frieze, just a boy's head, which very luckily I spotted.' But his examiners were giving nothing away and he came away worried. 'At the end – just as I thought they were going on to something else – Seltman said to Earp "Well what about going into the gallery of casts?" and Earp said "Oh I don't think we'd need bother – that's all right." Now does that mean I've got a certain first or so certain a second or third that it is hopeless to try and pull me up by means of the viva?'[45] He need not have worried. When the results came through, John had gained a first class in Part II of the Tripos with distinction in archaeology. He was also awarded the University Studentship at the British School at Athens and elected Beaston Scholar and Prizeman of Pembroke College.

Much to their delight, Bob Dixon was awarded a Craven Fund scholarship to study the 'same old dead languages' at the British School at Athens, though he was also elected to a Fellowship at Pembroke. In a letter to Darren Baillieu, Bob described the end of their final year. 'John Pendlebury drank more beer than anyone in the University, jumped six feet at Queen's and got a 1st in his trip – not a bad year.'[46]

'John had many brilliant contemporaries', recalled Rowe Harding later. 'Pembroke in his time was rich in Firsts and Blues, but no man of his generation had such amazing versatility – he could play the buffoon, or deliver an erudite lecture on the Egyptian Dynasties, or compose a string of verses or quote the classics with equal facility. As playboy, athlete and scholar he stood pre-eminent among his contemporaries, and I, who loved his humour, admired his athletic prowess and envied his wide learning and ease with which he carried it, am the richer for having known him.'[47]

3

October 1927–January 1928

ON OCTOBER 25th 1927, BOB Dixon was in Munich waiting for John. 'To-morrow John Pendlebury arrives', he wrote to Darren Baillieu. 'At 9.30 he will descend from the boat-train: at 9.45 we shall be sitting in the biggest Beer-palace in Munich drinking Münchener. The first toast I shall propose will be 'Ye Joyouse Companie and ytts firste Constable'.[1]

While Bob had spent a month in Berlin and Munich learning German, John had spent the summer touring Britain and Ireland with the Achilles Club, adding an international blazer to his trophies when he competed for England against France at Stamford Bridge. The British School of Archaeology at Athens had awarded John a Studentship and a grant of £100 to study in Greece, which was alternately awarded to Oxford and Cambridge. An Oxford graduate unexpectedly benefited when John declined the money, while still taking up the opportunity. Bob, having been awarded a grant from the Craven Fund, also planned to travel in Greece.

Armed with letters of introduction to museums from Alan Wace and Richard Dawkins (both former Directors of the British School), John and Bob aimed to travel by train through Vienna, Budapest, Belgrade and Sofia to Constantinople, from where they would sail to Athens, arriving in mid-November. They took Wace's letter to the Glyptothek and Alte Pinakothek, hoping to see the fine classical and Renaissance collections there, but found both museums closed. Munich left few favourable impressions on John, though their hotel was unlikely to forget him. 'A horrible incident this morning. I had a bath and – it being a fine morning – I was surprised to see the curtains were still drawn over the enormous window. These in high spirits and complete nudity I flung aside to find myself looking direct into the dining room which was filled with earnest but intensely interested breakfasters. Tableau!'[2]

They found Vienna more captivating. 'The Viennese are a great relief after the Germans – particularly their food! They seem much more casual and human. I suppose Austria must have been very severely hit by the war – at least their upper classes – because the Vienna of novels and one's imagination does not exist.'

They stayed with the Danube as far as Budapest, where they climbed up to the old castle of Buda to see the lights of the two cities, split by the river, stretched out below. Almost as splendid were the guests at their hotel – two fleeing Rumanian ministers and a 'most resplendent warrior in plumes and jewels and swords and a scarlet lined cloak.' Having been swindled out of some money by a man posing as a Bulgarian Consulate employee when they went to fetch their Bulgarian visas, they headed off towards Yugoslavia.

A slightly larger disruption to their plans was John's arrest as he got off the train in Belgrade without a transit visa. Bob displayed the diplomacy at which he would one day excel and eventually freed him from gaol, at which point a Serbian, who had befriended them on the train during a heated argument on European politics, took them under his wing. After introducing them to no less a personage than the Prime Minister, he led them on a Serbian pub-crawl through innumerable cafés, feasting on raki, garlic and ham. Before leaving, they introduced themselves to an ebullient Yugoslav archaeologist named Miloje Vassits, who was to make his name excavating at Vinca, a prehistoric site on the Danube near Belgrade, which produced finds very similar to those found in the Aegean. For two hours they talked of archaeology in rapid but broken French leaving just in time to catch their train.

They decided to give Sofia a miss after all the trouble with the visa, and headed from Serbia straight across Bulgaria. Crossing the border however was complicated by considerable ill will between the two countries – 'Each is raiding the other and we had great hopes of a battle on the frontier.' After Bulgaria had fought alongside Serbia and Greece in the first Balkan War to throw off their centuries-old occupation by Ottoman Turkey, Bulgaria had turned on her former allies to increase her own territory, resulting in her defeat in the second Balkan War. Seeing a chance to gain the coveted territories that were now part of northern Greece, Bulgaria had sided with Germany in the Great War, but was again thwarted. Skirmishes still occurred on Bulgaria's borders with both Greece and what was now Yugoslavia and there was a lingering mistrust of Bulgaria in the northern part of Greece through which John and Bob entered the country to cross east to the Greek-Turkish border.

They spent just one day in Constantinople, where they found their every move was watched. 'The police are horribly efficient, we were followed the whole time we were there.' It was with some relief that they sailed out of the city at dusk, through the Sea of Marmara and the Dardanelles, and out into the Aegean.

They reached the port of Piraeus on November 15th, where they found that Thomas Cook had lost John's trunk. So, with no more than the clothes he stood up in, John made his way with Bob up to the British School of Archaeology at Athens.

*

Athens at the time was a small and attractive city, its wide avenues, leading out of the central squares, lined with trees and elegant houses. Bustling cafés, humming with lively conversation, opened onto the pavements in and around Constitution Square. The School was on the fringes of Athens, perched on the slopes of Mount Lykabettos, looking out over the Evangelismos Hospital to the city. Beyond the Acropolis the Saronic Gulf stretched away to the south, framing the islands which had in antiquity been independent states, often at war with Athens.

Situated in beautiful grounds with a clay tennis court, which it shared with the American School of Archaeology, the main entrance to the British School was at the top of the garden on Odos Speusippou. To the east, Mount Hymettos rose up behind the Petraki monastery, in the olive grove of which the School had been built in 1886. The Upper House, which had been the original School, was a fine neo-classical house, surrounded by lawns and orchards. Founded to give students of the history, archaeology, literature, art and architecture of the Greek world the opportunity to carry out research in Greece, the School provided a forum for recent graduates and visiting academics alike. As the number of students increased at the end of the 19th century, an additional building for the students became necessary, leaving the original house as the Director's residence.

The students' hostel was built in a similar style in the garden below the Upper House. A path led down from the main gate to a clearing, where white marble steps led up to the heavy door. The door of the hostel opened into a hallway with a polished wooden floor, a fireplace opposite the entrance and a few Greek statues guarding the entrance. On the right of the hall was the Penrose Library, the walls of which were lined with books and journals covering every aspect of the classical world. It was lit by windows high up on the east side, through which the chimes of monastery bells could be heard, morning and evening.

The heart of the hostel was the Finlay, an elegant but comfortable library where students would relax or study in more comfort. The large stone fireplace faced two tall windows and a French window, which led out to a terrace overlooking the back garden. Well-thumbed leather and vellum-bound volumes lined every wall. These books had been the private collection of George Finlay, a friend of Lord Byron, who had spent many years travelling and amassing a library as varied in subject as his life had been in experience. Among many other books, he wrote a long and detailed history of the Greek War of Independence in which both he and Byron had played a part.

Opposite the Finlay was the dining room, where the students were joined at lunch and dinner by the Assistant Director and his wife, who also lived in the hostel. At the far end of the corridor a wide creaking staircase of rich dark wood led to the bedrooms and bathroom above. The hot water boiler in the bathroom was notoriously dangerous, having a tendency to blow its top. The top would then clatter down the stairs pursued by an alarmed and towel-clad student.

The hostel then had nine bedrooms, lining a dark corridor with a door at the end leading onto a terrace on the roof of the Penrose Library. Most of the rooms were long and narrow with a single shuttered window, and a small tiled fireplace across the corner for the cold winter evenings. The sparse furnishings gave each the clean austerity of a monk's cell. A double room – the first room on the right up the stairs – overlooked the front entrance to the hostel towards the Moni Petraki. This was where John and Bob were put.

The young men were rather unsure what to make of the School where they would be spending the best part of the coming winter and spring. The aura of learning only added to the rather monastic atmosphere. 'I only wish everyone wouldn't be so obviously learned to the eyebrows', John wrote to Herbert, 'It makes me feel such an impostor being here at all.'[3]

The School was the fullest it had ever been, largely with female students. They varied in age and purpose. There were schoolmistresses taking a year's sabbatical to see the country about which they taught; young graduates embarking on research projects at the start of archaeological careers; established academics in Greece for fieldwork; and one or two were, like Bob, there to explore the country and get a general knowledge of a subject before deciding on a profession. There was only one other male student, Oliver Davies, an Oxford Craven student studying ancient mines and metal sources, staying there when they arrived, but Bob commented acidly that the masculine minority was not much increased by his presence.

Bob found Winifred Lamb, Keeper of the Fitzwilliam Museum in Cambridge, clever but inhuman, and Sylvia Benton, 'an elderly school marm', as tough as nails and hard as a rock. Hilda White, the second of the schoolmistresses, on the other hand, made a favourable impression on John from the first. She reminded him of Vera Bayfield, the niece of their neighbour in Malvern, who married one of John's Cambridge friends, David Walker. 'The rest', he declared, 'are definitely sub-human.'[4]

Hilda was thirty-six, small and slim with an engaging smile and bright blue eyes. Her straight mouse-brown hair was cut in the short bob popular at the time, though earlier photographs show that long hair, piled on top of her head, suited her better, softening her features. She had gained a first class degree in Classics at Newnham College, Cambridge in 1915, and had gone straight into teaching. For the previous twelve years she had taught at St Bride's School, Helensburgh, near her home in West Kirby, the King Edward VI School in Louth and Bridlington High School on the North Yorkshire coast. By then a bored Senior Classics mistress, she had applied for a bursary to the British School and had arrived in Greece not long before John and Bob. Having formed a similar opinion of her fellow students, and feeling equally daunted, she was relieved at the arrival of two charming, intelligent and amusing young men. Born in 1891, her birthday a week before John's, she was thirteen years his senior.

*

The students at the School were each working on a specific project. All their trips were in some way tied in with their work: to see the remains of towns, cities or villages, and to track down the objects and pottery once in use there in the small district museums. For many of them it was their first experience of travelling in Greece, and of the difficulties involved in reaching the remoter sites in a country that had been at war for much of the past fifteen years. It was also their first chance to come to grips with modern Greek, which sounded utterly different from the classical Greek pronunciation that they had learned at school.

John's plan was to track down and publish all the finds of Egyptian origin down to 664 BC, the reign of the pharaoh Psammetichus I and the start of the 26th Dynasty. The chronology of Egypt up to that date, though still fluid, had more reliable 'anchors', established from ancient lists of the reigns of pharaohs. The sequence of Egyptian rulers had by then been quite well established from documentary sources and in excavation by, among others, Sir William Flinders Petrie. John's cut-off point marked the period when Egypt ceased to be so isolated from the other major empires of antiquity. Documentary evidence of campaigns against and within other civilizations around the Mediterranean and further east helped to fix with greater reliability the relative chronologies of the Mediterranean empires.

The dating of sites in the Aegean was less secure, so a catalogue of Egyptian pieces found on the Greek mainland and islands was essential in indicating a date for the deposits in which they were found. This could then be compared to other sites round the Aegean and a more secure dating system developed. It would only be an initial guide, for the finds could be misleading. For instance, an object could be an ancient 'antique', kept by later generations as a sort of heirloom. But where Egyptian finds occurred some idea could be gained of patterns of trade, and the cultural and artistic influences such trade connections brought. Wace had suggested the subject, not just because of John's growing knowledge of Greece and Egypt in the Bronze Age, but also because it was a work that was desperately needed by archaeologists in Greece. It was an important task and John found it daunting, as he admitted in the preface of the published catalogue, *Ægyptiaca*.[5]

Bob, meanwhile, had chosen to acquire a general knowledge of archaic Greek art, while Hilda was studying early red-figured vase-painting and Sylvia Benton Bronze Age routes and fortifications.

John, Bob and Hilda spent most of their first few days together. Within a week they had planned an exploratory trip up the east coast north of Athens towards Larissa with Margaret Rodger, the Oxford graduate from South Africa who had been awarded the £100 School Studentship that John had surrendered. Hilda had already, in her first fortnight in Greece, been broken in to the rigours of hill walking with the indomitable Winifred Lamb. In John's company, the experience of chasing vanishing paths, fending off vicious sheep dogs and the odd dubious shepherd, and arriving exhilarated if footsore, with only minutes of daylight left, at some remote inn or monastic hostelry, would prove invaluable.

Although the days were still warm, and often bathed in gentle sunlight, a sharp winter chill would settle as the sun disappeared. The large open fire was lit in the Finlay library and the students would flee from the bleak cold of the Penrose library, and gather around the hearth making their plans for exploring remote sites and long walks in open country.

Bob made a great impression on Hilda, and while John was struggling with the port authorities to retrieve his trunk, the two of them would go into town to the book club and have tea, or to the markets in Athens to buy supplies for the trip. 'He is a delightful and very brilliant boy,' Hilda wrote to her mother, 'and very beautiful to look at as well, with dark red hair and fair skin. You'd imagine that anyone with so many attractions would be hopelessly spoiled, but although he is a thorough young man of the world, and all things to all men, he's a delightful companion and noticeably considerate'.[6]

They began their trip at Chalkis and Eretria, the ancient enemy cities on the island of Euboea, across the narrow strait of the Euripos from the Boeotian coast. There was little left of Chalkis, which in early Hellenic times had been a great trading centre and port. There was more to be seen at Eretria, where they visited the remains of an ancient theatre, fortifications and harbour amongst the ruins of the city. The wealth of both cities had been founded on the local purple fisheries, but Chalkis had expanded further afield, setting up colonies in Chalkidiki and the western Mediterranean. John found an Egyptian alabaster vase in the museum, but like many of the Egyptian objects he found, its context was not certain, although it had been labelled as coming from a Mycenaean tomb in the area. The sight John found particularly appealing, though, was the

① GREECE

south Euboean Gulf, which separated the island from the mainland. Here, according to Homer, the Greek ships had once gathered around Aulis before setting off for the Trojan War.

The modern town of Chalkis had little to offer but a small picture palace, so rather than stay in their hotel all evening, they crept in to keep warm and watch the latest silent 'flick' to reach Greece. The hotel manager told them the boat to Volos would leave at eight the next morning, but they woke to find it had left at four – it was an old trick to get travellers to stay an extra night. So the following morning they awoke at four, and had to wait until eight. Hilda noticed that the locals treated such fluctuations in the timetable with equanimity. She wrote far more descriptive letters about the trip than either John or Bob, and described the scene to her mother. 'Here under the lamplight were gathered a little group of patient peasants with their bundles, waiting resignedly I suppose until some boat should be pleased to take them on board. Crouched under the lamp was a fisherman, as still as if he were carved in ebony, holding a long bending rod: the swirling water drew his line taut, and made hungry sucking noises round the steps and walls of the quay, but from over the dark water no sound came at all.'[7]

Eventually, out of the gloom, they heard the sound of oars in the water, and a small fishing boat emerged to take them to their boat to wait in more comfort. Bob and Margaret went to their cabins to sleep, but John and Hilda stayed on deck, spending the hours until they sailed singing songs like 'The Raggle-Taggle Gypsies-O', which John particularly loved because it reflected a freedom, an escape. To John, archaeology was rather like running off with the gypsies, sleeping under the stars and seeing places and things that others could only dream of.

'What care I for your goose-feather bed,
With blankets strewn so bravely-o,
Tonight I shall sleep in the wide open field,
Along with the raggle taggle gypsies-o.'

That Hilda loved the song too, and sang with him as they sat on the deck in the middle of the night, made a deep impression on John. Here, for the first time, was a woman who shared the outlook on life that John had first discovered on the trip with James Cullen, a woman to whom a life of archaeology was an exciting adventure.

The boat set sail at dawn, chugging slowly north past the ancient states of Locris, Phocis, Doris and Malis, past the narrow strip of land where 300 Spartan soldiers had fallen in battle against the Persian army of Xerxes at Thermopylae, towards the channel leading into the Gulf of Pagasae. As the day wore on and the sun rose higher, they basked in deckchairs. Soon their destination, Volos, came into view, a prosperous port, nestling at the foot of Mount Pelion, the home of Chiron and other mythical centaurs. The steep mountainsides were peppered with distant villages, which they set out to explore next day: to Dimini to see the Bronze Age beehive tombs, to the classical citadel of Pagasae, and up to the foothills of Pelion, overlooking the gulf below. Both Volos and Dimini had Bronze Age sites associated with them, and either could have been the site of the ancient city of Iolcos, the legendary kingdom that Jason left with the Argonauts in the *Argo* to search for the Golden Fleece. Wherever the student archaeologists looked they found some reference to the Greek myths to which they had been introduced by Charles Kingsley's *The Heroes*.

From Volos, they moved north-east through Thessaly, which had been won back from the Turks in 1881, towards the southern edge of Macedonia, retrieved by Greece in 1913 after the first Balkan War. Thessaly, legendary home of Achilles, was entirely surrounded by mountains, with only the Gulf of Pagasae giving access to the sea. Travelling slowly by train for most of the day, they arrived eventually at the small town of Kalabaka. The huge mass of the Pindus Mountains towered above them to their left as they approached, while in front, rising from the plain, the strange grey rock pinnacles of the Meteora loomed eerily out of the half-light of dusk. It was too late to find the monastery where they had hoped to stay that night, so they settled for a rather smelly little inn. Even the 'Flit' insect spray, with which Hilda had learnt to arm herself, did little to prevent the bugs making a meal of them.

Early next morning they set off with a guide from the village to the first of the monasteries they planned to see. Agios Stephanos and Agios Barlaam, like all the Meteora monasteries, sit high on the tips of gnarled fingers of grey streaked rock, their sheer sides worn smooth by wind and rain. For centuries, the only access had been in baskets, hauled up the side, until just after the Great War, when steps were carved out of the rock. The climb to the monastery was long and hard and they arrived at the top gasping, only to be told by the monk at the gate that entrance was forbidden to women. Hilda and Margaret Rodger were kept well supplied with ouzo, loukoumi and coffee, passed down to them in a basket, while John and Bob were royally welcomed inside.

Most of the Meteora monasteries were built in the 14th century, and their libraries were treasure houses of 10th- and 11th-century manuscripts of the Gospels and the Lives of the Saints. Alan Wace had compiled a catalogue of them in the past and had recommended that John and Bob try to see them. But the monks guarded them jealously and they were only given permission to see some of the less important examples. Bob had heard that Lord Curzon's father or grandfather, having bought some manuscripts from one monastery, was suspended in the descending basket in mid-air by the monks who regretted the deal they had made. John was rather more intrigued by all the relics of saints that they were shown – 'We saw the head of St Gregory of Nazianzus, the right hand of St Benedict and the left foot of St Chrysostom, all in jewelled cases'.[8]

On their monastic 'pub-crawl', John and Bob were presented with glass after glass of ouzo. Watched by the hospitable and eager eyes of each abbot, they could hardly refuse. The last two monasteries welcomed all four of them with open arms and open bottles as a cold grey mist began to wreathe itself around the rocks on which they stood. After five hours, four monasteries, three saints' relics and quantities of loukoumi, coffee and ouzo, they made their unsteady way across the Thessalian plain, and over the River Peneus by ferry to Larissa.

Catching the train at Larissa they arrived in the Vale of Tempe, cut through by the Peneus, flanked by willows and planes. Rising high above the river are the two mountains which it divides, Mount Ossa and Mount Olympus – the highest mountain in the Greek peninsula and legendary home of the gods. They managed to cross the pass, scrambling over rocky outcrops to avoid the railway tunnel, and sliding down the rocky face on the other side. The Athens train did not leave Larissa until the middle of the night, so they sat twice through another second-rate 'flick', and then sat in the station singing songs.

When they arrived back at the School in the first week of December 1927, William Heurtley, the Assistant Director, who had decided to excavate in the Chalkidiki peninsula, south-east of Thessaloniki, asked John to join him for the March season. John was delighted and wrote to his father, 'It has never been done before and ought to be very good fun. We are, I believe, apt to be cut off from all communication with the outside world for weeks, if the weather is bad. I am therefore at the moment sweating up the pottery liable to be discovered in the mounds, though as a matter of fact they don't really know at all what it will be like, except that it is rather Anatolian in character.'[9]

Deciding to leave their paperwork until the winter weather became too severe for walking trips, John, Bob and Hilda set off again, only days after arriving back from Meteora, heading for the Argolid and Mycenae. It was Sylvia Benton, the other former schoolmistress, who travelled with them this time. Hilda was rather wary of her. 'She is one of these terribly athletic people who always have to be better at things than anyone else: I don't take to her much, she's so very superior.'[10] Sylvia Benton was indeed a formidable woman, who had played hockey and tennis for Cambridge. She had infuriated the Director,

Arthur Woodward, when on her arrival she had climbed on her own the precipitous and dangerous Mount Taygetos in the western Peloponnese, although he had expressly forbidden her to do so. Knowing her own capabilities, she had simply ignored him; he responded by refusing to re-admit her to the School the following session.

At Mycenae the group stayed at the famous 'Belle Hélène', where John and James Cullen had lodged four years earlier. Hilda, on an earlier visit with Winifred Lamb, had described it in a letter to her family: 'The inn has a small verandah upstairs in front and a big one at the back and has big pepper trees almost hiding it in front. There is a yard at the back and another building where cooking etc. is done and where Dimitri and Constantine seem to spend a good deal of their time. The inn itself, on the ground floor, is one big bare room paved with black and white square slabs of stone, and with a door back and front and two big windows. It is high and very cool and airy. There are bunches of grapes, a melon or so and a few pomegranates hanging from the rafters making bright patches of colour. At one end are shelves filled with wines, mineral waters, cigarettes, tinned goods. A cupboard, three or four small tables and a number of kitchen chairs with rush seats complete the furnishing. The whole family serve at meals and chat happily meanwhile... Spiros is butler to the excavating party at Sparta each spring, so is a great man.'[11]

The family gave them a tremendous welcome. Dimitri Dassis was of Albanian descent, while his wife was from the village of Harvati, now generally known as Mycenae after the ancient city. Orestes, the youngest, was away doing his military service at the time. Helen, who was twenty-three, was a charming looking young woman, and became the Belle Hélène of the village. It was Spiros, however, whom they got to know best. As well as being an archaeological butler, he acted as a guide on long walks in the area. He was an intense looking young man, slim, with a fine, gaunt face, and considerable presence.

After dinner the four students went round the hill in the moonlight towards the citadel, and climbed into the 'Treasury of Atreus'. They took a candle with them and clambered down into the dromos. Deep in the dark, dank, silent tomb, they settled uneasily while John spun stories of ghosts and vampires, as Alan Wace had done before him.

Over the next few days, they explored what was left of the once powerful heart of the Mycenaean civilization. The magnificent citadel of Mycenae, still rumoured in classical times to be 'rich in gold', centuries after its demise, stood on a rocky outcrop between two river valleys in the low hills to the north of the Argive Plain. In the excavations carried out over the previous half century, the citadel had indeed yielded some exquisite works of art – ivory, silver, bronze, rock crystal and wall paintings, as well as gold. The site had also yielded Egyptian objects, particularly of 18th-Dynasty date, which had prompted Alan Wace to suggest the catalogue to John.

Looming high above the citadel of Mycenae to the east were two large hills, Mount Prophitis Elias and Mount Zara. From the citadel, its ancient defenders could look south from their stronghold, down the valley between Mount Zara and the low ridge in front of the citadel where the grander tombs such as the 'Treasury of Atreus' were built, towards the flat and fertile Argive Plain. Watchtowers high in the hills around would give warning of an impending attack, long before the enemy came near, and, for Clytaemnestra, notice of her ill-fated husband's imminent return. The Mycenaean strongholds of Midea and Asine were perched in the low hills around the plain, and others, like Tiryns, sat on the plain itself. They were all heavily fortified with massive Cyclopean walls, presenting a sheer and impenetrable mass of masonry up to seven metres thick, which still survived at Mycenae to a height of over eight metres, and higher still at Midea.

All the Bronze Age towns in the region were linked by ancient roads, guarded at intervals by forts. Traces of these roads could still be seen, so the two most energetic members of the party, John and Sylvia Benton, set off along one of them, following it for about ten miles and discovering forts on the way. John, tireless as ever, then climbed to the top of Mount Prophitis Elias to search for one of Agamemnon's recently-excavated watchtowers – from which the beacon announcing his return, after ten years in the Trojan War, would have been seen and the message passed to his waiting queen and assassin.

On his way back to the 'Belle Hélène', John trekked over the low Panagia ridge to see again by daylight the tomb of the night before and the eight other great tholos tombs that, along with many smaller ones, pierce the slopes of the surrounding hillsides. Even Sylvia Benton was hard put to keep up with him.

Miss Benton seemed a rather odd creature to the others. Fiercely competitive and a dedicated 'manager', she was not content merely to be involved in a trip, but had to take over its organisation. When Bob and John began changing their plans for the Argolid trip in order to escape an expedition, the planning of which had been totally usurped by her, Hilda felt she ought to try and steer Miss Benton away. 'I do see the point of view of the boys', she explained in a letter to her family, 'who are keen on paddling their own course and whose independence isn't so long established that they've ceased to value it extremely.'[12]

The forty-year-old Miss Benton had been a teacher since graduating from Girton College, Cambridge in 1910. Unlike Hilda, who was on a year's sabbatical, she had given up teaching to devote herself to archaeology. Her harsh and abrupt manner did not immediately endear her to those around her. In manner, very much a spinster 'school marm' of her time, she was domineering and yet, at the same time, rather naive and ill at ease. However, her diaries reveal an almost childlike pleasure and enthusiasm for things. At last out of the school life she had always known, she found herself in the company of an intelligent, attractive and enthusiastic young man, and she was completely *bouleversée*. She sought John's company at every opportunity, but he was embarrassed by her interest and tried, as unobtrusively as possible, to discourage her. In her diary of the Argolid trip she wrote, 'I arranged to go to the Argolid with four other people. What could be more prosaic? Four others resolved themselves into one very charming young man.'[13]

They all returned to Athens by different routes for Christmas. Hilda wrote to her mother, 'Athens really looks quite festive, with a good deal of coloured paper about and stalls with toys and oddments of all sorts along Aeolus Street, and carollers going from shop to shop with triangles and drums or pipes.'[14] In spite of this, they all felt a little homesick, including John, who while not particularly pious, did enjoy the more traditional occasions. 'We went to church on Christmas Eve to a Carol Service at the English Church, but on Christmas Day it was so packed that we couldn't get a seat anywhere at any service. It rather depressed me. But I hope the intention was counted to me for righteousness!'[15]

At New Year, the students went down to the quay at Piraeus to watch an ancient ritual – the dipping of a crucifix into the harbour to bless the waters. It was performed by the marvellously bedecked Archbishop of Athens, attended by a dignitary carrying four white pigeons with blue ribbons tied around their legs, which were loosed as the cross was lowered down to the water on a ribbon and submerged. At that moment a salvo was fired and all the hundreds of boats that had packed around to glimpse the ceremony sounded their sirens and whistles to welcome the blessing of the waters.

As soon as Christmas and New Year were over, the students got back to work. By now they had all settled in well, felt comfortable with each other and, as John wrote to his father, the society was very good indeed.

*

1928 brought cold weather and a renewed determination in John to get out to the countryside and complete the work for his catalogue. He still had to see the collections on the islands of Aegina and Crete; he hoped to do the first while attempting a walk not done for a hundred years, from Hermione to Poros. He had originally planned to do this on their first trip to the Argolid, but had slipped his knee at the last moment and so had to return early to Athens.

Curiously, the knee slip had loosened an old injury and allowed John more flexibility than he had had for months. As a trained athlete at his peak, he yearned for hard exercise, and playing tennis at the School did not quite fulfil the need. William Heurtley encouraged the students to play hockey at the nearby Panathenaikos football ground, and John, Hilda and Sylvia all joined in. However, it was the running and high jump that John missed most – until a mysterious announcement appeared in the local paper. As he explained to his father, 'Tomorrow I am taking my first gentle turn on the track. I have joined the Constantinople Athletic Club – an announcement of which appeared in the paper before I even knew there was such a club. My name was spelt Πεντμπερυ [Pentmpery]!'[16] This was a spin-off from a visit the Achilles Club had made to Athens the summer before, when its members had been offered honorary membership of a number of Greek athletics clubs. It delighted John to be back on the track, and he felt he had 'all the spring in the world'. 'I think that I shall have a good chance of the Greek record. It is only 6' or just under I think.'[17]

In the first week of January, John set off with Heurtley across the Isthmus of Corinth to the Argolid, where they joined Sylvia Benton in Nauplion. On their arrival, Sylvia noticed a difference in John's manner towards her. In trying not to encourage her, he had become rather awkward in her company. Miss Benton suspected that John was becoming increasingly fond of Hilda, but she felt that his cool manner was due less to that than to what the others might have said to him: 'Pendlebury, the Cambridge Blue... has thrown me over for another woman! I don't mind that but they must have told him something nasty for he had difficulty in being polite.'[18]

The atmosphere became more relaxed as they made their way across the peninsula from Nauplion to Old Epidauros. They took a car via the Mycenaean bridge and Hellenic fortress at Kasarmi, and on to Ligourio, planning to walk on from there with the help of a local guide. When they arrived they found the town celebrating the feast of Epiphany. 'Consequently', Miss Benton wrote, 'no one was very anxious to put off his black broadcloth and conduct us over the mountains to Kato Phanari. A man was found, but the bargain languished ('it was nine hours; we should be up to our waists in mud; it was an incredibly bad track'), when up spake an elder "I will take you for 100 drachs and start at once." So said, so done.'[19] Thus they set off with the guide and a mule to carry the baggage.

As dusk was falling they reached Ano Phanari, some two thousand feet above the sea far below, looking out across the hills of Methana and the myriad tiny islands to the hills of Attica beyond. Night had closed in on them by the time they reached their destination at Kato Phanari, a thousand feet down the other side of the mountain. Miss Benton was so delighted that, as she put it, 'I went fay and danced down, as Heurtley rudely said, like a wild goat'.[20]

They moved up a long valley, its slopes covered with arbutus, and down into a streambed, past a ferocious sheep dog, with, Miss Benton noted, 'fangs showing and just not daring to spring on the point of the stick Pendlebury held ready to receive it. I broke up the tableau by heaving a brick at it'.[21] Then they trekked upwards until they reached a gap in the hills.

Next day their walk took them down the coast to where the island of Poros was barely separated from the mainland. John wanted to see, among the ruins of Kalauria, the ancient temple to the sea god Poseidon, who was so prominent in John's favourite Greek legend, that of Theseus, born in nearby Troizen. Ancient Troizen had gone completely; it was thought to be beneath the picturesque village of Damala, which clung to the mountainside above the coast. Poseidon, 'earth-shaker' as well as sea god, was propitiated with good reason in the area around the volcanic Methana peninsula.

The historic part of their walk, from Poros to Hermione, took them next morning south-west high into the hills of the peninsula. The view was more breathtaking than John could have imagined. 'We went up a terrific gorge to the top of the ridge where we had the most magnificent view I've ever seen in my life. We could see Parnassos, Helicon, the Attic Mountains, Tinos, and the Cyclades, the hills of Arcadia, Cyllene and Chelmos and the whole length of Parnon right down to Cape Malea.'[22]

In the afternoon they descended to Hermione to meet their boat. They steamed past the south-east point of the Argolid, and after a brief stop at Spetses, 'A beautiful island where the brother of the headmaster of Tonbridge is trying to start a Public School', cut across to Leonidhi, up to Astros and finally reached Nauplion again.[23]

The next day Heurtley left for Athens while John and Sylvia returned in the same steamer, this time touching at Hydra and Poros, and passing the huge volcanic hills of Methana, which they had seen from far up in the hills a couple of days before. Hilda and Bob had planned to join them on the island of Aegina, but the Master of Pembroke, W.S. Hadley, had died suddenly on Christmas Day. As a Fellow of the College, Bob had to wait in Athens to see whether he would be summoned back to help elect a new Master. So Hilda went to meet them alone.

On Aegina, Miss Benton finally accepted that John was genuinely taken with Hilda, seeing how he opened up in her company in a way that he had never done with her. 'I never saw the boy happier or more charming than he was that evening, talking athletics and old Cambridge days.'[24] It was with some relief that John and Hilda saw Miss Benton off on her boat back to Athens, for they had spent little time alone together before. They took a small caïque with a triangular sail out onto the water for the afternoon, returning for dinner in the village and a rather soggy walk in the rain. The following morning they took a small steam yacht, which rolled all the way back to Athens in the swell. They sat out on deck, preferring the cold wind and spray on their faces to the grim interior where passengers were heaving along with the boat.

Back in Athens, they found that all the students of the School were to be invited to a party at the British Legation. 'After dinner John took me out to dance for a little in practice for the great dance. He dances well and is very keen on it. He is the one who is a Cambridge high jump Blue and a runner as well', Hilda explained to her mother, who had heard more about Bob than John up to this point.[25]

The dance was a grand affair, as John described to Herbert. 'We had the privilege of seeing the Turkish minister Djavid Bey and Madame Kapodistrias do a Turkish dance. They both weigh about eighteen stone but I've never seen anyone move so well.'[26] Also at the dance was the beautiful Ismene Atchley, the half-Greek daughter of Shirley Atchley, who worked at the Legation. Bob Dixon was smitten and soon afterwards they began an affair.

John and Hilda, too, began to spend more and more time together, going on long walks within Athens, and returning at the end of January on their own to Mycenae. 'We had a marvellous time', John wrote to his father. 'The family adopted us as one of themselves. I became Κυριος Τζον [Mister John] and Hilda, Δεσποινις Χιλδα [Miss Hilda].'[27] The plain of Argos was by now a fresh green carpet of young crops beneath the still snow-covered Mount Cyllene, and the weather was perfect for walking. In the evenings John and Hilda would stroll round the village, or up to the acropolis to watch the moon rise. One night they came across a dance around a large bonfire in the village square. Invited to join in, they were captivated by the enchantment of the firelit figures moving round, led first by one dancer and then another. In two of the dancers, John saw an echo of Socrates and Alcibiades. 'A man, very ugly but a beautiful mover, was leading the dance. He suddenly jumped into the crowd and pulled out a little boy whom he made to take his place. The child was just like a faun, jumping about and eluding him.'[28]

Such experiences drew the pair even closer, and John found himself falling for Hilda. She was charming yet tough, and she enjoyed travelling rough just as much as he did. However, for Hilda it was no more than a pleasant fling; she admitted in a letter to her family that she could not imagine there would be a future for them once they left Greece and the magic of the place wore off.

Hilda was so very different from John's two ideal women. She bore little comparison with the elegant, sensuous beauty of Nefertiti or the tall, slender, flaxen-haired Jehane St Pol, her icy cool exterior hiding a seething passion. But, although she could be rather difficult and catty, she was amusing and intelligent company. John was an athletic, intelligent twenty-three-year-old, attractive, yet not, according to Hilda, as striking as Bob, and he found her irresistible. His relationship with Hilda caused a scandal in School circles, not least because of the thirteen-year age difference, which led to suggestions that he was looking for a mother figure. Although the disparity in their ages made them a peculiarly matched pair, their very differences in temperament meant that they complemented each other well.

4

February–November 1928

'WE HAD LEFT PIRAEUS punctually, half an hour late. The ship was filled with soldiers who had never seen the sea before and never wanted to see it again. That night will remain in my memory as the most unpleasant I had ever spent.' John's first journey to Crete, in February 1928, did not start auspiciously. 'The soldiers lay about the deck in heaps, completely overcome. Some gave themselves up for lost and prayed to die; some were too far gone even for that and despairingly made offerings to Poseidon. We could not walk a yard without stepping on a face. There was one alone who survived; an Athenian policeman sat below one of the companionways and mocked them. It was a judgement, he said, for stealing a cheese earlier in the evening, and full restoration was demanded.'[1]

As they sailed into the port of Candia, or Heraklion as it was increasingly called, they saw a pretty town surrounded by Venetian fortifications. Mount Iuktas, a large outcrop of rock on the horizon behind, towered above the low rolling hills around, bounded to east and west by walls of mountains. Candia was the old Venetian name for both the town and the island but, since the ousting of the Turks, a more Hellenic name had been found in 'Heraklion'. The name Candia was an Italian corruption of the Arabic word *khandaq*, the defensive ditch around the town built by the Andalucian Moors when they had occupied the island 1100 years earlier. The Moors stayed a mere 137 years – a comparatively short time for Crete's invaders – until Nikephoros Phokas mustered enough forces to recapture the island for the Byzantine Empire and bring it under the aegis of Constantinople for another 243 years.

In 1204, the Venetians bought the island for a trifling sum in the carve-up of the Byzantine territories seized by the Fourth Crusade and held onto it for just over four and a half centuries. While the Venetians ruled in Crete, though, a new power was rising. Halfway through their stay on the island, the balance of power in the East shifted away from the Byzantine Empire, which eventually collapsed along with Constantinople in 1453. The new power in the East was the Sultanate of the Ottoman Turks. The Venetians resisted the Ottoman advance for 216 years, but finally relinquished most of Crete to its second Muslim occupation in 1669. After a twenty-one-year siege, the well-fortified town of Candia surrendered, its elegant and robust defences built largely of stone from the nearby ancient city of Knossos. It took another fifty years for the Venetians to give up the forts of Souda and Gramvousa at the western end of the island and of Spina Longa in the east.

The Turks held Crete until 1898 when, after war between Greece and Turkey was sparked by the violent struggle for freedom on the island, the Great Powers – Britain, France and Russia – intervened. Each occupied a part of the island, the British taking responsibility for Candia. When the violence continued Crete was granted autonomy under the continued suzerainty of the Ottoman Court, all Turkish soldiers were sent off the island and Prince George, the younger son of King George I of the Hellenes, was sent to Crete as High Commissioner. A Cretan Assembly was formed, the most prominent member of which was Eleutherios Venizelos, Minister for Foreign Affairs and Justice. This outstanding statesman played a leading role in Greek politics for the next three and a half decades. Prince George's rule, and the fact that the Cretans did not want to remain under the power of the 'Sublime Porte', led to an uprising on the island, resulting in the resignation and replacement of the Prince. The Cretans finally achieved *enosis* – union with Greece – in 1913, during the settlement at the end of the Balkan Wars.

When John and Hilda arrived in Crete with their friends, Vivien Whitfield and Margaret Rodger, only fifteen years had passed since the island had been united with Greece. Its Turkish past, however, was already being expunged methodically from the landscape, with the clearance of extensive acres of Muslim graveyards that had lined the road between Candia and Knossos, and the dumping of the gravestones.

*

John and Hilda found that, in spite of all the bloodshed of the recent past, the Cretans were warm and hospitable far beyond the level of common courtesy, and had a sense of humour that appealed to John. After dinner on their first evening, they met the British Vice-Consul in Candia, Mr M.N. Elliadi, whose old-fashioned manners Hilda found utterly charming. Elliadi and his wife invited them to go dancing at the Café Doré, assuring them that their travelling clothes were perfectly suitable. Elliadi became a good friend in later years and would try to teach John how to make his wartime cover as British Vice-Consul as convincing as possible.

Their journey to eastern Crete started in torrential rain, but they fired themselves up on the way with 'an early but necessary glass of cognac (a polite name for nearly raw spirits)'.[2] Bone-shaken and dazed from the appalling road, they arrived at the village of Chersonesos drenched, and headed straight for the small inn. This was to set the pattern for all John's later journeys: at the village wine-seller you could always learn about pottery, walls or other archaeological finds that might have turned up in the local vineyards. John could hold rather more alcohol than most and the Cretans were very generous with their light local wine and *raki*, the strong spirit distilled from pressed grape-skins, both of which John found very palatable.

The wine-seller built a fire of brushwood on the earthen floor, and they dried their clothes, huddling for warmth, while they ate potato omelettes and 'installed a little central heating' in the form of wine. As soon as they stepped outside they were mobbed by a crowd of small boys who had heard that the strangers were interested in local antiquities. John, whose love of things ancient did not extend to the Romans, was shown 'the most revolting mosaic pavement it has ever been my misfortune to see. Luckily the rest of the building to which it belonged has disappeared.'[3]

Descending through groves of carob and olive trees, they returned to the coast to splash around the rather washed-out site of Mallia, where a Minoan palace had been under excavation by the École Française d'Athènes since 1922. With its magnificent southern backdrop of the Lasithi Mountains, Mallia lay on the flat of the coastal plain, which every spring was thick with tall grasses and wild flowers. Now it was out of season so they had the site to themselves.

Although the palace at Mallia follows a similar design to that at Knossos (which Sir Arthur Evans and the British School at Athens had been excavating), it is very different in character. The warmth of the dark red soil gives an orange glow to the rocks and ground alike, while Knossos is as pale and silvery as the local clay – *kouskouras* – on which it sits.

An article John wrote gives a first glimpse of the hold that Crete was beginning to have on him, and of his irrepressible need to share his love of the island and its people. Near the top of a gorge they encountered a figure who might have walked straight out of an Edward Lear sketch. 'There fell in with us an old Cretan gentleman in all the glory of his native dress, his headcloth, his slashed waistcoat, a shot-silk sash round his narrow waist, his great baggy blue breeches and his high polished boots. I know of no sight finer than a well-dressed Cretan peasant, and with the dress goes a swing and a lightness of foot which always sets me thinking of the slim athletes of Minoan days.'[4]

This was John's first encounter with a true country Cretan. His picturesque costume and an agility that belied his years appealed greatly to John. So, too, did his humour, and 'the most beautiful articulation I had ever heard. We chatted for a little about the weather and then he turned and looked at the three ladies who made up the party: he considered for a moment or two and then said to me, "Are you a Turk?" This *mot* gave him the utmost pleasure and seemed likely to last him for a considerable time, as even after we had said good-bye we

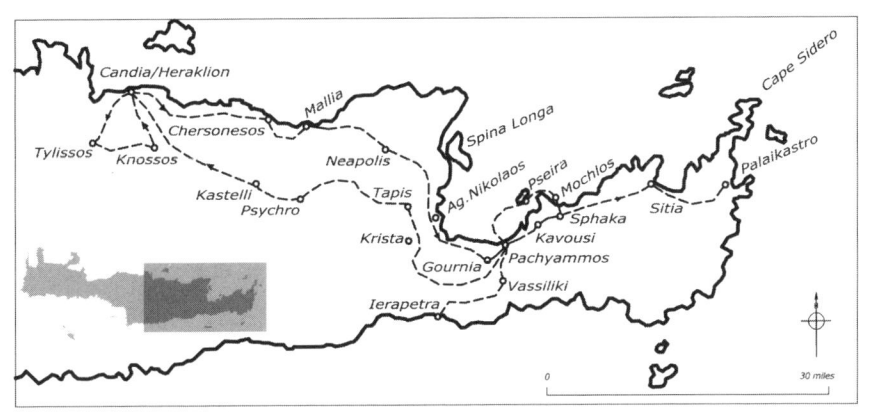

1928 ROUTE

could see him shaking with laughter as he walked away.'[5]

They walked on out of the pass and dropped to an upland plain full of flowers, with the town of Neapolis lying ahead. The town looked imposing from above, with its cathedral and tree-filled squares amid the red-tiled roofs, but close up they found it very odd. 'Persons of the female sex may not sit in the front of cars but modestly behind with the rest of the luggage. This is so that the chauffeur may not be distracted, though what is to prevent him from turning right round, and taking his eye right off the road, I do not know. Still I am sure vice has been stamped out in Neapolis. There are no night clubs (any more than there are in the rest of Crete); mixed bathing is not allowed (and private bathing is not much practised); cocktails are unknown (the favourite order being a double methylated).'[6]

They hired a car and driver and went on towards the small fishing town of Agios Nikolaos on the Gulf of Mirabello.[7] Eastwards from the southern edge of the Gulf, the coast was like a serrated knife of small coves and inlets with white cliffs, and in a letter to Herbert, John described it as one of the most beautiful walks of his life. A highway in later years sliced through this coast, but in 1928 the anemones were out beside the track that ran along the top of the cliffs. 'The water far out is that lazy violet colour which is the meaning of that resonant adjective οινοψ (wine-dark): closer in to the shore it turns into a deep peacock blue so clear that to see the stones thirty feet below the surface is nothing unusual. Tiny islands hang off the coast, broken from the mainland and tilted at strange angles, islands that have no life but the screaming gulls; islands that must have been the death of many a fine tall ship in the days when the sailor hugged the coast even when he had to travel by night.'[8]

Most of this coastline was terrible for farming, though they passed young boys out in scraggy fields, pushing rough wooden plough-shares through the hard, stony earth, pulled by 'a yoke of heavy swing-footed oxen', and piling the stones at the edge of the field. 'It is a sign of the unconquerable optimism of the Greeks that they have been doing this for countless generations, doubtless hoping to get down to stoneless soil. It is an unfounded hope. These stones were put there by some god as a primitive joke and he has not seen that the joke has gone far enough. The Greek peasant has more work for less reward than any peasant in the world. I will say that the grain tries to back him up as much as it can, and perches itself in incredible positions on rocks and half-way down cliffs, but even that cannot produce a really rich crop.'[9]

Soon they came upon a hollow where, cradled in a dip in the rock, lay the bones of the small Minoan town of Gournia. Between 1901 and 1904 the site had been excavated by the American archaeologist Harriet Boyd, of the University of Pennsylvania. One of the pioneers of Minoan archaeology, she eventually married the anthropologist Charles Henry Hawes, who had been studying the ethnic origins of the Cretans by measuring their skulls. Both had been in Crete at the height of the insurgence against the Turks, a very violent time for both communities.[10]

The Late Minoan town, which clings to the hillside, is a warren of small alleys and minor dwellings, tightly packed around a central miniature version of the Minoan palaces, known as the Governor's House. The houses of Gournia yielded in abundance the tools of the people who had once lived there – fishermen, stone masons, metal-workers, weavers and potters. It had been ravaged by fire at the same time as many of the other Late Minoan centres, in about 1450 BC. Though some inhabitants stayed on, the town was finally abandoned in about 1200, and gradually vanished from sight.

In its excavated state some of the walls stand over six feet, though there were no defence walls. Set back from the sea and protected by the hollow – or *gournia* – in which it sat, there was no need for the heavy defences common on the mainland. John found it a romantic place. 'The whole town must have given very much the impression of a modern Greek village except that at the top rose the castle of the local baron. You enter between houses and are almost at once in a network of streets. House is built up against house. There are no open spaces or courtyards. The street by which you have entered rises quickly by steps up to and beyond the long circling street that runs round the whole site about halfway up. The house fronts on this encircling terrace-road present a strangely modern appearance, with the steps up to the front doors. All the streets are paved with cobbles and between them grew anemones of every colour. Later in the year come the grasshoppers, which spring with a whirr as you put your feet down. Narrow little streets they are with hardly room for two to pass. A mule with much baggage must have been a great nuisance if it passed as one wanted to go out hurriedly.'[11]

They stopped for the night at the house of the late Richard Seager at Pachyammos, in the south-east corner of the Gulf of Mirabello. Seager, an American archaeologist, had been a close friend of Sir Arthur Evans. His work at Mochlos and Vasiliki had thrown precious light on the early stages of the Minoan civilisation, until his untimely death three years earlier in 1925. The house that he had built at Pachyammos, not far along the coast from Gournia, was a beautiful single-storey villa enclosing an open courtyard that gave shelter from the strong winds that blast through the isthmus of Ierapetra in late spring. The stone was softened by flowering bushes and shrubs, large geraniums and cascades of honeysuckle, and terracotta pots overflowed with plants. A cobbled path wound round the terrace leading to the rooms, each of which opened on to the courtyard. Seager had left the house to Nikolaos Saridakis, foreman of his excavations, on the understanding that Saridakis should always keep the house ready for visiting scholars. For many years it was a quiet and peaceful retreat after long walks round the island, and the welcome from Saridakis and his family, who lived across the plain at Kavousi, was always warm and generous.[12]

The following evening, the party arrived at Sitia in time to find a place to stay and a muleteer for the next day, but it was far from being a peaceful night. 'Of the night we spent I am not prepared to speak. Let me only say that by morning there was standing room only on me.'[13] John composed a rhyme in honour of his voracious companions, to be sung to the tune of the British Grenadiers:

'Some talk of being bitten and some of being bit,
By wasp or bee or hornet or by the humble "nit",
But of all the world's best biters you can commend to me,
The best of all is what we call the homely little flea.'[14]

When their muleteer arrived in the morning, they headed off again, climbing onto the high plateau of the east of the island. This limestone tract is far more wild and desolate than the rest of Crete. But every so often, towards the coast, it is cut by deep river gorges, brightened by oleander bushes even when the water is low.

They were making for the east coast, where the site of Palaikastro lay on the flat and fertile land between the plateau and the sea. Here, at the turn of the century, the British School, under the direction of Richard Dawkins and Reginald Carr Bosanquet, had excavated the remains of an extensive and prosperous Minoan town, a centre for the cult of Zeus. The town had overlooked the Kasos straits, one of the main sea routes between the Aegean and the North African coast, which separated the islands of Kasos and Karpathos from Cape Sidero, the north-eastern tip of Crete. John loved the wildness and isolation of the place. 'I have seen it from the sea on the way to Egypt', he wrote later, letting his imagination run free, 'and the impression is that of a new-discovered land, or a forgotten wilderness. It is thousands of years since the merchant princes of Palaikastro vied with the High King of Knossos in the possession of the finest painted frescoes and the most magnificent pottery; thousands of years since the Egyptian traders came creeping in with their fine spices and their proud tales of conquest. Though the Achaean sea-wolves never seem to have come raging and plundering into the place, Palaikastro dwindled and died when the power of Minoan Crete fell and seas were full of pirates, the bane of honest men. Sponge fishing is now the chief trade of the men of the east, and an arduous unprofitable job it is.'[15]

Unable to explore the site itself, as it had long since been reburied to protect the ruins, they went down instead to the rocks and the wide sandy beach only a few hundred yards away and bathed in the cool, clear water. As they swam, John's mind was full of the past, alive with the people who had once bustled through the busy town and on the now deserted shore, and he imagined how the water, now so still and quiet, hid the 'forgotten track of some old world galley'.[16]

On their way back west towards the village of Sphaka, the heavens opened. They plodded up the steep paths, drenched to the skin, towards the village where they had stopped on the journey east. John came across a dignified old gentleman standing in the doorway of the village *kapheneion*. When he saw John's bedraggled figure he came out and led him in to the warmth of the inn. Having heard that they were the same people who had walked through some days before, he took John by the hand again and drew him through the narrow streets to the family with whom they had stayed. 'I have never had such a feeling of dropping back through the centuries to the days of the Good Samaritan. He was disappointed that courtesy to his neighbour prevented him from doing all the entertaining by himself, but as soon as I reached George's house, he hurried out into the rain again, sent a messenger to bring the rest of our party along to the right house and soon returned himself, laden with bottles and jars of brandy and wine.'[17]

Their hosts welcomed them again with delight and found the soaked travellers some clothes to wear while their own dried. After a steaming lunch and time to dry by the fire, they set out again into warm sunshine. The wind that had raged through the night had died down by now, and they were able to find a caïque to take them across to the islands of Pseira and Mochlos. The waves slapped against the small boat's bows as it crossed the narrow strait, and an hour later they pulled in to the small cove that was harbour to the island of Pseira and clambered ashore.

The Minoan town, with its narrow lanes and tightly-packed houses, lay on the lee side of the island, scaling the hill above the tiny natural harbour, and was reached by a long stairway from the water.

John had a horror of small boats, and the journey to Mochlos had them all contemplating swimming to safety. 'It was a terrifying voyage. Our boat leaked at every seam,' he wrote to his father. 'I got as far as undoing my puttees once – and the girls were taking off their coats!'[18] But Mochlos, crowned with a small ruined fort, was worth the journey. The small settlement lay along the shoreline, while the Early Minoan tombs that Seager had excavated were over on the west side. The Mochlos Treasure that had come from the latter contained some exquisite jewellery and fine stone vessels of mottled blue, grey and white stone, quarried from the cliffs on the north side of the island.

Turning to look out to sea, John's exhilaration faded fast. 'Converging on us seemed to be all the white horses of the Aegean.'[19] During the journey back the waves grew enormous and the spray leapt fifty feet in the air, crashing against the rocks that seemed to get closer every second. 'First the stern rose high and we could see all around us; then for an instant the boat stayed level and the propeller snarled into space; then the bows rose and we seemed to be slipping astern into the next threatening giant.'[20] They came eventually under the lee of Pseira and into momentary calm. The crew began to sing 'what sounded suspiciously like a death wail', but Poseidon was kind and they chugged eventually into the haven of Pachyammos.[21]

Their final visit was to Lasithi and the Diktaean Cave at Psychro, a shrine at which rich votive offerings had been left from the Middle Minoan to the Geometric period, and which had been excavated at the turn of the century by D.G. Hogarth. Here a little Egyptian bronze statuette of Amen-Re of the 18th or 19th Dynasty had been found; it was already at least three hundred years old when it was placed in the cave as an offering. This highlighted one of the problems of the task John was undertaking. 'One must go cautiously in using the discoveries for dating purposes', John wrote in the introduction to the finished catalogue. 'Several stone vases of the Old Kingdom have turned up in deposits thousands of years later. Other objects too may have been kept as heirlooms or bought as "genuine antiques" in Egypt itself. Not all the scarabs which bear the name of Thothmes III date from his time. His name was one to conjure with, not only in Egypt but, for hundreds of years after his death, in Syria, where, like Richard Coeur de Lion, he was the bogey of children and the cause of all unknown fear. For Cyprus, too, which he may actually have conquered as he claims, hundreds of scarabs bearing his name were made as amulets more than a thousand years later.'[22]

There were several mountain routes up to the high upland plain of Lasithi, and they took the route via Kritsa and Tapis. On the way they found a small taverna, every wall of which was covered with pictures of old soldiers, brigands and statesmen. The majority of the pictures were of Eleutherios Venizelos, the Cretan statesman, who had retired from political life in 1924 but was soon to return to Athens to become, in 1928, Prime Minister of Greece for the fifth time. From Tapis the path climbed up and up. Far below they could see the small villages clinging to the slope, the Dionysiades Islands 'hanging off the crags like sea-gulls following a ship', and way off in the east, the plateau of Sitia that they had crossed a few days before.[23] The sun blazed on their backs, as the summit they were heading for seemed ever to recede from view. Hilda described it to her mother and sister. 'The first part of the walk was simply lovely – winding in and out above coves of the Gulf of Mirabello, and it was sunny and the water very blue. Then we began to climb and at about twelve we came to the mountain village of Tapis where we had lunch. We have been seeing the most wonderful anemones everywhere and this day saw some bright crimson ones – lovely things.'[24]

As they reached the shoulder of the Katharos Pass, flanked by Mount Dikte, the sun vanished behind a sudden, thick mist that enveloped them, cutting from view the world below. In no time, the mist had turned into a snow blizzard and, wrapping their coats more tightly round them, they walked harder in an effort to keep warm. They clambered along the barren and exposed path, across mountain streams and through the desolate landscape until they reached the upland plain of Lasithi, which was covered with a fine blanket of snow. 'The mountain paths are incredibly stony', Hilda wrote, 'sharp jags and ridges of rock so that you have to pick your way from jag to jag as there is no foot space between.'[25]

The icy wind penetrated every seam of their clothing as they plodded around the edge of the plain in search of the village of Psychro. The villages keep to the slopes around the plain, leaving the flat land for cultivation. The plain was peppered with the white sails of windmills drawing water to irrigate the fields along old Venetian channels, with the excess water draining through a natural swallow-hole at the edge of the plain. The main crop was potatoes, but the only things thriving in the bitter February weather were the almond trees, their pink blossom standing out against the background of white. 'John and I were behind and kept hoping that each village would be the one but it was a long way and about the furthest village. However, we got there in the end after splashing through endless muddy lanes.'[26]

Dusk had turned to night before they crossed the last hump-backed bridge by the village of Psychro. They were sorely tempted to swipe a bottle of cognac being nursed by a ragged urchin whom they asked for directions, but resisted, and finally came to the house to which they had been recommended. Doctor Kasapis was a Greek from Constantinople, who had come to live at Psychro with his German wife, when, some years before, he was, as a Royalist, made unwelcome on the mainland. His kindness, humour and generosity, often treating poor people at his own expense, soon made him and his wife well-loved members of the community. They had built a beautiful house up near the cave of Psychro, the Diktaean Cave, and it was there that John and the others were warmly welcomed with 'spotless rooms, scrubbed wooden platters, blackcurrant jam and home-made bread'.[27] John found that the doctor shared his love of telling stories, and they became firm friends. Over the years that friendship would grow stronger; and yet Dr Kasapis would one day be implicated by some in John's death because German soldiers forced him to identify John's body.

The Diktaean Cave, which legend held to be the birthplace of Zeus (competing with the Idaean Cave on Mount Ida for the title), was a vast, deep and intricate cavern opening into the mountainside some way above the plain. When they awoke the following morning the plain was still more deeply buried in snow. It would have been dangerous to attempt a descent into the cave, which was slippery with damp and chilly, even in the height of summer. So they decided to return towards Candia and make their way to Knossos in search of the spring sunshine they had left behind.

They chose one of the ancient passes out of the north-west side of the plain, leading past the swallow-hole, which would be a torrent of water when the thaw came, and up the gentle valley between Mount Louloudhaki to the north and Mount Bergadi to the south. Creeping up the belly of the valley, an ancient *kalderimi*, or paved way, followed the often dry stream bed up to the crest of the pass. With only a few steps cut into the rock on the steepest point of the crest, the path plunged down the other precipitous side, in tight twists and turns, towards the town of Kastelli, near the site of the classical city of Lyttos. The pass is still known for a cairn of stones by the side of the track, known locally as του Τσουλι το μνημα (the tomb of Tsouli). This was where a ruthless Turkish pasha, who had murdered, raped and humiliated countless of his subjects, had finally been captured by his enemies. The cairn on his grave was made of stones cast in hatred as a perpetual curse on his soul.

Back in Heraklion, John had hoped to meet Duncan Mackenzie. Mackenzie had been Sir Arthur Evans' assistant at Knossos since the start of work at the turn of the century. When in 1926 Evans had given the palace site and his estate at Knossos to the British School, Mackenzie was the obvious choice to become the first Curator. Mackenzie's careful and methodical work was the backbone of the excavation at Knossos, and his knowledge of the site and the finds from it was unparalleled. So it was to Mackenzie that John needed to talk about the Egyptian finds from the Knossos area. However, to his disappointment, John received little help from Mackenzie, who had only just managed to dock at Heraklion through a bad storm.

John's first trip to Crete had been a success and had whetted his appetite for the island, but there was a great deal more still to explore. While the Egyptian objects were mostly at Candia Museum, the sites at which they had thus far been excavated were largely situated in the central and southern parts of the island. It was clear to John that he needed to go back. Glad of an excuse to return so soon, he decided to make another trip the following spring. 'Crete is a wonderful country, much richer than Greece – the peasants finer men – more upstanding.'[28]

*

On their return to Athens, John and Hilda went for long walks together in and around the city, for there was no privacy at the School and they were by now deeply fond of one another. Neither of them divulged their feelings to their families, though each wrote of the other frequently, while the other students faded into the background. They had only a short time together before John was due to join William Heurtley on the five-week excavation in the Chalkidiki. The days went fast, spent unearthing objects for John's catalogue from the depths of the National Museum, while in the evenings they would play tennis in the School garden, or go dancing at the Caprice. Then, in a confusion of baggage and taxis, he was gone.

New students arrived at the School and made plans for journeys down to the Peloponnese, but Hilda admitted to her mother that she missed John's company very much. She was determined to keep busy while he was away and catch up with her own work, so that she would be free to travel with him when he returned. Not being particularly well off, she was also relieved at the chance to husband her resources.

*

'My darling Hilda,' John wrote in train-jolted handwriting, long before he reached Macedonia. 'We are fairly comfortable.... The carriage is swelteringly hot and the window is definitely possessed of the devil, for it continually raises itself when not watched.' Of the team he only said, 'The bees are quiet, all save the Queen Bee [Miss Benton], who is definitely suspicious.' Then, after some rather catty comments about his companions, he wrote: 'I do wish you were coming, dear. I do miss you terribly. Goodnight darling. Love from Jehan xxxxx.' They finally arrived at the Hotel Majestic in Salonika, where they were to stay for the first few days while gathering all their stores and equipment before moving to the site. John added a postscript: 'Can you guess what age Miss Benton registered as here? 22!!!! I caught the clerk's eye!'[29]

The mound, or 'toumba', they were to dig had been called Meceberna in classical times, but by the Middle Ages it became known as Molyvopyrgos, 'tower of lead', owing to the number of lead sling bullets found on the surface. It was spectacularly situated on the coast of the Gulf of Cassandra, where the 3000ft mountains to the north descended to the sea. Like Crete, this whole region of Macedonia had belonged to Greece for only fifteen years, and it had been bitterly fought over before and since, largely because of the strategic position of Salonika. It was bitterly cold, with a howling wind. 'Tell Dicky I haven't undressed for four days!', he wrote to Herbert, 'and if the Vardar wind continues to blow I have no intention of doing so for over a week!'[30]

John was extremely enthusiastic and, although he was joining a dig for the first time, was convinced that he alone could see the right way to do things. Already he had formed strong opinions on how a dig should not be carried out; the American excavations a mile and a half to the west at Olynthos, the most important classical site on the Chalkidiki peninsula, appeared to him to be the epitome of bad archaeology. It horrified him to see a legitimate excavation being carried out so casually. In writing to his father he vented his fury at the 'horrible mess' the excavator, Professor David Robinson, was making. 'He has destroyed a fine prehistoric site containing just what everyone wanted to know in the way of stratification. He is merely out for what will show well in a museum, employing over 190 men with no one to look after them. Twice a day he goes round asking the workmen – through an interpreter of course – what they have found! and where! It is probably the worst dig in history.'[31] When the report of the excavations was published in 1930, it turned out that John was not the only person to raise this criticism.[32]

On their own dig they worked from eight o'clock to midday and two o'clock to six o'clock, often collapsing into bed by eight-thirty. Heurtley's aims were to clarify the local chronological sequence, which had never been fully established. At first the results were unpromising. 'The settlement is very shallow and though we have dug trenches down to four metres nothing has turned up. All that is left now is to connect our trenches to a depth of two metres and collect the results. We then move on. Heurtley is quite satisfied. We have found pottery almost indistinguishable from Minyan but belonging to the early Iron Age, i.e. nearly a thousand years after its time.'[33] But the site had some surprises in store for them. 'We suddenly found a completely new stratum of Early Helladic pottery and are now inclining to the theory that we are discovering the origin of Minyan, not as we at first thought its grandson.'[34] The site's climate continued to make the working conditions unpleasant. 'Digging is rendered difficult owing to the appalling rain and cold which we have been enjoying. However, though the rain is worse it is now warmer, and I have been actually able to take a few clothes off at night, and (tell Dickie) I actually washed all over this morning, including the neck and behind the ears.'[35]

By law, the actual digging had to be done by local workmen, with the students supervising. 'The men are delightful. One old gentleman in my trench has adopted me and calls me παιδι μου [my child]! The others are more avuncular and address me as Mister John... We are surrounded here by the most extraordinary characters. The land is owned by a man called Palamides, commonly known as Fur Neck, from the collar of his coat. He is a complete vulture and has a collection of repulsive Hellenistic *anticas* [antiquities]. The other day he bought a coin of Lysimachos in exchange for a donkey – it is still a question which party got the worst of the bargain.'[36]

The team lived in tents but were allowed to use a nearby house for shelter. 'The house of which we have a room for the kitchen is owned by three incredible characters, known as the comic brethren – remarkable for their trousers – the seat of which extends well below the knee. They spend most of their time in bed, and if one goes into their room to get anything one is confronted by rows of heads in bed all talking. With them lives an old man locally called the Kaiser, from his moustaches. He sits over the fire all day, but emerges in the evening to take the animals for a walk separately – the mule, the foal, the pig, the goat, and lastly a couple of oxen on the end of a string from which they invariably break, which necessitates wild flanking manoeuvres. The old gentleman who adopted me has shaved his beard and has been named the Colonel, from his inflamed Anglo-Indian appearance. It is his habit when warm to divest himself of his trousers. Luckily displaying another pair underneath.'[37]

In early April they battled through floods to the 'toumba' site of Agios Mama, closer to Olynthos. The site lay on fertile land about one mile from the coast and was better protected from the weather by the Chalkidiki mountains to the north and east and a low ridge to the west. The site had once commanded the route into the interior of the peninsula and its inhabitants had grown wealthy on the passing trade and fertile plain, until Olynthos had eventually supplanted it. 'We are only making trial pits here, in order to see if it is worth excavating on a large scale next year. It is – well worth it – we have got some excellent stuff and even some complete vases which succeed in giving a lot of evidence for the Anatolian origin of the Greek race.'[38]

*

For Hilda, the cold, damp weather made Athens even duller without John, though as Easter drew near the School began to grow busy again. Just before John's return from Macedonia, Hilda heard that her financial problems had been solved by the death of an elderly relative who had left her some money. 'I'm sorry the poor thing didn't have more fun out of her own money, but it certainly removes any financial worries I was having, and is a very pleasant windfall.'[39]

John arrived back in Athens at the end of April 1928. It was Easter weekend, and Athens was flooded with candlelight as processions emerged from all the churches. 'Looking up at Lykabettos from time to time we could see a line of twinkling lights descending: the procession for the church of St George at the top.'[40] The following evening they went to the 'Christ is risen' ceremony at the Cathedral – the Metropolis. At twelve o'clock the bells were rung to signal the end of the fast, and people turned to greet each other before returning home, each bearing a candle, for their midnight Paschal feast. 'We were very lucky', Hilda wrote, 'as we once more met the extraordinary kindness which Athenians extend to strangers at their festivals. We were in Metropolis Street, tightly wedged amongst the people and with a view of only one corner of the stand, and none of the Metropolis door. A policeman was edging his way through the crowd and as he passed one of the people said to him that we were foreigners. He motioned to us to follow and going backwards himself, he drew us after him through the crowd explaining as he pushed his way that we were strangers and of course they must let us pass. He took us right under the ropes and through the line of police into the open space by the stand where we had a perfect view of everything.'[41]

Early on Easter Sunday, John and Hilda went out to Porto Raphti – a superb natural harbour along the coast from Piraeus. 'It was a perfect day and when we got to Porto Raphti about eight, the men of the village were dancing in the street to piping. I don't suppose they had been to bed at all after their Paschal feast. We left the car and walked through the village and along the shore where men were bringing sponges ashore from a little boat, and the dancing followed us.'[42] They spent the day on the beach, taking photographs of each other, John pretending to high jump or showing off how far he could stretch his leg in the air, Hilda sitting demurely in her tunic swimming costume.

*

John's catalogue was suffering from his inability to use unpublished finds, which included a considerable number of the Egyptian objects found in Greece and the islands. He had to choose whether to await their publication before bringing out his final catalogue, or go ahead without them. On his father's advice, he decided to publish sooner rather than later, and to update later as necessary. Herbert had always felt that the sooner John put something into print, the better would be his position in the archaeological world, where published work was required for many academic jobs. John agreed, though he was reluctant to produce a book that he felt would be 'horribly incomplete'.

Shortly after Easter John and Hilda made plans to travel in the Peloponnese, ending with a walk over the Langada Pass from Kalamata to Sparta. While they were sitting in the Finlay Library at the School after dinner, working out the details, William Heurtley, the Assistant Director, interrupted them. 'I'm sure there is going to be an earthquake. The sun was quite green last night.' 'We all laughed', Hilda wrote. 'But the extraordinary thing was that a few minutes afterwards came the first slight shock of the earthquake at Corinth and an hour later there was quite a bad tremor and a perceptible rocking: the long curtains in the Finlay waved about though the windows and shutters were closed. It was a most horrid feeling, the sensation of the earth trembling under you, rather like having an underground train passing directly underneath.'[43]

On their way to the Peloponnese they saw the effects of the earthquake. 'Corinth was a sad sight', Hilda told her mother. 'The railway station was all dismantled and showed a few cracks: most of the houses had cracks somewhere and a few had collapsed entirely, while others had lost their roofs: all the people were busy transporting their household goods to various places – open country mostly, it seemed, or the neighbouring railway stations where many of them encamped, so that there were sort of gypsy settlements all along the line.'[44] The rubble-filled roads were piled up with possessions that had been retrieved from the heaps of debris, and even the ruins of the ancient city were filled with tents to shelter the homeless.

They arrived a couple of days later at Kalamata, from where they started very early one morning to tackle the Langada Pass, the ancient route through the solid mass of the Taygetus range that John had walked with James Cullen. The road out of the town took them gently up into the foothills, passing villagers from the surrounding countryside flocking to market day in Kalamata. The path began to climb more steeply, high into wooded hills above a deep valley. As the magnificent view of the Messenian Gulf far below vanished from behind them, the peaks of Mount Taygetus loomed up large and snow-covered above them, accompanied by the roar of a torrent down in the valley bottom. They reached the plain of Sparta in eleven and a half hours, 'Half an hour under Baedeker's estimate', Hilda wrote in triumph, 'and out of that we had an hour's rest for lunch.'[45]

At the dig house in Sparta they were met by Spiro Dassis, of the Mycenae family, now in the role of butler to the School's Director, Woodward, who was doing some work there. Hilda took the one room left in the dig house, while John found lodgings in the flea-ridden local hotel, joining the others for meals.

John's feet, which had been badly bruised high-jumping before he left Athens, were in a sorry state after walking the Langada Pass. The next day's trip to the Menelaion all but finished him off. 'We had a bad time getting home', Hilda wrote, 'as the poor child had got to the hobbling stage before we reached the river again.'[46]

*

On their return to the School in Athens they found the newly-published second volume of Sir Arthur Evans' *Palace of Minos*. The massive book was in two parts and had the most recent plans of the site at Knossos, which Hilda spent the best part of three days tracing before they left again for Crete. This second trip was largely for pleasure, certainly for Hilda. John, however, was determined to corner Evans at Knossos and sound him out about the possibilities of archaeological work in Crete.

Passing through Heraklion and out of a gate in the massive Venetian fortification walls, they made their way towards Knossos. The road to the site took them south-east of the town and up onto the spurs of land that roll down from the foot of Mount Iuktas towards the flat land of the north coast. Passing the Villa Ariadne on the right, Evans' Cretan home, and a Turkish messarlik on the left, the road dipped down into the valley of the River Kairatos where the Palace of Minos stood. Deep beneath the slopes of the valley much of the Minoan town of Knossos still lay buried.

The general plan of the palace had by then been largely recovered, but the ruins were still rather confusing at first sight and spoilt in some places, John felt, by Evans' restorations. These Evans had undertaken since the start of his excavations, in order to protect the site and allow further digging. At the same time, he hoped to give the visitor some idea of what the palace might have looked like at its latest phase, using clues to the nature of the structure gleaned from the excavation. The restorations were anything but unobtrusive, but Evans had not intended them to be. His intention was to express the grandeur and beauty of the building. The stairway of the Stepped Portico climbed again to an upper floor, while frescos once more adorned the walls of the palace. Across the Central Court, in the east wing, it was possible for the first time in over three thousand years to descend four flights of the Grand Staircase to the Hall of the Double Axes and the Queen's Megaron.

Evans' colleagues appreciated the vision that had led to his restorations, though not everybody approved of them. While the skill of the restorers is beyond question, the restorations they created are very much of their time. They are typical of Evans' approach to archaeology, of his flair and imagination, his eye for detail and his determination to let others see the fruits of his discoveries. Knossos would have been a very difficult site to appreciate if it had not been for his rebuilding.

The original palace was built over a six-acre area, on five or six levels, moulded around the hill on which it stood (itself formed by successive layers of Neolithic occupation). It took advantage particularly of the view of the valley to the south, towards the distinctive outline of the sacred Mount Iuktas on the skyline. The impression of this, if nothing else, would have been lost on many lay visitors if it had not been for Evans and his team of architects.

The restoration work meant that there was little new excavation going on, but a large part of the site was already visible. With Hilda's copied maps in hand, they worked their way round the site with the expert help of the Curator, Duncan Mackenzie, who invited them to tea at the Villa Ariadne. Mackenzie was an old man by now, with a shock of white hair and a grey moustache. Walking back up the hill past vineyards and an old abandoned taverna, they reached a stone gateway and a drive leading through beautiful gardens that were showing the first signs of spring.

They found Evans sitting on one of the terraces of the Villa Ariadne with the British School architect, Piet de Jong, who was overseeing the restoration work. John broached the subject of working in Crete and found Evans very encouraging. 'There are certainly chances there', he wrote to his father. 'Evans suggested – secretly of course – either digging for Neolithic below the Central Court at Knossos or else going down to Komo on the south coast, which was the port on the Libyan Sea.'[47] Evans also intimated that his own excavations at Knossos would resume the following season.

Evans and Mackenzie insisted that John stay at the Villa when he had completed his work in the east, but Hilda was not invited. 'No women folk are asked to stay in that bachelor haunt', she wrote home, 'but a hostel is being built, and when it is ready, men and women students will be able to stay there and avoid hotels.'[48] The new hostel was to be in the abandoned taverna they had passed, but it was far from ready yet. However, the problem was less one of chauvinism than of old-fashioned delicacy on the part of the ladies. The Villa Ariadne, built in 1906, was falling badly into disrepair, as was its Curator, Duncan Mackenzie.

*

Following a few days retracing their steps in eastern Crete, John and Hilda returned to Athens. It was June 1928 and John would soon have to return to England. The weather was hot so they decided to hire a car and driver and make the most of their remaining time with some leisurely sightseeing and swimming in Attica.

Eventually, after a farewell dinner party with the other students, they parted ways. John caught the Orient Express back to London, while Hilda returned to Mycenae and the Argolid with the Professor of Greek at McGill University in Montreal, Professor Woodhead, and some other students.

*

While in Greece John had written to the Dutch archaeologist Henri (Hans) Frankfort, who had studied Egyptology under Flinders Petrie and Margaret Murray at University College London. Even though John was showing real interest in working in Crete, he was still very keen to get a foothold in Egypt. John asked Frankfort about the possibility of digging with him in Egypt, particularly at Tell el-Amarna, and possibly also Armant, both of which excavations Frankfort was now running for the Egypt Exploration Society. Frankfort responded favourably and suggested they meet, so when John reached London he went straight to see him. The meeting went well, and Frankfort invited John to join the team for the whole season, at Armant as well as at Tell el-Amarna, that coming autumn.

John now happily turned his attention back to Hilda. He was to take part in three athletics championships, including the AAA at Stamford Bridge. While he would be competing against athletes hoping to qualify for the 1928 Amsterdam Olympic Games, it is unlikely that he himself seriously expected to qualify. His priorities were changing, and only a year after his high jumping success at Cambridge, he accepted that his days of serious athletic competition were in the past. 'With all these youngsters coming on', he wrote later about the AAA, his last major competition, 'I felt like the title of a chapter in *Richard Yea-and-Nay*, "They Bay the Old Lion"'.[49]

John had invited Hilda to come and watch him high jump and afterwards join a party at the Hawks' Ball. She agreed and wrote to her mother to say she would be a little late arriving home, adding, 'You don't mind if I finish off my little fling do you – it is being very refreshing.'[50] Hilda did not give any indication in her letters that she felt more for John than this. She was certainly very fond of him, but John was in love with her.

So it must have been something of a surprise to her when, the day she returned to England, John proposed to her. At first she turned him down. Even though the thirteen-year age gap between them might not matter immediately, Hilda later confided to a friend that she had thought it would become more difficult as the years went on, for John was only twenty-four and Hilda already thirty-seven.[51] John would undoubtedly lead a very active life, and already few could keep up with him. But John persisted, insisting that the age gap made no difference to him, and eventually Hilda accepted him.

John wrote to break the news to his father. Apparently nervous of the reaction his news would cause, he used the words that Herbert had used to announce his remarriage. 'Your own style is best. "You will probably be surprised to hear that I am engaged" – to Hilda White, who got back today from Greece. I don't think there is any more to say because I can't catalogue her virtues! And you will probably like to come up to town and fall for her like I have. Please tell Dicky that although an archaeologist who took a first, she wears neither blue stockings nor horn-rimmed spectacles!'[52]

A few days later, John wrote asking Herbert if he could bring Hilda to Malvern for a couple of days. Herbert may have wondered what Greece had done to them, since John had just told him that Bob Dixon had secretly married Ismene Atchley. 'I suppose this is rather a shock! Briefly our plans are for me to come back after Egypt and for us to get married at the beginning of March and spend our honeymoon prospecting at Komo, and at several other sites in the south of Crete.'[53]

*

While John had an autumn season in Egypt to look forward to, Hilda had been invited by Winifred Lamb to join an excavation at Mytilene on the island of Lesbos. Although she was keen to work with Winifred Lamb, it would have meant a long and distant separation from John. John asked Frankfort if Hilda could come out to Egypt with him. Frankfort suggested that if, and only if, his own wife, Jettie, came out to the dig then so too could Hilda. John and Hilda decided to bring forward the date of the wedding to September and Hilda abandoned the idea of the Lesbos dig, choosing instead to study Aegean finds in Egypt as a parallel to John's *Ægyptiaca* catalogue of Egyptian finds in the Aegean. This meant that she would have work of her own to get on with in Cairo while John was down at Armant with Frankfort, and at least they would be in the same country.

As the wedding approached, John left Hilda at Caldy with her mother and sister, and went to spend a few days with his father and Dickie. He was busy preparing for their honeymoon walking and camping in Greece, and longed for it all to happen. 'My darling Lady, Yesterday I went and bought two camp beds – very smart! I do wish you were there to help me choose. Never mind though, only just over a fortnight now, dear love. It is wonderful isn't it. I still pinch myself to see if I really am awake.'[54]

On September 15th 1928 John and Hilda were married at the parish church of West Kirby in Cheshire, near Hilda's family home, with Pat Shackleton, John's Cambridge friend, as best man. 'It struck me as a very pleasant show', John wrote later, 'even though I was severely slapped on the hand for trying to produce the ring too soon! Pat was absolutely invaluable.'[55] After the wedding they travelled down to London, and dined at the newly refurbished Claridge's that night ('in state – being the only people there!'). The following day they boarded the Orient Express and set off on the three-day journey to Greece.

They stayed at the Hotel Majestic on Panepistemiou Street in Athens, with tall windows looking out onto the tree-lined avenue below. 'We are enjoying ourselves tremendously, though it has all been travelling and packing and unpacking so far', Hilda wrote home. 'It's all fun: John is such a dear.'[56]

At Mycenae, they picked up Spiro Dassis, who was to come not as their guide but, as Hilda put it, to 'buttle' for them, and no doubt as company for the guide whom he had chosen for them, leaving John and Hilda more time alone. Their journey from Mycenae took them across the plain to the beautiful village of Botsika, nestling on a hillside at the end of a long avenue of poplars. At the top of the village Spiro found them a place to stay. They were given the best room in the house, with a rickety balcony over the yard and chickens running in and out. They attempted to rig up their mosquito net, but without much success. 'It came down too close to our faces and we nearly had hysterics trying to crawl about under it without bringing it down', wrote Hilda, 'for the cat found no impediment in the balcony, and though we had a corner to corner search for the three skeleton kittens before we went to bed, we overlooked one black one, so in the course of the night John had several cat hunts despite which the cat ate the bread for the next day. We also suspected rats but that was apparently a distant earthquake.'[57]

At daybreak they climbed up above the village and headed westwards towards the Stymphalian Plain, with Mount Cyllene looming in the distance. Below them was the lake of Stymphalos – a mere of reeds and water fowl, with patches of grass in the shallows on which cattle stood chewing the cud. With menacing cliffs rising above them they skirted the plain to the western edge.

There the lake flowed furiously into an underground passage beneath the cliff, emerging at Argos more than twenty miles away. Passing the plain of Pheneos and Goura, they came eventually to Solos, surrounded by vineyards and chestnut trees on the slopes of Mount Chelmos. Nearby, the falls of the Styx cascaded down one of the faces of Chelmos. 'High up, below the crest, there is a sheer precipice and down its face a dark streak – the mossy background of the falls which gives them their modern name, Black Water. When the sun got the right position we could just see a silver line of water. It is certainly a very grim mountain, but it was such a heavenly day and the peaks had such a gossamer and rainbow veil of haze that we had to imagine what it would look like in a thunder storm or under a leaden sky to summon up the horror felt by ancients.'[58]

They ended their journey at Megaspelaion, a monastery in a vast cave, where they parted company with Spiro and the guide. John and Hilda headed up to Salonika to help sort the pottery from the Chalkidiki dig, marking sherds and trying to find joins – an absorbing puzzle, but monotonous. Much to Hilda's amazement, some actually enjoyed it, particularly Richard Hutchinson, nicknamed the 'Squire' for his imperious manner and dress sense. 'Hutchinson seems perfectly happy for hours with very little success to show, but he loves sherds for themselves I believe, and I haven't got to that length yet – I still only like the attractive ones.'[59]

Salonika was buzzing with activity as an International Fair was being held there. The narrow, dark streets were alive with the haunting tunes of street vendors and the vivid colours of their wares. The fair attracted people from all over the Balkans, elaborately and colourfully attired in their national costumes. 'There are about sixty thousand Jews in Salonika and their womenfolk have funny little flat head-dresses with folds falling down behind and little jackets with an edging of squirrel fur round the neck and each side of the front.'[60] Before two decades had passed, Sturmbannführer Adolf Eichmann would ensure that this colourful population was virtually wiped out.

5

November 1928–February 1929

THE *KHEDIVIAL MAIL* docked at the port of Alexandria early in November 1928. After the cool sea breezes of the Mediterranean, John and Hilda stepped off the ship into the chaotic and stifling heat of a 'howling, picturesque mob' on the quayside to battle through lengthy customs queues, bustled and pushed from one official to another. The noise and confusion of the scene were at once fascinating and daunting, especially after such a long journey.

Out of the seething crowd, a young Englishman emerged and made his way towards them. Introducing himself as Stephen Glanville, he explained that he was one of the Egyptologists who would be working with John at Armant and had been sent to meet them. Glanville was a quiet, humorous and intelligent young man, four years older than John, who had fled to Egypt originally as an English teacher for the Egyptian Government Education Service in the Delta after getting a fourth class degree at Oxford. It was a time of great political unrest amongst Egyptian students following the 1919 riots and his students were 'sullen and unruly youths'.[1] When on leave over Christmas in 1922, Glanville had travelled down to Luxor where he met Francis Newton, the architect who was running the excavations at Tell el-Amarna. The tomb of Tutankhamen had only recently been discovered, and Newton arranged for the young teacher to see inside. From that moment Glanville was hooked. He joined the excavation at Tell el-Amarna in 1923 and continued teaching in the Delta only long enough to learn ancient hieroglyphics and German before in 1924 applying for and securing a job as an Assistant Keeper of Egyptian and Assyrian Antiquities at the British Museum. This job now allowed him to spend his spare time excavating in Egypt, first with Newton and Griffith at Tell el-Amarna, and then with Hans Frankfort at Armant.

Once outside the port, Alexandria, advertised in the 1920s as the Deauville of the Orient, had a coastal freshness. But they found this entirely lacking in Cairo after the long hot train journey southwards, late in the year though it was. The hot, heavy atmosphere brought Hilda down with a bout of the malaria to which she was occasionally prone. Determined not to miss anything, she had brought quinine with her and recovered quickly, so that night Glanville whisked them off to see the pyramids by moonlight.

Cairo was a dirty, dusty and noisy city, but with a charm that overcame its decay. The old quarter of the city had changed very little since medieval times. Small streets were lined with old mosques and madrasas, houses and warehouses, and the dark arched recesses of the old covered markets, their entrances half-buried by the accumulation of centuries' worth of dust and rubbish. As in medieval Europe, each quarter of the market, or *suq*, sold specific goods: pots and pans or baskets, woodwork or metalwork, cloth or leather. The small arches of the ancient shop fronts were overflowing with their wares, hanging off or piled onto every available surface. In the small winding passages and dark doorways of the spice *suq*, sacks of spices spilt over from the confinement of the interior into the dimly lit lanes with splashes of rich colour, filling the air with the aromatic, choking dust of chillies, cumin and ginger.

John and Hilda sauntered down past the workshops and warehouses of the Sharia Khayyammiya – the Street of the Tentmakers. Here, behind wooden-latticed oriel windows, high up the walls, and in hidden courtyards behind imposing, dilapidated arches, men and women produced the brilliantly coloured ceremonial tents for which Cairo had long been famous throughout the Middle East. This, one of the oldest roads in Cairo, led to the massive 10th-century gateway of the Bab Zuwayla where, in Mamluk and Ottoman times, criminals were executed and their heads displayed on pikes.

The Street of the Tentmakers led them to the Mosque of Ibn Tulun, the only surviving part of the older city of al-Qataï. Medieval and post-medieval houses clustered still around the walls of the mosque though, within a decade, all but two of these would have been demolished.[2] John and Hilda climbed the steps spiralling up on the outside of the minaret to the small open-sided room at the top. There before them were set out the streets and alleys of the old quarter of Saida Zeinab below, and far in the distance on the western horizon, like vast ghosts from the far more distant past, they caught again a glimpse of the Pyramids of Giza.

On meeting them at Alexandria, Stephen Glanville had informed them that there would be no space for Hilda at the Armant camp until after Christmas. Hilda had planned to return alone to Cairo for a short time anyway in order to do her own work, but only temporarily. Now not only was she unable to join John on the dig, but she could not even visit him before Christmas. It was a lonely prospect to spend a month in Cairo without John. At least he would be with other people his own age, and busy with the sort of work he had dreamed of so long. Postponing the separation as long as possible, they decided to travel together down to Luxor for a couple of days before John went on to Armant, and Hilda back to Cairo.

John's cousin Kathleen Hargreaves, who lived in Cairo with her husband,

Lionel, took Hilda under her wing. Kathleen was a warm and generous woman, but 'how very 'English' and tough Lionel is!' John wrote to his father.[3] The couple lived in Zamalek, on Gezira Island on the River Nile, the most British area of Cairo, in a country that was largely run by the British. It was quieter and cooler than the rest of the city, close to the river, its streets lined with trees.

Kathleen helped Hilda to find a pension on the island and invited them to one of the city's high social milieus, the Gezira Sporting Club. Here the *jeunesse dorée* of Cairo played polo, tennis, cricket and hockey or a more genteel game of croquet before a dip in the pool. Kathleen enrolled Hilda as a temporary member, but it was not the sort of atmosphere in which Hilda was at ease. Much frequented by British officers stationed in Cairo, or on leave from some other less agreeable corner of the Empire and by British officials in the Egyptian government, it was said that the officers were tested for military efficiency and fitness for command on the polo grounds, and the officials for their civil service suitability on the tennis courts.

In spite of the dusty charm of the old city and the crisp freshness of the Gezira Club lawns, this was not the Egypt John had been dreaming of for so many years, so they drove out to Giza. Even to a casual visitor who knows little or nothing of the history surrounding the Pyramids and the Sphinx, these structures are staggering, breathtaking in their immensity and antiquity, ancient even to the ancient world. From Giza they went to the necropolis at Saqqara, accompanied by a local dragoman or interpreter, two camels, a white donkey, a camel driver, the camels' owner and two camel boys. John photographed and made notes on each monument they visited: what reliefs were to be found in each tomb and temple, how much bakshish had to be paid to get into the less visited tombs, and bibliographical references.

John's notes, made wherever he travelled, are factual and unembellished. However, they record an increasingly thorough knowledge, and with a growing command of the languages involved, he developed a profound understanding of the people with whom he came into contact as well as the archaeology and history of where they lived. Hilda, meanwhile, was more descriptive than John and observed the details of contemporary Egypt, recording sights and traditions that are themselves now history.

'The three pyramids and the Sphinx were on our right as we started,' she wrote to her family, 'the former were just coming out of a morning mist, but the Sphinx was quite clear with blue shadows and blazing sun. There is always a cool breeze in the desert so we were not too hot. I found a camel trot very tiring at first but we did a good deal of walking, the result being that it took us nearly three hours to get to Saqqara. Our way lay between the inundation, beyond which and out of sight was the Nile, and the low hillocks of the desert. There were millions of wild duck on the water, and we saw some ibises, passed one Bedouin encampment and soon came in sight of the Abusir pyramids and just afterwards the step pyramid of Saqqara... The sunset was incredibly lovely. I do wish you could have seen the reedy, bird-haunted stretches of the inundation lit with the most delicate and lovely opal colours, and later with violet and rose.'[4]

*

It was early morning when, having travelled down to Luxor by train, John and Hilda arrived at their hotel. The Savoy Hotel was a long, elegant building, fronted by a cool terrace and set amid beautiful shady gardens of palms and flowering shrubs that stretched down to another terrace at the edge of the Nile. Across the wide river the Savoy faced the west bank, whose cliffs hid the tombs of the pharaohs and their queens, lit to a deep scarlet every evening by the setting sun.

Luxor had once been the ancient capital, Thebes, city of Amen. The pharaohs of the 11th Dynasty had made Thebes their capital in preference to the old capital at Armant (ancient Hermonthis) where John was soon to dig. Their city with the main temples occupied the east bank, while the tombs and mortuary temples were situated on the west bank. By the 17th Dynasty, Thebes had become the capital of the whole Egyptian Empire and remained so for 500 years, with a slight hiccup when Akhenaten abandoned the worship of Amen and founded his new but short-lived capital, Akhetaten, at Tell el-Amarna.

Centuries of pharaohs had left their mark at Thebes, creating a feast of Egyptian art and architecture at the temples of Luxor and Karnak, Medinet Habu and Deir el-Bahari, and the tombs of kings, queens and nobles. John devoured as much of it as he could. His once exclusive passion for Egyptology was now influenced by the Aegean, and he particularly sought out the sites whose carved and painted reliefs gave clues to the identities of other peoples in the eastern Mediterranean of the second millennium BC. Among the most interesting to John were the tombs of four nobles – Rekhmara, Menkheperrasenb, Senmut and Useramun. On the walls of their tombs were pictures of men bearing objects as gifts or tribute. Many of the objects were clearly Aegean in inspiration and probably origin, or more particularly Cretan. The Egyptologist Gerald Wainwright had, some years before, written an article identifying the figures, said to be from Keftiu, as Cilicians.[5] The subject was still hotly disputed, but John felt that Wainwright's arguments had been either refuted out of hand or merely ignored. John was convinced that there were Minoan Cretans amongst the figures, and, though he disagreed with Wainwright, John believed that his ideas deserved more detailed examination and began to research the subject for an article that would launch him simultaneously into the academic worlds of Egyptology and Aegean prehistory.

*

Hilda made her way back to Cairo alone while John settled down to life on camp. The Armant accommodation was rather luxurious compared to that of the Chalkidiki dig. The site was archaeologically rich, the team good-humoured, and the Director, Hans Frankfort, witty and enthusiastic. Frankfort was in a good position to advise John on his work on the *Ægyptiaca* catalogue, and would generously refer to John's 'forthcoming work' in his own book, *The Mural Paintings of El-'Amarneh,* published in 1929. He recognised that John had great ability, was keen and hard working, and helped him as much as he could to learn the job fast and well.

The site at Armant was a vast and important one. A honeycomb of underground chambers and passages had been cut through the soft desert rock for the burial of the sacred Bucchis bulls. The bulls were held in very great honour during their lifetime, each individually named and buried amid great ceremony and wealth on their deaths. The belief in the sacred power of the bull was held far and wide, and the fact that pilgrims such as Alexander the Great, Darius I of Persia and several Roman Emperors recorded their visits on large slabs of stone erected at the site is evidence that it stretched beyond the boundaries of Egypt. These 'stelae' record the names and details of the succession of the Hermonthis bulls and were a very useful tool in working out comparative chronologies for different countries in the ancient world.

'The rock is so bad that instead of being able to follow up the underground passages we have to cut down to them, which means a long slow job. Yesterday we thought we had the thrill of an untouched burial – but although the lid of the sarcophagus was unbroken we found on going down that it was a unique one with a door in front which had been effectively opened. Inside on the wall was a handprint left by one of the robbers. At the moment however it seems that we can not only add a completely new chapter to Egyptian religious history but also will probably be able to rewrite the history of the Ptolemies and the Romans from the point of view of Upper Egypt.'[6]

John was too busy and involved with the dig to write to his father more than occasionally. Even then the letters were packed with queries about names and places and dates that he wanted his father to look up, or with books that he asked him to procure. 'If you could suggest any Roman Emperors of the period who might correspond to 'Miuksymn', 'Miukrimys' and 'nrs clutsiun', we should be very happy'. Written in haste, his letters communicate John's enthusiasm. 'The dig is going very well. We have made some very reasonable discoveries and disproved Howard Carter's dictum that we should find nothing but shrewmice. *The Daily Telegraph* has all our news in it. Tell Dickie I wash all over every day in hot water! Up at six every morning and bed at 8.30-9...I have made my mark on the dig by discovering a completely new use of a hieroglyph which has curiously enough enabled us to decipher the name of the Bucchis bull Ba'her-khat or 'soul before body'. (In confidence) we have found stelai of Darius the 1st and Alexander the Great and two Roman ones we are puzzling over. They seem to be Macrinus, Maximian and Valerian.' But the letters also give away just how much Greece had got under his skin. 'I still hanker after Greece though.'[7] Hilda, writing to her mother from Cairo, confirmed this. 'I do hope that John does get a chance in Crete as he would love that above all things, I know, and so should I.'[8]

Hot days gave way to very cold nights. One evening, about a fortnight after John's arrival, a huge storm began to brew. Building in strength as night came on, it blew down the mess tent while they were all eating dinner in it, and several of the other tents succumbed around them. 'We spent the night in the one which seemed most secure, and a pretty miserable night it was. I'm glad to say that my tent survived by some miracle, though of course it was simply filled with sand.'[9] Sandy or not, everyone piled into that tent for the rest of the night and next morning deserted the camp to spend their day off in the comparative oasis of Luxor.

Although less diligent about writing to Herbert, John always managed to find time to keep in touch with Hilda, writing to her every day. The pain of being apart was exacerbated for her, he knew, by her loneliness. Her work was initially hindered by the French Director of the Cairo Museum, Henri Gauthier, who made it difficult for her to get the necessary passes to work in the museum. But she found allies in the Keeper, Rex Engelbach, and the Egyptologist Battiscombe Gunn. Engelbach helped her find relevant references and gave a lot of his time to discussing her work proposals with her.

Hilda's pension, the Villa Mouso at 6 Sharia el-Amir Tusun, was owned and run by a 'warm Yorkshire body' called Miss Salmon. Around her, Gezira and the other European areas of Cairo were being developed, the buildings reflecting the streamlined geometry and modern simplicity of 1920s Art Deco, all surrounded by the trees and gardens of the popular Garden City ideal. 'This house is very charming and Gezira itself, though it is being built up, is still very pretty, with lots of open spaces, trees and flowering bushes and two minutes away the Sporting Club with its polo fields etc. which is very pretty indeed.'[10]

As winter drew on, the pension began to fill up and Hilda revealed more than a touch of snobbery about those she found herself sharing with. 'I don't much like the people here at present,' she wrote home. 'Two sisters from the Port Said hospital who are quite nice but a bit common and a very "bright" couple who talk too much: he is a man who has risen from the ranks and got a swelled head in the process and is a terrible bore and very silly into the bargain: she is charming. Miss Salmon is very kind and nice and I have Kathleen very near and anyway I haven't much time for people. But the meals here are rather a trial in the way of conversation as the Captain monopolises it and snaps at his wife if she tries to prevent his being too blatantly ridiculous as the poor woman sometimes tries to do tactfully. However I mustn't be a cat. Still he is dreadful.'[11]

Hilda spent the sharp, chilly evenings before dinner wrapped up alone in a rug in her unheated room. This was the time when she was at her lowest and would begin to feel that she could not stick it. She was counting the days until she could go down to meet John in Luxor, cheered by the news that she would be able to spend a short time with him at Armant as well as the two days leave John had for Christmas.

*

'I wish we could be home for Christmas', John wrote to his father. 'I should much like a proper English one again, as well as a little English beer!'[12] Originally Hilda had been told that the propriety of the camp would mean John moving out of his tent for Hilda and sleeping on the mess tent couch. This would have made it impossible for Hilda to stay at the camp for the fortnight after Christmas and before the Amarna dig started. Then Stephen Glanville decided to leave after Christmas, meaning that John could put his tent together with Stephen's, making room after all for Hilda. Her relief was enormous as her time alone in Cairo had seemed to pass so slowly and she had been dreading going back after only a few days with John at Christmas.

When Hilda arrived in Luxor she found the suntanned John 'looking splendid'. They spent the day strolling around the town catching up on their news. They wandered out to see the temples at Karnak by moonlight before returning to Luxor to dine amid the splendours of the Winter Palace, the epitome of 1920s glamour in Egypt, where they danced throughout the evening. A conjuror performed tricks for the audience in between dances, extracting a small fluffy chick from the inner pocket of John's jacket. The ancient Luxor Temple was floodlit, and the lights of the elegant and luxurious two-tiered passenger boats moored on the banks of the Nile gently illuminated the more modest silhouettes of the feluccas.

The following morning John took Hilda back to Armant with him to meet the rest of the dig team. The camp was busy with the preparations for Christmas. 'Hussein, the head servant, and his assistants had decorated each of the tents with boughs of bougainvillaea, and the mess tent between its two posts had a triumphal arch of oranges, tangerines and bananas with green leaves. When we dined at night we had many candles in Chianti flasks with red bows round their necks, and there were red and white crackers to make the table look gay.'[13]

The Egypt Exploration Society (EES), in the person of Armant's wealthy benefactor and original excavator, Robert Mond, had sent two huge hampers from Fortnum and Mason, overflowing with delicious hors d'oeuvres, preserved fruits and chocolates. But the pièce de resistance was a proper Christmas dinner of roast turkey, for which one of the camp turkeys had been volunteered.

That afternoon, all the villagers who worked on the dig gathered near the site. A local band played what seemed to Hilda something akin to a 'welcome to royalty' when the team of archaeologists arrived, and then the fun could begin. The children ran races – 'the little boys were so terribly keen and also had to be watched to prevent their cheating like mad' – and buried their faces in soup plates of flour to find coins with their teeth.[14] As the music played, some of the men picked up quarterstaffs to display their considerable skill in stick fighting. This display of so medieval a sport appealed greatly to John, who was soon learning how to use the quarterstaff himself. The last part of the show also deeply impressed John, who was no doubt already dreaming of the Saracens of the past. A man arrived on horseback, *galabiyeh* and scarf flying, and began to display some excellent horsemanship, with whirlwind changes 'that ended abruptly in a flurry of sand as the horse was pulled up short in about a yard'.[15] When he had galloped off in a cloud of dust, the excavation's water man rode in on his shabby little old donkey parodying the first rider to great acclaim, also rounding off his display in a cloud of dust as he fell off. After the show, the men had a huge feast and sat listening to the band until late into the night.

Work began again a couple of days after Christmas and Hilda had her first experience of archaeological life in Egypt. The work was rather like watching a beehive at its busiest. There were four basket-carriers to each digger, small boys moving in a constant ebb and flow to take the soil away in small round baskets, which they carried on their heads or shoulders. They would empty the baskets into dump trucks on a small hand-operated railway, which would run out along the spurs of the vast ever-growing spoil heaps to dump the soil. Meanwhile the little boys, under the eagle eye of the *ra'is* or overseer, would run back with their baskets by a different path.

The team worked on a shift system, taking it in turns to go down at 6.30 for a couple of hours before breakfast, one of the most strikingly beautiful times of the day in Egypt, as the sun begins to touch the desert with colour. 'After breakfast we go down to the dig until 12 or sometimes I wait up here until the post comes and only go down for an hour before lunch as I am tracing some plans of John's to send to Mr Heurtley.' Water was brought regularly from a well in the cultivation a mile from the site, carried in an earthenware jar or *zir* by a man on a donkey, and then boiled before drinking. 'After lunch work goes on again until 5 and we generally spend all afternoon there and have tea at 3.30. The camp boy, Amin, brings it down in thermos flasks. When we come back to camp there is generally a few minutes' hockey before dark, then baths in flat saucer baths (*tishts*), then dinner at 6.30 and after that work or talk or letters until bed time.'[16]

Hilda revelled in the companionship and the dusty but sophisticated charm of the camp. She would dress every night for dinner, saving her best silk stockings for trips into Luxor. John bought her a pair of Japanese black silk pyjamas decorated with dark red flowers and a long silk coat, which she would wear over a dress in the evenings, with her satin shoes gradually becoming more and more scuffed in the sand.

When not on site, Hilda began to make a home of the two tents that they had put together as bedroom and sitting room. 'I spent the morning arranging our first house... The bigger tent is our sleeping tent and we each have a little washstand and a set of shelves, and I got some pretty striped stuff from Luxor and made curtains and also have a curtain under which to hang clothes. The other tent is a small sitting room with a spare camp bed as a couch and a deck chair. We have two little tables which are always getting crowded up because there are so few places to keep things, and it is marvellous how soon chaos exists if one doesn't take care.'[17]

John was delighted to have Hilda with him again, and announced to his father that she had brought great luck to the dig. 'Immediately she arrived finds simply began to roll up right and left.'[18] They both wrote home about the characters on the team: Hans and Jettie Frankfort they liked very much. 'Mrs Frankfort is another very versatile person', wrote Hilda, 'a wonderful linguist and very clever draughtsman, and a very entertaining person with a pleasant sense of humour. With regard to the last, so is Frankfort. He's not such a good linguist though very good indeed, but he is I should think more imaginative and impulsive.'[19] In fact, they both spoke English, Arabic, French, German and a little Italian besides their native Dutch. Very much a member of the family was a small puppy, Bucchis, acquired at the start of the season.

Alan Shorter, the philologist, was not well liked by the team. John's description of him reveals as much about himself as his subject. 'Shorter is a terrible example of an only child who has become an Anglo-Catholic. In spite of his mother having been a nurse he has been taught to take a pride in the physical infirmities of his youth which were apparently manifold, with the result that I have never seen a more useless body in my life. He is slower in the uptake than anyone I have ever seen and almost criminally negligent on occasions. He is willing at almost any time to make the table blush by bad quotation of poetry or foreign language. Reticence is unknown to him and Religion draws him as "iron draws the hands of heroes". He has little or no humour but considerable good humour. Great power of working hard but no power of getting results.'[20]

Stephen Glanville, who had met John and Hilda off the boat at Alexandria and had now returned to England, was considerably more popular. 'Glanville is greatly missed', wrote John. 'He has a fine sense of humour, immense knowledge – gained in a short time and in spite of bad sight, a weak knee and a liability to internal ailment, is a very fine athlete and hockey player. He nearly got his blue at Oxford.'[21] Glanville's overcoming of ailments gained far more respect from John than Shorter's apparent submission; illness and infirmity were the things he feared most in himself and hated most in other people, which resulted in a gross intolerance of weakness, especially if exploited. After all, he had overcome the loss of an eye. John was a great believer in the idea that it is no shame to fall, but to lie long.

Brian Emery had been on the excavations with Robert Mond at Armant since 1927, before Mond had given the concession over to the Egypt Exploration Society. He was 'a tall rather weedy man' who struck John as, 'intensely bigoted in his views and convinced that all that need be known is Egyptology.' John admired his very fine draughtsmanship and his skill as a practical engineer, but was surprised to see how little Arabic he had learnt, though he had been coming to Egypt for some years. 'His wife's life is one continual spoiled wail.'[22] Hilda, however, found Brian and Molly Emery, 'a kindly pair with a touch of vulgarity but a lot of good heartedness'.[23]

Nevertheless, they all got on well together and there were few undercurrents of bad feeling. Though Shorter was openly the scapegoat, he did not appear to care much and usually any excess irritation or tension amongst the team was dispelled by a game of hockey after work.

Even out in the desert opportunities were beginning to arise for John, not least the possibility of following the direction that Glanville had taken. He and Frankfort were both eager to help John make the most judicious move at a time when he still had all his options open. Before he left, Glanville had asked John whether he would be interested in standing for a job as Assistant Keeper in the Department of Egyptian and Assyrian Antiquities at the British Museum the following year. This gratified John in some ways, but the job would have serious drawbacks. The post would certainly give John the security inherent in a 'proper job', but he would be on probation for the first two years, precluding him from going on any digs in Egypt during that time and with no guarantee that the Museum would let him do so after that. As for digging in Crete, that would be out of the question.

On the eve of 1929, John and Hilda visited Chicago House, the centre of American research in the area, where Glanville's brother-in-law, Tony Chubb, was working. It was a different world and Hilda was amazed at the conspicuous wealth of the place. It was 'a beautiful dig house complete with every luxury including badminton courts, built by the Americans who are copying the reliefs and inscriptions at Medinet Habu. We had lunch there, finishing up with ice pudding, and then worked in the library for a couple of hours.'[24] The living conditions in the Armant camp, though a far cry from the luxury of Chicago House, were very good compared to the hardships imposed on teams by archaeologists such as Sir Flinders Petrie. Hans Frankfort's approach was more along the lines of 'any fool can be uncomfortable'.

The dig was wound up in mid-January and the team began to pack up. Plans had to be finished, photography of objects completed, last minute finds lifted from the ground and tidied up for photography, and all the pottery and objects drawn. John had done most of the official photography and the report in *The Daily Telegraph* was illustrated by his pictures.[25] Hilda, who was not part of the team, did what she could in the end-of-dig turmoil and filled in the rest of her time learning hieroglyphics.

Before they left, they had a surprise visit from neighbours of Herbert and Dickie in Malvern. The Perrins family – of Worcestershire Sauce fame – were cruising down the Nile in the *Scarab*, a luxurious Thomas Cook *dahabiyeh*. After visiting the camp for lunch they invited John and Hilda to join them for dinner on board. The crew of the *Scarab* ferried John and Hilda down river, singing a rowing song on the way, and deposited them on the landing stage of the Savoy Hotel where they could change for dinner in comfort. Their hosts, Dyson Perrins and his wife, were travelling with two friends and no fewer than nineteen servants, crew and engineers to look after them – 'So you can imagine what a trip like that must cost!' Hilda declared to her mother. 'John thought about £1000 and we decided that if we had a £1000 to throw away we wouldn't do it like that, though it looked a fascinating way to travel.'[26]

John and Hilda spent the night at the Savoy before heading back to camp for the final packing up. The poor dig Ford was packed to its limits, 'With Todros the camp postman sitting sideways by the driver with his feet hanging overboard, and long planks loaded on each foot board and across from the windscreen to the back of the car and baskets and packages all over us. The carpenter was busy at the camp making cases for the finds and the car had to bring out as much material as possible each journey it made.'[27]

Frankfort was well pleased with the success of the dig at Armant and with the publicity it had received in *The Daily Telegraph* and *The Illustrated London News*. The latter provided large spreads of text and photographs, bringing archaeology to a wide public, and, as the Egypt Exploration Society depended entirely on donations and subscriptions for the funding of its excavations and other work, this coverage was essential. There were several wealthy benefactors who contributed regularly but this could not cover the entire cost. Every year, the EES exhibited the finds of the season and copies of objects that the Cairo Museum kept. But the most crucial funding came from museums, mainly in Britain and the United States. In return they claimed a proportion of the finds directly comparable to the amount of money they had contributed. It was an imperfect set-up, not improved by the way in which the division was carried out. All the finds of the season would be laid out on tables in the Cairo Museum, the Director of which would pick out the best pieces. The rest were then shipped back to London to be shared out between the benefactors.

When the camp was all packed up and John and Hilda had moved back to Luxor and the Savoy Hotel, John's knee, which he had scratched a fortnight before leaving Armant, suddenly swelled to such proportions that they had to call off a planned trip to Quseir, on the Red Sea. Hans was in no doubt as to the cause of the festering. 'Mrs John, in the authority of newly married wife, had never wanted anybody to touch it, and done for weeks on end the wrong thing. Smith [John's doctor] taught her better and all is going well now, but it was a bit of a fright.'[28] Not only did John have a knee twice its normal size but he also caught flu, sending his temperature soaring. The forced inactivity was torture for John who hated disability in himself far more than in other people, largely because he had spent most of his life making sure that he was physically resilient.

Though John and Hilda regretted the cancellation of their trip, it was their guide, Hassan Sherreif, who was most disappointed. 'It was a great thing for him to be chosen as guide,' Hilda explained to her mother. No sooner had they wired to him that the departure was delayed as John was ill, than he turned up in person. 'A very picturesque figure, standing at the door of the hotel. He had come all the way from Quft to see how John was.' He was greatly concerned that the deposit John had given him for the camels had already been paid and he was terribly worried that he had not yet succeeded in getting it back. 'He is a very fine man and extremely honourable.'[29]

Hassan Sherreif was a fine man in appearance also, with his scarf wrapped round in the Egyptian fashion, and with his long flowing *galabiyeh*. '*Al Hamdulillah!*' (God be praised), he exclaimed on seeing that John was not at death's door. John thought that the population of Quft would think his illness a judgement on his failing to say the customary *Inshallah* (If God wills it), when one of the *Qufti* diggers asked if they were going to Quseir. It shows a certain tendency towards superstition in John that forever after he always used the phrase in some form, often just as DV for the Latin *deo volenti* – God willing – before expressing hopes or plans.

John and Hilda passed their enforced spare time in further study of the ancient Egyptian language. If he were to apply for the job at the British Museum then his language would need to be extremely good. 'I can't claim to any scholarly acquaintance but only to a fairly useful working knowledge.' He had plenty of time to mull over the advice he was getting on taking the British Museum job. He was less than inclined to go for it. His father and Hilda agreed with him, but Hans did not. 'Frankfort is all for accepting it if it is offered,' John told his father, 'because he says one can walk out at any time like Griffiths. But I can't see that. In any case it would mean that I should have to work so hard at the language that I should practically have to drop contact with the Aegean. What I am going to do though is to use it as a lever. I am going to write to Evans and ask his advice and if he does think I am worth keeping in the Aegean world he will at any rate have to show his hand. I also wonder whether a hint dropped at Cambridge might have any effect. However, of course I can't say anything definite until I hear from Glanville.'[30]

Charles Seltman, University Lecturer in Classics at Cambridge, was the first on the Aegean side to reply to John's leverage tactic. He tried 'to dissuade me from having dealings with the powers of darkness – ie the BM… and is moving heaven and earth to prevent it. I hope to get the same result from Evans and the rest… This possibility of the BM is more useful as a lever than I dreamed.'[31]

Now that the season was over the team went their separate ways. Brian and Molly Emery went on to their camp at Gourneh, where Emery was copying the exquisite reliefs in the tomb of Ramose, while the others, after some time off, were to go on to Tell el-Amarna. Hilda had come to like the Emerys, and they came several times to visit John. 'We have got on with them very well. Emery especially is a very pleasing character. We shall miss him at Amarna, especially at hockey.'[32]

Hilda nursed John attentively, frightened by the suddenness of his illness. John was more stoical, glad that it had happened in Luxor rather than on site. The knee was mending, but slowly. John was confined to his room and balcony, and was getting thoroughly bored – 'I read and write and eat and sleep'.[33] So he was glad of the visits of the cheerful doctor, Seth Smith, who brought a newly arrived member of the Amarna team. Seton Lloyd was a young architect who had trained with Sir Edwin Lutyens. He had no previous experience of archaeology and had not the slightest intention of becoming involved. In fact his presence in Egypt was as much a surprise to Hans Frankfort as it had been to Lloyd himself, for he had only taken the place of a friend at the last minute. A mutual friend in Cairo arranged the introduction to Seth Smith, whose father was also an architect. 'I got in touch through him with almost all the archaeological crowd here... I think it is being terribly good for me to find myself deposited among this congregation of classical scholars and literary professionals.'[34]

As Hans and Jettie Frankfort had already gone to Amarna to set up the camp, the visits of Smith and Lloyd provided some relief for Hilda. Rather than stay with John all the time, she took Lloyd round Luxor, and they visited the tomb of Tutankhamen which had just re-opened. John was under orders from Hans to stay still until his knee was completely healed, and then go to Aswan for a few days.

Meanwhile news began to filter through of changes at the British School at Athens. Arthur Woodward had decided to resign as Director, a move which made many hope that the way would now be open for the next generation, ending what John called 'the discouragement of the young' in a world dominated by old men.[35] Woodward, now forty-five, had been Director for six years and felt it was time for someone younger to succeed him. In giving notice to the Chairman, George Macmillan, he emphasised how important it was for the new Director to be a reasonably good Greek speaker, 'able to correspond in, attend lectures profitably in, and take part in discussions in the tongue.' It was first and foremost an administrative job, and would mean sacrifices by anyone who saw the job as an archaeological opportunity. 'And he will soon realise that getting a thing done in England and getting a thing done in Greece are two very different processes. And after all this he will find that the post has its unique compensations.'[36]

The committee's first choice for new Director was not, as anticipated, William Heurtley, the Assistant Director. Instead they approached a young Oxford classical scholar called Humfry Payne. Payne had also been offered a job by Merton College, Oxford, and was hesitant about accepting the Athens job, for it meant being separated for most of the year from his new wife, who wrote as a journalist under her maiden name, Dilys Powell. Dilys Powell was tied to a job in Fleet Street, and would have, at most, a couple of months leave each year to come out to Greece to join her husband.

Hans was delighted at the news of the imminent change in Athens. 'I just heard that Woodward resigned in Athens,' he wrote to Glanville, now back at the British Museum. 'If you can do anything to push Payne you will save the face of British Archaeology in Greece. For the other candidate is Cuttle, a flat-footed plebeian with a red nose, goggles and no brain. Please go carefully, but Hall might easily do something useful, via Forsdyke or alone. In time, with Payne for classical and John for Minoan stuff, Athens might become again worthwhile.'[37]

*

Finally John and Hilda escaped to Aswan. They stayed at the beautiful Cataract Hotel, with a verandah overlooking the river, and revelled in the hot and cold running water that would be denied them for the next two months.

The following day, four boatmen, singing all the way, took them by boat to the ancient temples of Philae, drowned by the original Aswan dam. 'The tops of the pylons and the capitals of the columns stand above the water now. We were rowed around to get a general view and then landed on the top of the architrave of one of the courts and climbed from there to the larger pylon and from there had a lovely view of the great rocks and hills all round the lake.'[38] At the dam itself, a little trolley car pushed by two boys took them along the upper edge of the dam, the water far beneath them forcing its way through the partially open sluice gates.

Refreshed and full of anticipation, John and Hilda set off to join the rest of the team at Tell el-Amarna, a place that would captivate John's heart for years to come.

6

February–April 1929

MALLAWI WAS A SMALL, attractive town, with a faintly European air beneath its coat of fine dust. Like many Egyptian towns of the time it was very cosmopolitan, its grocery stores run largely by Greeks and French, so John could indulge his penchant for beer and Greek wine.

When, in mid-February 1929, the train from Aswan spilled its passengers onto the platform after the eight-hour journey, John and Hilda were met by the camp postman and some of the men from the dig. There was no car, so a slow procession began, led by six men carrying their heaps of luggage, stopping often to shift loads or retrieve something dropped twenty feet off a flood dyke into a field below. After a precarious mile along the narrow causeways they reached the Nile, where a decrepit felucca was moored. This boat had served the expeditions to Tell el-Amarna for many years, and had been repaired so many times that it appeared like some patchwork toy. The tall stepped mast, tapering elegantly, was wound up in the bound sail. As they set off, a gentle wind picked up and the large triangular sail was unfurled. For an hour and a half, the felucca took them southwards upriver against a strong current. Rounding a bend in the river, they passed the north headland of the city of Akhenaten and Nefertiti, which had briefly been the capital of one of the greatest empires in the known world and which John had often imagined since his first fascination with its most unorthodox of Egyptian rulers. Here the cliffs pulled away from the river's edge to a depth of three miles, creating a roughly semicircular plain like a strung bow. Hemmed in by the cliffs of the high desert on the curved side of the plain to the east, the Nile formed its seven and a half mile long western edge.

From the river, fields of brilliant green, shaded by palm, lemon and mulberry trees, hid what lay beyond. The boat stopped at a small landing stage from which a narrow path led up the bank before vanishing into the cultivation. One by one, they filed along the narrow path, twisting through dappled greenery, past a blindfolded bullock turning a wooden water wheel. Emerging into the late sun, they followed the path through a gap in a large ruined wall and a dusty, rippled landscape opened up before their eyes.

The ripples were the buried mudbrick walls of the ancient city, made more visible by the long shadows of the afternoon, and John and Hilda found themselves at the northernmost tip of the still mostly buried city of Akhetaten, the city's ancient name, meaning 'Horizon of the Aten'.

The historical background to the Amarna period was still in the process of being worked out. Every new discovery added to the picture of this extraordinary episode in Egypt's history. John was later to write a book on Tell el-Amarna, in which he set out his own view of the 18th Dynasty Amarna pharaohs, together with a putative chronology. Akhenaten was born Amenhotep IV, son of Amenhotep III and Queen Ty. They belonged to a dynasty whose first king was Pharaoh Ahmose in 1539 BC, opening the period which became known as the New Kingdom. Ahmose and his three successors, Amenhotep I and Thothmes I and II, rid Egypt of the non-Egyptian Hyksos kings – the 15th, 16th and 17th Dynasties that formed the Second Intermediate Period. 'When they were driven out at the beginning of the 16th century BC the pursuit did not stop at the frontier, but extended on and on into Asia. The great Pharaohs of the early XVIIIth Dynasty regarded their conquests as the continuation of the war with the invader.'[1]

The early pharaohs did not care to hold on to the lands they conquered. They collected the tribute they wanted from the vanquished during each season of campaigning, but left the conquered lands to their own devices in between. Then came the great Queen Hatshepsut who used her reign not to campaign but to build up Egypt into a secure and prosperous country. This infuriated her nephew, later Thothmes III, who longed for the campaigns of her predecessors. 'Much as Thothmes III hated her memory, he must have acknowledged to himself that, thanks to her, he had greater resources and a better organised country behind him than any of his predecessors. The administrative training which he had had during the weary years of peace also stood him in good stead, for his purpose was an empire, not a hunting-ground for spoil.'

Thothmes III conquered the eastern coast of the Mediterranean and inland as far as the Euphrates, setting up a system of government as he went. 'Egyptian residents were appointed in every important city. Travelling inspectors made their rounds. The local kings sent their sons to Egyptian Universities. In many ways the Empire resembled the Native States of India, with their English advisers and their heirs to the throne at Oxford and Cambridge.' Egypt had become a great empire, which the two succeeding pharaohs, Amenhotep II and Thothmes IV, maintained and even enlarged a little. The Pharaoh of Egypt developed diplomatic relations with his 'brother' of Babylon and his 'royal cousin' of Mitanni. Mitanni was an empire in the north of what is now Iraq and Syria, which acted as an important buffer state between the Egyptian dominions and the hostile Hittite Empire in what is now Turkey.

When Amenhotep III ascended the throne in c.1411 BC, his empire was assured and secure. Tribute came in from all his predecessors' conquests.

'Amenhotep III did not even have to lead the military parade usual for a new king', John wrote. 'In the fifth and sixth years of his reign he fought in Nubia, claimed to have made fresh conquests, returned home and devoted the rest of his life to the pleasures of the chase and the court.' It was left to his queen to maintain the confidence of the empire's outposts. Queen Ty was, unusually, not Amenhotep III's sister, nor even of royal blood, which was stranger still. She was the daughter of Yuia and Tuyu, who were both greatly enriched by her marriage.

The Egypt in which Amenhotep IV grew up was a country not of war and battles, but of hunting and leisure. But these pastimes left the young man cold, even when he became pharaoh himself, co-opted onto the throne, as John and others thought at the time, alongside his father in about the 25th year of the latter's reign (c.1386–4 BC). 'His main preoccupation was with religion', John wrote of the younger pharaoh. Egypt had for centuries worshipped her own pantheon, with many gods specific to particular regions of the country. But when she became a single country and the pharaoh the King of the Two Lands (Upper and Lower Egypt), two dominant gods emerged. Amen, king of the gods, was at first local to Thebes (Luxor) and the Theban 18th Dynasty pharaohs lavished the spoils of their conquests on his temples. The cult of Ra, the Sun god, was centred on Heliopolis, north of what is now Cairo. The vast priesthood of these two gods wielded great power and immense wealth. But around the time of Amenhotep IV's grandfather, Thothmes IV, a more international god emerged. This was the 'Aten', or sun disk. 'It is not surprising', John explained, 'that with the growth of internationalism, symbolized by the entrance of Pharaoh into the council of kings, a god should arise whose appeal was more universal.'

Where Amenhotep III acknowledged this new god up to a point, he still considered Amen to be paramount; but he was old now. Queen Ty, who was largely in charge of the running of the empire, perhaps saw some diplomatic advantage in this less parochial god. However, his son, Amenhotep IV, and his wife (and sister), Nefertiti, embraced the new god to the exclusion of all others, and 'to the new king the Aten was the one sole god through whom all life comes. The other gods were devils and were to be proscribed. Here indeed was a revolution.' Only Ra, as a sun god, retained some favour, but as the young pharaoh's very name honoured the god Amen, he changed it to Akhenaten, meaning 'It is well with the Aten'. John described Akhenaten and Nefertiti as religious maniacs, with the determination of zealots to convert those around them, and the power to enforce it.

All about them in Thebes, however, were monuments to the old religion and the conspicuous wealth of Amen. Akhenaten wanted his capital to honour only the Aten, and to be untainted by the old religion. So, in about the fourth year of his reign, he began to search for a new site to build his capital. Two hundred miles to the north he found it at a spot that later became Tell el-Amarna. In the cliffs surrounding the semicircular plain, Akhenaten ordered vast stelae to be carved, defining the boundaries of his city and declaring what he planned to build there. A city of mud-brick and rubble sprang from the sand, the ordinary buildings whitewashed to look like stone, the more important ones thinly faced with stone. Speed was essential for the impatient pharaoh, resulting in some very poor quality construction. There were not enough skilled craftsmen, and many of those carving inscriptions were illiterate, and needed rough examples in plaster as a guide to lettering.

*

As John and Hilda emerged from the cultivation, they saw, a hundred dusty yards ahead, an ancient house that had been rebuilt on its 3300-year-old foundations to become the North Dig House. Behind it loomed the north cliffs, just before they met the river's edge, taking on the reds of the sinking sun. In that light the colours at Amarna intensify and the plain takes on a rich beauty unimaginable in the blank and flattening light of midday.

The North Dig House was surrounded by desert but the tops of felucca sails were visible above the palm trees as a reminder of how close the river was. 'This house is delightful', Hilda wrote. The rooms led off a central courtyard with four stone bases where pillars had once supported a roof, clerestory windows giving light and cool air to a central room. In front of this, another courtyard had originally been a loggia, a covered area with an open colonnade on one or more sides. 'It is all of mud and mud-brick with wooden beams and bamboo or reed roofing and is most attractive. John and I have two rooms opening one out of the other and are beautifully comfortable.'[2]

In the dining room, two more bases had once supported plastered wooden pillars and now left little room for the table. A door led off to a small sitting room and another to a similar small room with shelves for the finds. The bedrooms were ranged along the east side of the house and the plastered mud-brick walls kept the rooms cool by day and warm by night. 'We've caught a few mice in our sitting room but they are too well behaved to come into our bedroom.'[3]

There were four modern villages in the plain, all along the river bank. Et-Till was the most northerly, and its full name, et-Till el-Amarna, derived from the Bedawi tribe, the Beni Amran, who had settled the area in the early 18th century. There was never a 'tell', in the sense of a mound formed by successive layers of occupation, but an early foreigner's mistake stuck and the site was known ever after as Tell el-Amarna.

The full importance of this extraordinary site had been understood only

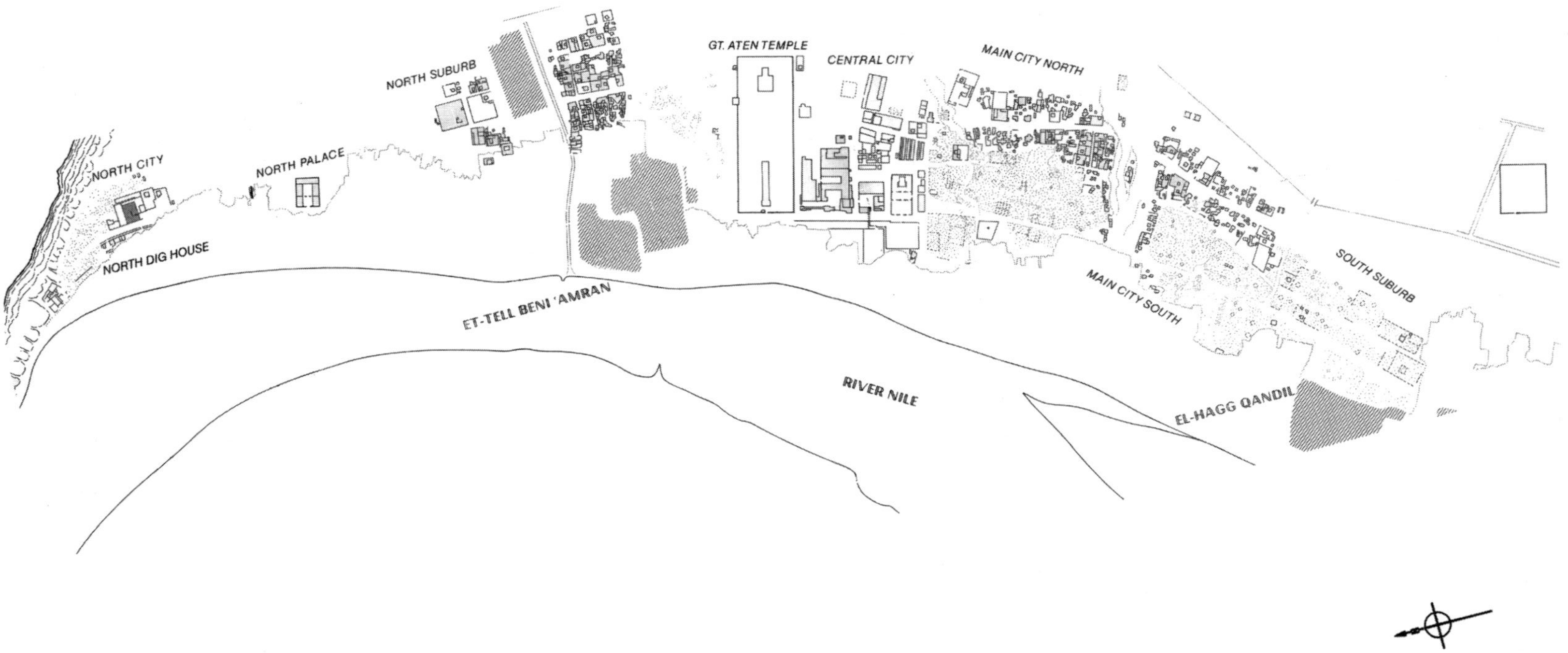

After Kemp & Garfi 1993 Copyright Egyptian Exploration Society: Reproduced with permission

3 TELL EL AMARNA : THE MAIN CITY

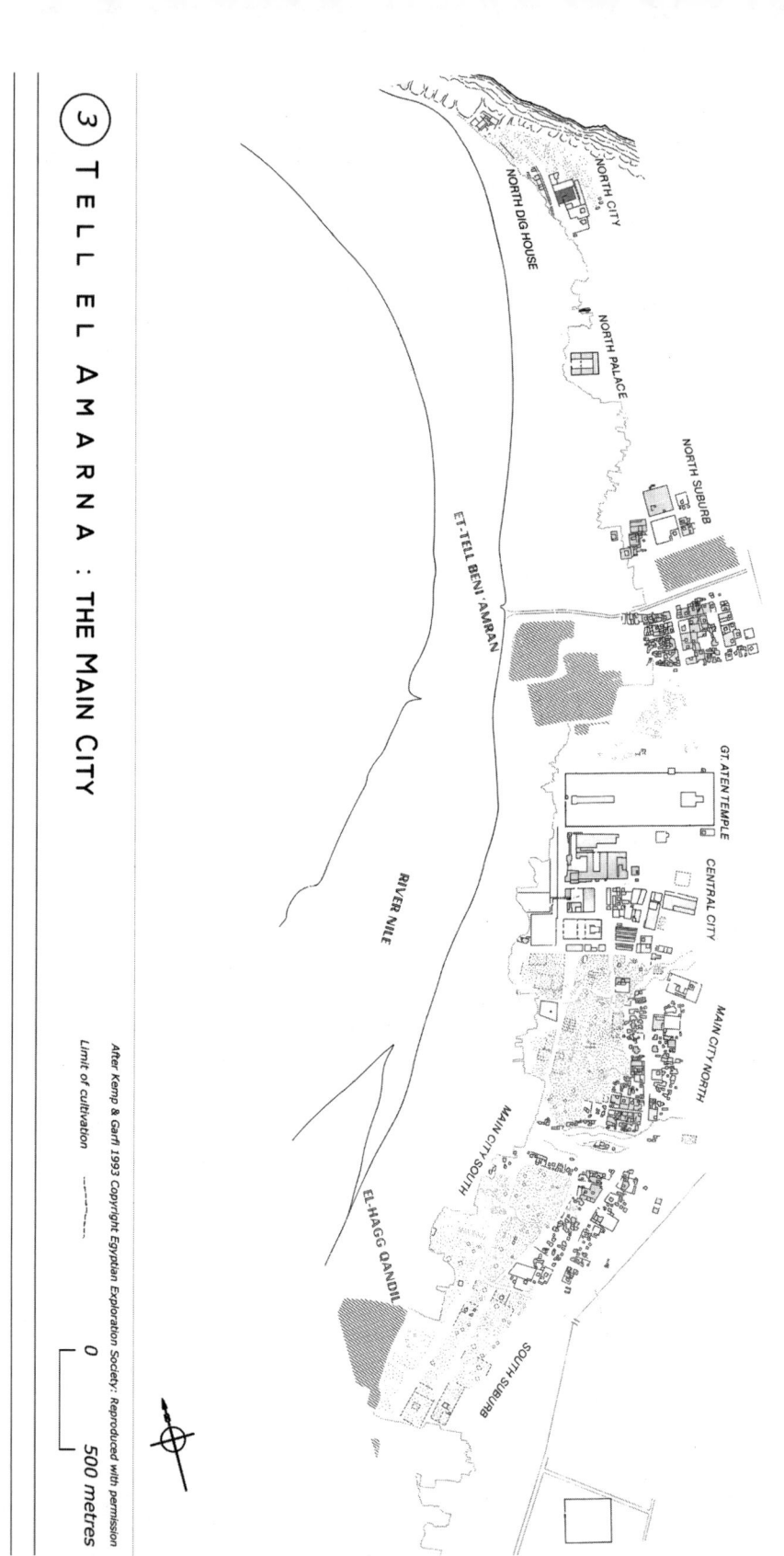

after the chance discovery in 1887 by an old peasant woman of more than 300 hard-baked terracotta tablets, which she proceeded to hawk around the local collectors. Eventually someone recognised that the tablets, the 'Amarna Letters', were inscribed with the cuneiform writing of the Akkadian language and were dated to the second half of the second millennium BC, when Egypt was ruled by the pharaohs of the 18th Dynasty. It turned out that the Amarna Letters had come from the ruins of the 'House of Correspondence of Pharaoh'. In 1891–2 Flinders Petrie had carried out the first excavation of the ruins, the results of which were published in 1894. John later wrote to Petrie, 'I should like to thank you for the inspiration to archaeology your books gave me when I was still at school'.[4] In a single season, Petrie found the Records Office from which the Letters had come, a great temple to the Aten, and a palace, which he called the King's House, as well as parts of the official palace. He also uncovered some of the large private houses of the pharaoh's officials in the central and southern parts of the widespread site. Following Nefertiti's death in c. 1367 BC the city had been largely abandoned; it was the only capital of ancient Egypt not to be buried under a modern city, but was covered by 3300-years-worth of wind-blown sand and alluvial deposits.

The concession to dig the site had passed in 1907 to a German team under the direction of Ludwig Borchardt. They carried out an extensive survey of the plain and systematically excavated the city until 1914, when the Great War prevented further work. Their greatest find remained largely unknown until after the war. The painted limestone head of Nefertiti, with her exquisitely fine features and sensual elegance, became one of the most famous objects of ancient Egyptian art, an icon of beauty and grace. John acquired a picture of the sculpture from which he would not be parted. As a Cambridge friend would later remember, 'he had a very special affection for Nefertiti, and did not encourage any rude remarks about her neck and forehead'.[5] The Egypt Exploration Society had taken over the concession to dig the site in 1921, under the direction first of Thomas Peet, Professor of Egyptology at Liverpool, and then of Leonard Woolley in 1921–2. When, in 1923, Woolley abandoned Egypt to dig at Ur of the Chaldees in Mesopotamia, the excavations were continued by Francis Newton, who had worked as architect for Evans at Knossos in Crete, by Francis Llewellyn Griffith and finally by Hans Frankfort.

*

The site of Tell el-Amarna and its setting could not have been more different from Armant. Set out in a band along the east bank of the Nile, the remains of the city extended far to the south of the dig house, which was at the northernmost end of the plain. That season's dig was to take place in the North Suburb, about two kilometres south over soft sand. The route to the dig took them past the North Palace, which had been excavated between 1923 and 1927, revealing fishponds and aviaries. The floors and walls were beautifully painted in a style unique to Tell el-Amarna, depicting birds and other wildlife in marshland. When the palace was completed, Frankfort moved the excavation to the North Suburb, revealing roads lined with large, prosperous houses interspersed with a mass of increasingly small, poor buildings away from the roads. The 1928–9 season was continuing this work on the west side of one of two main north-south roads in this part of the city (West Road), and it was becoming clear that they were finding predominantly merchants' houses.

Further south lay the Central City, where all the most important administrative buildings of the ancient city had been, as well as the Palace and temples to the Aten. Just south of these was the Main City, the principal residential area. Further south again, five to six kilometres away from the North Dig House, was the wealthy South Suburb. The houses in this area were magnificent, and the people who lived in them were the very wealthiest and most influential officials of the city after the royal family themselves. The great houses of the North and South Suburbs and of the later North City had been surrounded by estates of gardens, stables, granaries and bakehouses, the larger ones with their own wells. In between these estates the very poorest inhabitants managed to fit their simple homes, using the walls of surrounding houses wherever they could. The modern villages of el-Haj Qandil and el-Amariya lay near the South Suburb, where, as with the North Dig House, the ruins of one of the largest ancient houses had been rebuilt to house the German excavators of the South Suburb.

One kilometre beyond the southern extent of the ancient city, near the southernmost of the modern villages, el-Hawata, where the cliffs once more drew close to the Nile, were the remains of the Maru-aten. This lavishly decorated royal residence, with its beautifully painted plaster floors, walls and pools (the latter painted with fish), has long since vanished beneath fields. John later described it as the most important of the king's residences outside the city, the 'precinct of the Southern Pool', a 'pleasure-palace or Paradise'.

*

The main workforce for the work in the North Suburb came from et-Till, the village closest to the site. But there were one or two Haj Qandilis as well, and the proportions changed the closer the work got to the central and southern parts of the city. The main bulk of the city lay between the villages of et-Till and Haj Qandil. Carrying out the more difficult work were the *Quftis*, skilled diggers from the town of Quft near Luxor, their families trained originally by Sir Flinders Petrie.

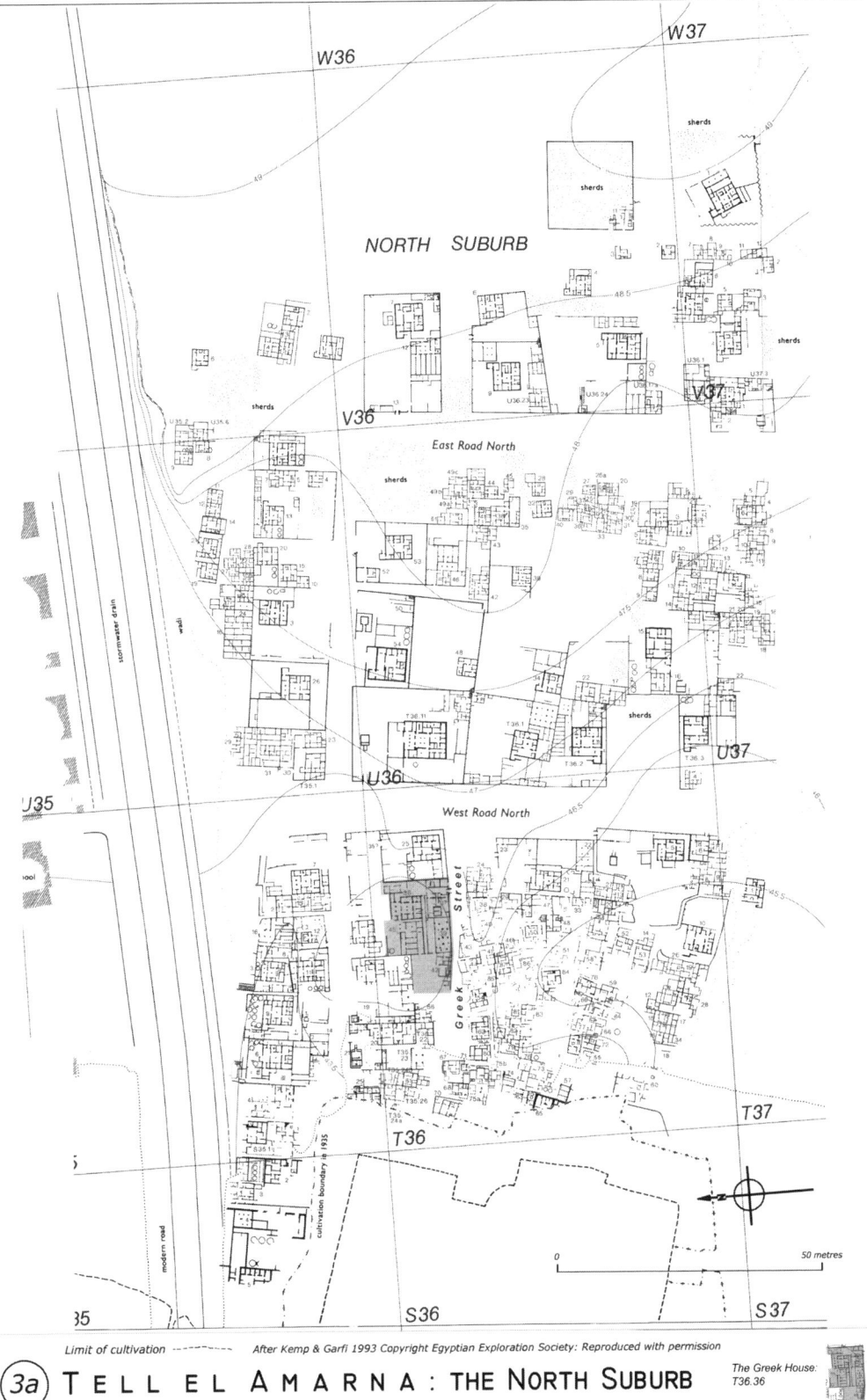

(3a) TELL EL AMARNA: THE NORTH SUBURB

After Kemp & Garfi 1993 Copyright Egyptian Exploration Society: Reproduced with permission

The Greek House: T36.36

As at Armant, each digger had four or five child basket-carriers, who would carry away the excavated soil in small straw baskets to the nearest dump. Over all these presided the *ra'is*, who ensured that everyone was working efficiently, usually, as Lloyd recorded, 'with long straps'.[6] The Amarna dig was known for the chanting of the children and workmen as they worked: 'O, the Baths of Alexandria' was one chorus that Lloyd particularly remembered. In overall supervision were the team members such as John, checking that everything was carefully excavated and the finds properly collected. Lloyd, as site architect, measured the emerging plan of the suburb.

The team was much the same as at Armant, including the now 'great lolloping puppy' Bucchis, with the exception of the Emerys and Glanville and the addition of Hilda and Seton Lloyd. Hilda described Lloyd as a 'long slim youth with a quiet voice, a pleasant humour, and a discriminating taste in books, as well as nice manners and disposition', and he had fitted effortlessly into his unexpected job.[7] Hans was not in the least disconcerted at the unplanned change in personnel. 'Lloyd is a great success, a nice fellow, well read and keen.'[8] Lloyd, in his turn, described the Pendleburys as 'unequivocally English'.[9]

The work of that season was entirely on domestic buildings of the North Suburb. Frankfort had begun excavating this area the previous season, his first as Director, two years earlier. The large houses here belonged to the wealthy rather than to the nobility, who lived closer to the palace in the South Suburb. The North Suburb was set between two wadis running into the Nile from the High Desert to the east. Further divided by two ancient north–south thoroughfares, known as the East and West Roads, the suburb remained almost intact, with only the western edge now covered by the cultivation, and provided a complete residential unit of the city that could be entirely excavated in only a few seasons.

The house of a rich family in the city of Akhetaten was typically set in its own enclosed estate, often with its own well and beehive-shaped granaries to hold grain brought from the family's agricultural estates. Many families had land on the other side of the Nile, but the grain could also have come from their other estates elsewhere in Egypt. Ancillary buildings were slightly separated from the owner's more elegant domain, as was the small, brightly painted private chapel which some of the largest houses had. The chapel was usually set in a garden of trees and shrubs, separated from the house by a wall, for which the fertile Nile mud was brought in.

The houses were of a standardised form, with bedrooms and a bathroom off a central pillared room. A smaller, usually two-pillared room, facing west or south, supported the columns of the floor above, with its outer wall almost open to the elements in the form of a loggia, where the family could sit and enjoy the fresh air and the view. The central room was the most important in the house and was often the most decorated. It was cool because it was surrounded by an insulating shell of rooms, and its clerestory windows, raised on three sides above the height of the surrounding rooms, trapped the breezes without letting in the direct heat of the sun. In one corner of the central room one of the doorways led via a staircase up to the roof, and to the upper room or loggia. Evidence for these loggias only survived in the smaller column bases and traces of plasterwork which did not belong to the rooms below in which they were found. The decoration was simple, consisting mainly of a frieze depicting fruit, flowers and birds. The beams of the roof too would have been plastered and painted with geometric designs.

It was the personal details that made Tell el-Amarna so different from the standard Egyptological world of tombs and temples. There was still an echo in every house of the people who had lived there. In one whitewashed, stone-lined bathroom, a low wall isolated the bathing area which was lined with stone slabs to make it waterproof. A stone floor in this cubicle allowed the water, presumably poured over the bather across the low wall by a servant, to drain into a vase or out through a drain. Next to this was another slab with depressions carved into its surface, in which lay the traces of aromatic substances. 'Beside this lay a stone stool,' John wrote later, 'and evidently the master of the house was rubbed down after his bath with the preparations of which the grease and crystals still remained in the bowls. Beyond the bathroom was the closet. Here was a pierced limestone seat, hollowed out for comfort and supported between two brick compartments containing sand. In one case pottery dippers were found in these. Below the seat was a vase.'[10]

John instantly fell in love with Amarna. It touched something in his imagination which Armant had failed to do. Glorious though the burial chambers of the sacred Bucchis Bulls had been, here at Tell el-Amarna was a city which had once bustled with people and echoed to the sound of voices, and it was the daily lives of these almost tangible and often named people that was revealed rather than another clue to the chronological sequence. It was archaeology at its most intimate, both rewarding and inspiring. 'We have found the house of a master painter,' John described to Herbert. 'Though my suggestion that the presence of wine and food jars in every single room was due to the fact that he had been told by his doctor only to drink at meals, and therefore ensured that there should be a slight meal wherever he wanted one, was treated with contempt. As also was my explanation of the two human skeletons found there as those of physicians who had ordered him to cut out drink all together.'[11] The wine jars were marked in hieratic script with the origin, vintage and quality of the wine, such as 'Wine of the House of Aten. Year 3. GOOD; wine of the Southern Pool. Year 7. GOOD GOOD'.[12]

The mud-brick houses, cool in summer and warm in winter, often had stone lintels, jambs and thresholds of doors, which the richer and more pretentious owners would have elaborately carved to show off their position and status. Wood, a rare and expensive material in Egypt, was used sparingly for columns and doors, though termites devoured what the inhabitants did not salvage when the city was abandoned, and it was rarely found in excavated buildings.

Furniture was never found, because it had all been taken away when the city was abandoned. However, the furniture of the time survived well in the tomb of Tutankhamen and other tombs at Deir el Medina. It only took a small leap of the imagination to place the high elegant beds into the platformed niches of the bedrooms of these houses at Amarna, with their extra thick walls to keep the room cool and support wind-catchers. The wooden couches, stools and chairs, so well illustrated in the finds from the tomb of Tutankhamen and in wall paintings, were draped with embroidered covers, the floors strewn with rugs and animal skins. 'The inside of the house', John wrote later, 'though simple and rather austere, must have been a glow of colour with the patches of bright paint and the gilded or polished furniture. The windows seem small, but the sunlight is so intense that large windows were unnecessary, and besides they would let in the dust and sand, since there was neither glass nor oiled parchment which the Minoans used.'[13]

Even the styles of the clothes and jewellery worn by those who lived there were known from the representations of Tutankhamen and his young wife, Ankh-sen-pa-aten, third daughter of Akhenaten and Nefertiti, and the same queen – later renamed Ankhsenamen – whose plight had come to light in the Amarna Letters. Both men and women would usually wear a fine linen robe. The women's robes, often represented as transparent, fell to just above their ankles in close-fitting pleats, lightly bound above the waist to accentuate the figure. The arms were always left uncovered except by heavy bracelets and torques, and their hands were bejewelled. Over their breasts they would wear either a heavy collar-type ornament of gold and precious stones, or a lighter and cheaper version of this in coloured faience. It was the small beads that made up these elaborate composite necklaces that were the most common finds on the site. Made of brightly coloured faience in tiny moulds, these were shaped into all sorts of fruits and flowers. 'In many of the tombs of the nobles at Thebes,' John described, 'we can see the merrymaking and the wild parties that must have gone on in such houses. Laughter in Egypt is never very far from the surface and this world was so good a place that the next must be like it, for nothing better was possible.'[14]

'We hope to finish our little block of houses in about a month', John wrote to his father, 'when Hilda and I may be sent up to the hills to look for the hitherto undiscovered and probably unplundered tomb of Smenkhara, the successor or rather co-regent of Akhenaten (this is confidential) while the rest go to the Great Temple site and try and rescue some architectural details from the mess which Howard Carter made of it when digging for Petrie.'[15]

The tomb in question was some two hours walk away across the high desert. Some locals had reported to Frankfort that there was a tomb there. Hilda described what they found at the end of the journey. 'It was an impressive place, where huge column drums had been carried and then abandoned at the mouth of the valley.'[16] They identified where the ropes had been secured — holes were carved out of the rock as if to pass the ropes through for the hauling up or letting down of some large object. Nearby they saw what could have been a filled-in pit. Frankfort was intrigued by what they had reported and determined to investigate it further one day, though they were aware that it could just as easily prove to be the remains of an ancient quarry as of an ancient tomb.

The team's days off were spent exploring the vast area of the plain, the deep wadis that had been gouged out of the cliffs further east and south, and the high desert above the cliffs behind the house. From the latter, they could see the north end of the site laid out before their feet, with the pattern of the houses and roads of the ancient city sharply visible through the dust and sand. Along the eastern edge was what would once have been a bustling riverside. Ships bringing goods from the Levant and Asia would have been a familiar sight, alive with the chattering of different tongues from the Aegean, the Hittite Empire, and the Mitannian State in northern Mesopotamia, as well as Nubia and the other regions south of Egypt.

To the west, across the river, the far larger plain was the garden and grain basket of Akhetaten. Boundary stelae were set up to define the limits of the new city, enclosing vast tracts of fertile agricultural land to support the incoming citizens. Now the silver band of the river with its midstream islands was bordered by only a narrow strip of cultivation as it curved about, meandering east and west on its journey north and flecked with the sails of feluccas.

The high desert was very different from the dusty plain below. The high, steep limestone cliffs had been eaten away and undercut by centuries of wind, and loose rubble scree covered the foot of the cliffs, where a narrow path wound steeply up behind the house. The high desert was a plateau that stretched as far as the eye could see, cut at stages by deep wadis created by occasional sudden and torrential downpours and gouged by quarries. Over the whole rocky surface were strewn boulders of dark chert, some perfectly spherical. In the Stone Age, this had been an ideal source of stone for tools and the flakes left from their manufacture still lay everywhere. The darkness of these rocks and the blankness of the landscape made a desolate sight.

Far to the east, across this stony desert, was the Red Sea, but there was nothing in between but the fading tracks, as forgotten now as the trade towns on the Red Sea coast that they had once linked with the Nile. In the city's heyday, the 'Mazoi' or 'Medjay', the police of Akhetaten, would patrol the tops of the cliffs, which formed the eastern boundary of the city, looking for outlaws hiding in the maze of wadis.

*

'We are being very successful here', John wrote to his father, 'more in the architectural line than in the actual finds.'[17] The majority of the finds were small and often broken. Following the death of Akhenaten and Nefertiti, the city had been abandoned by the wealthier courtiers, and the inhabitants given time to gather their possessions. As a result, the objects left behind tended to be small, such as beads and pendants, which had been overlooked or broken and discarded. Such beads were strung together for displays in London or Cairo, but the result was usually a stringy, rather insignificant and unconvincing necklace. There were also flat pieces of faience, sometimes decorated with lotus flowers, which appeared to be fragments of inlay, possibly used in decorating furniture. Yet the lotus pieces had a strange arrangement of holes cast beneath the surface of the design, which remained a mystery.

Then, one day, hidden beneath a couple of bricks in the courtyard of a house they were excavating, was found, wrapped in linen, a complete necklace, though somewhat jumbled up. Hans' wife, Jettie, spent the entire afternoon lying on the ground, gently blowing sand away from the tiny loose beads and gathering them up. The garland was of faience, moulded into the shapes of a variety of fruit and flowers, then fired with different glazes to produce vivid combinations of colours. Hans was overwhelmed by the find and immediately wrote a long, nearly illegible scrawl, covered in scratchy sketches and scribbles in the margin, to Stephen Glanville.[18] Suddenly he could see that the pieces of white faience tinged with the subtle green and blue of the lotus flowers they represented, were not inlays for furniture at all, but the end pieces of garland necklaces. The unusual holes set at different angles were to gather up to six strings of beads while sitting flat onto the skin of the wearer, at the same time acting as a counterpoise. Likewise, the small pendants, smaller than a fingernail, were not to be strung together as one single line necklace, they were simply one row of a much larger necklace.

It was the task of the London office of the EES to make sense of these hurried messages from the field, and present them as an interim report. It fell to a young woman, Mary Chubb, as assistant secretary, to decipher the barely legible screed. Mary was the sister of Tony Chubb, who had been in Egypt with Chicago House copying inscriptions at Medinet Habu. Stephen Glanville was married to their sister Ethel, so there was already a strong Egyptian connection.

Frankfort had gone to the trouble of typing his report this time, but even this gave Mary the impression 'of having been done while going over rough country on camel-back.' It began, 'Nekclace offaience7/8, consistingof 2 POlychrome end)pieces in the shape of?xxxlotus-fowlers.'[19] After some hard deciphering, Mary read back the description of the necklace. The first row was of cornflowers in blue and green. Beneath this was a row of mandrakes or poppy leaves, and the third was of bunches of vivid blue grapes. The fourth row combined white flower petals with a yellow base alternating with long blue cornflowers on green stems, while the fifth was a row of petals or dates – two blue, one green, two red, one green, two blue and so on. The last row was of long lotus petals with blue tips.

Along some of the rows, in between the above beads, were tiny ring beads and cylinder beads, filling in the spaces to hide the string. These continued beyond the front of the necklace to vanish on each side into the lotus-flower counterpoises. These fell down over the back of the shoulders to balance the garland in place, and out of them one string emerged from the point of the lotus flower to carry a single row of lotus petals across the back.

Mary was captivated. 'I stopped typing and looked across the table at the secretary... No Field Director ought to have to waste time typing these reports... Wouldn't it be wonderful if one member of each dig did nothing but this sort of work... They might send someone who was on the staff already.'[20] So began Mary Chubb's involvement with Amarna, a time of which she would later write so vividly.

It fell to Hilda to re-string the complicated design, which took the best part of two days. Hans asked John to model it for a photograph, for it would very likely have been worn originally by a man. But John was tanned only from the neck up, which rather spoiled the effect, so they also asked one of the local boys, Amin, to pose in it – 'We thought of browning John with cocoa but it wouldn't be very pleasant.'[21]

The registration of finds – drawing, describing and measuring – was done by the team around the dining room table after the evening meal had been cleared away. The small repetitive finds such as amulets, beads, ring bezels and pendants were organised into a typology to avoid recording every one. 'John's help in all these matters is invaluable', Frankfort wrote to Glanville, 'and I feel ashamed that he should only get his keep and the inefficient lubber [Shorter] fifty quid and his trip.'[22]

The unfortunate Shorter was still at the receiving end of the team's teasing, something John enjoyed very much. 'I had some pleasure yesterday with Shorter', John wrote to Herbert, 'to whom all things written are sacred and to be treated with the most distinguished consideration'. John gave Shorter a piece of his site notebook with what he said was the transcription of an inscription from a piece of painted plaster. 'The trained philologist spent three hours on it and then gave up in despair saying that it must be some curious prayer addressed to the Aten or to the King. I then got him to transliterate it – when it read very simply "You big stiff!"'[23]

The dig on the east side of West Road had now reached the wadi that defined the northern limit. The two wadis defining the north and south limits of these blocks were both ancient, so for the first time they were able to have a complete unit of the city, as it had been built, opened up before them. As the dig moved to the other side of West Road, the houses were increasingly small and crammed together, and they had to dig as much as ten feet down to reach the buildings, leading to vast quantities of spoil and the problem of where to dump it. But the area proved productive. 'We have found what John desired,' Frankfort announced to Glanville in his peculiar English. 'The harlots' quarter. At least we found a place which is a conglomeration of small square rooms (cubicles), a magnificent steatite Bes, 15cm high, on an alabaster pedestal, more Chinese than anything I know. Unfortunately he lost his tool and his tongue, which were both, no doubt, red jasper and prominent. That (viz: the loss) had one advantage, namely that he could be displayed, an hour after discovery, to James Henry [Breasted] with Mr and Mrs JD Rockerfeller [sic] and party. It was a delightful visit, for all were keen and extremely interested and the R's incredibly and noticeably relieved at, for once, not being dragged through tombs and temples, but seeing stuff of real life people. I had hastily the faience garland necklace brought up and also the monkey chariot. The first was simply glorious in the sun and stunned them completely. I am sure there will something come from this for us which is good.'[24]

The Rockefeller party had left their yacht on the river and arrived on site on 'a gaggle of decrepit donkeys, accompanied by secretaries, valets, detectives, cameramen etc.', Lloyd wrote to a friend. 'I had the job of showing Mrs Rockefeller round – and eventually of building her back onto her mount in a welter of large white legs and flannel underclothing.'[25]

For Hans something good was to come of the visit. James Henry Breasted – 'the Grand Old Man of American Egyptology' – was a wealthy and influential American academic specialising in the archaeology of Egypt and the Near East. The real reason for his visit had been to recruit Hans Frankfort. 'James wants to hatch young men and wants a chair for that in Chicago, combined with fieldwork and me in the chair.' He was looking for a likely candidate who could both teach and lead a major fieldwork project in Iraq, the site of Eshnunna, which had just been discovered in the desert east of Baghdad. Frankfort was more than hesitant at the idea of living and working in 1920s Chicago. 'I feel already rather self-conscious about the 'Dr' but that at least came from a university founded in 1575 in a town which had lived on rats and its aldermen for months during a siege. But Chicago...!'[26]

The work began to close down at the end of March, and as the excitement of the dig was over they began to plan their travels afterwards: John and Hilda dreamed of a couple of nights of luxury at Shepheard's in Cairo. Hilda succumbed to the inevitable Egyptian trial – 'We've most of us had our turn at 'Gyppy tummy' and it's mine now. I feel much better today though I'm still eating interesting things like dry Force and plain boiled rice. John and Hans are shut in the dark room with the photographs they have just taken. Shorter is poring over hieratic inscriptions on jars recording epoch-making remarks like so many measures of good wine, or so many lbs. of meat. Lloyd is busy in the drawing office with the plan of the site and I think Jettie is washing the statuette's face with delicate care.'[27]

John's spare time had been spent finishing off his *Ægyptiaca* catalogue, making alterations, checking for errors and creating the index. Henry Hall, Keeper of Egyptian and Assyrian Antiquities at the British Museum, had agreed to write the foreword, which would give the book extra academic weight. So all that remained was the section on Rhodes, which they could complete in the following months, and the illustrations, which Hilda was to do.

*

News had meanwhile arrived from Greece that Humfry Payne had been made Director of the British School at Athens. This opened up a possibility in John's mind. 'With regard to Greece and the School, I think if Heurtley does resign as he well may (since he and Payne don't get on over well), that I might have a good chance of keeping the prehistoric flag flying!' Now, with the remote possibility of applying for the BSA Assistant Directorship, it was clear to John that he did not want the British Museum job. 'I wired (and wrote back) that I was sorry but I could not apply in spite of the certainty.'[28] The next favourite, Alan Shorter, would now get the job.

John had been waiting to hear from Evans, who had been occupied sorting out the aftermath of the robbery of his coin collection. It was not until after John had turned down the British Museum job that he finally got word from Evans: 'Today came a letter from Evans, emphasising the lack of opportunities in the Aegean and advising me to take the BM job. There's nice encouragement for you!' Frankfort was determined to help John, so he wired to the new Director recommending John as his '2nd in command'. 'There might well be a chance of the post as Heurtley can hardly (worse luck) stay on after this and they can hardly put an older man under Payne – who is only twenty-six.'[29]

John was wrong. Heurtley did decide to stay. The British School's secretary, W.R. Le Fanu, wrote to Woodward of John's enquiry about Heurtley's post: 'Pendlebury has apparently found the Egyptian climate too much for him, and seeing Payne's appointment as your successor wired to his father to enquire if Heurtley's post was vacant too, as he would apply for it if so, as he wishes to "devote himself to Aegean archaeology". Macmillan wrote to Mr Pendlebury (senior) explaining that the Assistant Directorship is not vacant, and making instead a provisional offer of his new studentship.'[30]

George Macmillan, the School's Chairman, had decided some months earlier to inaugurate a new studentship at the School in Athens. The studentship was to be open to a British Man (stressed by Macmillan), with an Honours degree in Classics, who had shown a 'special knowledge of some branch of Greek Archaeology, History, Art or Language'. Initially for a period of two years, with the option of a third, the student would receive between £200 and £250 per academic year. The condition was that the Macmillan Student stay for a minimum of eight months in Greek lands and, while carrying out his own research, be completely at the disposal of the Director.

John wrote immediately to Le Fanu to find out more. 'I have just heard from Pendlebury from Egypt,' Le Fanu recorded, 'enquiring for the terms and regulations of the Macmillan Studentship, and if, as seems likely, he applies I have no doubt that the Committee will appoint him to it.'[31]

If he had been at all discouraged by Evans's initial attitude, John was greatly reassured by Alan Wace's response. Wace wrote that John would do better to go for the Assistant Directorship after Heurtley's next three-year stint, travelling and learning in the meantime. He had been asking around Cambridge on John's behalf, trying to find a sinecure position to allow him the freedom to do this. He also thought John should get in touch with Carl Blegen, an American archaeologist, and ask to join his team for a while. Frankfort disagreed with this advice as he thought Blegen was selfish from the digging point of view, although he was good at exploration. Finally, Wace suggested that John enter his catalogue for the Hare Prize for unpublished research. John was not keen on this, as the next award was a year away and he had made arrangements for publishing the catalogue with the Cambridge University Press.

John preferred instead to try for the Macmillan Studentship. The disadvantage of the Macmillan was that it would put him entirely at the disposal of the Director and force him to stay in Greece for eight months, at the expense of continuing to work at Armant and Amarna. However, he felt refusing the Macmillan would alienate him from the School's Chairman, and give out the message that he turned work down. To take the Macmillan would also put him in a better position to apply for Heurtley's job when it became available. So he sent in his application.

*

John and Hilda spent the last day at Amarna going up to the Eastern Village. This had been dug in 1922 by Leonard Woolley, but he had missed a wall painting under a layer of plaster. John and Hilda had noticed it on a walk the day before, and went back to try to make a copy of it. 'Hilda traced and painted a marvellous scene of four figures of Bes – the lower half only unfortunately – which will undoubtedly be one of the features of the exhibition in July. It really was great fun – and the only tragedy is that the rest of the thing is not there and that Glanville has just published definitely the fact that figures in wall painting only occur in royal palaces!'[32] The day was tinged with sadness when Bucchis the puppy died, having contracted pneumonia and distemper. 'We all miss him', Frankfort wrote to Glanville. 'He was a nice brute.'[33]

The next morning, John and Hilda retraced their steps back through the cultivation and then downriver by felucca to catch their train at Mallawi. 'We had a very nice send off from the Frankforts. He really does seem to think I have done some good', John wrote to Herbert. 'He wants to meet you and find who gave me my memory (mine! that you used to curse!!).'[34]

Back in Cairo, John and Hilda treated themselves to two nights of luxury at Shepheard's Hotel. While they had been away, the Egyptian Museum had opened its exhibition of the treasure from Tutankhamen's tomb. The boy king had grown up at Akhetaten, and the landscape they had left behind had been familiar to him, although three thousand years separated them. The treasure showed the people who had inhabited the ancient city, such as his pretty wife, Ankh-sen-pa-aten. When her parents had died, the priests of the old order pressurised the young couple into returning to the old capital of Thebes and the old religion. Their names were changed from Tutankhaten to Tutankhamen and Ankhsenamen, to signify the end of the Aten religion. The echoes of what they left behind of their childhood home could be glimpsed in the objects that the

Museum was now displaying for the first time.

The staggering artistic skill of the ancient goldsmiths was for the first time fully comprehended. But the very objects, and the traditional manner in which the young king had been buried, were a witness to the failure of the dream that Akhenaten had realised on the plain of Tell el-Amarna. How did the king come to die so young? One of the most poignant of the Amarna Letters was a missive from Ankhsenamen, following the death of her husband Tutankhamen, to Suppiluliumas, the powerful Hittite king. Both sides of the correspondence survived in Egypt and at Hattusas, the heart of the Hittite empire in central Turkey. Though there was hostility between the two powers, she begged him to send her one of his sons to marry, as she would not marry one of her subjects. She trusted few of the people at court around her, and she risked everything by doing this. The Hittite king was not surprisingly shocked at the request and refused, convinced that it was a trick and that his son would only be murdered. She persisted, and finally the Hittite king agreed to join the two dynasties. The tragedy is that the young Hittite never did arrive, and from that point Ankhsenamen was never heard of again. So the last vestiges of the Amarna age fell silent with her. Only the systematic destruction of every image of Akhenaten and Nefertiti and the dismantling of every temple they ever built disturbed that silence.

In Tutankhamen's treasure John and Hilda could see the wealth of the people whose city they had been unearthing. The objects with which Ankhsenamen had buried her young husband were breathtaking, and brought the people who had lived at Amarna 3300 years ago into vivid picture.

Perhaps after Armant John may have been tempted eventually to sacrifice Egypt in favour of working in Crete, but Amarna took a hold on him every bit as powerful as Crete. He was keen to return to both sites, and Frankfort was equally keen to have him back, but the acceptance of the Macmillan Studentship would preclude him from returning to Egypt the following season. John's future, though full of possibilities, particularly in the Aegean area, was very uncertain.

(Above) John Pendlebury aged nine, 1913.
(Below, left) John, aged five, with his father, Herbert Pendlebury.
(Below, right) John and Hilda's children, David and Joan Pendlebury, at Cromer in Norfolk.

(Above, left) John, the athlete, Pembroke College Cambridge 1923–4.
(Above, right) John competing in the Oxford v. Cambridge hurdle relays, 1925 (with Cleckley of Oxford beside him).
(Below) Bob Dixon, Hilda White and John Pendlebury on the boat to Chalkis, Greece 1927.

(Above, left) John and Hilda Pendlebury on their wedding day, September 15th 1928. (Above, right) John and Hilda at Broughshare, Caldy, on their way to their wedding night at Claridges in London. (Below, left) Hilda at Olympia, Greece 1928. (Below, right) One of many visits to the Imperial Airways yacht, *SS Imperia*, stationed at Spina Longa, Crete 1932. Left to right: Rosaleen Angas, unknown, Skipper Poole, Seton Lloyd, John Pendlebury and Mary Chubb.

(Above) The 3300-year-old North Dig House, North City, Tell el-Amarna, 1931.
(Below) The Villa Ariadne, Knossos, built in 1906 by Sir Arthur Evans as his home in Crete.

(Above, left) Sir Arthur Evans, c. 1930.
(Above, right) Mr Elliadi, the British Vice-Consul.
(Below) Reconstructing the Throne Room, Knossos, 1930.

(Above) John fencing on the front terrace of the Villa Ariadne, Knossos, 1931.
(Below) John arriving at Mallawi Railway station, 1931–2 Amarna season.

(Top) Rosaleen Angas and Hilda Pendlebury on the Great Wall in the North City at Amarna, 1931–2. (Below, left) Work in progress at Amarna, with children in the background emptying the baskets of spoil 1931–2. The man at the front centre was nicknamed the 'Soldier of Fortune' by the team. (Below, right) Mary Chubb giving first aid to one of the basket girls, Tell el-Amarna 1931–2.

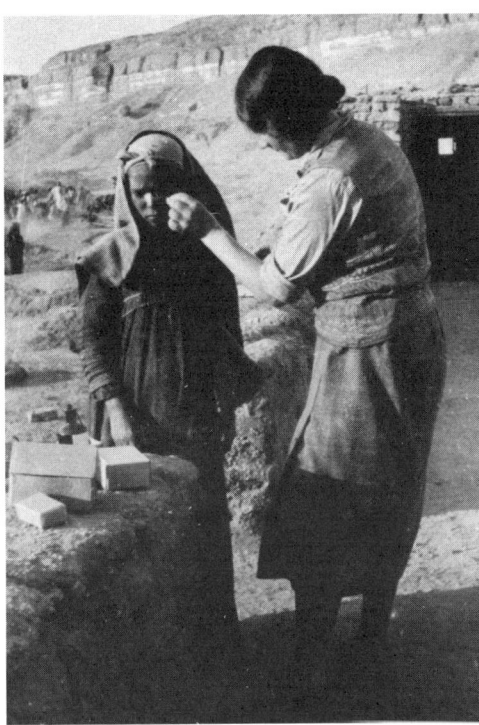

(Above, left) The Taverna, Knossos, after renovation by Ralph Lavers.
(Above, right) John on horseback at Khafaje, Iraq 1933.
(Below) Rachel Jacobsen, Jettie Frankfort and John at Khafaje, Iraq 1933.

7

April–December 1929

THE IDIOSYNCRATIC ENGLISH of the regulations for cabin-class passengers on the Rumanian package boat from Alexandria to Piraeus delighted John. 'Electric lambs in salon to be extinguished at 24 Midnight', they declared. 'Electric lights ventilators to be taken down while passenger leaving cabin', and 'Not to touch piano if can not play well'.[1] It was April 1929 and John, Hilda and Lloyd had been invited by Charles Seltman, one of John's tutors at Cambridge and a collector of antiquities, and his wife Isabel, to join them on a yachting trip round the Greek islands. They met the Seltmans and their hostess, an American lady and fellow collector called Mrs Emmett, at the small port of Phaleron, east of Piraeus. Their boat turned out to be a small steamer, built on the Clyde in 1898, which Mrs Emmett had chartered for the cruise.

Their voyage to Tinos and Delos was straightforward, but then the weather deteriorated. The April winds whipped up the seas about the boat for most of the nine hours it took them to reach Samos, leaving all on board drenched and wondering how long it would be before the boat sank. While the rain and sea-spray were welcome after months of dust and desert, nonetheless they were not sorry to reach harbour. They set off to explore and stretch their legs. 'Walking in Greece after Egypt', Hilda mused, 'makes one feel as if one had wings'.[2]

When the weather cleared, they sailed on to Chios and then Lesbos, guided for part of the way by dolphins through narrow straits, past wooded shores and tiny coves. Eventually the weather caught up with them again, tossing them between Mykonos, Paros and finally the volcanic island of Thera, where the Minoan town at Akrotiri had yet to be discovered. The houses, painted with scenes as fine and vivid as those of Minoan Crete, still lay under the metres of ash and pumice thrown up by the volcano's last violent eruption – a Minoan Pompeii. John would have loved the place but he never lived to see the excavations that were carried out a quarter of a century later by Spyridon Marinatos, with whom John would cross swords before the year was out.

No sooner had they caught sight of Phaleron again than their hostess's son contracted mumps and they were all declared in quarantine. Woodward asked them to keep away from the School until they were clear, so they holed up in a small Athens hotel learning German. The School's new Director, Humfry

Payne, was also in Athens making preparations for a dig that he wanted to start that June at Eleutherna in Crete. He planned to look over the site and find lodgings and workmen and asked John and Hilda, if they were clear of mumps, to join him on both the reconnaissance trip and the excavation.

John was by now despairing of getting a project of his own under way, particularly as it became clearer to him how the BSA committee operated. 'I have found that it is not that Evans is no power in the land', he explained to Herbert. 'The trouble is that he alone *is* the Committee and that my enthusiasm for Kommos has roused his fears and started him definitely vetoing prehistoric. So there is no hope from that quarter. This I know for certain.'[3] Demoralised by what smacked of an old man's jealousy of the young, particularly after putting so much faith in Evans's initial enthusiasm, John hoped to get more encouragement from Payne. By the end of April, the mumps had failed to materialise so John and Hilda accompanied Payne to Crete.

Since their last visit, Evans had purchased an old taverna at the roadside below the Villa Ariadne. So instead of lodging at the Hotel Minos in Heraklion, both John and Hilda could now stay at Knossos in the house that is still known as the Taverna. 'It is a charming little house', Hilda wrote, 'with a roofed verandah on the west, from which the roof slopes down slightly to the west side, so that it is like half an ordinary pitch-roofed house. At the south end is a large sitting room with cupboards stocked with household things for people who stay here when the Villa is shut up, and a larder. To the north are the two bedrooms and a really decent lavatory and a tap where extra water can be drawn for any purpose. It is quite self-sufficient.'[4]

Evans was in residence up the lane, along with Duncan Mackenzie, Piet de Jong and Emile Gilliéron, the fresco restorer, so they all ate together at the Villa Ariadne. This gave John the opportunity to tackle Evans and Mackenzie directly on his hopes of finding a site of his own to dig. John's concerns began to evaporate as the subject of his prospecting Kommos was raised by Mackenzie and the general feeling was voiced that he would likely get the Macmillan studentship. Evans, too, was more approachable, probably because of Payne's presence, and took them on a tour of the palace. This had changed a good deal since their previous visit. 'It really is becoming a most habitable affair,' Hilda observed.[5]

The following morning Payne, John and Hilda started out to Eleutherna by car towards the north-eastern foothills of Mount Ida, along the new road that was being built between Heraklion and Rethymnon, from where they planned to continue on foot. Evans had provided them with a basket of the kind of luxury foods that he felt it impossible to travel without. Their guide had gone a day or so ahead of them with a couple of mules, bedding and tents and met them at the end of the unfinished car road at the village of Marathos. They packed the mules and set out on a glorious Cretan spring day, over hills covered in spring flowers, wild rose bushes and trees resounding with nightingale song.

The site of Eleutherna stood high above steep valleys, its acropolis reached by a causeway. They set up their camp on a terrace of olive trees and for two days explored the site, developing the best excavation strategy. Byzantine remains in the form of a fortification tower were already known there, but Payne suspected that the site was considerably older and the excavation was intended to find out how long the acropolis had been in use before the Middle Ages. The experience was good for both John and Payne, as it was the first time either of them had had to carry out such a reconnaissance and decide how best to tackle a new site.

They eventually left Eleutherna and crossed over the western foothills of Mount Ida, staying en route at the monasteries of Arkadi, Asomaton and Agios Ioannis, heading towards the south coast. A gorge below Agios Ioannis brought them to the shore where they took a fishing boat belonging to the monastery, planning to sail to Kokkinos Pyrgos via an ancient site at Keramai which was best reached by sea. The fishermen were so busy fishing illegally with depth charges along the way that it was nearly dark by the time they reached Keramai.

With the light failing, the three of them had only just enough time to scramble up the steep slope to the acropolis of the remote site. They gathered some of the pottery scattered on the surface and made notes on the foundations that were still visible before darkness forced their return to the boat. They found just enough to see that it could be what John, as romantic as ever, described to his father as 'a Mycenaean pirate base'.[6] The fishermen had lit a fire on the beach for a fish supper, so the others added what to them was the obvious accompaniment. 'They were much impressed', Hilda wrote, 'by our cooking potatoes – chipped potatoes – and if they had any doubts before that we were "lordi" (English Lords), that settled it, potatoes being superior food.' After the meal they sailed on through the night, arriving at Kokkinos Pyrgos in the early hours of the morning. Exhaustion and a strong and parching sirocco wind thwarted their plans to sail on to prospect Kommos, but by this time the Keramai site had captured John's imagination too much for him greatly to care. The freshness of the Villa Ariadne was like heaven after the south coast. 'The garden of the Villa is a mass of honeysuckle and other flowering bushes and the nightingales are singing day and night.'[7] John's enthusiasm increased when he found that the site at Keramai provoked none of the reservations in Evans that his interest in Kommos had.

*

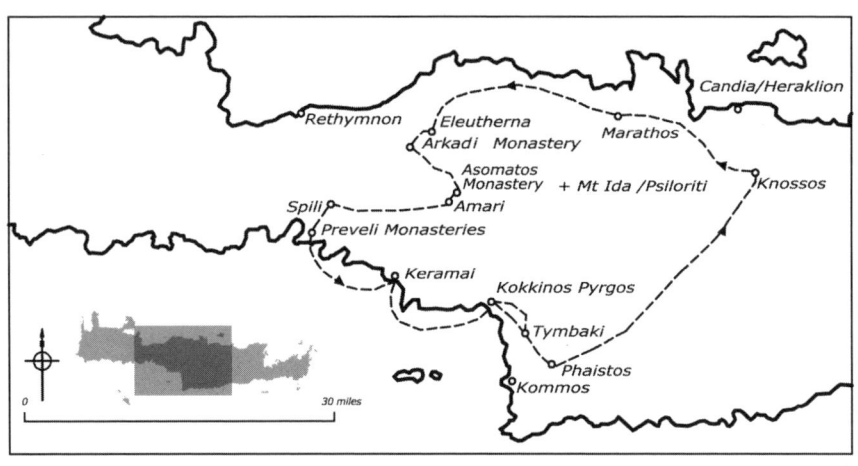

1929 ROUTE

A letter from John's father, however, managed to take the edge off his excitement. Herbert had strongly suggested that John apply for a job that had just come up, lecturing at Cambridge, though in what subject is not recorded. John respected his father's advice but was adamant that this job was wrong for him. 'First. Don't forget that I must have freedom.' His real objection, though, came from having found Keramai. 'Second. I have found a site to dig next year which I think even Evans can hardly condemn... It is the ideal place to dig. Payne is very keen on my putting in for a permit, so I shall do so formally to him.' Yet he still felt the need to justify his lack of enthusiasm for the job and came up with every excuse he could think of for avoiding it: he might after all get the Macmillan Studentship; the job would make the dig at Keramai impossible; he felt, probably with some justification, that he was unsuited to teaching subjects outside his range of interests and would have no time to put any course material together. But it all really came down to one reason and John had already made up his mind. 'Having worked and got on so far with my real interest – i.e. practical archaeology', he wrote, exasperated, 'it would be madness to fling it over just when I most need to be on the spot, and it would mean flinging it over since I have to be out here roughly from November till June. As you know, I <u>don't</u> <u>want</u> an academic life... I have written to Jock [Lawson] explaining that though I know the advantages etc. of a University position, I am unsuited in every way for this.'[8]

*

John and Hilda returned to Athens for a few days before catching another boat out of Greek territory to Rhodes where John had some final research to do for his catalogue.

Rhodes is the largest of the Dodecanese islands, an archipelago stretching along the eastern edge of Aegean. The islands had been under Italian occupation since Italy had seized them from Turkey during the Libyan War of 1911–12. Italy clung to them through the Great War as a useful foothold in the Near East and as a bridge for closer contact with the Levant, until her claim on them was upheld in the Treaty of Lausanne in 1923. It was then that the island of Castellorizo, off the southern coast of Turkey, was also ceded to Italy, which was to give the Italians an important hold in the eastern Mediterranean in the Second World War.

When John and Hilda arrived on Rhodes they found the town and harbours alive with activity and festivity, in preparation for a much-publicised visit by the King and Queen of Italy. This piece of propaganda, showing Italian popularity in the islands, was clearly successful. The Rome correspondent of *The Times* wrote that, 'All the accounts insist upon the essentially popular character of the celebrations, which is naturally interpreted here as proving that there is no genuine desire on the part of the islanders to belong to any other Power than Italy.'[9] However, affluent Rhodes was the exception to the rule. Large-scale emigration from the Dodecanese islands during the Italian occupation was drastically reducing the native population, by as much as two thirds on some islands by 1929. A little more than a decade later, with Italy at war with Greece, John would be among those trying to get the islands back for Greece, supported by a large expatriate Dodecanesian population.

Rhodes could not fail to work its magic on John. 'The old town is thrilling – like all the medieval castles of Europe put together', he wrote to Herbert, revelling once more in a world of knights and pageants. Hilda gave a more detailed description. 'The battlements are simply fascinating with inner and outer walls, bastions and keeps and machicolated parapets and a huge underground aqueduct all in good repair. Inside the wall for the most part is the old Turkish part of the town, with minarets and overhanging oriole [sic] rooms and masses of orange and pomegranate trees… We came back through the market of the old town where Arabic, Italian, Greek, Turkish and Yiddish all flourish'.[10]

When the island returned to normal, John managed to get his work finished in three days while Hilda found parallels in the local pottery with pieces she had been studying in Cairo. The museum staff were enormously generous with their Egyptian material, unusually allowing John full permission to publish the finds in his book although they were as yet unpublished by the excavator. They left the island feeling warmly towards the Italian archaeologists, who could not have been more generous.

*

John was not in the least prepared for the news that awaited him back at the British School. He wrote to his father explaining what had happened. 'Yesterday I got a wire – unsigned – from Knossos saying that in the event of Mackenzie retiring in the autumn would I carry on at a slightly reduced salary and slightly shorter period of residence, and that it would not interfere with the Macmillan – the whole strictly confidential – so not a word! I presumed it was Evans and not Payne who had sent it, so I wired back to Evans "Received wire unsigned answer affirmative". It seems a pretty good show. Also I heard from Payne that Evans seems quite happy about my digging at Keramai, so that I should be looking for funds for the dig.'[11]

This turn of events, though sudden for John, was the result of a situation that had been building up over the previous two years. There had been a great deal going on at Knossos of which John and Hilda, and to some extent even Duncan Mackenzie himself, were totally unaware – hence the clandestine nature of the telegram. In December 1928, Piet de Jong had been asked to compile a report on the state of the Villa Ariadne and the estate under the Curatorship of Mackenzie. The results were not good, nor were his observations on Mackenzie's health, both physical and mental.

It was Mackenzie's job as Curator to keep the house in good repair as well as supervise archaeological work and a great deal more besides, a job he was finding increasingly difficult to cope with. The School's Director, Arthur Woodward, forwarded de Jong's findings to Macmillan, stressing how filthy the house was, 'plagued by mosquitoes, which bred in an unsatisfactory outdoor WC at the back of the Villa'. There was a desperate need for repairs in both the house and garden, but for months no effort had been made to tackle them. 'I must record my conviction', he added, 'that if the Villa is to be used by Students of the School, it should be more adequately looked after. I should dissuade women-Students from going, and should certainly not take my wife to stay there, till matters improve.'[12]

Over the course of the following year, Mackenzie's daily visits after work to Loukas' *kapheneion* in the village had turned more and more into serious drinking bouts. Yet Evans and the School committee knew they could not just fire a man who had given twenty-nine years to Knossos and still devoted his life to the site. The cause of his decline in health was generally believed to be a descent into alcoholism, but it is quite possible that this was a symptom of a graver mental illness. Many believed that his decline could be traced back to the death in 1927 of one of his oldest and closest Cretan friends, the Muslim foreman of the site at Knossos, Ali Basitakis. One way or another, Mackenzie, by now nearing seventy, could no longer cope with the job and the committee had to get him away from Knossos before the house, estate and reputation of the School suffered further.

The eventual loss of respect amongst the local villagers was the saddest blow of all for a man like Mackenzie. Over the past decades, he had become more involved with and loved by the local Cretans than the more distant Evans, as the latter later described in a posthumous tribute to Mackenzie. 'The simple surroundings of his earlier years gave him an inner understanding of the native workmen and a fellow-feeling with them that was a real asset in the course of our spadework. To them, though a master, he was ever a true comrade... No wedding ceremony, no baptism, no wake was complete among the villagers without the sanction of his presence, and as sponsor, godfather, or "best man", his services were in continual request.'[13]

The matter was passed to the old guard of the British School – Macmillan, Evans, John Forsdyke (Keeper of Greek and Roman Antiquities at the BM) and Theodore Fyfe (formerly Evans's architect at Knossos). All of them had known Mackenzie for many years, but they were unable or unwilling to take the obvious steps to solve the situation until it was nearly too late. They decided to wait until 'his health broke down utterly (as is quite conceivable) or he were convicted of some serious misdemeanour'.[14]

It was only when, early one morning, Evans found Mackenzie in a drunken slump at the dining room table at the Villa that any action was taken. They had their 'serious misdemeanour' and Mackenzie's removal was swift. He was sent to Candia and staff at Knossos were told not to let him return to the Villa Ariadne or Taverna in any circumstances. Evans felt he had 'saved Mackenzie's face' by calling his departure early retirement, and perhaps with certain people he had. But he had taken from Mackenzie the one thing he had left to live for, Knossos, at the same time as making it plain that Mackenzie's 'friends' were behind this treatment. They had no choice but to dismiss him, but they showed him little, if any, compassion.

When John and Hilda arrived back in England in early June 1929, both Wace and Forsdyke confirmed the offer of the Curatorship at a salary of £150, involving three months annual residence at Knossos. This unexpected windfall was gilded by John's being awarded the first Macmillan Studentship. The announcement of the award in *The Times* was spotted by John's old house master at Winchester, F. P. David, who wrote delightedly to Herbert Pendlebury. 'The Aegean offers a fine field, and I suppose also a larger one; and there is always the Egyptian work and knowledge as a foundation. But after his visit to Athens, I was prepared to bet that Greece would secure him. I should hardly think, though, there are many archaeologists thus double-barracked as John is. It is a fine distinction.'[15]

*

The Macmillan Studentship obliged John to return to Greece after the summer for the new School session, which ran for eight months from November to July. This made a further season in Egypt impossible. Any disappointment John might have felt about being cut off from Egypt for a while was lessened when news came that the 1929–30 Amarna season would probably have to be cancelled due to lack of funds.

What John did not expect was that Egypt was not prepared to let him go quite so easily. No sooner had John secured the Macmillan and the Curatorship at Knossos than he received a letter from Stephen Glanville. Hans Frankfort had accepted the offer of the new professorship at the Oriental Institute in Chicago. With the job came the opportunity for Frankfort to direct an excavation at Tell Asmar in Iraq with a very large budget, but this meant that he would not be able to continue his work at Tell el-Amarna and, with the short notice, the 1929–30 season would have to be cancelled. This left the EES without a Director at Tell el-Amarna for the 1930–31 season. On Frankfort's strongest recommendation, Glanville offered John the chance to take over the running of the Amarna dig.

This changed everything. John's steadfast, many would have said stubborn, efforts to keep both his areas of interest alive, in spite of frequent discouragement and setbacks, had at last paid off. Without hesitation he accepted Glanville's offer. He now held more leverage than he could ever have hoped for, and set out his own terms to Glanville. 'My Aegean duties are: 1929–30, eight months in Aegean of which three are to be in Crete as Curator. 1930–31 ditto. 1931–32, three months in Crete. These months in Crete will be usually from the middle of February or the beginning of March onwards. This means I should have to dig early in Egypt. Also, and this is a point I must make, I may have to apply for the Assistant Directorship in 1932–33. Actually I hope that Heurtley will be staying on and that I can apply for the Directorship direct three years later. But I must make that clear. On the other hand I could resign the Macmillan easily next year and so only have my time at Knossos to worry about in 1930–31.'[16]

Mary Jonas at the EES was delighted to hear of the new Director. 'You cannot be more pleased at the prospect of working for us at Amarna than I am at the idea of securing you for the Society's work, and I only wish we had known in time to secure you for this season and save very much of the trouble and worry that we have landed into lately.'[17]

It is probable that John had only ever dreamed of achieving so much in both fields so early in his career. This combination put him in a truly unique position in the archaeology of the eastern Mediterranean. At the age of twenty-five he had secured two extraordinary and important sites. 'Amarna means a real chance of making a name – and what is more a definite position and hold on both sides. It is a great and famous site and it is the biggest compliment I have ever been paid to be asked to succeed such celebrities as Petrie, Borchardt, Peet, Woolley, Griffith and Frankfort… It is a great show.'[18] If ever there was an annus mirabilis for John, this was it.

8

January–November 1930

WHEN SIR ARTHUR EVANS invited John and Hilda to stay the weekend at his Victorian mansion, Youlbury, in Boar's Hill near Oxford, he knew nothing of John's appointment as Director at Amarna. John took huge pleasure in keeping the news quiet 'from the Aegean world' until he had met personally with Glanville, but it must have been torture not to give the slightest clue to Evans or his other guests – all stalwart members of the British School committee.

The weekend gave Evans the chance to brief John on the real situation at Knossos and Mackenzie's state of health. But things were about to get much worse. Not more than a month after Mackenzie had been dismissed he was found in a 'pathetic state of derangement' in a small hotel in New Phaleron. He was taken to a nursing home but was in a terrible state and penniless, and the British Vice-Consul in Piraeus was called in to try and and find out about family or friends who could be contacted. But Mackenzie was beyond giving a coherent response.

It was a difficult situation for the British School, which was morally bound to take responsibility for Mackenzie. The new Director, Humfry Payne, was still in London. John, by now officially Curator at Knossos and therefore a school officer, was first back in Athens and took charge of the situation. He wrote to Mackenzie's sister, who was married to an Italian civil servant in Modena, asking her to come and fetch him. As Acting Director of the School, John could get the funds necessary for medical and travel expenses.

For the best part of the next year, one problem after another arose. Mackenzie's sister was afraid to travel with him because of his increasingly unpredictable and sometimes violent behaviour. The School had given him a very small pension, on the grounds that he would then be unable to afford to drink. John, however, felt that this was not enough and later wrote to Payne, 'I should like to have my salary reduced this year so that my salary and Mackenzie's expenses and pension = £250. I feel with my "pluralist" position this is the least I can do, but please make it plain to those concerned that it is anonymous and in no way to be acknowledged. Next year we can see how things pan out.'[1] Eventually Mackenzie died in penury in Italy in 1934 at the age of seventy-three, his pension drained away by full-time medical care.

*

Meanwhile, with reasonable fieldwork experience and travel behind him, John felt it was time to develop ideas arising from the research for his *Ægyptiaca* catalogue. He chose to join the debate on some hotly disputed tombs at Luxor and whether the people they depicted bearing tribute to the pharaoh were Minoan or Aegean. John had already voiced his views in the conclusion to his catalogue, but aimed to assess more fully the archaeological evidence available to date for relations between Egypt and the Aegean. He sent an article entitled 'Egypt and the Aegean in the Late Bronze Age' to the editors of the *Journal of Egyptian Archaeology (JEA)*.[2]

The article was a discussion of a paper published by the Egyptologist Gerald Wainwright in the *Liverpool Annals* in 1913.[3] John felt that Wainwright's theory had been dismissed out of hand and not yet 'been paid the compliment of the detailed examination which it deserves.'[4] Wainwright had looked at the question of whether the place referred to in Egyptian and Near Eastern texts as Keftiu could be identified with Crete. Alternatively, he suggested that Keftiu could have been in Asia, while the Cretans were known as the 'Peoples of the Sea'. His conclusion was that the identification of Keftiu with Crete could not any longer be upheld, giving as evidence reliefs in four key Egyptian tombs depicting foreigners bringing tribute to Egypt. John knew the tombs in question and very ably took Wainwright's points one by one and dismissed them.

John approached the debate as if it were a battle between honourable knights. It is a courteous and good-humoured piece of writing that reveals his pleasure in joining the fray. In one instance, Wainwright had insisted that a particular text made it certain that Keftiu had to be close to a place called Gebail (known to be Byblos in the Levant). John approached the argument rather differently. The quotation in question was, 'Men do not sail northwards to Byblos to-day. What shall we do for cedars for our mummies, with the produce of which priests are buried, and with the oil of which (chiefs) are embalmed as far as Keftiu?' John felt this text very clearly separated Keftiu and Byblos. 'If Keftiu were in the Gulf of Issus, it would be as if someone in Devonshire wrote: "Men do not drive northwards to London today. What shall we do for newspapers, with which the minds of (men) are lightened as far as Hampstead?"'[5]

John had an extremely good grasp of the evidence, not only the artistic elements from the tombs, but also the archaeological parallels in Crete for objects depicted in the tombs. If anyone had doubted the depth of his knowledge in the two fields, then this article certainly put those doubts aside. When he had reassessed the evidence John then began to interpret it. He concluded that the timing of the collapse of the Minoan world was reflected in the absence of references to Keftiu after the reign of the 18th dynasty pharaoh Amenhotep III, father of Akhenaten, when before this they had been frequent. This was mirrored by a seal of Queen Ty, wife of Amenhotep III, which was the latest extant find of Egyptian origin in Crete. Until that date Egyptian objects had been common on the island, and afterwards they stopped. The process worked in reverse in mainland Greece, leading to the conclusion that with Minoan Crete out of the picture, Mycenaean Greece had taken over the trade with Egypt.

John's imagination did not however let him stop there. In the sudden, and still largely unexplained, demise of Minoan Crete John saw an uprising by the other islands of the Aegean against the long Minoan colonial dominion. This, he ventured, may have been the origin of the myth of Theseus, who represented the oppressed Aegean people, leading an uprising against the Minoans, represented by the dreaded King Minos, who exacted the annual tribute of boys and girls to dance with death in the bullrings of Knossos. 'Was there a great sea battle in which the galleys of Minos were overwhelmed by the long ships of the Men of the Isles? Was the power of Knossos already broken by an earthquake? Was there treachery and a rising of the populace? We shall never know. But after that wild year Crete lay in the dust, and desolation reigned from Agia Triada to Palaikastro, and her destroyers sailed away, as two hundred years later departed the ravagers of Troy. Surely that is how it happened.'[6]

This was not the only legend that John drew into his conclusion. He felt there was perhaps some echo of truth in a theory recently put forward that the sudden and total collapse of Crete was at the core of the Atlantis myth for, to all intents and purposes, Minoan Crete had vanished from the consciousness of the civilised world. There was evidence that a collapse in unity amongst the Aegean islands and the mainland led to their ill-advised invasion of Egypt and the consequent cessation of her valuable trade. This cessation in turn led to a need for them to look elsewhere for sources of wealth. Could the Aegean islands and mainland perhaps have looked instead towards the Black Sea? Was this, he mused, the origin of the myth of Jason and the Argonauts? Was their search for the Golden Fleece an allegory for searching out new and lucrative trade routes?

Several generations after peace and trade were re-established with the Egyptian Empire, Egypt was again invaded by the 'peoples of the sea'. John outlined the state of current thinking on this point. 'The leadership of this second invasion has been attributed with great probability to Agamemnon, the son of Atreus. This not only fits in with the accepted date of the Trojan War, but, as I hope to show, goes far towards explaining it. What however nothing will explain is the more than Pelopid stupidity of these two invasions.' The invasion was a failure, so yet again Egypt withdrew its trade. John thought it likely that the 'peoples of the sea' looked back towards the Black Sea, where a new power, Troy, had since arisen to guard access to it. 'I have very tentatively suggested that the stupid and violent rupture of these hard-won relations with Egypt was the direct cause of the Trojan War and ultimately of the downfall of the Achaean power.'[7]

This article is an essential piece of John's writing. It shows how his imagination drove his passion for archaeology. It was not unusual at this date, however, to draw on the myths and legends of ancient Greece to inform, and in turn to be elucidated by, careful archaeological work. His arguments in the main body of the article are clearly thought out and well-expressed. His conclusions show his passion for the romance of the world in which he found himself. It was the world of Theseus, Jason and Agamemnon that inspired him, that was a foundation of his love of Crete and the Greek world. John was determined to approach archaeology as scientifically as modern methods of excavation would allow, and to push forward the boundaries where he could, but not at the expense of his imagination. Nevertheless, the article certainly caused a stir and eyebrows were raised in British Museum quarters.

Stephen Glanville, as editor of the *JEA*, advised John to 'tone down his conclusions' before publication. 'He and Hall', John told Herbert, 'have been over it and jotted down suggestions. They can't want much alteration or they would never have sent it to be put up in print.' John could not understand their resistance. 'I do not see why facts that have been assumed for years, eg Theseus and Crete, Agamemnon raiding Egypt, the date of the Trojan War (all of which are in an article of Miss Lorimer's in the present *JHS* [*Journal of Hellenic Studies*] should not be scrutinized.[8] I have already suggested in 'Æ' what I have here worked out. There is not one fact that can be contradicted and it is the first attempt that has been made to give an adequate consecutive account of Crete and Troy. I stand to it.'[9]

Glanville and Hall, however, continued to block John's article, but without – much to John's annoyance – specifying what it was exactly that they objected to. There was, in fact, a huge gulf between the world of Bronze Age Aegean archaeology and the world of Egyptology and there was little love lost between the two disciplines. The subject of Egyptology was seen as concentrating on tombs, temples and texts; Aegean archaeology was very different. The two forms of written language of the Bronze Age Aegean had so far eluded translation. However, there was a wealth of vernacular literature, legend and tradition that had come through the civilisations of classical Greece and Rome that was thought to throw light on earlier ages. It was also true that there was a greater understanding of domestic and cultural development in the Aegean available from extensive excavation of cities such as Palaikastro in eastern Crete. This was lacking in Egypt because the main cities of ancient Egypt lay beneath modern ones. Only the case of Tell el-Amarna and the workmen's villages provided any evidence of domestic practice. But neither of these examples could be seen to represent the long and continuous habitation of ordinary villages, towns or cities.

John's article crossed the barrier, not so much because he was drawing parallels with well-known myths and legends, but because it was to Egyptologists that he submitted it for publication. 'Stephen's remark about Orthodox Egyptology I simply don't understand', John fumed in a letter to Herbert. 'As they have said: everything as far as the beginnings of my conclusions are OK and always has been. Surely I am justified in giving my conclusions when they do not conflict with tradition, archaeological evidence or probability, and when they form the only connected and reasonable explanation yet given. Am I to give the evidence (which I have already done in *Ægyptiaca*) and leave it to someone else to form conclusions or am I, after piling up all this evidence, to finish off with a half suggestive line (which again I have already done in *Ægyptiaca*). My theory is not fantastic. Every remark made I can and have quoted chapter and verse for. If I try and make it attractive by the mere addition of epithets, is that a fault? However, it stands. I feel strongly about it because when I mentioned it to Stephen originally he was all for it. So was Hans and so is Payne.'[10]

Then, amidst all the wrangling with Hall and Glanville, John received a letter of support from a most unlikely quarter. Thomas Peet, Professor of Egyptology at Liverpool University was, according to John, 'the most sober and, in fact, pessimistic of archaeologists, not to say damping'.[11] His letter then came as a complete if welcome surprise, and John copied it out in full to send to Herbert.

'I do not see you have any cause to be perturbed by anything that H and G may have said about your article. [This] is extremely useful and it is the first time anyone has taken the trouble to do it. What pleased me more still was to find someone really analysing W's method instead of merely quashing him with an ex-cathedra pronouncement. As for the constructive part of the paper, which I gather is what H and G dislike. I see nothing unreasonable in it. Archaeology is not an exact science but goes about its business mainly by the help of hypotheses. Clearly a hypothesis which fits none of the facts (and we get plenty such in Egyptology) is a waste of time and paper. But a hypothesis which does fit the known facts is for the time being valuable, even if later facts should arise which lead to its modification or even rejection. So far as I can see you do give a very reasonable explanation of a group of facts which no one, I believe, has previously taken the trouble explicitly to verify, much less to explain. For my own part I shall certainly adopt your point of view as a working hypothesis unless or until some one else makes out a better case for another.'[12]

Much to John's delight and amusement, Peet added, 'Your proof came back to me through Glanville. Hall had made one or two small verbal alterations in the proof, not however in the least modifying what you had said. If I remember rightly, I accepted three of them, as they all went for greater clearness of expression, and (between ourselves) rejected one or two others which I thought were not improvements'. 'And that from the sceptic Peet!!', he declared triumphantly to Herbert.[13]

Hall backed down on many of his criticisms, largely, John suspected, because of Peet's intervention — 'Peet must have written him a real scorcher!'[14] When he also received an offer from Alan Gardiner, another eminent Egyptologist, to use his library, John began to feel a little less alienated. Payne then invited John to present his ideas in an illustrated talk at the Open Meeting of the British School at Athens. 'Payne said he wanted to make certain that the theory had a hearing before it was possibly mucked about by the BM people.'[15]

In the event, the notorious article was well received. Herbert wrote to John approving of the final appearance, complete now with Hilda's drawings. Hans Frankfort was typically irreverent in his support, 'congratulating me on my robust style and the jocular kicks on the bottom I gave Wainwright.'[16]

But it was Wainwright himself who proved that the article had hit its academic mark. 'I had yesterday a lovely letter from Wainwright saying what a nice article it was but why bring in Keftiu! Particularly as it made more work for him since he had just finished an article on the subject and now had to begin all over again. He has devoted an appendix to my article, which he said he was picking to bits, going over each sentence and giving his comments! He said it was a pity I should uphold an outclassed view and that while he hoped always to be quite nice, yet he hoped to deal faithfully with the subject! (That obviously means abuse).'[17]

John was not in the least worried by this response, indeed he took it as a compliment that he was himself now considered worthy of such an academic duel. 'I wrote back saying that at any rate he could not complain now that he had no straightforward facts to stand up to (which had been his wail), that I was looking forward to seeing his article and correcting any mistakes I might have made and that I looked forward to much fierce and honourable controversy.'[18]

*

With the first days of 1930, John and Hilda explored the classical remains of Sicily, travelling back through southern Italy. On their return to Athens, they found a copy of John's first book, *Ægyptiaca*, waiting for them, 'with as far as I can see only one misprint, "EGPYT" for Egypt!'[19] This cheered him up after the article problem and he began to relax a little, teaching Hilda and some students how to fence. Among them was Nick Hammond, a new student at the School, a small young man with a large personality and piercing blue eyes. Every bit as tough a walker as John, in December 1929 they had walked to Thebes, in time to catch the Orient Express as it passed through the town on its way to Athens. At three o'clock one morning, joined by Heurtley and another student called Theodore Skeat, they had crept out of the sleeping School and set off by moonlight. John maintained the lead, followed close behind by Nick Hammond, while Heurtley battled on bravely and Skeat, who was known as 'the Horse' because of his slow but determined plodding, did all he could to keep Heurtley in sight. John sprinted the last mile or so to try to delay the train for the others. When Hammond arrived, just in time to catch the train, he found John sitting there 'fresh as a daisy and having consumed most of the beer in sight'.[20]

In the middle of March, John and Hilda returned to Crete for John to take up the Curatorship at Knossos. There had been an earthquake since their last visit, and though the damage was minimal, John had to wire 'frantically to reassure Evans'.[21] John found that reassuring Evans would be one of the more frequent and tedious aspects of his new job.

The Villa Ariadne was to be their home for the time being, but after years of neglect under Mackenzie they had a lot of work ahead to make it habitable. John's first act was to create a proper archaeological library, starting with a spare copy of his own book that his father had sent out, along with duplicate copies of archaeological, topographical and classical works that they had at Malvern. *Ægyptiaca* was now in circulation and John was pleased to hear that the eminent German professor Georg Karo was already using it in his work on the shaft graves at Mycenae. 'The book seems to have made a very decent impression generally'.[22] The 'sceptic Peet' commented favourably on the book, though he said he would have preferred it to be volume one, with a further one to come on the Egyptian finds in Syria and Palestine. He did pick up some inconsistencies in the text and pointed out where greater clarity could have been given, but his review in the *Liverpool Annals* was kind. As John related proudly to Herbert, Peet concluded 'that the book has put an important if small branch of Egyptology on a new footing and that the tables and indexes are beyond praise while the book is a beautiful piece of printing and very cheap.'[23]

Wainwright's review of *Ægyptiaca* was published in the *JEA* as his response to John's article. It started off favourably: 'Mr Pendlebury has given us a book of the type so necessary to the student – a collection of all the material

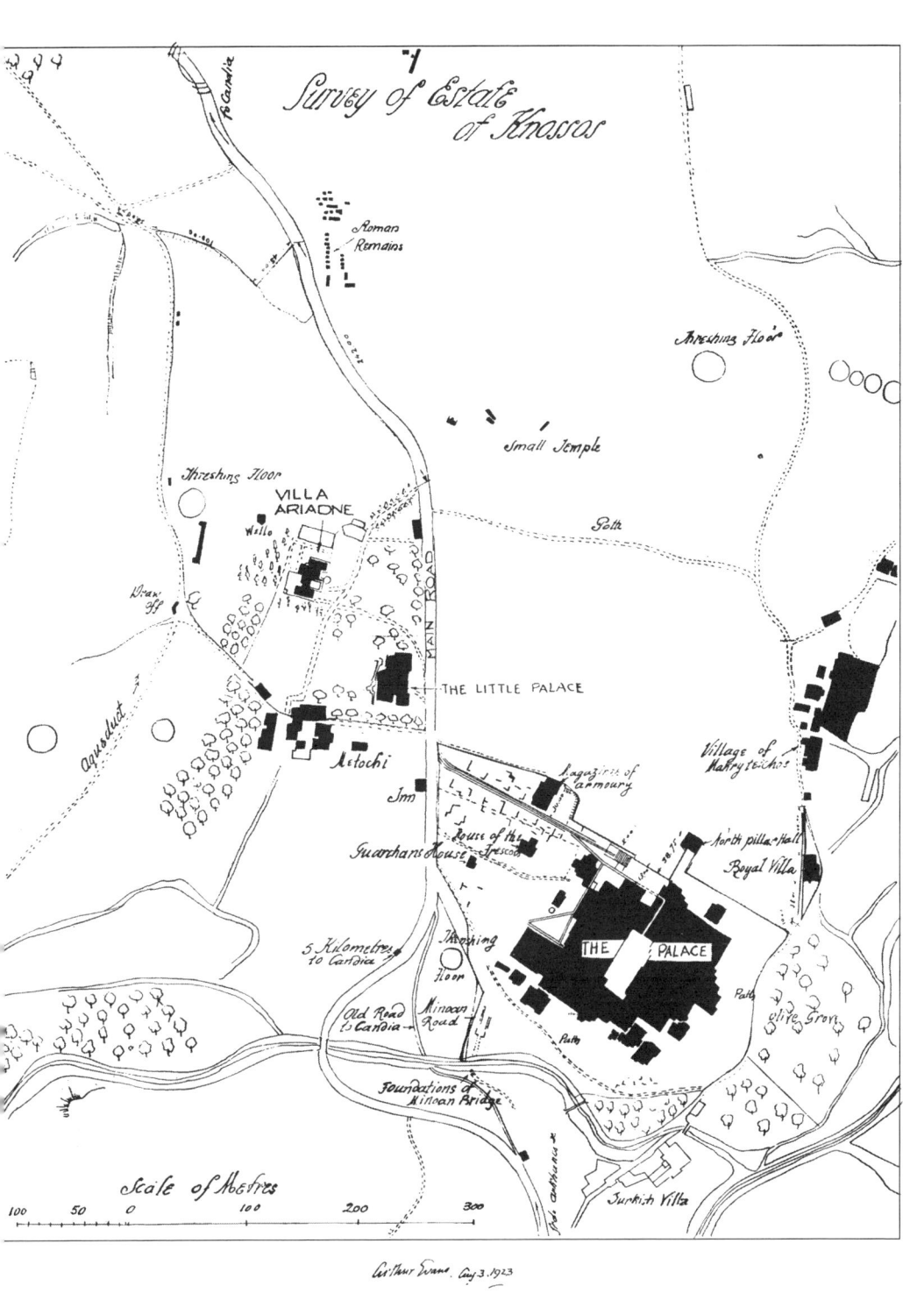

Survey of the Knossos Estate, 1923.

(*Copyright of the British School At Athens. Reproduced with permission*)

bearing on a definite branch of archaeology.' He continued that John's work had raised some valuable questions, not only about the available evidence, but also about the surprising lack of evidence in certain areas. Why was there so little evidence of Minoan settlement in western Crete and so few Egyptian finds, while the east of the island was so rich in finds? He also questioned the lack of Egyptian finds from the hinterland of Ierapetra, which as a modern port seemed the most likely situation for a Minoan one. 'But trade seems to have ignored it', he mused, 'and to have made for the little Minoan port of Komo, near Phaistos and its group of ancient sites.'[24]

John's study brought out clearly that Minoan archaeology was still very much in its early childhood, if not its infancy. The gaps in the archaeological evidence were due to the limited amount of excavation that had gone on thus far rather than to a lack of ancient activity. This was particularly true of western Crete, which has since proved to have rich Minoan remains. Likewise, Kommos proved to be a far more substantial Minoan port than could be guessed at without excavation in 1930.

*

John was now learning to manage the Knossos estate, helped in the supervision of the Villa Ariadne and gardens by Kostis Chronakis and Manolis (Manolaki) Akoumianos. He was also in charge of returning the palace to good repair, free of weeds and particularly of animals, which had been allowed to roam freely. 'I have given orders that any animal found there shall either be taken up to the Villa where I shall demand money for its return (if I do not eat it for dinner) or else turned away and tethered in a fine field of corn near the palace, so that the owner can have a bit of trouble with the farmer!'[25] Unfortunately, the girl detailed for the job misunderstood the message and drove the animals into their owner's cornfield, 'where I saw them later destroying their master's crops as hard as they could. That will teach him!'[26]

The accounts for the whole estate had to be balanced from the income of its produce to meet some of the costs of maintenance. The productivity of the vines and olives on the land depended on a good tenant who would not exhaust the soil for short-term personal gain. Although John had more energy and enthusiasm for the work than his predecessor, he lacked Mackenzie's experience and knowledge of Greek and was forced to learn a whole new vocabulary for renting, subletting and trespass.

All this had to be achieved within the short period of residency between mid-March and mid-August, in between guiding visitors round Knossos. While this would leave him little time for archaeological research of his own, it was an opportunity to get to know the island, as well as to become acquainted with the objects and pottery found over nearly thirty years of excavation while compiling a reference list. The bonus was that he would be required to assist in and report on further excavations at Knossos, should Humfry Payne as Director so wish.

John was fortunate in having a Director in Athens very close to his own age and with whom he got on well. One letter from John to Payne shows the level of banter that they enjoyed. 'I still have £21 in hand out of the £50. But please to send your humble servant more that was always honourable and a truth Backsheesh ya Khawaga! For know honoured sir – Mr Payne – that I await an increase of 20 to the hungry mouths of my family on or about the 4th day prox, and where food to come from I not know. Also wine barrels empty, bad men and robbers have carried away whisk and the soda bottle he burst with pride at having served the Honourable Director. Have mercy – sir – Mr Payne. How shall I keep the satyr from his mate or dilemma from his horns?'[27]

John was soon forced into a more serious tone of correspondence following an incident that happened within a fortnight of his taking up his post. Payne had come to Crete for a few days to see how John was getting on. Also staying at Knossos was Dorothy Hartley, who had been a fellow student of John's at the School in 1927. Payne and John went to see some vases in a house in Candia. They turned out to be proto-Geometric – the period Miss Hartley was studying. Their driver, Myros, took her and John to see where the vases had originally come from, while Payne returned to Athens. John wrote in a postscript to his light-hearted letter: 'It seems very disappointing. Usual striated cliffs, with one or two holes that may have been tombs (one has a bench left at one end). But practically no pottery... Not worth digging.'[28]

The vases had been found some years earlier and the then Director of the Candia Museum, Stephanos Xanthoudides, considered them of little value and allowed the finders to keep them in their house. But while Miss Hartley was photographing the vases the following day, the police burst in. They confiscated the vases and arrested Myros and the owners of the pots, while John was questioned by the police and Miss Hartley's boat to Athens held in the port until she had told her story to the police.

The police were perfectly satisfied that there had been a mistake, and that an over-zealous informer in the village had misinterpreted the viewing of the vases. Myros told John that the present Director of the Candia Museum, Spyridon Marinatos, had declared 'that the English had tried to buy the vases and that they had gone to all lengths to find a site to dig unknown to him and step in his way'.[29] John was livid, a mood not improved by a 'very rude and insulting letter' from Marinatos.[30] To make things worse, the following day the local paper accused the British School of 'wishing and trying to buy the vases and of dealing on a vast scale'.[31] John felt Marinatos was behind it. He wrote an equally strong letter in response to Marinatos, stating that there had been no question of buying or selling, and clearing the letter with the British Vice-Consul, Mr Elliadi. Elliadi, a gentleman of the old school, was furious and felt that an official apology was required or steps would have to be taken at a higher level. The owners of the pots themselves wrote to the newspapers, explaining that the vases had been found years ago and shown to Xanthoudides.

By early May the Geometric pot incident appeared to have breathed its last. 'The row with the Museum has ended by Marinatos apologising to me and I hear from Payne that the Ministry of Archaeology at Athens, to whom we appealed, has sent him a real stinker telling him he has degraded not only himself but the whole Greek Archaeological Society.'[32] Following this Marinatos handed in his resignation. 'We are waiting hopefully to hear if it is going to be accepted.'[33]

Marinatos was, like John, fairly new in his job. Like John he had followed an illustrious and highly admired predecessor who had left a huge task to his successor. Marinatos's predecessor, the highly esteemed Stephanos Xanthoudides, had failed dismally to halt the growing illegal export of stolen Cretan antiquities. Marinatos was determined to stamp out the trade, and equally determined not to be influenced, as he felt Xanthoudides had been, by the good reputation of men like Evans or Mackenzie. He had already crossed swords with Evans and Payne and the American School the year before and wanted to bring the 19th-century system of patronage into the more official system of the 20th century. He was adamant that every procedure should be carried out to the letter, with no exceptions, and felt that John should have informed him of the situation before taking it further.

John, just as much as Marinatos, revealed too great a tendency to speak in anger, and it is more than likely that the incident did neither of them any favours with their superiors. They were both volatile young men, eager to prove themselves in their new professions, who believed passionately in what they were doing and in their own integrity. It is not surprising, therefore, that when the dust had finally settled on the incident, John Pendlebury and Spyridon Marinatos went on to develop a very good working relationship, with considerable mutual respect.

*

The Villa Ariadne and the Taverna were beginning to look more presentable, just in time for the descent of a tour group, the Hellenic Travellers. With spring well under way, the tourist season had begun. After dealing with a party of 100 Poles one day, then groups of Americans and Swiss who dropped orange peel all over the palace, John and Hilda were beginning to realise that this requirement for mass entertainment at short notice was to be a fairly common occurrence. Among the Hellenic Travellers were the historians Gilbert Murray, HAL Fisher, Liddell Hart and Ernest Gardner and John found them 'a much more intelligent crowd than usual!' Evans arrived in Crete shortly afterwards, in time for a visit the following day from Eleutherios Venizelos, the Greek Prime Minister, who had asked specifically to visit Evans and the palace.[34]

When he was not escorting the tourists around the palace John sought out a place at the palace to house the pottery collection. He decided to use the Throne Room's antechamber to store the pottery when the roof was complete. 'With Evans' permission', he ventured to Payne, 'I want to bring out a catalogue and with his or anyone's money I want to build a museum S[outh] of the Priest King fresco.'[35]

The problem would be lack of time, though, not money. With Evans's arrival, John found himself supervising pockets of excavation all over the palace. Although he was delighted to be digging, these sometimes sizeable excavations produced even more finds and pottery to be sorted and less time in which to do it. One small excavation was by the Theatral Area at the north end of the palace, which led to the discovery of a previously unknown complex of pavements and retaining walls, predating anything they had yet found. But it was when they began to excavate some deep, lined pits (*kouloras*) on the west side of the palace that the problem began to get out of hand. These *kouloras* were filled to the brim with pottery. 'If you imagine a room twenty feet long, fifteen feet broad and fifteen feet high filled with pottery, you can imagine how much came from one walled pit!'[36] Then, at the bottom of two of these, they found the remains of two houses, 'well plastered in red with a lot of complete MMIa vases'. Nearby, they found another house with a wonderful collection of the MMII polychrome pottery known as 'Kamarais Ware', after the site where this extraordinarily elaborate pottery was first discovered. All these houses had been demolished to enlarge the court, along with the original boundary wall of the oldest part of the palace of the same date, 'complete (we hope to see tomorrow) with ramp and fortified entrance'. It was an important find and Evans gave John and Hilda the opportunity to publish the work together in the *Annual of the British School at Athens*, as well as describing it himself fully in Volume IV of *The Palace of Minos*.[37]

John was working himself into the ground. 'I am having a fairly strenuous time 6am–6pm solid on the dig trying to do three people's work. My own, De Jong's, and Mackenzie's left over from many years. The dig goes well, very interesting, but much too much for me alone to look after, even though Hilda does do the pottery almost alone.'[38] He hoped that next year would be quieter. By early June, they both needed a break and escaped ten miles west along the north coast for a weekend, where in perfect isolation and free from Evans' constant badgering, they camped on the beach near Almyro with only the sounds of the sea and the gulls ringing in their ears.

Evans did have his good moments; he clearly enjoyed being back at Knossos, and was in great form, as long, John commented to his father, as he had not had champagne the evening before. He approved of John's idea to create a proper archaeological library at Knossos and donated fifty pounds. He then tackled the domestic arrangements, and began lavishly furnishing the Taverna, so that it could be self-sufficient. John found out how awkward Evans could be, though, when he tried to set a date for returning to England. He and Hilda wanted to be back by July 20th, but Evans kept throwing work at John, determined that he should stay longer.

Evans was clearly annoyed that John had not only started on the job a month later than Mackenzie had in the past, but was also trying to leave a month earlier. John tried to explain the return date to his father. 'Evans has no conception of honesty and his one idea now he has got someone to work for him is to keep him working, irrespective of other duties. I really often feel that it would be better to go definitely over to Egypt, keeping say three months of the year free to keep up with what's happening in Greece. However, I shall wait and see. Evans is obviously itching to get my time here extended. That I will not have. Three and a half months is enough for anyone, cut off from society, besides when one's work is definitely on Eg[yptian] Gr[eek] Connections it's a mug's game giving up one of them.'[39]

As Evans had been working on both the proofs to Volume III and the content of Volume IV of *The Palace of Minos*, it occurred to John to write a smaller, more accessible guide to the palace. For, as John subsequently described in the preface, 'the fortunate possessors of *The Palace of Minos* have hesitated before hiring the pack animal necessary for the transport of that monumental work round the site'.[40] John enjoyed writing. There had been little leeway for humour in a catalogue like *Ægyptiaca*, but a more approachable way of writing about archaeology was very important to John, and it was a style that he did very well. In describing to Herbert how he planned to voice the guide, he found that the more naturally he expressed himself the better it read. 'Have decided to use "You" throughout. "One" is so lonely while "We" gives the visitor the impression that he is not alone and may cause him "to turn his head uneasily as though a fearful fiend doth close behind him tread"'.[41]

John rounded off his first season in Crete by succumbing once more to his passion for costume. He had admired the clothes worn by Cretan men since his first visit and now had himself fitted out in dark blue baggy breeches and waistcoat over a white shirt. Over this he wore a hooded cloak, with edges embroidered in black and lined with scarlet, and the effect was finished off with tall white boots and a black scarf or *mavromantili* to wrap round his head in the local fashion. 'Perfectly gorgeous', he wrote to his father, 'a great show.'[42] Photographs of him in this costume show him standing proud, like the formal images of the old Cretan warriors who had fought against the Turks. In his imagination he was probably already one of them, and this image of him would, indeed, one day intrigue his enemies.

9

November 1930–February 1931

THE FRENCH GROCERY STORE of Jules & Henri Fleurent in Cairo (established 1878, purveyors of wine, spirits, beer, mineral waters and general provisions) stocked many familiar brands of marmalade, pickles, spices and anchovy paste – Tate and Lyle, Crosse and Blackwell, Libbys. 'Flit' insect repellent topped Hilda's expedition shopping list, followed by rice, tea, dried and tinned fruits, baked beans, tinned meats, dried food stuffs, cake ingredients, cheeses, herbs, spices and six packets of the rather nasty sounding 'Force food'. Only the occasional luxury – six tablets of Bournville chocolate, a bottle of Johnny Walker Red Label whisky and fifteen okes of fresh apples – crept in. Messrs. Fleurent would despatch the order (worth 1990.5 piastres) by goods train to Deir Mowas station across the Nile from Tell el-Amarna and would be further delighted to deliver two pounds of unsalted butter every Monday and Thursday starting from November 6th 1930. Meanwhile, John paid a visit to Sinclair's English Pharmacy, Est. 30 years (opposite Shepheard's Hotel). Here, it was proudly announced, could be found pure drugs and chemicals, perfumes, toilet requisites, surgical goods, English, French and American proprietary medicines. John bought Palmolive and carbolic soap, soloid of potassium pomanganate for scorpion bites, bandages, oiled silk, eye drops and antiseptic gauze, all of which hinted at less enjoyable times than Hilda's fare.

The new team had arrived in Cairo in early November, and were put up at the Victoria Hotel on the Sharia Nubar Pasha. John and Hilda, meanwhile, stayed, at their own expense, at the Continental Savoy Hotel, one of the more luxurious hotels. The Victoria, though cheaper, was relaxed and comfortable, and John preferred its simple comfort to the 'splendours of places like the Continental', so the choice was evidently Hilda's. She felt that an appropriate distance should be kept between the Director and his wife and the team, and she once again became known, without much affection, as 'Mrs John', the nickname Frankfort had given her when, newly-married, she fussed over John. She misjudged John in this and failed to realise that her attempts to create a hierarchy would not work when John was surrounded by people of his own age with whom he got on well. John, on the whole, managed to avoid such a hierarchy, and ever after he and Hilda stayed at the Victoria with the rest of the team.

On their first evening, John invited his new team to dinner at the Continental. Mary Chubb, the twenty-seven-year-old assistant secretary at the

EES who had had to decipher Frankfort's reports, had finally managed to reach Egypt herself and was to act as secretary to the expedition. A small young woman, with dark hair often tied tightly back, she had a keen intelligence and a wicked sense of humour akin to John's. As a talented sculptor, she observed the people around her very carefully. Many years later she wrote a book, *Nefertiti Lived Here*, amalgamating into one the two seasons that she was to spend at Amarna, which revealed her acute perception.[1]

During dinner, Mary had a chance to observe John properly for the first time. She found him quite tall, 'but with a breadth of shoulder that seemed a little to diminish the impression. Otherwise he had the slim build and – I had already seen – the springing step of the trained athlete... Yet already there was a hint of the increasing weight which maturity so often brings to the athlete.' In contrast to the 'tow-headed, brooding, rather formidable' man she had seen from time to time in the London office, she now saw his 'easy, light-hearted manner, as he told us of an encounter of the afternoon which had amused him'. But she sensed a 'controlled and concentrated power, even while he laughed.'[2]

The new site architect was Hilary Waddington – a tall man of twenty-eight with mischievous blue eyes, who gave the impression of being considerably younger than his years. Seton Lloyd had been poached as excavation architect in Iraq by Hans Frankfort, but he had arranged to come out later for a month, to prepare to build a model of a typical Amarna house for the Chicago Institute and to help Waddington take over the work as seamlessly as possible. The third new member of the team was John Bennett, a young philologist who had been recommended to John by Stephen Glanville. He was the only member of the team with a degree in Egyptology, but, like Mary and Hilary, this was his first experience of working on an excavation in Egypt. His job was to deal with any hieroglyphic or hieratic inscriptions that might be found, as well as helping with recording and supervision of the workmen along with the others.

John was probably apprehensive about taking over such an important excavation, just as Frankfort had admitted to being at the start of his first season. Though he had worked with a team in Egypt before, John had never led one. His work as Curator of Knossos had been very different. In addition to this, his team was inexperienced.

After a few days in Cairo, they travelled to Tell el-Amarna. John settled in well to organising the *ra'is* and workmen, and work began three days later with fifty local people, thirty of the more skilled Guftis and 240 children. John appointed one of the Guftis, Umbarak, as head *ra'is*, with Ali Sherraif, Mahmoud and Abderrahman Umbarak, and Hussein Sawag each in charge of their own 'company' of workmen. 'They seem to be very happy and contented – so far.'[3]

John, like every member of an excavation to Egypt, had learnt a certain amount of Arabic prior to his first season and had picked up a lot more in the months at Armant and Amarna. It would have been virtually impossible for him to take up the Directorship and deal with the workmen and house staff if he had not been competent in the language.

On the first day of the dig, John emerged from his room a very different vision from the smart man that they had hitherto encountered. Dressed in navy shorts with a belt of multi-coloured twisted leather, a pink shirt, and with his hair verging on the unruly, John was back in his element. Hilary, meanwhile, appeared proudly dressed in full bush khaki, complete with solar topee, and with a gun in his pocket, the very image of the intrepid African explorer and fully prepared to act the part. John's attire put Mary and Hilary at their ease and they began to feel more like the group of adventurous twenty-somethings out on an expedition.

They began work where Frankfort had left off nearly two years earlier. A large wadi, or dry riverbed, defined the north edge of the North Suburb. Two parallel roads running north–south survived on both sides of this wadi, called the East and West Roads. The North Suburb did not extend much further east than the houses on the eastern edge of East Road. It became clear during the season's work that the eastern bank of the River Nile had been further east than the present day. The western houses excavated along the north wadi edge were deeply buried, and the remains of the houses were found to be practically at river level. The proximity of these ancient buildings to this earlier bank showed that there had been no cultivation on this side of the river in Akhenaten's day. The evidence was beginning to show that there must have been another major road further to the west of West Road along the bank of the river serving the river traffic, though it was inaccessible under the present cultivation.

Hans Frankfort had excavated the entire area east of West Road, as well as the large houses along the western edge of West Road, known as the corn merchants' quarter. He had also excavated the larger houses running along the southern edge of the large north wadi as far west as the edge of the cultivation. This left a large area sandwiched between the houses on West Road and the cultivation. This area, actually comprising three residential blocks separated by two small east-west lanes, Straight Street to the north and Greek Street to the south, was one of John's main targets for the 1930–31 season.

They began on the western edge where the foundations were deeply buried, two to three metres below the present ground level, and therefore likely to be the most time-consuming part of the dig. John estimated that it would take a good four weeks to excavate. The depth at which the houses were buried led to the problem of where to dump the soil that was being lifted. They had to avoid areas where they were intending to dig, and yet also needed time to measure and draw the buildings thoroughly. The area proved to be so densely built up that, in order to take some of the pressure off Hilary and to avoid delays in excavation, John decided also to excavate two large houses on the north side of the north wadi.

The excavation of the west end of the block between Straight Street and Greek Street produced few finds, but these were interesting. They included a leaf-shaped knife with a wooden handle, a good relief of the king (legs only and kilt), a Mycenaean pot, a fine carnelian ring bezel 'engraved with the figure of the king, squatting with his hand up to his chin' and a 'smiling' clay hippopotamus.[4] The houses yielded valuable evidence of painted interior decoration, and the whole of this western area produced a great many fish hooks and fish amulets. This, together with its proximity to the ancient river bank, suggested that it was probably a fishermen's quarter.

The most unusual house was found at the east end of the block, behind one excavated the previous season. 'I can say with certainty that we have got the house of a big Mycenaean merchant.'[5] Though the house by and large conformed to a standard Amarna house, with a central room with rooms leading off on all sides except to the loggia, it also had many peculiar characteristics that were more reminiscent of the Aegean. It was set in large grounds with a private chapel, what appeared to be a shop, a bakehouse, cornbins, animal stalls and storage magazines. John was certain that the house had belonged to a rich merchant, perhaps from Rhodes, who lived at Akhetaten – 'the inevitable Greek grocer of his day'. 'In several little details he unconsciously betrayed his origin. For instance the couch in his sitting room was not set symmetrically at the centre of the back wall, as an Egyptian would have had it, but in a corner, as in the 'Room of the Plaster Couch' at Knossos. Again in true Aegean style he was forever plastering and replastering his bathroom, once a year at least.' One of John's favourite finds, though, was a complete Rhodian pilgrim vase containing traces of a solidified resin or unguent, which he was sure was used for resinating the merchant's wine. Another was a face moulded in plaster, which 'can only be described as a counterpart in clay of the Gold Masks from the Shaft Graves of Mycenae – though these are of course several centuries earlier in date.'[6]

Although the dig was going better than John could have hoped, he was having less luck with his new philologist. From the beginning, Bennett had declared that, as the sole 'real' Egyptologist on the team, he should be treated as more than a mere junior member. John had hoped he would improve as the dig went on, but he only got worse, challenging John's authority at every turn.

John had no choice but to report the matter to Glanville, who had recommended Bennett. When, only a fortnight into the season, Bennett developed a fever, thought to be paratyphoid, and had to be sent to Mallawi, their sympathy for him had run very short. John remarked that the illness was 'due partly to excesses in Cairo' and also because he had not been fully inoculated.[7]

Life in the camp lightened during Bennett's absence. From early morning to dusk (at around five) they were busy on site or in the house. Then they would play hockey until the sun finally set, when they would retire to the house to wash and change before dinner. The lamps were lit at dusk, illuminating the rooms with a warm glow while the distinctive smell of kerosene pervaded the house. Dinner, prepared by Abdellatif Abu Bakr, was usually splendid and John added an air of ceremony to it by donning his newly acquired Cretan cloak. Beer, kept cool in a tin bath or *tisht* of water, accompanied the meals, with wine from the Greek grocer in Mallawi on special occasions.

*

Every Thursday was pay day, and the workmen would congregate at the North Dig House to claim their money. Each produced a ticket recording any extra bakshish earned that week from a particularly good find or the quality of their work. It was hoped that this would prevent some of the more marketable finds vanishing into the pockets of their *gallabiahs*. The money was never kept on site for obvious security reasons, but difficulties sometimes arose if the cash for some reason did not arrive. 'We had quite an unpleasant time last pay day,' John related to Herbert. 'The bank manager had gone away ill and no one knew how to open the safe to get our money. So they had to send for someone from Minya, all of which took a long time. Meanwhile we were waiting with all the workmen grouped round, frightful stiffs. Every now and then someone would go frantically down to the river and look for the boat. We didn't finish pay till after dark and even then the bank had not sent the right change and we had to pay in half piastre pieces!'[8]

Not long afterwards Seton Lloyd arrived back from his first season in Iraq with Frankfort. At the same time, Bennett returned from the clinic in Mallawi. During his absence, John had been doing Bennett's work on the hieratic scripts. On discovering this, Bennett 'later spent a day rubbing out my transcriptions in the graffiti book and substituting his own handwriting! *El hamdulillah, huwa zey magnoun* [Praise be to God, he is utterly mad].'[9]

Occasionally, John and the others were invited to a meal with a local *Omda*, or head of a village. Part of the village of Et-Till lay on the west side of the river, and one day the *Omda*, inviting them for lunch, sent donkeys to pick them up. 'I had a beauty that was almost the size of a horse, with a splendid embroidered saddle and reins. At the Omda's we had to wait about 5 hours for lunch which lasted from 2.30 till 4 about 15 courses, 10 of them meat. My eyes were bubbling by the finish and we are all going for a walk by moonlight on the high desert to walk it off.'[10] To Glanville he described the experience more graphically as a 'bowel-racking proceeding'.[11]

*

The area to the south of Greek Street was very different to the affluent neighbourhood that enclosed it. It had clearly been used for rubbish pits when the larger, more important houses were first built. Gradually the pits had been filled in and the land claimed for smaller houses. In between these the poorest inhabitants began to build what was one of the most depressed areas of the ancient city. 'The houses themselves', John explained in his first despatch for *The Daily Telegraph*, 'form a bewildering labyrinth of slums, with narrow alleys, and blind corners, and refuse pits everywhere.'[12]

Many of the ancient walls had all but disappeared. After the city had been abandoned, the poor who could not afford to leave moved out of the slums into the empty houses of the wealthy. They reused bricks to build partition walls in the spacious rooms or brick pillars to support the ceiling, replacing the valuable timber columns that the rich had been careful to take with them. In subsequent centuries the walls were mined for the valuable ancient mudbrick to use as fertiliser on the crops. In unravelling these layers of change and decay, the team laid bare for the first time an entire suburb of a major ancient Egyptian city, 'with its roads and streets and squares, its official buildings and its merchants quarters, its rich houses and its hovels.'[13]

In one of these tiny hovels, the men found a jar (*zir*) set into a corner of the back yard. These *zirs* were commonplace in Amarna and were used to store water and keep it cool. Nonetheless, each jar was cleaned out on site under supervision. John described the scene. The pot was lying on its side and was lifted only after it had been photographed in situ. 'As the bowl over its mouth was removed there poured out a flood of gold, ingot after ingot as bright as the day they were buried, and after that silver, rings and bars and bent and broken cups, and last of all as though he were guardian of this treasure a tiny silver figure of a Hittite god with a gold cap. Eight pounds of gold and three of silver poured out while the workmen looked on with open mouths.'[14]

The bars of gold and silver had been roughly cast in the sand, suggesting that stolen objects had been hurriedly melted down for easier disposal. The robber's hoard led to the hovel, otherwise known as building T.36.63, being renamed for the papers as the 'House of the Crock of Gold'. Although archaeologists dread any find that hints at 'buried treasure' for the trouble that it can cause locally with illicit digging, the discovery was a useful publicity coup, reported first by *The Daily Telegraph*, then by *The Illustrated London News* and even on the BBC.[15] In the final publication of the site, John added a footnote. 'The vase was lying less than a foot below the surface. A chip had been made in the lid by the tethering stake of a local worthy. His feelings on hearing what he had missed are recorded, but inconvenient to print.'[16]

Nearby, in another house, a tiny painted limestone head of a girl was found. It was barely more than an inch high and the carving was extremely fine. Her beautiful face was painted terracotta, with her eyes lined in black, and the whole framed by her black, short plaited wig. The figure bore a striking resemblance to Ankh-sen-pa-aten, third daughter of Nefertiti and Akhenaten and wife of the ill-fated Tutankhamen, as depicted on a chair found in her husband's tomb. This small piece, though less sensational than the hoard, was infinitely more charming, as John's description betrays. 'The rather broad face, with its delicate mouth and its beautifully modelled eyes, its firm chin and slim neck are unmistakable. What an amazing figure it must have been when it was complete.' For the team this was undoubtedly one of the best finds of the season. 'Her expression,' Mary Chubb described to Mrs Hubbard, the American sponsor who had made the season possible, 'is a curious mixture of youthful amusement and regal dignity, which makes her utterly charming.'[17]

*

John was already planning where to dig next. In a reconnaissance of the Palace in the Central City and the South Suburb, he was dismayed by what he found. 'There seems to be some promising stuff, but our predecessors, the Germans, Woolley, Peet and Griffith have 'hogged' the place so much by digging only the big houses instead of working scientifically through it that there is a lot of difficulty in finding out where they actually did dig.'[18] The richness of the areas between the large houses in the North Suburb was evidence that the whole story could not emerge through cherry-picking.

Shortly after the discoveries in the North Suburb, the last member of the team arrived, long overdue. Gilbert Phillips, an American volunteer recommended by Henry Hall of the British Museum, stayed only two weeks, which proved more than enough. Phillips took it into his own hands to publicise the hoard, writing to *The New York Times* offering to send them a piece about Amarna with photographs. Naturally the paper was interested – however, Phillips had omitted to secure permission from the EES. Phillips had implied to John that he was keen to sell in order to earn a little money because he had to get back to the States, but John told him to contact Glanville for permission. In doing so Phillips lied to Glanville that John thought 'very well of the idea and feels that the Society would derive very desirable publicity'.[19] Glanville was alarmed that this unofficial publicity would not mention the EES, thereby upsetting the Society's sponsors. When John heard of this from Glanville he was livid and wrote back, 'We must apologise for him. He is utterly illiterate and ignorant and came out here for a bit of a thrill. After doing a certain (a very certain) amount for a few days he got bored. He made no attempt to learn the language or be anything but the vulgarest type of tripper... In any case, he is the last man to be allowed to talk about Amarna... Let him go, he's a bloody man'.[20]

Meanwhile the excavation moved north across the wadi. The houses here were larger and better appointed, suggesting that their owners were wealthy and influential people. The walls of these houses had survived to a greater height than those of the North Suburb, in spite of their proximity to the wadi. The most splendid was the House of Hatiay. Bennett proved some worth by associating the name inscribed on a large and elaborately inscribed lintel over the main entrance with Hatiay, Overseer of the King's Works, whose tomb was already known at Thebes, modern Luxor.

Hatiay had clearly used his position to get quantities of stone for his house, for every door was lined with limestone jambs painted dark red. One lintel showed that he could also draw on a very high quality of craftsmanship, something that was at a premium in a city with so much public building being undertaken in a short time. The interior of the house had also been elaborately painted and for the first time they were able to reconstruct the design scheme from the fallen fragments. Elements that had fallen from upper rooms gave the first clues as to their form and Seton Lloyd began to construct a model of a typical Amarna house for the Oriental Institute in Chicago, which would be loaned for the EES summer exhibition.

The inscribed lintel had been sabotaged before it fell. Akhenaten's name had been chiselled off while those of the Aten and Nefertiti were left unscathed. This was the latest in a number of clues of a rift between Akhenaten and Nefertiti towards the end of Akhenaten's reign. The evidence of the lintel and the greater occurrence of the queen's name on smaller objects at the north end of the city began to suggest that that area was her stronghold. Much was still to be discovered about the history of the city and its inhabitants, from royalty to poverty, but that was its appeal. Even the tiniest details from the smallest houses revealed something of the city's past.

It took fifty men to carry the vast lintel back to the North Dig House. It was a tremendous procession with the men chanting *Wallah negib* (By God we're bringing it) to the beat of their feet as they carried with seeming effortlessness the cradle they had created for their load. John led the way with what Mary noted was an unmistakable expression of 'elation and pride' on his face.

After a Christmas celebrated with bottles of Greek Mavrodaphne wine, the excavation moved back to the North City, where the North Dig House was. The Dig House had been the largest private house in the city, and the excavations around it showed that the whole of the North City was full of large important estates. Another substantial estate was uncovered contiguous to that of the North Dig House, and although not quite as large, it still boasted walled gardens enclosing a private lake, a chapel (unusually built in stone rather than mudbrick), stables and coach house, servants' quarters and seven corn bins. The house was typical in form, though on a grand scale, but there seemed to John to be considerably less privacy than was normal in an Amarna house. He came to the conclusion that the estate must have been an official residence. One clue came from the stone chapel, the only one known at Amarna. John was sure that it had been the North City residence of the High Priest, particularly as there were striking parallels with the official residence of the Priest Panehsy near the Great Temple excavated in earlier years.

He described what they had found in a letter to Seton Lloyd, who had already returned to Tell Asmar in Iraq. 'Up here we've had some wonderful developments. All that stuff you saw is merely "grounds" belonging to the houses to the west; but the biggest of those looks like a residence for the Bishop of Akhetaten, with a stone chapel, approached between two huge brick pylons. Only the foundations remain of the enormous building itself.'[21]

Finally, John began an investigation of the massive wall that ran along the other side of the Royal Road from the large group of estates around the North Dig House. He thought it might be some kind of fortification wall, but what they found was totally unexpected. It turned out not to be one thick mass of walling, but a double wall, the two skins five metres apart. As for the dip in the wall through which they had so often walked on the path from the river to the house, 'Oh Boy!', John exclaimed to Lloyd. 'The place we have always been walking over was a vast gate, wonderfully painted. We have covered it up until next year, but the little we have got out is simply first class. It can't have stood for more than a year and there is masses more, with figures and animals. We are leaving it here until we get advice as to its preservation, as it is all lying on its face and the backing has been eaten away.'[22]

Towers flanked the gateway, with stairs leading up to the top where more fragments of wall painting were found. 'For the most part they consisted of friezes composed of flowers and fruit. At intervals, however, or perhaps on another level, occurred festoons and chequers. But the two gems, promises of future discoveries, were first the head of a pigeon and secondly the forearm and waist of a man wearing an elaborately embroidered kilt. The paint is marvellously fresh, contrasting with the weathered appearance of the fragments from the tower.'[23] Two false doors flanked the gate, and fragments of sculpture showed that statues of the royal family had once gazed down from above these. The elaborate form of this gate made John wonder whether this might be the 'Window of Appearances' which was so often shown in tomb reliefs and from which the royal family distributed gifts to their subjects. Nobody had ever convincingly located this window, though it had to be somewhere in the city. At the very least John had found a contender for the role.

By the end of the season they had traced the double wall for nearly three hundred metres, with no hint of a return. It clearly enclosed a major building and further evidence from inscriptions on broken doorjambs and lintels showed that it must have been a royal building. In the tomb of May, Royal Chancellor, Overseer of the Soldiery and Bearer of the Fan on the King's Right Hand, which was cut into the cliff on the edge of the plain, there was a representation of a palace that fronted onto the river. This could not have been the Great Palace in the Central City, which was separated from the river by several major buildings. It was this North Riverside Palace that they had found on the doorstep of the North Dig House.

*

By the middle of January the season was wrapped up and they returned to Cairo. Exhausted after the excavation, John succumbed to flu, not helped by the inevitable tension prior to the division of finds. Although he was fairly optimistic after going through the objects with Rex Engelbach and Battiscombe Gunn, he knew it was up to the Cairo Museum's Director, Pierre Lacau, to make the final decision. John had worked hard throughout the season to keep the Museum well informed of the progress of the dig. In this he was helped enormously by Mary Chubb, who had kept the accounts and records up to date, as well as working on the excavations and registration of the finds, where her artistic talents resulted in some beautiful drawings. The EES got fewer updates than John would have liked as a result and he wrote to apologise to Glanville. 'It has been an abominably hard season owing largely to worries due to inexperience and the fact that I never felt I could be away from the dig a moment.'[24]

The regular reports to Cairo and Mary's catalogue of all the objects and photographs paid off. Lacau was far better disposed to them than was usually the case. 'The division has gone excellently. We have: half the gold – more than half the silver. The princess's head. A nice wooden box lid. Bronzes galore. Plenty of nice faience, the Mycenaean mask, a gold ring and some bronze ones. Moulds of stone and pottery. They have taken the lintel, the lavatory seat, the

3b TELL EL AMARNA: THE NORTH CITY

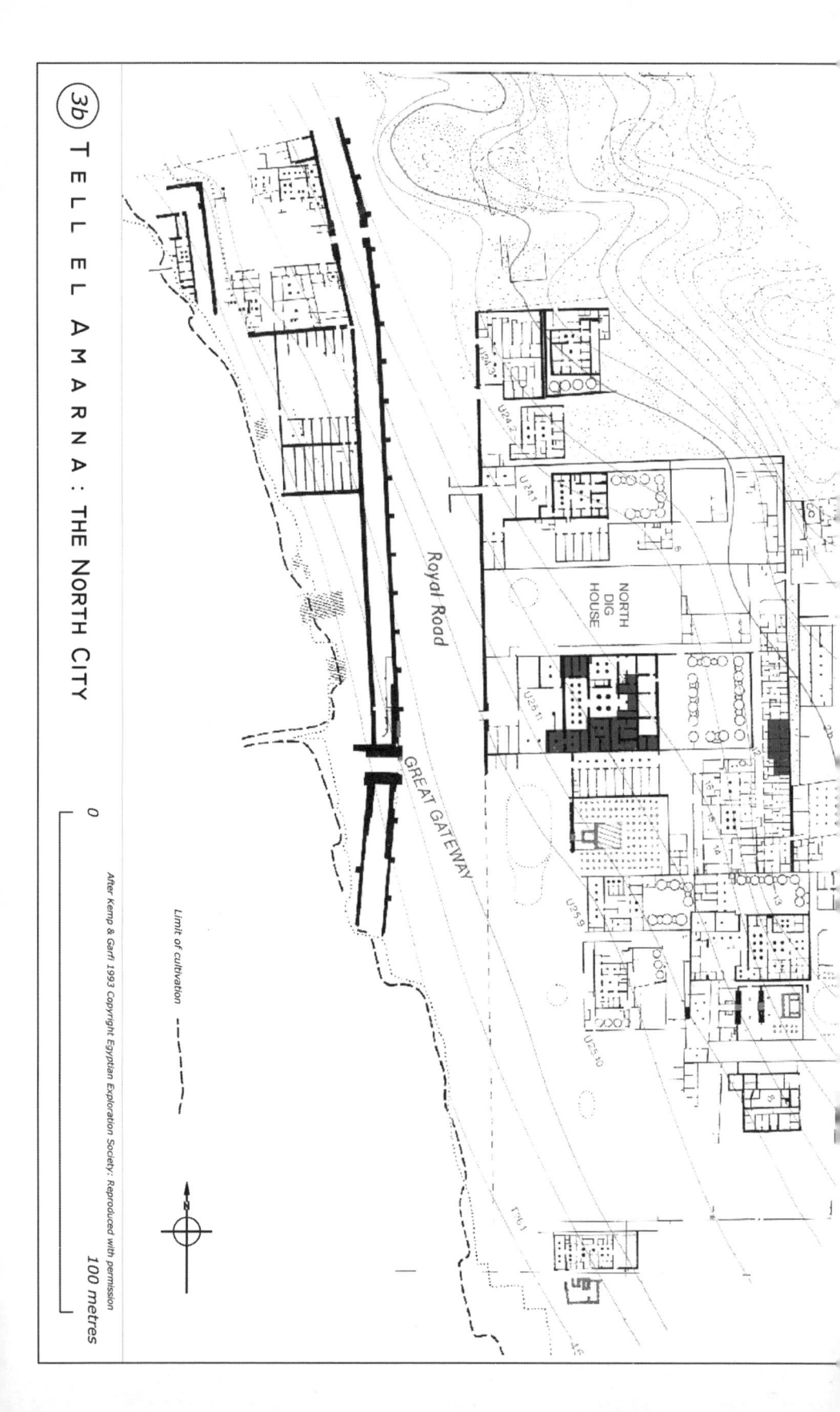

Royal Road

GREAT GATEWAY

NORTH DIG HOUSE

Limit of cultivation

0 — 100 metres

After Kemp & Garfi 1993 Copyright Egyptian Exploration Society. Reproduced with permission

lovely glazed brick, and a goodish amount of faience and bronze. They are making us a replica of the glazed brick, a cast or two of the rear seat and a reproduction of the little Hittite god from the crock of gold.'[25]

Before leaving Cairo, John and Hilda received an invitation to dine with Rex Engelbach and Battiscombe Gunn. Gunn was about to leave Cairo for the States and they sounded John out about taking over his post, 'viz. practically 2nd in command of the Museum beginning at £E 900 a year!' He declined the offer because of his involvement in the Aegean. The thought of taking a museum job in only one of his fields did not appeal to him, and he was unwilling even to consider the idea for another five years or so, but he was delighted to have been asked. 'Don't mention this to anyone', he urged Herbert. 'It was strictly unofficial although Lacau – the titular French Director of the Museum – had asked them to sound me. This was entirely due to having published things and I can't ever be grateful enough to you for spurring me on to do so!'[26]

This was not the only job that John had been approached about during the season. He confided in Glanville that he had had 'a roundabout offer' of a job in Palestine, setting up the new British School of Archaeology in Jerusalem. He would probably have accepted it if it had not meant abandoning work in Greece.

*

John and Hilda now headed for Greece. They had invited Hilary and Mary to travel with them in the Argolid. Bennett went to join the team at Abydos, from where he wrote to John asking if he could come back to Amarna the following season and complaining that he felt John had had a grievance against him. 'I wrote back a reasoned letter saying that I had had no grievance against him. I had naturally been annoyed at his not learning Arabic and that any atmosphere had been created by his own curious change of temper on his arrival... I of course had to tell him then of the number of occasions when in the face of great desire I had refrained from more than a very mild comment.'[27] The season had proved to John that one architect on site was not enough, and he told Bennett that it was unlikely there would be space for a philologist, as there were so few inscriptions that needed immediate interpretation.

But the problems of the season were soon forgotten and John could only marvel at the success of the dig. 'On the whole I think we can look back on a really wonderful season. A Mycenaean House. Gold and Silver. The Princess's head. A splendid house belonging to an already known official with a magnificent painted lintel. Excellent small finds. Bronzes which should clean up as well as those Cairo has kept. A stone chapel with the second biggest house at Amarna. The finest wall paintings ever waiting till next year. A palace waiting likewise... If that doesn't bring in the money, what will?'[28]

10

February 1931–February 1932

BEFORE LEAVING EGYPT AT the beginning of February 1931, John drew a map in Hilary's site notebook to show Hilary and Mary where they were to meet up with him and Hilda in Athens, including instructions of where to find the British School, and, most importantly, John's favourite haunt, Loubier's in Stadiou Street. This beer house-cum-restaurant was 'a cheerful place to gravitate to as evening fell and the early spring air grew chilly', Mary wrote later. 'The beer was pale and cold and memorable, and there was always a plate of savoury snacks thrown in for good measure... Loubier's always seemed to be brimful of laughing Greeks.'[1]

The next day the four of them stocked up on chocolate, insect repellent and film for their week-long trip and set off by train towards the Peloponnese. They were met at Mycenae by a Spiro grown so thin and sick since they had last seen him that it was impossible for him to act as their guide. What they did not know was that he did not have much longer to live. The family welcomed them to the Belle Hélène inn and, Mary remembered, they 'settled down for the first of those perfect evenings which happen when you are travelling the hard way through the countryside of Greece'.[2]

It was arranged that the youngest of the Dassis brothers, Orestes, would accompany them on the trip as butler and guide, though he had none of his brother's experience. Next morning, they walked up to the citadel of Mycenae. 'John moved forward towards the small modern rail-gate which barred the way in', Mary observed. 'The guard in the village had handed him over the key, as he was a privileged archaeologist. He made a proud face. "I feel very majestic holding the key of Mycenae in my hand." He spoke banteringly; but I was sure that, as he often did, he had thrown his inflection like a light cloak round a thought which was anything but frivolous.'[3]

After the flatness of Amarna, the vertical tracks of the Greek hills and mountains were hard going. They walked from dawn till long after dusk, getting lost and sliding down steep valley sides on their backsides to regain the right track high on the far side. The beauty and tranquillity of the villages they stayed in, whether down on the coast or high in the mountains, made up for the sore feet and exhaustion.

John was good company on walks, particularly during the rest breaks when his companions could finally catch up with him. Since childhood, he had acquired an extensive repertoire of popular songs, including Victorian music hall songs. This love of bawdy light entertainment he had inherited from his father. Mary had noticed at Amarna that John was often singing softly to himself, usually *Lillibulero*, the tune that he loved best and which his friends associated with him ever after.

They returned to Athens via Perachora, where John photographed the latest finds for Payne. From there John sailed to Andros with the Byzantinist Romilly Jenkins, who was to succeed Heurtley as Assistant Director at the School. On his return, he and Hilda joined Payne and his wife, the writer Dilys Powell, on a walking trip along the southern edge of the Pindos Mountains.

Early March was not the best time of year to tackle these mountains, and though the weather held as far as Delphi, it scotched their plans to walk down the Mornos valley to the ancient site of Naupaktos, and the Gkiona pass proved impassable. They turned instead north-west to the town of Lamia and then down the coast to Thermopylai. They passed Chaironea, Livadia, and the ancient site of Orchomenos on the edge of the flat plain that was all that remained of the ancient Lake Copais. On an outcrop was the Bronze Age fortress of Gla, which had once formed an island in the middle of the lake that was now drained and cultivated. Dilys Powell, unused to the type of walking trips now familiar to John, Hilda and Humfry, and attired in entirely the wrong clothes, stayed back from the rain-soaked Gla trip and Humfry stayed with her. 'Hilda, I morosely reflected, would never have drifted into such a situation. Presently the Pendleburys returned with streaming mackintoshes and glowing faces.'[4]

Over those ten days, Dilys Powell got used to watching the figure of John from afar, 'always ahead on any walk'. She saw a man who would 'jump straight to the top of some little wall where anybody else would have stepped up.' In conversation in the evenings or during picnic lunch stops, she noted how he talked. 'Clear, vivacious, quick without haste, the syllables precisely enunciated.' She remembered how he looked, too, when he talked. 'One felt his glance fixed on one. Sometimes I found his manner daunting, but that, I fancy, was merely due to his looking at the world with one eye instead of two.' Like Mary Chubb and others before them, she noticed how his travels in search of sites through the roughest of landscapes satisfied both his passion for history and a love of hardship. 'The conditions of travel added a flavour of uncertainty. The discomforts of the trip were minimal, indeed non-existent in comparison with the exhaustion he would later inflict on himself in long walks in Crete. But everything joined to strengthen his idea of himself as an explorer, a figure in a continuing adventure.'[5]

*

After the trip to Pindos, John and Hilda returned to Crete where the Paynes joined them. John concentrated on writing his guide and organising everything before Evans descended. At Knossos, before the storm of Evans' arrival, Dilys Powell was able to see another side of John as he revelled, as she saw it, in domesticity. 'Through everything John wore an air of contented authority. He was not only the explorer. He was the explorer with – I am sure he liked to feel – a solid family background.'[6]

John found it easier to work without the diminutive but energetic Evans breathing down his neck, so was glad of the news that his arrival had been delayed by earthquake damage to the railway in Serbia. Then bad weather put him off sailing, giving them another three days' grace.

Evans wasted no time after his arrival in getting excavation under way to the south of the palace on the west side of the road to Archanes, cut into the slope of Lower Gypsades. A large gold ring, which typically Evans called the 'Ring of Minos', had been found in a vineyard on the site, and Evans hoped that they might at last find the burials that must have existed somewhere in the vicinity of the Minoan palace and town, and perhaps even a royal tomb. The hillside was steep, but soon they found a structure far more astonishing than they could have hoped for.

John was in day-to-day charge of the excavation, and his excitement was obvious. 'We have got what certainly looks like a royal tomb with side chapels and pillared halls.' They uncovered a roofed pavilion, reached through a short entrance passage, with a portico opening into an open paved court. A door led from the court into a small inner hall, off to one side of which a staircase led to an upper level. A doorway at the end of the hall led into a larger pillar crypt with the two pillars surviving to their original height. 'We are still a good six feet from the bottom and the top of a door leading further into the hill has just appeared. It will be about the highest piece of ancient walling preserved and should be a magnificent monument.'[7] The evidence on the jambs showed that the door could be locked from the inside, eliciting the comment from the workmen, 'dead men do not lock themselves in', and the conclusion that there may have been a trap door in the ceiling.

The doorway in the hillside opened into a small passage leading to a subterranean chamber cut into the bedrock off the north-west corner of a pillar crypt. This paved square chamber had a single pillar in the centre. 'It is about twelve feet square with a square gypsum pier in the middle surrounded by the usual depressions in the gypsum paving, and lined with upright slabs of gypsum about six feet high. These slabs were held back at the corners and in the middle of each side by key slabs. These in their turn were kept in position by two huge cross beams which ran across the central pier. The roof was originally the rough rock. It was painted a deep Egyptian blue so that the dead man lying back would, as it were, see the heavens through a square window.'[8] Progress was slow because of heavy rain and the need to shore up the roof, which had collapsed on excavation.

The tomb had been built in the Middle Minoan III period (c.1700-1550 BC), contemporary with the greater part of the surviving palace, but had been destroyed by earthquake and after repair used for multiple burials. The whole structure ran very close to the road – John was concerned that Evans would do a 'lot of tunnelling and then clear off leaving me to deal with infuriated road inspectors.'[9]

Even before the excavation of the 'Temple Tomb', as Evans called it, was finished, Evans imposed his interpretation on it as the tomb of Minos, erected as a sort of cenotaph to the king whom legend held to have died abroad. As he always did, Evans immediately began the restoration of the structure as such, 'really playing about with the tomb in an abominable way', ignoring the possibility that there was any other interpretation.[10] In his guide John would make clear without comment that much of the restoration was done by bringing in 'old blocks from elsewhere'. As for the horns of consecration, he wrote that they 'may have crowned the façade or have stood within'.[11] Evans had ignored the uncertainty and re-erected them as he saw fit. John was not alone in his views, though Evans was impervious to most criticisms, and John was delighted when a visiting Belgian professor declared loudly that they were the worst he had ever seen. 'That incident has lasted ever since as a topic of conversation.'[12] The icing on the cake came later when Evans was given an award for the excavation. John merely wrote to his father, 'I see Evans got the Petrie Medal for our tomb!'[13]

Even worse was Evans's interference with John's guidebook. He wanted it 'miserably short and cheap', and to control the content. Though John resisted, he had a job convincing Evans' old friend and ally, George Macmillan, who published *The Palace of Minos*, of that fact. Macmillan and Evans wanted the guide to be described, prominently on the cover, as an offshoot of *The Palace of Minos* and Evans' work, and to be written under his direction. 'This seems to me to be the very negation of what I intended', he wrote to Herbert, 'and in such a case I won't do it. First, as I shall point out to him, the actual guide part is entirely my own. Secondly such a description on the title page would debar me from any personal opinions or disagreements, thirdly that if that is what is intended, any précis writer could boil down the P of M.'[14]

John's list of publications was growing rapidly. With *Ægyptiaca* and the *JEA* article behind him, he was busy writing up both his and Frankfort's work on the North Suburb at Amarna to appear in an interim report in the *JEA*. He was also co-authoring the official EES publication of the excavations with Frankfort, *City of Akhenaten II*, which was nearing completion. With Hilda, he had begun work on a guide to the Stratigraphical Museum at Knossos, and an article in the *British School Annual* (*BSA*) on the excavation of the *koulouras* was due out soon. Then there was the guide to Knossos.

Eventually, John got Macmillan to take his idea of the guide to the Macmillan committee by insisting that as the Knossos dig was a British School excavation, the proceeds from the sales of the guide should go to the School. But it was the end of May by the time John heard again from Macmillan, who was using every delaying tactic he could come up with. Macmillan blamed his publishing partners, saying that they didn't see any profit in a guide. John was sorely tempted to take the guide to another publisher and reproduce the plans, the copyright of which was what tied him to Macmillan, at his own expense. The existing plans were far too complicated for a guidebook anyway. If Evans did not like it, that was his problem. 'You have no idea how puffed up the old man is and what a lot of harm all the intense flattery he has received has done him.'[15]

Meanwhile, John had finished the task of sorting thirty years' worth of pottery excavated at the palace. 'All the boxes of pottery are stored and plotted on the plan of the Palace. The houses outside the palace I have drawn in a notebook and plotted on them their respective boxes. All this in English and Greek for the foreman's benefit.'[16] Whether he got any thanks from Evans he does not say, but the eminent American archaeologist Carl Blegen was certainly impressed at John's success in creating order out of chaos.

As the season in Crete drew to an end, the issue of John's departure date again loomed. He felt that again Evans was merely inventing work for him, and did not see why he should stay on merely to 'dance attendance on him and, quite uselessly help de Jong with reconstructions I don't approve of.'[17] He was beginning to suspect that the job as Curator was scarcely worth the trials he endured with Evans, and he confided to his father, 'I really don't see how we're to stand him even another year.'[18] John's determination to get home may have had something to do with the fact that Hilda either knew or suspected that she was pregnant. They eventually travelled back to London in comfort on the Orient Express and spent a quiet summer divided between Hilda's family in Cheshire, John's in Malvern and in Cambridge.

*

In September John and Hilda returned to London to join the other members of their team in setting up the Amarna section of the Egypt Exploration Society exhibition. Their venue was the Wellcome Historical Medical Museum in

Wigmore Street, in which they had three exhibition rooms. During preparation, these had been roped off to discourage the public from coming in before time but, in spite of this, they received a surprise visitor. 'Suddenly', Hilary Waddington recalled, 'Sir Arthur Evans came down the short flight of steps and took a flying leap over the rope. We had a horrible feeling he was going to catch his toe in it, but he didn't.'[19]

John had prepared a series of lantern slide lectures on Amarna, and the team attended the exhibition regularly to talk to visitors about the dig, inspiring at least one child – Cyril Aldred – to become an Egyptologist. Fifty-seven years later he would write his own book on Akhenaten. The Amarna element, in which they exhibited the finds they had gained from the division that season, was a great success. They also exhibited modern jewellery alongside ancient jewellery on loan, and they had a thousand visitors in the first five days. John had some postcards made showing the discovery of the crock of gold and other scenes. 'We have decided to open on Saturday afternoons in future and made quite a good bag yesterday.'[20] When the visitor numbers grew to over four thousand, they decided to extend the exhibition another month.

However, in spite of the success of the exhibition, the EES did not gain the subscriptions or donations on which the financing of the expeditions depended. 'Had it not been for the National Crisis [the government's abandonment of the Gold Standard]', John's father, Herbert, wrote to the EES's Mary Jonas, 'I feel sure that the finances of the Society would have gained considerably. But everywhere is the cry 'I can't increase my subscriptions, I must cut down.''[21]

There were just enough funds to get the team back to Amarna and, towards the end of October 1931, John and Hilda arrived back in Cairo, where the team spent a few days at the Victoria Hotel. Mary Chubb and Hilary Waddington, by now archaeological architect to the Palestine Government, joined them again. John had employed another architect – a slight, handsome man called Ralph Lavers with tousled brown hair and a fondness for tank tops – and had also borrowed a philologist called Herbert Fairman from the Armant project. The last new member was Stephen Sherman, who had been with the RAF in Egypt.

At Amarna, they began by recovering the remaining fallen paintwork that they had buried at the end of the previous season, but were disappointed to find that no complete stretch survived in situ on the walls. Lavers realised that this was because it had come from a room over the gate, not from within the gate itself, which appeared to have been undecorated. Gradually, by piecing together the fragments and recording how and where they had fallen, the pattern of the room above became clearer and Lavers managed to make a reconstruction of the whole gateway. They also seemed to be right in interpreting the building to the west of the great wall as the palace where Nefertiti had lived after falling from grace at the end of Akhenaten's life, for they found quantities of wine jar sealings bearing her name alone.

John, meanwhile, sent another team to begin investigating the estate of the North Dig House, which, it now appeared, had been only partially excavated in 1923 by Newton and Griffith. The ancient staircase of the house had never been cleared, and none of the ancillary buildings. 'Corpses in the outhouses', John noted in the dig diary, 'fear ancient scandal.'[22] It was frustrating trying to re-dig a badly recorded excavation, particularly when on one occasion two hours of meticulous work were spent lifting some fallen paintwork from the North Dig House before they discovered a note at the bottom of the deposit saying it had been re-buried. 'Evidently monkeys dug this house with their tails. Rot them', John recorded.[23]

In the North Suburb, the remaining houses north of Hatiay's were excavated, completing the excavation of the suburb. Many of these buildings proved to be incomplete, suggesting that the city was still expanding in this suburb at the time that the town was abandoned.

*

This was a much happier season than the year before, for everyone was far more relaxed with each other, and they all shared a similar sense of humour. When John declared that he and Hilda had decided to found a dynasty, he asked the others to come up with a motto while he invented the coat of arms. Mary came up with 'infra dig' – *infra dignitatem*, meaning 'beneath one's dignity' – and it stuck.[24]

Mary, like John, had a talent for writing or adapting light verse. Between them they adapted poems from Flecker's *Hassan* to life at Amarna, so Ishak's poem became:

Thy dawn, O master of the dig, thy dawn.
The hour the Gufti eats a spot of brawn.
The hour the water bints go to the river.
The hour that brother Peanut has a liver.
The hour that old Umbarak blows his whistle.
The hour that Philips sate upon a thistle.
O Master of the dig, the Amarna dawn.
That dawn, O master is completely dirty.
The water bint will ne'er again see thirty.
The villagers, who dig, in trenches lurk.
The boys who carry sand are lashed to work.

For thee the ferry of et Till is drawn,
Bearing thy beer at night, thy tea at dawn.[25]

Dawn was a magical time at Amarna. The team on the early shift would walk down to the site in the freezing darkness, wrapped in their thickest winter clothes worn over their summer clothes. In an unpublished short story written a few years later, John described a typical early start on site.

'A cold January morning at Tell el-Amarna. The mists still hung over the palm trees that fringe the Nile and extended far enough into the desert to make the static supervision of the dig a perishing job. The workmen were sluggish, I couldn't blame them, they must have been freezing in spite of layers of clothing and shawls wrapped so tightly round their heads that they couldn't hear a single direction. Their hands were numb, grasping the dripping hafts of their clumsy mattocks or turiahs. To each workman went a couple of children – boys and girls – to carry away in their small round baskets the sand he excavated. They too went listlessly and the only activity was shown by the foremen – the *ra'ises* – with their busy switches. Quite suddenly the mists dispersed. Over the rim of hills which enclose the plain of Amarna the sky turned green, then red and like a flash the edge of the sun showed above a gap in the cliffs. '*Oy Devs Oy Devs deh! L'Alla tantost veh*'. The dawn at Amarna is a never failing wonder and many people must have misquoted Flecker's poem, "Oh Master of the World, the Amarna dawn". With the first gleam of the sun an astonishing change took place on the work. Omar Ali of the golden voice began the high pitched song of the dawn, his first line followed by a crash of sound as the whole body of men, boys and girls joined the chorus.

Ya Fattah! Ya 'Alim!
Ya Fattah! Ya 'Alim!
Ya Rehman! Ya Rehim!
Ya Fattah! Ya 'Alim!

'That sound of singing at the work has never lost its fascination. The hammered rhythm beats out over the still desert for miles. A stroke of the turia, drop the haft of the turia on the foot, raise the basket to give to the boy, pick up the turia, next stroke. We sing many songs on the dig, comic, amorous, topical, but not one has ever given me that same thrill. It seemed that in that moment the whole aspect of the work changed. Though most of my energy was spent in assisting the sun to restore my circulation, it was easy to see how the children began to run instead of slouch, how the wrists of the workmen became supple and how jokes began to fly. Within a quarter of an hour the work was running on oiled wheels.'[26]

John now moved the main body of men down to the Central City to start the excavation of the royal estate, beginning with the Small Aten Temple. Known in the glory days of Akhetaten as Hat Aten, the 'Enclosure of the Aten', it was entered originally from the Royal Road, still called the Sikket es-Sultan, on the west through massive pylons or gateways, surviving in places up to fifteen feet high. These led into the first of three courts, in the midst of which stood a great altar surrounded by rows and rows of mud bases. John thought they were bases for some sort of awning, but they later turned out to be small individual altars for offerings.

The entrance to the second, smaller court was flanked by another set of pylons, inset with recesses with stelae depicting the royal family. Traces of another altar were found within the court as well as a house for the priest. The innermost court was the largest and contained the inner sanctum, and a 'sanctuary court', planted with rows of trees. This temple was remarkably different from the Egyptian temples of the old religion. Instead of an enclosed temple, which would get darker and darker as the worshipper approached the inner shrine, the temple to the Aten, the sun disc, was completely open air and flooded by the rays of the Aten so charmingly depicted on the reliefs of the period. 'The dig goes excellently… The Temple is one of the most important sites ever dug here as well as one of the most difficult.'[27]

Separating the Small from the Great Temple was the residential part of the palace, which had been partially excavated by Flinders Petrie some forty years earlier. A beautiful fresco of two of the daughters of Akhenaten and Nefertiti, now in the Ashmolean Museum in Oxford, had been found here, and Mary managed to recover some more fragments of the fresco. The substantial base of an ancient bridge across the Royal Road linked this building with the large official buildings of the palace, much of which remained to be excavated to the west.

The residential buildings were nothing like the standard Amarna houses that had been excavated thus far. When they found six identical rooms, John was convinced that these were the bedrooms of the six daughters of Akhenaten and Nefertiti. In another room they found two paint brushes, complete with lumps of paint and fish bones which seemed to have been used as quills. A splash of paint could still be seen on the floor where the painter had wiped his brush. John fancifully supposed that this might be the personal painting set of the artistically minded Akhenaten.

'The house was surrounded by a terraced garden', John described in *The Illustrated London News*, 'approached from the north by an elaborate gateway flanked by flower beds. From the garden ran the bridge to the official Palace, where the state rooms and reception halls would be. Although we did not completely finish the excavation of it this season, we obtained evidence to show that above the central gate of the bridge was a room with painted walls, which must almost certainly have been a Window of Appearance, from which the king showed himself to his people.'[28]

A series of magazines or storerooms on the east side of the building yielded a set of sculptors' trial pieces, on one of which the craftsman had been practising hieroglyphs, while another showed the normally clean-shaven Akhenaten with stubble on his chin. A large alabaster vase found was all the more remarkable for being carved with the names of Queen Hatshepsut, around 150 years before Akhenaten's time.

John was very conscious that publicity of the finds was the only way of gaining and keeping new subscriptions to keep the work going. As well as writing popular accounts for *The Illustrated London News*, he also took packets of the EES postcards with him which, on quiet evenings, the team wrote to those who had subscribed at the exhibition on the progress of the work. As he wrote in the report for the EES, 'if we cannot interest people in our work the sooner we stop the better'.[29]

Meanwhile, John began to prospect the Royal Tomb. The Department of Antiquities was considering a proper excavation of it following the discovery that a mummy, long assumed to be that of Akhenaten, found in the tomb of his mother, Queen Ty, was probably that of Smenkhara. Smenkhara was one of the more mysterious figures in the tale of Amarna. As John understood it, Smenkhara was made co-regent with Akhenaten at the end of his reign, marrying his niece, Akhenaten's oldest daughter, Meritaten, and eventually ruling with her too. But on Akhenaten's death, it was not Smenkhara but Tutankhamen who became pharaoh.

The Royal Tomb lay deep in the large wadi that sliced through the eastern cliffs and above which the sun rose. Some four miles into the stark and barren riverbed, another wadi branched off to the north. This was where the Royal Tomb, thought to be Akhenaten's, was cut deep into the west face of the valley. It had never been properly and scientifically excavated and John was very keen to dig it, though it was outside the area of the EES concession. In the dig diary, he noted that they found – on the 'wayside' – the upper part of a granite ushabti of a king, 'probably that of Smenkhara', and a gold earring just outside the tomb. 'Tomb evidently originally for the King. Then converted into Tomb of Maketaten [Akhenaten's second daughter] and disused.'[30]

Hilda was now seven months pregnant and beginning to find life at the camp arduous. She had caused ripples in the otherwise happy season by insisting on John's position as Director being fully appreciated by the rest of the team. But John made light of it in an article about the season, describing it as the pleasantest dig imaginable. 'To begin with, we were all more or less of the same age, so that the natural hesitation of a newcomer to address the Director did not enter into the matter, though, speaking personally, I think they might at least have pretended that he had a white beard!'[31] However, when Hilda told Ralph to get out of John's chair at the dinner table as it was the 'Director's chair', it caused embarrassment all round, not least for John.[32] Hilda was clearly getting tired and fractious and it would have been unwise for her to stay until the end of the season, more than a month away. Before her return to England, John held a fantasia in her honour, 'during which several very primitive and "folklory" songs, dances and plays were performed – as I suspect to ensure a male child!'[33]

John accompanied Hilda northwards as far as the boat at Port Said, and she was given an impressive send off. 'A fairly royal progress. First as we were going down river a very nice farewell song by the boatmen, then an official send off for her by the local Lord Mayor and the presentation of a very nice Roman gem. Then – getting onto the Port Said train at Cairo – people turned out of the small half compartment for our benefit so that we should have it to ourselves and finally on getting on board she was specially met and given a de luxe cabin!'[34]

On his return to Cairo, John met Rex Engelbach who invited him to dinner and persuaded him to stay on for another day to see Pierre Lacau, the Director General. Lacau, as John had hoped, granted him permission to dig the Royal Tomb '(which is not only outside our concession but also forbidden by law!)... It is a remarkable privilege.'[35] On top of this, the Antiquities Service was to pay for the project so it would not disable the other work at Amarna.

In spite of this, John was miserable and ill-tempered when he got back to Amarna. He had not been separated from Hilda for any length of time since their first season in Egypt, and he must have worried about her travelling while so heavily pregnant. She was forty by now, and it must have taken a great deal out of her to carry on working in Egypt. But in starting a family, John and Hilda were exposing themselves to increasingly frequent and lengthy separations, and in many ways the halcyon days of their early married life were drawing to a close. Perhaps part of John's misery was an awareness that some part of this idyllic life with Hilda, shared between Crete, Egypt and England, getting the best of seasons in all places, could not survive the arrival of children. He distracted himself by organising men to take up to the Royal Wadi and morosely took off alone with two *Quftis* and ten local workmen. He slept in a tent while the workmen made their own shelters to sleep in and kept to himself.

Mary Chubb had arrived back at Amarna while John was in Cairo, having gone to meet an Irish friend of hers, Rosaleen Angas. Rosaleen was effectively taking Hilda's place on camp, but she was to all intents and purposes there as a chaperone for Mary, not just in the eyes of the Egyptians but also in Hilda's. Mary felt that Hilda had been greatly relieved at her suggestion that Rosaleen come and stay for the remainder of the season, and that she felt less uncomfortable about leaving the largely male camp, and John, with two women rather than one.[36]

John camped up at the Royal Wadi for three days and nights before Hilary took over until Christmas. It was extremely cold at night, and the tomb was dark and dank by day. But John took advantage of his solitude to work things out and wrote a letter to Mary apologising for his behaviour. 'I really must thank you for getting me out of the slough of despond last night. I have been rather at a loss since Hilda left. So forgive previous bear's heads. I am quite all right, so Lavers needn't come down at all unless he must. The other two certainly must not. I do hope Walary [Hilary] sticks to it. We really do need the stuff he is doing very badly. God save you, John.'[37]

He followed it up some time later, still feeling bad about having let things get to him. 'Again Mary, I can't thank you enough for all you did at Amarna. We couldn't possibly have carried on the happy camp we did without you, and as for me – I just couldn't have a-born it without your soothing influence! Do tell Lavers how sorry I am if I gave him the impression of being fed up with him. I was absolutely horrified to hear of him asking what sort of a temper I was in. I didn't know I could scare anyone, and it is awful doing it without meaning to. I know I behaved like a bear with a sore head – but it was a wedged one in great tightness!'[38]

While Hilda had arrived back in London on December 25th to spend a lonely Christmas on her own at the Frankforts' flat, the Amarna camp received the customary large hamper from Robert Mond. That afternoon they held a fantasia which lasted right through to late evening. The *Omda* sent over a turkey, a goose and oranges, which was just as well as John had noted in the dig diary that the camp turkey had 'lost several pounds in weight owing to a fierce two hour fight with its reflection in a mirror'.[39] John got on well with the new *Om*da, who invited the team over to play tennis on his new sand court: 'Not so bad when you get accustomed to it.'[40]

Sherman took over the work up at the Royal Tomb after New Year's Day 1932 and John returned to his old self at the camp. 'The tomb (Royal) dig has gone wonderfully well', he wrote to Herbert. 'We have found that Amenhotep

III had a daughter called by his own name "Neb maat Ra" whom he married and whose alabaster "gut holder" was in Akhenaten's tomb.'[41]

The excavation of the tomb was very successful, yielding quantities of fragments of relief, both decorative and inscribed. It would take a long time to put these fragments together before any substantial information could be gained from them, but at last there was a proper record of the tomb. The tomb had never been completely finished, and even the huge dolerite and diorite pounders that would have been used to level the floor of the chambers had just been left where they were last used. Only one chamber appeared ever to have been used. This was for the burial of Maketaten, the second of the royal couple's six daughters. 'Perhaps', John mused, 'the King lost interest in the tomb after his daughter's death. Perhaps he deliberately tried to put the idea of death from him and would no longer allow work to go on there once Maketaten's chamber was finished. We shall never know.'[42]

There was no evidence to say whether or not Akhenaten was ever buried in this tomb. Though the canopic jars to hold his vital organs were there, they appeared never to have been used, and yet *shawabti* figures inscribed for him, which would only have been put in a tomb at the time of a burial, were found. 'They may, of course, have been used for the princess,' John wrote, 'whose death must have come unexpectedly before her funeral furniture could be prepared. But it seems best to assume that Akhenaten was laid here as he intended and that his sarcophagus and probably his very body were broken up by order of his successors.'[43] The tomb revealed that Akhenaten had also introduced changes in funerary practice. From the hundreds of fragments of several pink granite sarcophagi scattered all about the tomb, it was clear that the carved figures guarding the four corners were of Nefertiti rather than the traditional goddesses.

Just before the end of the work, Engelbach came to visit the site and inspect the Royal Tomb. He was delighted with the work they had done, despite the fact that one or two of the EES committee had expressed doubts amongst themselves that 'Pendlebury and his team' were up to so important a job.[44] They were proved wrong.

For John, archaeology was exciting, in spite of the often slow and careful work required. To him, the passion felt by archaeologists should be shared and not hidden in a mass of worthy publications. One of the joys of working at Amarna was the personal element of the site, its extraordinary nature and the people. If he, as the archaeologist, could not communicate this, then he had no business digging at all. 'Theoretically... the indexing, cross-referencing, photography, noting, and numbering of objects is soullessly endless on the perfect excavation. In practice, however, we may remind the prospective field archaeologist that such terrors do not loom so large. The trouble with so much of modern fieldwork is that it makes efficiency an end in itself, that it tends to regard the formation of a corpus, whether of pottery or of anything else, as the be-all and end-all of its labours. Excavators in their publications are too fond of publishing their notebooks, and while no doubt it is excellent that every piece of information should be put on record for the use of students, it is often the case that the grisly tables and charts which form the bulk of ideal excavation reports merely result in the complete refusal of anyone to read them.'[45]

For Amarna there was another very good reason for bringing the city to life in print. The mudbrick from which the city had been built had largely decayed back into the dust from which it was made, making it very difficult for visitors who were not familiar with the site plan to appreciate the magnificence and beauty of the buildings that had once stood there. 'Mudbrick is not a very romantic material', John wrote in his guidebook to the site. 'But once you put behind you the expectation of splendour, you will find an equal pleasure in exploring these homely remains.'[46]

The spirit of the place resonated with him, and he tried to explain it further. 'It is not merely that the famous head of Nefertiti was found here, nor yet that Tutankhamen began his reign here. There must be, I think, some inherent romance in the idea of a royal city, built at the whim of a Pharaoh in a hitherto uninhabited spot, founded, inhabited and deserted within the half of a generation and left a wilderness again to this day. It was for its short span of life the capital of the greatest empire in the world. It was the scene of a fantastic experiment in monotheism while that empire was going to rack and ruin. In its streets were represented all the nations of the known world, Minoans, Mycenaeans, Cypriots, Babylonians, Hittites, Jews and a score of other races, while in the background the old life of Egypt went on unchanged and unaffected.'[47]

11

February 1932–March 1933

THE IMMINENT BIRTH OF his first child brought John hurrying home to a snowy February in Hampstead, where Hilda had gone into a nursing home. John, after a hectic if successful season, was tired and unwell, so Hilda sent him home to rest. When she unexpectedly went into labour there were complications, and Hilda was given an emergency caesarean. On February 26th 1932, David John Stringfellow Pendlebury was born.

The emergency operation was distressing to both Hilda and John, but they were nonetheless delighted with their new son. However, John's father, a surgeon himself, was furious, both with the surgeon for not letting John know in advance and with John for not telephoning him instantly with the news. Dickie let slip his feelings to John, whose happiness, tinged with tiredness, illness and worry for Hilda, quickly turned to rage. Two days after David's birth, he wrote to his father, struggling to remain polite. 'I certainly would have wished to know but I did not know what is medical etiquette. Actually of course I never heard until I went into the room next morning and Hilda told me, when I promptly informed you. That was the first I heard of it. If you wish to blame Lane Roberts [the surgeon] that is one thing, but I do not see why we should have the happiest moment of our lives spoilt like this. Hilda of course knows nothing about it – I hope I shall not have to tell her.'[1]

Herbert was every bit as stubborn as his son. He would not let the matter rest, and neither would John. Five days later John felt compelled to write again. 'Since it seems to me of some importance whether you consider me to be a large and rather inefficient liar, I'd be glad if you would let me know whether you would prefer to ask Lane Roberts yourself as to whether he informed me of the operation beforehand or whether you would like *me* to ask him to write to you giving the details. I quite understand that your professional pride prefers to believe that he did do so but I think you will find that whether you ask me, him, Hilda or anyone at the nursing home they will tell you that I was not informed. In any case you will realise that I refuse to pass the matter over and will not drop it until you realise the truth.'[2]

John refused to meet his father until he apologised. When he eventually did, John was immensely relieved that the rift was mended. 'I had been terribly sad last week and am rejoicing it's all over.' John could now express the pride of the new father – 'Don't you think the infant is a credit?' Their first choices to 'stand gossip', or act as godparents, were their old Pembroke friend, Old Man Comber and, curiously, Sir Arthur Evans. Both expressed their gratification at the request but refused.[3]

It was three weeks before mother and baby were allowed back to their temporary home at the Frankforts' flat in Hampstead. 'Both are flourishing. David is strong in forearm and leg and lung. I expect Hilda will be taking him up to Caldy about April 2 for ten days before leaving for Crete... I have just begun to receive incredibly flowery letters of congratulation from Egypt, many pages long.'[4]

*

John went ahead to Crete, where he finished the *Guide to the Palace of Knossos*. Hilda and David arrived a month later, in time for the Greek Easter, and John planned a fantasia on the roof of the Taverna in David's honour. They had a pleasantly quiet season without Evans, whose absence meant, much to John's relief, that there was no excavation. Instead, he finally completed the catalogue of two thousand boxes of sherds from the Knossos excavations, which Payne agreed to publish in the next *BSA*. He then began to compile a more detailed catalogue giving the date of the contents of each box, with which Hilda helped him. John decided that they should also have a little light relief from work available and began to build a tennis court on the hillside above the Villa Ariadne.

He planned only a couple of trips, not wanting to leave Hilda alone too often. However, he took Stephen Sherman, who had joined them, on a marathon walk down to the south coast and over to the east of the island. Travelling south down past Kommos, Matala and Kaloi Limenes, they cut back through the Asterousia Mountains past a Neolithic site at Miamou. Visiting Pyrgos on the way they headed up the slopes of Mount Dikte to Viano and Amira. Passing round the south-east of Dikte, they visited Kalamafka, 'a beautiful place and a very fine Minoan site', before reaching Lato, 'an archaic Greek site in one of the most magnificent positions ever seen'.[5] At Spina Longa they lunched with Captain Pool and his Imperial Airways staff on the yacht *Imperia* before taking a bus back to Knossos, with Sherman driving some of the way.

His next journey was up Mount Ida in the company of a 'wandering botanist' named Jekyll, formerly of the Natural History Museum. Their route took them through Axos and Anogia, and from there to the Nida Plain and the Idaean Cave, and on up to the summit, returning down to Nida for the night. From Nida, they went to Kamares, visiting the famous cave site, then to Gergeri and Prinias. They ended up at Krousonas, where they picked up their car. 'We were very lucky in our weather and were able to sleep out every night. The shepherds of Ida too are a most interesting and kind lot of people.'[6]

John heard that his guidebook had finally met with Evans' approval, so he began to develop ideas for another book. The idea started as a bibliography of ancient sites in Crete, but soon grew into a 'magnum opus', a proper archaeological guide to Crete, 'which will take some years. However it will be worth it.'[7]

Meanwhile, Stephen Glanville wrote with another suggestion. The British Museum, together with the Victoria and Albert and London Museums, wanted to start a new series under the general title of 'London the Treasure House'. 'It is to be a series taking history in periods and showing what material there is in London. I should be doing Mespot [Mesopotamia], Egypt and the Aegean. I have accepted, while saying I know nothing about Mespot or indeed Egypt, but that I'd be pleased to learn! It does seem a good opportunity of learning something about Mespot.'[8]

*

John, Hilda and David left Crete for England at the end of June, travelling again on the Orient Express. 'I am thinking of either hiring a baby or getting a very lifelike doll when David grows up. It makes such a difference to the ease with which one gets through customs and passports!'[9]

In London, they stayed at the Wigmore Hotel, near the Egypt Exploration Society exhibition. John had been worried for some time about the quality of the exhibition. It had been organised at the last minute due to delays in the finds arriving from Egypt and there was a shortage of money. However, it was even worse than he had feared. 'A very inferior show, space inadequate etc. Really it's hardly worthwhile going on with a Society which takes so little interest in its most important job!'[10] John's lectures at the Royal Society were, however, very well attended, and film footage shot at Amarna by Hilary Waddington over the first two seasons was a great success.

The lack of funds that had resulted in such a poor exhibition began to have further repercussions. Although the Belgian Egyptologist Jean Capart was working hard to squeeze some more money out of the Brooklyn Museum for the Amarna dig, it came too late in the day. Small amounts were coming in, including the proceeds from the EES's share of the treasure horde from the first season. The Society had been given permission to sell the gold, as it had no stamps and was seen to have no archaeological value, and eventually added £256 to the Amarna budget. But this was not enough to keep the team together. With the extra cost of publishing the second volume of the *City of Akhenaten* on the North Suburb, which John was writing with Frankfort, the EES could no longer afford to keep Mary Chubb on the Amarna staff. Hans Frankfort recruited her to work with his team in Iraq.

When he received news that both Sherman and Lavers had also been approached by Chicago, John observed to his father that Amarna was becoming a prep school for Chicago. 'Frankfort, Lloyd, Mary Chubb, Lavers, Sherman in three years is not bad.'[11] But it was bad. Mary Jonas explained the problem to their loyal sponsor, Mrs Hubbard. 'It is impossible for a poor Society like ours to vie with the Chicago Institute, and it really seems as if we had become a training ground for recruits for Chicago... We are extremely fortunate in having Mr Pendlebury who is not tempted with the golden bribes as Director and we hope to retain him, but it is disappointing for him if he is always having to train a fresh staff.'[12] 'So far', John joked to his father, 'Hilda and I are the only ones considered undesirable enough not to be approached!'[13]

Sherman and Lavers were offered a starting salary of $2000 a year. John felt no bitterness; in the financial climate of the times, he could understand how important the money was, particularly as it was so rare in archaeology. It was the short notice that made it a difficulty. So it was an enormous relief when Lavers and Sherman refused their offers, deciding to stay at Amarna that season after all. John planned only a short excavation that year, because of the the uncertainty of funding. Bearing in mind Glanville's book proposal, he decided to use the spare time on a trip to Iraq to visit Frankfort's team, returning via Palestine.

While in England, John wanted to concentrate on sorting out somewhere to live. They had been renting a house in Barton Road, Cambridge, but were looking for somewhere better, and found the perfect house at 21 Madingley Road. 'It has a very nice hard tennis court. The owner is letting us have it cheap as she is going away and doesn't want to shut it up or sack her maids.'[14] With a home that they could call their own, albeit rented and short-term, John and Hilda were at last in a position to entertain their Cambridge friends, giving small dances and dinner parties. David appeared to relish the attention. 'I think he enjoyed his time at Cambridge. He certainly was a success and often used to have a small escort of celebrities when out for a walk.'[15] John and Hilda took up horse-riding at the end of the summer. John knew that there was good riding to be had in Iraq across the Diyala desert and he wanted to be ready for it. It was a brief but happy time before the inevitable separation, as Hilda and David were not to accompany John out to Amarna. Hilda had decided to stay with her family at West Kirby and take lessons in hieroglyphics with Thomas Peet, Professor of Egyptology at Liverpool University.

*

John arrived in Cairo at the end of November 1932 and spent his time sorting out the fragments of four or five granite sarcophagi that had been found the previous season in the Royal Tomb. 'I think... that we shall be able to restore one more or less complete and the whole of one side of another. I have also been handling a lot of the Tut stuff looking for re-used things.'[16] He hoped that among the objects deposited in Tutankhamen's hastily prepared tomb would be some made during Akhenaten's reign. The nature of such objects and the names carved on them could hold further clues to the complex period that they were trying to unravel, and when the various co-regencies had occurred.

Fairman had already gone ahead to Amarna, while Sherman went to Armant to pick up a light railway for dumping the spoil. Hilary, now happily married and ensconced at the survey camp at Athlit Castle in Palestine, was planning to use his leave to work at Amarna. Ralph Lavers and one of the two new members of the team met up with John in Cairo. Tony Chubb and Stephen Glanville had recommended another of the Chubb family, Philip, as a photographer. Philip had been close friends with Glanville since the age of five, and John soon got on as well with him as he had with Mary and Tony. The other new recruit was a young New Zealander by the name of Charles Brasch. Brasch was an aspiring young poet who had fled the commercial world of his wealthy father to live in England, during which time he became a member of the EES and joined the Amarna team. 'I was to go, informally,' he later wrote in his memoirs, 'as a kind of unpaid cadet, to learn and to make myself useful.'[17]

Cairo was alive with activity as the Egyptian king, King Fuad, was due to arrive in the city that week. Egypt was very unsettled in the period between the death in 1927 of Zaghloul, leader of the Wafd party, and the Anglo-Egyptian Treaty in 1936. The Wafd party had a great deal of support in its wish to throw the British out of Egypt, propounded as forcefully by Zaghloul's successor as leader, Nahas Pasha. This anti-British feeling was manifested in frequent demonstrations leading often to riots, particularly in the capital, as well as strikes, and there was always a fear that this unrest would turn into a massacre of the British, as had happened in 1919. That was still a vivid and bitter memory for many of Cairo's sizeable British population.

Brasch's first impression of the Nile Valley was of isolation. 'South of the Delta, which is indeed a different country, you see nothing and can imagine nothing that is not Egypt. Your horizon is the rough-broken line of cliffs enclosing the valley, which is in most parts between two and six miles wide and nowhere more than thirteen. Climb the cliffs and you see nothing except endless desert hills, utterly barren. The sky overhead is always the same blue clear sky of Egypt. The river, higher or lower, is the one everlasting Nile. It seems that this is the whole world, that nothing else exists.'[18]

The team took the train as far as Mallawi, 'where the engine driver and fireman were said to visit the prostitutes who lived along the street opposite the station, brazen women sitting bare-headed on the doorsteps of their steep narrow houses in capacious robes of purple or red with heavily painted faces and big gold ear-rings'.[19] The slow journey up-river on the felucca gave John and the other Arabic speakers, Fairman and Sherman, a chance to catch up on the local news since the previous season, as well as all the gossip and rumours from other digs. But at Amarna there was little evidence of the political turmoil of the capital.

While it was still dark on the first day, the two supervisors chosen to take the early shift were woken up with a cup of hot sweet tea. Setting off into the cold darkness, they arrived at the Great Temple enclosure or Gem Aten, where work was to begin and where the villagers awaited them, sullen, sleepy and cold.

The Great Temple was the heart of the ancient city and its most important building, dwarfing the Small Aten Temple. It was for this temple of the new religion that the city had been founded on virgin ground. The heart of the temple was the sanctuary, but John had to delay plans to start there while they waited for the light, hand-operated railway to arrive. The small tipper cars would allow them to shift the spoil well away from the site. So John began to excavate the temple enclosure. Petrie had put down a few trial pits in this area, but no thorough investigation of it had yet been undertaken.

The enclosure was vast, measuring three hundred yards in width by nearly half a mile in length, almost as long as the city was wide. 'Before, however, even the boundary wall was built some dedication ceremony must have taken place. The foundations of a ceremonial gateway, later razed to the ground, were discovered just within the main entrance. In front of this were a number of plaster receptacles, sunk on the main axis, for liquid offerings, while a mud paving was laid all over the area. From here an avenue of sphinxes led eastwards, to be replaced by trees after some hundred yards.'[20] The speed with which the city went up led to a serious compromise in the quality of the buildings and their decoration. Even this temple, the greatest building in the city, around which everything else was laid out, was done with more haste than panache. As John wrote later, this temple was to be 'the crowning achievement of the whole venture. It was to be the centre of the worship of the new god all over the world. To this Temple the eyes of the Nubian and of the Asiatic were to turn for inspiration for their local sun temples at Sessebi and Jerusalem'.[21]

Now that John could ride, he couldn't resist heading out on horseback over the flat expanses of the Amarna plain, dressed appropriately. 'I got over two Arab horses today and went for a ride with Philip Chubb. The caparisons of mine, being silver and blue went very well with my Cretan costume but the saddle which they covered had a huge pommel in front with pistol holsters and a great chair back behind. The stirrup irons were solid the length of the foot below and the leathers were set right back so that it was impossible to get either one's feet forward or one's heels down. The horses, or at least the stallion I was riding, have nothing between a jog and a full-out gallop, they can neither trot nor canter and the pommel and the stirrups prevent one from getting forward properly when galloping. However my horse was very fast, quite tireless and very sure-footed as well as looking exceedingly nice and being lent free of charge whenever I need it.'[22]

Back in the Central City the dig was going well, but difficulties arose because, after the final abandonment of the city, it had been thoroughly dismantled. 'Practically every stone was taken from the buildings', John wrote in the preliminary report.[23] They did however have substantial clues as to what it had looked like in a stylised representation of the temple in the tomb of Meryre, High Priest of the Aten.[24]

Gradually they began to piece together the plan. 'We have got some quite interesting architectural details hitherto unknown in Egypt, such as huge concrete platforms flanked by thirty rows of thirty-five square brick piers, but the whole thing has been very wantonly destroyed. Our only find of note is a very nice sandstone head of the king to be used as an inlay.'[25] When they came across what appeared to be row upon row of open courts with statue bases standing four deep on each side with platforms all around, John concluded that Akhenaten and his architect were 'quite barmy'.[26]

Eventually, the work took a turn for the better, with a collection of fine finds in trenches where the walls had been robbed out. 'Apart from the one German year when they got all those heads, there has never been such a year for first class finds. Plaster mask of Nefertiti, Plaster Mask of Akhenaten, the best trial piece ever seen of Nefertiti. One of two royal heads. A small group consisting of an ape sitting on an altar and a cross-legged scribe below – absolutely brilliantly done.'[27]

But the best find came from the south part of the city. Hilary had noticed that in between the excavated areas was a part that for no apparent reason had been left unexcavated. They were walking over it, past some exposed walls, when Hilary's new wife, Ruth, dislodged a mudbrick and revealed part of a plaster head. When they looked more closely they discovered that there were other fragments, but of worked stone. If news of the discovery got out, the site was sure to be looted over the summer, so John sent Charles Brasch and some of the workmen down to help them excavate the spot.

What they found were two or three small houses, which seemed to be related in some way to the house Petrie had excavated in 1892.[28] The German excavation had ended only a metre or two away and appeared to have missed parts of the sculptor's workshop where the famous Berlin head of Nefertiti had been found. It was here that Hilary's group found the unfinished quartzite head of a woman, possibly Nefertiti, possibly one of her daughters.

There is a rare, haunting beauty in this piece of sculpture, which, though unfinished, has a gentle, sensitive quality that makes it now one of the finest Amarna pieces in the Cairo Museum. The slightly upturned face is still marked with the setting-out lines for the features and, though the eyes are blank, only lined with black, the exquisitely carved mouth had already been touched with red. There is a passion in this simple act of the sculptor's, colouring the lips before the head was finished. John felt that it was the most human face he had ever seen on a sculpture, and it became one of the iconic images of the Pendlebury years at Amarna. John, who had loved the more famous image of Nefertiti for so long, was moved to write a short love story based around a woman who resembled this piece.[29]

The men were just as pleased with the find, particularly as they were given a reward for their work. 'The entire dig shouted out it was "bakht Mr Dafid" – luck of Mr David and there is a song about him stating the number of his children and how his grandchild shall be mudir.'[30]

The season had been a remarkably successful one. Philip Chubb had turned out to be a first-class photographer, and John hoped that he would become a regular member of the team. He was worried that Philip might be tempted to join his brother and sister at the Oriental Institute of Chicago, and decided to get money from the EES to build a proper photographic studio.

John arrived back in Cairo at the end of January, 'after a terrific send off from Amarna in which thirty people were concerned'. John knew that the Cairo Museum would be delighted with the finds: 'I very much doubt whether they will part with any of the best stuff. It is all too good.'[31] Of course Cairo did want to keep all the best pieces. John commented to the EES, 'How Brooklyn will take that I don't know!'[32] This highlights a major concern. If the EES did badly out of a division and had little to take back to England, the sponsoring museums might feel they had not had a good return on the money they had donated, which could result in their withdrawing support the following season. The EES could get casts made for their exhibitions, but without the support of the American museums they would be in trouble.

*

On February 8th 1933 John flew from Gaza to Baghdad, where he had arranged to meet Hans Frankfort. John explored the markets of the city of Haroun al-Rashid, the medieval Caliph of Baghdad depicted in Flecker's *Hassan*, a favourite subject of John's doodles. Here he found, 'what I really wanted, a huge sheepskin coat which smells like a polecat but is very warm'.³³ He was less impressed with the Baghdad Museum, which, although it contained some interesting pieces, he found gloomy and sad. Then Frankfort took John to see some of the ancient sites. Though a migration of the Shamar tribe and their camel train prevented them visiting Kish, they did get to Babylon: 'a most impressive place of which very little has been dug. The walls are standing in places up to about 40 feet'.³⁴

Eventually they drove out to Tell Asmar where Frankfort was directing the excavation of a vast palace and temple complex of the ancient city of Eshnunna. The city site of Eshnunna was, at four thousand years old, more ancient than Amarna, and had been under the control successively of Ur and Elam before being destroyed by Hammurabi. It was very different to Tell el-Amarna, not least because, unlike Amarna, it was a genuine 'tell', a mound built up over centuries by layers of successive occupation, with considerably deeper and more complex stratigraphy than the short-lived city of Amarna could boast. Both buildings and objects were better preserved, and the finds were not just rich but extremely plentiful.

John stayed for ten days at the camp where he found himself in familiar company, with the Frankforts, Seton Lloyd and Mary Chubb. The rest of the Tell Asmar team consisted of Thorkild Jacobsen (philologist and archaeologist), and his wife Rigmor (site photographer), and the conservator Rachel Levy.

The remote excavation house was an impressively large creation of mudbrick with a gatehouse, designed by Seton Lloyd as his first job in Iraq. At forty to fifty miles across the desert from Baghdad, and twenty from the nearest cultivation, it had to be as self-sufficient as possible. 'It was indeed an ambitious affair', Lloyd wrote in his autobiography, 'grouped around three courtyards, of which the largest had accommodation for the staff, including tiled bathrooms and a library. Drawing office, conservation laboratory and antiquities magazine surrounded the second, with servants' quarters and garages in the third. Water, brought from the nearest canal-head by truck, was pumped to tanks in a tower over the arched entrance, over which a beacon light was installed.'³⁵

In fact the expedition house catered for two major excavations, Tell Asmar and Khafaje, which was nearer to the Diyala River, and the two teams were as closely connected as the twenty miles distance between them allowed. During excavation the American team at Khafaje, led by the French archaeologist Pierre Delougaz, lived on site, returning once a week to the Tell Asmar expedition house.

In the late afternoons and on days off, the team would relax and sometimes go hunting. There were four horses stabled in camp, three of which had been bought locally by Jettie, Rigmor Jacobsen and Seton Lloyd as a means of escaping the isolation of the camp from time to time. The fourth was the camp horse used for urgent journeys to Khafaje or Baghdad when heavy rains made the roads impossible for the cars. So John borrowed Lloyd's horse and went riding with Mary, Rigmor and Jettie over the dunes and along the beds of ancient dried out irrigation channels with the distant view of the mountains to the east separating Iraq from Persia, and to the Diyala valley near Khafaje.

The camp was a very relaxed and happy one, particularly at the end of each week when the Khafaje team returned to the Tell Asmar fold and played Fred Astaire and other popular American singers on their portable gramophone. On John's last night at Tell Asmar, Frankfort organised a more traditional Arab fantasia, with singing and dancing in one of the courtyards. 'The locals can't either sing or dance', John noted, 'but the Northerners and Kurds have some very good national dances.'[35]

When Mary Chubb had a chance to talk to him privately, she asked John very tentatively how things had gone at Amarna with her brother, Philip. John had nothing but good to say about him and was even thinking of lending him money, so he was rather shocked when Mary said that she felt it was time to alert him to the fact that Philip was thoroughly unreliable and untrustworthy. It was not just Mary and her family who held this opinion of Philip, but Stephen Glanville, too. After the Bennett and Phillips fiascos, John felt that he was a fairly good judge of character and would not believe the insinuation against someone he had come to like. Indeed, he was angry with Mary for 'betraying' her brother when he was not there to defend himself. When John left, Mary felt that her attempt to warn him had somewhat soured his visit.[37] She did not even refer to John's stay in her published account of the excavations at Tell Asmar, *City in the Sand*, though he appears elsewhere in the book.

John was missing Hilda and David, whose first birthday had come and gone, and was longing to meet up with them on March 11th in Athens. However, he still had a long way to travel. He took the Nairn bus for the epic 500-mile journey across the desert on an unsurfaced track from Baghdad to Damascus. At Damascus, he visited the museum to make notes on its collections and then crossed the mountains of the Jebel esh-Sharqui to the river valley on which the ancient site of Baalbek stood. Crossing over Mount Lebanon, John was again on the shores of the Mediterranean. Using Beirut as his base for a few days, John visited Byblos, stopping at Dog River on the way back and seeing stelae which had been set up by various conquerors, from Ramesses II and Sennacherib to Napoleon and Allenby.

He worked his way south down the coast through Sidon and Tyre to

Haifa, and then on via Megiddo, site of a famous battle between Pharaoh Thothmes III and a Syrian warlord, to Jerusalem, where William Heurtley (former Assistant Director of the BSA), was soon to be based as the new librarian at the museum. 'Having only two days there I decided not to site see (or sight see) but merely to wander round. The Dome of the Mosque on the site of the Temple is a really gorgeous affair and the El Aksa Mosque, converted from a basilica of Justinian. The city walls too are very pleasant to wander round. At the moment they are mostly Arab, Turkish and Crusader work but they go down below the present level over a hundred feet in some places to really early stuff.'[38] John visited David Iliffe and his staff at the Jerusalem Museum before heading to the Crusader castle at Athlit, just south of Haifa, where Hilary Waddington and his wife were based. Then from Haifa he took the train to Alexandria, and sailed to Athens to be reunited with Hilda and David, 'grown out of recognition', adding proudly that he 'really is a fine young tough'.[39]

12

March 1933–March 1934

THE THREE PENDLEBURYS SAILED to a Crete in full spring glory only to find that their new home was uninhabitable. The Taverna at Knossos had developed huge cracks in the masonry and was too dangerous to live in, and Ralph Lavers, who was staying with them, advised them that it would be cheaper to pull the whole building down and rebuild, giving them the chance to add an internal staircase. So they moved into the Villa Ariadne while the work was carried out.

John's guidebook, *Handbook to the The Palace of Minos, Knossos, with its Dependencies*, came out in the early spring of that year, 1933, and John was dismayed to find that Macmillan had sent out only fifty copies, though John was sure he could sell at least two hundred a year in Crete. Evans, typically, began his foreword, 'In fulfilment of my own desires, Mr Pendlebury has excellently carried out the plan of a summary guide to the House Of Minos and its immediate surroundings'.[1] He then went on to write about the restorations without further reference to John. Shortly afterwards, another publisher, Methuen, approached John to write a book on the archaeology of Crete. Methuen was to publish a series of archaeological guides under the general editorship of Professor Arthur Cook, who had taught John and Hilda at Cambridge. They wanted John, not Evans, to write the one on Crete and it took little persuasion. 'I had already started! It will really be my Index to Sites made historical instead of topographical. I ought to be able to get quite a lot of new facts and some I hope unacceptable ones.'[2]

John had been planning several exploratory trips over the island during the season. This added new purpose and at Easter, John and Hilda set off for Mt. Ida, walking west from Knossos to Agios Myron, 'the ancient Rhaukos, of which nothing remains – and Krousonas the brigand village, one of the "Gates of Ida", where we were very hospitably entertained.' Here John met some of the old brigands, the *kapetanoi*, who had fought against the Turks. It had been one of the centres of Cretan resistance and would remain so. John would later draw on their experience when he recruited Satanas, one of the *kapetans* from this village. It would be in trying to reach his own brigand recruits at Krousonas that John would be captured. On that spring trip, however, all talk of bandits and brigands seemed to be mere nostalgia, and their minds were far from war. 'The next day we did what I hoped was going to be a monastery "pub crawl" north-

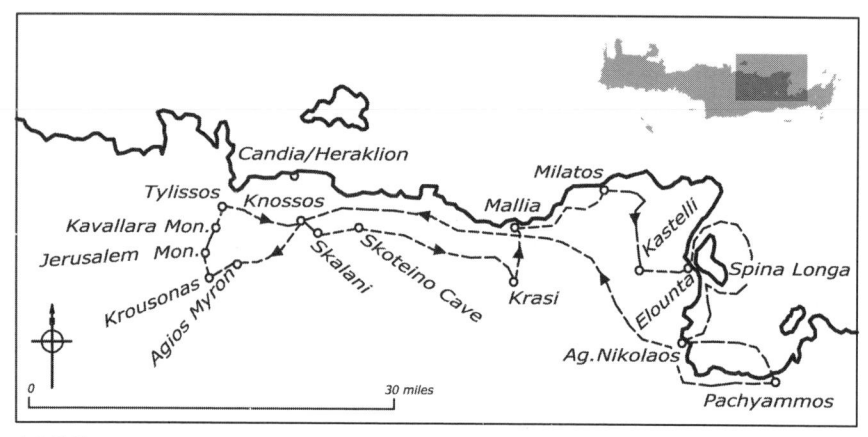

1933 ROUTE

wards via the Jerusalem and Kavallara monasteries to Tylissos. Unfortunately all the monasteries are deserted and ruined.'[3]

Mary Chubb and Rosaleen Angas arrived in Crete soon afterwards to join John and Hilda on a walk east of Heraklion, and were met at the mountain village of Krasi by Seton Lloyd and his wife Joan. They were led by the muleteer Kronis Bardakis, with his trusty mule Arabella, who had accompanied them on so many walks. Kronis, known affectionately as the Old Krone, was to become, like Manolaki, one of John's right-hand men in more troubled times. They travelled thence towards the magnificent cave of Skoteino which, like most caves in Crete, had been an important Minoan shrine, and there they spent the night on a threshing floor. The angular Lloyd still had to get used to sleeping on the hard gravel – 'all right', he remembered wrily, 'if one has dug a small hole for one's hip bone'.[4]

After a night on the beach near the palace at Mallia, they walked up from the coast, past the site of Milatos, mentioned in *The Odyssey*, where John was delighted to find that there was a rich site. Climbing up over the northern foothills of the Diktaean range that separated the Gulf of Mallia from the Mirabello Gulf, they passed lines of windmills on the ridges or saddles between crests, and descended to the small fishing village of Elounta and the Imperial Airways base at Spina Longa. From the hills above, the Venetian fortress, on its own small island north of the Spina Longa peninsula, was like a jewel on a bright blue enamel background. Captain Pool entertained his guests with his usual style. 'For all of us', Lloyd recalled, 'it was like a miracle to be given hot showers and cocktails before a very good dinner. For the Captain too, it must have been a change to have three pretty girls for the night, and a good deal of alcohol was drunk. He admitted that there were many times when he wondered if the boat were not by now "aground on empty bottles"!'[5] The following morning, a little the worse for wear, John and his friends left Elounta and walked on to Pachyammos to recover on the sheltered terraces of Seager's house.

The trip had been both successful and enjoyable for John, but it was clear to their travelling companions that Hilda had not been happy. She was finding it increasingly hard to keep up with John on these walks. Even with a nanny taking some of the strain of caring for the baby, Hilda was trying to cope with returning to work and found the walks had become tests of endurance. Increasingly she lagged behind, often in tears. John, who was usually far ahead, did not appear to notice. Mary remembered him hectoring her over something as pointless as forgetting to pack the butter, failing to see how this added to her misery.[6] Lloyd's enduring memory of John on that walk was of him 'striding across the Cretan landscape with an occasional glance at his stop-watch, and of his poor wife's brave attempts to keep up with him'.[7]

John and Hilda spent the rest of the season in a combination of work on the dating of the Knossos pottery and walks with various visitors, though Hilda often stayed at home to look after David. By the time they returned to London, John could look back over a season full of discoveries of ancient routes and sites. Hilda, though, was finding her limits.

They arrived back in London in early July 1933, in time for the EES exhibition. It was a huge success, with visits from such luminaries as the sculptor Jacob Epstein. Hilda had gone straight to Caldy to leave David with her family before rejoining John in Cambridge. The establishment was beginning to take an interest in John, and not only was he asked to join the committee of the EES ('About time an excavator gets onto it'[8]), but Alan Wace put his name forward to the Society of Antiquaries.[9]

John's departure from Crete did not mean that the problems of the job were left behind. The limited time that he could spend at Knossos was beginning to cause difficulties, and whilst he had suggested that Manolaki take over the administration of the estate, John felt that he still needed overseeing. It is unlikely that John was unaware that this suggestion threw into question his own position, and it is probable that it was an intentional move. Though John was far more effective administratively than Mackenzie had been, there was little doubt that the Curator was needed on the spot for a greater part of the year. The job had not proved to be as attractive as John had hoped, and the advantages of being there when Evans was not were tempered by the total lack of excavation in his absence. This was not the career in Minoan archaeology that he had envisaged. Although John's explorations and his research into ancient routes and topography offset the disadvantages of the Curatorship, he felt that it was only a matter of time before these, too, would be frowned upon in favour of estate administration. The committee was soon to reach the same conclusion.

In the meantime, John was content to finish the laborious dating of the Knossos finds, and, thanks to Hans Frankfort, he managed to acquire a new recruit, a young woman called Mercy Money-Coutts, who had originally approached him to work at Amarna. Mercy was a tall, slim woman with a good brain, a keen determination to learn and shining blue eyes. Though she appears rather gawky in photographs, she had a smile that lit up her face, and an attraction not captured by the camera. The villagers of Tzermiado, who call her η Μονιχουτση (*i Monihoutsi*), still remember her swiftness of foot over the mountains, and she was the only one of John's walking companions to keep pace with and even overtake him. 'She seriously wants to take up archaeology – field archaeology', John wrote to his father. 'I've advised her to apply to be admitted to the School for the coming session. Hans thinks she should be encouraged.'[10]

*

Each return to England involved the hunt for a house to rent the following summer, as it was not worth their while maintaining a home all year round. Hilda was pregnant again and John was relieved when he found one that suited them in Cambridge. 'We saw over a splendid house today which would suit us next year down to the ground. It's in Herschel Road. They will want six guineas a week and we should have to supply some of the linen and plate. It would probably need three maids. It's got absolutely everything we want, and finance permitting seems just the house for us next July to September.'[11]

Leaving Hilda and David again, John travelled by the Orient Line to Egypt in the second week of November 1933. The funding for the Amarna excavation had appeared promising for once; but then one of the subscribing museums withdrew its offer. When the Copenhagen Museum had offered around three hundred pounds, it was on the understanding that this would put them at the top of the list in the acquisition of any finds. Then a minor typing error suggested that Brooklyn had outbid them, and Copenhagen pulled out completely.

John was fed up with the lack of any concerted fundraising effort by the EES. 'Can't the committee for once do something – make a real appeal. After all this is the best year we've ever had. People generally are interested in Amarna and a series of letters to *The Times* and *Telegraph* etc. from eminent folk (as was done before the first year at Armant) would work wonders. If the EES stops digging, it had better leave out the second E!'[12]

When the team arrived at Amarna, the North Dig House had undergone a massive facelift since the previous season, under the supervision of Stephen Sherman. Now, instead of the individual metal *tishts*, they could have proper baths, the water from which drained onto a garden of tomatoes, cucumbers and rose trees donated by the Mamur of Mallawi. John had also had a brand new studio built for his photographer, Philip Chubb. However, the triumph was undoubtedly the new lavatory block which, in keeping with the local flair for eccentric building design, looked more like a sheikh's tomb.

The only thing the photographic studio lacked was its photographer. No sooner had they arrived in Cairo than Philip Chubb was recalled to England immediately by the EES and relieved of his obligations to the Amarna dig. Apparently a cheque had been drawn in Chubb's favour and subsequently stopped. Hugh Last wrote to John trying to explain their actions. 'After this affair, in which entanglement with the police has only just been avoided, it is obvious that we must not delay in hearing Chubb's side of the case.'[13] Although the exact nature of the misdemeanour remains a mystery, it was serious enough for the committee of the EES to demand that no further money be given to him and that John buy his ticket for him, in case Chubb should vanish with the money. The situation could not have been worse for John, who felt bitterly let down. He vented his anger and disappointment to Mary Jonas. 'I know you could not have told me anything off your own bat and loyalty to a member of my staff, recommended to me by a family for whom hitherto I have had a certain friendship, prevented me from taking notice of hints. But quite frankly I do feel that it is a bit hard when the rogue of the family is passed off on one with no warning as a presumably estimable character while that family sits back holding its breath till the person in question does one in the eye! That's three people now I've taken on other people's recommendation. Bennett on Glanville's, Phillips on Myers' and Philip on his family's. I now shall stick to my own people!'[14]

John turned his concentration back to the excavation. Having cleared the vast enclosure of the Great Aten Temple the previous year, he now began the clearance of the sanctuary, the heart of the temple. There were good representations of it in Amarna tomb paintings, in spite of the destruction that had followed Akhenaten's reign, and John was developing an idea in his head of what Akhetaten might once have looked like. He did his best to bring it to life in his writing, determined to communicate what he felt about the site to visitors who might be put off by the flat, almost featureless plain in the harsh light of a midday visit. Few casual visitors stayed until sunset, when the buried remains sprang into sharp relief, framed by the glowing, crimson cliffs around. The team members saw it every evening and never ceased to be awestruck by its beauty. It made the sacred nature of the site, so tied to the movement of the sun, easier to comprehend.

'Now we will proceed as if we were of the Royal Party entering the

3c TELL EL AMARNA: CENTRAL & SOUTH CITY

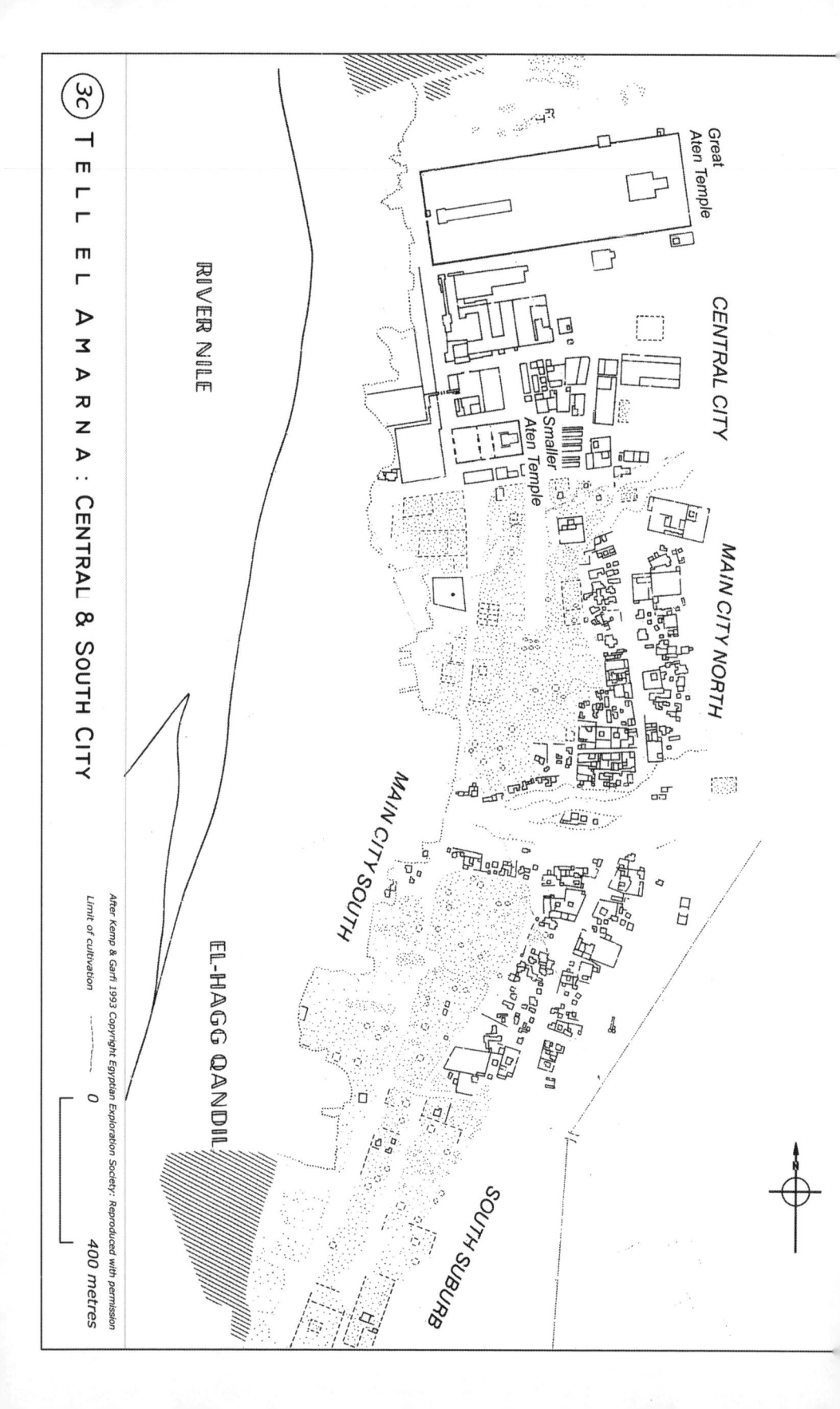

Great Aten Temple

Smaller Aten Temple

CENTRAL CITY

MAIN CITY NORTH

MAIN CITY SOUTH

EL-HAGG QANDIL

SOUTH SUBURB

RIVER NILE

After Kemp & Garfi 1993 Copyright Egyptian Exploration Society; Reproduced with permission

Limit of cultivation

0 — 400 metres

Temple to worship. The party has dismounted from the chariots, to which the grooms are attending. They enter between the tall pylon towers. On their left is a columned pavilion, its massive concrete foundations sunk to a depth of over three feet, since all this approach is "made earth". They pass on to the entrance to Per-hai, the House of Rejoicing. Here again are tall pylon towers of mud-brick faced with stone and fronted each by five tall flagstaffs with fluttering pennons. The doorway has no lintel, for that would block the passage of the sun. Per-hai consists of two colonnades flanking the central passage, which is open to the sky. There are two rows of four columns on each side whose position has been determined by the marks left on the vast platforms of concrete on which they are set. Each colonnade has an altar of fine limestone at the East end, carved with the usual representation of the King and Queen making offerings. Behind the altars a short flight of steps descends into chambers in the thickness of the pylon towers which flank the entrance into the next division of the Temple, Gem-Aten – the Finding of the Aten. Here we enter something quite new in the way of temple architecture.'[15]

As with the smaller Aten Temple, the progression was always into sunlight, the reverse of earlier Egyptian tradition, which led from sunlight into increasing darkness. The sanctuary at Amarna was, as John put it, a true sanctuary of the sun with airy courts open to the sky. The pathway through the last courtyard would have been flanked by rows of offering tables, leading towards the main altar. 'Here are heaped the fruits of the earth and the meat of many cattle, for the Aten, like Pharaoh, seems a good trencherman!'[16]

As the discoveries continued to rise, so did the number of visitors. The peculiar charm of the North Dig House and John's lively and eccentric hospitality – he still presided over dinner wearing his Cretan cloak – were as much of a draw as the enthusiasm he brought to conveying the atmosphere of the extraordinary site. Representatives of the subscribing museums came and stayed, as did David Iliffe, head of the Jerusalem Museum. Many were welcome as friends, but some were entertained for reasons of expediency. 'We are threatened with Capart and three of his harem for twelve days', John moaned to Herbert. 'Rot him.'[17] The Belgian Jean Capart was Professor of Egyptology at Liège as well as Director of the Belgian Musées Royaux du Cinquantaire, but he appeared to wield influence far outside his own country. He was a passionate advocate of the Amarna excavations, though it was not always clear for whose benefit. His presence meant hard work in persuading him to convince the Brooklyn Museum, with whom he had great influence, to give more money to the excavation.

The workmen were now divided between several different areas of the site, some working on the temple and palace and related buildings, others re-excavating the houses dug by Petrie in 1892, including the Records Office, from where the famous Amarna Letters had come. Here they found bricks stamped 'The Place of the Correspondence of Pharaoh' and, in time to impress Capart, came the discovery of more fragments of the baked clay cuneiform letters – 'mostly', John noted, 'in the part which Petrie claims to have exhausted completely!'[18] It was the tablets that really fired John's imagination, particularly in the absence of any papyri at Amarna. He arranged to have a cuneiform expert from the museum in Jerusalem look over the letters before the end of the season. 'I hope they turn out to be something nice – the fall of Knossos or something.'[19] Then, a week later, news of a linguistic breakthrough gave him hope of something similar from Crete itself. 'I see in *The Manchester Guardian* someone has read Etruscan – now for the Minoan scholars!'[20]

Capart was greatly impressed with his visit and 'has promised to get Brooklyn to see the job through to the bitter end'.[21] Capart himself later wrote of his visit. 'I had the privilege of spending a fortnight at el-Amarna in the spring of 1934 and I must describe briefly the atmosphere of happy activity and conscientious work which prevailed on site and in the thousands-of-years-old house restored to house the diggers. These people, up with sun, did not return until the sun set quickly on the horizon. Then it was time for the attentive examination of the finds and a discussion about the architectural plans. Pendlebury, in his Cretan shepherd's cloak, which he donned after shedding the stubborn dust of the dig, was truly a leader of an expedition, conscious of his responsibilities to the demands of the science.

'Nor can I forget the diligent pains of the courageous Mrs Pendlebury who gave up numerous hours of her day to attend to the essentials of everyday team life, at the same time working on the finds inventory and drawing potsherds and small bits of enamel: rings and amulets of a rich variety on this site.'[22]

Theft was always a problem on such a large site, and often the guards, or *ghaffirs*, were involved. When some pots were stolen one night, John had a huge row with one such guard, Abd el Megelli. Three days later, John noted in the dig diary: 'pots stolen restored in night – not all the same ones. Abd el Megelli says that the Almighty is wise to him – so am I.'[23] But this was nothing compared to what they found at the Royal Tomb when Sherman took Capart up to the scene of the previous season's work. The tomb had been comprehensively smashed up in the intervening time and a large number of reliefs hacked out to be sold on the illicit antiquities market. Even though the EES had not been responsible for guarding the tomb, it was depressing for the team who had worked so hard on recording it. John wrote of the vandalism to Herbert, adding that following the thefts the tomb had 'been filled in by the inspector presumably to cover up knowledge of the true extent of the damage!'[24]

By the end of January, John's exhausted and understaffed team had fallen victim to a host of illnesses – Brasch with jaundice, Sherman with malaria and Lavers with flu. Given the loss of Philip Chubb and the need for Hilda to take things more easily, John was under an enormous amount of pressure to keep the dig running smoothly, particularly in an area of the Central City so full of promise. 'We seem to have got the Army or the Police GHQ. There are long rows of dormitories, stables with special mangers outside for the stabling of the "flying squad" and a nice house for the CO, a gentleman who was so fond of his wine that he actually surrounded the name of the vintage on his jar stoppers with a royal cartouche!'[25]

The dig was wound up at the end of the first week of February. Usually important areas excavated were backfilled immediately, but John and Sherman between them had managed to arrange for the Royal Egyptian Airforce to take aerial photographs of the site first. It was an inspired idea and, in the resulting images, the entire plan of the city stands out in vivid contrast to the surrounding plain.

Meanwhile, Hilda returned to England alone in time for David's second birthday, while John stayed on in Cairo for what turned out to be a disappointing division. John thought the Director, Pierre Lacau, had picked out all the prettiest objects for Cairo like a magpie, leaving the less glamorous objects for the contributing museums. It soon became clear that this may have been due to Capart's stirring during his recent visit to Egypt. Capart acted as a sort of broker for the Brooklyn Museum, from whom the Amarna excavation got most of its money, and it is likely that he was trying to influence what the Cairo Museum kept and what it left to go to the EES. Not surprisingly this had annoyed Lacau and his colleagues.

Thankfully, Capart seemed satisfied with the finds that the EES could keep and suggested that, as a token of the financial help that Brooklyn had given the Amarna excavation over the years, the expedition should become known as a joint EES and Brooklyn project. 'He absolutely agrees that the Society must keep complete control and that the "joint" idea is in name only. But he is equally convinced that we ought to write at once suggesting it as he wants to shove in his recommendations soon but after we have made this step.'[26]

What none of them suspected was that various members of the EES committee were already planning to shut down the work at Tell el-Amarna in favour of a new site in Nubia.

13

March 1934–April 1935

JOHN RETURNED TO Crete in early March 1934, desperate to get up into the mountains again and begin the exploratory work that would underpin his next book. He thought he would have more time to travel as Evans, now in his mid-eighties, had stayed in England to write the fourth and final volume of *The Palace of Minos*. 'I only hope he does finish it', he wrote to his father, 'and that I'm not left with it, expected by the learned world to finish it off.'[1] But an initial trickle of visitors to the palace turned into a torrent. John found himself tied to Knossos, showing round the endless mass of people – including a 'perfect spate of German tourists who have been flooding the palace like the Gadarene swine. They are an unattractive race.'[2]

Despairing of getting away from Knossos, John ploughed on with the dating of the palace pottery, assisted by two eager British School students: Mercy Money-Coutts and Edith Eccles. The cataloguing and dating of thirty years' worth of pottery excavated at Knossos would be a huge achievement, useful to those working not just at the site itself, but all over the island and wherever Minoan pottery was found around the Mediterranean. The sequence at Knossos, though representative of an important but limited locality, provided a basis for dating which had not been sure before. 'When I publish these I shall have given justification (or not!) for Evans' dating of each bit [of the palace] and shown people where to look for sherds of any particular date they want to study.'[3]

It was April before John managed to escape the monotony of Knossos. Evans had asked him to revisit a tomb at Kalergi in the Pediada district, just to the west of the Dikte range. Accompanying him were Mercy Money-Coutts and the foreman of Knossos, Manolaki.[4] This was followed by a week-long exploration of central Crete, following an ancient route south from Knossos, passing along the east side of Mt. Iuktas, and into the Messara Plain from the east. This time they were joined by Edith Eccles and, for part of the way, by Ralph Lavers, who was in Crete to work on some plans for John.

However, John soon began to feel exhausted by the students' earnest enthusiasm. Even the library proved no sanctuary. 'Here with two voracious students it is difficult to browse at the books one wants.' For the first time in Crete, John found himself in the position of teacher. 'I think I shall send them off on a trip of their own. They are both too nervous of talking Greek in front of me. I know that feeling very well and a trip by themselves would give them much more confidence.'[5] So they took off round the Peloponnese looking for, and finding, new sites themselves and learning to speak Greek. When they returned, John sent them off to explore for sites in the Malevizi region around Knossos. Now it was their turn to search for rumoured remains of ancient walls and interrogate villagers about finds turning up in the vineyards and olive groves. John then offered to let them write up their findings along with his own in a joint article in the *British School Annual*.[6]

Free of his charges, John was just about to set off on a trip to the east of the island, when Seton and Joan Lloyd turned up out of the blue, accompanied by the writer Captain GR (Dick) Wyndham and the artist Tristram Hillier. Once they were safely ensconced in Seager's house at Pachyammos, John invited them to join him on his trip east, stressing that it would not be for the fainthearted. Evans had lent John his diaries from the 1890s and John had set himself the task of revisiting the sites that Evans had found but, not having dug yet in Crete, could then only provisionally date. John was now in a better position to date them than anyone.

It was a tiring journey, taking eleven days, which began with the sheer climb to the remote cliff site of Kavousi. 'An hour of steep climbing', John wrote of the trip, 'through some of the wildest country in Crete brings one suddenly to the beautiful fertile valley of Avgo... On leaving the valley, the country became very wild as far as the village of Roukkaka. Here to the South of the village is a small Roman site. Captain Wyndham discovered this by sitting down heavily on the sharp point of a sherd.'[7] Skirting round Mount Thriphte, they came to Peukous, where they spent the night in preparation for the next morning's two thousand foot climb to a cave known as Latsida. 'Although no antiquities were reported as coming from here it was evidently worth visiting, the more so since there is a certain amount of evidence to show that the Dictaean cave is not that at Psychro but should rather be looked for in these mountains. This cave must be one of the most extensive in Crete, rivalling that at Skoteino. The entrance is a practically sheer drop of some 20 feet and two galleries open off it. These widen out into great halls of stalactites, which stretch an unknown distance into the mountain.'[8]

Their route then took them through the district of Praisos to Sitia on the north coast. Here John hired a boat to take them round Cape Sidero, the northeast tip of Crete, via the Dionysiades Islands to the north and Elasa Island to the east. 'Unfortunately the boatman was a rogue', John complained to his father. 'The motor broke, he couldn't mend it, didn't want to sail, couldn't row and it eventually came down to using horrible language and threats of violence to make them row us into a bay by the lighthouse on Cape Sidero.' After five

SPRING 1934 ROUTE

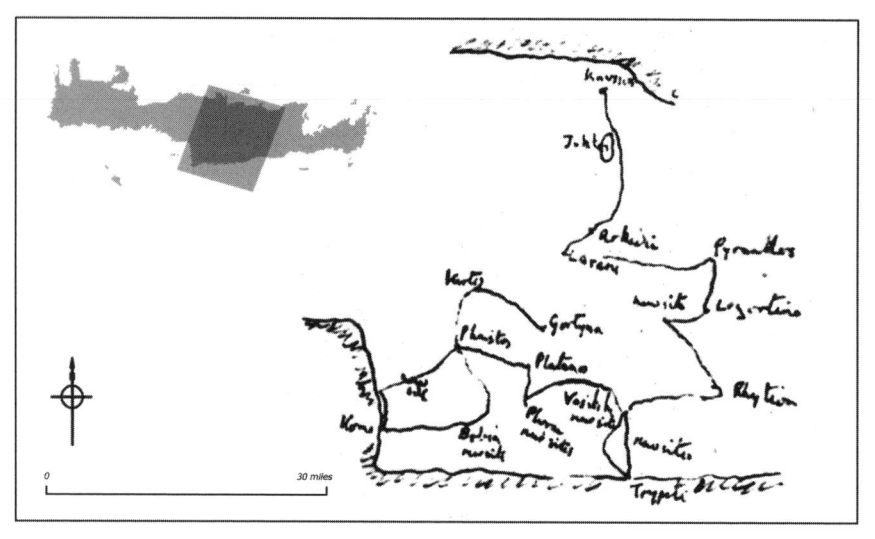

hours of argument, they finally landed, only it was some considerable distance from where they had arranged for the muleteer to meet them with their baggage. So they had to borrow a mule from the lighthouse men to carry 'Joan Lloyd and the lunch' to the monastery of Toplou where they were to spend the night. John meanwhile tore off towards Eremopolis to find the muleteer. '10 miles in one and a half hours over really rough country isn't bad going! I got to Eremopolis in time to look over the ruins and to go on, still ahead, to Toplou Monastery to prepare for them.'[9] The abbot looked after the exhausted band with 'true monastery hospitality and a chicken to take on with us.'[10]

After visiting Palaikastro and Zakros on the east coast, they followed a good coastal track to the plain of Xerokampos, thought to be the site of the classical city of Ampelos mentioned in Pliny. 'The whole of the plain as far as the village is littered with cut stones, some re-used in modern walls.' At the north end of the plain they came across a small fort or Minoan guardhouse similar to many such that they had encountered along their journey. After doubling back to Zakros, they headed this time up the gorge and onto the plateau. 'The country inland from Zakros and Ampelos is wild in the extreme, until the fertile plain of Zyros is reached.'[11] The plain had appealed in ancient times too, as it was littered with remains of buildings and a road system. They only had time to look over another fort with Minoan walling before heading down to the south coast at Makrygialo. Now a tiny fishing village, there had been a sizable Roman settlement on a promontory to the west of Makrygialo, but much of this was masked by the now burgeoning corn of a Cretan spring. John and his companions kept to the south coast as far as Ierapetra and then turned northwards, up the isthmus, full circle to Pachyammos and the comfort of Seager's house. Here John left the Lloyds and Dick Wyndham with their friend Tristram Hillier, who had sprained his ankle just in time to avoid what he had justifiably considered likely to be too tortuous a journey.

John returned to Knossos alone on foot to find a letter from the British School committee. The letter informed John that the School had changed the rules applying to the Curatorship. Whether he was in residence or not, John was to be responsible and potentially available to supervise any work or deal with any emergencies. Cutting to the chase, they declared 'therefore he is not expected to undertake direct responsibility for independent archaeological work out of reach of Knossos'.[12] The meaning was plain; the Committee was making him choose between Knossos and Amarna.

John wrote to the chairman of the BSA, Sir John Myres, for advice, but he already knew what the outcome would be. 'I have said', he explained to his father, 'that I quite realise that now the School has taken over the cultivation of the vineyard itself that a business man ought always to be in residence or at any rate on tap in Athens. That the two most important things – the first digging and the collecting of the crop – are well outside my three months (or Mackenzie's six for the matter of that). That I felt I should not be justified in giving up my work in the Near East outside Crete to tie myself to administrative work. I said that I wanted to help the school as much as I could and did he think it would be easier for them if I resigned at once or finished my term of office next year and meanwhile coached my successor.'[13]

Though John felt that the School might have shown him the courtesy of discussing the matter with him in person before forming a sub-committee to decide, he thought that it was as well to leave on these grounds as any. 'Sooner or later', he wrote to his father, 'I should have had to leave and this gives us a chance of leaving gracefully for a particular reason. I have now got Knossos into order and my only regret is that we shall be leaving the Taverna so soon after we have made it look so nice.'[14] It was indeed his only regret. The job had not proved to be what he wanted and he would now be free to devote all his time in Crete to exploring sites, ancient routes and landscapes. More importantly, he was free to start looking for a place that he himself could dig, unencumbered by Evans. The publisher, Methuen, was in no particular hurry for *The Archaeology of Crete*, preferring that it be as complete as possible, and told John to take as long as he liked.

Myres and the School did not respond immediately, and John, who was soon to leave for England for the birth of his second child, had to assume that he would not be coming back as Curator. He was determined that everything be left in good order for his successor, whoever that may be. 'I am pointing out in my report at the end of the season for their guidance (whether they ever see it is another matter) that things are happening agriculturally here from October to August and that there is no closed season for antiquities to be found. If they hope to get someone who, while nominally here for three months and paid for that period, will either stay here for ten months (and go barmy) or be permanently on tap in Athens, they will be pretty lucky. Actually I think they are trying to crack the whip – they don't realise a. that I have cracked too many whips myself to be impressed, b. that it may serve with a lazy horse but with a lively one that's doing its job they will be thrown!'[15] Ironically, the estate had turned over a larger profit that year than it had done in years, even though John had spent a great deal of money on securing its grounds.

The School finally decided to make the changeover of Curator with immediate effect. They chose R.W. Hutchinson, 'The Squire', a lanky man with a very colonial taste in clothes, which mainly consisted of white trousers and navy blazer or a white suit. John had worked with him on his first excavation years before in Macedonia.

John arrived back in London just in time to be with Hilda for the birth – again by caesarean – of their daughter, Joan. Herbert made sure that he too was in town, ostensibly in case John did not get back in time, but probably because he did not want a repeat of the events surrounding David's birth. David was brought in soon afterwards to meet the new baby, but 'seemed very disappointed at finding only one sister. He searched all over the room for more!'[16] In June, John, Hilda, David and Joan travelled down to Great Malvern to take up residence at Winstanley. Herbert Pendlebury had, like so many others at the time, been suffering financially and had decided to let Winstanley while he and Dickie lived somewhere smaller. John and Hilda, keen to do anything to prevent Herbert and Dickie from having to sell up, had decided to rent the house in Malvern rather than one in Cambridge. 'The mountains of luggage (about 30 pieces) arrived safely! The house looks very nice and Dicky has done the place proud with flowers.'[17]

The family spent a happy and leisurely summer at Winstanley. For David it was to be an opportunity, increasingly rare, to spend time with both his parents together. John's life and work being as it was, David and Joan would grow up far more in the company of their grandparents than their father. To a lesser extent the same was true of their contact with Hilda.

When the summer was over, the young Pendlebury family moved back to London for the annual EES exhibition and lecture tour. It was here that John first began to hear rumours that the EES were thinking of giving up the Amarna concession. Among those rumoured to be keen to finish the dig were Capart, who had been John's guest at Amarna, and Percy Newberry, with whom John had spent the weekend earlier in the summer. John and Newberry had talked then about 'schemes for an institute in Cairo on the lines of the BSA, amalgamating the EES and the BS [British School] in Egypt.[18] Nothing, however, can be done till old Petrie and Miss Murray are out of the way I'm afraid and at the moment it's all very secret.'[19] Newberry had said nothing, however, about wanting to close down the Amarna dig. John decided to challenge Hugh Last, the honorary secretary of the EES, with the rumours, but Last thought the whole thing 'fantastic' nonsense. 'So that little conspiracy has been squashed', John wrote to his father with unfounded confidence.[20] Though John did not know it, it was his friend Stephen Glanville who was most keen to bring to an end to the Amarna project. Years later, Glanville told his sister-in-law, Mary Chubb, that it was because of Hilda's unpopularity on site, but it is unlikely that this was the entire reason.[21]

Oblivious to the seriousness of the threat to the Amarna dig, John began cheerfully to look ahead. Hilda had decided to accompany him first to Amarna and afterwards to Crete, leaving the children with Herbert and Dickie. It must have been a difficult decision for Hilda, particularly as Joan was barely six months old, but to be with John and to be intellectually active were in the end more important to her at that stage. She would be away for seven months and John for eight, as John wanted to take Hilda to visit Syria or Palestine or Frankfort's team in Iraq, with perhaps a stopover in Cyprus on the way back to Crete. 'It will make us much happier', John wrote to his father, 'to know we're leaving the brats in good hands.'[22] In the autumn of 1934, John and Hilda set sail on the Orient *SS Oronsay* for Alexandria.

Their arrival in Cairo was very different from their first visit six years earlier. Now John and his work were known they found themselves bombarded with invitations, but they escaped as soon as they could to the relative tranquillity of Amarna.

John wanted to concentrate on digging in the official part of the palace, on the opposite side of the Royal Road from the King's residence which they had excavated two years earlier. It was at the heart of the city and arguably one its most important buildings. Petrie had done limited excavations, but as soon as they began to re-excavate, it was clear that they could not totally rely on his records. 'If my idea is correct – we shan't know till we have a complete stamped brick – only fragments have hitherto turned up – the great pillared hall (certainly an extension to the south) was the coronation hall of Smenkhara. Here we found a quantity of complete faience tiles – the first found hitherto – very William Morris!'[23]

Then the Antiquities Service offered John the opportunity to return to the Royal Tomb and clean it out completely, to remove any temptation to thieves. In addition they invited him to re-record the reliefs on the walls of the tomb – 'an unprecedented honour for any private Society I am told.'[24] The walls had been drawn before but not to a high enough standard, yet John was not sure that the committee would allow the work. 'As the tomb is about to be closed finally when we've finished', John wrote, trying to convince Hugh Last, 'Lacau has offered me the right of copying the wall carvings (again a bit of a privilege) and even hoped to be able to give a bit towards the publication of them. It will have to be a very quickly done job I fear. Lavers is perfectly competent and we have three others (my wife and the two Shermans) who can do a bit of tracing to help him. Whether the whole can be done or not depends on a lot of things but at least the inadequate existing publication can be completed and corrected – Fairman and I can do the checking. It seems to me that this would be a bit of a feather in the Society's cap (it has been refused before). Could you put it to the committee or to the executive members of it? If there was another first class draughtsman as well as Lavers it would lighten things – I don't like to ask Miss Calverley and we can't afford to pay anybody specially for it.'[25]

Hilda had been working up at the house on the *ostraca* and finds, where she now did much of the philological work with Fairman. She visited the dig daily, but was still taking things quietly. John admitted to his father that, although they were both fit and happy, they were badly missing the 'brats', as John invariably but affectionately referred to them. Amarna was not a safe place for children, and it is not surprising that John and Hilda, while happy to take David to Crete, never considered taking him to Amarna. 'A boy was bitten in the jaw by a scorpion today, which had been nesting in his clothes', John wrote, describing one typical incident. 'When he came up, no one knew what was the matter with him and I thought he had put his jaw out and in again very quickly by laughing too much. However, the scorpion stung him again and revealed itself. Luckily it was a very small one and the boy had an immediate injection, so he is none the worse.'[26]

Christmas at Amarna was as lively as ever, with a grand fantasia in the afternoon, 'in the course of which a casual gentleman turned up and did some quarterstaff with our champion. He too was a champion and had a really beautiful wicked face like a fallen angel. On being asked where he came from he said 'from Gehenna' (ie Hell!) Though it was later discovered that this was the name of a village near Sohag, it cast a gloom over the proceedings particularly as some are now ready to swear that he walked straight up a vertical wall casting no shadow – also no photograph taken of the contest came out.'[27]

'I'm glad to hear of the infants' Christmas', John wrote to Herbert. 'All sorts of good wishes were sent from here including hopes for a long life for David and a good marriage for Joan. Also a special fusillade of shotguns in their honour. The number of times their name has been used to conjure an extra piastre a day is astonishing.'[28]

Work resumed after the holiday in an area close to the cultivation and consequently very deeply buried, in some places by as much as 12 feet. The work was slow and often frustrating, as Petrie's records time and again proved to be unreliable. When Mary Jonas forwarded a letter from Petrie in Jerusalem, complaining of some 'omissions' in the *City of Akhenaten* II, John was furious and wrote back to her with typical irreverence: 'Tell Petrie to go and bury himself. a) Anyone but a pink-eyed moron with flat feet would be able to fit the detail plans into the general survey. He's barmy. b) The absence of a scale on each detail plan is a justifiable criticism and shall receive attention. The scale is, however, mentioned in the list of plates. c) There is an index as large as life and twice as good as any he's ever produced. Could you write and ask him if he's found any omissions – I'm always glad to hear of those but to say there's no index is ullage. d) Let him wait till he sees what I've got to say about his plan of the palace.'[29]

The slowness of the work on the palace began to put John under increasing pressure. He was in danger of running out of time and money, particularly with the work to do at the Royal Tomb, which would deprive him of at least three members of staff for more than a fortnight. In addition, it was always at the back of his mind that there might not be another season, that he might not get to the essence of one of the most significant buildings ever to be excavated in Egypt, let alone at Amarna. This threat drove him ever harder, and he was regularly on site for twelve hours a day, and expected a similar dedication from his team. This stress and his consequent tiredness began to show in his attitude towards both staff and workmen.

One day, he decided that he should take on more workmen and children, but when some of the prospective workers ran across the site, stepping on some paint on the way, John lost his temper. The result was that he only heaped more work upon himself, as he described to his father. 'The enquiry as to who did it took a long time and resulted in my refusing to take on anyone from a particular village. Then I spent the rest of the day heaving about heavy stones onto camels to transport to the house so that the disappointed village shouldn't have a chance of damaging them. By the time I got back and did some photography

I was ready for bed. Yesterday was my early morning and meant from 5.30 to 5.0 on my feet.'[30]

John desperately wanted to do Amarna justice before having to leave, should it come to that. There was clearly envy amongst Egyptologists that such a rich and important site was being excavated by a man who himself professed to be a field archaeologist and not an Egyptologist. As far as John was concerned, he was an 'authority on the relations between Egypt and the Aegean', 'quite an authority on scarabs', 'a good excavator' and 'no more of an Egyptologist than that if one excepts a smattering of hieroglyphs'.[31] But envy there was, and it is probable that this was behind the moves to close down the dig at Amarna. It was also seen in the relationship between John and Fairman; when John overruled Fairman on several occasions, Fairman did not like it.

One of the areas over which they came into conflict was the Harem quarter of the palace, where Petrie had discovered a beautiful painted pavement, showing birds in the marshes. Petrie had constructed a shelter to protect the pavement, and visitors had swarmed to the site to see it. Unfortunately, they had trampled the crop of a local farmer, who, in 1912, hacked the pavement to pieces. What remained was taken to the Cairo Museum, where it is to this day. John reasoned that Petrie would have recorded the now empty room with greater care and attention than elsewhere and it could, therefore, be used to dump spoil. Fairman and Lavers disagreed, but John over-ruled them.

With rumours of dissension in the camp, Stephen Glanville, now Honorary Secretary of the Society, took the opportunity while in Egypt to visit Amarna and talk to the staff. John and Fairman would later each write down for the record their side of the story when they returned to London. The tension did ease, but nonetheless, the opportunity of sending half the team to work at the Royal Tomb was probably something of a godsend. After successfully getting permission, Fairman, Lavers and Sherman went to camp up in the Royal Wadi and began copying the surviving reliefs.

This left John very short-handed back at the Central City, and, with a spate of misfortunes, the pressure grew: John fell into a pit, putting out a couple of ribs; Hilda came down with a violent temperature; and Charles Brasch fell down a dump and sprained his ankle. 'The curse of Tutankhamen!' John quipped.[32]

John was forced to rest while his ribs mended, but it gave him the chance to catch up with work before they began investigating another tomb in the hills. John had heard of the tomb from a man who had apparently found some steps leading down into the high desert. He was terrified of telling anyone and had somehow been scared off carrying out an illicit dig. He had agreed, however, to show it to John, who was greatly excited by the possibilities. 'It would be fun if we did find the untouched tomb of Akhie. It certainly hasn't been touched for thousands of years.'[33] Lacau came and visited the tomb with John and gave his permission to dig there after the rest of the work was done.

This necessitated an urgent fundraising effort, and Mary Jonas' letters were full of ideas. Mary was ruthless when it came to extracting funds for Amarna because, as John once wrote, one needed 'the tongue of angels to coax money' for excavations. On hearing of the death of the husband of their loyal and devoted supporter, Mrs Hubbard, Miss Jonas couldn't help commenting that perhaps now she would have even more money to spare on Amarna. Or: 'A Mrs Cambridge (wife of a retired doctor) came in the other day to ask how to get to El Amarna. She said she had spoken to Mrs Pendlebury when she was at the Exhibition... She looked expensively dressed, but one never knows!! Anyway her fur coat looked worth an SD [substantial donation] to the Society.'[34] Eventually, Brooklyn gave a supplement of two thousand dollars, but unfortunately it was too late to use it for the current season.

Mary Jonas had a soft spot for the Amarna team, and clearly enjoyed corresponding with John. He often threw in silly stories or bawdy limericks at the end of his letters, which occasionally put Mary in an awkward position. 'It's all very well for you to tell me your letters to me are for the edification of the Committee and then to add such a ribald rhyme at the end. What about the blushes of the ladies on the Committee if I showed it? Next time put the signature above the scandal!'[35]

The season finished with the discovery, on the last day of the dig, of two granite heads. A great many fragments of monumental sculpture had been recovered over the season, and the chance of finding more the following season (if there was one) tempted John to keep some of the finds back, so that they could work out if there were any joins. Lacau agreed. 'Lacau who stayed here one night was tremendously impressed and promptly confiscated a big piece of land for us to dig under the cultivation.'[36]

The other members of the team went their separate ways after the most difficult season that John had yet had to deal with. Lavers and Fairman left in style by plane, which, much to the excitement of the staff, made a special landing on the Amarna plain to pick them up. John and Hilda, meanwhile, stayed on to make a final investigation of the Royal Wadi. 'If two dreams I've had are anything to go by we are going to find two tombs with a lot in them!'[37] In the end there was no sign of another tomb, but it was a happy time for John and Hilda. 'The weather up in the hills is perfect, though a bit windy at night. It's all right for us with a tent but the men in their rough shelters must get a bit cold. However they're all very cheerful and sang a long song in honour of David's birthday the day before yesterday, hoping that the small Pasha would become a big one one day and that Joan would make a good marriage!'[38]

By the end of the season, John's book, *Tell el-Amarna*, had been published; but when a copy arrived at Amarna it turned out that the printers had managed to mis-spell Amarna on the spine. 'I wired at once to them about the inexcusable error of ARMANA on the cover. They can't let it go out like that. The paper cover too is pretty bad – particularly when I think that Lavers offered to do them a really decent design.'[39]

Reactions to the book were mixed. Mary Jonas had heard from Percy Newberry that he had thought it very good. Engelbach, who had seen the book in proof form, thought the first chapter rather too 'flowery'. 'I suppose', John responded, 'it's the Amarna spirit working in me.' According to John, Capart simply hated the historical side of the book, while Glanville's response was that although it was 'propaganda in the wrong direction he's bound to admit it's good propaganda!' Generally, though, it was very well received. Alan Shorter reviewed it for the *Journal of Egyptian Archaeology*. 'This useful and attractive little book fills the need, long felt, for a popular and inexpensive account of the famous site which has provided so much of our knowledge of the daily life of the ancient Egyptians, and which otherwise can only be studied in the technical memoirs of the Society and of earlier excavators.'[40] He added that the author was to be congratulated on having provided a most readable description of the site, on which John was very well qualified as Director to write, and that it was enlivened with humour and imagination. Aylward M. Blackman, reviewing it in the *Liverpool Annals*, wrote: 'This pleasantly written little book will surely be welcomed by those – and they are by no means very few in number – who are interested in Akhenaten and all he represents. Mr Pendlebury deals here not only with the history of the el-Amarna period and the art, architecture and religion of Akhetaten, but he has also much to tell us about the daily life of the inhabitants of that ephemeral city.' He concluded, 'the two chapters on the public buildings and private houses are excellent and supply the ordinary reader with just the information he desires'. Reviewing *City of Akhenaten II* in the same journal, Blackman wrote that it was a 'valuable contribution to the history of domestic architecture'.[41]

John's skill in making his work accessible to any audience was not, as Alan Wace admitted later, one common amongst archaeologists.[42] When the Italians published the results of their excavations at the Minoan palace of Phaistos in Crete, John was infuriated that it was 'on such a scale that no private individual can buy it!' His philosophy was simple. 'If archaeology is to become a mumbo-jumbo of esoteric mysteries then the sooner it stops the better. We dig for the enlightenment of the world, and while it is obviously a crime to cheapen the importance of antiquity by modern sensationalism it is equally a crime to pretend that it is a secret not to be understanded [sic] of the people. The "people" are desperately interested, and interested in the right way. They have only been scared on the one hand by those who "write down" to them, and on the other by those who write in a language peculiar to their little coterie and intentionally above the heads not only of the "man in the street" but of the average archaeologist also. After all, any one can read an interesting history, and what is archaeology but the providing of the bones and sinews of history?'[43]

14

March 1935–April 1936

WHILE JOHN AND HILDA were in the Royal Wadi, the political situation in Greece had erupted into a Republican uprising against the threat of the return of the monarchy. Crete, staunchly Republican and home of the elder statesman Eleutherios Venizelos, was heavily involved. The uprising was led by General Plastiras, already a veteran leader of *coups d'état*, and Venizelos. Not only had rebels taken over the model barracks in Athens of the Evzones, famous for their costumes, but the Military College as well. They soon surrendered in the face of 'point-blank artillery and machine-gun fire'.[1] Simultaneously, the naval arsenal on Salamis had been seized and the warship *Averoff*, light cruiser *Helle* and several other ships were commandeered and sailed for Crete. Venizelos had retired to Crete in October 1934, and refused to return to Athens until those behind a recent assassination attempt on him were punished. Now he set himself in charge of the rebels in Crete, of which there were a great number, and he even declared the island's independence. Crete rose to the defence of the Republic which, though fervently defended by the followers of Venizelos, was in its political death throes. Crete was bombarded by government planes, but the Cretans rose to the call to arms, and veterans of the fight for freedom from the Turks raised their old rifles to shoot at the planes.

'With old Venizelos up in arms like this and all access to and exit from Crete, and according to some rumours Greece too, forbidden, it doesn't look as if we shall be able to get there for a bit – if at all this year.' This brought home to John the wisdom of leaving the Curatorship in the hands of someone who could be there at such a time. 'It's a bit of luck we did give up Knossos; not only would it have meant that there was no one there to look after the property, but also even if we had got there, business and travelling would be impossible. I don't know whether Hutchinson and his mother have had any trouble or whether they have had brutal and licentious soldiery billeted on them. It does seem a mess.'[2]

Before they left Cairo, John wrote to the Greek Consul there to find out whether it would be possible to travel in Crete. 'Probably my Homero-Cretan will be like Chaucer-broad Lancashire to him!' After a fortnight, the rebellion was quashed. Venizelos escaped with his main followers to the Italian Dodecanese island of Kasos, off the north-east coast of Crete, and the Royalist

Prime Minister, Tsaldaris, got his wish, with the restoration of the monarchy later in 1935. The large Greek community in Egypt gave good coverage to the uprising, though they were biased strongly towards the government, and were very angry that when the trouble died down Venizelos and his fellow leaders of the rebellion went without punishment, 'while the dupes are court-martialled.'[3] The following November there would be an election, the results of which would defy belief in an honest ballot. 'I particularly enjoyed the Greek Government's statement that only 100 votes out of 8000 were cast against the Restoration [of the monarchy]. That rather casts doubt on the whole of that Plebiscite. 8000 is about the right total number of votes and 100 is about the right number of votes for the Restoration I should say.'[4]

At last, John and Hilda could leave Egypt. 'The division of spoil is over and is to my mind just. The number of things they have taken, contrary to expectation, is equalled by the number of things they have left us, also contrary to expectation.'[5] They snatched a few days of holiday in Palestine and visited the Heurtleys in Jerusalem, then flew back to Egypt, caught the boat to Athens and sailed to Crete.

The island had quietened down by the time they arrived and everything seemed to have returned to normal. Evans was in residence at the Villa Ariadne for what would prove to be the last time, having come out for a festival in his honour in Candia and Knossos. John and Hilda arrived for the last of three days of festivities, which culminated in the erection of a bronze bust of Evans at the entrance to the palace at Knossos.

It was John's first visit since resigning the Curatorship, and it was awkward when the house staff kept coming to him or Hilda for instructions. This wasn't helped by the Squire's vague nature and his aged mother's refusal to learn any Greek. John had kept in regular touch with the Squire from Egypt, helping and advising where he could, but here in Crete, he had to let the new Curator find his own feet.

'Of course it is frightfully easy to criticise one's successor (as one's predecessor) but it is rather annoying to see the Hutchinsons putting their foot in it right and left with Evans in spite of the fact that I told Hutchinson all the ways and traditions and got him to write it down. However, we hold our tongues. It's lucky Evans leaves on Monday. There would soon be an explosion.'[6]

For the first time a full excavation of a Roman building was being undertaken at Knossos. Crete had been a provincial Roman colony and some of the remains were superb. The first to be discovered lay in the grounds of the Villa Ariadne, and became known as the Villa Dionysos; it was producing some extraordinarily fine mosaics. Until John had travelled to the Levant, where there were superb Roman remains, he had been no fan of the Romans. However, even he was dismayed by Evans' lack of interest at the discovery.

Evans, though, looking back over his life in Crete, wished to concentrate on the Minoans, not the Romans. He had finished the final volume of his magnum opus, *The Palace of Minos*, and he had been honoured by the Cretans for his work. Now it was time to leave. Though John was frequently exasperated by Evans, he had nonetheless represented a different era, when pâté de foie gras was commonplace in a picnic hamper on journeys round the island and visitors – at least the most important or interesting ones – were welcomed and entertained at the Villa as guests. So when, on April 22nd 1935, Evans left Crete for good, John found himself regretting the passing of his world. 'There has been a sad break in the continuity of splendour since our day. It was rather depressing.'[7]

*

John's travels around Crete were more extensive even than those of Evans and his contemporaries. To John, the purpose of these journeys was not just to 'bag' as many sites as possible in one season, though he did relish the count as it grew. Neither was it an attempt merely to knock a couple of seconds off the existing record, despite Seton Lloyd's memory of him far in the distance, stopwatch in hand. Though his fitness and speed were John's only real vanity, he felt that he had to compare with a runner of the ancient world in the prime of fitness.

John wanted to understand the way the landscape reflected how the islanders had developed throughout history. Settlements of the Neolithic period – though, as at Knossos, they occasionally coincided with Minoan ones – were very different from those in use during the Minoan period, just as Minoan settlements differed from those founded after the Minoan collapse. John's walks were a means of understanding how people communicated with each other at various times in the past. 'Only those who have actually walked the mountains', he wrote, 'can tell how misleading a map may be, and the maps of Crete are in any case woefully inaccurate. Who would think that from Souia on the South coast to Lakkoi South of Chania is as long a day's journey as from Tsoutsouros, the ancient Priansos, on the South coast to Amnisos on the North coast? Distances are useless. Times alone matter.' The times he eventually published were almost entirely recorded by him and represented in his estimate 'about half-way between a running messenger and an ordinary party of merchants'.[8]

For his book on Crete, John hoped to combine his own extensive knowledge with that of earlier explorers of the island, including sources from the ancient world on routes, times and distances involved between centres of population. He wrote, asking his father to find an edition of the *Geographi Graeci Minores* and enquiring about the 'Peutinger Table' – 'This I believe is a sort of map of the ancient world made in Roman Imperial times'.[9] John wanted his book to be more than archaeology. He loved contemporary Crete as much as its past. He realised that every hill, valley, escarpment or even pile of rocks had a name that would soon be lost, as the modern world encroached relentlessly on the island. Local words and names were fast becoming obsolete, so he used his trips to pick up variations in the Cretan dialect. Place names were often clues to the topography or history of an area, and some reflected long-forgotten or almost forgotten legends. Crete was rare in that, preserved in its dialect, were words that only occurred in Homer, as well as a rich admixture of Moorish Arab, Italian and Turkish from its rich if troubled past. 'I believe I could now go to the mainland of Greece – speak correct Greek and yet be quite unintelligible!'[10]

With a muleteer to carry the baggage, John could go anywhere on the island, from the most impenetrable gorge on the coast to a shepherd's hut high in the mountains. He came to know the island, as the Cretans said of him, *patousia me patousia*, step by step. After interviewing John, a local journalist admitted to being ashamed that the Cretans themselves did not know their own island as well as Pendlebury. John did not find every site on the island, but he found more than anyone else. Even John's fellow archaeologist, Tom Dunbabin, while undercover in Crete during the occupation, had to admit that exploring in Crete was 'ill-gleaning after Pendlebury'.[11]

Their first walk of the season, at the end of April 1935, was to the west of the island. It was the longest single trip they had yet undertaken, free of any responsibilities other than to roam. They only ended the journey when the mules could take no more. The car dropped them at Tylissos, the beautifully situated remains of a Minoan villa on the slopes of the Ida range. Here they picked up their muleteer and two mules – 'the mare is unfortunately likely to drop a foal any day now!' – and skirted round the northern edge of Mount Ida, heading through the highland villages of Gonies, Anogia and Axos. At Melidoni they came across a cave with 'stalactites literally like curtains with all the folds', but it had a grisly past as the place where the Turks had trapped 370 Christian Cretans and smoked them to death. By this point, John had already discovered three more sites.

John was again following in Evans's footsteps, looking for possible sites that Evans had heard of forty years or more earlier. They cut back down to the north coast to spend a night at Rethymnon, and walked parallel to the coast westwards as far as Souda Bay, in the middle of which was a small island crowned by a Venetian fortress. Here, overlooking the bay, they scouted round the site of Aptera, 'one of the largest in the island with good Greek walls and

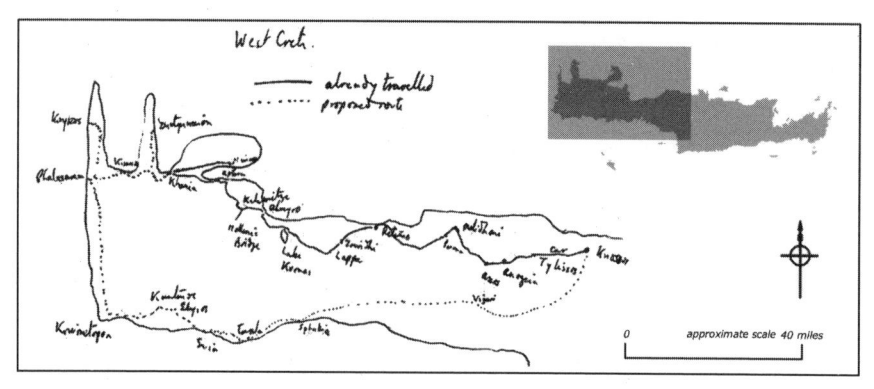

SPRING 1935 ROUTE

some very magnificent Roman cisterns'.[12] Tired and dirty by the time they reached Chania, they indulged in a good hotel for a couple of days while they waited for Edith Eccles to join them. But as soon as they were rested, they headed out prospecting for sites along the promontory that divides Souda Bay from Chania, following the north coast of the bay. From the west end of Souda Bay there is a spectacular view back along the north coast of Crete, with the White Mountains in the middle distance and the coast stretching far to the east. John would have approved of the fact that this is where he was finally buried.

Chania was a lively place and, as the island's centre of administration and foreign consulates, it was here that the trials of the rebels from the uprising two months earlier, were being held. 'There is a whole gang of rascally attorneys at the hotel. My feeling is that old Venizelos ought to have made the gesture of offering to come back and stand the racket if they'd have let the others off. He's come very badly out of this.'[13] He added later, 'West Crete is full of the cry τουφεκιζουνε τα κουπελια (they are shooting the boys) quite a sort of Irish "They're hanging men and women for the wearing of the green".'[14] It was this spirit that John loved in the Cretans, and he would not forget this glimpse of how they reacted when something was imposed on them against their will.

At Chania, they were joined by Edith Eccles, and continued westwards with her to the monastery of Gonia. Here they took a boat north up to the Diktynnaion promontory, overlooking the Gulf of Chania. John, Hilda and Edith then walked back down as far as Kastelli Kissamou, where Edith left them again, and across to the ancient port of Phalasarna. 'At some time in the sixth century [AD] a great submarine movement took place which tilted the whole island as if on a pivot. As a result the West end was raised in places as much as twenty-six feet out of the water so that the artificial harbour of Phalasarna on the West coast is now well above sea level and some 150 yards inland, while a corresponding subsidence in the East has caused the disappearance of many of the stretches of sand on to which the ships were hauled and has swallowed up parts of the ancient towns.'[15] But reaching Phalasarna was significant for John for another reason – 'I've now been on foot from end to end of Crete!'[16]

When they reached the village of Mesogeia, they found that the local police sergeant and the head of the village had been warned that John and Hilda were heading their way but with no idea of what time they would arrive. When they did turn up at half-past four in the afternoon, both men were happily ensconced in the village pub, 'with a heavy meal waiting for us and "very nicely thank you!" having filled in the time with some good wine. We were given wine here twenty-one years old'.[17]

Following a very wild and windy track down the west coast, they rounded the south-west corner of Crete and encountered no one for the next six hours of their walk. Zigzagging between the coast and the hills, they eventually came to Sougia. While the muleteer took the mules on ahead by land, John and Hilda rested for two nights before rejoining them by boat at Poikilassos. They had then hoped to go up the Samaria Gorge to the Omalos Plain, but the mules had by now had enough. Instead they skirted the west side of the White Mountains back to Chania and took a car back to Knossos.

It was not long before Hilda had to return to the children, having already missed Joan's first birthday, while John stayed on in Crete. He, the Squire and Mercy Money-Coutts met up at Neapolis and headed up into the mountains enclosing the Lasithi Plain. They skirted round above the north side of the plain, 'through quite some of the wildest country I've ever seen, quite the worst paths – no water to be found and about 90 in the shade and over 4000 feet to climb!'[18]

John loved the wildness and remoteness, and there were some very interesting sites, as he described to Evans, who had explored the area in the 1890s. The one that had most grabbed his eye was in a village at the north edge of the Lasithi Plain, called Tzermiado. Nearby was a cave, known as the Trapeza cave. 'We found a lot of EMII – MMI, MMIII, LMI and Hellenic sherds. I am going to apply for a permit to dig it next year, as it seems to supply exactly the evidence lacking at Psychro.'[19] Psychro was the village just below the Diktaean Cave, legendary birthplace of Zeus, and a centre of worship for the Minoans. If John could prove that the Trapeza Cave had been used as a place of worship before the Diktaean Cave, it would be a very significant discovery. Although Professor Dawkins had carried out some excavations in Lasithi, the plain was rich in sites of all periods, and John was beginning to see that it had huge potential for future work.

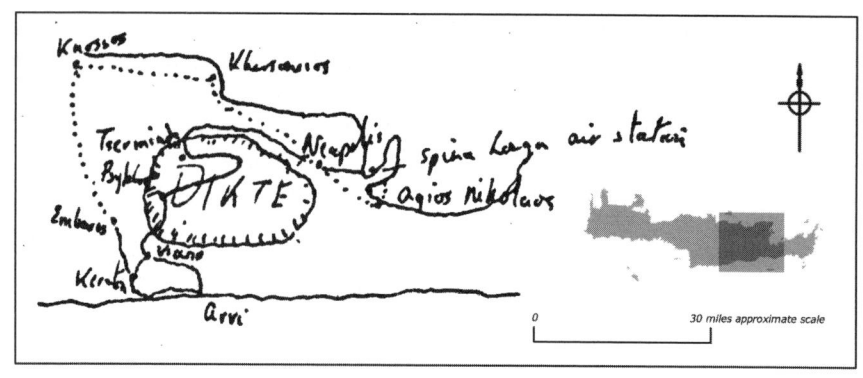

LATE SPRING 1935 ROUTE

'On the Friday we went up over the other rim of the plain and down to Viano. It was very hot but in contrast to the N side of Lasithi it had a good road and plenty of water on it, so one was able to keep cool by turning oneself into an evaporating machine. I have gone the colour of the background of a Hawks tie!' On the way, John managed to twist his ankle and 'for a bit had to break my record and ride a mule for the first time in Greece.'[20]

Back at Knossos, John was not about to let the ankle slow him down: 'I've been skipping in the morning early before breakfast, bathing at noon and playing tennis in the evening so I'm just about as fit as I've ever been in my life – and probably lighter!'[21] After only a week's 'rest', John set off, again with Mercy and the Squire, to go up Mount Ida from Krousonas.

*

John was finding the Squire's mother difficult to cope with. 'Mrs Hutchinson will I fear soon have to be put out of the way', he told his father, 'she is quite impossible. The 'Squire' himself is a dear but totally vague and, when loaded with a mother who – if she had four times as many brains would be nearly quarter-witted – is quite incapable of doing the work. I feel it would be a very nice thing if she went one day – quite quietly – into a nunnery and stopped there.'[22] He added later, 'Anyone who happened to find her on the edge of a cliff would be doing a very good service if he stumbled against her accidentally.'[23]

*

Meanwhile, Hilda had arrived back in England after months away. She picked the children up at Malvern, where they had been living with Herbert and Dickie, and took them to her mother's house in Caldy; there she again left them to go and sort out their home in Cambridge. They were renting a house from A.W. Lawrence, brother of T.E., but it was too big for Hilda to manage alone, so she took on two servants. 'I have had rather a horrid time getting the house ready', she wrote to Mary Jonas, 'as I couldn't get maids until the day before the family arrived, but I was lucky to get them as quickly as that and I had the Lawrence's faithful "charwoman" every afternoon to keep things clean.' Soon after, her sister Dora and the children's nanny, Miss Bevan, brought David and Joan to Cambridge. 'The family arrived on Friday looking very well and happy and we are settling down and getting things into running order…At the moment I am feeling rather flat and a bit exhausted but that won't last long.'[24]

*

John's mind could not have been further from such domesticity. He had had a very successful season and, together with those from the previous year, he had now discovered ninety-eight previously unknown sites. He wanted to fit in just one more trip, nominally to try and make it a round hundred, but, as he confessed to Mary Jonas, 'travelling in Crete is too good to be true after Egypt. One can stretch one's legs over the mountains.'[25] He now felt he was justified in claiming that he knew the island better than anyone in the world. Few Cretans would have denied it, though Manolaki, who had often accompanied first Evans and then John, had probably seen more of it than any of his compatriots.

John landed at Croydon airport in mid-July 1935, and settled down with the family in Cambridge. They now had a home that they could spend money on, and as well as redecorating, they spent nearly five hundred pounds on carpentry, new electrics and kitchen facilities. They bought china and furnishings, carpets and curtains, kitchen implements, and even built a tennis court, which cost twice as much as the one at Knossos.

It was a peaceful summer, but for John it may have been overshadowed by the impending enquiry by the Egypt Exploration Society resulting from Fairman's complaints the previous Amarna season. This took place at the end of September 1935. The official documentation of the enquiry summarised the 'criticism of the Society's work' under three sections. The first of Fairman's arguments was that the staff employed at Amarna was 'too large and for the most part unqualified; that it was an amateur dig, since the Director was unpaid'. The second was that 'Mr Pendlebury's attitude to his staff in camp had caused much discontent with consequent lack of efficiency'. The third of Fairman's accusations was that 'Mr Pendlebury had committed serious archaeological blunders, which could have been avoided if had listened to his subordinates'.[26]

The committee of the EES took full responsibility for the first accusation, 'whatever truth there may be in [it]', and did not consider it worthy of an official response. As for the second, the interviews had been carried out on site. The situation had arisen as Hugh Last was handing over as Honorary Secretary to

Stephen Glanville, so Last's request that John talk to his staff was overseen in the event by Glanville. Given the opportunity to talk to Glanville privately, each member of staff had willingly accepted that John be present. The problem of 'personal difficulties in camp was discussed with great frankness on both sides'. The report nevertheless concluded that there was 'no purpose in wasting the time of the Committee with details of misunderstandings which, there is every reason to believe, will not occur in the future. It is sufficient that the three members of the expedition (including Mr Pendlebury) who will still be free to work for the Society, are convinced that nothing stands in the way of harmonious co-operation next season'.[27]

The third accusation was solved by John and Fairman presenting their differing opinions in writing to the committee. Glanville did not consider these of 'sufficient importance to place before the Committee, but it was the wish of both that this should be done, and a statement by each is appended to this report'. He concluded that even this difference of opinion would in no way affect the 'satisfactory conclusion reached on the personal side'.[28]

*

John was back in Cairo by mid-November 1935, this time without Hilda, who felt it impossible to leave the children again for so long. The team still included Fairman, as well as two new members, an English Egyptology student, T.W. Thacker, and a German, Günter Rudnitzky, both of whom were to arrive later with Fairman and Lavers. John meanwhile indulged in Cairo's social scene with Sir Thomas Russell Pasha, the commandant of the Cairo Police Force, who had lived and worked in Egypt since 1902.

Russell Pasha knew the country well and was a useful source of information at a time when anti-British sentiments were rife. John wrote to reassure his father that he was not in danger of the riots that took place on November 13th, 'which I gather were very much exaggerated in England. I saw nothing of them and heard nothing, though I was within 200 yards of one of the worst all morning. I gather they would have been nothing at all if the police had been allowed to prevent instead of to cure. However, all now is quiet'.[29]

The riots were only one of the problems that faced the British in Egypt at the time. Italy had just invaded Abyssinia, which shared a border with Egypt. John wrote home: 'Egypt is filled with English war planes and Alexandria with British warships. What trouble we shall have I don't know. No one knows the truth at all. The best solution would be for both parties to wipe each other out. They are an unpleasant lot of blighters both Italians and Abyssinians.'[30] However, this lightened the tension within Egypt for the British, who were generally seen to be keeping Egypt safe from the Italians.

Things were, however, safe for the time being and the season at Amarna went ahead as planned. After the furore of the previous season between John and Fairman, John's first act was to remove the dump that had caused so much trouble and dig beneath it. He described the results to Mary Jonas, unable to suppress the triumph and vindication he was feeling: 'Below the famous – or infamous dump was nothing at all! We only had to clear a couple of metres to see that. A gamble failing by two metres of nothing and causing all the "kulla bulla"!'[31] Though Fairman had returned to the dig under John's direction, there was little real rapport between the two men anymore and it is unlikely that John was able to hide from Fairman his satisfaction at the outcome of the whole affair. According to Günter Rudnitzky, Fairman seemed to get his own back throughout the season, infuriating John with some of the archaeological decisions he made in John's absence.[32]

Thacker and Rudnitzky, on the other hand, were both a success. Rudnitzky later described Thacker as 'friendly, calm, gifted and discerning', qualities he may well have had to draw on more than usual during such a season.[33] Thacker had studied for a time at Berlin University and he and Rudnitzky got on well together. John saw in Thacker 'a bit of a genius' while Rudnitzky struck him as rather quiet and serious, but of both of them he said that they had the right spirit.[34] Rudnitzky, looking back sixty years later, wrote of John: 'At that time I did not ponder over the character of Pendlebury and found him too singular to view him against a national background. I simply enjoyed his presence and felt a difference in the atmosphere when he was present or absent. Looking back, I would say he charmed with amiable radiance, well-poised liveliness and quick-brained astuteness.'[35] There is little doubt that the presence of these two placid students calmed what might otherwise have been a volatile season.

As always, money was a constant worry. Communications were such that news of the state of funds took time to filter through to John on the dig. He wrote to Mary Jonas in exasperation: 'You see I don't know how much has come in from places like Oxford and Cambridge. Mrs Hubbard I suppose is in Fiji still. That is a nuisance because I am sure she was going to carry on her subscription – or so I gather from the very nice letter I had from her shortly before leaving. I have written to Capart asking him for more already since these damn Yanks take such a sin of a time.'[36]

Mary Jonas, writing from London the same day, was equally exasperated: 'I am sorry that Mrs Hubbard has not come up to scratch. I have written to Prof. Newberry but have received no reply. Mr Raphael has subscribed £50 to El Amarna on Mr Glanville's request, and the Ashmolean has supplied the £40

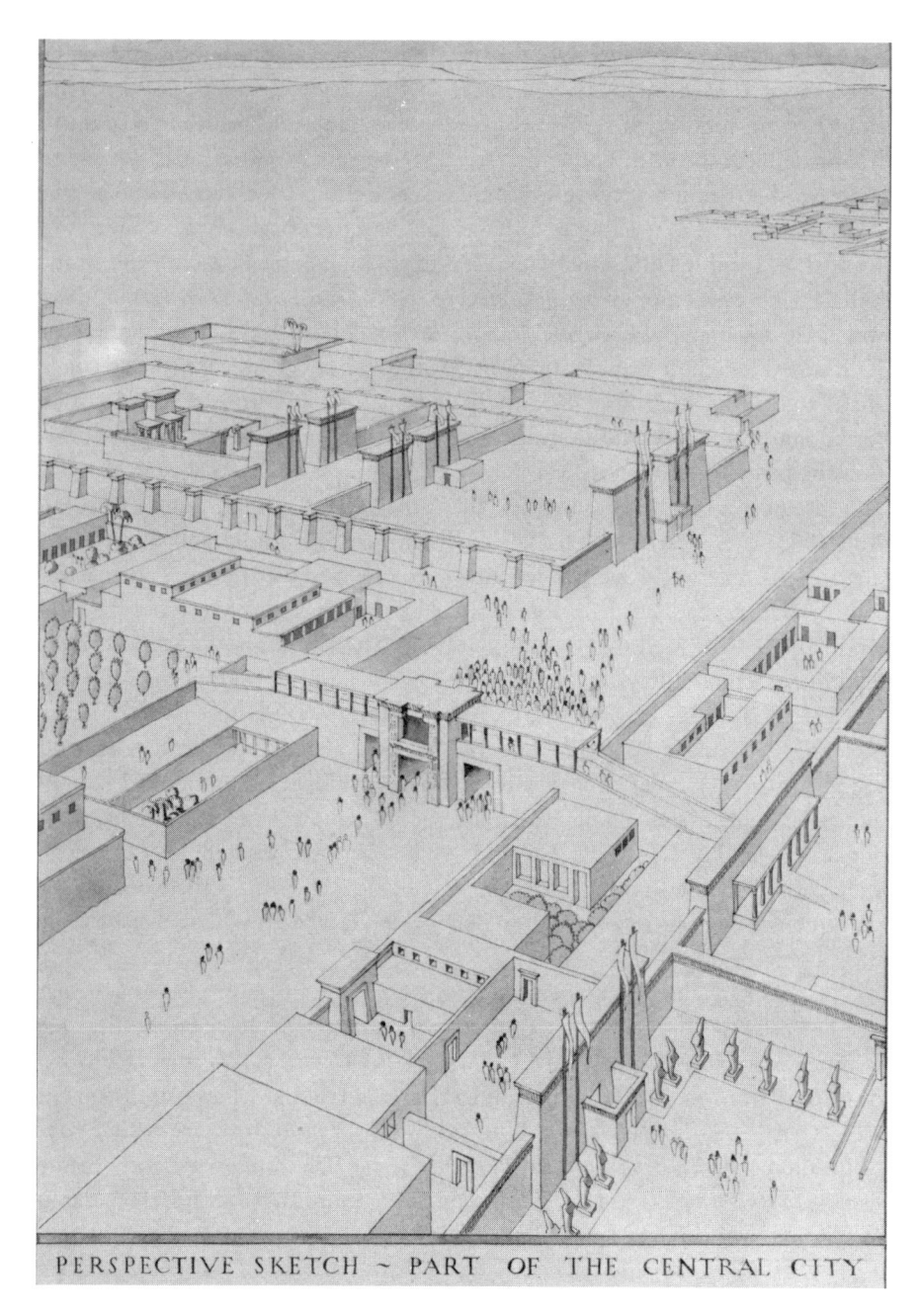

Sketch of Tell el-Amarna by Ralph Lavers

(Copyright of the Egypt Exploration Society. Reproduced with permission)

promised (it came today) but our Hon. Treasurer will not draw cheques on "possibilities", hence the cable which I sent off for him yesterday. I do not know if he has written as well, but on looking at your figures he thinks you must deduct the Hubbard £200. I hope that you might be able to get a promise from Capart for something to balance this, so asked him to add the last words, "unless extra money comes". I wish to goodness I could think of a gold mine, but I have never been a "gold-digger"!'[37]

John's frustration was fuelled by the importance of what they were uncovering. The form of the Palace was at last beginning to make sense and the deliberately smashed and widely scattered fragments of inscriptions and colossal statues of the pharaoh could now be assigned to their original positions. 'The coming fortnight should see most of the Palace as shown in Petrie completed and a good slice taken from the projection westwards.'[38]

They had begun by completing the Weben Aten, where so many of the fine trial pieces had been found during the previous season. They then cleared the Broad Hall, a vast space which appeared to have been surrounded by the colossal statues of the Pharaoh. 'The plan of the Palace', John reported to the EES, 'is completely symmetrical as regards the main state halls, and must have been a most impressive building, its general plan being grander than that of any other single building yet revealed by excavation in Egypt. The Broad Hall itself, originally intended to be a gigantic colonnade, but later for reasons of economy confined to an open court surrounded by statues, is approached from the south by a series of monumental entrances, themselves fronted along the main axis by a colonnade. These entrances are from a higher level from the south which is itself crossed by a series of causeways leading from the large buildings to the south and from the Bridge to the King's House.'[39]

The architectural details that they managed to recover were sufficient to be able to form a reconstructed view of their original appearance. The columns were made of limestone, sandstone and quartzite, some inlaid with brilliant faience. The most exciting element was the complete symmetry of the building plan. John was sure that if they could have just a few weeks to finish the palace plan the following season, then the 'palace in its entirety can be accurately planned down to its smallest detail, including the variations of elevation'.[40] The finds, too, were extraordinary. Sculptors' trial pieces were abundant, hinting perhaps that with so many stone masons required, some were forced to learn on the job.

That Christmas, John abandoned the camp to go off hunting ibex in the high desert with the Russell family. 'We had a whole patrol of the game patrol with us amounting to about twenty camels and men. We went up some thirty miles into the desert. I must say it really was an education to see the trained trackers at work and to learn how to distinguish from droppings and tracks the length of time since the animal had passed. By three bits of bad luck we didn't see a single ibex. On the first day a group caught our wind and were off ten minutes before we arrived, on the second day an untrained dog showed himself on the skyline and scared off the same group, on the third day when there was a thick fog as I was coming down the same group again were crossing our path and of course hared off. However it was a magnificent trip. I found that a proper riding camel is a very nice ride and one can do six hours or more at a stretch at a slow trot of five miles an hour without any stiffness. Of course the whole district was disturbed at Russell's arrival and for the whole period the house was filled with Omdas – Mamurs – police officers and everything.'[41]

John managed to glean some information from Russell Pasha on the deteriorating political situation, as he described to his father. 'We shall know within a month about wars and rumours of wars (so I hear officially but secretly and confidentially). Also we expect a spot more trouble here internally but both will be over one way or another by the end of the month... If you'd seen as I have our power here by sea, land and air – you wouldn't think our Italian friends would try anything on. Also we have Crete promised as a base.'[42]

The only thing actually holding up the Italian invasion of Abyssinia, though, was the weather. 'I hope to goodness these rains hold things up in Abyssinia long enough for some sort of peace to be patched up. Otherwise I'm convinced we are for it. And a war on behalf of Abyssinia does seem silly. However I suppose if the Italians want it they must have it in the neck. Egypt will be taken over by us which may make things easier here... The latest remark attributed to Haile Selassie: "Mussolini – my Enema – my Douche."'[43]

The threat to the region added urgency to the financial constraints already jeopardising the completion of the Palace excavation. John and his staff were working flat out to achieve as much as possible: 'The dig has taken such a strenuous turn that I've really only been able to pour myself into bed at night. The plan we are getting has turned out to be that of the finest and most impressive secular building ever found. It beats Knossos and the Mespot buildings into a cocked hat. As I had vaguely suspected it is a gigantic symmetrical building with great halls, and colonnades over 200 yards long with vast approaches and pylons. We are desperately trying to get to the spot to which it all leads up before the money runs out...The finds too are good but pale beside the plan. I don't suppose anybody will ever take any notice of it but it's nice and satisfactory to know it's done.'[44] John asked Herbert if he could find out the dimensions of Buckingham Palace, the Louvre, Versailles and the Vatican. 'Buildings only – not grounds. It would make an interesting comparison, but I think a building of about 1100 yards by 330 takes a bit of beating.'[45]

The season finished in the middle of February, and had resulted in the excavation of an extraordinarily large and impressive building. Nevertheless, John was very careful in what he recommended to the committee of the EES for the completion of the work the following season. He calculated that it could take as much as eleven weeks. 'This would complete the official quarters of Amarna and enable all tests to be undertaken so that the Society – even I admit – could leave it with a clear conscience that nothing more – short of the expropriation of large tracts of cultivation for this purpose – can be got out of it.'[46]

At the end of his interim report, John added with questionable diplomacy, 'before closing I should like to pay a tribute to the staff – particularly to the new members. Mr Fairman and Mr Lavers need no commendation. The plans and information recovered are sufficient tribute. But Mr Thacker and Mr Rudnitzky arrived on their first excavation to find the most puzzling kind of work imaginable in progress. I need only say that after a few weeks I have never had to hesitate before leaving them in charge for a short period, being assured that their knowledge of Arabic is sufficient for them to give all ordinary orders and that their appreciation of the difficulties of the dig and their sense of values is sufficient for them to know when to decide a matter themselves and when to ask advice elsewhere.'[47]

John was elated that the season had gone so well, and felt it was 'certainly the best bit of work I've ever done'. They were all exhausted but happy. John told his father 'my hair is half way down my back – full of nits and will remain so for another ten days.'[48]

In the middle of March, following a division that amply provided for the next exhibition, Hilda met John in Cairo to help sort through the fragments of sarcophagi from the Royal Tomb. The city had still not settled down completely, and John, sounding more and more like his fellow members of the Turf Club, told Herbert, 'the miserable Gyppies still are squabbling about things they don't understand. I expect we shall have a few troubles in Cairo. I expect you saw that some students were silly enough to demonstrate in front of the Turf Club the other day – whereupon ten or twelve of the hardest cases in the Near East left the bar – sallied out and paved the streets with the unconscious victims before returning to their pink gins. One – on hearing cries of "down with England", said "What I've always said. I'm a Scotsman".'[49]

This reaction to the anti-British riots in Cairo reveals an attitude to Egypt and the Egyptians that John would never dream of applying to the freedom-fighting Cretans. It is clear that Egypt never really found as deep a place in

John's heart as Greece – and particularly Crete – had done. At Amarna John was the *mudir*, the Director, and there was a distance between him and the villagers working on the dig. Beyond his patriarchal role at Amarna, he never felt inclined to explore and become intimately familiar with the country outside the site, perhaps because the physical challenge did not compare to that found in Crete. As a result, his knowledge of spoken Arabic was considerably less than his command of Cretan Greek. Though John loved the Egyptians' sense of humour, he was never attracted by the formal culture of hospitality in Egypt, preferring the easy conviviality of Crete, liberally lubricated by wine and raki.

15

May 1936–August 1939

ON MAY 2ND 1936, JOHN arrived at the Cretan village of Tzermiado, which nestled in the shadow of the 300-foot high plateau known as Trapeza (table), on the northern side of the Lasithi Plain. Armed with a permit from the British School to excavate the Trapeza Cave, John, Hilda, Mercy Money-Coutts and Ralph Lavers set up a dig house in this, the largest village in the Lasithi Plain. It is always colder and wetter on the plain than it is nearly 3000 feet below on the coast, and spring was still little in evidence through the rain when the team arrived. 'The people here are a most affable lot and I'm sure we shall enjoy our stay, particularly as there are a gratifying lot of mountains to climb on Sundays.'[1]

With the team, as foreman for the first week of the excavation, came Manolaki, on whose extensive experience Sir Arthur Evans had thought John could draw. Then, for the rest of the dig, Spyridon Marinatos lent his own foreman, Ioannes Meliarakes, who, as a man of Psychro, had even greater experience than Manolaki in the excavation of caves and the local archaeology. Evans had discovered the cave back in 1896, one of several in the rocks around the village.

The Trapeza Cave was small and cramped compared to the Diktaean Cave across the plain at Psychro, but was otherwise commodious. Protected from the heavy rain outside, the cave was nevertheless cold and damp. Luckily for the seven or eight workmen digging at a time, it was fairly well ventilated, so that the fumes of the petrol lamp were not a problem.

The opening of the cave led into a steeply sloping passage, which evened out before turning at right angles into a deeper chamber. They divided the cave into sections, according to its natural rock divisions, and took each section down in stages, keeping a lookout for any surviving natural stratigraphy that they could then follow. The deposits were much deeper than John had imagined, but they failed to find what the locals assured them they would. Tradition had it that a great treasure, in the form of a golden sow and her seven golden piglets, was buried in the cave and was guarded by three ghostly black men (Αραπιδες). This legend was common to many ancient sites, but it still enchanted John. Unfortunately, belief in such myths was the driving force behind the pillaging of many sites, and Lasithi was no exception. The cave had already been thoroughly dug over, and most of the bones and skulls they found had been mixed up. But there was enough evidence to suggest that some bodies

SKETCH MAP OF THE PLAIN OF LASITHI

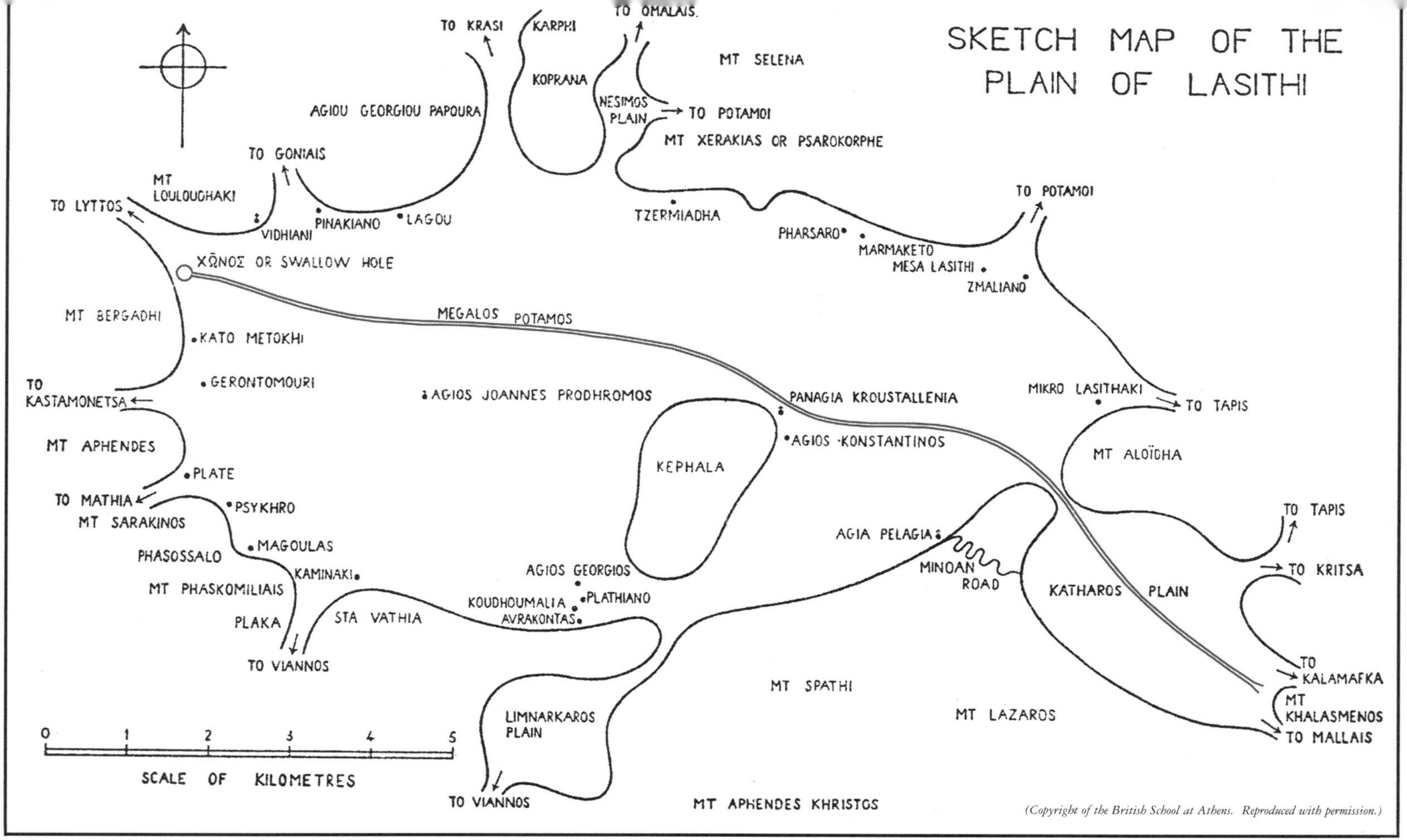

may have been buried on stone shelves and that older bones were swept aside to accommodate new arrivals. 'It has gone amazingly well up to date and I think another week should see the end of it. We've got an entirely new type of EMI (Early Minoan I) pottery which has never been found anywhere else and which must be autochthonous to Lasithi – also a new type of bone figurine which must also be Lasithiote. Quite a number of stone vases, knives etc. In any case it will add quite a lot to our knowledge of the Early Bronze Age. Quite clearly it was the original Diktaean Cave, as the deposit stops short at the moment that the famous one begins.'[2] The villagers, when they were told that Trapeza was a sacred cave that had been in use long before the Diktaean Cave honoured Zeus at Psychro, decided that it must be the cave of Zeus's father, Kronos. John was delighted to have found something so revolutionary at what seemed to him to be such a late stage of Cretan archaeology, but commented to his father, 'It means the devil of a lot of rewriting of the book, curse it!'[3]

As John's first truly independent excavation, though it only lasted a fortnight, the Trapeza dig had been a promising and impressive start. Marinatos promised to give them a large case at the Candia Museum for their finds, and they could now contribute a good photographic display to the British School's fiftieth anniversary exhibition in London.

However, the euphoria of their first Lasithi season was seriously marred by some news from the British School at Athens that cast a deep gloom over everyone. The Director, John's friend Humfry Payne, had died suddenly. 'He was only thirty-five and apart from bad asthma about as fit as anyone could be. It will be a terrible loss for the school and for archaeology in general as well as for his friends.'[4] At first doctors at the Evangelismos Hospital in Athens had thought a pain in Payne's knee was due to rheumatism, but it later emerged that a simple graze had become infected with a staphylococcus germ. An antidote did exist and American friends of Payne's in Athens had tried everything to obtain some for him but failed to get it in time. More than fifty years later, their failure still brought them to tears.[5] John was deeply affected by his friend's death. 'We shall miss him a lot', he wrote to his father. 'Our friendship throve on insult and abuse. I'm very glad to have known him particularly on trips. "My God, to think we're paid to do this!" on a very good day when we had found Perachora and were sitting on the hills above... He is buried, I'm glad to say, at Mycenae – with another good friend of ours – Spiro from the hotel.'[6]

John had been captivated by the Lasithi region and the warmth and enthusiasm of the people of Tzermiado. Lasithi had in abundance everything John loved about Crete – wild, beautiful mountains, a proud, strong people with a fascinating and diverse history and archaeology, both secluded from the rest of the island and yet in touch with it, for even Trapeza Cave had yielded objects of Egyptian and Sumerian origin. 'We've got a programme for years here. It is so cut off a place that it has all sorts of queer survivals. Even nowadays they use more Arabic words than anywhere else and have Turkish gestures. There are most interesting sites of all periods and from surface and chance finds all of them seem to be first class and rather different from elsewhere.'[7]

Fuelling John's increasing fascination with the vernacular Cretan dialect was the islanders' talent for *mantinades*, improvised rhyming couplets in a meter of fifteen syllables which were the essence of every song and poem in the island from at least as far back as the Middle Ages under the Venetians. It was the same form as the island's most famous epic poem, the *Erotokritos*, a Renaissance tale of knights, tournaments and courtly love, which many on the island could still sing or recite by heart. Particularly among the shepherds the use of oral poetry to maintain and tell stories was common, and the Homeric resonances could not fail to appeal to John. Most Cretans could create reams of *mantinades* to suit any occasion, and John, who was not unused to cobbling light verse together, took to the form easily and enthusiastically.[8]

They were people of mischievous humour too, and were an appreciative audience for John's pranks. John described one incident to his father in a letter which might as easily have come from the little boy at St George's School in Broadstairs. 'I sent round to the police station here today a bogus arrival form of Benito Mussolini – parentage unknown – religion *Satanolatreia* [Devil-worship] – profession: white slaver. The commandant tells me it took him in for a quarter of an hour and has fined me a dinner to pay for the cost of a wire to all the ports for information.'[9]

When the team had finished sorting the finds, John and Hilda headed off for a three-day walking trip across the Lasithi Plain to Psychro on the south side of the plain, where they stayed at the house of one of the Trapeza workmen, old George Markogiannakis and his daughter-in-law, Ourania. 'George had a delightful village house', Hilda later wrote, 'with a terrace and courtyard: our beds were spotlessly clean but I shall never forget the rasp of Ourania's homespun sheets on my chin.' Old George was a larger-than-life character who during the excavation had supervised the pot-washing girls, most of whom came from the village of Tzermiado. But Lasithi was a small community and the ties were complex. The girls, most of them no more than sixteen, 'teased and plagued him with their frivolous ways'.[10] The old man felt more comfortable going on an expedition, and he and another of the Trapeza workmen, Nikos Paterakis, were to act as guides to John and Hilda.

They spent the first morning in climbing Aphendis Sarakinos, the mountain which rises steeply on the south side of the plain. From there, every peak surrounding the Lasithi Plain stood out clearly, and old George could name every one. Such was the advantage of taking an old guide. The men of Lasithi were incredibly fit, and shepherds from Tzermiado, even in very old age, would regularly walk between Mallia on the north coast, nearly three thousand feet below Lasithi, and the mountain pastures. They rested after a lunch prepared by Ourania, before beginning their climb of Mount Dikte, which towers above the south-east of Lasithi. A pass led up from near the village of Agios Georgios under the sheer and vast west face of the mountain, before emerging into a smaller upland plain, a vision of fresh grass and spring flowers at the end of May. This, the Limnarkaros Plain, was dominated by the impossibly high, sheer cliffs of Spathi. There in the midst of this domain of shepherds, was a very small Byzantine church, then dedicated to St George.

'The chapel would have provided shelter if mountain mist and rain had come down on us', Hilda late recalled in her unpublished account of the walk, 'but we were lucky. There was a fresh breeze blowing and we were glad to have our supper with the chapel between us and the wind, but by the time we were ready for bed and our lilo mattresses had been pumped up, the breeze had fallen and it was warm and still with a misty moonlight. Some time later we heard far off the clink of stones on the hillside and the sound of voices as our two mountain guides came to join us after their day's work was over. A quiet word of greeting and they sank down at the edge of the cornfield at a little distance and pulling their brown woollen cloaks about them went off to sleep.'[11]

At half-past four the next morning they moved on, passing a spring called Arvasami, until they came to a *mandra,* or shepherd's hut. These huts, built out of dry stone and usually circular, were used during the long summer months when the shepherds took their flocks up to the high pastures. Roofed with branches covered in turf, the *mandras* were often divided inside, half used for eating, sleeping and making cheese in cauldrons perched over an open hearth, the other half used for storing the cheeses. Outside were stone-walled enclosures, where the sheep would be kept for milking, shearing or slaughter. Some of the *mandra*s were a few hundred years old, but many were probably considerably older, with no change in their use or appearance over time.

The one they entered belonged to Georgios Krasanakis of Agios Georgios. John and Hilda had never been inside a *mandra* before. 'We were invited to enter and bending low crept inside. The place was full of smoke and as soon as we could see we found that a number of hairy shepherds were busy at cauldrons scalding the milk of their flocks preparatory to making it into cheeses. A fire of boughs was quickly kindled on the earth and rock floor of the hut and round this we sat and steamed, and were given our second breakfast of cheese and bread, and wine in great quantities. In this atmosphere it was not long before we were dry. At intervals someone would peep out from the low door and report on the weather.'[12]

As soon as there was a pause in the rain, they headed off to climb the Christos peak, accompanied by two of the sheep dogs from the *mandra*. With mist and drizzle closing in around them, they could hardly see where they were walking. 'At one point we passed very close to the edge of some great gulf, climbing over rocks that ended abruptly on our right in a sort of window or gateway opening onto a space filled with a billowing sea of mist surging through the opening in great waves, a grim and chilling memory.'[13] The descent was dangerous, without any view of guiding landmarks. The guides split up, one to go ahead and the other to stay with John and Hilda. But their guide had eventually to admit that, in the thick fog, he was lost.

In one of the few recorded instances of Hilda writing about John, she said that he 'enjoyed himself in a situation like this and pitted his brains and determination against the difficulties. He and the guide began to argue about the points of the compass and were each of a different opinion as to where the South lay.' She admitted that she was hoping John would be right ('he was determined enough and the guide was in something of a panic'), but does not say how he might have taken being wrong. A sudden gap in the mist solved the problem in John's favour to reveal the south coast and the town of Ierapetra bathed in sunlight far below. The guide now got his bearings back and led them quickly to the comfort of the *mandra*. 'Soon', she recalled, 'we were safe back in the warm smoky interior, drying off for the second time, and being supplied with more central heating in the form of wine and food.'[14]

They set off into the mist again soon after towards another *mandra*, called Lakanida. 'Soon after leaving it we suddenly walked into another world; the change from cold grey mist to bright warm sunshine was as sudden as if we had walked through a door from one to the other.' They had a better guide this time, who had walked every inch of the mountain since he was a small boy. They were aiming now for another upland plain, larger than Limnarkaros and more accessible. 'We crossed a river at the approach to the Katharos Plain and the last downhill stages before we reached the regular path across the plain were through trees and very pleasant. At last we arrived at Sgouroprinos, a tiny wine shop under the dark pine trees and a threshing floor amongst the crops where we camped, rested, ate our supper and slept under the stars.'[15]

The next day took them on the last leg of their journey, across the Katharos Plain to Kritsa, taking in the Hellenic fort on the hillside at

Akhladies and a place known as the Kitten's Cistern, mentioned as a Minoan site by Sir Arthur Evans in the notes on his *Travels in Crete*. By ten o'clock they were on their way back to Tzermiado by way of the Alexena saddle.

Once back at the village, they packed up the excavation and threw an end-of-dig *glendi* or party for the village, with singing and dancing to the music of the lyra, drum and *askimandoura* (a type of bagpipe made from a sheep's stomach). 'A very pleasant show marred only by the political difficulties of various of our friends which made it impossible for them to meet each other socially.' The finds were loaded onto mules, which proceeded past the windmills on the north-western edge of the Lasithi Plain and down the steep mountainside to the world below. As there was no bone specialist in Crete, John was told that he had to send all his boxes back to Athens. 'I shall probably be arrested for some particularly grim form of trunk murder.'[16]

*

When they arrived back in England, John was surprised to receive an official invitation to stand for the Directorship of the British School at Athens. Humfry Payne's sudden death had left a vacuum, which had been filled temporarily by the Assistant Director, Peter Megaw. When Megaw left Athens to take up a new appointment in Cyprus, Alan Blakeway, an old friend of Payne's, was appointed as temporary Director. The School took its time making a decision. John was not the only candidate, and while he was a good one, he had made it clear that he would not give up what he had heard would be his last season at Amarna for the British School Directorship.

When John bumped into Seton Lloyd, he was told that there was a possibility that the Metropolitan Museum would be interested in continuing the work at Tell el-Amarna, which raised John's hopes enormously. After all, they already had an important collection of Amarna artefacts, and had long been generous subscribers. He also told John that the golden days of Chicago House might be over. 'The Chicago people are having a thin time. After living in the lap of luxury they now find Rockefeller has withdrawn his support owing to their extravagant habits.'[17]

John had plenty on his mind as he set off on holiday with Hilda and the children. They had decided on Cromer in Norfolk, where John had often gone as a child. But his mind was elsewhere and he kept in regular contact with Mary Jonas, to whom he confided his dilemma. 'I've had an official request to enter for the Directorship of the BSA – not that that means anything. As the duties wouldn't begin till Jan 1, by which time the Amarna dig would be over, I've said I would take it on but only if they can't find someone else which I'm sure they can.'[18]

As the holiday progressed, the idea of the Athens job began to weigh more heavily on him. 'If I'm forced to take the BSA', he wrote to his father, 'which I expect to hear any day now, I should aim at getting to Athens as soon as the Amarna dig finishes to take over from Blakeway, say the last week in December.' The weather turned bad, and as the rain poured down outside on the seaside resort, John became increasingly restless. It was likely that he would have to support the Cretan dig himself to a large extent and, with the distinct possibility that he would not have a job, John was beginning to cut costs. 'Tell Dickie – though she won't believe it – that no alcohol has passed my lips since I got to Cromer, nor have I had it injected elsewhere!'[19] This sacrifice cannot, however, have improved his mood. Meanwhile, John was busy convincing himself that the School Directorship was not the solution. 'No more news from the School – I gather in a roundabout way that they want me but don't want to have to ask me! The more I think about it the less I want it. a) It's not my pigeon – diplomacy. b) It will interfere horribly with my work – a peripatetic Director can't do his job and a stationary myself equally can't do it.'[20]

John's despondency increased, and he seemed to be counting the days until they could go home. Hilda was far more settled into parenthood than John, and perhaps differences were starting to appear between them over what each wanted in life. His description of the holiday to his father was, 'we merely vegetate here'.[21] He was beginning to realise that he would never want a settled life. He had thought about it when the Budge Fellowship at Christ's College, Cambridge had come up, but it was unlikely that he was very sorry when someone else got it. The reality of his life was sinking in and, however much he loved Hilda and the children, he could not change what he had become. It seemed that becoming ordinary was the thing that frightened him the most, and even when he was back at home in Cambridge he was dining in Hall or out alone more and more frequently. Even the Athens job meant stable family life, a mundane routine in an office with little variation. He didn't like the social whirl of the diplomatic and expatriate circles. John was quite simply most at home on site or in the mountains, and that meant being a long way from Cambridge. It was a depressing end to the summer.

This despondency and his uncertainty about his future direction were exacerbated by the BSA's announcement that they were to postpone their decision on the Directorship until the autumn. The delay in the BSA's decision was caused by the death, at a similar age to Payne and from a similar cause, of Alan Blakeway. The School was reeling from the deaths of two of their best, brightest and youngest so close together. Then, just before John's departure for Egypt, the BSA came to a decision about the new Director and appointed George

Mackworth Young, a retired civil servant, on a year's contract. The brief victory of the younger generation over the old was over. It appeared that the older man seemed the safer option. The temporary appointment did not ease John's mind, and he began instead to worry that they were just biding time until he had finished in Egypt. 'In any case it is a breathing space. I couldn't have started off really straight away. Mark you it is pure theory that I was considered at all.'[22] The decision left John's mind clearer for Amarna. Dows Dunham, Associate Curator of the Egyptian department of the Museum of Fine Arts in Boston, had worked his magic on the Trustees' Committee and squeezed five hundred dollars out of them: 'Will you please notify Pendlebury,' he wrote to Mary Jonas, 'and tell him that I am personally mighty pleased to have been able to arrange for this contribution. I hope it will be enough to be of real help in the coming season.'[23] Soon after, the Brooklyn Museum also stumped up a thousand dollars. The final season at Amarna was at last provided for.

*

In the hope that the Metropolitan Museum of Art would take over the concession to dig at Amarna, John began the soul-destroying process of calculating the value of whatever household equipment in the North Dig House could be sold off to them. It was the end of a very happy part of John's life. Worrying John most, though, was what would happen to the *ghaffirs* (guards), some of whom had worked for the Society for many years and he tried hard to negotiate a future for them.

As always, cash flow for Amarna was a problem, for no money given for the excavation went directly to the dig funds. Not for the first time, John used his own money as a guarantee until the Society paid him back. John's father was now acting as John's financial manager, as, with John putting a great deal of his own money into digging in Crete, he needed someone to keep an eye on everything in England.

John and Ralph Lavers shared a cabin on the Orient voyage out to the steamy heat of Alexandria. Lavers, however, fell seriously ill, and spent most of the time in bed, emerging only occasionally when they were in port. So John was left largely to his own devices. Had he known that Ralph was also suffering from streptococcal poisoning he might have been more concerned. As it was, he enjoyed the voyage enormously, palpably glad to be returning to the challenges of life on site. 'I managed to get as fit as I've ever been in my life on board. I hold a record which will take a bit of beating of twenty-nine sets of deck tennis in one day.'[24] John went on shore trips to Pompeii and elsewhere with some of his fellow passengers, one of whom was Molly Hammond.

Mrs Molly Hammond was a vivacious and attractive young woman travelling with her three small children. Her husband, Martin, had gone ahead to Cairo, taking over the solicitor's office from John's cousin by marriage, Lionel Hargreaves. She and John got on well together, and he invited her and her husband to come and visit the work at Amarna. Ralph survived, despite being treated for several illnesses before being correctly diagnosed, and was able to join John for dinner with the Hammonds during the few days they could stand the sweltering heat of the city. But he remained weak for some time, increasing the pressure on John when they got to Amarna, for the lack of funds meant that the expedition was already short-staffed.

Unfortunately, the rumour of the Metropolitan's interest in digging at Amarna proved baseless, so John tried to arrange for the house staff to be taken on by the Sudan expedition. After all, the much-loved Hussein abu Bakr of Abydos had been with the Society for thirty years and Abdellatif his brother for twenty years. It was not a question of money but of prestige for the family.

The dig at least did not disappoint, but at times John could barely suppress his anger at the EES's decision to give the site up. 'I think we shall be able', he commented to Mary Jonas, 'thoroughly to save the Society's face and leave a clean field for our successors.'[25] They managed to complete the palace, to the north of which they had found houses that had clearly belonged to the more important palace servants. The houses were reminiscent of a typical workmen's village, on what John described as the 'county council plan'. The rest of the work was largely a case of tying up any loose ends, and it looked like they would finish ahead of the allotted time.

The success of the Cretan dig probably saved John from sinking too deeply into bitterness, for at least he had somewhere challenging to move on to. This showed in his attitude to the work; for whatever he felt about the EES committee, John was far more relaxed on site than he had been for some time, and instead of letters about quarrels with the workmen and the EES, he reverted to his storytelling. 'Did I tell you of the new arrival in Egypt – a corporal in the Worcesters – who found a torpid snake in the desert one day. He had always heard that the thing to do with vipers was to nourish them in the bosom and accordingly put it kindly into his shirt. Naturally it bit him. Well his companions, equally newly arrived, had heard that the thing to do for snake bite was to souse the victim with whisky and not let him go to sleep. Five days later the unfortunate victim was found suffering from DT and lack of sleep having drunk about four bottles of whisky a day and having been marched up and down and pinched and pummelled by his devoted companions.'[26]

They offered hospitality to a large number of visitors that season, making the most of the final season and the charm of the North Dig House. Among them were Molly Hammond and her husband Martin. John went to meet them at the station in Mallawi towards the end of November, and put on a typical Amarna fantasia for them in the evening. They had planned to stay for a few days, but Martin had to leave on business after only two days. Molly stayed on, as other guests were expected after a day or two, and it made sense for her to leave with them instead.

One of John's other guests was Gayer Anderson, a keen collector of Egyptian and Islamic antiquities. On his retirement from the Egyptian Civil Service, he persuaded the Egyptian government to give him two fine but dilapidated and sub-divided houses, one 16th- and one 17th-century, joined by a bridge over an entrance to the Mosque of Ibn Tulun in Cairo. He restored them with interiors and objects salvaged from houses elsewhere in Cairo and the Middle East which were being systematically destroyed. The condition of the government's permission was that on his death the houses were to become a public museum. Gayer Anderson had a deep love for and understanding of Egypt, and though he died before he could long enjoy his creation, he managed to save something of the domestic architecture of old Cairo and to gather into a book the legends that surrounded the two houses and the mosque. John had visited him in Cairo, and would not have missed the fact that the old name of the house was the Bait al-Kritliya, which had been translated by some as the 'House of the Cretan Woman'. After this, his last visit to Amarna, Gayer Anderson wrote to John that he held his visit there, 'next only to his view of the undisturbed tomb of Tut'.[27]

Though the dig was going well, the funds suddenly began to dry up, as promised donations did not materialise. John sent urgent telegrams to the EES for more funds. Mary Jonas tried to explain the situation to John. 'I am sorry the Committee could not see its way to send further cash, but after all the Schweich Fund won't even be granted till the new year, Mrs Hubbard seems silent as the grave, and up to date no promises have come from America. As to the future of the guards or workmen I am hoping that Glanville has been able to suggest something, it is very difficult for the Committee to make decisions, and the Society is not really able to make pensions to native workmen. If they did, what sort of sum would be regarded as of any help? I personally have no idea, and how many of them do you consider it would be policy to recompense?'[28] Finally, Mrs Hopkins Morris sent the necessary £50 to finish the dig and John completed the Central City, which was unique in that no other official quarters of a capital had ever been dug. But what pleased John almost as much was that the Sudan dig agreed to take Hussein Abu Bakr.

In thanking Mrs Hopkins Morris, John could not hide his irritation at the attitudes of the sponsoring museums. 'I'm sorry Museums don't want scraps. It always seems funny that they are willing to buy things in the market for hundreds of pounds – yet if they subscribe to a dig a fiver they expect a Nefertiti head. It may be of interest to know that one of those pieces was valued by a dealer here (not in Paris) at over £50 merely for its Amarna connection. The present part of the city is of course the least profitable. Our successors on private houses will have a fine crop. Anyhow... the Society will need fear no recriminations from any who follow.'[29]

At the end of the season, John wrote to Mary Jonas. 'In spite of all lack of subscriptions I have finished with an effort that's nearly left me dead.' Though he did not mean to take it out on Mary personally, he expressed all the pent-up frustration that working for the Society had involved when he heard that they were still quibbling about a pension for Hussein Abu Bakr. 'As I have said ad nauseam our only real obligation is to Hussein who has been with the Society for 30 years although "We have no legal obligation towards him" is a favourite phrase of the Society's. In any case he is going to the Sudan - unwillingly, but on my personal request since they have had a row there and sacked their *suffragi*. I know I'm silly but having worked with people for years – taken them out of their normal employment and so on, I hate leaving them flat. But others will come to dig here who will no doubt discount the legal obligation side and behave as I have wanted to and as I have been, and am, ashamed not to behave. I hate leaving with a nasty taste in the mouth.'[30]

John's departure from Amarna for the last time was extremely difficult. In a letter to his father, he wrote, 'Please excuse the alcoholic-looking writing which is taking place in the train to Cairo. I've had a very sad departure from quantities of weeping workmen, all of whom waited on the platform, and a fine escort of all the Sudani police who have ever been camp guards with us. And Amarna is over. Well I've done a reasonable bit of work there and had some of the happiest times of my life – so I can't complain.'[31]

John's mood was saved by a happy Christmas spent with Molly and Martin Hammond at their apartment in Sharia Seray el Gezira, on the edge of the Zamalek end of Gezira Island, near the palace built by Ismail Pasha for the Empress Eugenie. They soon managed to lift the gloom that leaving Amarna had cast over him. As John described to his father, 'we had great fun at Christmas with the children here – aged seven, four and one, and I attended my first Christmas service for ten years. We had a very pleasant little dance in the flat after dinner and are hoping to repeat the performance on New Year's Eve... The Hammonds have been very kind in taking me out to see Cairo, which I'd never done properly before.'[32] What Hilda made of such effusive enthusiasm when neither she nor their own children were around is not hard to imagine.

John later confided to Mercy Money-Coutts, when she asked him if he'd ever been involved with anyone else, that he had once fallen for a married woman in Cairo. Mercy met Molly when she and her family came to stay in Crete the following summer. She felt from the knowing looks she often caught on Molly's face that there had been something, some attraction between them.

*

As soon as spring arrived, John and Hilda left the children again and headed out to Greece where they planned to spend the whole season together. But as soon as they got to Crete towards the end of April 1937, Hilda found two lumps on her stomach, and immediately flew back to England. Two consultants had seen her in Crete, and both pronounced that the lumps were benign, but ought to be removed as soon as possible. Both felt it made more sense for her to be seen by her own doctor, Lane Roberts.

John wrote to Herbert to ask him to look after the arrangements. 'Can you kindly foot the bills? I mean for operation and nursing home. Owing to the restrictions in Greece one is not even allowed to write to one's bank (!) without a special permit from the Bank of Greece! All letters bearing the address of a bank are destroyed! A good start for the new regime… This is all frightfully sudden and unexpected so please forgive me if I've missed out any details. It's all very worrying.'[33]

Hilda's operation took place in early May 1937 and was successful, but both she and John decided that it would be best if she did not travel out to Greece again that season. Hilda's family had offered to look after her at Caldy, but John preferred that she go as a paying guest to the Frankforts in Hampstead. 'Healthy – friends – stimulating conversation – and a chance of doing some quiet work in Hans' library.'[34] Sadly for the children, she was not considered fit enough to recuperate at Malvern where the children were again being looked after by Herbert and Dickie.

*

So John stayed in Crete alone. The team would be a small one without Hilda. 'It's tragic she can't be out here.'[35] John and Mercy were joined instead by Marion Pascoe, a student at the British School, and by Manolaki (Manolis Akoumianos), again as dig foreman. Marinatos had also asked John if he would train his new assistant at the museum in excavation methods. John deeply appreciated the 'compliment and kindness' and the respect from Marinatos that the request showed.[36] They took their time reaching Lasithi, exploring the north coast to the east of Milatos, another area that John found had been missed by archaeologists. They stopped for an evening on the yacht at Spina Longa and then, via Pachyammos and Kalamauka, made their way up into the mountains to Tzermiado.

John was thinking ahead to a long-term association with Lasithi and his strategy for the 1937 season reflected this. He wanted to get a broad idea of the nature and dates of sites in the area around the village, so planned to carry out a series of exploratory excavations dotted around the area. They explored two small caves, the Skaphidia to the north of the village and the Grymani, little more than a cleft in the rock near the Trapeza Cave. The Skaphidia Cave proved to have been a Neolithic burial place, 'the first ever to be found on Crete.'[37] They also opened sixteen test pits on and around the Kastellos, a flat-topped hill projecting from the slopes of Psarokorphe to the east of Tzermiado, which dominated a minor route into the Lasithi Plain. Though they did find evidence of buildings on the Kastellos, the top had been so denuded over the centuries that it seemed only worthwhile to carry out selected test pits rather than a full excavation. John had hoped to find a settlement site of the richness of Gournia, but here at least he was disappointed. 'At the moment we're on a quite well preserved building of MMIII date which is producing quantities of pottery of a distinctly local fabric. Luckily the proprietors of the land are very obliging. As a matter of fact we are doing them a good turn by making new fields for them with our dumps and they are only too keen on our not having to fill in again as we are strictly speaking bound to do. Also I think they are rather proud of having antiquities to show on their land.'[38]

The village was extremely proud of its newly-uncovered heritage, very much encouraged by the local schoolmaster, Mr Sphakianakis, who not only took his pupils to see the excavations on a regular basis, but wrote enthusiastically about every find in the local newspaper, Ανατολη [The East]. The schoolmaster had a great influence on the local perception of the archaeology and managed to persuade his fellow villagers that the provenance of finds was of paramount importance. Until then they were continually bringing casual finds to the team thinking they would be interested in buying them. On the other hand, those with objects they had found quite innocently hesitated before coming forward because they were certain John would report them to the police. So fully and proudly did the villagers engage in the excavations that they were considering naming a street in the village 'Pendlebury'. Not only had their finds covered every period except classical and Roman, but there was still a great deal more to dig, particularly high up above the village at a site called Karphi. This outcrop of rock– its name meaning 'nail' – hung off the edge of the mountains north of Lasithi, from which it was separated by another, higher upland plain, the Nesimos Plain. Above this plain were a number of tombs on the slopes leading up to Koprana. As well as the occasional golden eagle, huge eagle vultures soared up on the thermals from the sheer drop below the outcrop of Karphi, circling over the site and often emerging out of the clouds in alarming proximity.

It was a steep two-thousand-foot climb to reach Karphi from Tzermiado. Mercy could not only keep up with John but, to the delight of the workmen, often outstripped him. 'As for the donkey that takes up the spades – shovels – picks – mattocks – baskets etc. I don't know what it thinks.' The Assistant Director of the Candia Museum, a man named Petrou, whom John was to train, found it a terrible strain though. 'He is a nice lad but wants a good kick on the behind to make him turn up in time on the dig. However he will at least have seen an organised dig and if he takes in half of what I've told him he'll have learnt a bit.'[39]

In the saddle between Karphi and Koprana were the ruins of a settlement which had been found by Evans in the 1890s. One area had a large quantity of pottery on the surface. It was right on the edge of the outcrop, with a gateway through the rock leading to a sheer drop. It was here that John opened up his last excavation for the season and found a site totally new to Cretan archaeology. 'Our final find was quite unique: a Sub-Minoan – Protogeometric Temple on a peak about 4500 [feet] up with all sorts of cult figures – dove goddesses etc. which show the continuity of culture up here. There were also a number of tholos tombs or rather of square tombs with a beehive above arranged in a row – a sort of early Iron Age Appian Way.'[40]

Now, with some unique finds local to the immediate area, Sphakianakis had the idea that a small local museum be established to house them. On occasion, though, he got carried away by his enthusiasm and caught John out in the local paper. 'Of course the Schoolmaster has fixed on the one point on which I know I have made a mistake. I was wondering what was the ancient name of our big Geometric-Roman site, which is the 4th biggest in Crete. I was reminded this year that a coin of Akontion had been found nearby. I tentatively suggested this might be the name of the place. This was of course leapt on by the local population. After I left however I remembered – and confirmed – that it was Koite or Akoite of which I was thinking – Akontion being in Boeotia!'[41]

When the dig was over, John went back up to the Limnarkaros Plain to spend the night at the little Byzantine church, before climbing the three main peaks of the Dikte range the following day. On his return, the mules were packed up with the finds and equipment and sent in a long convoy down the precipitous mountainside. John, Mercy and Marion stayed behind, crossing the plain to spent the night at Psychro, on the far side of the Lasithi Plain, with the genial Doctor Kasapis and his German wife. He, like John, had a passion for amusing stories, and now that John was working in Lasithi on a regular basis, the two became firm friends. John and Hilda had first met them nine years earlier on their first trip to eastern Crete, but since then Kasapis had spent some years out of the country because of his royalist sentiments. He and his wife had returned with the restoration of the monarchy. He was a generous man, much loved in Psychro because he refused to charge his many poorer patients.

As soon as they arrived back at Knossos, John was off again to do a new route up Mount Ida with the Squire and Mercy. 'I want to see how quickly Ida can be climbed when one is really fit, and with ordinary luck one should be able to put up a good time now I know the way and do not have to wait for my active but aged local shepherd.'[42] This was John's penultimate possible route up the mountain and one that was impassable for mules: 'Record time to the summit too'.[43]

The quantities of fragments of terracotta figurines from the shrine at Karphi had been taken straight to the Candia Museum, where conservators pieced together one figurine from 489 pieces and another from 300, with fragments of seven more. 'They are quite astonishing, and with crowns of alternating disks and birds, and feet projecting through a sort of window in the skirt they are really unique.'[44] Marinatos was delighted as he had just written an article about such figurines, comparable examples of which had been found at Gazi, west of Candia. 'I thought it would only be a fair return for his help to suggest that he included these as an addendum even before we published them.'[45]

In a letter to his father, John professed to feeling rather homesick: 'I'm beginning to long for the fleshpots of England. A nice bit of fish and some really good meat – some sherry, some claret and some real beer would do me a lot of good.'[46] But he felt desperately in need of a holiday which had no archaeological motive. The School Committee had announced that they wanted George Mackworth Young for another year and John, though still not keen on the job for himself, was disappointed at the news. 'Rather a bad thing I should say. He hasn't been the success I expected. But I expect the Committee are keeping him as a warming pan for Dunbabin whom the Oxford members are determined to have sooner or later.'[47]

John arrived back in England in the first week of August 1937. After some time in Cambridge and London, John and Hilda went up north to walk from Corbridge to Carlisle along Hadrian's Wall. 'We stayed at a very decent pub called "The Angel" at Corbridge. Next day to Chesters (Cilurnum) a very fine fort, then getting out of the car at Shield-on-the-wall we walked along the best part of the wall to Housesteads (Borcovicius), also a good camp and on to the "Twice-Brewed Inn" where we picked up the car and went on to Birdoswald (Camboglanna) and so to Carlisle. I think we saw the best of the wall and every type of camp, milecastle and turret as well as the station at Corbridge and very fine abbey at Lanacost. Next day we got to Buttermere and Derwentwater, where I climbed Maiden Moor and Cat Bells, lunched at Rossthwaite and back to West Kirby by Thirlmere, Windermere, Newby Bridge, Lancaster, dining at Preston.'[48] They picked up the children from Hilda's mother in Caldy, but no sooner had they brought them 'home' to Cambridge than John's mind was off again, with thoughts of a holiday in Kenya with Hilda. Herbert and Dickie had investments there in a coffee and sisal business run by Dickie's brother, Will Webb, at Kia Ora, Ruiru. However, the business was in such a bad state that Herbert had finally to sell Winstanley.

It did not occur to John that it might be an inconvenient time to go out and stay with Will, and he was very embarrassed when Herbert pointed out the possibility. 'I hadn't realized I'm afraid that Will might be embarrassed. He gave such a warm invitation to us both not only when he was last over but also when we very nearly went in 1935 that I'm afraid I'd rather taken it for granted. But there is an absolute certainty and that is that Hilda ought to have a holiday away from everything and as you know we have never had the chance together and also we have, during the last few years, been separated rather a lot.' Herbert doubted that Hilda was up to such a difficult trip, but John was certain that she was as resilient as she had ever been. 'With regards to Kenya being a bit tough, of course you having been there know much better than I can, but from descriptions, both yours and others', it seems not only comparatively luxurious compared with Amarna or Crete but also just the simple sort of thing we both like. Should the journey up through the Sudan be too tiring, there is always the return of either the *Mantola* or the *Malda* to Port Said – whence to Crete.'[49]

Even with John in the same country as the children, Hilda had to take David and Joan to Hunstanton without him as he had to finalise the typescript for the Crete book. It was not until November that Herbert received the triumphant, 'the book is finished!'[50] Before long John had also completed most of his work on the official Amarna publication, *City of Akhenaten III,* and he told Mary Jonas that he would come into the EES office and return all the notebooks, 'now thank God done with forever'.[51]

Christmas 1937 was John's first at home in ten years and the first he had spent with his children. It was a cruel irony that David and Joan both came down with flu, so all their parties and celebrations had to be cancelled.

John and Hilda had planned to go to Kenya at the end of January 1938, but at the last minute Hilda decided not to go, saying that she would prefer to meet John in Cairo on his return journey and go on to Crete with him. As the trip had already been paid for, John decided to go alone. However, it was not ideal as the whole point of the holiday had been for them to spend some time together. John, though, could not help but look forward to the trip and the only thing that appeared to concern him was whether people wore stiff collars with soft evening shirts in Kenya.

By the end of the month John was on his way to Mombasa on the *SS Mantola* of the British India Line. It was, perhaps, John's first real holiday, and included a six-day safari to the Serengeti game reserve in Tanganyika and a tug of war with a lion ('the lion's end of the rope being baited with a leg of game. The lion won!').[52] It culminated in a journey in various land and water craft – including paddle-steamers – to the Murchison Falls, during part of which John shared a cabin with an American surgeon and a box of fifty live chameleons he had collected for the San Diego zoo.

At the Murchison Falls, John parted company with his host, Will Webb, to travel up the White Nile. 'Certainly the whole thing has done me a lot of good. I've been enjoying it thoroughly from beginning to end. It is a wonderful country.'[53] When they reached Kosti at the end of the voyage, he transferred to a train through Khartoum and on to Wadi Halfa.

As soon as John reached Cairo, he headed straight out to the district of Maadi where Molly and Martin Hammond now lived. He returned to central Cairo that afternoon to meet Hilda. Keen to avoid the more tedious invitations in Cairo, John and Hilda escaped to the famously exotic Mena House Hotel near the Pyramids at Giza. 'It was the one thing apart from climbing the Great Pyramid I hadn't done.' Next day he remedied that too. 'Well worth it. A magnificent view.'[54] It was not quite the holiday together that Hilda or John might have hoped for, but it was all they had time for before moving on to Crete.

*

They reached the island at the beginning of April 1938, exchanging the increasingly suffocating heat of Egypt for the freshness of early spring in Crete.

John and Hilda covered most of eastern Crete before joining Mercy Money-Coutts to climb up to Lasithi from the south-west, 'via Phrati – Embaros – Erganos and Limnarkaros – a new way into the plain which must have been used quite a bit in antiquity.' The weather was atrocious and it was in driving rain that the season began on May 10th 1938. John had rented a new dig house at Tzermiado, 'very palatial, four good rooms, kitchen, outside lavatory, two good terraces on which to work'.[55] The house was, indeed, a fine one, with a view out across the whole Lasithi Plain. However, as a direct result of John's association with this house, which in the years since has stood empty, the

Germans were to use it for the brutal interrogation of many of those villagers who were now working with John.

There was a grand welcome back for them on their first evening in Tzermiado, where they were greeted by five village elders 'suitably liquored up for the occasion'. The elders spoke earnestly on how the excavation had benefited the district. 'It made one realise', John commented to his father, 'what the reception of a Proxeny or a Presbeia must have been like in classical times.'[56]

Two new recruits had joined the excavation. Vincent Desborough was a student of the British School, while Frank Thompson had just left Winchester, and was filling in the summer before going up to Oxford. 'The two new members of the dig are quite acquisitions. Desborough is rather of the elderly Oxford type (aged twenty-five I should say). He makes me feel very young. He is very good at his job. Thompson – an ex-College man – goes up to New College in the Autumn and combines puppyish lunacy with a good deal of common sense. His father is the writer on India. He talks exactly like Seton Lloyd in intonation and phraseology.'[57] Frank Thompson was a poet who shared John's love of silly verse. Marion Pascoe was back on the team, and Ralph Lavers was joining them briefly to draw up a plan of the site. It was a relief for him to get away from Syria, where he had been working with Sir Leonard Woolley on the Hittite site of Carchemish. It was not Woolley who had been the problem, but his wife, as John described to his father. 'He is not going back to Syria and frankly - hearing his fantastic stories about Lady W – (who must be a complete bitch) – I'm not surprised. Few people last even a season. Woolley has this damnable Minoan obsession which is ullage. It is a pity as he is clearly the best excavator living.'[58] With Hilda back on the team too, it was a much more sizeable team than in 1937.

However, the clouds hanging over Karphi were not the only ones to darken the mood of the team. The news from Europe was not good and the possibility of war was increasingly becoming a probability. Hitler's Third Reich was gaining in strength and territorial greed, and though the British Prime Minister urged peace and appeasement, everyone, wherever they were and whatever work they did, had half their attention on the worst that might happen. John was no exception. 'With the prospect of a good many pleasant seasons here it would annoy me to have to begin trailing a pike in the Low Countries.' Nevertheless, by the end of the summer he would be drawing on all his contacts to do just that. The young Frank Thompson would do likewise, and though their paths would not cross again, they were to follow very similar roads with the same end.[59]

It was far too wet to start high up on Karphi, which could vanish in the clouds within seconds, even when the plains below were clear and dry, so John decided to start digging lower down the mountain, where they excavated an Archaic house at Kolonna. But as soon as the weather improved, John moved the excavation up to Karphi proper, and was soon writing excitedly to his father about the results. 'We are going to get a sort of robber baron's Amarna – one of the first connected town plans ever found – or rather dug – in Greece. Luckily most of the ground is uncultivated, and by throwing the earth carefully over rocky parts we can make fields which amply compensate the owners for the small loss of pasture occasioned by leaving the excavated houses uncovered. It is a good dig for an architecturally-minded person – not only a town plan but also built tombs of a unique type and so far all different.'[60]

The site continued to yield remarkable buildings, including 'fine large houses', a 'probable barracks' and a 'big five- or six-roomed house with walls standing eight foot high'. Not only did it have a cemetery, 'eight large built tombs' of which they had already excavated, but also what John thought could be a 'palace'. What mattered most was that they could retrieve the whole town plan. Though finds were rare, pottery survived in profusion – 'very nice pottery which is the ideal stuff for the period we are christening Intermediate, i.e. that usually know as Sub-Minoan – Protogeometric – the real Dark Ages.'[61] John could not help referring back to Amarna, for they had in common – though for different reasons – a scarcity of finds. 'The site having been deserted – not destroyed – they naturally took all their valuables with them. If only they hadn't been so tough and had been beaten up by the Dorians we should probably have got some first class finds.'[62] Herbert told John that he referred too liberally back to Amarna, which could have no relation to such a site as Karphi. John replied vehemently. 'No – I'm not being obsessed by Amarna – but as I say it is nice to find a similar site where one can concentrate on a cross section in the history of a people without being concerned with a complexity of periods.'[63]

*

John's book, *The Archaeology of Crete*, was delayed until at least the autumn, but John already had two new projects in mind. The first was in the same vein as *The Archaeology of Crete*, but this time concentrating on the Cyclades, 'which I hope to visit in the course of the next few years. Nobody seems to have tried to pull them together either and certainly their prehistoric stuff is in a good mess.'[64] He got as far as an outline for this book, but never had the chance to write it.

The second project was to produce a book about the Crete that John himself had grown to know, whether talking with old soldiers in remote village wine shops or walking with shepherds, learning their stories and what they called each rise and fall of their mountain ranges. John was particularly captivated by Lasithi, and he planned a special section or even volume on it alone, covering not just the archaeology, but the regional dialect and folklore. For this last section he wanted to bring in Professor Richard Dawkins. Dawkins had carried out studies of the dialects of Greek Asia Minor before the Great War and the exchange of populations. It was an extraordinary work not just from a linguistic point of view. He recorded the traditions of storytelling from one village to another, at a time when few could read or write. What was so valuable about his work was that he recorded the differences in the words each village used to tell the same stories.

John was very keen to carry out the same sort of study in Crete. After discussing the possibility with Dawkins, he planned to collect 'snatches of songs about as many villages in Crete as I can. They will be a pleasant addition to my and Dawkin's volume on Modern Crete.' The way of life that Dawkins had recorded in all its richness had already gone, and though Crete appeared under no immediate threat, John saw that there was a risk that the richness of the island's language was in danger as influences from outside grew. He also wanted to include a section on the geology and botany, and got as far as sending two passing botanists up Mount Dikte with a guide and 'orders to bring back all modern flower names. They are going to write it up and let me have an article to combine with my general history of the Diktaian area.'[65] But as with the first project, war would intervene.

*

Once the dig was running smoothly, John and Hilda left for a few days to go and meet Molly and Martin Hammond and their three children in Candia. The Hammonds had rented the Seager house for four months from the end of May, and as there is no mention of Hilda meeting the Hammonds in Cairo, this was probably her first opportunity to meet the family with whom John had spent so much time. They found on arrival that Martin Hammond had been delayed in Cairo for a while, so it was just Molly and the children who turned up. John and Hilda took them all back to Knossos for a night and on to Seager's house the next day. Once Molly and the children were settled in, Hilda returned to Knossos, while John, planning to walk back to Tzermiado early the next morning, stayed with them at Pachyammos.

In John's absence the work had gone well, revealing one of the best finds they had had to date. Found in a deposit dating to the 5th century BC, the object depicted a dolphin with a man on its back carrying a child. 'The child rules out Arion', John appealed to his father. 'Can you think of or find any classical legend of a man and infant being carried by a dolphin?'[66] Herbert did his best and asked around. But when he replied that a friend suggested it must be Arion, John told his father to tell the friend, 'that when I see a cithara with a navel and testicles I'll believe my find represents Arion. Till then not!'[67] Some of the pottery, too, was wonderful, including objects that were familiar from Minoan sites, such as bull's head rhytons and anthropomorphic figures.

With such new material, John was suddenly faced with the problem of how to describe what he was finding within the terminology that already existed. 'Both Sub-Minoan and Proto-Geometric are revolting terms. Here at Karphi, while we have two or three typically Proto-Geometric sherds and a number of PG shapes of vases, the whole feeling is Minoan. Therefore I am adopting the term Intermediate for the Period and keeping Sub-Minoan and Protogeometric as descriptive of Style. As I see it 1) c.1400 sack of Knossos and all Cretan cities. But purely political – no colonisation or real domination. 2) c.1230 Achaian Empire. Crete parcelled out to Achaian baron (Idomeneus). Domination of island by small number of housecarles. 3) c.1100-1050 Enter Dorians. Independent Minoans under Minoanised Achaian rulers take to the hills – best example is Karphi. 4) c.900 Geometric Period begins and Crete enters the Hellenic world.'[68]

In the middle of June, John wrote to his father that life on the dig was 'enlivened' when Molly Hammond came up to stay with the team for four or five days, leaving her children with their German governess, Else Doorn, at Pachyammos. Else had been with the Hammond family for two years in Cairo but, nonetheless, they were aware that, as a German woman, she had obligations to the fatherland. 'While in Cairo', Martin Hammond recalled later, 'she was always very fussed if, for any reason, it was inconvenient for her to have her usual half-day off. She explained that if she did not go at least once a week to the German Club, she got into trouble. She told us of the activities of this Club, how all German women and men met to exchange views. Again while in Crete she would come to ask if she might have a few hours off if there was a German boat anchored in the harbour – she simply must go to see them on board, which, of course, we allowed her to do. I feel that these girls, perhaps unconsciously, were all part of a system by which bits of information were picked up and passed on to higher authority to be pieced together. Some of them possibly knew what they were doing and there must have been one or two members of the Club or the ship who were trained in gleaning information, but Else was, I think, an unconscious medium. She caused a little trouble in Crete.'[69] This did not stop the Cretan police from summoning Else and Hammond to Ierapetra to explain to a magistrate why it was that Else was still on the island while there were so many Cretan girls who could look after the children equally well.

Mercy, seeing Molly on the dig with John, was convinced that there was something between them from the way they seemed utterly at home in each other's company and the comfortable familiarity with which Molly looked at John.[70] It could have been that Mercy was highly sensitive, as she herself was already falling in love with him. A photograph taken by John of Molly, Martin and Hilda less than a month later shows Molly looking relaxed and sexy, even when wind-blown on the top of a mountain. There is no evidence that John and Molly were having, or had ever had, an affair, but there is no mistaking, in the same photograph, Hilda's look of discomfort.[71] However, it is clear from the affection with which Martin Hammond writes of John in his unpublished memoirs that he was under no such impression.

By the second week in July, the team at Tzermiado had packed up the dig. They were given a grand send off, with a civic banquet at which John made a long speech. They left the following afternoon, accompanied by the mayor and town council as far as the next village. Hilda and John then made their way up to the Katharos Plain, staying near a hut owned by an old friend. After a night on the high upland plain, they descended the Diktaian massif to Pachyammos, where they were welcomed by the Hammonds. 'Two days later', John wrote, 'we dragged them loudly protesting up the highest mountain in sight – Aphendis Kavousi - and on to Stravodoxari, Oreino and Skinokapsala. Four new sites including two of the date we are digging and a fine Minoan fort called "The Dragon's Gate".'[72]

John and Hilda returned to England at the end of July, and organised a family holiday with the children. But it wasn't long before they packed the children off again to stay at Malvern. By September 1938, the situation in Europe was, as John observed to Herbert, looking 'pretty black'. Hitler was demanding the Sudetenland from Czechoslovakia, and the Prime Minister, Neville Chamberlain, had flown over to Germany to try and gain an assurance that no other territorial seizures would be made. 'I suppose these blasted Germans are working up for another beating. They ought to be abated as a nuisance. As long as we don't throw Tanganyika to the wolves as a sop.'[73] John checked that his health certificate was safe and sound, just in case he could get into one of the services. He had already offered his services to Naval Intelligence.

At the end of the month, Chamberlain came back from his meeting with Hitler at Berchtesgaden, waving his famous piece of paper, allaying public fears for a while. John was happy to keep the children in Cambridge for the time being, knowing they could be moved to Hilda's family in the north if necessary. He wrote to Herbert: 'If it should still come to a war I should naturally hope for a job in the Near East, but I think Mussolini is obviously ratting hard which means I take it that the war would be pretty well confined to Europe. No local news here. Everyone digging fine trenches and provided with gas masks.'[74]

Even under the shadow of impending war, John managed to find humour in the situation. He passed one Air Raid Protection (ARP) story to his father. 'A large London firm was issuing gas masks to its employees but first gave them a questionnaire asking if they suffered from certain specified diseases which would make it impossible to wear a mask. To their surprise all the girls said they suffered from Claustrophobia. On enquiring of the lady who looked after the girls they were advised to read the definition of Claustrophobia in the English Dictionary in the Canteen. This read: Claustrophobia. Fear of Confinement!'[75]

While he waited for the proofs of *The Archaeology of Crete* from Methuen, John had an unaccustomed lull in his workload, which he filled by walking ten to twelve miles every afternoon and making plans. He had decided to build a spring on the north side of Karphi, on the path descending the Lasithi mountains. It was to be his gift to the villagers of Tzermiado, who had welcomed them with so much affection. 'Donald Robertson – Professor of Greek – has written me a very nice little poem for our spring near the dig.

Ω ξειν', ευ μεν πινε, χαριν δ'εχε τοισι το πιστρον
δειμασιν; χημιν ην στομαθ' αναλεα.
Ενθυμιον των Αγγλικων Αρχαιολογων.'[76]

John's translation of the poem read:
'Stranger drink well, and thank as you pass by
The fountain's builders. Our mouths too were dry.'[77]

The translation of the last line is ironically ambiguous, meaning both a 'reminder of the English archaeologists', which is what was probably intended, or 'memorial to the English archaeologists', which is, in fact, what it turned out to be.

John wanted to call the spring 'Vitsilovrysi'. *Vitsila* was the local name for the Eagle Vultures – 'or I believe ornithologically an Egyptian Vulture' – that regularly soared up and around the site. 'The name has a faintly Italian ring to me', John wrote to Herbert. 'I can't find any ancient Greek word it's connected with... I have got Eric Gill to design it for a most moderate fee. In spite of being the best letterer in the world it seemed to appeal to him that no one would probably ever go and see it!'[78]

As Christmas approached there was snowfall a foot deep. It was only John's second Christmas with the children and again illness dominated when David succumbed to a mild case of jaundice. If David's illnesses were psychosomatic in order to gain the attention of his father then few would have blamed him. Even John felt the coincidence, but whether it was his son he was feeling for is ambiguous. 'It would be bad luck if two Christmases running – and those the only two I've been at home – he was in bed.'[79] Thankfully, David recovered fully, and with a stream of friends coming and going, it was the best Christmas they were to have.

The new year of 1939 brought the welcome release of the final Amarna publication to the Oxford University Press ('a great load off my chest'), as well as the long-awaited publication of *The Archaeology of Crete*. Even at the proof stage, those who read it were effusive. 'It is evident to anybody', enthused Forsdyke of the British Museum, 'that this is an extremely important book – full, practical and first hand. And excellently produced. It seems to me to be quite different from any archaeological work that exists: a happy and proper conjunction of the old and the new style of exploration and research.'[80]

Arthur Cook, John's former tutor at Cambridge, who had initiated the series to which John's new book belonged, was very pleased. 'Sound, straightforward work, strictly scientific and yet interesting throughout, with few (perhaps too few) excursions into the realm of hypothesis, and a laudable absence of unnecessary capitals! Oxford must sit up and take notice.'[81] If Hugh Last, of Brasenose College, Oxford, was anything to go by, Oxford did. Last, who was now on the Committee for the Oxford University Craven Fund, which was contributing to John's Lasithi work, was equally effusive. 'To me at least it seems just the right sort of book, where learning is alive.'[82]

John sent a copy to all those who had been influential and encouraging in the early days, including Monty Rendall, his headmaster at Winchester, who still followed John's work, and had been to stay with him in Crete. 'I am delighted that you have done a work which, I suppose, no one else could do: for no one else has visited about seven hundred sites and spent hours and days with the peasants of Crete. It is truly a magnum opus.'[83]

It is clear, though, that many thought John could have achieved some academic post by this stage in his career, and his old headmaster was no exception. How many people he had told of his reluctance to become involved in the academic system is not known, but many thought he deserved better. 'I hope', Rendall continued, 'the book will bring you a full measure of the recognition which your work deserves and carry you to some high and important post. A young OW [Old Wykehamist] and great friend of mine John Ward Perkins has just been appointed Professor of Archaeology in Malta. Cyprus wants a wholetime English Director, though Dikaios, working under Megaw, is doing great things.'[84] Few realised that it was John's own choice not to have taken the academic path, as others of his generation – and younger – had. But John's book proved that the way he had chosen to approach archaeology had worked.

Professor Dawkins, who had himself excavated in Lasithi many years earlier, wrote to John: 'I am pretty sure no one could have written it but you, and I admire very much the closeness of the texture and the abundance of material; and the arrangement, everything seems to find a place. In particular I like the clearness of what you have to say about the periods and how far they are real time divisions and how far they are local or even just stylistic. There is some good stuff too on that most difficult question of LMIII. In fact your book is just what was wanted and I congratulate you on having produced it; the amount of work must have been enormous. The lists of sites with references is a good idea. Altogether my warm congratulations.'[85]

John was receiving praise from all quarters, and it was hugely satisfying for him to have pleased the grand old men of archaeology at the same time as producing a work that was so innovative. Evans' letter would particularly have pleased him. 'I do thank you very much for your very useful work and fruit of so much travel in the island as well as your own digging. I have only had time just to look through it but I see how much useful material you have packed into it and I am glad to find you so much in agreement. Thanks too for your kind references to myself. It is satisfactory to feel that the Minoan classification as a whole has so far stood the test of continuous discovery. Åberg's attempt to upset as you have pointed out is wholly unwarranted by our stratification and indeed is a model of wrong-headedness! For a general knowledge of Cretan archaeology your book will be most serviceable and your personal knowledge of Cretan geography serves you everywhere in good stead.'[86]

By March, John was back in Athens and headed off directly to Kimolos and Syra to gather information for his next book on the Cyclades. On his return, he found a curious stranger in his bed. Some of the students, led by Frank Stubbings, had taken the bust of Homer from the Finlay Library at the School and put it on John's pillow, while the extremely tall Oswald Dilke hid under the bedclothes with his feet sticking out well over the end of the bed.

John gave a lecture on his Lasithi discoveries at the Open Meeting of the British School in Athens, attended by King George II of Greece and his family, who talked afterwards to John. The event was a great success. 'I met a lot of old friends at the lecture, which being the first for three years was very full indeed. Everyone seemed interested. The Squire came over from Knossos and gave a very short, chatty and garbled account of the new Tholos.'[87] Within two years, John was to meet the King again - in very different circumstances - when the monarch and his government went into exile with the advance of the German army on Athens.

John seemed to be cramming in every opportunity for travel that he could, perhaps sensing that the chance would soon be gone. As soon as the meeting was over he went off to explore the Cycladic islands of Naxos and Paros, 'finding a lot of new sites, new words and good wines. A lot of the inhabitants are Cretan in origin. Got back yesterday morning at five and saw the midnight service outside the Cathedral. I hadn't seen it since 1928.'[88]

After Easter John was about to leave for Crete when news arrived that the American archaeologist Carl Blegen had just discovered a Mycenaean palace at Pylos, 'with a lot of inscribed tablets'. John headed off immediately, spending a night on the way at the Belle Hélène at Mycenae for the first time in nine years, and visiting the grave of his friend, Humfry Payne. 'Blegen has got a Palace apparently of the Homeric period – really Nestor's! – and 185 clay tablets inscribed in a form of the Minoan script – though it seems to me probably not in the Minoan language, since the combinations of signs aren't the same as in our Knossian ones.' When a hundred more tablets were found soon after, John commented, 'Very literary old bird Nestor.'[89]

Political unrest was making itself felt, even among old friends. 'The unfortunate Iliffe has been badly shot in Jerusalem. What a world.'[90] It was just the beginning.

When John arrived at the Taverna in Crete, the place was quiet and Mercy was the only other member of the School staying. 'I have already got through a lot of work in the Museum', John wrote home, 'and, *Marte volente,* hope to do a trip or two and then get up to Lasithi in a month's time. But I don't like the look of things. However, I am where I shall be most useful.'[91]

April 1939 appeared to bring the growing international unease rather closer to Greece, with the Italian invasion of Albania. In spite of President Roosevelt asking for the assurance that Germany would invade no more European countries, Hitler continued to demand Danzig from Poland. John had spoken with the Legation when he was in Athens, and they had advised him to go to Crete as planned. 'I propose to listen in to Master Hitler in Candia. Owing to the censorship I do not say more.'[92] The following day Hitler denounced the non-aggression pact that he had signed with Poland in 1934, and again demanded the 'return' of Danzig.

John was clearly of a mind that war was coming, it was only a matter of when, and he wrote to his father about settling his affairs. 'In case of trouble I purposely leave all arrangements with you at home. Is there any way of extending a Power of Attorney indefinitely? If so let me know and I will have an affidavit signed before the Consul. I'm not panicking but I do want everything absolutely straight.'[93]

To distract their minds, John, Mercy and the Squire went on a trip to the extreme north-west of the island. They found a good many sites on the way to Chania, where they picked up a Consular Agent from the Swedish embassy by the name of Naxakes, before continuing to Kastelli Kissamou, where they saw a site that John had discovered and which had since been excavated. Within two years, this whole area would be in the thick of the battle against swarms of German paratroopers descending on the island.

They took a boat round the north-west prong of Crete to Gramvousa, where a magnificent Venetian fortress on an island was a reminder of an earlier invasion in Crete. This fortress had withstood the Ottoman invasion for more than twenty years. John was well remembered at Phalasarna, and was given a riotous reception, although it was four years since he had last been there with Hilda. 'It is a fine site with its slipways sixteen feet out of the water owing to the 525AD earthquake.' Taking many photographs, they returned via Platanos Mesogeion, Polyrrhenia and Rhokka, 'where a slightly tight policeman took us for spies and on my suggestion that he rang up the King or the consul to vouch for me said it would cost 25 [drachmas] and it was cheaper in the long run to let me take what photos I wanted!'[94]

When they arrived back at Tzermiado, they discovered that John's old friend George Markogiannakis, father of one of the house staff at the Villa Ariadne, and the man credited with discovering the Diktaean Cave, had died. At least he would not have to witness the occupation of his beloved plain.

The carving work on the fountain at Vitsilovrysi was well in hand. 'Our memorial plaque has been carved with the inscription I sent you. Very nice. All the letters well done individually but with rather a nice irregularity in the alignment. I am taking up our old mason to put it in place and on the most inconspicuous part of the fountain I shall have carved the names of Robertson, Gill, myself, the carver and the mason.'[95]

Though the situation had temporarily quietened down, the presence of Italian troops in Albania made the Balkan countries very ill at ease – particularly Greece. John felt, 'The worst feature to my mind is that one is beginning to wish to God it would come soon and not hang over our heads.'[96]

Again, the weather was too bad to start at Karphi, for while it rained down on the plain, Karphi was within the clouds and, archaeological exigencies aside, zero visibility was not advisable on a site that sat on a rock projecting over a sheer drop of several thousand feet. So excavation started on some of the tholos tombs on the southern slopes of Koprana. They also began to build the trough for the spring and fountain, only to find that there were traces of ancient walling on either side of it. The villagers did not have a good water supply and were hoping that once the water was collected in a tank of some sort, they could pipe some of it down to the village.

Mercy and Marion were back, joined for a short while by another of the School students, Vronwy Fisher, 'a Cambridge hockey blue'. The work was initially slow because of the unexpected depth of the soil covering the site. 'I think I have got reasonable evidence now that it was under Achaean leadership that the Minoans fled here. We have also got what is the first inscription of the period – at least the scratches on a stone spool are very reminiscent of Minoan writing.'[97]

John began to build a hut at the saddle between Karphi and the rest of Koprana, where they could lock up stores and equipment and shelter in bad weather. John was determined to build it in the way traditional to the area, though the builders were 'two gigantic purple masons straight out of Chaucer. I have had wished onto me two Albanian wife murderers who escaped when Zog opened the gaols. One can speak practically no Greek but got the shock of his life when I repeated to him the first Sura of the Koran. Also a sheep stealer from Ida who is a bit lame and wasn't quick enough on his feet to avoid arrest.'[98]

Meanwhile, John wrote an article on the history of Lasithi for the festschrift of Sir John 'Johnny' Myres. 'I was going to write… on the ebb and flow of Minoan population but have abandoned the idea and have written rather a jovial article on the history of Lasithi – one which can't properly be put into a dig report but which I think is eminently suitable for a volume like this, particularly when it is for someone like him – "Take care of the theories and let the facts take care of themselves!"'[99] The article pulls together the results of all John's walks, his excavations and research, into a short history of the Dikte Mountains. 'The district of Lasithi comprises the range of mountains known in ancient times as Dikte. The plain itself lies nearly three thousand feet above sea level. Although the surrounding mountains seldom rise less than a thousand feet above the plain it is accessible from all directions by tracks which are passable for pack animals even in the worst weather. Thus, it is not surprising that throughout its history Lasithi should have been enough of a self-contained unit to have developed very strong local peculiarities and characteristics yet at the same time not to have been impervious to outside influences which reached it from every direction. This is especially true of the Minoan period when it lay in the very centre of the then populated part of Crete.'[100]

John demonstrated in the article the ease with which he could convert the results of excavation into a readable story. His grasp of Cretan archaeology went far beyond the purely Minoan. Having recently written *The Archaeology of Crete*, he had the history, archaeology and topography of the island imprinted deeply on his mind. Every mountain, every route he tried, every new site he visited or found, contributed to a picture of the past. His ability to turn it all into an appealing story was what made him stand out. He found echoes of the ancient Cretans in the people he met and knew. John loved the spirit of the old men in the tavernas talking of seizing their weapons in times of trouble in the low-lying coastal lands and heading off into the mountains to the high pastures to fight from their mountain strongholds. Most recently, in 1935 and before then against the Turks, all within living memory, they had done just that. In Karphi, John could see the Lasithiotes of the past doing much the same. 'Karphi in Lasithi is not the only site of this type. It may be higher, 4000 feet above sea level, but Vrokastro, Kavousi, Kourtais of excavated sites, are as high, comparatively above the surrounding country, and of unexcavated ones Kandilioro near Vianos, Kastri near Stavrokhori and Ellenika near Oreino are almost higher.'[101]

John saw represented at Karphi the collapse of the Bronze Age civilisations in the Aegean to a race known as the Dorians, who used iron rather than bronze. Though it was the site most extensively excavated to date, it was also the nearest inhabited mountain fastness to Knossos. They had found elements, such as the shrine, which were typically Minoan in tradition, and yet the architecture of the town, particularly the largest building, which John called the Great House, was of Achaean form and construction. 'May it have been the capital of the old regime? Did some grandson of Idomeneus fly hither? Did he still call himself the Minos of Crete? And did he bring with him the mixture of Achaean and Minoan culture we find on the site?'[102]

John suggested that the Achaeans had come to Crete in around 1250 BC. Although they had taken over the island, they had adopted many of the Minoan styles as their own. 'Then comes the Dorian invasion. Achaeans and Minoans together fly to the hills and found a new settlement. Perhaps the very strong Achaean influence indicates some influx of refugees from elsewhere as well. The Achaean has the chance to build the type of house he has always wanted to build. He does so, except for the roof. He cannot find the joiners or masons to build him a gable.' John added as a note, 'I have just built a house on Karphi and I know.'[103]

*

When John's 'house' was completed, he held a topping-out ceremony. 'To stamp down the *lepida* or waterproof earth for the roof I had a dance at mid-day on the roof. Very alarming for those below but productive of some very good photographs.'[104] John's photographs of the party are – intentionally or otherwise – a curious throw back to the Bronze Age, the men dancing round the musicians, their joined hands raised high above their heads as depicted in so many terracotta models across the eastern Mediterranean. The backdrop was stunning, the mountains giving way to a distant glimpse of the Lasithi Plain.

The spring of Vitsilovrysi too was nearing completion. 'The masons wanted to do an inscription for themselves – so with great care we wrote out – carefully spaced:

Δ. ΡΟΜΠΕΡΤΣΟΝ ΜΕ ΣΥΝΕΓΡΑΨΕ
Ε. ΓΚΙΛΛ ΜΕ ΕΣΧΕΔΙΑΣΕ
Ν. ΑΠΟΣΤΟΛΑΚΗΣ ΚΑΙ Μ. ΚΑΡΥΩΤΑΚΗΣ
ΜΕ ΕΚΤΙΣΑΝ
ΙΟΥΝΙΟΣ 1939

This translates as: 'D. Robertson wrote me/ E. Gill designed me/ N. Apostolakis and M. Karyotakis/ built me/ June 1939'. It is interesting to note that John did not credit himself for conceiving the idea. 'The first effort of the masons was sheer nonsense – neither words nor letters bearing any relation to fact. The second at least made sense, though it rather implied that Robertson was the composer of Gill. The third which we had to accept is in what I should call the 'Fringed style' and dates approximately to 1100 BC.'[105]

The last visitor of the season was the head of the Cyprus Museum, Porphyrios Dikaios, who was to contribute so much to the knowledge of Bronze Age Cyprus. 'Unfortunately he is liable to indigestion and found a twelve- hour day a bit long – also the 1200-foot climb was beyond him and meant a mule for him. However – he enjoyed himself and – for the first time since LMII, Cypro-Minoan relations have been re-established – to the profit of Cyprus and Crete.'[106]

On June 24th 1939, John threw a *glendi* for the village. It was St John the Baptist's day and therefore John's 'name day'. 'It was the best we have had up to date. I really felt the village father! – pretty near 1000 people and dancing from 9–3! Total cost of making the whole village tight £7!' The next day they were honoured guests at the last day of term at the school, 'with lots of recitations and prizes. I'm giving one in the future for the best essay on the history of Crete and particularly Lasithi.'[107]

John had grown to love the villagers of Tzermiado as much as they had him. It was a very happy time after the disappointment of leaving Amarna. Here at Tzermiado everything worked. The team was a happy one, the work fascinating and revolutionary, the landscape mountainous and the support, interest and enthusiasm of the villagers sincere. It was a charmed season, heightened, perhaps, by the suspicion that it would be the last. Mercy and John had begun to spend more and more time with each other, always going on walks together, working together. It was perhaps inevitable that they would succumb to the atmosphere of the place. Even today, whenever John is mentioned in the village, so too is Mercy. Hilda was seen as a bit of a battle-axe, whereas the η Μονιχουτση, Mercy Money-Coutts, is still talked of with great love and affection. Nobody who saw John and Mercy at that time doubted that there was something between them. Manolaki, Marion and the villagers, all felt it, but did not judge, did not question. Marion, who shared a room with Mercy that season, recalled that Mercy never once slept in their room. Mercy put it all down to the magic of Crete working on them a little too well and felt that it would be of no interest to anybody but them.[108] What actually went on, how much John did succumb to Mercy, who loved him so much, and what John actually felt for Mercy – the answers to all these questions have died with them. Mercy's love for John, though, was enough to bind her to Crete long after John died. Her Cretan husband and children ensured that she, too, became enmeshed in the history of the island.

The site of Karphi had been a magnificent one, and its situation ensured that the final photographs of it would be stunning. John's last piece of work was to connect that season's excavated area with that of the previous season. It was not a simple matter by any means. 'We are in the throes of expropriating land – which, though small in extent, seems to belong to about forty different proprietors. These refuse to grant a power of attorney to one of their number – though they are all the same family – on the ground that he would probably sell their houses and their wives, their fields and their wells, their gardens and their sheep.'[109]

Given the success and good atmosphere of the dig, the full impact of the last but abiding incident was all the more bitter. John arrived one morning by the newly-finished fountain to find 'our marble plaque chipped and the stone with which it was done lying beside. I was nearly sick on the spot. I sent for the Mayor, the schoolmasters and the police. Except for one of the schoolmasters the general attitude seemed to be that now they'd got the fountain out of one it didn't really matter... As a result I sent the whole village to Coventry – except for necessary routine – and refused all hospitality. This frightened them out of their wits and into a sense of guilt – but no effective steps were taken to find the culprit. The most likely theory is that the large and savage family of Spanakes had a grudge against one of the masons and were infuriated that his name should appear on one of the corner stones – as is usually done. They got someone to go and damage this. He probably made a mistake as to which plaque was meant and damaged the wrong one. What a people – they can't even wreck properly! However all Crete seems to have heard of it – not from me – and Tzermiado is in for a bad time.'[110]

John, as usual, was writing in the heat of the moment. He felt so hurt because he genuinely cared deeply for the village. Whatever he said, he always felt closer to the people of Tzermiado – and they to him – than anywhere else in Crete, even Knossos. And when he returned in very different circumstances just a year later, the whole incident had been forgotten and their mutual affection and respect was all that survived.

*

When John returned to England, he and Hilda took the children on holiday to the Isle of Wight. John wrote to Herbert from there, preparing for the worst. 'The position is really as follows: Should I not get an immediate job I should stay in Cambridge where I could do temporary work and be in touch. We have offered to take in evacuated infants and Hilda, now that we have a reliable maid who has promised to stay whatever happens, has undertaken to be available for part-time Red Cross. I am taking it that the percentage of safety is so nearly the same at Malvern and Cambridge as not to enter into the question. So at least people seem to think. We shall stay here as proposed. If the crisis develops in the next few days, travelling for the first day or two will be clearly impossible. On the whole I think it is very nice of the Germans to let everyone have their holiday first this time!'[111]

16

3 September 1939–6 June 1940

'I REMEMBER HIM coming out of a pub in the morning', John's son, David, remembered years later. 'We were on our way back to Cambridge from the Isle of Wight and had stopped for lunch and he told my mother, sister and myself that the war had started. That evening the sirens went and not knowing what to expect, the whole family put on gas masks and went into a reinforced room in our house. I can remember that he and I rolled a tennis ball across the room for what seemed like hours.'[1]

By the time Neville Chamberlain, sounding tired and beaten, had come on the air that day, September 3rd 1939, to announce that Britain was at war with Germany, emergency measures had already been put into practice throughout the country. Through the BBC Home Service, Pathé News at the cinemas and the newspapers, every family had been told how to protect itself against bombs and gas attacks. More than any other threats in the war ahead, the images of the aftermath of enemy air attacks had been graphically brought home to the British public.

Families were advised to reinforce a room in their house as a makeshift bomb shelter, at least until more public shelters could be built. Window-panes had to be crossed with sticky tape to minimise the danger from shattered glass should a bomb explode nearby, and every window and door had to be draped in thick blackout material to prevent light escaping which could be seen by enemy bombers on night-time raids. For the same reason, all street lighting was extinguished and no cigarettes were to be lit up out of doors after dark, as the light from a single match could be seen up to a mile away.

The following morning John and Hilda emerged with the children from their shelter, having missed the all-clear signal and spent the whole night in there. No sooner had John crawled into a hot bath than the drone of the air raid sirens began again. 'No sound of bombs or firing – but quantities of planes – all as far as I could see ours.'[2]

Long before, when Chamberlain was meeting Hitler in Berchtesgaden in September 1938, John had approached Naval Intelligence Department (NID) to tell them of his knowledge of Greece, Crete and the Aegean as a whole and to offer his services. John knew that his old Pembroke tutor Jock Lawson's Greek language and experience of travelling and researching in Greece had been called

(Above) John Pendlebury on top of Aphendis with local Lasithiots, looking out across the Lasithi Plain. (Below, left) John walking through a village in Crete. (Below, right) John, Stephen Sherman and Hilary Waddington outside the Royal Tomb, Tell el-Amarna, 1936.

(Above) Hilda, Mercy Money-Coutts and R.W. Hutchison, the 'Squire', with their local guide on the summit of Mt Ida, Crete, 1936.
(Left) Martin and Molly Hammond with Hilda on the summit of Aphendis, Crete, 1936.

Opposite page: (Top) Agiou Giorgiou Papoura – Armos site, 1937.
(Bottom) The Spanakis family, major Tzermiado landowners around Karphi. John annotated it 'St Spinach day'.

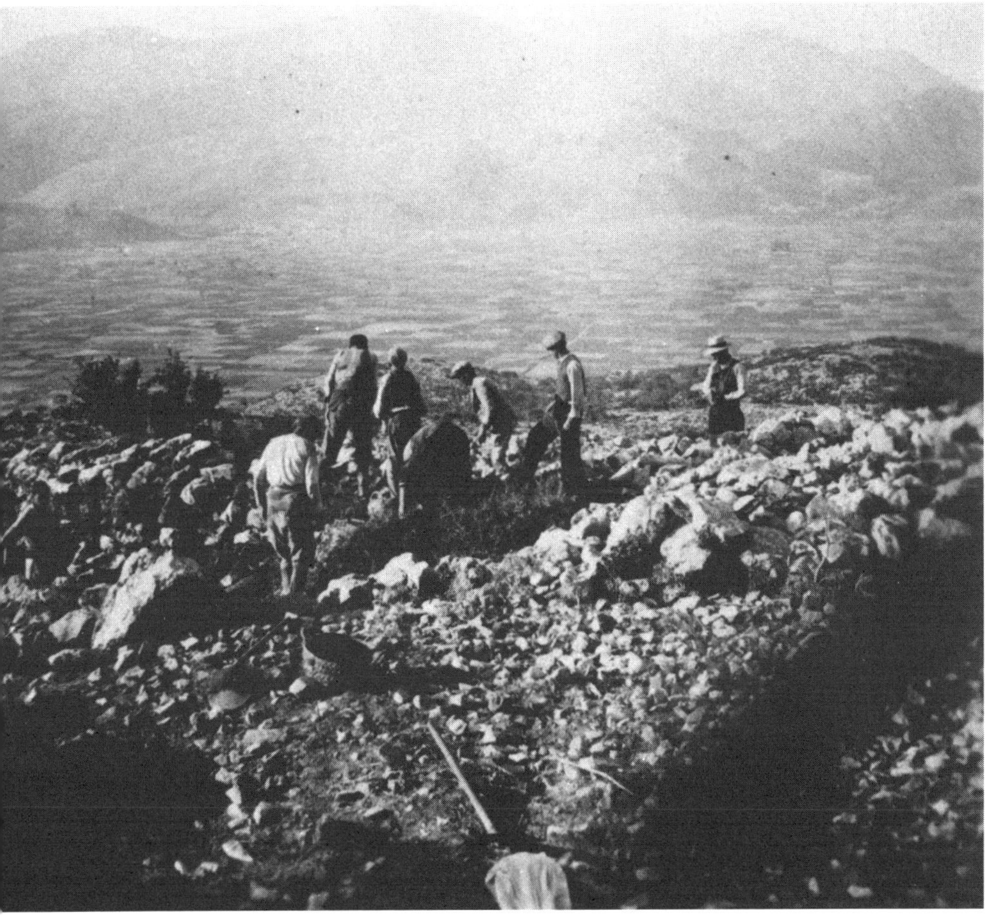

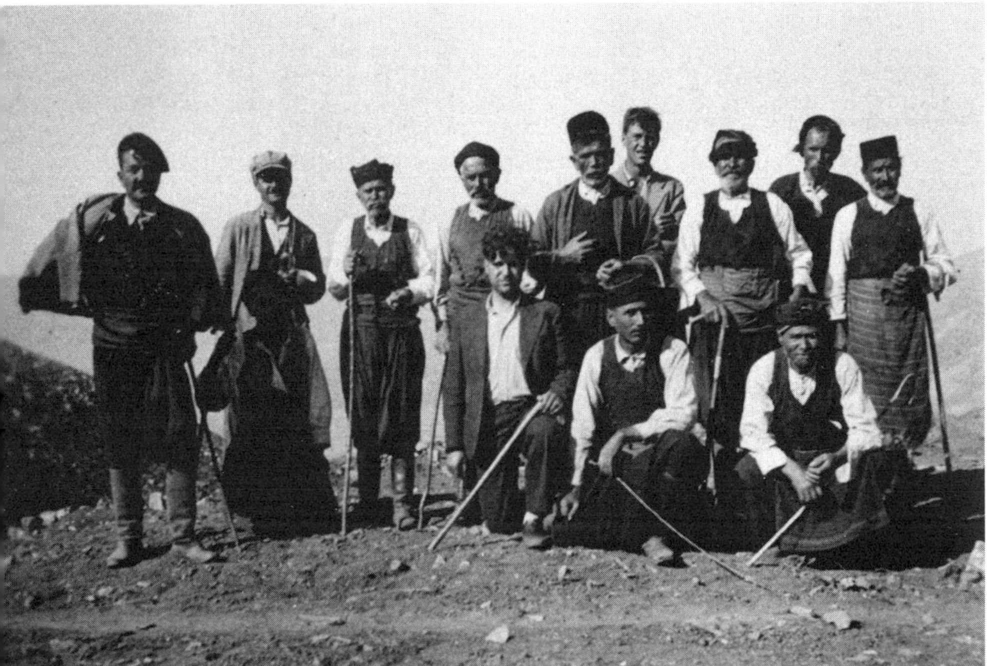

(Above) Karphi at the end of the excavations, looking south towards the dig hut and Mikre Koprana.
(Left) Dance (or *glendi*) at the end of the Karphi excavations, July 8th 1939.

(Above) Left to right: Kronis Bardakis (the 'Old Krone'), David Bowe of Field Security and Manolis Akoumianos (Manolaki - 'the Old Wolf') near John's wartime HQ, Heraklion, November 1940 – March 1941. These two Cretans were John's right-hand men. (Below, left) Kapetan Antonis Grigorakis, known as Satanas. Though an old man by 1941, he was a formidable resistance leader, and looked to John like an Elizabethan pirate. Here he is in uniform, probably during the Venizelist rebellion of 1935. (Below, centre) Kapetan Petrakogiorgis, one of the most steadfast of Cretan resistance leaders. (Below, right) Kapetan Manolis Bandouvas, who was brave, but reckless and indiscreet.

(Above) Unloading bombs for the RAF at the harbour, Heraklion, 1940. John acted as Liaison Officer between the British forces and the Cretans.

(Below) John at target practice with his .38 revolver, under the guidance of Lt Col Stephen Rose of 50 Middle East Commando, November 1940 – March 1941.

Some of the situations in which John was called on to liaise between 50 Middle East Commando and the local Cretans: (Left, top) Left to right: Bill Burton (Company Commander), McFie (with back to camera), Symons, Nicholl ('Nick the NOIC'), the Captain of the *Derby* (with his bull terrier) and Ken Hermon (DLI Company Command) on the mole at Heraklion harbour. (Right, top) Fusilier George Williams, bodyguard and batman to Lt Col Stephen Rose, 50 ME Cdo, with an unexploded sea mine containing about 500lbs of explosives. It was rolling around dangerously on the beach at Matala. He is holding a gun cotton charge with which to blow it up. (Left, centre) 50 ME Cdo training with requisitioned landing craft in Sitia Bay before the attempted landings on the Dodecanese island of Kasos in January 1941. (Left, bottom) Decanting red wine from the barrel for 50 ME Cdo's Christmas dinner, Heraklion, December 1940. (Right, bottom) December 1940. Procession to Heraklion Cathedral for a Thanksgiving Service after the first major Greek victory against the Italians at Argyrocastro during the Albanian campaign. Here, John and Lt. Col. Stephen Rose parade past the 50 Middle EastCommando.

(Above, left) The *Dolphin*, the armed caïque crewed by Mike Cumberlege, Nick Hammond *et al*. John became an honorary member of the crew. (Above, right) German parachute regiments being dropped by Junker 52s into Crete at the start of the Battle of Crete, May 1941.

(Above) A street in Heraklion showing the devastation of the German bombing. (Below, left) Heraklion mole and harbour after severe German bombing, looking towards the quarter where John's HQ was. (Below, right) Official ceremony at John's grave, 1947. Hilda is to the left of the cross.

on by the Navy in the First World War, as had that of Sir John Myres, and he was certain that Naval Intelligence was where his knowledge would be of the most use. He had written again before leaving Greece in March 1939 and approached the Naval Attaché, Captain Parker RN, in Athens on his arrival there. In May 1939, Parker wrote to the Director of Naval Intelligence (DNI) on John's behalf, but they intimated that John's services would not be required, in spite of the strong personal recommendation from Parker. John asked him if there was another department to which he could apply, so Parker suggested, on the advice of the Military Attaché in Athens, that he try Military Intelligence.[3] 'Meanwhile', he wrote to his father, 'I have offered my services as a stretcher-bearer to the ARP (Air Raid Precaution) folk. Anyhow thank goodness they've raised active service age to forty-one so that in any case I should sooner or later trail a pike.'[4]

The evacuation of children from the major cities, planned long before, was put quickly into action, as the threat of air raids became more immediate. John and Hilda took in a twelve-year-old French girl from the Institut Français in Kensington. 'Collette Mille by name and bilingual by nature, which in some ways is a pity.'[5] The family tried hard to cheer her up and make her feel at home, though she never really settled. Her mother came frequently to visit her, and breaking all the rules insisted on taking her back to London for days at a time, so she never had a chance to get to know and like the family any more than they did her.

Writing up Karphi provided John with some distraction at least from waiting for news of a war job, but his preoccupation with the war still came out in the report. He had been advised to maintain the pressure if he wanted to get involved early on. 'Badgering I'm told is the only hope. Pity I'm bad at it.'[6]

When John had no response to his application to the War Office, he asked for advice from Sir Montague Butler, then Master of Pembroke College, Cambridge, and father of the Conservative MP and John's Pembroke contemporary, R.A. 'RAB' Butler. Following this, on September 14th 1939, John put in yet another application to the DNI. 'I know Crete and most of the Aegean Islands intimately', he added, 'as well as most of the mainland of Greece. I have many personal contacts all over the Aegean which should be a good source of information, since, particularly in Crete, I am known to a great part of the population.'[7]

An official had annotated the application with the comment, 'Recommended directly to DNI by R.A. Butler. Seen and seems tough and generally desirable'.[8] John was called to a meeting in London, and wrote with great relief to his father on his return. 'Thanks to the Master, his Right Honourable son has succeeded in ramming me down the Admiralty's throat. I went up on Thursday, was promised very quick attention and that previous failure should be looked into. London is a queer place with very little traffic and a surround of balloons.'[9]

On September 17th, it was announced that the Soviet Union had invaded Poland, bringing a new dimension to the war. John believed even more strongly that the situation in the East would deteriorate, though any news about the progress of the war was strictly monitored and controlled by the newly-established Ministry of Information (MOI). The MOI took its responsibility to often ridiculous lengths. When, on the outbreak of war, the RAF had dropped leaflets over Germany ('I like the idea... It is treating them like NW frontier tribesmen! As indeed they are.'[10]), the story went round of an American journalist who wanted to get a copy of one of these leaflets. The Ministry apparently refused on the grounds that it might fall into the hands of the enemy.[11]

Cambridge, in contrast to the almost deserted capital, soon doubled in population, mainly due to the exodus of Londoners. The University absorbed the students evacuated from the London colleges, who revelled in the opportunity of playing pranks on and with the Cambridge undergraduates. 'The medical students from Barts caused some amusement at John's by putting up a notice to the effect that all freshmen must present themselves at Addenbrookes to be inspected for venereal disease. About eighty duly did!'[12]

Step by step the government brought in more security measures. Each person was issued with an identity card to be carried around at all times. Apart from the need in wartime for the authorities to be able to challenge anyone acting suspiciously, it had the added advantage of making it easier to identify anyone killed or wounded in a raid. But though the precautions increased, little else seemed to be happening, least of all air raids. 'Everyone here seems very cheerful, but anxious for the war really to begin. I have finished all I can do for the Crete publication so now await better times to finish it.'[13]

Finally, on October 14th, two days after John's thirty-fifth birthday, news came from the War Office. Immediately he contacted his father, 'Subject to sending a copy of my birth certificate, they are enrolling me as an emergency Intelligence Officer... It does not prevent me carrying on with the Admiralty – which of course is much more likely to need me. I think it as well, though, to have two strings to one's bow.'[14]

In the meantime John found work with the Cambridge Joint Recruiting Board, checking the credentials of would-be recruits and sending them to the specialist board to which their abilities were most suited. At least it gave John 'a spurious feeling of doing something!'[15] Though the job lasted only until mid-

November, John then heard from the War Office that he would soon be called up to London for an interview.

The weather got worse as winter closed in, and apart from doing some interviewing in Greek for the linguistic board of the War Office, John could only wait. John's papers had certainly been doing the rounds. First the NID passed them to the Secret Intelligence Service (SIS), which had no vacancy for him, and they in turn passed the papers to Military Intelligence (MI 1A). 'The Admiralty have shoved all my papers over to the War Office and seemed surprised I wasn't already there. Meanwhile I'm taking advice as to whether I am allowed to enlist in the ordinary way with any active unit, or whether I must wait.'[16] As the work on the Joint Recruiting Board came to an end, John was unbearably restless. 'If I don't join up at once may I come down for a bit to get fit on the hills? I've had no exercise for ages except long Sunday walks on the flat.'[17]

Then, on December 17th, John heard from a Captain Brunyate in Military Intelligence. Subject to his being passed Grade 1 in a medical test, he advised that John take a course with either the cavalry or infantry Officer Cadet Training Unit (OCTU), recommending the cavalry as probably the more interesting option. Brunyate explained, 'It is now generally accepted that a potential Intelligence Officer requires some military training in addition to his special qualifications.'[18] This attitude that military training was not of much importance for Intelligence Officers was soon to be proved seriously outdated. The course was to begin on January 19th 1940, and John leapt at the idea of joining the cavalry. However, he felt certain that his glass eye would affect his medical grading, so he did not raise his hopes too much until the examination results arrived.

When they did – 'They were very nice about it, but according to printed regulations they had to put me IIa (vision), though they put in red ink all over that I was absolutely fit for any service and the other eye was perfect – this after I had read them some minute letters at a considerable distance. They said they didn't think it ought to make any odds. I have sent the paper up to the WO and pointed all this out strenuously. So I hope to hear by tomorrow.'[19]

Then at last, ten days into the New Year, John got the news he had been waiting for. 'The calling up notice came this morning. I am to report on Jan 19th (Friday) at Weedon, Northants. to 110th Officer Cadet Training Unit (Cavalry). I have been given at once the rank, pay, and allowances of 2nd Lieutenant which seems all wrong now that everyone goes through the ranks. However, I'm in! The sheet says "On probation for three months", so I imagine that is the length of the course. I gather it depends on the Near East whether I finish the course or not. If nothing is doing there, *Inshallah* France about May. I have been busy ordering uniform and – I may say – a sword is still part of our equipment. I must be about the last person to be issued with one. Tell Dickie her Kikuyu elephant sword won't do!'[20]

John tried to find out more details about how long the course would last and what it would involve, but few people seemed to know for sure. 'It takes I gather four to five months, but I suppose I might be called on earlier if a job arose. Pay is 11/- a day and 6/- family allowance. Uniform allowance, forty pounds, which doesn't go far. I went up to town on Monday to get a few things at the Army and Navy including a gigantic sword. I am taking Gibbon's 'Decline and Fall' with me. It seems a good opportunity to read it right through which I have never done.'[21]

*

The camp at Weedon, built in 1805 at the height of the Napoleonic wars, was an imposing sight. A branch of the Grand Junction Canal stretched between and under two elegant clock towers raised above portcullises at either end of the main camp. The terraced hill behind, covered in the barracks, led up to the School of Equitation at the top. Though it was in an attractive stretch of undulating countryside, the camp looked desperately bleak and forbidding on that cold grey January day, but John was excited to be taking the first step towards doing something positive towards the war.

They were to follow the ordinary cavalry course, though somewhat more hurriedly. 'We are a motley collection', John wrote to Hilda on arrival. 'Ten of us have commissions, the rest (some fifteen) are ordinary cadets. All have some hopes of the Intelligence. In addition there is another large section of cadets not intelligent. I have six companions in my room. Luckily all are very nice. There are, as far as I know, no huntin' shootin' fishin'. Three or four at least have hardly ever been on a horse and we are being definitely graded tomorrow.'[22] John knew one of his room-mates, a fellow Wykehamist called Pearson, and in the next room was an Egyptologist from the EES, Peter Fell. 'Four of the people have been in the fighting in Poland and among our six are twelve languages.'[23]

In barracks, the commissioned and non-commissioned cadets were all treated the same, doing their own cleaning and making their own beds. Outside, the officers amongst them were allowed to remove the white cap band that marked them as cadets and be treated as regular officers.

'We feed well on the whole', John wrote to his father, 'though high tea at 5.30 makes most of us have a later supper in the canteen. We have about three months here and then possibly a course more specialized in Cambridge. Finally we have been promised active employment. We begin serious work tomorrow.

I gather I shan't be quite the worst horseman so that is something. We seem to be kept fairly hard at it, though owing to the weather the first parade is not till eight am. Eight three-quarter-hour periods a day. Saturday afternoon and Sunday off and a fortnight's leave at Easter. So we shan't be so badly treated.'[24] He finished his letter to Hilda, 'I think it is going to be great fun!'[25]

The ferociously cold winter and the general belief that army training camps were hell on earth led one concerned family friend to suggest sending out relief clothing. John was touched by the gesture but suggested that his life was not as hard as all that and she could probably find someone more deserving. But the weather wreaked havoc on the organisation of the military authorities. 'All leave was stopped this weekend; owing to the weather last weekend quite a lot of folk all over the Southern Command were held up for over twenty-four hours. The thaw seems to have started good and proper. It is raining like mad and I expect we shall be knee deep in mud before long.'[26] Soon the cadets also succumbed to the cold. 'My voice is only now returning. We have an appalling epidemic of colds and coughs from which the younger seem to suffer. Our troop is down from twenty-five to eleven.'[27]

In mid-February 1940 John received an urgent message from the War Office to come to London so that they could assess his linguistic abilities. His examiner for Greek turned out to be a veteran of the Aegean campaign in the Great War and an old student of the British School at Athens, Stanley Casson.[28] 'The Arabic is tomorrow', John wrote to his father, 'so [I] have to stay up with no clothes or razor and the problem of getting off a pair of field boots! A job will eventuate but I expect I shall be finishing the present course first. Luckily my voice has come back a bit. This laryngitis isn't bad but it's so beastly tiring.'[29]

The routine of the course was broken from time to time whenever John could get leave to go back to Cambridge or Hilda came to stay the weekend with him in Northampton. All the time he was getting fitter and riding better.

As the end of February approached, weather, tempers and riding improved. 'Now that the weather is so much better we are all feeling much more uppish. We are getting out more and doing mounted tactics and things. Today for the first time we had to groom our horses and do everything for them. The horses seem to take it much more kindly than I should have expected.'[30]

Only occasionally did archaeology enter his new life, but it was not well received. He adored being a soldier, 'I've forgotten all about being an archaeologist'. John was offered the chance to apply for a job in Athens that he does not specify, but he brushed the idea aside. Archaeological jobs seemed even more unsuited to him now than they had done before the war.

The course passed very quickly and eventually the time came for their progress to be judged. 'We were inspected by the Inspector General of Cavalry yesterday when my horse insisted on jumping the "grid" two bars at a time.'[31] The cavalry course eventually finished in early May and John returned to Cambridge. He had been sent by MI L(b) to attend an Arabic course at Christ's College and was reluctantly in the middle of this when he was summoned. He scribbled the news to his father at once. 'I have to go up to London tomorrow to the War House – No inkling of what it may be. If it means a sudden call to go out I'll let you know at once.'[32]

It did. John had been selected for 'special employment'. The military training, such as it was, was over and it was time for the intelligence work to begin. He requested leave to absent himself from further attendance of the Arabic course, feeling it to be a waste of time. 'We strongly suspect that the WO paid for the course a long time ago and are determined someone shall take it. Myers, who dug for the EES at Armant, is on it. In contrast to Weedon I am the youngest but two! I hope to goodness this call does mean a bit of action. I don't want to spend the whole war doing courses.'[33]

There was, however, one more course ahead, and a reunion with the man with whom John had set out in the middle of a night in 1929 to catch the Orient Express in Thebes. Nick Hammond had spent the intervening years walking around Albania and Northern Epirus in between teaching Classics. Hammond remembered their first wartime encounter, in London. It was in a 'dingy dark and depressing basement room in the WO', while the retreat from Dunkirk was in full flow.[34] John stayed at the Oxford and Cambridge University Club for the duration of the course, writing to his father: 'Here I am and here I shall be for a short or long period as the powers may decide before being shipped off somewhere to be horribly wicked. More I can't say.'[35]

Both John and Nick Hammond had been summoned for special duties, and Hammond later wrote about those days of late May 1940: 'The mists of unreality, which had enveloped me after my first experience of Red Tabs and the hocuspocus of "Special Service", were dispelled by the sight of John poring over the latest maps of Crete. He had already a firm grasp of the situation. In his mind's eye he was planning the organisation of Crete for resistance with a clarity of purpose and a care of detail which were fully-fledged. He hated that vague hovering around the fringe of the subject which is not uncommon in staff officers far removed from the scene of action and which is infinitely discouraging to volunteers for "Special Service"; and so he had swooped onto the practical details of planning with unbounded energy and enthusiasm. He talked to me of swordsticks, daggers, pistols, maps; of Cretan *klephts* from Lasithi and Sphakia, of hide-outs in the mountains and of coves and caves on the south coast; of the power of personal contacts formed by years of travel, of the geography of Crete, its mules and caïques, and of the vulnerable points in its roads.'[36]

They conferred with each other whenever they could, whether in the War Office, John's club, or by telephone, when, for secrecy's sake, John spoke in Cretan dialect and Nick in the broader vowels of the dialect of Epirus in northern Greece. They were only in London for a few days, during which they learnt to fire detonators in a conference room at the War Office and used gelignite to blow up 'mud and angle-irons in a suburban gravelpit'. Nick admitted later that they learnt very little, but the course was cut short by events.

By early June 1940, the war was not going well for the Allies in their first major encounter with the German forces. It had proved impossible to stem the German flow into Belgium and Holland in mid-May, and the Allied troops had been surrounded and backed into a corner around the French harbour town of Dunkirk. Their only chance was evacuation by sea back to England, and so began Operation 'Dynamo'. Although losses to shipping of all shapes and sizes were great, 220,000 British and 120,000 French troops were successfully evacuated to the North and South Forelands of Kent, from where John had watched the actions of the earlier war as a child. 'Queer thing', John wrote to his father, 'the way the Army seems to be at its best in a retreat. Even Mons and Corunna seem to be put in the shade.'[37]

John and Nick were nevertheless inspired by their instructor, an officer in the Royal Engineers, who had fought in the Norwegian campaign in April 1940. They were further galvanised by the sorry sight of the surviving soldiers returning from Dunkirk.[38]

On June 2nd 1940, John was put on twelve hours notice. He finalised all the financial arrangements that would ensure Hilda and the children would be comfortable, whatever might happen to him. 'I do feel it's essential in these times that Hilda ought to be able to lay her hands on a bit at a moment's notice. Things move so quickly!'[39] At the same time he gave his father power of attorney over his property.

It was inevitable that while John felt exhilaration at the thought of leaving, those he would be leaving behind felt only fear and unease. All too conscious of this, John made light of the situation in his letters to his father. 'Nice bit of irony. I went out with someone the other day to ride in Hyde Park and the first thing my horse did was to try and climb a tree! Result I've had two stitches in my elbow... Hilda's gone back to Cambridge today. She'll come up for a night before I leave. She's going to take Joan down to a farm in Wales and let the house. Rather better I think.'[40]

When the time came to say goodbye to Herbert, with no certainty even of arriving safely at his destination, there was no chance of making the situation easier to bear, so John kept his notes to his father brief. 'Well if I don't see you before I go off, Good bye and good luck – and thank you for everything.'[41] The War Office was to let Hilda know of John's safe arrival and Hilda would then tell Herbert. Then on June 5th 1940, 'I leave tomorrow evening or the next morning. Address will be c/o Room 367 – the War Office. They will forward through the bag. But – as I know I needn't say – don't mention my job or what I am or even hint. Diplomatic bags can be opened! Rank – when hostilities begin Captain – GSO3. Until you hear from me it is still Esq.'[42]

Just before John's departure Hilda came down to join him in London at the Oxford and Cambridge Club in Pall Mall. They had only a couple of hours together. When Stephen Glanville and Mary Chubb, John's friends from Amarna days, heard that he was at the club, they decided to go and find him. There was luggage in the hall, and when they asked for John at the reception they were told that he was leaving that evening. The porter pointed them to the bar where John and Hilda were sitting. It had been years since Mary had seen John, and that last time had been soured by the bitter misunderstanding over the conduct of her brother, Philip. Although it had all been cleared up a long time ago, they had lost touch when Mary went to work in the States. Now, Stephen and Mary intended only to say a few words to John and then leave, not wanting to intrude. But both John and Hilda stood up and insisted that they join them for a farewell drink.

Mary was acutely aware of the awkwardness of the situation. 'Hilda must have hated us intensely for interrupting at that moment, or perhaps it eased some of the unbearable tension of the situation.'[43] They chatted for a while and wondered how the war would affect each of them in the months or years to come, and whether any of them would not come back. As soon as they could, Mary and Stephen took their leave. Half an hour later, the Pendleburys said goodbye to one another on the steps of the club and John left. Hilda never saw him again.

17

6 June 1940–October 1940

JOHN AND NICK HAMMOND had been recruited by MI(R) – Military Intelligence (Research), a branch of the War Office. Along with a handful of other recruits with a similar background of work and travel abroad, they set off late one night in the first week of June 1940, destination unknown.

John was light-hearted in his letters to Hilda. 'We had a very amusing journey – beginning by getting lost at midnight in the New Forest!'[1] They had made their way to Victoria Station, guided by a splendid Guards officer in full dress uniform, and then, by way of the New Forest, finally reached Poole harbour on the south coast. Early next morning, they embarked on a Sunderland flying boat, which took a circuitous route around the Southern Mediterranean to avoid flying over the Italian mainland, for Italy's entry into the war on the side of Germany was expected any day. In contrast to those he had left behind, John was happy and positive. Nick Hammond remembered John's approach some years later, when he had not just the advantage of hindsight but a wartime's experience of intelligence work behind enemy lines. 'Of the party of experts that set off on a fine June morning for the Middle East, none was more optimistic than John and none knew his terrain more thoroughly; for Crete was in his blood and he knew its mountains, as the Greeks say, stone by stone. It was inspiring to feel that our special knowledge and experience would be put to effect in one form or another.'[2]

Greece, still neutral, feared Mussolini's designs on the Balkans with good reason. From June 11th, when Italy finally announced her intentions to become Hitler's ally, Greece suffered one provocation after another as Italy tried to draw her into a reaction that would compromise that neutrality.

As the Sunderland flying boat wove its way across Southern France to Corsica, down to Tunis, up again to Malta and over via Corfu to Phaleron near Athens, John grilled the other MI(R) recruits travelling with him, to ascertain the depth and nature of their knowledge. They had all been chosen for their special experience of areas in the Balkans; but other than the fact that they were all to report to MI(R) in Athens, none of them knew to exactly which part of Greece they would be sent. However, at that time Albania was the cause of most immediate concern in the Balkans. It was feared that Italy, having invaded Albania on April 7th 1939, would try to advance from there into northern Greece or Yugoslavia. Making up the five recruits on the Sunderland, apart from John and Nick Hammond, were David Hunt, J.M.F. May and Arthur Viscount Forbes. 'John was eager to learn all that the experts among us knew of Albania', Hammond recalled, 'which looked like being the first scene of any subversive operations – and he certainly intended to be in the first line.'[3]

John had expected to find the same high standard of accuracy in the others that he demanded of himself, but was dismayed to find that some of their information was as much as twenty years out of date and of little practical use. It was clear to Nick that John had a far greater grasp than any of them as to what their role would involve, asking what the harbour facilities were like, the local population's attitude towards Italy, the minorities in Northern Epirus, the mountain routes and where the vulnerable points were on the routes from Greece into Albania. 'Before leaving England he had studied the recent Italian maps which showed the construction of new roads in South Albania, and he consulted me and the others about their significance. His firm grasp of practical detail and his insight into the character of Balkan peoples made his conversation inspiring and his proposals sensible.'[4]

When their plane arrived on Corfu, they came within view of southern Albania. Looking out across the water, they talked of the harbours at Santi Quaranta and Butrinto, and of the harsh inland Kurvelesh lying at the feet of the Acroceraunian Mountains. John, however, was not to be sent to the Greek/Albanian border, though some of the others, in the coming years, would make it to that region. This time, only John was allowed to disembark when they arrived at the small port of Phaleron, from which he and Hilda had sailed with the Seltmans on their wild-weather cruise so many years earlier. The others, whose covers as businessmen were deemed less credible than John's, who appeared to be travelling as himself, were sent on to Egypt.

'It's very funny coming to a place where there is no blackout.'[5] Athens in June 1940 was little changed from pre-war days. John went straight up to visit the British School as soon as he arrived. There were a few familiar faces – British School students, such as Frank Stubbings, whose thesis John had been reading, Helen Thomas and Vronwy Fisher, all of whom were now working in the Legation. Also there was George Mackworth Young, the elderly and rather serious Director. John was delighted to get a rise out of him by announcing that he was going to call on the German School.

With Young also working for the Legation, the School was extremely quiet, as Compton Mackenzie had found it twenty-five years earlier while embarking on a mission not very different from John's, but in another war. Mackenzie had found that there was 'about its emptiness the air of a small Cambridge court or Oxford quadrangle in the heart of the Long Vacation. The bedrooms which in times of peace were used by students had the austerity of bedrooms in a college... The photographs upon the walls of temples, theatres, and mountains; the faded groups of student archaeologists in old-fashioned straw hats, who in bygone years had sojourned here for a while and hence sallied forth to excavate some classic site; the library of Hellenic scholarship and research; the long table in the deserted dining-room; the subtle air of learning which permeated the whole place with a faint dusty perfume; all these spoke of a life ruthlessly interrupted by the war, and all in their so utter desolation seemed to diffuse a dread about the sensitive mind that the life thus interrupted might never be resumed. The tranquil statues and viewless busts upon their pedestals had taken this house for their own, and sharp was the reminder of art's length and life's brevity.'[6]

John did not have to linger long in Athens. On June 11th, the day the Italians finally declared that they were joining the war on the German side, John's future was settled. 'So the balloon has gone up! I leave for Crete today as Vice-Consul for the whole island.'[7]

*

John arrived back in Crete on June 12th 1940, and returned to his old home at the Taverna in the garden of the Villa Ariadne. John and Hilda's furniture was still there, including their bed ('the Great Bed of Ware') in the downstairs bedroom. The Squire and his mother were still ensconced at the Villa, which was lit only by petroleum lamps and candles, as it had been since the house was built by Evans in 1906. Everything looked the same, but nothing was.

The Vice-Consulship was now John's formal cover. His real job had to remain secret to everyone. This was easier said than done, for, as John had pointed out in his application to the NID, he was known to a great part of the population. Added to this, the Cretans have a relentless curiosity to know everything about their friends, and to discuss what they find out, whether fact or fiction.

As MI(R)'s sole representative on the island, John's first job was to discover which Cretans were pro-British and which pro-Italian or pro-German. He had then to organise groups of resistance fighters who would fight from the mountains in the event of an invasion of the island, whether by Italy, which seemed the more likely at that point, or by Germany. John's MI(R) boss in Athens was Bill Barbrook, who had arrived in Athens just before John's return to Crete. His public face was as the Assistant Military Attaché at the Legation. John was to send fortnightly reports and details of his plans to Barbrook, who would forward them to the General (Research) Headquarters (G(R) HQ) in Cairo, run by Adrian Simpson, the man whose job it also was to keep an eye on any movements the Axis powers might make in the East towards the Suez Canal and India. There was, however, another Intelligence organisation in Athens, called D Section, which covered similar territory but was under MI6 control.

D Section had to be considerably more secret than MI(R), as its work would undoubtedly be seen as defeatist. D Section's aim was to prepare for an enemy invasion – training agents and planting supplies of weapons and explosives, so that its agents could carry out sabotage after the event behind enemy lines. It also oversaw propaganda and whispering campaigns. Heading D Section in Athens was a British businessman called Sinclair, who had worked for many years in Greece. His codename was 'Mark' and he had three colleagues from the British business community in Greece, who were codenamed Matthew, Luke and John – collectively, they were the Apostles. Between them they had a network of Greeks who could call on some very tough characters. Second-in-command of D Section in Athens was the charismatic Ian Pirie. Although Pirie's cover as adviser on Air Raid Precaution (ARP) was less secure, it enabled him to obtain detailed plans of public utilities and other industrial works in Athens as potential post-invasion targets of sabotage. It was vital that the Greek Government, assured that he was advising them on ARP measures and fire control, did not suspect the true nature of his interest in them.

Barbrook's cover as Assistant Military Attaché, on the other hand, involved collaborating closely with the Greek Government and General Staff. This meant coordinating future activities with them behind enemy lines during an attack on Greece and doing on the mainland what John was doing on Crete, building an organisation to carry out guerrilla warfare against the occupying forces after an invasion.

Though John's cover in Crete was more public than Barbrook's, Ian Pirie later commented that John's 'exact functions and indeed his membership of MI(R) were not however disclosed to the Greek Government, and in this he approximated more closely to a D representative.'[8] What little is left of John's communications with MI(R), in the form of Barbrook and Simpson, would suggest that John found himself largely on his own. Details of his brief and the plans and reports he sent back from Crete have mostly disappeared. Later, it was to become clear to Cairo and John that Barbrook had not been forwarding John's reports to Cairo as and when he should have done. Consequently, G(R) in Cairo had little idea of what John was up to, and he had precious little feedback from them. D Section, though, were well aware of John's value, as Pirie was later to acknowledge. 'In due course, owing to his great knowledge and popularity in the island... he represented both organisations there.'[9] In fact, if not in label, John had become adopted by D Section.

Nick Hammond's description of John's ability to assess what needed to be done in Albania rang all the more true of Crete, and John wasted no time in getting down to work. Crete was dominated by three main groups of mountains – the Lasithi or Dikte range in the east, the Ida (Psiloriti) range in the middle and the White Mountains in the west. Each of these three ranges had its own fertile upland plains, which commanded the major routes and passes in the area. Historically, these plains had always been hotbeds of resistance, difficult to reach and hard to attack. The westernmost one, the Omalos Plain, was the subject of one of the most famous resistance songs in Greece, an unofficial anthem. Dating back to the struggle against the Turks, this powerful song, with its uncompromising words, was used again against the Germans.[10] It was to these plains that John went first to find the support he needed.

The Cretans had a social system very much like that of the Scottish clans: family loyalty and honour were all-important. Though this could lead to vendettas lasting for years, if not generations, it also provided a solid basis of trust and co-operation amongst a large group of people. John knew many of the key figures in these clans and he sought them out. Once the leaders or *kapetans* were convinced, the loyalty of the rest would follow – not that the Cretans needed much persuading. John was very encouraged by the reaction he got from the Omalos Plain, Anogia and the Nida Plain – the part of Crete that he knew perhaps least well. 'Anglophily is rampant!', he wrote to Hilda. 'I hope DV [deo volenti – God willing] to go up to Lasithi as soon as the Squire gets back from Athens.'[11]

Soon John's travels did bring him back to Lasithi and to Karphi, where he looked more earnestly than ever at its potential as a place of refuge in an island under occupation. After the last dig season in 1939 John had not thought to return for a long time and had worked hard to finish writing up his work on the site for publication before going into active service. Karphi had bewitched him and, although weighed down by a war that was biding its time, John had allowed a touch of Karphi's magic to show through in his final report. 'In the uncertain shadow of war it is like looking into another world to recall the days of the dig, the torch-lit dances we gave the village and that last grand dance given to the workmen and to the fathers of the village on the windy saddle of Karphi itself. The ground shook to the beat of the long, winding dances, and the red wine passed round the halls of the city as three thousand years ago in the wild days of the Iron Age Lords.'[12]

Now, back again and charged with the task of doing all in his power to prepare Crete to resist occupation again, John was in his element. But it was also painfully clear to him that England at the time was far from safe. The news was scarce and not at all encouraging, with France fallen and Britain left alone against the Axis forces. 'I hope things aren't too depressing at home', he wrote to Hilda. 'Here we sadly lack news but at all events the one thing we know is that we shall never give in. First', he wrote, echoing the rallying cry of the *kapetan*s, 'θα παρομεν τ'αρματα να φυγωμεν στην Μαδαραν!' [We shall take our weapons and go into the high pastures!] If England was overrun we'd fight from the colonies I know.' He signed it, touchingly, 'With all my love my darling, your loving husband.'[13]

The *kapetan*s were the old fighters, the heads of their clans and widely respected. They varied both in character and temperament, but were all tough and had proved their courage long since. To gather them under a single banner was no simple matter. Old feuds and self-importance were the more obvious obstacles. They had to be treated with enormous tact and patience, and they tried this patience often.

One *kapetan* who particularly stood out was Antonis Grigorakis, with his air of calm authority. 'He is a very dignified old gentleman who looks like an Elizabethan pirate.'[14] His nickname, Satanas ('Satan'), betrayed his piratic background. There are several stories about how he came by this name – that he had pulled the beard of the village priest during his baptism, provoking him to exclaim, 'You little devil!', after he had asked the child's name; or that only the devil himself could have survived the number of times that he had been shot. His benign, time-worn face belied the strong fighter inside, who had fought hard in the Venizelist rebellion in Crete five years earlier, during which he had apparently been badly wounded.

There was no such benignity about the appearance of another *kapetan* who came to work with John. Manolis Bandouvas courted controversy. His photograph shows a heavy face, with a thick handlebar moustache, a solid frame and shrewd eyes. A wealthy peasant, he had vast flocks of sheep, hence the codename Bo-Peep given to him later in the war. He was a good businessman but stubborn, narrow-minded and self-important when it came to dealing with his fellow *kapetan*s, and positively garrulous when it came to handling confidential information. He was as unreliable as he was brave. But he had influence, so was needed.

The last of the three *kapetan*s of the Heraklion province whom John picked out was the impressive Petrakogiorgos. His face was dominated by a prominent hooked nose and deep-set, penetrating eyes. A brave and honourable man, he also commanded a sizeable business in olive oil and foodstuffs, so his code-name was Selfridge.

These three men and their attendant bands eventually became known to the Germans as 'Pendlebury's Thugs'. John organised a network of such contacts to cover the region and tried to get them all armed, though few Cretans of that era were without their own weapons – many very antiquated but still serviceable. The vendettas made outlaws and banditry so rife that the Cretans from remote mountain villages would always travel armed on long journeys down to the main villages or coastal towns. Given the scant military training that John had received before leaving, it is likely that he had far more to learn from them on the handling of weapons than they from him.

John's closest and most trusted aide was his old muleteer from pre-war treks over Crete. Affectionately called the 'Old Krone', Kronis Bardakis was loyal, discreet and dependable. He, like the *kapetans*, was a striking figure in full Cretan costume, with a silver dagger in his cummerbund. The image was perfected when on the outbreak of war with Italy he sported a British General Service cap badge, complete with lion and unicorn rampant, on his astrakhan pillbox hat.[15]

Life at the Villa Ariadne at Knossos, however, was as if caught in a time warp. The Squire, still officially Curator of Knossos, and his mother doggedly remained in Crete. As his contribution to war work, the Squire was working part-time with a man named Rolston at the Cable and Wireless Company office in Heraklion. The company was used by the British as a fairly reliable line of communication in the region, so it was from here that John despatched his reports to Barbrook in Athens.

Meanwhile, the situation in the Mediterranean was deteriorating, with Italian attacks on Greek shipping building up. Italy had a navy of considerable size and ports under her control in Libya and on the Italian-held Dodecanese islands to the north-east of Crete, as well as her own naval bases in Italy and Sicily. The Dodecanese had been granted to Italy after the Paris Peace Conference of 1919, but the islanders were deeply unhappy with their Italian masters and so many had emigrated that the population had dropped by as much as three-quarters on some islands in the intervening years. Italy's forces were also responsible for pushing the British back into Egypt in the North African campaign, so it was Italy which was the main threat at this stage in the Mediterranean rather than Germany, and the Italians were far from popular. 'There is an old Italian skipper here with two ships who is getting very annoyed at people (I'm afraid at my instigation at first) going up to him and asking how it is that with Italy mistress of the seas, he doesn't go away!'[16]

But this was not quite the 'action' that John had envisaged. He was frustrated at his own comparative inactivity and the feeling that he had somehow got the easy way out compared with those in Britain at the time. To a large extent this inaction was due to one of two complications in MI(R) business. The first, in Albania, had no impact on John; the second, in Crete, did. In July 1940, a Greek agent, codenamed 'Sphinx', was landed on the island by submarine without John's or Barbrook's knowledge.[17] His mission had been to contact General Mantakas, a noted Cretan anti-Metaxist, to plan a revolt against the Metaxas government in Athens should it yield to pressure from the Axis. However, the 'garrulity', as Pirie put it, of the Cretans made his task impossible and he was discovered and arrested by the Metaxas police within a week of his arrival on the island. The British Consul, Elliadi, somehow managed to get him released and he was sent on to Egypt, but the damage had been done and all MI(R) and D work had to be halted for a while to protect their other agents. The Apostles stuck to their normal businesses while Pirie took on full-time ARP tasks, 'lecturing the Athens Fire Brigade, installing shelters at various neutral Legations and the like', though quietly helping D Sections active elsewhere in the Balkans.[18]

John, meanwhile, was one of the victims of this enforced inactivity and his discomfort crept into his letters to Hilda. 'I hope everything has been peaceful in your part of Wales. It's dreadful sitting here not knowing. I suppose I am doing some good. It makes me very jealous to hear of what people are having the honour to do in England and Africa.'[19]

On a clear day, it is possible to see from the east end of Crete across the Kasos Straits to the island of Kasos. Beyond lay Karpathos, called Scarpanto by the Italians, who had one of their major airbases on the island. Italian aeroplanes scoured the narrow Straits, one of the most important and most dangerous sea routes in the Eastern Mediterranean. This made the Dodecanese Islands of great strategic importance. In the autumn of 1940, the Royal Navy and the RAF launched a simultaneous sea and air attack on Italian military targets on the islands. The British ships probably had little idea, as they passed through the Kasos Straits from Alexandria, that – as John put it to Herbert – the 'whole population of the east coast crowded the hills and cheered them on!'[20]

John visited Athens only once during this time, in mid-September 1940, for a conference with Bill Barbrook, the MI(R) man at the Legation. Changes had been made within D Section in Athens, and Pirie had become the section's number one, replacing Sinclair (the Apostle Mark). Pirie got on better with Bill Barbrook and the two worked more closely together in Athens. It seems that this collaboration extended to controlling John's work. It appears that Barbrook ceased sending John's reports to Adrian Simpson in Cairo as John became involved more in D Section work. Barbrook's cover was known to only a few Greeks, who believed that he was an expert on anti-Fifth Column work; this allowed him to keep in close contact with the hated Maniadakis, the Minister of Home Security, who was known as the 'Himmler of Greece'. Pirie, too, could maintain contact with Maniadakis, as ARP matters fell within the remit of the Home Security ministry. Together with the contacts held by a British businessman called Bowman, they could keep a pretty close eye on how the Fascist Metaxas dictatorship might react when the crisis came.

MI(R) took over the responsibility for arranging sabotage behind enemy lines when Metaxas gave the Greek responsibility for it to Maniadakis. Though D Section had set the programme up, supplied and funded it, there was a danger that the Greek government might have learnt of D Section's existence, so Barbrook took charge in Athens and John in Crete.

Meanwhile, the Director of the British School, Gerard Mackworth Young, had been made Director of Publicity when the School closed. He was a fellow old Etonian of the British Minister in Greece, Sir Michael Palairet, so had close contacts with the Legation. Young advocated initiating whispering campaigns, but his assistant, the Press Attaché David Wallace, was against this. Their job mainly involved propaganda, for after Rumania and Bulgaria had acceded to German demands few were convinced that the Fascist Metaxas regime would not do the same. When, in August 1940, the Italians blew up a Greek light cruiser, the *Helle*, in Tinos harbour, the gravest of a series of cross-frontier raids that the Italians made to goad Greece into the war, Young's team realised they need waste no resources on anti-Italian propaganda. Instead, they channelled their resources into countering the considerable German propaganda and espionage at work in Greece at the time.

John, meanwhile, had complaints from Hilda that she had not been receiving letters from him. John wrote to reassure her that he had been writing. 'I hope the letters are coming through now all right. I haven't had any from you since the one big batch but there may be some waiting in Athens.'[21] There was a good reason why the letters had been going astray. The Germans, still on peaceful terms with Greece, had a relatively free rein in Greece and had been intercepting letters. They did not, however, understand all that they received. After John's trip to Athens in September 1940, the Squire had written a letter to England, in which he described the state of the School in Athens. The German spies read it as referring to Knossos and reported it as such. 'At the Archaeological School in Knossos, the excavations have become only ancillary. Mr Hutchinson, who in Pendlebury's absence had taken over the leadership of the School, writes home on September 26th 1940: "The British School for Archaeology really functions no longer as a school, as the Director and three students are all busy on official affairs."'[22]

The torpedoing of the *Helle* did not create the climate of fear or retaliation for which Italy had hoped. The Cretans had already made up their minds which side they were on and were eager to get started, never wanting to miss out on a good fight. 'I am thinking of applying to the German and Italian governments for a life-saving medal', John wrote. 'The numbers of offers received to cut the throat of every German and Italian in the island is amazing.'[23] Yet Greece still clung desperately to her neutrality, much to the irritation of Mussolini.

Though he wrote to Hilda that the trip to Athens had been constructive, John came back with little news on when action in the Mediterranean could be expected. He was deeply frustrated by his own position and uncertain of when anything might come his way. 'I suppose one is doing some good here but one feels rather small living this peaceful a life. My God, I do take off my hat to England.'[24] The situation did not appear to bother the occupants of the Villa Ariadne, however. 'The Squire and his mother haven't yet really realised there is a war on. It infuriates Rolston and myself.'[25]

As autumn drew on, the thrill of being 'the most bogus Vice-Consul in the world' was wearing thin for John, except for the occasional highlight. 'I had the honour of being able to help four of our airmen at Sitia the other day — I've never seen such enthusiasm as the Cretans showed. Presents showered on them. "In fact", one of them said, "we might be conquering heroes instead of bloody fools!" The Italians of course are furious about it and the contrast with their own men, who had to be smuggled through in a plain van at night!'[26]

The less than friendly Cretan reaction towards the Italians was not surprising in the light of stories, whether true or not, emerging from the Dodecanese island of Kalymnos at the time, as John described to his father. 'The Italian soldiers broke into the convent and started raping the nuns. The abbess pulled out a pistol and shot four. Her head was cut off and stuck up over the gate.'[27]

In the middle of October 1940, the situation grew steadily worse. 'I think things are coming our way soon and that we shall soon be trailing a pike. If it takes any pressure off England then the sooner it comes the better. But it will take bigger and better and more Germans than there have ever been to get England down.'[28]

18

28 October–31 December 1940

ON OCTOBER 28TH 1940, the Italian ambassador in Athens delivered an ultimatum to General Metaxas, the Greek dictator. It made false accusations about fictitious breaches of Greece's neutrality, and demanded settlement. Without hesitation Metaxas turned down the excessive demands with a simple 'Όχι' (No). Italy formally declared war on Greece, though Italian troops had already crossed the border. Mussolini had finally lost patience. He was determined to prove to Hitler that he could initiate and maintain a campaign without his help or involvement. But he underestimated the Greeks.

Hilda received a telegram – 'Greece behaving grandly. Very proud of Crete. Reverted to my proper rank.'[1] The disguise had been dropped. John took his uniform out of its box and walked out as Captain Pendlebury, with a silver dagger tucked into his Sam Browne belt, to add a Cretan dash to the British uniform, and carrying a swordstick instead of the regular army issue swaggerstick.

All of a sudden the island began to hum with activity. The entry of Greece into the war brought Crete's importance as a strategic naval and airbase covering the Eastern Mediterranean to the fore. In their efforts to maintain neutrality, the Greeks had prevented the British from using the naval base at Souda Bay in Western Crete. Now they opened the island to them. The British had gained an ally. The Greeks had always been very sensitive about Crete, which had only been part of Greece since 1913, and had preferred the French to tackle its defence. The fall of France that summer had made that impossible and the Greek Government conceded its defence to Britain, having originally feared her tendency to support Crete's claims to independence.

The Navy were the first to move in, temporarily taking charge of all forces on the island, shortly followed by the 2nd York and Lancaster Regiment. At the same time, a small body of 'experts' was sent from Egypt. With them was a cipher officer, Patrick Savage, who maintained their contact with Athens and Cairo. He recalled that the experts had been sent to reconnoitre the island and to make recommendations on whether and how Crete might be held against possible enemy attack. With a lack of foresight and common sense that was common with the confused bureaucracy and insularity of the different wartime intelligence departments, no one had informed them of John's work or suggested that they call on his knowledge of the island. Likewise, there was no preparation for liaison between the various intelligence groups that were to appear on Crete in the following few months, though this was more often the fault of the heads of department in Cairo than of the agents on the ground.

On November 6th 1940, shortly after the first contingents had arrived, more of the army was landed, commanded by Brigadier Oliver Tidbury. Tidbury assumed command of all British forces on the island and was based at the island's capital, Chania. In liaison with the Greek military commander, he had to initiate the defence of the whole island, and most importantly the naval refuelling base at Souda. The island was not easy to keep supplied. All shipping coming from Egypt had to get to the harbours on the north coast, which meant taking either the hazardous, though faster, route through the narrow Kasos Straits between east Crete and Italian-held Kasos, or the narrow passage between west Crete and Kythira. Both routes were highly vulnerable.

John reported to Brigadier Tidbury at Chania immediately after the latter's arrival.[2] Technically he now came under the command of 'Creforce' – the codename for British forces on the island, and, though John was still the representative on the island of MI(R) and D Section, his job had to be adapted to the additional demands of Creforce.

Meanwhile, Adrian Simpson of G(R) in Cairo, who was supposed to be running MI(R) in Greece, was getting annoyed at the lack of information he was receiving from Barbrook in Athens. 'You will see that a definite directif was laid down with a view to plans being submitted to Middle East for approval... but the fact remains that NO specific plans, if they exist, have ever been submitted to Middle East from Athens.'[3]

As early as September 1940, it had become clear that an invasion by Italy was only a matter of time, so D Section had shipped in five tons of stores by cruiser from Egypt to Crete. With the stores had come two Greek-speaking British officers, who were partly to set up post-occupation demolition and partly to assist John. These men were Terence Bruce Mitford and Jack Hamson. It had been decided by Brigadier Whiteley of GHQ Middle East that D Section should only work on the mainland and 'not repeat not operate in Crete'.[4] However, he forgot to take the islands of the Greek archipelago into consideration, so D Section chose Souda Island, just off the coast of Crete in Souda Bay as a dump for the ammunition and other stores. Souda Island was also to function as a 'boarding school for saboteurs', training the steady flow of Greeks who had volunteered to act behind the lines. The island, capped with a Venetian fortress, lay off the north coast at the west end of Crete. There was already an anti-aircraft battery there attached to Creforce, but they kept quiet about D Section's activities, so the Greek authorities were never suspicious. John was put in charge of the new arrivals, and he was able to call on them or supplies from the dump if he required them. He forwarded some of the dump to Athens, using one of their Dodecanesian caïques, the *Taxiarchis*, while another load was sent direct to Piraeus from Alexandria on D Section's own vessel, the *Dolphin*, at the end of October. The *Dolphin*, a small auxiliary schooner, would reappear in Crete a few months later with Nick Hammond on board.[5]

Following the Italian attack on Greece, D Section began to assume that the mainland would eventually be lost. They did not think that Crete too would be lost; indeed, they were optimistic that the Allies would keep hold of it for the duration of the war. In the meantime, Cairo determined that Hamson and Mitford should 'get down at once to the job of building up a D organisation on the island', which had 'hitherto been left to Pendlebury of MIR'.[6]

In mid-November, the Commander-in-Chief of Middle East Forces, General Sir Archibald Wavell, visited first Athens and then Crete to survey its defence preparations. In Athens, Wavell met Pirie of D Section and Barbrook of MI(R). It is very possible, then, that in Crete John also met Wavell. All that John could report back to his father was that they had had an old Wykehamists' dinner during Wavell's visit to Crete, and Wavell too had been educated at Winchester. Herbert understood that to mean that the two had met and was further persuaded when a photograph appeared in *The Illustrated London News* of Wavell landing in Crete and being met by someone who bore a remarkable resemblance to John, complete with swordstick.

The more significant result of Wavell's visit was that the Cretan 5th Division was sent from Crete to the Albanian front, as had been agreed at a conference in Athens, to fight against the Italians. The gap left by their departure was filled in part by the arrival in central Crete of another battalion of the 14th Infantry Brigade, the 2nd Black Watch, and the 50 Middle East Commando.

The controversial commando unit used unorthodox methods for their equally unorthodox activities, and in consequence were somewhat frowned upon by the conventional military authorities. Initially, Adrian Simpson in Cairo was also in charge of the commando unit's forays into enemy territory, though they came under the more immediate orders of Creforce in Crete.

Part of the commando unit had already arrived along with Tidbury. With the arrival of the balance, the two halves met up in Souda and made a hair-raising journey to Heraklion on board the ship *Fiona*, surrounded by the potentially highly explosive combination of a cargo of bombs and a deck-full of leaky petrol cans. They were met off the boat at Heraklion by John, who found them quarters in an empty school, the tobacco factory and the barracks at the aerodrome.[7]

To the 'Troopers' of 50 Middle East Commando, John was instantly recognisable as a wartime officer. He greeted them on the quay at Heraklion wearing a stiff cream mackintosh over his uniform, his cap not quite straight and carrying a leather-covered cane – his swordstick. This commando unit, unlike some of the others, was largely made up of regular soldiers from before the war, and commanded by Lt.Col. Peter Symons, who had fought in the infantry during the Great War.

John's official task now was to act as liaison officer between the British military authorities on Crete and the Greek military and civilian authorities, though he also persevered (in the increasingly restricted time available to him over the following months) with his own MI(R) work. Mitford and Hamson had largely taken the D Section work back from him, leaving John more time to go back to consolidating groups of resistance to fight after an occupation. He took advantage of the presence of the Commandos to learn more about, and take part in, their work. He went with them on trips throughout the island either gathering supplies, or detonating mines that had washed ashore and acting as interpreter to explain to the Cretans the dangers and inevitable risks of damage to property that could result from uncontrolled explosions. Stephen Rose, second-in-command of the 50 ME Cdo, recalled that there was a tumultuous reception wherever they went with John and their staff car would be piled high with fruit and flowers.[8]

Another man, Harry Burr, who was in Field Security in Chania and occasionally visited Heraklion and John, witnessed the same thing. 'From the first days of our landing, his knowledge of Crete and the Cretans was invaluable both from the point of view of the higher staff and our humbler pleasure in knowing where and how to buy the best wine and eggs… His good friends were everywhere and to go about with him was a rather Bacchanalian Progress of Cretan hospitality. His love for the island seemed to be the great passion of his life and he made everyone share it.'[9]

None of those on the island who knew him well at that time had any idea for whom John was working, or what work he was actually involved in. The officers of 50 ME Cdo would witness some of his work while travelling round the island with him, how he would take advantage of the trips to take some of the villagers aside for confidential talks. But they were not aware of the significance of what he was doing or that he was working for Intelligence.

But soon after the arrival of 50 ME Cdo at Heraklion, one of its officers walked into the men's mess in Heraklion, set a battered-looking instrument on the table and asked, 'Anyone know what that is?' A young corporal said 'Yes, it's a theodolite'.[10] Then, asked if he knew how to use it, he replied that he did, and the officer took it away. The next day, the men were up in the hills near Heraklion on a training exercise, when a truck came up to take Corporal Maxwell Tasker-Brown back to Heraklion. On the way down he was told that he was to report to Captain Pendlebury, who had a job for him.

Corporal Tasker-Brown made his way through the back streets of Heraklion, not far from the port, to a small house across the alley from the school in which some of 50 ME Cdo had been billeted. 'I found the house without any trouble – a door in a high wall that opened into a small yard... My knock was answered by a small man in Cretan costume with a GS cap badge in his pill-box hat, and a silver dagger in his cummerbund. He beckoned me to follow up the stairs, knocked on a door, opened it, said what I thought was 'Cheerio Corporal' and left.'[11]

John, who was sitting at his desk, stood up and, holding out his hand, introduced himself – 'Rather an un-Captain-like action'. John told him a little about who he was, that he had been an archaeologist before being trained as a cavalryman and becoming the Vice-Consul. John struck Tasker-Brown as a fairly tall man, a little under six feet tall – 'a handsome man with an engaging smile, always fizzing with energy. Very alert, quick in his movements and physically tough'.[12]

All John told Tasker-Brown of the work on which he was now engaged was that it was to do with 'local security'. John mainly needed Tasker-Brown to answer the phone ('I can still remember the number – *pente dodeka*, 512'), do some map-drawing, keep the house secure and keep people out – mostly the 50 ME Cdo officers, who kept dropping in to see what was going on in there. Without any knowledge of Greek there was little else that John could give him to do. Though John could tell him little about what all this work was really for, one thing was very clear to the young corporal from the first moment, 'that anything this man wanted done I would "bust a gut" to do it really well... It took only a day or two to recognise in JP the archaeologist, the scholar and the gentleman – kind, considerate and with a sharp wit and a great sense of fun.'[13]

The house was a simple two-up two-down affair, with the front door and staircase in the middle. Tasker-Brown was given one of the downstairs rooms as his own. The room opposite was a 'reception room', basically furnished with a couple of old chairs and a rather incongruous Victorian chaise-longue. This was the room into which Kronis, who had met Tasker-Brown at the door, would put any visitors until they had been checked out. One of the upstairs rooms belonged to John, while the other was his office, with a desk, a couple of chairs, a standing cupboard and an old, rather impressive safe.

'Kronis brought me a camp bed and I was laying out my blankets when

JP came in to tell me that he had got hold of a big table for map work.' Then he saw the blankets. 'Have you no sheets?', John asked him. 'He did not seem to know that soldiers did not have sheets. Next day Kronis put a pair of lily-white sheets and a pillow on the bed. Later, JP gave me a Cretan cloak to use as an extra blanket and suggested that I should wear it if I was out late at night.'[14]

John explained the Cretan situation to his young assistant, and how it had all arisen, saying that there were still Germans and some Italians in Crete, but that they were generally known to everyone and always watched.

One of the first jobs that John asked of him was to become a routine one, to visit the Harbour Master in order to make a list of all the berthings and sailings that had taken place that day. This way they could keep a check on who left the island and who arrived, and what cargoes were being shifted. 'The Harbour Master was a happy soul. He had the idea that soldiers drank at any hour of the day. It took a few visits before I managed to explain that coffee was preferable at nine o'clock in the morning.'[15]

At first the office work that John had mentioned seemed to be little in evidence. The safe contained a few letters, copy letters, cables, code-book, pistol ammunition and maps. 'He gave me the spare key, with instructions that any messages delivered should be locked up. I was also given a list of telephone numbers where he could be contacted – also to be locked up. It was only when he got down to the maps that I realised what he was really doing. He told me about his "hill men" – *Ghaffirs*, he called them [after the Egyptian guards at Amarna], how he was trying to organise them into fighting groups and train them, explaining that since the Cretan Division was in Albania, the island's defences were pretty thin on the ground. The problem with the Greek maps was that they were of poor quality, badly printed and too small in scale. In addition, most of the hill men could not read a map properly or give a grid reference. He therefore needed enlargements of certain areas and additional landmarks. Later I did panoramic drawings to match up with some of the map sections... On occasion several copies of a section were needed. All maps were put in the safe when the house was left... The range of his influence and contacts – i.e. geographical, was in the early days a mystery to me. After a while I could begin to measure it just by plotting on the map the places he went to. Most were within thirty to forty kilometres of Heraklion, though often he made longer trips.'[16]

Tasker-Brown's work developed as time went on, and he spent time out in the town with the two Field Security NCOs based in Heraklion, Sergeant David Bowe and Lance Corporal Ralph Stockbridge, picking up whatever useful security information they could. Tasker-Brown found Stockbridge a charming and friendly man with a quiet, dry sense of humour. He was building up some useful contacts, having learnt modern Greek very easily. Bowe was a large man, who 'worked hard at being larger than life and almost succeeded'. A great eater and drinker, he was also a great talker and John nicknamed the pair 'Castor and Bollocks'. Though Tasker-Brown was not sure how much his wanderings about town contributed to John's work, John encouraged them. When one of the commando's officers implied that it was 'inappropriate' for a L/Cpl to be wandering around the town late at night while the rest of the unit were tucked up in bed, John provided Tasker-Brown with a pass, which said simply, 'Any time, any place, any dress', and signed it as Station Staff Officer.[17]

*

John also spent time with the other members of 50 ME Cdo, and the situations he got into with them were often on the bizarre side. Stephen Rose once found John outside their HQ by his house near the harbour, holding a goat whose udder, torn on some barbed wire, was being sewn up by the commando's Medical Officer, Dr Pedersen, as John gave a running commentary of the proceedings in Greek to a very attentive crowd. On another occasion John was dragged off by Dr Pedersen to the Heraklion red light district to translate as Pedersen carried out his standard army brothel check for venereal diseases – 'A necessary affair', Rose commented, 'whenever British troops found themselves in strange and uncharted places'.[18]

Others began to notice that John's work, involving long journeys around the island, was taking its toll on him. Patrick Savage, the cipher officer who was based at Creforce HQ at Chania at the other end of the island, had been billeted just outside town on the upper floor of a farmhouse, with the animals inhabiting the lower floor in traditional Cretan style. 'Pendlebury would sometimes saunter in, exhausted and bedraggled, and after a chat and a drink he would go fast asleep on the floor. He would have disappeared by the time I woke up in the morning.'[19]

As Stephen Rose and Tasker-Brown had noted on first meeting John, he was not a military man. The course at Weedon had done little to prepare him for what was expected in Crete should an invasion take place, and he knew it. Rose helped him to practise handling weapons, such as a .38 revolver, more effectively and took the photograph of John looking out of a cave during practice. Tasker-Brown also gave freely of his experience as a regular soldier. 'He had an insatiable need to learn all that he could to be able to turn his hill men into a fighting force. He asked endless questions about weapons and explosives – particularly the latter. All I could do was to explain, largely by diagrams, the use of gun cotton – wet and dry, fulminate of mercury detonators and the use of fuses, how to cut down trees and poles with gelignite necklaces and how gelignite rolled in a newspaper could be burned as a flare without exploding. What pleased him most was that all of this stuff was relatively safe as long as it was kept separate. It meant that his men could carry it about without blowing themselves up.'[20]

In return for the doors John opened for them, 50 ME Cdo was pleased to help wherever it could. With all his contacts, John could arrange anything from interpreters for a detached company, to laundry services carried out by nuns at the local convent or requisitioning fishing boats in the harbour. 'Sometimes,' Rose recalled, 'negotiations took place in the streets, attracting a crowd of onlookers and barefooted boys chanting "*Zito Hellas – Zito British*" (Long live Greece – Long live the British).'[21]

The commando unit thanked John by making him an honorary member of the Officers' Mess, which was initially in the Heraklion Chamber of Trade until they could find a suitable house to requisition. 'Only one out of the many we looked at had a WC as opposed to an EC [earth closet] or just a hole in a marble slab. It was then I first heard from JP "Isn't Nature wonderful!" – heard many times later on!'[22]

John was also brought in on a farmhouse enterprise that the Commandos had dreamed up. They had found, with John's help, a small farm in the hills to the south of Heraklion in order to have a place where they could spend their spare time rather than being stuck in the mess. They gathered some animals there and took turns to tend them when they were off duty. Stephen Rose bought some carved Cretan furniture, including chairs, a table and a heavy chest in which they would keep quantities of wine and huge cheeses.

Though Greece was openly at war with the Italians, she was not yet so with the Germans, and as John had explained to Tasker-Brown, a number of Germans still remained freely on the island. In November 1940 it was estimated that there were fifteen still at large, but there were no grounds on which they could be asked to leave. The general of the Cretan Division, General Papastergiou, felt that the patriotism of the Cretans was far too fervent to allow Fifth Column work to be a serious problem, though occasionally John would feel the need to send cables to Cairo asking for a check to be made on the reliability and political soundness of certain individuals. Ironically for Papastergiou, this patriotism, in which he had placed so much faith, was to backfire on him. Only five months later, he would be murdered in Crete for returning from the Albanian front without a single one of his men of the Cretan 5th Division, all of whom had been ordered to surrender to the Germans. It was agreed eventually that all the Germans on the island should be shadowed, and it fell to John to see to it that this was carried out.

How much the Germans learnt of the army's and John's activities at this stage is difficult to say, though a later German report on his work showed that what knowledge they had they only managed to glean after they had taken the island. If there were German spies on the island at this time, and it seems from the German records that there were, they appear to have picked up remarkably little in the way of useful intelligence. In a classic piece of propaganda literature, their description of John's office conjures up an image of a den of iniquity. 'Dark beings settle themselves in here. Munitions and explosives are stockpiled. Pendlebury's office soon becomes the crystallisation point of all British interests, and comprehensively ousts the real Consulate.'[23]

They believed that he had been terrorising the pro-German Cretans by lining them up in rows on the street and telling them: 'You are traitors to our common cause! In England traitors are hanged! We'll do exactly the same with you!' The report added: 'These threats against Greek citizens resulted in a protest from the Prefect of Heraklion to the Athenian Government. "Crete belongs to Greece! It is no English Protectorate, in which the British can say or do as they like", wrote the faithful employee.'[24]

This sort of propaganda was not unusual. But in spite of the Metaxist Prefect's complaint, John still had more of a job holding back the Cretans than urging them on. It was, after all, only a few years since the Cretan rebellion against the dictator Metaxas, so any supporter of his was less than popular. Metaxas, meanwhile, still insisted that they were fighting the Italians, not fascism, and it was all that D Section could do to try and convince the regime that they were fighting fascism as much as the Italians. Government censors made sure that journalists did not attack fascism and if any attacked dictators they were liable to be arrested. However, since the Greek resistance to the Italian attack, every political party was behind Metaxas in this situation. D Section had been actively encouraging the Greek government to reinstate Venizelist politicians and soldiers, but some were more welcome than others. On his return to Greece in this amnesty, one politician, Professor Panayiotis Canellopoulos, showed his good faith by enrolling as a private in the army. Maniadakis showed his 'good faith' by sending him straight to the Albanian front. The Venizelist soldiers were not, however, allowed to re-enlist to defend their country. Among these was a Colonel Bakirdzis, known in Greece as the Red Colonel (implying he was a social democrat, not a communist), who had an outstanding military record. Under the codename Prometheus, he became one of D Section's best recruits, trained at the 'sabotage boarding school' on Souda Island. His codename was chosen, Pirie noted, because 'for a period he was to be bound, then, after one month of occupation he was to throw off his chains and go into action against the occupying authorities'. Only after the German occupation had settled down would the group be able to ascertain the security measures against which they could then act, and in addition 'have a better chance of distinguishing quislings from patriots'.[25] Prometheus eventually nominated his equally impressive successor Prometheus II, also a graduate of the sabotage school on Souda Island, when his opportunity came to return to the regular army.

*

Meanwhile, the commando unit was ordered to carry out reconnaissance of all beaches and possible airborne landing places in the provinces of Rethymnon, Candia and Mirabello. They were then to produce a report and map showing defensive positions or posts recommended for preparations needed to delay any enemy trying to land on the north-east or south coasts. This was one of several such defence reconnaissance reports to be undertaken between June 1940 and May 1941 — all done independently and without reference to each other.

Although it has been said that the commando unit was sent to Crete to help with the defence of the island, this was not entirely true. The unit was only small and had been sent to Crete for clandestine offensive operations against the Dodecanese. Without transport, tools or earth-moving equipment they could not possibly have made any worthwhile contribution to the defence of Crete in the longer term. It would have taken several Royal Engineer construction units with sophisticated equipment to make a difference to defences around Heraklion and its airfield.

Given the military situation, by the end of November 1940, Barbrook was so tied up with his cover work as Assistant Military Attaché that Ian Pirie had to take over his MI(R) work.[26] So it may well have been Pirie who was behind a raid into Dodecanese waters that was planned by the commando unit. It was intended as a small scale raid to capture an Italian caïque that used to deliver the post to all the islands. The lack of specialised landing craft compelled them to attempt to capture this caïque for use on pirate-type operations in and around Kasos and Scarpanto. They had requisitioned all the Cretan caïques that could be spared and had already improvised their landing techniques to adapt as well as they could to such a motley flotilla. John, as liaison officer to the commando unit, was called on to find some men who could be used for this raid.

It is in the recording of such incidents as this that one sees most clearly the complexity of the historical process as it works in Crete. In the case of this raid, the only surviving accounts are those written by the Cretans who were involved. The problems arise when trying to discover who was involved, in what capacity and to what extent. According to the *kapetan* Manolis Bandouvas (whose 'Memoirs' were dictated to a ghost-writer shortly before his death), it

④ THE DODECANESE ISLANDS

was he whom John chose to lead the band. According to a nephew of Satanas, Haralambos Giannadakis, it was Satanas whom John chose.[27] Bandouvas' long and elaborate account of this incident (as with many others) is a triumph of self-aggrandisement and consequently deeply unreliable.[28] It is seen by other Cretans to be closer to fiction than to fact. Giannadakis' account is not much more reliable.

The question of Cretan storytelling (or perhaps myth-making) needs some explanation. An incident that involves people or events that are important to the Cretans is often embroidered and elaborated in the retelling. There is a tendency for a storyteller to work his way into events in which he took no part, and to put himself in places where he could not have been, with responsibilities and status he would not have been given. Such details can creep unnoticed into each retelling and, when well-received, remain. For it is the telling of the story that is important, not the detailed recording of an event for posterity. This is what makes the Cretans such superb storytellers. It is how they keep alive the tales of their island's past. It is not universally true of Cretan writers, but there is a strong tendency towards it in the Cretan memoirs dealing with the Heraklion province during the war published to date. The Cretans will always tell you of fellow raconteurs, 'They are all liars – except me'.

In his book, Bandouvas recounted how John called on him to choose and lead the men, including the older and far more dependable Satanas. Bandouvas claimed that he was told that the reason for the raid was to capture an Italian officer from the island of Castelorizzo in order to glean information from him. The account is over long and melodramatic, full of doubtful tales that increase the stature of Bandouvas at the expense of those around him. His view of events does, however, give a valuable insight into the sort of man Bandouvas was, and that, however brave he was, secrecy was not his strongpoint.

According to Bandouvas, the men were told by John to bring pistols, knives and four days' rations. When Bandouvas asked why they could not take larger guns, he was told there were none to give. John had for some time been trying to procure ten thousand rifles for his men, but so far without success. Bandouvas told John that they would have to retrieve the weapons they had handed over to the police in the amnesty following the Cretan uprising of 1935. John apparently told him this was impossible as nobody must know about this business. However, this demand for secrecy did not (by his own account) appeal to Bandouvas. How could they go on a mission without telling anyone that they were serving their country and not just smuggling? Stubbornly he declares, 'That is not to happen, it cannot happen. Find other men. I am not going!'[29]

He says that after a couple of days John relented, and Bandouvas went to get the weapons from the police only to find that they had no bullets – because he and his 'clan' had not handed them over when asked. So he decided to go to the Greek Garrison Commander, where he also found the Metaxist Prefect mentioned in the German report. Not surprisingly they were curious to know why bullets were needed for guns they were not supposed to have. Bandouvas obligingly told them about the whole business. The news spread fast and the presence in the British wartime records of the result records that the authorities were not at all amused.

> 'To: British Consul Candia   Nov. 30 0800hrs
> From: Creforce.
> Most Secret and Urgent for OC 50 Middle East Commando.
> British Minister ATHENS has been informed that a British expedition starts for coup de main in DODECANESE at 0800 hrs today. From that it is evident that a leakage of information is taking place here in CRETE. I suspect Pendlebury's hillmen. Please confirm that you are carrying out no such operation against DODECANESE or territorial waters at present. Otherwise I wish to see you and Pendlebury forthwith. I must, as I emphasised yesterday, be kept informed of any operation contemplated not less than 24 hrs beforehand.'[30]

In a long cable to Middle East HQ in Cairo on the subject, Creforce reassured them that they had denied all knowledge of the incident. Although Brigadier Tidbury knew that the commando had other work than that given them by Creforce, he was angry that such a raid should have been undertaken without his knowledge. He wrote to Cairo, 'As I knew that a raid by Commando men in a caïque manned by Cretans had started on night 30/11 with task of capturing an Italian caïque I have ordered that our caïques shall not enter DODECANESIAN waters. British Minister considers that he should be fully informed if operations against DODECANESE were intended but I think that under those circumstances secrecy would be impossible.' Not aware of the original culprit, they thought the Prefect, Tsousis, was to blame. 'Consul and I agree that if Prefect of CANDIA had merely referred his information and suspicions to the Governor General (Sphakianakis) instead of also telegraphing to ATHENS the storm in a teacup would have been avoided. But the Prefect is a Metaxist, which may be cause of trouble. I understand that the Governor General is taking action.' The cable ends with Tidbury recommending 'strongly that 50 ME Commando and all other loose individuals here be placed under my orders and that all operations be ordered from this HQ in consultation with NO i/c [Naval Officer in Charge].'[31]

The Germans later seized on this incident and elaborated it beyond all recognition for a propaganda report published in 1942. 'The British envoy in Athens had to apologise for the over-reaction of his subordinate. But a few months later the Prefect was withdrawn. Supposedly because some members of a State Youth Organisation, which he had encouraged, had greeted him publicly with raised right arms. Henceforward it was common knowledge who had the say on Crete.' As far as the Germans were concerned the Pendlebury rot had now set in. 'Greek official circles very quickly took this into account. The new Prefect of Heraklion, the Mayor of the city, the Director of the Greek Secret Police, the holders of military power, showed themselves as true friends of England's and became Pendlebury's trusted associates, with whom he had no problems. Officials who brought him information received gold watches from him, "for faithful service". Public opinion was bought by Pendlebury, and each one of the newspapers published in Heraklion received up to 100,000 drachmas from his bribery fund. The English Vice-Consul had more power than any Greek Government organisation on Crete. He had the population behind him, he disposed of unlimited sums of money, and now he begins to set up his own armed Praetorian Guard.'[32]

It was men like Bandouvas, who had no conception of the meaning of secrecy, who made John's job so difficult. Fortunately they were rare. But John needed Bandouvas, as those who followed him when Crete had been taken would need him, even though often against their better judgement. He was to continue to cause trouble for the rest of the war because of his need to be top dog. According to Haralambos Giannadakis, John later told Satanas, 'Bandouvas is a good man, but judgement and discretion he does not possess'.[33]

*

At the beginning of December, John's work was redefined again within the structure of Creforce. The Commander of 50 ME Cdo, Lt. Col. Peter Symons, had worked between the wars as a mining engineer in Rhodesia, and had been a sapper in the first world war. At forty-seven he was rather old to be in charge of a unit such as the commandos, and by all accounts he was a tiresome and difficult man, who was unpopular with his men, the Cretans and John.

In mid-December, Symons was assigned the duties of Commander of the Heraklion Area, including the province of Candia and the remainder of Crete to the East. John was appointed his Station Staff Officer. Between them they were to deal with the local administration of all British Military Troops in the area, and the supervision and co-ordination of the local supply of perishable rations, selection of billets and the fixing of rents in conjunction with the civil authorities, and finally, discipline.

Jack Hamson, who had become a good friend of John's, was not well-disposed towards Symons and deplored his demands on John's time. Hamson was D Section, which, as an offshoot of SIS, had recently amalgamated with MI(R) to become SO2, unbeknown to its agents in the field. Hamson and Bruce-Mitford's work of stay-behind sabotage was still kept very quiet, as its work was seen as giving in to 'defeatist behaviour'. As John himself expected to stay behind whatever happened, they worked closely together, in particular on Dodecanese operations.

Hamson was deeply impressed by John and believed that he might have achieved so much had he been given more of a chance to put his ideas into action. Writing as a prisoner of war, Hamson referred to John as Duncan for security reasons, but his real name has been reinstated here.[34] 'John was so nearly a great man that almost he is inexcusable not to have attained that greatness conclusively and effectively. But he allowed himself to be imposed upon by brigadiers and such like; he permitted himself to be recalled to Headquarters and put in charge of Q movements, to be made the pantry boy of the silly little colonel in charge of a commando (a commando, that under that leadership, God help it).'[35]

Symons, the 'silly little colonel' referred to, was something of a scapegoat and the butt of the men's jokes and occasionally of the Cretans' as well. In Heraklion, many of 50 ME Cdo got to know the Cretans well, and were asked to act as godfathers to their children. Symons wanted to do this, but rather than waiting to be asked, he put himself forward as godfather to the latest infant to be born in the local hospital. It turned out, though Symons did not know and nobody told him, that the child was that of one of Heraklion's most notorious prostitutes, father unknown. It caused endless amusement behind the scenes when Symons turned up at the christening in full uniform and in his staff car. 'He really has put his foot in it this time', John remarked.[36]

The Harbour Master of Heraklion had a sense of humour as wicked as John's, and Symons had caused him a great deal of trouble since his arrival. When Major General Gambier-Parry, who had succeeded Tidbury in the command of Creforce, visited Heraklion, he was presented with a large natural sponge, examples of which were found in profusion off the Cretan coast. Symons made it clear to the Harbour Master that he, too, wished to be presented with such a gift. The Harbour Master promised to arrange it, and in due course presented Symons with a miniscule sponge no bigger than a walnut – cruel, but not entirely undeserved.[37]

Symons, though, was not the only cause of problems. John was still under the impression that the plans for what he thought needed to be done and reports on work achieved were being passed by Major Bill Barbrook, the MI(R) representative in Athens, to Adrian Simpson in Cairo as arranged.

On New Year's Day 1941, Simpson wrote to John, having just received his reports for the first fortnight of December. John had written, 'I am presuming that my regular reports through the Military Attaché Athens are in possession of Middle East', adding that the reports covered the period from June 14th to the outbreak of the Italo-Greek war. Simpson wrote directly, 'Actually we have not received a single one of these reports, but this is probably due to the peculiar arrangement which obtained under which Barbrook had been instructed by the War Office to report direct home.'[38] The reports have never been located since.

So for six months John had effectively been working entirely independently of any Intelligence organisation. Cairo had gone five months without remarking on the apparent silence from John in Crete, and John had received no feedback and no direction from anyone, except perhaps from Ian Pirie of D Section in Athens. Simpson promised that from then on they would keep in close touch with his activities.

As was apparent to those who knew him, John did not much care for the authorities, whether military or civilian. Once, on a visit to the British Consul in Chania, Geoffrey Meade (to whom John gave the Homeric epithet 'the palely-smiling Meade'), John dumped a shapeless sack in the porch. 'What's in that?' the nervous Consul asked. 'Oh just some grenades,' John replied casually. 'But won't they go off?' 'Not unless the sun reaches them'. The poor Consul sat through lunch nervously watching the sun creep nearer, and just as it became perilously close, John got up, taking his sack and his leave.[39]

The departure of the Cretan Division to the Albanian front had left Crete rather more vulnerable than was desirable. Though some more troops were brought in, they, like the commando unit, did not have enough equipment to make a significant difference in the actual defence. John's idea had always been to arm the Cretans themselves, and he had requested over and over again that some ten thousand rifles be sent to Crete for this purpose, and to get his men into a reserve division. His requests seemed to fall on deaf ears, so he sharpened them up a bit.

'I am making a grand collection of tickings off,' he confided in a letter to Hilda, 'usually beginning "In future you should NOT repeat NOT". As far as I can see the authorities are not unlike Greek grannies and are apt to stand on roofs scolding people. Every Government cypher or code has obviously been made up on the assumption that the recipient of any signal either has been, is, or will be doing something wrong. My best rebuke was for using the word bastard in a wire to the Minister. In reply I pointed out that as it was in the code book the word was obviously meant to be used, and that the Minister was old enough to know the facts of life and that it was the only word that fitted the individual it referred to.'[40]

Part of the reason why the requests for rifles were not fulfilled was that the factories where they were made had suffered severely in the bombing of Coventry, and though some three thousand rifles were sent to Crete from America, these did not reach John.

In December 1940, Tasker-Brown saw a new face appear at John's house. A tough stocky man, dressed, as always, in a blue suit, he was the captain of one of the caïques requisitioned by John. With his white hair and moustache he was always known as Agios Georgios – Holy George. 'He had a fierceness about him – should have been a pirate.' The caïque had both sail and engine. The latter was extremely noisy and had started life in a Leyland lorry. The crew of the caïque included up to three fishermen and a signals sergeant with his radio who loathed being out on the sea. 'A number of trips were made – East and West of Heraklion – checking out vulnerable bits of shore with the map and making a few drawings. We also checked out look-out points. There were a number of these on high points. They were supposed to be manned and most of them were fairly alert. On some occasions Holy George insisted that they were drunk and asleep and wanted to borrow my rifle to wake them up.

'JP was a bit concerned about the noisy engine and designed a most ingenious silencer. It was a small oil drum stuffed with wire pan-scrubbers. Somebody – probably Kronis – must have scoured Heraklion to get so many. It worked quite well, except that it "sooted up" easily and every now and then it blew a pan-scrubber out of the pipe.'[41]

Christmas arrived and the authorities allowed everyone to send home a free single-sided letter. It was two months since the last letter Hilda had received from John and it was packed with all the news and stories he could squeeze onto his one side of paper. He told her of a tour of villages on which he had been taken – presumably another 'Bacchanalian Procession'. 'I have been carried shoulder high round five towns and villages and have been blessed by two bishops and have made a number of inflammatory speeches from balconies. The spirit is amazing!'[42]

Many of the villagers already had family members fighting on the Albanian front and some even claimed to have two sons, two donkeys and all their bed linen serving too. The Cretans, as always, were spirited and courageous fighters, and the Italians fairly paled at the sight of them. 'Did you see', John wrote home, 'that Mussolini has complained that a) the sword and bayonet are barbarous weapons which only Greeks would use and b) that they have been sending savages from Crete. But I'm sure nothing to the savages that can be sent.'[43]

Just before Christmas an expedition was launched into the hills to find turkeys for the commandos' Christmas lunch. While plum puddings of a sort could be concocted out of army rations and a little imagination, the turkey had to be the real thing. John, Stephen Rose and Rose's batman, Fusilier George Williams, took the unit's three-ton truck and a haversack stuffed full of drachma notes and headed off along the dirt tracks that were still the only way of getting around the interior of the island. They scoured the countryside, visiting even the smallest farmsteads in the search, and eventually returned with some three dozen birds, 'which gobbled all the more going over the bumps and potholes in the tracks'.[44] The final touch to the lunch was a huge vat of wine donated by the people of Heraklion, which they drank from tin mugs.

When writing to Hilda, John still emphasised the light-hearted and familiar: 'All old friends here are very well, either twirling their moustaches (the vine disease got into mine and I had to have it out) or relating catastrophes. The puppy called Satan [which he had been given by Kronis when he had returned to Crete] is now the size of a moderately well grown calf and shows no signs of stopping growing. I am extremely busy as everyone who comes has always heard I'm here and has had instructions to get into touch with me. Result is I have to deal with everything from girls to drunks. The old Squire and his dam continue their peaceful unhurried way, unconscious of wars.'[45]

The final note of the letter is defiant and optimistic. 'This is hardly a Christmas letter but do know that I am thinking of you all and hoping that you have as happy a one as you can. Goodness knows where I shall be. However, since we shall win – mainly thanks to you people at home and to the Greeks – it doesn't matter. Well, a very Happy Christmas to you all and all my love from here, John.'[46]

The Greek army was doing well and had repeatedly pushed the Italians back into Albania throughout December 1940, in spite of a bitter winter. Metaxas declared that the success of the army was due to his re-organisation after the coup of August 4th 1936. The army resented this association and the credit that Metaxas was taking for their achievements, declaring that they only supported the Metaxas of October 28th, not the Metaxas of August 4th. Pirie later noted that when the average soldier returned on leave from the front to find himself 'being given the Fascist salute by a smirking member of the Neolaia [The Metaxist Youth movement], his chief inclination is to kick his backside'.[47] Metaxas and the Neolaia took note of British warnings and ceased to mention that date. Though the dictatorship and the youth movement that it spawned were hated, particularly in Crete, there was no escaping the fact that they were now united against a common enemy.

Italy's failure was increasingly indicating a likely move by the Germans to come to their aid. On New Year's Day, Simpson wrote to John. 'As developments in your part of the world are more likely to take on a more active form in the near future I am anxious that you should have more time at your disposal to assist in planning and supervising, where necessary, any para-military activities which may be decided upon, as I know that you have a very intimate knowledge of the subject as well as a personal knowledge of the individuals who are likely to be of use to us for various operations. In these circumstances I am arranging to send Captain T. E. H. Davies to you in the near future to act as your assistant. You will, of course, employ him as you think best, but I suggest that you may find him useful to relieve you of a certain amount of your routine staff duties.

'Davies speaks Greek fluently and has a thorough understanding of the Greek mentality, so I think you should find him useful. He has been one of my GIIIs [staff officers] for the past six months and consequently knows all about our work.'[48]

In Athens, meanwhile, Pirie was heard to comment, 'I expected to eat my Christmas dinner in Athens, but where I shall eat my Easter egg, goodness knows!'[49]

19

1 January–early March 1941

AS THE OFFICER in charge of G(R) on Crete, John took responsibility for Souda Island and Section D's equipment and explosives and was put in charge of Hamson and Mitford. As well as being a depot for storing explosives, the island served as a training school for Greek agents working for D Section in Crete, on the mainland and anywhere else around the eastern Mediterranean where they could be useful.

Section D had been defined at a high-level conference at its HQ in Cairo in November 1940 as a 'network of Greek Nationals who have been selected for the purpose of carrying out individual, isolated acts of sabotage of plants, ships etc. in the event of the Occupation of Greek territory by the enemy.'[1] For as long as Allied forces were on Cretan territory, any guerrilla or sabotage operations would be organised by G(R) in Crete. But should Crete ever be taken by the enemy then Section D was to arrange for a sabotage group to remain on the island. In those circumstances, Section D would become entirely independent from G(R). It was this preparation for action in the event of a German occupation that was the reason for keeping Section D secret from the Greek authorities. It was considered by those in higher authority as defeatist behaviour which might consequently have a damaging effect on Greek morale.

The conference also decided that any guerrilla or sabotage operations to the Dodecanese taking place from Allied territory would be a G(R) responsibility, and that the Dodecanese was as high a priority as Albania. It was in this capacity therefore that John became involved with the Dodecanese raids, along with Hamson and Bruce-Mitford. Nick Hammond was by now also heavily involved in D Section work. Using contacts amongst the numerous Dodecanesian societies that had sprung up abroad, particularly in Alexandria, Hammond was involved in buying a number of caïques to start up trading connections between Greek ports and the Dodecanese islands. This would allow D Section to keep in closer contact with the islands and so gain more up-to-date intelligence.

John's assistant, Tom Davies, arrived in Crete on January 5th, and in the following weeks John badly needed him to take on the more mundane routine tasks dumped on him by Symons. Plans for raids on the Dodecanese, for which 50 ME Cdo had been sent to Crete, were beginning to take a more concrete form.

An unknown but 'reliable' source provided information to help with any nocturnal landings, and once assessed by MO9, this was passed on to the commando unit. They added advice gained from their own experiences. 'Bays are usually best avoided. They are the easiest to cover with fire, economical to defend and obvious places for submerged wire. Our limited experience at home inclined one, with raiding parties, to avoid "good landing places" like the plague! Each time we tried it, it paid hand over fist to go for the bad landing places. Better to have to swim ashore unopposed than to keep a dry shirt and walk into machine-gun fire – to say nothing of wire!'[2]

The codename for the Dodecanese islands was 'Mandibles', and the man who was most keen to use 50 ME Cdo in raiding operations against them was the Commander-in-Chief Mediterranean, Admiral Sir Andrew Cunningham. He felt that priority should be given to the capture of Kasos, off the north-east tip of Crete, to set up guns along its coasts, with the dual purpose of securing the Kasos straits for allied shipping and harassing the Italian airfield on the nearby island of Scarpanto.

Two Naval officers were attached to 50 ME Cdo. The intended raids would be amphibious, so co-operation with the Navy was essential. The officers were Commander Nicholl, who had the distinctive feature of a sliced-off ear, and as Naval Officer in command was known as 'Nick the NOIC', and Lieutenant McFie.

The Navy agreed to provide a ship for the raid, now fixed for the night of January 16th/17th, but the vessel inspired little confidence. She was an ancient mine-sweeper called *HMS Derby*, run on coal and with funnels that spat out fiery sparks like a noisy metal dragon whenever she was stoked up. In fact she was anything but the sleak stealthy vessel one would expect for such clandestine nocturnal operations.

The first raid was a reconnaissance trip to find landing beaches and exits from the beaches, which usually involved a stiff climb up a cliff. But on the night, the main problem they encountered was not beach-shelving or wire, but the lack of specialised landing-craft. Instead they had to use their motley collection of locally requisitioned boats, the only way into which, from the *Derby*, was down rigid wooden ladders. Not only did many of the small boats leak, but one or two even sank gently beneath the surface the minute the men attempted to board.

This lack of appropriate equipment was the major bugbear of the commando unit, for a workman is only as good as his tools. The other bugbear was the incompetence, indecision and appalling sense of timing of those ultimately in charge of such operations, sitting far from the scene of action in London or Cairo offices. It was certainly felt by the men in the field that the operations were conceived by people who had no notion of the practical difficulties, but just thought up outrageously grandiose schemes, taking the credit for successes but distancing themselves from failures.

Just as the commando had completed the tricky transfer to the rowing boats, the order was sent through that the operation must be halted then and there. London had decided that for the time being there was little to gain after all from 'stirring up the Italians through pinprick raids in the Dodecanese'.[3]

In the meantime, Davies, though sent to assist John, was being waylaid by Creforce HQ, while they decided to whom he belonged officially. Everyone had to have their place in the scheme of things, even if it was only on paper and bore no relation to their designated brief. More time and more energy wasted.

The frustration at the failure of this first operation was compounded when a ban was put on all minor operations against the Dodecanese. The CO of Creforce wrote to Cunningham saying that there must be more training in the meantime, so that the same clumsiness with the boats should not be repeated when eventually the ban was lifted. His main concern was the reliance placed on *HMS Derby*, as the operations had to be calculated as accurately as possible beforehand and *Derby* was not built for precision timing. The exercises were to be carried out off Sitia Bay at fortnightly intervals to give the men a chance to get accustomed to the idiosyncratic *Derby*.

On February 15th, it was decided that Operation Blunt would be given another chance. They were rather more cautious this time, yet doubts about *Derby* lingered. 'Considering the dependence on *Derby*'s ability to carry out four, repeat four, days extremely tightly timed programme unduly hazardous especially as rehearsals of landings have shown original timings were over-optimistic. Accordingly have instructed OC Commando (Symons) to abandon immediately should possibility of obtaining surprise be lost.'[4]

Accompanying the raid this time were John Pendlebury and Jack Hamson. Later, while languishing in a prisoner-of-war camp, Hamson wrote about the operations he had witnessed and his account, written with hindsight and embittered by later events, is vivid and critical.

The poor organisation was a handicap from the start. Hamson had been brought, by boat plane, from the base on Souda Island to Heraklion. Once on board the *Derby*, he was told that he was to go ahead of the advance party with the guide to locate the right landing spot – at night in a place to which he had never been before. Then he was asked if he had a map as they had found that the commanding officer, Symons, did not. Hamson was livid at the mess that had led to so much being left to the last minute. All this reconnaissance could have been done long before. 'I could have gone, I or any other man with some sense and a little courage (Pendlebury went later), with two or three first alone to see, to make plain, to arrange: and if we perished, well, we perished, just too bad. But now they hazard the attack with five hundred (too many and too few) on an ill-founded guess, in a flurry, with little hope of success.'[5]

They sailed in the bright and sunny mid-afternoon on the *Derby* – 'Dirty, covered with soot, littered with men and cases and equipment and rations.' There were in fact closer to three hundred men on the raid rather than the five hundred quoted by Hamson, and the plan was to land them in stages, using the small boats. 'Boats – leaking tubs, the oars don't fit, of all shapes and sizes – assault landing-craft are on order somewhere.'[6]

It was night when they reached Kasos. Hamson was summoned to the bridge where Nick the NOIC and Symons were puzzling over the map, trying to work out where they were. John was talking to the guides he had brought. What had happened was that Nick the NOIC had brought only Italian maps with Italian names, which meant little to the guides, who were local fishermen and knew only the local names. All this was only found out at the last minute as the boat lay, engines turning, off the enemy coast.

As more time was wasted on trying to sort this out, the moon began to rise. Their position became increasingly dangerous as the minutes passed. A decision had to be made, so the Naval Commander said to the Colonel: 'Sir, I have brought you to the point you showed me on the map. It is already past the hour agreed for the landing. I must ask you either to land here now or to return with me. I can no longer endanger the ship.'[7] The Colonel replied that they could not possibly land that night and would have to return with *HMS Derby*. So after lingering off the coast of an enemy-held island for over an hour, they slipped away as noiselessly as the spark-spurting *Derby* would allow, to repeat the attempt the following night.

On the afternoon of the following day, they set off again. On this occasion Hamson went off in one of the small boats with a local boy as a guide, while the *Derby* stayed as close in as her captain dared put her. There were eight men rowing the 'great lumbering tub', as well as Lieut. Commander McFie, Hamson and the boy.

In the pitch black they had to scout around until the boy could recognise the landmarks needed. The navigation however had been mishandled again, and they were some two miles away from where they should have been. The boy finally found an identifiable landmark, confirming that they were way off course. In the slow creaking boat it had taken nearly an hour to get to that spot and it took almost as much again to regain the ship. But they still had to find the right place and land the men in the leaky tubs, so that they could carry out the operation they were there for. Dawn was not far off and the moonrise was closer still. The sea was beginning to rise badly and this made the small boats even more awkward to handle and speed was becoming essential.

'Sir', Hamson was addressing the Captain, 'We are now precisely at this spot, nearly opposite the village. There is a beach there, and it is practicable. This is the part of the island which is reported to be heavily guarded; but we were not fired upon nor, so far as I know, observed. The spot you indicated for the landing is two miles further east. I do not know whether the beach there is practicable. The boy says that, so far as distance goes, he can take the advance party before dawn up to the position they are to attack from this beach here, equally well as from the original spot. He says that the beach here is better. He seems to know the place well, and to be very level-headed and reliable. The sea is rising and our boat was becoming difficult to manage.'[8]

The Commander decided it would go down better with his superiors if he stuck to the original plan and the original beach. So they went out to sea again and came back towards the coast two miles further east. It was now the Naval Commander who was livid. 'This is where I brought the ship in the first instance.' The boats put out again to look more closely. It was an impossible landing place and McFie told Hamson, 'Man alive, I cannot get you ashore there: in this boat and in this sea, have a heart. Well, I can get you ashore perhaps, but none of us will get off.'[9]

The incompetence and ineptitude of the whole exercise caused enormous frustration in every one of the men concerned, 'soured not by failure merely but by fiasco.'[10] For the Commander had decided to turn back yet again. The small boats could not have landed anybody in that place — let alone several hundred men with equipment and rations for four days.

One of the officers on board, a Lieut. Michael Borwick, had a rather more light-hearted memory of the return journey, albeit of another near disaster. 'The captain of HMS *Derby* had a very unpleasant bull terrier which bit me in the backside and started to bark its head off just as Commander Nicholl was returning from a reconnaissance. The clouds rolled away and there was a large gun emplacement waiting for the unwary. The Royal Italian flag was hoisted by the *Derby* as a ruse de guerre and we sailed away to Crete.'[11]

The failure and confusion of this Kasos raid led to the diversion of Admiral Cunningham's attention to a different Dodecanese island — Castellorizo. It lay off the south coast of Turkey, some distance from Crete, and plans for its capture (Operation Abstention) were carefully laid to help impress the Turks into helping the Allies.

The Greeks, reacting to pro-German propaganda, were becoming nervous about the amount of practical help that Britain would be prepared to give, should the Germans decide to join Italy in her obviously struggling attempts to take Greece. So Sir Anthony Eden, General Sir John Dill (Chief of the Imperial General Staff), General Wavell and Air Marshal Sir Arthur Longmore (Air Officer Commanding Middle East) went on a diplomatic tour of the Eastern Mediterranean to sort this out at the same time as attempting to persuade the Turks into the war on the Allied side. With Anthony Eden, as a junior diplomat, was Pierson (Bob) Dixon, John's friend from Cambridge days. The conferences began in Cairo with the Commanders-in-Chief of the three forces. 'During these conferences', Dixon remembered later, 'the C's-in-C showed themselves surprisingly enthusiastic for an expedition to Greece.'[12] Details of what lines they would suggest could be held against a combined Axis attack, what troops could be spared and how and where they could be transported to Greece, were all agreed upon in Cairo. Then Eden, Dill, Wavell, Longmore and Dixon flew to Athens. They were met by Sir Michael Palairet, the British Minister in Athens, and Harold Caccia, and taken in secret to the king's country home at Tatoi, in the woods of Attica. Greece made it clear from the start that she would fight Germany whether she had help from Britain or not.

A month earlier, on January 29th 1941, the old dictator General Metaxas had died. Many felt that the fascist government could not survive without him, but it was vital that the right person take over. A new Prime Minister was found in Alexander Koryzis. He agreed with the suggestions brought from Cairo about which lines to defend, but maintained that it was finally up to the military, headed by the Greek Commander-in-Chief, General Papagos, to decide. The result was an agreement to hold the Aliakmon Line. This was further back into Greece than the Albanian front currently being held against the Italians, but it was stronger. No one was in any doubt that Germany would be a considerably more formidable adversary than her Italian ally. The delegation returned to Cairo and orders were given to raise the force to send to Greece. They had now to approach Turkey, so they flew from Cairo to Adana on February 25th 1941. It was with this visit that 'Operation Abstention' was designed to coincide.

Fifty ME Cdo set off on Operation Abstention – to capture the Dodecanese island of Castellorizo – on February 24th. This was a larger operation than the two against Kasos, and involved two Royal Navy destroyers, *HMS Decoy* and *HMS Hereward*.[13] Everything went well to begin with. The men of 50 ME Cdo were successfully landed, though more slowly and erratically than intended, and with the help of the gunboat *Ladybird*, which blasted the Paleocastro Fort at the centre of the island, the Italian garrison was forced to surrender.

Daylight brought Italian retaliation in the form of Savoia 81 bombers based on Rhodes. Three of these were shot down, but the *Ladybird* was hit. She limped back to Cyprus and the commando was left without support on the island. The destroyers had already left for Cyprus after unloading the men, to pick up the relief force which would hold the island once it had been secured by 50 ME Cdo. But before they arrived a small force of Italian torpedo boats and E-boats shot their way into the harbour, rescued the Italians hiding there and left again.

Yet again poor communications began to control events: 50 ME Cdo had but a single faulty wireless set with them, so a message sent to the approaching *HMS Hereward*, that the enemy had surface craft in those waters, was unclear and misunderstood. The warning to be careful was taken as a signal of real and immediate danger. In dangerous waters, and with inadequate time before daybreak, the landing of relief forces was considered too risky, so they withdrew, but not just to Cyprus. The whole squadron went all the way back to Alexandria to refuel, and the men of the commando were left high and dry on Castellorizo and completely unaware of the fact, as they were not in radio contact.

Italian aircraft bombarded the island throughout the following day, while the commando tried to curb the looting of the jubilant islanders, free now, as they thought, from the long Italian occupation. The commando unit expected the reinforcements that night, not knowing that they would scarcely have reached Alexandria by then, twelve hours away by sea. The Italians, on the other hand, were only two hours away on Rhodes, and were loath to lose Castellorizo. When their counter-attack came the next morning, they had more and fresher troops, naval and air back-up, and more ammunition. The commando unit abandoned the lower parts of the island and retreated up to the Fort, while the troops they awaited to relieve them were still only three hours out of Alexandria.

Decoy and *Hero* arrived in the middle of the following night, and landed fifty men of the Sherwood Foresters. They expected the island to be in the commandos' hands, until they found the first dead commando trooper, and a couple more cut off from the main group. Then it soon became plain how desperate the situation was, and it was decided to abort the operation and take the commando unit back to Crete and the rest to Alexandria. But, as with all evacuations, some were left behind, and were either captured or attempted to swim to Turkey. Some of those who swam were lucky enough to be picked up, others never made it. They had been too exhausted before they had even set out.

Though John had not been involved in this raid, Tasker-Brown had.

'When I got back he was waiting for me, eager to hear what had happened. He had judged, quite rightly, that I would be hungry and thirsty. We rarely kept food in the house, but he produced wine and cake. By the time the cake was eaten and the wine drunk, I must have fallen asleep. I eventually awoke to find myself on my bed, tucked up in the Cretan cloak and he had even bothered to take my boots off.'[14]

Needless to say, few people were impressed by Operation Abstention. The planning of it had been a disaster, but 50 ME Cdo were at least free from any hint of blame this time. It was the Navy which had much to answer for, but the report that confirmed this was designated 'Most Secret', and it took thirty years for it to be released. In the meantime, the commando unit was generally thought to have been responsible, and at the beginning of March 1941 was ordered back to Cairo.

The order included Tasker Brown. 'When the time came for 50 [ME] Commando to leave for Egypt, no one bothered to tell me. I asked JP what he thought I should do. After a long discussion he eventually said I ought to go. I remember feeling that had I been able to speak Greek the question would not have arisen.' Tasker Brown was devastated at not being able to stay with John. '"The Uncrowned King of Crete" – as the commando unit got to call him – proved that, soldier or not, he was a leader, and real leaders are rare, especially among soldiers.'[15]

20

7 March–5 April 1941

IN THE SPRING of 1941, contact between Britain and Crete was at best erratic. In the first week of March, John was still only receiving letters from Hilda that she had sent the previous September. He could only hope that the letters he had managed to send, through more official channels, were reaching Hilda more reliably. 'Try HQ Middle East next time', he suggested. 'Captain please!... My letters have been irregular – but so has my life!'[1]

John's work, involving long journeys of days away at a time, was beginning to wear him down. 'I have been having a bit of bother with blood poisoning – Nothing to worry about but annoying when one can't sit down and get over it.'[2] Having seen two friends of his own age – Humfry Payne and Alan Blakeway – die of blood poisoning, this was no small concern, however lightly he brushed it off.

Heraklion maintained its calm and relaxed atmosphere. The other British carrying out security work in Heraklion, apart from John, such as the Field Security Unit, were enjoying the welcome peace of the island. 'What our duties were, in this farcical unit to which I belonged, I, at least, never clearly understood', wrote Ralph Stockbridge, the Field Security officer with whom, along with his colleague David Bowe, Tasker-Brown had spent a lot of time around the town. 'I interpreted mine as the identification of pro-Germans in the town. There were probably not more than a score of these and all of them, I suspect, harmless people with business or family connections with Germany. Meanwhile we enjoyed Heraklion... Coffee-housing was then, as now, a favourite pastime, and Regginakis' establishment in the main square, facing Morosini's beautiful Venetian fountain, our favourite rendez-vous.'[3]

John's work was rarely so relaxing, though from time to time he went out to spend some time in the peace and quiet of Knossos, leaving 'the old Krone' to look after his 'discreet establishment'. 'Occasionally I manage to get a peaceful day up at the Villa and have a bath.'[4]

There is a wistfulness in John's last letter to Hilda as he asks after 'Little Arthur, Myres, Mercy, Marion and all the rogues of yesteryear?'[5] He was tired, and perhaps a little disillusioned by the apparently chaotic planning epitomised by the Dodecanese raids. But he was also aware that this period was the calm before the storm. A week earlier Hitler's troops had crossed the Danube into Bulgaria from Rumania. Soon Thrace and Macedonia too would be threatened. Yugoslavia was the next potential target, and no one yet knew how she or her ruler, the Prince Regent, would react. Her decision to capitulate or to stand would greatly affect the speed and strength necessary for the defence of Greece.

The Eden delegation had now settled with Greece that they would hold the Aliakmon line together, should Germany declare war against Greece. Greece was now hearing from all sides that Germany intended to attack her, in spite of reassurances from Hitler to the contrary. This prompted George Vlachos, the editor of the newspaper *Kathimerini*, to write a powerful open letter addressed to Adolf Hitler. The date was March 8th 1941. It summed up perfectly all the promises, assurances, let-downs, lies and U-turns that characterised Germany's dealings with Greece up to that time. It was a deliberately naive letter, putting each point clearly and logically as to why the Germans could not possibly intend to attack Greece after all they had said and promised. It talked of Britain sending men and planes to help Greece against the Italians, when Britain had scarce enough to defend herself. But Greece was not now going to turn out those men just to please Hitler, if that was all that was going to stop him. The final sentence is superbly Greek in its defiance and drama: 'We shall see this torch light a fire that will light this little nation, which has taught all other nations how to live, and will now teach them how to die.'[6] The letter had a deep effect on all Greeks. It voiced the feelings of dismay and defiance felt by the whole country.

*

Cairo, the heart of Middle East operations, was also the centre from which Balkan operations were run. A strange oasis, it was worlds away from the desert war, though its streets were teeming with uniforms of every description. It was a haven of luxury to many of the soldiers on leave from fighting in the desert, and to agents on leave from their harrowing work in occupied territory. However, it was thought by many that the authorities, who were based there in Middle East Headquarters, were so cosseted by the colonial life that they could never fully grasp what was happening in the field, or appreciate the difficulties that had to be overcome (Cairo itself being the source of so many of those difficulties).

Bob Dixon, though he was not coming from active combat, was still taken aback by the lifestyle in Cairo when he attended a large cocktail party given by General Wavell in early March 1941, 'shattering illusions that Cs-in-C live in a tent in the desert drinking camp coffee out of billycans.'[7]

Jack Hamson and Terence Bruce-Mitford were recalled to Cairo at the same time, on the grounds that it was impossible that Crete would fall to the enemy so their services were no longer necessary. Hamson was not so much surprised by the situation he found in Cairo as incensed. Having witnessed the results of inadequate planning in the Dodecanese, he was appalled to see how much time was spent by the headquarters' staff partying and drinking gin at Shepheard's Hotel. The fact that these people, who, he felt, were wasting the talent, energies and lives of men in the field, could sit around in clubs and bars and dance late into the night, before a trip to the seedier parts of old Cairo, seemed absolutely unjustifiable. However, the organisation for which John was working, MI(R)/SOE, and the one for which Hamson and Mitford worked, D section, did not appear to take much notice of the experience gained by their agents in the field. In fact, any suggestions, based on hard-earned experience in the field, of how things could be made to work more efficiently in Crete, were swept aside in favour of far-fetched and impracticable Cairo-initiated schemes.

The various intelligence departments working from Cairo did not enjoy much harmony in their relations with each other – a state of affairs which fortunately was not found in the field. All were originally looked upon with misgiving by the military authorities, and there was a struggle for whatever practical support could be extracted from the regular forces.

Hamson, writing later in a prisoner-of-war camp about his experience of Cairo in March 1941, expressed his anger at the way in which John had been treated. 'John [was] continuously harassed by Cairo and by local brigadiers, kept without supplies, without encouragement, checked in his every undertaking; John, to whom a single rifle from Cairo was treasure-trove. It would have been heroic in Terence and myself to have disentangled John and given him the occasion he so obviously required, the occasion to which it was so almost certain he would have risen. Not merely to have appreciated the soundness of his plan – that was easy enough, except apparently in Cairo – but to have made the plan a feasibility, when we ourselves were subject to the same ineptitude of Cairo and had our own little businesses to attend to at their behest.'[8]

John's ideas both for the defence of Crete and for raids against the Dodecanese were hampered by the lack of arms, yet his requests for these were always referred. Fifty ME Cdo had at one point done what they could for him. Stephen Rose had, a few months earlier, taken him to the commando storerooms to look for a box of rifles for John, saying that if anyone asked what had happened to them he would claim that they were 'lost in battle'. John took one box to give to his men. The Greek governor found out about this and kicked up a fuss, but John kept the guns.[9]

There was a lack of vision and decision in the way Cairo managed affairs. 'I judged them to have been petty and mean, ignorant and without insight', wrote Hamson, a perceptive and discerning lawyer by profession. 'I did not judge him [John] to be that, but rather a man I respected and admired... With a man his equal at Cairo, no better, no worse, John would not I think have failed in Crete. It was the headquarters we had at Cairo which made it necessary for John to be a man of outstanding greatness in order to succeed in Crete. It was John's defect – and ours – which failed to find that degree of determination, of insight and of decision which should have carried us effectively even through the morass of Cairo. But if there was fault and defect in John – and I think there was – it pales into insignificance, quite, beside the nastiness, the sloth, the nullity of Cairo.'[10] Although many, including Hamson, became embittered by this, John at least remained optimistic about the chance of success when the moment to act finally came.

*

'At present we seem as safe as you, though by the time this gets to you we may not be so!', John wrote to Hilda in March 1941.[11]

By March 20th, the Germans had completed their troop movements and General List's 12th Army was now amassed and ready on the Greek-Bulgarian border. They were waiting for Yugoslavia to give in to them. Yugoslavia had been the centre of a diplomatic tug-of-war for some time. Bob Dixon wrote in his diary: 'A very strenuous week, attempting to retrieve the Yugoslav situation, which grew steadily worse, the Germans finally winning.'[12] On the 25th, Prince Paul of Yugoslavia's Prime Minister and Foreign Secretary went to Vienna and signed the Tripartite Pact with Germany and Italy. This did not mean that Germany had secured her as their military ally, but as a non-participant neutral with a bias towards the Axis, allowing supplies and stores to be carried through the country in sealed trains.

The Yugoslavs were livid at this weakness, and within forty-eight hours the Prince Regent had been ousted and the government toppled. The pact was now null and void. But Hitler had no intention of bargaining further or of forgiving this move. Yugoslavia had become as much a target as Greece.

Hamson's departure to Cairo had meant the closing down of Souda Island and the dispersal of the local guides who had worked with him and Mitford there. The stores of ammunition and explosives were to be locked up and saved for later use. Meanwhile the guides came under John's orders in addition to his own men.

In the middle of all the work and preparations brought on by the imminent invasion of Greece by Germany, the British authorities still chose to quibble about John's rank. He had a right as an MI(R) officer to take on the rank of Captain on the outbreak of hostilities, but no one at MI(R) had mentioned this to anyone else, so he came under the 'perusal' of the Customs Force. John, in his letter to Hilda, had expressed doubts as to whether the information had ever sunk in. 'I have a strong suspicion that I am still being paid as 2/Lt though I should have had pay and all allowances – including staff allowance – as a Captain from June 4.'[13] A month later, the Army Pay Office finally learned that John had been appointed as British Vice-Consul, and wasted no time in writing to the Foreign Office, fearing that they had both been paying him at the same time. They even asked the Foreign Office if they could claim any money back from over-payments. They were assured that the Foreign Office had never paid John a penny. As to sorting out his rank for John's benefit, that was to take them much longer.

The stores on Souda Island were for Hamson and Mitford to use in sabotage should Crete fall into enemy hands. They were strictly for D Section use – i.e. for sabotage on no longer allied-occupied territory. John had been put in charge back in November of arranging safe custody for them. He could not have found a better place than Souda Island. It lay at the entrance to the large natural harbour of Souda Bay, and was crowned by a Venetian fortress. It was an isolated and beautiful place. Jack Hamson, in one of the lighter moments of his account, remembered the sea path there. 'Past the Venetian fort and down to the water in the night, in the still night seemingly more luminous than day, brilliant, with a full moon picking out the snows of the White Mountains, the darkness of the cliffs of Kalami, the blue and purple of the sea, yes and the blades of grass at our feet as we went in silence with equipment and rifles and bombs and knives through the ruins of other wars.'[14]

The store included flares, rifles, detonators, clothing, food and medical stores. When Hamson and Mitford had left for Cairo, John had to sort out the stores and dispose of perishable goods such as food and medical supplies to those who could best use them. He managed to get some of the pistols and all the rifles to his store in Heraklion, to await the day when they might be needed.[15]

Hamson's men were paid and some of them retained either as guards or because they had special knowledge of the Dodecanese islands. All had their permits and identity cards retrieved and burnt as a security measure. Plans for raids against these islands had not yet died. Hamson had been, and John still was, determined to carry out a successful scheme against them. After the mess due to bad organisation, they were certain that good planning would bring the right results. John would soon meet others who had 'some sense and a little courage', and saw his ideas as workable. A local boat, the *Eos*, shipped all the stores off to their various destinations. What had to be sold was sold and the proceeds sent to the Consul, the 'Palely-smiling Meade', in Chania.

On March 28th 1941, John set off on another journey, to the east end of Crete – the only journey on which he made notes. It was ironic that he would cover much of the same territory as on his first trip to Crete, such a different Crete, back in 1927. He made his way around the coast setting up or checking observation and communications posts, such as the one Tasker-Brown had been shown from the coast by Holy George. He checked what weapons they had and whether more were needed, how easily they could identify enemy aircraft and ships and then report their findings to central points, and the number and reliability of the men holding the posts. He chose places from where the widest and clearest views along the coast and out to sea could be achieved. The men he used were mostly local policemen, often only two per post with a single rifle between them. As the days passed, getting increasingly warm, many of the posts could be moved up to higher ground and better vantage points.[16]

Starting at Cape Drepani, John worked out the range of vision from each place and chose the next one accordingly: from Drepani, down to Agios Nikolaos and Kritsa, then further to Hierapetra on the south coast, along eastwards to Agia Photia, inland via Stavrochori to Kavousi, and along the north coast to Sitia; from there to the north-east tip of Crete, Cape Sidero, down to Palaikastro, then to Zakros, across to Kouphonisi, the small island off the south-east of Crete, along westwards to Cape Goudouras and back to Ierapetra; then further west again to Myrtos, slipping inland to Gdokia and Kalami, then west again to Arvi on the coast, and further to Tsoutsouros and Kaloi Limenes, up to Matala, Kokkinos Pyrgos and back to Heraklion. At these locations, and many in between, he set up observation posts, many of them near gorges leading to the sea, with high, not easily accessible cliffs. The number of men at each post varied, and their vigils, night and day without leave, often led to strain. John would make a note and try to find a way of getting them relieved. He had to work out how they could be supplied and sheltered, especially those in high, exposed places, obvious to attacking aeroplanes from Italian-held Scarpanto. They had to be advised on what to do should a landing party or raid be launched from the Italian-occupied islands.

Old soldiers, veterans of the fight to end the Turkish occupation, were keen to help guard these posts, as the young men of fighting age were all still up in the north fighting off the Italians, bracing themselves for the imminent German attack. These small bands guarded what could be good landing beaches to minimise any delay in dealing with an incursion. All were given compass cards to determine the direction in which ships and planes were seen travelling, and codes for the different types of aircraft they might see – whether friendly, enemy or unknown, and what type. These could then be phoned through to the main regional exchange using the pre-arranged code. In addition, John gave them silhouette cards so that they could tell the nationality of an aeroplane from a distance by its shape.

The Neolaia, the Metaxist youth movement run on Crete by Colonel Papadakis, acted as volunteers around the island. Perhaps their flirtation with fascism had died with the old dictator, but more probably the fascist message had meant little to the majority of young Cretans who had been encouraged to join up. There was now no question of where their loyalties lay, and where there were no local police or old soldiers, the Neolaia would keep the watch, in some places led by the local priest.

Some of the posts lacked all these means of detecting the enemy, and had to rely solely on judgement of the height at which the aeroplane was flying to determine its nationality. Complaints were made that the telephone operator at one exchange would not answer quickly enough, if at all. John was trying to create as efficient a network as possible, considering the obstacles, between men who could be trusted and were dependable. But the problems that had to be overcome were legion.

The telephone system was supposed to work by the men ringing each other to synchronise timing – however, they would often just ring up when they felt like it. In some areas they could not hear the telephone – or anything said through it – when the sea was bad or the wind was up. 'They look as if they are never going to be relieved!', John noted, remarking their occasional despondency and boredom.[17]

Papadakis of the Neolaia helped as far as he could to get them better organised. But the Cretans did not always appreciate the dangers that faced them – 'Slit trenches dry, but no one goes in to them at Kritsa', John noted. 'Telephone had been removed as they thought there was no danger.' In other places he stressed their keenness and willingness. At one post, on the island opposite Agios Nikolaos, he wrote: 'Suggest they should all be armed unless it is thought this would provoke retaliation.'[18] This was a constant worry of John's. He knew that the Cretans would resist an invasion, whether they had guns or not. His determination to get those ten thousand rifles was entirely because he knew they would stand a better chance if they were armed with guns rather than with farm tools and their own hands. The Military Attaché in Athens, Jasper Blunt, had estimated as early as May 25th 1940, before John's arrival in Greece, that the Cretans had two thousand Manlicher rifles hidden away, but told the War Office that another five thousand rifles and ammunition would be needed for arming irregulars.[19] Whether they were ever provided is unclear, but it is unlikely, given John's preoccupation.

John's plans for general defence were more tied up with what the army was doing. He thought little of the schemes Symons had thought up before his departure, as they depended on the use of lorries – but these were constantly being requisitioned or disabled. 'Symons never answered this question', he noted dryly.[20]

'Patrolling of beaches done by police, and ex-soldiers, field guards and Youth Movement. Only 1 & 3 armed (ie Police and Field Guards – *Agrofilakes*). Keen as mustard. Suggest stock of arms deposited to be distributed to various police stations at discretion of Papadakis for use by ex-soldiers. May be against rules of war but otherwise there will be a massacre, since men, women and children will fight without arms.

'Suggest some form of Home Guard given uniform among ex-soldiers who will NOT be called up till the moment'. This John felt would avoid the risk of their being shot as *franc-tireurs*. But in the event the uniforms could not be found. 'Most important this (Home Guard) should be under their own elected chiefs – e.g. each village has its "Captain", each district its "leader". These should all be responsible to Papadakis, but the local police would act as Staff Officers to convey orders to each "party" from HQ.' Conscious that this use of civilians might be misconstrued, he added, 'Would this be allowed?'[21]

The guards on these posts were all enthusiastic, and many others came forward to offer their services. Frequently they were thrown on their own resources to get round the problems – setting up, in one case, a bonfire system in case the wires should break down. Air raid warnings were most often given by church bells.

Sometimes, however, a certain amount of rivalry emerged, as John noted in Lasithi: 'I have given orders to our men to work better with the police. At the moment there is jealousy, which is tragic as both are desperately anxious to help. On the whole the blame lies with those admirable men Papadakis and Christakopoulos who, while willing to do anything for us, are, not unnaturally, annoyed with people of their own nation who feel bound by personal ties to one of another.'[22]

Difficulties were also encountered when people did as they were bid and reported immediately – all at the same time: 'At the moment it seems in the Province of Lasithi that the keenness and enthusiasm of the authorities have overdone things. It is all very well for every village to telephone at once, but if each police post does this there will be chaos.'[23]

The system of lookout posts was essential, as the bulk of the Allied forces were concentrated around the main towns, leaving these outlying areas otherwise unguarded. John was trying to create a system that would work as quickly and efficiently as circumstances would allow by delegating the work carefully to avoid an overload of the system. He had been trying to persuade the first Brigadier on the island, Brigadier Tidbury, to adopt his plan, but Tidbury was reputedly unimaginative, and the fact that it was not military, but done on a local basis probably gave him the idea that it would be impossible to implement. John's notes and observations show that there would, of course, have been difficulties, but that the keenness and determination of the people involved would have made it work. Hamson wrote of how John had, 'preached in season and out to ears wholly deaf' on the 'very high courage' of the Cretans' and how effectively they could be organised.[24]

The toughness of the country Cretans and their dedication to such a task amazed and inspired those who witnessed it throughout the occupation. They did whatever was necessary to keep a post going. In order to keep one post supplied, the local Cretans would walk for twelve hours to reach Sitia, with no mules to help them with the supplies on the return journey. At another post, they had to pay for a donkey themselves in order to transport their supplies, but they never complained. The island of Kouphonisi was particularly vulnerable. Valued for its view to the Dodecanese and its lighthouse, it was very hot with little shade. The men there requested a machine-gun to stop the theft of their sheep, for several of these small islands off the east coast of Crete were vulnerable to raids from the Italians, who came over on fast boats and stole their animals. Even where guns were available, they were often antique and without ammunition. As with many of the posts, there was no change of shift for the crew and no leave. The lighthouse crew included one old man who should have retired long since, but stayed on to do his share of the watch.

Some places, such as the Vianos region, were well-armed and were already on the lookout for parachutists before the Germans invaded – three weeks before the Germans' first use in Greece of parachutists at Corinth. Somehow word must have got around that Crete might be invaded this way.

Nick Hammond, who had been drawn into MI(R) work at the same time as John and knew the problems it entailed, was impressed by John's contacts. '[They] were all personal acquaintances from the time of his travels and they owed him a deep personal devotion; they had been selected with an insight which none other than John could have brought to bear, and they covered the majority of mountain and coastal villages.'[25]

John spoke to no one of his work. His closest friends on the island, even those involved in other Intelligence work, knew nothing of what he was doing or even for whom he was doing it – though it has to be said that those for whom he was working were not clear on this themselves.

'In preparing future guerrilla bands', Nick Hammond wrote, 'it was necessary to choose the key personnel with the greatest care and to ensure that their activity did not become known; for before the time for action they had to be trained in weapons, explosives and organisation. The selection of hide-ups for dumps of stores, the reconnaissance of roads and of coves, and the choosing of targets had all to be done with the maximum of security. In preparing for the planting of agents with suitable cover in cities, where they could maintain wireless communication, collect intelligence and undertake sabotage under eventual enemy occupation, nothing was more vital than secrecy.'[26]

Even the Germans were to concede in a later report on John, 'The few collaborators of Pendlebury's who may perhaps become known as a result of further investigations are hardly likely to give important information, as Pendlebury, even vis-à-vis his closest collaborators, was very secretive. It must be said of Pendlebury that he carried out his activities, from the point of view of Intelligence information, in the most excellent way.'[27]

21

6 April–c. 17/18 May 1941

ON APRIL 6TH IN THE early morning Germany struck, simultaneously invading Greece and Yugoslavia. For the previous month the British, New Zealand and Australian forces had moved up through Greece to hold the Aliakmon line, while the Greek troops continued to hold the Metaxas line they had fought so hard to keep. The Germans reached the Metaxas line first, but were pushed back by the Greeks, who put everything they had left into the fight.

Whereas the Greek army had been through one of the severest winters fighting the Italians, the Germans were fresh and rested. As the bitter cold lingered, the Greeks withstood the harshest bombing and shelling the Germans could throw at them. They engaged some two hundred of the elite paratroops and bested them. All that the Germans tried on the Metaxas line at first failed. But the security of the line depended entirely on the co-operation of Yugoslavia, and though the government that had made the pact with Germany had been overthrown, the Allies had failed to secure the alliance of the new one, and Yugoslavia's defences were not strong.

Within a short time, the Germans were able to defeat the Yugoslavs in the Strumitsa Pass and bypass the Metaxas line altogether. The British delegation to Greece in the previous two months had tried to bring this possibility home to General Papagos, but he had been loath to withdraw his men and simply give up land so sorely defended for months. The wisdom of the British suggestion was now clear.

The following day, the Germans hit in the heart of Greece – her main port of Piraeus. A bomb with a timer device had been placed in the *SS Clan Fraser* in the harbour. When it blew, the entire cargo of munitions and TNT went sky high. The repercussions were felt as far as the centre of Athens, yet the toll in the harbour was even more devastating – six merchant ships, sixty lighters and twenty-five caïques were destroyed. The port buildings were severely damaged, and an ammunition train and the barge it was unloading were ignited, setting off equally destructive subsidiary explosions.

On the day of the invasion John cut short his trip round the observation posts and returned to Heraklion. He began to concentrate on what should be sabotaged should the Germans get as far as Crete and to plan the 'stay behind' campaign. Although staying behind in enemy-occupied territory was officially a task for D section and aimed purely at sabotage, John had no intention of pulling out.

'It had always been his intention to stay in Crete', Nick Hammond wrote later, 'and lead the resistance, and he never talked as if any other course was possible... John's plan was original and daring, and given his personal qualities as a leader in a limited area with a more or less homogeneous population, the plan was full of promise. It required more resolution in an Englishman to stay behind voluntarily and be submerged by the German tide than to return later as many did when the ebb was likely to set in. But for John the choice did not exist; he felt himself a Cretan and in Crete he would stay until victory was won.'[1]

Anything that could prove to be of military use to the Germans would have to be destroyed. Now, more than ever, the arrival of the Germans seemed to John to be only a question of time. The telegraph facilities of the Cable and Wireless office would have to be dealt with, the instruments smashed, the building burnt (John made a note to 'give them a lesson in pyrotechnics'), and whatever could be used in the hills would have to be taken.

He chose three men who would each take a wireless set and go to Mount Ida, Mount Dikte and East Crete. They were all English and had worked in the Eastern Telegraph Office before. Their names were Sharp, Edmonds, and Rolston, the last being the man with whom Hutchinson had been working at the Cable and Wireless office in Heraklion in the summer of 1940. He had also done what he could to help John with some of the more mundane parts of his work at the same time.

Three others would stay behind after the wireless operators had left, to destroy the equipment. Foster, who had lived in Heraklion for many years, was one of these. He and Rolston were the main men with whom John dealt in the telegraph office. Foster was an eccentric character, described by Ralph Stockbridge as an 'elderly and bibulous' gentleman, who had once, in a fit of enthusiasm, stuffed oranges into the mouths of the lions on the Morosini fountain.[2]

Other targets for demolition were the harbour (which would be a job for the Sappers), the power station, railway sheds, telephone and automatic Exchange, emergency telegraph station, all cold storage and crucial roads and bridges. This required the dispersal of explosives to the areas where they would be needed, the likely source of which was the store of munitions on Souda Island. They were still kept there under lock and key and John was responsible for them while Hamson and Mitford were in Cairo. Even the eventual necessity of sabotaging the water supply was considered, though very much as a last resort. However, all these measures depended on getting adequate prior warning of the first attack in order to have sufficient time to carry them out. This was never given.

John searched for outlets for equipment to take into the hills at short notice – blankets and wireless sets and a means of recharging the wireless batteries. Cairo had seriously underestimated the budget needed for such post-occupation work, giving it no more than five or six thousand pounds a year, an amount that Pirie described as 'ludicrous'.[3] According to Pirie, they made no provision whatsoever for wireless transmitter contact after the occupation, a fact that seemed inconceivable to those such as Ralph Stockbridge who would make their way back into occupied Crete as wireless operators.

John knew that the men would need some sort of supply line to keep them alive in the mountains, where spring would arrive far later than on the coast. He counted on getting seven trucks for transport to the different regions, though this estimate also proved over-optimistic, far exceeding the number of vehicles that were eventually available. His plans were now concentrated on central and eastern Crete, including the Ida range, which was perhaps the most secure stronghold on the island.

He thought that, if he could get them, it would be best to have one wireless set above Krousonas, in the foothills of the Ida range, and another up on Karphi – how remote now were the days of the dig and the 'beat of the long, winding dances'. Two other possible sites were above Kavousi, overlooking the Gulf of Mirabello on the east side, and Khonos, on the easternmost rocky plateau of Crete before the land falls away into the sea. But most important of all were the weapons that still had to be found somehow.

Krousonas was John's centre of operations and the home village of many of the people he could most trust – notably Satanas. The village was comparatively large, nestling in the foothills of Mount Ida, and had a sizeable population. It is ironic that this village should have produced some of the best men that John recruited, and yet was later to be the source of some of the worst traitors – mainly due to inter-village rivalry.

Meanwhile, the Germans were moving down through Greece. Salonika fell on April 9th. Some of the German troops that had gone into Yugoslavia swung round to cross the Greek border at two more points, bypassing the Greek positions. Four days later, the Allies withdrew to the Thermopylae Line and began to consider evacuating their forces from mainland Greece. The battle was clearly already lost. Their manpower, equipment and communications were totally inferior to those of the invaders. Their main gain in the campaign was to delay the advance of the Germans.

The German army was closely supported by the airforce, with devastating effect. The concentrated daytime bombing meant that as the Allied troops withdrew to the Thermopylae Line, they could only move by night if they were to avoid heavy losses. But this in turn led to many accidents on the roads. The whole effect was deeply demoralising, but by April 20th they had secured their positions on the Thermopylae Line.

*

Chaos had meanwhile taken hold in Greece. Piraeus had been all but destroyed in further air raids and then the Prime Minister, Koryzis, committed suicide in mysterious circumstances. The Greek army in Epirus capitulated without warning on the 21st, and its evacuation became an immediate necessity. It was planned to begin on the night of April 24th and continue for three nights. Those who could not be embarked in the main exodus were to make their way to the Peloponnese in the hope of being taken on board there.

So the evacuation of the troops to Crete and Alexandria began. The threat from German fighters and bombers was formidable, yet many of the Hurricanes that had survived the Greek campaign, and might have helped to cover the evacuation, had been destroyed on the ground at Argos the day before the evacuation began. Around Greece's southern coasts, twenty-three small and medium-sized ships were also destroyed, limiting the means of transport to Crete. Where troops were able to find a ship, there was no guarantee that they would make it to Crete. They were fired on mercilessly if the Luftwaffe caught them in daylight. Instances were reported in which one or two ships would turn to help another that had been seriously damaged by enemy fire, only to be sunk themselves. It is scarcely surprising that those troops who did finally make it to Crete were shattered and their spirits low. A large quantity of their heavy armament and their own personal weapons had been lost or left behind and destroyed. It was a pitiful gathering on Crete and could have done little to inspire confidence in those already on the island.

King George II of the Hellenes had left for Crete with his government on April 23rd. He had done little to inspire the confidence of his people since Greece had entered the war and was a poor figurehead, often, Pirie noted, appearing bored in public and making no attempt to visit the front. It was Prince Peter who, as a liaison officer to the British Military Mission, had visited the Albanian front and received a very warm reception from an army otherwise resentful of the Royal Family. The new Prime Minister, Tsouderos, was chosen partly with the evacuation of the government to Crete in mind and in large part by Pirie and D Section agents. They had to have someone who could bring members of other parties into the government if Greece were to maintain any sort of cohesion against a German invasion. The mainland government of

Metaxas had been deeply unpopular in Crete, not least for its antagonism towards the ideas and ideals of the Cretan Venizelos and his followers. Tsouderos was chosen for his milder image. Members of his cabinet who were seen as more confrontational, such as the Greek Himmler, Maniadakis – the cruelty of whose secret police aroused the hatred of the Cretans, were hurried on to Egypt.

As the Germans were consolidating their hold on mainland Greece, they began to develop plans to take Crete, which, up until this point, they had not seriously contemplated. Their preparation of the airfields on the mainland began almost immediately.

Meanwhile, a meeting was called in Crete on the last day of April by Wavell, who had come over in order to assess how the defence preparations had been going until then, and how best to use what little time was left to them. The Generals Wilson, Weston and Freyberg were there to represent the land forces, and Wing Commander Beamish and Air Vice-Marshal D'Albiac, the RAF. Wavell gave Freyberg command of Creforce and told him above all to deny the airbases on Crete to the enemy. Freyberg thought that a combined attack from air and sea was most likely, and yet the available RAF air cover was woefully inadequate.

From Chania, Brigadier Chappel was sent to Heraklion to establish the headquarters of the 14th Infantry Brigade. These were the first troops to be based in the Heraklion area since 50 ME Cdo had left in March. They comprised the 2nd Battalion York and Lancaster and 2nd Battalion Black Watch, the 2/4th Australian Battalion (three hundred men) with the 7th Medium Regiment Royal Artillery (two hundred and fifty men), now set up to act as infantry, two Australian light anti-aircraft batteries and a section of the 15th Coastal Regiment, again of the Royal Artillery. Two Greek Battalions would arrive a little later, along with the 2nd Battalion Leicestershire Regiment. They had two Matilda tanks and six light ones. Time was limited, and they had to work fast to get the defences into order to protect the airfield and the town two and a half miles to its west. At the end of April, the RAF still planned to keep one fighter squadron at Heraklion, but through early May the aeroplanes were lost one by one while warding off constant attacks against both shipping and the aerodromes.

The arrival of the King of Greece caused great excitement, and he stayed temporarily at the Villa Ariadne. The King met John there, and he was to speak of him with admiration following the war when he went to Cambridge to receive an honorary degree.

*

There is a strange tale dealing with John's activities at this time, which takes the art of Cretan myth-making to extremes. The author, Theocharis Saridakis, is thinly disguised in it as a 'schoolboy', who, he claims, related the story to him.[4] More fiction than fact (and greatly inflated fiction at that), it purports to record conversations at the Villa Ariadne between the King of Greece, Sir Michael Palairet – the British Minister, and John, who is given the epithet of 'Consul-Warrior', amongst many other adulatory adjectives, most of them invented by the author.

The author describes how he accompanied John on a night-time ambush, following the road along the coast west of Heraklion, as far as the River Giophyro, where they met up with a band of seven English soldiers and a Cretan from the Consulate. Taking cover in the reeds at the mouth of the river, they waited until, just after midnight, 'They saw the black shadow coming in from the mute waters of the sea. He neared the shore. With great care the silent shadow drew in onto the beach. He left the water and got out onto the marshy land. With quick movements the man opened the plug of the rubber dinghy and it deflated with a quiet hiss. He folded it and buried it in the sand. An army bag awaited him next to a small suitcase on the beach. The moment he went to pick it up the Consul [John] and two of the Cretans knocked him flat. The relentless blows threw him down onto the sand without a noise. With his hands behind his back and a dagger in his heart, he let out no word, no death rattle... The new arrival was wearing the dress of a Greek major. He had the regular papers of an officer, a lot of money in his clothes and more in the suitcase. He also had several strange things in his bag. The young Cretan remembers a strange mirror which folded, a long and powerful lens, a heavy pistol with a wide barrel, maps, a compass, a camera and a suspended leather map case. He also had several photographs in a large wallet.'

He goes on to describe how John searched the allegedly German corpse, finding, to his delight, a long roll of paper covered in code, amongst other incriminating personal papers, before burying him nearby.

His praise and admiration of John are boundless. 'The heroic patriot. The English Gentleman. The Consul. The Captain. The leading protagonist of thriller, John Pendlebury. [He rarely gets fewer than five adjectives – mostly superlatives – at each mention.] Impeccable in appearance, cheerful and kindly, smart in the fine and festive uniform of a British officer, with the imperial emblems, the holster, the revolver in its cloth case, and the twisted leather stick in his right hand, freshly shaved and resplendent.' As Patrick Leigh Fermor, one of the later Liaison Officers in the Cretan Resistance, commented on reading the account, 'My word. John Pendlebury would have been embarrassed by this'. Embarrassed possibly – amused certainly.

*

On May 14th 1941, Jack Hamson returned to Crete to join his colleague Terence Bruce-Mitford. Their chief in Cairo had withdrawn them from the island on the assumption that there was not likely to be an invasion of Crete and therefore their services were no longer deemed relevant. Only when forced by the overwhelming evidence of an imminent invasion did they grudgingly reverse their decision. When he got back to Heraklion, Hamson found that even John was downcast. This may have had something to do with the fact that Hamson and Mitford had effectively been put in charge of John, though all three men were the same rank.

On the same day, Nick Hammond turned up in Heraklion, having arrived in Crete with Pirie, Pawson and others at the end of April. Nick had, like John, been adopted by D Section, though in his case it was a full transfer. D Section had failed to leave any wireless communication with its groups on the mainland. The Salonika group felt that wireless transmitter (W/T) sets would compromise their security, while those sets intended for the Athens groups had been demanded for use in Yugoslavia as being of a higher priority. Only a few days before the Germans marched into Athens, D Section got two W/T sets into the city, but the key to the codes they were to use were lost when the boat that had carried Pirie and the others to Crete, the *Irene*, was sunk. It was only thanks to another of the Souda Island trained agents that new codes could be delivered to the Prometheus group in Athens, who could then re-establish W/T contact and get SO2 (formerly D Section) up and running again. This was achieved by the suitably code-named Odysseus, after a truly Homeric epic journey following the fall of Crete.

Nick Hammond had been busy on the mainland trying to carry out sabotage in the face of the German advance, including the blowing up of warehouses of cotton and cotton seed at Lake Copaïs, where John and Hilda had walked with Dilys and Humfry Payne so many years before. This was no simple matter, given the steady flow of retreating Allied troops.

He and John had not seen one another since the journey from England in the Sunderland flying boat just under a year earlier. 'The intervening months had taught us a great deal about the difficulties of our job. The department for which we worked had not at that time acquired the full recognition of the regular branches of the services. It was necessary for the man on the spot to win the personal confidence of the local naval and military officers, who at first regarded his nose as false and his schemes hare-brained. John had succeeded to a remarkable degree in winning this confidence; his unique knowledge of Crete, his personal charm, his tenacity and determination, and his aggressive views had overcome most opposition. During the winter, when I had been arranging to send caïques to the Dodecanese, Naval Intelligence officers at Alexandria had spoken with enthusiasm of John Pendlebury as a man they trusted. And I found the same respect for him at Souda and Heracleion [sic], when I landed from Greece.'[5]

Hammond had just joined the crew of a variation on the Greek armed caïque theme, built in Haifa – *HMS Dolphin*, D Section's boat. Her skipper was a wonderful character called Mike Cumberlege. He wore a single gold earring, having pierced his own ear with a sail needle at a party just before the war to convince a beautiful young woman that it was not painful. When he yelped in pain the lady was so touched that she gave him her earring, which he wore ever after. Hammond described Cumberlege as a 'natural buccaneer of superlative courage', and he and John took an immediate liking to one another.

Cumberlege and Hammond had met when it was decided that the best way to blow up the Corinth Canal was to sail up it with a six-day delay action mine slung under the *Dolphin*. Under the orders of the Naval Attaché, they had sailed westwards through the canal towards Patras dragging a dinghy filled with eight depth charges and a limpet mine with six-day delay fuses attached to each. The detonation of one would set off the rest, some two and a half tons of explosives in all. On April 26th, they had returned and sunk the dinghy about 350 yards to the east of the only bridge crossing the canal, where there was a natural fault in the north bank. The mine slipped about sixty yards further east. Destined to go off on May 2nd, they did not stay around long enough to know the outcome. Thereafter, Crete became the gathering point of D Section personnel and stores to use back on the mainland.

For Hammond, it was easy to understand why John and Cumberlege were instant friends. 'Both were men of vigorous speech and independent ideas, with great force of character and abundant humour; and both possessed that clear-headed audacity which undertakes the apparently more dangerous course after a detached study of the advantages and disadvantages. They possessed too a simplicity of motive in facing or inviting danger, something much more spontaneous and automatic than the ordinary man's sense of duty, a rare quality which I only met once again during the war. This virtue, this "arete", made them incomparable leaders of limited numbers of men such as subversive operations envisage.'[6]

Mike Cumberlege's cousin, Cle, was also on the crew as the gunner. He had fled the monotony of a desk job to get a look in on something more exciting. Then there was able-bodied seaman Saunders, who possessed 'the efficiency and humour engendered by seventeen years of service on the lower deck'.[7]

Saunders and Hammond had been firm friends since their first meeting in an air raid in Athens, during which Hammond had been driving a truck, carrying in the back a magnetic mine – on top of which Saunders was perched. Lastly, there was Jumbo Steele, a South African private in the Black Watch who had a taste for adventure and was a crack shot.

The crew had brought the *Dolphin* from the mainland with the main flow of the evacuation and under constant attack. But finding the situation at Souda Bay little better, they went on to Heraklion to give their engines a badly needed overhaul. Hammond immediately went in search of John through the narrow streets above the harbour, to his small office up a narrow flight of stairs. Mike Cumberlege described it in a letter to Hilda shortly afterwards: 'I shall never forget John's office with its two Lear watercolours and a somewhat rickety wardrobe filled with guns of all sorts, piles of paper money bundled in with every sort of other paper etc. We used to foregather there to work out our plans.'[8]

To Hammond, John seemed far more alert to the imminence of the danger to Crete than they were. They had relaxed after their ordeals on the mainland, while he saw how ill-prepared the island was to face that danger. Though some men had managed to get away and were filtering back to Crete, the whole of the Cretan division had been surrendered in Epirus by General Papastergiou, who had returned to the island without a single Cretan beside him. Back on the island the Cretans were outraged at this betrayal of his men. Almost as soon as he had set foot on the island he was murdered at Kastelli Kissamou. John felt as strongly about this as the Cretans. He was convinced that the older islanders should be better provided with weapons, to fill partially at least the gap left by the absence of the young fighting men of Crete, so many of whom were now prisoners or struggling to return to the island. But the weapons were simply not available.

That evening John told Hammond of all the preparations that he had made and the organisation he had set up, and the following day John went down to *HMS Dolphin*. Within no time, John and Mike Cumberlege had planned another raid on Kasos. 'It was going to be a terrific party', Cumberlege thought, 'and stood considerable chance of success.'[9]

The idea was for the *Dolphin* to take John and a group of his Cretans across to Kasos after dark, to attack an Italian post and take prisoners. These, they hoped, would divulge details of the German plans to invade Crete. But they had to take into consideration that the post in question might have been reinforced, for the attack was certainly not far off, yet the *Dolphin* could only carry some fifteen men in addition to her crew. Nor was she the fastest boat on the water, and there was a strong probability that she would still be out and vulnerable in the Kasos straits when the sun rose. But they had their guns and it was considered worth the risk by the naval and military authorities, as well as the crew. The plan appealed to John as it would give his men the chance to develop their 'offensive spirit.'

Before the operation could take place, though, the *Dolphin* crew had to reconnoitre the south coast for the Navy, to note any beaches where supplies and reinforcements could be landed during an invasion, without the ships having to run the gauntlet to the north coast. Mike Cumberlege took the opportunity to check out beaches and coves where a boat could put in secretly should the island come under enemy control, and so keep John and his men supplied. Helping them was one of John's men, whom they met in the tiny quiet harbour of Sphakia: 'A good sailor', Cumberlege reckoned, 'and, neither inquisitive nor talkative, he was the right type and he knew the dangerous south coast well.'[10]

John went with them as far as the pass leading down into the Messara, and suggested suitable places. He asked Hammond, an explosives expert, to take a look at some sites he had set up for laying charges to demolish certain bends in the road to the south coast. 'He had already driven some bore-holes for camouflet charges, and he had trained men in the neighbouring villages.'[11]

John's trips round the south and east coast were already bearing fruit. The men he had chosen were sound and dependable. In one of the villages to the east of the Messara Plain, John introduced Hammond and the others to one of his leading men. 'A bald-headed giant with a ferocious moustache and a large family of sons', Hammond remembered. 'He breathed blood and slaughter and garlic in the best Cretan style and marched us off at a fast pace to the inlet of Matala. The cliffsides of the inlet are riddled with caves, and the colours and style of the approach are reminiscent of smugglers' coves in Cornwall; a picturesque place but too obviously suitable for use as a secret base. From Matala our guide took us on to the shelving beach of Kokkinos Pyrgos, suitable for beaching light craft, and to Ayia Galene, where the water was so clear that we dived to gauge its depth; for it seemed possible that ships of moderate draught could be brought close inshore.'[12]

While the crew of the *Dolphin* were tied up with these reconnaissance trips, John went back to Heraklion. It was not known what form the German invasion would take, but it was thought that it would most likely come by air with some sort of back-up by sea. Information gleaned from Ultra (the intelligence gained from the decoding at Bletchley Park of German naval dispatches encoded on Enigma enciphering machines) had indicated that the airfields were the most likely target, as the key to the Germans' success was the quick and easy landing of supplies and reinforcements. However, the source was so secret at that stage that even General Freyberg would later refrain from putting the information gained from it into practice, lest the Germans discover that their code had been broken. But the Germans had undeniable air superiority, and it had seemed fairly certain, even as far back as the winter of 1940, that their main targets would be the major airfields, and that they would perhaps also try to land forces elsewhere inland.

Consequently, Jack Hamson and Terence Bruce Mitford were sent up to the large upland Nida Plain beneath Psiloriti (Mount Ida) to consider the possibility of enemy aircraft landing there. They produced a brief summary report, which concluded that, although access and communications were difficult (with Krousonas six to seven hours, and Anogia four hours away by foot), there were three possible runways on the plain – each more than a thousand yards long. These were all on the east side, where the sandy soil was remarkably level and covered in short springy grass with very few loose stones lying around. The western side, however, was studded with scrub and rocky outcrops so could not have been used. Also on the eastern side, they noted tongues of turf that ran up between low rocky promontories, where aircraft could be stowed away, concealed beneath camouflage nets.[13]

The Nida Plain belonged to the village of Anogia, and from mid-March to mid-December some five thousand sheep grazed there, during which time the shepherds would live in the half-dozen *mandras* that were set around the plain above the level of the floor. With an abundant water supply from the spring below the Chapel of Analipsis (Ascension), it was a bountiful place.

Having made the report, John sent some of his men from Krousonas up to Nida with Hamson and Bruce Mitford, to strew boulders on its surface to prevent aircraft landing. As the main targets were known to only a limited number of people, as a contingency plan this was not as far-fetched as it might seem. For while it would be difficult for any sizeable force to break out of there easily or with any speed, it might provide an opportunity to land supplies and refuel for fresh attacks on more significant targets.

Hamson was very unhappy that he and Bruce Mitford had been put above John: 'I considered myself his hand merely and his representative, whatever view authority might take of our ranks. It was he whom I went to see at Heraklion on May 16th before I went up into the hills – it was an act of well-nigh incredible imprudence and stupidity on the part of authority to have sent us over his head – and yet in spite of his disappointment and his sense of the ineptitude, he made available to me the whole of his resources. It was by virtue of his knowledge, of his power, and in his name that I was enabled to do in the hills whatever I succeeded in doing. And his name was indeed one to conjure with in those hills. "I am sent by Mr John, Mr John says, Mr John suggests, Mr John requires": Those were my infallible passwords. Though he was absent, it was upon his strength that I relied; and more, present or absent, it was to him that I instinctively turned for guidance and for inspiration, or rather to that phantasm or concept of John which, magnified in the mind of men, grew upon me also in those hills. It was essentially his business, his proper work, which by accident and by twist of fortune I was called to discharge, and which I endeavoured to discharge essentially as his. It was he who primarily committed to those men; it was in his principal name that they obeyed me. I was to them a casual stranger; he had lived with them and knew them. It was to the echo of his voice that they listened and could respond; and that there was in my voice this echo I am proud and glad.'[14]

Hamson and Mitford were based up at Krousonas, and the Krousoniots were the men who would hold the plain. John planned to join them there as soon as things began to happen, to organise them to fight where they could do most good.

Meanwhile, back in Heraklion, John had a brief chance to relax. Whenever there was a chance to vex someone who was being awkward or difficult then John would rise to it with relish. If he could pretend, in his guise as Vice-Consul, also to be a 'Squire'-archaeologist, oblivious to the existence of a war, then so much the better. An occasion arose one day in Heraklion: the victim was an American journalist with the Associated Press named Robert St John. He had arrived in Heraklion after following the story of the evacuation from the mainland, along with two other journalists – one English, one American – and he decided that he wanted to see the British Vice-Consul.

They found him. 'His chief interest in life had always been and still was the ancient ruins of Minos, which were only a few miles out of Heraklion, at Knossos. He'd written a book years ago about the ruins. He wanted to talk about both the ruins and the book. I tried to point out that, as the Australian officer had said, hell might break loose on Crete any minute. But Atherton [the English journalist] got interested in the ruins. The Vice-Consul presented Atherton with a copy of the book, at cost plus postage. He even autographed it. Then Atherton autographed something for the Vice-Consul. Hill and I were getting impatient, and when the Vice-Consul finally persuaded Atherton that he shouldn't miss this opportunity of going out and spending an afternoon looking over these relics of the oldest ruins in the world, we had our first row with the Balkan Correspondent of the London *Daily Mail*.

'We said we'd seen the ruins of enough cities already. Modern cities. We weren't interested in ancient ruins right now. Atherton grumbled a bit about how all Americans lack any real appreciation of art, history and archaeology and other things that really count. But he backed down, and we left the Vice-Consul. A little later we ran into someone who said the boy king of Yugoslavia was staying on the estate of an English millionaire near Knossos [Villa Ariadne]. Now Atherton had a double reason for wanting to take the afternoon off. He thought we could get an exclusive interview with Peter as well as see the ruins. But Hill and I argued that down by pointing out that we had too much news already. What we needed was some way of sending it.'[15]

The German raids were increasing in strength daily over the harbour and the airfield, hinting at an imminent invasion. Every dawn and dusk some thirty German planes would drone overhead. The British planes faced them out as best they could, though it was clear that they stood no chance of reducing their numbers significantly, and they suffered severe losses they could ill afford as a result.

When the *Dolphin* crew was given orders to go round to Ierapetra on the south coast and judge the feasibility of salvaging the valuable cargo of a ship that had sunk just offshore, the planned Kasos raid had to be postponed. The sunken cargo contained ammunition, light anti-aircraft guns, machine-guns and small arms – 'A cargo that might have turned the scales in the defence of Crete', Hammond noted.[16] Before the ship had even left Alexandria, the Germans had found out about her cargo and torpedoed her en route. She had managed to get as far as the coast near Ierapetra before she was finished off by German bombers. But the shallow waters in which she had sunk gave hope that her cargo might be salvaged.

It was hoped that the salvagers of the wreck of *HMS York* in Souda Bay might help, as heavy bombardment there made it impossible for them to continue their work for the time being. So the Kasos raid was put off, provisionally, until the night of May 20th; the *Dolphin* aimed to pick up John and his men on the evening of May 19th.

'Before leaving for Ierapetra John gave us dinner at the Officers' Club overlooking the harbour', Nick Hammond remembered. 'He insisted on Saunders coming who, as a regular seaman, was somewhat abashed but greatly delighted at dining in an Officers' mess. John was in tremendous spirits, keyed up by the increasing tempo of the German raids on Heracleion aerodrome and harbour during the last few days.'[17] That evening, John had gone down to the harbour to do a stint on the *Dolphin*'s machine-gun. As the Luftwaffe, flying low over the town, let out bursts of machine-gun fire at the harbour, John opened up on them from the mooring close by the quayside. The local fishermen lost no time in gathering up the fish concussed by the bombs, and the

Dolphin crew – including John, now an honorary member – dined on fresh fish that night, with lamb, cheese and wine besides.

'John was confident', Nick recalled, 'that if Crete were lost his Cretans could be depended upon to carry on guerrilla warfare in the hills. He had received a considerable supply of stores and ammunition since our arrival at Heraklion, and there was a large dump on one of the islands at Souda Bay which could be moved to suitable hide-ups. His main shortage was in small arms, but he had sufficient with which to start operations; and from his discussions with Mike he knew that communication could probably be kept open by sea from the south coast to Africa.'[18]

After dinner, they talked over their plans for Kasos, and John broached the subject of Hammond joining him to stay on the island after the attack on Crete had begun. Mike Cumberlege was not keen on the idea as Hammond was the only Greek-speaker in the crew and he wanted to hang on to him. Within a couple of days, D Section, now safely in Cairo and officially renamed SO2 as part of SOE (Special Operations Executive), would send a telegram to London with the same suggestion, but by then it was already too late.

22

20–22 May 1941

THE WRECK OFF the coast at Ierapetra was not the only ship full of badly-need munitions to be destroyed before it could reach its destination. From the beginning of May to the start of the invasion, half the guns that had been sent from Alexandria, and more than half the stores, were sunk either in the open sea or in the harbour. Souda Bay was congested with wrecks of all sizes to the point where any more would have rendered it impenetrable to shipping altogether. The obvious vulnerability of the Souda anchorage led to a special formation of Royal Marines being brought in, at all but the last minute, to defend it. They were known as the Mobile Naval Base Defence Organisation (MNBDO).

The pressure from the daily attacks meant that the ships could only be safely unloaded after dark, and men were grabbed wherever they could be found to act as stevedores and speed up the unloading of vital supplies and rations. But the process was still too slow and many ships had to wait offshore, exposed to raids, before a quay was free for them.

In their attempts to ward off the enemy from the harbours and the airfields, the thirty-six RAF aircraft on Crete fought with great skill and courage, but against overwhelming odds. Though they managed to bring down sizeable numbers of enemy aircraft, their own numbers were rapidly depleted to the point where only six survived that could achieve anything at all in the air. However keenly it was recognised that the key to holding the island lay in the Allies' ability to join in combat in the air, it was obvious that these six planes would make not the slightest impression on the hundreds that the Germans had at their disposal. Finally, the decision was taken to withdraw them to Egypt where they could at least survive to fight at better odds another day. On May 19th they left. The order should then have been given to demolish the three main airfields at Heraklion, Rethymnon and Maleme. But the time for that had passed.

On the morning of May 20th, shortly after daybreak, in the far west of the island, the airfield at Maleme and the Naval base at Souda Bay were subjected to the most intensive bombing they had yet witnessed. At Maleme the air was so thick with dust from explosions that the soldiers on the ground did not for some time realise that the first German gliders had quietly slipped down to earth. The shortage of weapons on the island meant that many of the gun crews had no more to defend themselves than the artillery they manned. Once the fighting came too close to use them they were in trouble.

The German troops inside the gliders formed the leading element of the Assault Regiment. Each load emerged in tightly organised units, about ten to a glider, ready to set up their field guns and join up with other units in the minimum amount of time. Most of them were wiped out immediately or shortly after landing, but enough survived to cover the next wave of the attack – the slow, deep-humming formations of Junker 52s. Had the RAF been there they could have dealt with them easily, but they were not, and all that those on the ground could do was watch as each aircraft opened and specks of bright colour flashed across the sky and gently floated down to the ground.

After the first moments of spellbound wonder at the sight of hundreds of different-coloured parachutes falling out of the sky, the Allies began to shoot. While suspended in mid-air, the paratroops were sitting ducks. The Allied soldiers soon realised that if they aimed at the feet they stood a fair chance of hitting their target. Alternatively, they could send up incendiary devices and set the parachutes alight.

The German losses at this stage were very high, and the parachutists' chances did not improve much on landing. If they avoided getting caught in trees, there was no guarantee that they would land close to their equipment and weapons, which were dropped by separate parachutes, or that they would not drop into the middle of the enemy soldiers. The Cretans acted quickly. As John had predicted, they grabbed any tool or implement that they could lay their hands on and joined the battle. The Germans were totally baffled by this, having been assured that their reception from the Cretans would be one of open arms and friendly alliance.

However, not all the parachutists met with bad luck. Many got to their weapons and managed to break lines of communication between Allied units early on. They landed with everything that they could possibly want, except water. Each man carried an automatic pistol and a jack-knife (in case he should have to cut himself free of his parachute in a hurry), rations for several days, thirst-quenchers, cigarettes and contraceptives. Spare vests, socks and pants were rolled into their trouser turn-ups.

Many fired guns as they came down from the Junker 52s, though this gave them even less than the little control they had over their descent. The uniform was camouflaged and specially designed for the purpose, and the parachutes colour-coded for units, supplies and munitions. The first wave even included doctors, with all their surgical tools, drugs and bandages. Every last man had a caffeine-based solution, which could be self-injected to keep him awake and alert and to quicken his responses and senses. They had planned everything down to the smallest detail, but it was hot and they had to get water. Many suffered heatstroke from the sun and from the weight of their uniform.

The greatest danger in such an attack was the haphazard nature of their descent onto the scene. Though they were dropped in carefully planned groups and each man knew exactly what to do when he landed, they were inevitably dispersed, dropping in olive groves, river beds, ditches and fields. Though the danger of this was as great if not greater for them, it did enable them to act as snipers and open fire where least expected, making life even harder for the Allied runners who were the only alternative to the broken communication lines.

*

Nobody in Heraklion or Rethymnon had the slightest idea of what was going on in the west. It was remarked that the lines of communication were down, but this was not unheard of in normal circumstances. Here, in central Crete, the morning of May 20th seemed like any other day, except for the lack of the routine bombardment. It was 4.25pm when the bombers came. They wasted no time in making up for their earlier absence. In the worst bombardment yet, the Germans pounded relentlessly away at Heraklion for an hour, causing immense damage.

Throughout the previous three weeks, through the daily bombardments, only the anti-aircraft guns had been allowed to open fire, in order that none of the other guns, painstakingly hidden and camouflaged, should give away their positions. This meant that as much as possible of the armament would be intact when it was most needed, when the German troops began to land.

The heavy drone of the troop carriers followed on from the deafening racket of the bombardment. They came in tight formation, in two waves, from the north and north-west, two hundred of them. They flew low over the land – no more than three hundred feet above the ground – and from them emerged multi-coloured clouds of parachutes.

The parachutes floated down in five main groups. One landed to the west of Heraklion and another just to the south of it. These first two groups were backed up by another group further to the west, beyond the rivers Giophyro and Xeropotamo, to ensure that nothing came at them unexpectedly from Rethymnon to their rear. Others came down to the east of the town, either side of the road to the airfield and in a valley further east beyond the aerodrome itself.

The Allied forces in the Heraklion sector comprised mainly the original British forces that had held the island since November 1940. Added to these were an Australian Battalion and a Greek garrison. While it was the Greeks' responsibility to hold the town and the land immediately to the south and west of it, the 2nd Yorks and Lancs. and the 7th Medium Regiment held the east of the town, and their positions also acted as the west side of the defence perimeter centred on the airfield. Going round eastwards to the south of the airfield were the 2nd Leics. and the 24th Battalion of the Australians, whose territory covered the Babali road and the twin hills known to Cretans as the 'Duo Aorakia' and to the troops as the 'Charlies'. The Black Watch covered the airfield itself and the East Hill to the south of it.

The headquarters of the 14th Infantry Brigade was in a cave in the rock outcrop to the east of Heraklion, above the so-called West Wadi (the Kassabanos River). From here, Brigadier Chappel co-ordinated the defence of the Heraklion sector, and it was a hive of activity on that first day as people came in and out getting their orders. Amongst them was a young officer of the British Military Mission, which had been set up to report on the military situation in Greece to the Middle East, until it had been evacuated to Crete with the other troops at the end of April.

For this officer, Patrick Leigh Fermor, one man stood out from the others who went in and out of the cave that day. 'I only met him twice, and it was actually during the battle. I was enormously impressed by that splendid great figure, with his rifle, as opposed to an ordinary officers' service revolver, and the swordstick he carried; I remember him stooping to come down the stairs that led into our Brigade HQ, in a deep cave, supported by a pillar in the middle, between Heraklion and the aerodrome. He had a Cretan guerrilla with him, festooned with bandoliers. John Pendlebury made a wonderfully buccaneerish and rakish impression, which may have been partly due to the glass eye. Anyway, this dismal cave was suddenly full of noise and laughter... He had a great reputation for knowing Crete and the Cretans backwards, being an indestructible force in the steepest mountains, and had a tremendous capacity for drinking strong Cretan wine without turning a hair, or only now and then. The great thing was that his presence filled everyone with life and optimism and a feeling of fun. Everyone felt this, and it hung in the air long after his death. I saw him so little, and you can see what an impression he left.'[1]

When the first troops landed to the west of Heraklion, the west gate of the town – the Chania Gate – was held by Cretan recruits who had been armed with whatever spare guns could be found and roughly organised into companies. This was done to compensate in part for the absence when it was most needed of the Cretan 5th Division. Many of them came from the village of Krousonas, and they fought furiously to keep the Germans out. Satanas was there and so was John. John had already gathered the group for the proposed raid on Kasos, and his visit to Brigadier Chappell's HQ was to find out where he and they could be of most use. It was presumably Chappell's idea that they go to the Chania Gate. At the last minute some arms were supplied, and the Cretans proved time and again that they were excellent shots.

The distribution of the guns had been undertaken by Satanas. He had taken them up to his village of Krousonas, and according to a nephew of his he handed them over to the sergeant of the gendarmerie, saying, 'I will send you men with my signal and you will give one to each man and keep a note for me and a register'.[2] John kept a receipt for each weapon and the ammunition that went with them, usually a hundred rounds apiece, and the men signed for them in whatever way they knew how.[3]

This nephew of Satanas, Limonakis, who had been away all this time in northern Greece with the Cretan 5th Division, remembered his uncle and another man, Apostolos Xomeritakis, telling him about some intelligence information obtained from the Germans in the form of a topographical map of the area around Heraklion. The map indicated where there were springs outside the walls of the city and on the more central roads. These springs were essential to the parachutists if they were to avoid dehydration. Limonakis told how one such spring lay just outside the Chania Gate, 'exactly on the spot where today the Plateia Koraka lies and where the roads of Therissou and 62 Martirou join.' Here there was a small eating-house, and the spring was just outside it. Just before the battle began, John allegedly took Satanas to the spring and told him: 'All the German soldiers who will fall to the west of Heraklion will be drawn by that spring. Therefore we must fortify that point. One can see it exactly opposite the Venetian walls so we can hit them from there.'[4] The top of the Chania Gate and the flanking Venetian walls formed a superb lookout point for the western approaches to the town and an ideal point of defence. It was manned mainly by the Greeks, the older Cretan recruits and fifty British troops.

The parachutists who landed there were one half of the 3rd Battalion of the 1st Parachute Regiment (III.Bataillon, Fallschirm-Jäger-Regiment 1). They were under the command of Major Karl-Lothar Schulz, one of the champions of the paratroops. It was the task of Regiment 1 to capture the town and airfield of Heraklion. The overall commander of this eastern sector of the offensive (Orion sector), was Colonel Braüer. He had landed some two miles to the east of the airfield with his staff and the 1st Battalion of the 1st Regiment, in the Vathianos/Gournes area.

In all areas, the resistance was fierce and unexpectedly strong. Nothing had prepared the parachutists for the opposition they encountered. Their reconnaissance intelligence had not detected most of the gun positions so well camouflaged, which had not opened fire until the order was finally given as the troop carriers came in. This tactic paid off, for the Germans had expected far fewer numbers of men and guns. Chappel's defence worked well. The half of the 2nd Battalion of Regiment 1 that landed inside the Allied perimeter of the airfield was completely disabled. The few that escaped had to do so by sea.

Many of the difficulties that the Orion Sector of the German forces faced were made worse by the muddles and delays that had preceded their departure from the mainland. The first wave of Junkers did not return soon enough or in good enough condition to start off again on the second wave at the appointed time. There was a great deal of last minute reshuffling of men, and some were left behind for lack of transport. The departure was further delayed by the dust clouds that the planes churned up as they took off, which took ages to settle. This disrupted the close formations in which they were meant to fly. Finally they had taken off three and a half hours late. This left them little time to get themselves organised and in contact with other groups by nightfall, let alone take the town and airfield, which was their original objective. The landings in this sector were made far more dangerous by these delays, as the fighter planes, which had been intended to protect the Junker 52s as they dropped their loads, could not stay over the area any longer than originally planned, and they could not resynchronise with the delays of the Junkers.

Schulz's group, split between the areas to the west and south of the town, had fallen late of their target time and somewhat dispersed. They had been sent in with heavy weapons, but came under a lot of fire from houses and high vantage points around them. The Battalion, advancing for the attack on the town, got as far as the outskirts, but as they approached the town wall, with darkness falling, they were repulsed by the strong defence they encountered. Attempts to break into the town during the night failed. Major Schulz accordingly disengaged his men and occupied the ridge five hundred metres west of the outskirts of the town.

The group to the west of Schulz's lot was part of the II Battalion of the 2nd Regiment, seconded temporarily to Colonel Braüer's regiment. They had landed ahead of Schulz, and had met with no resistance, as they were outside the area protected by the Greek Battalions. In charge of this group was Captain Gerhard Schirmer, and he proceeded to ensure protection from the west and south. 'It wasn't long, however, before the first attacks came,' remembered Schirmer, years later. 'The 3rd Battalion Paratroop Regiment 1 attacked the town of Heraklion, but the western edge of the town was magnificently defended by the English. There was an ancient ten-metre high town wall, in which there were few gates, and it was impossible to get in.'[5]

By the end of the first day the Germans had failed to capture any of their targeted airfields. It was essential that at least one should be taken, so that they could begin to fly in reinforcements. It was decided that the only one that could feasibly be captured within the time limit was Maleme, and from this point the incoming forces concentrated on the airfield there.

Originally the plan for the Heraklion attack had been to ship in Mountain Troops as reinforcements from the mainland, using two Light Ship groups under escort from the Italian Navy. The first was destroyed north of Chania. The second, carrying a battalion of the Mountain Troops, was spotted off Milos by the British Navy. The Italians created a smoke-screen to allow the German troops to get away, so none of the reinforcements ever arrived. 'We had to carry on alone in Heraklion', Schirmer recalled. 'That was an unbelievably difficult situation, especially as the losses were very high.'[6]

*

On the dawn of the second day, May 21st, the German communications in the Orion sector were very poor. An order sent by Colonel Braüer to put all the forces in the area towards an attack on the airfield was not received by the two groups to the west of the town under Schulz and Schirmer. Schulz did, however, intercept a message that the VIII Air Corps were planning a heavy bombardment of the town between eight and nine o'clock that morning. He decided to make the most of this by pushing against the town in the wake of the bombardment.

Dividing his troops into two storm-groups, taking some of Schirmer's to boost numbers, Schulz sent one lot to attack the Chania Gate and the other to take the northern gate on the sea-front. The southern group at the Chania Gate failed completely to get through and was forced to join the northern group. Schulz was determined to capture the town, clear it of Allied resistance and advance on the aerodrome from the west.

However, they met with tougher resistance than they had expected. This and their lack of heavy weapons hampered their attempts to get to the harbour and occupy it. They tried and failed to take the Venetian fort, which the Greeks were holding tenaciously as they were tending their wounded there. The fighting in the streets was desperate, as the Cretans and Greeks refused to give up ground. It was rumoured that the Germans used Allied prisoners as shields in their advance.

*

Oblivious of what had hit Crete, Mike Cumberlege and the crew of the *Dolphin* were, at the time, rounding Cape Sidero at the north-east tip of the island. 'I was in the Kasos straits hurrying back to tell John we should have to lie low for a bit due to the extraordinary amount of air activity in the vicinity. We had no idea that the attack on Crete had begun. We put into Sitia and landed to telephone John that we should be in that evening but for some reason, at the time inexplicable to us, we were unable to get a message through so we left the message to be passed as soon as the line was mended. During that day we were continually fired on from the shore – not an unusual event for us but rather tiresome.'[7]

Cle Cumberlege and Nick Hammond took guns with them just in case, a Mauser each, and cautiously approached the landward end of the mole where the Venetian fort stood guarding the entrance to the inner harbour. 'As we came up to Heraklion in the dusk we noticed a large fire and clouds of smoke and found the harbour wall deserted of its usual guard', Cumberlege remembered. 'Even then we didn't realise what was happening but made fast at the tip of the mole with our engine running whilst my cousin [Cle] and Hammond went to ask for permission to enter.'[8] Nick Hammond continued the story. 'We saw that machine-guns were covering us from the embrasures. To our right we could see nothing, being bounded by a high sea wall: and then we saw the Nazi swastika flying on the electric power station not far off. In the inner harbour there were a number of British dead and in the street ends which abutted on the harbour we could see Greek soldiers firing from cover.'[9] The fort was still held by the Greek soldiers protecting their wounded. Many of the British troops had been moved across to the east to help defend the aerodrome, while the Greeks and the Cretan civilians continued to defend the west side of the town in some vicious street fighting.

Then, at around four that afternoon, an unknown Major in the Greek army and the Mayor of the town apparently offered the surrender of Heraklion. But they had no authority and no support to do so, and it came to nothing. The Germans assumed that the British were forcing them to fight on, but the fierceness of the fighting showed otherwise. By the time it was dark the stormgroups had got nowhere and were forced back out of the town to the place from which they had started to the west of Heraklion.

The accounts of John's movements at this stage vary, owing to the general confusion. He and Satanas were involved in the fighting at the Chania Gate on the first day. The late arrival of the parachutists in this sector left too little time after the visit to the caves and the fighting at the gate for John to have left the town in daylight that day. It was early on the second day when, as Schirmer described, the Germans had been pressed back to the ridge five hundred metres west of the gate, that some say John and Satanas, either just before or during the first bombardment of the town of which Schulz took advantage, agreed to try and make it by different routes back to the men in Krousonas.

There is no doubt that it was a dangerous move. John clearly thought that it was important enough to take the chance. He had been to see Brigadier Chappel, who must have given him some idea of where and how he and his men could best contribute. The Cretan men at the Chania Gate were well organised into battalions under the command of British and Greek officers in the area. John's responsibility was not to stay with them but to get to the hundred or so men he had organised up at Krousonas and more elsewhere. He could have stayed in Heraklion. He knew, and was certainly told by others, that he would be taking a dangerous risk to go, but he and Satanas agreed that they must try.

In going by different routes, at least one of them might stand a chance of breaking through. So Satanas headed south via Knossos and then cut westwards across the rippling spurs of land to Krousonas. This was the longer route, and the more arduous due to the constant ups and downs involved in crossing the spurs of land. Given the concentration of parachutists landing close to the coast, this might have seemed a reasonable route. The parachutists reinforcing both Schulz's and Schirmer's groups had been seen landing south and west of the town at different distances from it, but how they manoeuvred themselves once they had landed nobody could see from the town. What directed John's choice of route is not known – did he feel that he was sending Satanas, an old man, by the safer route, or was his judgement impaired by his tiredness and perhaps lingering illness? There are no certain answers, only conjecture.

After they had parted at the Chania Gate, John went back to his office to fetch another gun. Before leaving, he gave a message to Manolaki to take up to the village of Skalani, just to the south of Knossos, and to contact the men he had organised in that region. They were to hold the Prophitis Elias ridge running from the villages of Spilia and Skalani in the south, towards – and overlooking – the low land occupied by the airfield in the north. It was territory familiar to Manolaki, as the west face of the ridge overlooked the palace at Knossos down in the valley (where Manolaki, like many of the villagers of Knossos, had taken his family to spend the previous night, feeling Evans' reconstructed palace to be safer than their own homes), and faced the Villa Ariadne on the opposite hillside. Also in the valley was the important north-south road running through Knossos, which was being guarded by a British detachment. But the ridge was the strategic vantage point commanding the whole airfield that was the most urgent to defend. It also provided an excellent view over the town of Heraklion and much of the land east, west and south of it.

John then drove out of the town with one of his men, Myron Samarites. He did not take the main road west to Chania, but the southern fork that splits off just beyond the Chania Gate. This took him away from the open ground and to the spurs of the Iuktas foothills, where he dumped the car. It was found later by Captain Max Balli, of the Field Security unit. The driver's door had been wrenched off and John's uniform cap was on the seat. Mike Cumberlege was told that there did not appear to have been signs of any struggle. It had not been a particularly good idea to take the car, as John soon realised. Speed was not as important as cover.

Cumberlege heard from Samarites, who came out of Crete with him much later, that John had volunteered to 'clean up a farmhouse where some parachutists were hidden. It was during this attack, which I understand was led by John with his famous swordstick, that he was severely wounded'. During the fight, John and Samarites managed to kill several Germans, among them Hitler's cousin, a Major Hitler: 'He has his revolver and cap badge as proof.'[10]

John must have judged that he had a chance of getting through at this stage, before more waves of parachutists made the route impenetrable. Schulz's group had been forced back, as far as could be seen from the Chania Gate, to the ridge five hundred metres directly west of the Chania Gate, so to try and cut through to the south-west of them might well have had a chance of working. John knew the land that he had to cross like the back of his hand. The paratroops did not. It was a fair assumption that he had a better chance of succeeding than most. Though there may have been a certain lack of judgement on his part, he saw the risk and decided to take it.

Hamson later speculated on what John may have been thinking at that time. 'I have often wondered what was in John's mind as he went out to make that reconnaissance, looking towards the south-west where, on the horizon, his eyes were confronted by the hills of Ida. The business in hand of the parachute troops, no doubt, but merely that? I think perhaps that then he too may have been led away by a declamation, by an inability then (in the crisis which he foresaw, against which he had not been permitted to provide and which was now upon us) to attain to any other alternative but the doing of what was immediately to hand; and went seeking in this business his escape also – his escape, I mean, into death. Perhaps he went gaily, with interest in this new turn, for he liked adventure and danger. But more probably he went, I think, in the sadness of his heart, with sense of the pity of it, with sense of the waste and ineptitude behind him, with sense of his failure.'[11]

There are as many different versions of what happened next as there were (and are) people to tell them. But there are enough common elements to be able to piece together events from the web of Cretan folk-tales and second-hand fictionalised fact.

At this point another man enters the picture, a reserve soldier who had been called up to fight on the Albanian front, but was back on leave after being wounded. The fact that parachutists figure so largely in his account could mean that he was remembering not the second day — when if anything was dropped it was supplies, not men — but the first day of the battle. This would imply that it was on the first day that John left Heraklion.

However, according to Polybios Markatatos of Goniais, it was on the second day that he saw John. When the attacks had begun, his company had been defending an area to the west of Heraklion, straddling the car road to Chania. His platoon, stationed on the rising ground to the east of the bridge over the River Giophyros, had set up their machine-gun nearby in the area known as Kaminia. Markatatos was the 'sighter' on the gun.

Around mid-afternoon on May 21st, a swarm of Stukas began intensive low-level bombing, backed up by their gunners, of the districts around Heraklion. Markatatos remembered parachutists being dropped after an hour or so of bombing. After a while his platoon was forced to withdraw to better positions. 'I remained at my post and continued to fight against the parachutists falling on all sides. Suddenly I saw above me an officer whose face was unknown to me and for a moment I was alarmed. Seeing my fear he calmed me, telling me to have courage and not to lose my head, and at the same time he began to fire, standing upright with his revolver, at the falling parachutists. In the meantime, four parachutists came into very close quarters with us and then began a hand-to-hand struggle with them in which the unknown officer succeeded in killing three with his revolver and I the fourth.

'Immediately after this, he told me to fire with my machine-gun in the direction of the car road, so that we might be able to advance farther westward. He went first and, crouching at the corner of a cottage which was a little way in front, he fired continually at the Germans who were in sight ahead of us. In this position he was wounded through the right breast, and seeing this I ran to bring him help, and when I asked him what was the matter he answered, "It is nothing; only give me some water." I could not do what he asked because I had no water, and it was impossible to find any because of the constant threat of Germans all round. I asked him again what we were to do and he said, "Stick to your post; don't lose your head." Then, because of the impossibility of taking the wounded man anywhere, and because of the hazardous position in which we were, I continued to fire at the Germans until my ammunition was exhausted, when we were both taken prisoner.'[12]

After his capture, Markatatos was beaten up before being taking to Tsalikaki Metochi, a makeshift prison some three kilometres to the west of Kaminia, where the Germans were holding all their prisoners while the battle still raged. As they took him away he saw his wounded companion being taken into a neighbouring cottage. It was only when he reached the camp that he found out that the wounded Englishman was John Pendlebury.

When Markatatos had first encountered John, he was alone and on foot. He had his swordstick with him (which was not as much use as he had hoped, since many of the parachutists had weapons that they could fire on their way down), two pistols – one strapped on each side – and a rifle slung over his back. John had insisted that they try and break through the lines to Krousonas to get reinforcements. All the time the sky was full of Stukas bombing and strafing the area with machine-gun fire from no more than fifty feet above them. John was shot in the chest while unslinging the rifle from his back. It was not clear whether the shot came from parachutists on the ground or the Stukas firing from the air.

There is another story, however, in the official SOE archive report, which was written by the head of D Section in Greece, Ian Pirie.[13] This account involves a woman called Aristea Drossoulaki. The story she gives in this account was gathered in the early months of the occupation. The version she recorded later varies quite a lot.[14] Pirie recorded that George Drossoulakis, one of John's men trained on Souda Island, was with John during the fighting through Heraklion. He had been trying to deliver a message to Hamson and Bruce Mitford up on the Nida Plain. George was killed and John seriously wounded 'through his back and chest'. John, having been captured, was taken by German parachutists, unbeknownst to him or his captors, to the house of his dead comrade. Mike Cumberlege's version says that at this point his captors took John's identity disc and left. As they never return in any account, it is safe to assume that they were killed. George's wife, Aristea, 'put Pendlebury to bed and attended to his wounds as best she could'. When Aristea asked John what had happened to a couple of officers called Jack Hamson and Terence Bruce Mitford, John was taken aback. He asked how she knew of them, so she told him that her husband had worked for them. It was an unexpected moment of relief for John, to find himself in what seemed to be a safe house, and though he now had to tell Aristea that her husband was dead, he could at least tell her that he had died 'fighting like a hero'.

The Pirie account begins on the day of the German invasion, May 20th 1941.[15] Aristea told the questioner that John's condition did not improve that day, so she went into town in search of a doctor. 'On her way she was stopped by a German soldier and asked where she was proceeding. She made some excuse about fetching some water from a place further on but he told her to turn around and draw water from a nearby well and would not listen to her pleadings that it was not drinking water. She made further efforts that day and finally got a doctor, who said that the case was much too serious for him to deal with and that he would send an ambulance and a military doctor.' He meanwhile gave instructions on how to deal with the patient, which Aristea and her sister followed for the next two days.

This brings the story to May 22nd 1941, which Aristea described as the third day, when everything began to go badly wrong. When a truck carrying a small group of German soldiers pulled up outside the house, John and the sisters were apprehensive but did not suspect too much amiss. Aristea did not want to take any risks with her children, though, and sent them off to a relative via the back door. John begged the two women to leave too in case they got into trouble for helping him. If they should somehow find out who he was, they would be in serious trouble. Both, however, refused to leave John. Aristea was convinced that one of the Germans would be the doctor promised, and so as soon as she had let the soldiers in to where John was lying, she went to the kitchen to heat some water for John's wounds.

She realised she was wrong when she heard her sister scream. Running to the bedroom, Aristea saw the soldiers throwing her sister roughly from the room. She tried to get past them into the room and could just see John trying to get off the bed, protesting at the women's treatment, before she too was roughly ejected. They heard loud angry voices inside the bedroom and several gunshots. John's body was then carried out to the truck and taken away.

Next morning, the German soldiers returned and arrested Aristea for having harboured a British officer. Luckily for the sisters, the soldiers seemed to believe that John was a regular soldier rather than an agent. After twelve days in the prison at Tsalikaki Metochi, she was released and made her way home. It was a gruesome walk, along a road lined with bodies. Scanning the corpses from the centre of the road, as no one could go any nearer, she found the body of her husband, George Drossoulakis. Then, drawn to a shirt she recognised as one of her husband's which she had lent to John, she found John's body too.

What soon became clear was that the Germans had no idea whom they had shot. Either those who had carried out the shooting had been killed themselves and been unable to report whom they had shot, or, as Mike Cumberlege's account suggests, they had simply not known who it was that they had killed. For some months afterwards, having found Pendlebury's card on her husband's body as well as his own identity card, the German authorities repeatedly threatened to shoot Aristea if she did not tell them where John Pendlebury was in hiding. They refused to believe her when she told them they had shot him as he lay wounded in her house.

Meanwhile, Aristea tried to discover where they had buried the body she knew to be John's. She finally located it at Gergeri, but when she got there it had gone. The Germans had become so desperate to find John that they had all the recent graves between Archanes and Heraklion opened in the search for a body with a glass eye. They had used local youths to do this, forcing them to stick their fingers in the eyes of every corpse.[16] They then reburied John with the rest of the British dead, satisfied at last that they had got their man.

Aristea's later story was that she was inside her cottage with her sister, Theonymphe Manoussakis, who was married to another of John's men. She had no idea of their husbands' whereabouts in all the confusion of battle. 'About ten Germans came into the house and after first searching they asked if there were English in the house: they wanted, we discovered, to bring in a wounded man. We gave them a blanket and together with two Greeks whom they had taken prisoner, Elias Papaeliakis of the village of Gergeri and Konstantinos Loukadakis from the village of Daphnes, they carried over from the other side of the road a wounded officer: we noted, and the two Greeks also assured us, that this was an English Captain.'[17]

They put John down on a bed and went out. While the Germans were out of the room, Aristea approached the wounded man to ask him who he was, and if he knew Captains Hamson and Mitford, for whom she knew her husband had been working. 'Hearing the names of the two Captains he was amazed and asked me who I was. I answered him that I was the wife of Georgios Drossoulakis and that willingly I would give him what help I could. Then he told me that he was the English Captain John Pendlebury, a thing which terrified me because I knew of his activities from former conversations with my husband. I asked him what had happened to my husband and he told me that he was all right and was taking a message to the village of Krousonas to the English Captain Hamson, and at the same time he asked me to get a doctor, and water.'[18]

Their search for a doctor was unsuccessful but, at about eight in the evening, three Germans turned up. One of them, a doctor, cleaned and bandaged John's wound. John talked to them in German until the bandaging was done and they left. Aristea asked him what they had been talking about. John explained. Knowing that the Germans could treat him as a *franc-tireur*, since his bloodied uniform had been removed, he was aware also of the danger to the sisters for harbouring him. In order to prevent this he had told the Germans that the two Cretan sisters should not be harmed, because it had been Germans who had brought him into their house in the first place. They had told him that they must put on a light in the house to escape bombing (though how putting on a light would prevent bombing is unclear), and that they would return later.

At around ten-thirty that evening, another German doctor arrived and gave John an injection. He assured him that they would fetch him the following morning to transfer him to a hospital for better treatment.

'All night I and my sister and the two Greeks mentioned before, who in the meantime had been set free, tended the wounded man with all the means at our command. He sought to calm us and gave us frequent thanks for our care, and encouraged us, telling us to keep calm: victory would be ours.'[19]

*

Despite the many discrepancies in these accounts, even amongst those told by one woman, Aristea Drossoulaki, the essence of the story remains the same. Mistakes, misremembered details were passed back to Cairo and then to Hilda and Herbert, but the core and the outcome do not change. The Germans who killed John had found an English soldier in Cretan clothes and with no means of identification.

Aristea Drossoulaki finally refined her story in 1947. She said that she saw the Germans prop John up against a wall and three times shout a question at him, which she probably could not understand. Three times he answered 'No'. They ordered him to stand to attention and then opened fire. Hit in the head and the body, he fell.

Again it is necessary to stress that in Crete stories develop with the telling. There is nothing cynical in this, only a sincere desire to captivate an audience. Truth – perhaps something they understand rather better than the rest of us – is always subjective. John, as well as the events that surrounded them all at the time of his death, was and remained deeply important to those who came close to him. Dilys Powell tried twenty years later to talk to Theonymphe Manoussakis about those few days in 1941 and she found that 'the horror was still alive for her'. 'In their prison camp, she said, the women wept despairingly. "Where is my husband?", they cried; some of them scratched their names on the wall. At last the "fortress" was opened and they straggled back to their homes. "There was no light", said Theonymphe. "There was no water. There was no food. Nobody had any money. Everybody was in rags. You could hear nothing but women crying. Human corpses lay on the ground among the bodies of dead mules."'[20]

23

May 24 1941, onwards

THE ORION SECTOR UNDER Col. Bräuer now put all its forces into taking the airfield. RAF bombers and fighters flying from Egypt as support during the battle were still able, up until May 24th, to land at Heraklion within the British perimeter, and though the concentration of the invasion had shifted to Maleme, it was still essential to stop the British landing in Heraklion.

So on the night of the 25th, Schulz's and Schirmer's groups moved round the south of Heraklion over Allied-occupied ground. At dawn they attacked the ridge of Prophitis Elias, four kilometres to the south of, and overlooking, the airfield. They established themselves in this position and managed to make contact finally with Bräuer. Several counter-attacks were made to dislodge Schulz's group from the ridge, with a simultaneous approach by a small British force on one side, and a Greek force led by Manolaki as a guide from the other.

During one of these counter-attacks Manolaki was killed. 'It was Phyllia – she was a girl still in her teens – who, when the fighting had died down and families were returning to their homes, went up the hill to look for her father. She found him lying on his face; he was dead. A little earth from the explosions of battle was scattered over his body and its Cretan clothes. His hands were at his sides, slightly curled, palms upward. One hand still held his summer straw hat.'[1] It was not until more than a month later, when Miki Akoumianakis, Manolaki's oldest son, had managed to make his way back from the Albanian front, that the family managed to bury Manolaki, near a small Byzantine chapel that he had excavated himself on the west face of the ridge of Prophitis Elias where he had died.[2]

Meanwhile, the Germans had gained ground but had not succeeded in taking the airfield any more than they had in taking the town. Then, during the night of May 28th, the Germans noticed that ships were coming and going nearby. The next morning revealed a deserted airfield. The Allies had gone, evacuated during the night to Egypt.

The surprise was as great at Rethymnon, where the German troops had failed in their objectives. The die was cast far to the west at Maleme, where some of the fiercest fighting of the war had been going on to take Hill 107 overlooking the airfield. Lack of communication and the consequent lack of coordination had allowed the Germans to take Hill 107 and defend their aircraft as they landed on the airfield. This was seen to be enough to declare the pointlessness of carrying on defending when the battle was as good as lost by this one loss of ground. They could not possibly have known that the Germans were on the point of calling off the invasion as their losses were far beyond their expectations and their timing was completely awry.

The evacuation from the west of the island was far more harrowing than that from Heraklion. The men had to march south across the island to the tiny harbour of Sphakia before they could be taken off by boat. All the way along this road they were bombarded by German aircraft without mercy. When they reached Sphakia they were still under fire, only there were fewer places to take cover. The ships were too full and many men were left behind. Those who did manage to get on board a vessel were hounded all the way to Egypt by the Luftwaffe.[3] It was a nightmare that compared with Dunkirk.

*

So the battle was lost and the occupation began. But it was also the birth of the most stubborn resistance the Germans were to encounter during the war.

Thousands of Allied soldiers were left behind without being caught. Ralph Stockbridge, the Field Security officer working in Heraklion under Harry Burr, stayed hidden in the mountains until he could get off the island. Returning later, as a wireless operator working under the Inter-Services Liaison Department (ISLD), he spent longer in occupied Crete than any other agent. He and others managed to escape into the hills where they were hidden by the Cretan villagers at great personal risk. Others, like Jack Hamson, Harry Burr and a young officer called Jack Smith-Hughes, were taken prisoner. Jack Smith-Hughes happened to be locked up with Papadakis, the head of the Metaxist youth movement in Crete, the Neolaia, and with him managed to escape and hide in the mountains. Hamson and Burr were not so lucky and spent the rest of the war in prisoner-of-war camps in the heart of German-occupied Europe. Also taken was Maxwell Tasker-Brown. Fifty ME Commando had been sent back to Crete at the height of the battle. Having fought the rearguard action at the west end of the island, many of them were taken into captivity.

Some of the stragglers hiding in the mountains formed a deep bond with the Cretans who protected and fed them. By the time they were evacuated by, among others, John's old friend Skipper – now Commander – Pool, they were already determined to return. Martin and Molly Hammond, having met Skipper Pool in Crete in 1936, got to know him much better when they were all in Cairo subsequently. Eventually they learnt what he was up to when he vanished from Cairo for periods of time. 'Dressed as a Cretan, with high boots, baggy trousers, multi-buttoned black waistcoat, silk shirt, black turban and possibly a flower behind his ear, he was landed off a submarine at some deserted spot on the coast where the Cretan partisans (members of the Cretan underground movement) had a donkey and a goat waiting for him. He would ride away on the donkey, with the goat tied behind and wander about the island selling cigarettes and oranges in German camps, etc. One can picture him arguing the toss in Greek with Germans who understood no Greek but probably spoke English! In the meantime he would, somehow, get in touch with the men in hiding and arrange to take them off in the submarine. We were told that in this way he rescued some hundreds of our men. He had to make a number of these trips and well deserved the DSO awarded to him.'[4] Among these hundreds of stranded soldiers were the first to return to the occupied island, Ralph Stockbridge and Jack Smith-Hughes. Commander Pool used these trips to Crete as an opportunity to find out as much as he could about John's fate, but already a veil of myth was settling over him, and it was not always easy to distinguish fact from fantasy.

*

Meanwhile, the crew of the *Dolphin*, having hurriedly put to sea under fierce fire from Heraklion harbour on the 21st, had made their way in a stolen caïque to the south coast. Mike Cumberlege wanted to get in touch with one of John's agents, Solakakis, and find out where John's hideout might be. Then Cumberlege would be able to supply him secretly from Egypt. But before they could do this they were attacked by a Messerschmitt 109. Jumbo Steele took to the guns, but Saunders and Cle Cumberlege were killed and Mike wounded before, as it came back to finish them off, the Messerschmitt was shot down by Steele. They returned to Egypt determined to get back to supply John as soon as possible, unaware of what had happened to him.

*

When Aristea Drossoulakis was released from Tsalikaki prison she saw bodies laid out along the side of the road. Amongst them, as she said in a later statement, she saw the bodies of her husband, George Drossoulakis, and Captain John Pendlebury. She recognised John by the shirt that she had given him to wear. He was buried not long afterwards near the main road to Chania.

For a long time afterwards she was regarded with suspicion by the Germans, who had found John's message on George Drossoulakis' body. He had never reached Krousonas. They threatened to execute her if she did not tell them where John was hiding.

In the confusion of the battle, none of the standard procedures for reporting details of action could apply. The first concern was to stay alive for as long as possible – longer at least than your enemy. Both sides were exhausted and drained by one of the fiercest battles of the war. The Cretans had fought viciously – men, women, priests and even children. If a parachutist got caught in a tree, or somehow strayed from his company, then he would be lucky if he survived the rage of the Cretans. For they had had only thirty years free from the foreign occupations which had covered the previous thousand years of their history. They were not going to give up lightly what they had fought for throughout those thousand years and had only just achieved. The Germans failed to grasp this, preferring instead to blame outside intervention, if only for the sake of propaganda. 'It is undoubtedly to be attributed to Pendlebury's activities that large numbers of the population turned guerrilla. It is also perfectly clear that Pendlebury's intelligence network will one day be put into operation again by his subordinate *kapetans*.'[5]

The German forces would not believe that John was dead, denying categorically that they had shot him in cold blood. Those who had done it most likely never lived to tell the tale or knew anything of the man they had shot, as for some considerable time after John's death Berlin sent out bulletins in newspapers and on the radio about John and his work. Mike Cumberlege heard a couple of them declaring that 'the bandit Pendlebury will be caught and he can expect short shrift when he is found'.[6] Then, as people filtered back to Cairo from Crete, rumours came too from those who had seen John during the battle or heard of him since. These were picked up and passed on as current news of him. Even Reuters in Cairo came out with a bulletin that appeared to many people who knew John, in Cairo and England, to describe him. 'The small force of British, New Zealand and Australian troops who have evaded capture in Crete and are conducting vigorous guerrilla warfare against the Germans, are commanded by a British officer well known to the islanders. He moves freely about organising raids on German posts, depots, and aerodromes, and spurring the islanders to continue their resistance. Many Cretans have joined the Imperial troops and are helping to fight and obtain food and ammunition.'[7] At first it was thought that the confusion arose because Jack Hamson was still on the island, and had a similar stature to John and also had a glass eye. But Hamson had already been taken prisoner. It could be that the Cretans led the Germans to believe that John might still be alive and causing them trouble from the hills.

Stories about John began to circulate at around this time. He had been seen fighting at the harbour, he had been fighting throughout the eight-day battle at the Chania Gate, he had been killed on the first day, he had been tended by the sisters for twelve days, he had died slowly in a field hospital set up in his old home at Knossos. Nobody knew and yet everybody had their own version of events, preferring to pretend knowledge of such a man than to admit they were not there themselves. Over time they began to believe the stories that they told, with a little more elaboration each time. Each storyteller would weave himself into places, company and events in which he originally had no part. It was the tradition of the island and John would have been delighted that the magic was worked on him. It also served a useful purpose in that the Germans had no idea what had really happened to John.

Other stories were beginning to make their way out of Crete which told in less attractive terms how the Germans had baptized their occupation. Eventually, on October 11th 1941, an article appeared in *The Times*. 'There is much that is shocking, but nothing that is surprising in the account of German atrocities in Crete issued this morning by the Greek Government. German military practice and teaching have always emphasized the necessity for "ruthlessness" in the treatment of populations which do not submit with becoming docility to the invader. The German Army committed many infractions of the laws of war as laid down by international conventions during the last European struggle; but those misdeeds were not comparable with the crimes which the Nazified militarists and the Gestapo – who follow them like hyenas in the track of the larger beasts of prey – have committed in this war in every country where there has been the slightest popular resistance to their aggression and their depredations. When their armies suffer ill-fortune, as sooner or later they will, we shall no doubt witness an unedifying attempt of the soldiers to put the blame on the Gestapo for these excesses. For the present, however, they are regarded as normal accompaniments of totalitarian warfare by the leaders of the "Herrnvolk".

'The case of Crete is particularly distressing', it went on. 'Hitler has praised the Greek armies for their valour; he had expressed his admiration of the Greek contribution to civilization. He had said that a nation which submitted tamely to conquest was unworthy to survive. The Cretans are Greeks of pure stock. When their island was invaded they formed extemporized bodies of Home Guards and resisted the invader with the valour that added to his difficulties and losses. German fury at this "Barbarity" knew no bounds. There have been executions, often accompanied by torture and insult, wherever the invaders have penetrated. The statements made by the Greek Minister of War have been confirmed by British, Anzacs, Greeks and Cretans who have since escaped from the island. Not content with executing members of organised bodies of volunteers in flagrant violation of the Hague Regulations, they have reintroduced the savage practice, unknown in Europe for generations, of killing non-combatants who refused to give them information. The result of these crimes has disappointed their perpetrators. Numbers of Cretans have taken to the mountains and are waging guerrilla warfare against their tyrants. It is to be hoped that we shall be able to give them something more than sympathy in their struggle against savage oppression.'[8]

The Daily Telegraph published Berlin's reply to these allegations of their 'shameless and brutal' methods in Crete. 'Here the British put themselves seriously in the wrong by inciting and carefully organising the civilian population, long before the beginning of the German attack. In Crete unlimited gang warfare assumed fearful forms. The British in particular prepared this by a generous distribution of arms of all categories. The main work in this respect was carried out by Captain John D. S. Pendlebury, who was sent to Heraklion in June 1940 as British Vice-Consul and representative of the Intelligence Service. He was fully aware that his activities contravened international law. His diary contains the sentence: "This may be a breach of the law of war." The documents of the consulate which were found in Crete provide the German Government with incontrovertible evidence for all these actions.'[9]

They did not confine their search for more information about John to the island. In the evacuation of the Allied forces from Crete, which began on May 28th from Heraklion and Sphakia on the south coast, there were those who were left behind either because of their wounds or by lack of transport. Hamson was amongst those who were captured and taken to a prisoner-of-war camp in Germany. The Germans fortunately had no idea of his connection with John or D Section, and he was taking no risks. Though he wrote copiously and secretly about his experiences in Crete, he always referred to John as Duncan in his writings.

Another officer captured in Crete was Captain Harry Burr of the Field Security Unit, who had described going round with John as a Bacchanalian progress of Cretan hospitality.

Burr had broken a leg some months earlier and had to be left behind in a field hospital. He was taken by the Germans to the German Base Hospital in Vienna, where, kept incommunicado, he was interrogated by a Major Freunde of the German Intelligence Service. 'He was convinced that I was closely connected with John Pendlebury and doing the same job, which was not correct.'[10] But Freunde could not shake the idea from his head, and was determined to get what he considered the truth out of Burr. 'Burr has so far declined to give further information with regard to his activities as an officer. As soon as he is again capable of being questioned, he will be interrogated further, and it is to be hoped that he will at least be able to give some further information about his own and Pendlebury's activities, since he must remain under the suspicion that he allowed Pendlebury's activity regarding the uprisings of the population on Crete to take place.'[11]

The Germans eventually came to believe that John was dead, following the excavation of the graves by the young Cretans. On finding the body with the glass eye, they took a Greek doctor to identify the corpse. It was Dr Kasapis from up in Lasithi who in 1927, with his German wife, had welcomed the cold and exhausted John and Hilda in from the night 'to warmth and food and kindness, spotless rooms, scrubbed wooden platters, blackcurrant jam and homemade bread'. He and John had become great friends during John's work in Lasithi before the war, and revelled in telling each other outlandish and funny stories. For what he was now forced to do, though it must have caused him considerable pain, he was later imprisoned for collaboration. But the Cretans subsequently released him, considering him to be an honourable man who had been coerced into helping the Germans.

Far away in Vienna, Harry Burr heard of the exhumation indirectly from Major Freunde. 'Before seeing me he told the interpreter the details... and as he was the officer in charge of the exhumation he gave other details about the heat and his glass eye which made me fairly convinced that the story was correct. I, of course, heard from the interpreter who, having a passion for tea, was rather a friend of mine. It is wonderful what you can do with a Red Cross parcel!'[12]

A particularly gruesome account of the exhumation is given by Theocharis Saridakis, the fanciful poet, who claimed to have witnessed the exhumation. He told of a man called Hartmann, who worked with the local Gestapo and took part in the exhumation. He propped up John's body and shot it several times, so that, after so long a search, he could say he had shot Pendlebury. Without knowing whether or not this is true, it is hard to say which would be worse, the truth of it or the fabrication of it.

In Crete, a rumour was circulating that all the trouble that the Germans had taken to find John's body was because Hitler could not sleep until he had John's glass eye in Berlin as proof of his final demise. John would have been greatly amused by the trouble he had caused them.

John was reburied at Stavromenos, as the original grave was considered too obvious a focus of resistance for villagers. This move served little purpose; when Commander Pool, a few months after the battle, sailed a boat to occupied Crete with Jack Smith-Hughes, Ralph Stockridge and Satanas, he found that the Cretans still put fresh flowers on John's grave every day.

Burr discovered that John's death, which he had not known about while on Crete, had greatly impressed the Germans, and that John had helped the Greeks on the west side of the town when they were hard-pressed and tried to reach reinforcements for them. The Germans continued to believe that he had died of his wounds, but they really did not know one way or the other.

But in their propaganda literature they chose to portray a different image, finding a certain irony in the circumstances leading up to his death and demanding sympathy for the innocent paratroops, his victims, who were after all only trying to help the Cretans, if they could only realise it, between bombardments. This final version, written from the viewpoint of John's killers, is worth repeating:

'It is a strange arrangement of fate that Pendlebury, who had aroused the Greek population with lies and calumnies against the German paratroops, should die in the arms and in the care of just these paratroops... The men, who had experienced the cunning of the guerrillas, who had seen many comrades fall in the fire of the aroused civilians and had stood in the olive groves with teeth clenched by the horribly mutilated bodies of their comrades, these men knew nothing of a Mr Pendlebury. They did not suspect that all the inhuman events of the last hours were the work of this English Captain there before them in the dust of the road. They saw a wounded foreign officer who needed care. And they provided this with the natural readiness to help of the German soldier even towards his foe. They brought the wounded man out of the firing line into the house which offered better shelter. It was the house of one of the notorious *kapetans* of Pendlebury's! There they came across a woman whom they asked to look after the wounded man and to stay with him.

'The woman refused. If other German soldiers were to come, then she would be shot because she had sheltered an Englishman. The calumnies which Pendlebury had allowed to be disseminated about German soldiers now turned themselves against their own originator! Only with difficulty could the Germans make clear to the woman that nothing would happen to her. They promised the Englishman they would send a doctor to examine him and give him treatment.

'The doctor came. It was a German military doctor. He dressed the wounds of the man and gave the woman instructions for his care. Despite the harshness of the battle, although they were cut off on all sides as a small band in forlorn posts, the German soldiers did not hesitate to help the wounded enemy. None of them came to the thought of doing to the helpless opponent what had been done to them by the brutalising guerrillas. This is the way German soldiers behave.'[13]

Before John died, he had written letters to Hilda and to his father, which the Germans found after his death. They were so impressed that they told Burr they were sending them to John's home via the Red Cross. Burr, who was writing about this to Bob Dixon after his release in March 1944, did not expect the letters to arrive until after the war, as, 'I have heard many stories of promises or good intentions by individual officers with regard to personal papers and all seem to get to Berlin and stop there.'[14]

Sadly, that is exactly what happened, for neither Hilda nor John's father ever received their letters. The Germans took them to use as evidence against him, in a posthumous attempt to justify their actions. In their report on him, written in October 1941, they wrote: 'From Pendlebury's notebooks and farewell letters, which have been captured, it is clear beyond doubt that he did not fear death but was ready to give his life for England on Crete because he felt himself to be a Cretan and because he felt responsible for the fate of these people in the framework of the British Empire.

'The numerous notes give a picture of the exceedingly varied and prudent activities of this man, who developed such restless activity in a fanatical way that barely allowed him to rest, and led to the fact that in the last weeks before his death he had become extremely strained and could only keep going with difficulty.'[15]

There is a grudging admiration for John in this report. Apart from the obvious scoring of propaganda points, they clearly thought very highly of him. But again they underestimated the Cretans by imagining that they could be led like lambs to the slaughter. 'Pendlebury himself was a great idealist and a glowing friend of Crete, who placed all his intentions at work in using the love of freedom of these people for England's purposes. It is obvious from his farewell letters to his father and to his wife, that he had absolutely no scruples over his activities. He regards himself as a shining beacon of love of his country, and carried out unceasing work in the service of his country.

'The extraordinarily varied activities of Pendlebury have given a sort of aura to this man. The naked facts indicate that he has done his duty as an English officer and Intelligence agent, that he played during the whole of this period in the most unscrupulous way with the lives of the population, and that international agreements were no more than paper to him by comparison with the assumed rights of the British Empire.'[16]

The report ends on a rather ominous note. 'Further investigations will be made into the network he left behind, and in particular into the *kapetans* who have disappeared, and it remains to be hoped that these efforts will also be crowned with success.' It was signed on behalf of the Chief of the Supreme Command of the Wehrmacht.[17]

Though the Germans surely knew of John's activities long before war was declared between Greece and Germany, they seem to have discovered very little as a result. What they did know, they found out for the most part after they had shot him. Though they intercepted several of his letters, they found out little that they could use. They portrayed him as an empire-building envoy, planning to claim land for the British Empire and paint the Aegean pink. As far as they were concerned he sent his Cretans, 'with false words and invented horror stories to stir up and maintain hatred against Germany and Italy. On May 5th 1941, he is able to write to his wife with satisfaction after seven months of activity: "The spirit of the Cretans is wonderful. But where are the soldiers of Crete? They are still carrying on, as I am told, a guerrilla war in the Peloponnese. I wish I had them here. Now our *kapetans* will nevertheless carry on fighting in the mountains, and even the women and children, if it has to be, just as they did in the battle of Pindar [sic. – Pindus more likely]. It would be a great achievement to reconquer Greece and the islands, and to conquer the Dodecanese – my dream for many years, as you know."'[18] This letter was sent by John two months after the last letter that Hilda ever received from him, leaving her with nothing more than the anxiety of waiting to hear through official channels and wondering what was happening.

After the battle, the Germans sent in a special unit to try and capture documents of the Greek Government in Crete, but instead they found John's office at the British Vice-Consulate. 'In Heraklion, the largest town of Crete, in the office of the two British Vice-Consuls, there hangs a remarkable picture between those of the King and the Queen. It shows a man of about thirty-five, with unmistakeably English features, in Cretan national dress; high boots, wide stockings like a skirt, a close-fitting black waistcoat, heavily embroidered cape and a black cap. This picture gave us our first aquaintance with Mr John Pendlebury.

'Who was this Englishman?'[19]

The 'Sonderkommando von Künsberg' found a notebook and papers that John had been keeping. It revealed some of his movements, and some of his men's names. Those who had been closely involved with him took to the hills as planned when the British had evacuated Crete. Those who felt that his death might put them at risk managed to get off the island. Satanas did so, to return a few months later with Commander Pool, Jack Smith-Hughes and Ralph Stockbridge. Others, like George Drossoulakis, had died in the battle. It was foolish of John to have kept a notebook or indeed any record. Perhaps it was, after all, his archaeological training that led him to keep some sort of reference. It was sheer luck that the people mentioned by John were not harmed, luck and the fact that John had told them nothing. 'The few collaborators of Pendlebury's, who may perhaps become known as a result of further investigations, are hardly likely to give important information, as Pendlebury, even vis-à-vis his closest collaborators, was very secretive. It must be said of Pendlebury that he carried out his activities, from the point of view of intelligence information, in the most excellent way... Four of Pendlebury's co-workers were able to be taken prisoner; interrogation of them, however, has not shown that they are in any way to be accused – as mentioned above, Pendlebury confided little in other persons.'[20]

Though many returned to the island to look for John, they found only stories of how he had died. Mike Cumberlege, trying again later to track down John's agent from Arvi, Solakakis, and get information about John's death, found out that Solakakis had himself been murdered by another Cretan with a grudge – 'This man I removed.'[21] Nick Hammond never returned to wartime Crete, but worked thereafter on the occupied mainland. A year later he wrote to Hilda of John: 'This time last year his spirit was a great inspiration to me and those with me, and the memory of it lives... His influence remains strong and will inspire them too when the time comes. I and those I was with, who are now scattered, would like to tell you how much we treasured and respected him... His is the spirit which will finish this war.'[22]

Tom Dunbabin, who was to spend a long time in occupied Crete, contributed, along with Hammond, to a memorial book for John. He wrote that many of those evacuated from Crete believed that John had remained behind on Psiloriti to carry on the war beside his men: 'And in a sense he did. His friends were the first to take to the hills in the traditional Cretan manner, the first rallying-point of the people who were still stunned with the speed and success of the new form of war which the Germans had carried out in Crete. The Cretans gave a good account of themselves during the occupation. They preserve the simple patriotism and old-fashioned qualities implanted in them by their long struggles against Venetian and Turk.

'They had leaders, like John's friend Satanas, who had fought against the Turk, and the younger men had the same spirit. The development of operations did not call for large-scale guerrilla action in Crete, but there were before the end many thousand men in the hills, and every Cretan looked forward to the day of reckoning. If John had indeed remained among them to organise them immediately, to tell them what to do, to keep in touch with Egypt by wireless and by small boat as he had planned with Mike Cumberlege, they might have given the Germans even more trouble than they did. For one of their weaknesses was that they had no single leader, and few of them were known outside their own area of a few villages. John was known from one end of Crete to the other, could talk to each man in his own dialect and ask after his family and gossips. The Cretans would have accepted him as one of themselves. Most of the men who rose to command the little guerrilla bands were the men he had chosen, and with them he could have used the first precious months, when the Germans had not yet clamped their hold on every corner of the Cretan coastland, to organise a strong and united force.

'As it was, he made the task of those British officers who took up the fragments of his work immeasurably easier. It was enough for any Cretan seeking to introduce himself to one of them to say: "I am a friend of Pendlebury. He stayed in my house. Here I have this paper from him." The unshaken loyalty which those officers found in the Cretans, not only in their close associates but in the great mass of the population, which could conceive no other than a British friendship, is the best tribute to his memory.'[23]

Hilda admitted to Mary Chubb that life was very grey without John. She had to wait as each clue to John's fate filtered through from friends in Cairo, sometimes raising her hopes and then eventually dashing them. Her life could never be the same without him. She never returned as an archaeologist to Crete or Egypt. Her life instead revolved around her two children and a growing interest in amateur theatre and local archaeology. The children already knew their grandparents better than they had known their father, but David was now faced with an almost impossible act to follow. It was bad enough that his father was almost a stranger to him, but to have him held up as the ideal of manhood must have been very difficult. Between John's father, Herbert, and Hilda, there must have been enormous pressure on David to excel. Had John lived, it is probable that he himself would have continued to compare David's progress with his own at the same age, as he had done all along, but at least David might eventually have realised that his father was fallible.

Mercy Money-Coutts found out about John's death by other means, but was unable to pass the information on to Hilda or anyone else. Mercy was working in the Diplomatic Section of Bletchley Park, based at Wavendon Manor. Also working there as a code-breaker was Charles Brasch, the aspiring New Zealander poet who had worked at Amarna with John. The intercepts of the Auswärtiges Amt, the German Foreign Office, may have included von Künsberg's reports from Crete. The fact that Brasch, who had access to the German Diplomatic decodes, and Mercy, whom he knew to be a close friend of John's, were both stationed at the same location, implies that this was probably where Mercy heard the news.[24] This was confirmed, years later, by Edith Clay, former Secretary of the British School and a friend of Mercy's. She was with Mercy when news of John's death came through. She recalled how Mercy silently fell apart in front of her when she heard that John was dead, holding her head in her hands before taking herself quietly to an empty room.[25] Mercy had not confided to Edith that she loved John, but Edith suspected, as did many of their contemporaries.

Mike Cumberlege, who would himself be executed in the German concentration camp at Flossenburg two days before the German surrender, wrote to Herbert: 'We all loved and respected your son and I feel it a privilege to have been able to work with him. I can assure you that for us they were very happy days filled with work and excitement. Both Commander Pool and myself have a particular love for Crete since the years before the war and I think perhaps more than anyone we consider it a privilege to carry on the war of liberation, the spirit of which lies in the memory of John held in the hearts of those worthy old mountain men.

'In finishing I should like to put you in mind of the opening stanzas of Lord Byron's *Siege of Corinth*; it was in that fashion that we all fought the battle of Crete.

"Never we men for a day stood still
Whether we lay in the cave or the shed
or stretched on the beach, our knapsacks spread
As a pillow beneath the resting head
But some are dead and some are gone
And some are scattered and alone
And some are rebels on the hills
That look along the Cretan valleys
Where Freedom still at moments rallies."'[26]

A fellow Pembroke man, the Reverend G.E.M. Gardner-Brown, who only encountered John once, on one of his many boat trips, set up a cross over John's first grave. It was inscribed:

RIP
Captain John Pendlebury
Intelligence Corps
Archaeologist
and
Scholar of
Pembroke College, Cambridge.
Killed in action 20th May 1941.[27]

The Cretans put fresh flowers on the grave every day and when Hilda went out in 1947 to visit his next grave herself, the then Director of the Heraklion Museum, Nicolas Platon, gave a moving tribute:

'Αγαπημενε Φιλε! Η Κρητη θα διατηρησει την μνημη σου αναμεσα στα πιο ιερα της κειμειλια. Το χωμα που εσκαψες με την σκαπανη του αρχαιολογου και ποτισες με το αιμα του πολεμιστη, θα σε περιβαλλει παντοτε με ευγνωμοσυνη.'

'Beloved friend, Crete will preserve your memory among her most sacred treasures. The soil which you excavated with the archaeologist's spade and watered with a warrior's blood will forever enfold you with gratitude.'[28]

John Pendlebury's legacy in Crete, however, is that of an archaeologist. There is a small, insignificant street named after him just outside the Chania Gate in Heraklion, but even its inhabitants, when asked, did not know who 'Tzon Mpetlempouri' was or what he had done. As his generation dies out, his memory is the preserve of archaeologists and historians. Only in the villages of Knossos and Tzermiado in Lasithi is he remembered vividly and with great respect and affection. Even so, thanks to Dilys Powell's book, *The Villa Ariadne*, written in 1972, John's grave is one of those most frequently visited by tourists (including royalty) to the beautifully serene British war cemetery at Souda, looking out over Souda Bay.

Inscribed on his grave is the first line of this stanza from Percy Bysshe Shelley's elegy on the death of his friend, John Keats, *Adonais*:

'He has outsoared the shadow of our night;
   Envy and calumny and hate and pain,
And that unrest which men miscall delight,
   Can touch him not and torture not again;
From the contagion of the world's slow stain
   He is secure and now can never mourn
A heart grown cold, a head grown gray in vain;
   Nor, when the spirit's self has ceased to burn,
With sparkless ashes load an unlamented urn.'[29]

Notes

Chapter 1 1904–1923
1. Information courtesy of the Royal College of Surgeons; *Who's Who*, 1911.
2. Pers. Comm. Rose Mary Braithwaite.
3. JP/L/18, 5.2.16, John to Lily.
4. JP/L/30, 11.6.16, John to Lily.
5. JP/L/44, 12.11.16, John to Lily.
6. JP/L/36, 8.10.16, John to Lily.
7. JP/L/32, 2.7.16, John to Lily.
8. JP/L/46, 26.11.16, John to Lily.
9. JP/L/65, 20.5.17, John to Lily.
10. JP/L/66, 27.5.17, John to Lily.
11. JP/L/80, 4.11.17, John to Lily. By this time, though, the stress of Herbert's job had begun to tell on him; he developed a severe inflammation of the parotid gland in his face, and for some weeks could barely open his mouth. When the inflammation subsided, his colleagues found that he had a benign tumour, which they managed to remove. His recovery was slow and he was invalided out for the rest of the war. TNA: PRO WO 374/53310.
12. JP/L/92, 17.2.18, John to Lily.
13. JP/L/94, 4.3.18, David to Herbert.
14. JP/L/95, 7.3.18, Mary David to Lily.
15. Morgan 1970.
16. JP/L/110, 16.5.18, David to Herbert.
17. JP/L/122, 23.6.18., John to Lily.
18. JP/L/125, 7.7.18, David to Herbert.
19. JP/L/131, 10.8.18, David to Herbert.
20. JP/L/259 [sic.], miscatalogued, John to Lily.
21. Pers. Comm. Christopher Hawkes.
22. Pers. Comm. Gerry Dicker.
23. JP/L/224, 30.3.20, David to Herbert.
24. JP/L/173, 10.6.19, David to Herbert.
25. JP/L/199, 23.11.19, John to Lily
26. JP/L/232, 22.12.20, David to Herbert.
27. JP/L/233, 13.3.21, John to Herbert.
28. JP/L/237, 21.12.21, David to Herbert.
29. The original letters relating this journey do not survive. They were, however, transcribed and pasted into a photograph album by Herbert Pendlebury, but are not catalogued within the main BSA Pendlebury letter catalogue.
30. Wace 1943.
31. Wace 1964.
32. Mackenzie 1931.

Chapter 2 1923–27
1. Pembroke College archive.
2. The Reverend Percival Gardner-Smith, Dean of Jesus College, Cambridge. Quoted in Marshall 1994, 58.
3. JP/L/241.2, 25.4.23, Comber to Herbert..
4. Wace et al. 1943, 7.
5. Wace, op. cit.
6. Uncatalogued letter from Arthur Willis to Hilda Pendlebury, 5.2.49, BSA archive.
7. Wace et al., op. cit., 8.
8. Papers of Rose Mary Braithwaite. Courtesy of Rose Mary Braithwaite.
9. Uncatalogued letter from Rowe Harding to Hilda Pendlebury, 11.2.49, BSA archive.
10. Letter from John to Sir Flinders Petrie, 8.6.30, Petrie Museum of Egyptian Archaeology at

NOTES

University College London. Quoted in Janssen 1996, 59. Petrie 1894.
11. Wace et al., op. cit., 7.
12. *The Sporting Life*, 10.11.23. Cambridge University Athletics Club archive.
13. Minutes of the Pembroke College Debating Society, Pembroke College archive. Courtesy of David Baillieu.
14. *The Cambridge Review*, 3.12.24, 155.
15. *The Times, Sporting News*, 29.11.24. CUAC archive.
16. Research courtesy of Carol Grundon.
17. Uncatalogued letter from Rowe Harding to Hilda Pendlebury, 11.2.49, BSA archive.
18. Hewlett 1900. This book was also a favourite of TE Lawrence.
19. Papers of Pierson Dixon, courtesy of Piers Dixon; Uncatalogued documents in the BSA archive.
20. Papers of Sir Pierson Dixon.
21. ibid.
22. Uncatalogued document. BSA archive
23. *The Cambridge Review*, 6.11.25, 79. CUAC archive.
24. Uncatalogued letter from Rowe Harding to Hilda Pendlebury, 11.2.49, BSA archive.
25. SC Roberts, Wace et al., 1948, ix.
26. Personal account of Rosalind Bayfield. Courtesy of Stephen Rose.
27. Papers of Darren Baillieu. Courtesy of David Baillieu.
28. Correspondence between John Soper and the author.
29. *The Pem*, Pembroke College archive.
30. *Pembroke College Gazette*, Pembroke College archive.
31. Uncatalogued letter from Arthur Willis to Hilda Pendlebury, 5.2.49, BSA archive.
32. Papers of Darren Baillieu. Letter from Darren Baillieu to Hilda Pendlebury, 1951. Courtesy of David Baillieu.
33. *The Cambridge Review*, 12.3.26, 332.
34. Pembroke College archive.
35. Butcher and Gill, 1993.
36. Uncatalogued and undated letter from JDSP to HSP. BSA archive.
37. Uncatalogued and undated letter from JDSP to HSP. BSA archive.
38. Uncatalogued and undated letter from JDSP to HSP. BSA archive.
39. *The Sporting Life*, 28.3.27. CUAC archive.
40. *The Bystander*, April 1927.
41. Uncatalogued and undated letter from John to Herbert.
42. Uncatalogued and undated letter from John to Herbert.
43. Uncatalogued and undated letter from John to Herbert.
44. Uncatalogued and undated letter from JDSP to HSP. BSA archive.
45. Uncatalogued and undated letter from JDSP to HSP. BSA archive.
46. Papers of Pierson Dixon. Letter from Pierson Dixon to Darren Baillieu, 1927. Courtesy of Piers Dixon.
47. Uncatalogued letter from Rowe Harding to Hilda Pendlebury, 11.2.49, BSA archive.

Chapter 3 October 1927–January 1928
1. Papers of Darren Baillieu. Letter from Bob Dixon to Darren Baillieu. Courtesy of David Baillieu.
2. Uncatalogued and undated letter from John to Herbert. All the letters relating to this trip are similarly undated, so their content was used to date them approximately. BSA archive.
3. JP/L/268, 20.11.27, John to Herbert.
4. ibid.
5. Pendlebury 1930.
6. JP/L/270, 28.11.30, Hilda to her mother and sister.
7. ibid.
8. JP/L/271, 30.11.27, John to Herbert.
9. JP/L/273, 4.12.27, John to Herbert.

10. JP/L/266, 6.11.27, Hilda to her mother and sister.
11. JP/L/263, undated, Hilda to her mother.
12. JP/L/278, 16.12.27, Hilda to her mother and sister.
13. Papers of Sylvia Benton. Courtesy of Lady Helen Waterhouse.
14. JP/L/279, 24.12.27, Hilda to her mother and sister.
15. JP/L/281, 26.12.27, John to Herbert.
16. JP/L/283, undated, dated later by Hilda to 3.1.28, John to Herbert.
17. JP/L/284, undated, dated later by Hilda to 4.1.28, John to Herbert.
18. Papers of Sylvia Benton. Courtesy of Lady Helen Waterhouse.
19. ibid.
20. ibid.
21. ibid.
22. JP/L/286, undated letter, John to Herbert.
23. ibid.
24. Papers of Sylvia Benton. Courtesy of Lady Helen Waterhouse.
25. JP/L/287, 10.1.28, Hilda to her mother and sister.
26. JP/L/288, undated, John to Herbert.
27. JP/L/289, undated, John to Herbert.
28. ibid.

Chapter 4 February–November 1928
1. Pendlebury, *First Trip to Eastern Crete* (1928), in Wace et al. 1948, 14.
2. Pendlebury in Wace et al. 1948, 15.
3. ibid., 16.
4. ibid., 18.
5. ibid., 19.
6. ibid., 20.
7. Imperial Airways had a sea-plane refuelling base here on the route between Europe and Africa.
8. Pendlebury, op. cit., 22.
9. ibid.
10. Hawes' evocative manuscript account of working during the Insurgency is in the Pendlebury archive of the BSA, partly in his own handwriting and partly transcribed by Hilda Pendlebury.
11. Pendlebury in Wace et al., 25.
12. Happily, this tradition continues. Seager's house now accommodates the American Institute for Aegean Prehistory and Study Center for East Crete (INSTAP-SCEC).
13. Pendlebury, op.cit., 35.
14. JP/L/295, undated, John to Herbert.
15. Pendlebury, op. cit., 37.
16. ibid., 38.
17. ibid., 39.
18. JP/L/295, as above.
19. Pendlebury, op. cit., 43.
20. ibid., 43.
21. ibid., 44.
22. Pendlebury 1930, xvii.
23. Pendlebury in Wace et al., 46.
24. JP/L/294, 16.2.28, Hilda to her mother and sister.
25. ibid.
26. ibid.
27. Pendlebury in Wace et al. 1948, 47.
28. JP/L/295, as above.
29. Uncatalogued and undated letter, John to Hilda, BSA archive.
30. JP/L/301, 18.3.28, John to Herbert.
31. ibid.

NOTES

32. Liverpool Annals
33. JP/L/301, as above.
34. JP/L/303, 26.3.28, John to Herbert.
35. ibid.
36. ibid.
37. JP/L/303, as above.
38. JP/L/305, 2.4.28, John to Herbert.
39. JP/L/304, 1.4.28, Hilda to her mother and sister.
40. JP/L/310, 23.4.28, Hilda to her mother and sister.
41. ibid.
42. ibid.
43. ibid.
44. JP/L/312, 4.5.28, Hilda to her mother and sister.
45. JP/L/313, 10.5.28, Hilda to her mother and sister.
46. ibid.
47. JP/L/314, undated, John to Herbert.
48. JP/L/313, as above.
50. JP/L/310, as above.
51. Pers. Comm. Mary Chubb.
52. JP/L/316, undated, John to Herbert.
49. Undated, uncatalogued letter, John to Herbert, BSA archive.
53. Undated, uncatalogued letter, John to Herbert, BSA archive.
54. Undated, uncatalogued letter, John to Hilda, BSA archive.
55. JP/L/318, undated, John to Herbert.
56. JP/L/320, 20.9.28, Hilda to her mother and sister.
57. JP/L/326, 26.9.28, Hilda to her mother and sister.
58. ibid.
59. JP/L/335, undated, Hilda to her mother and sister.
60. ibid.

Chapter 5 November 1928–February 1929
1. Unpublished MS: Brief biography of Stephen Glanville. Courtesy of Mary Chubb.
2. The Beit al-Kretliya, combining two houses – one 16th-century and the other 17th-century – into a single house, spans one of the main entrances to the mosque. This extraordinary house was acquired in 1935 by a member of the British-run Egyptian Civil Service, RG 'John' Gayer-Anderson Pasha, who collected interiors from other threatened houses around the Middle East to restore the Beit al-Kretliya to something akin to its former glory. Gayer-Anderson acquired it on the understanding that, on his death, the house would belong to the Egyptian Government as a museum. It remains to this day one of the most interesting and evocative places to visit in Cairo.
3. JP/L/343, undated, John to Herbert.
4. JP/L/345, 11.11.28, Hilda to her mother and sister.
5. Wainwright 1913.
6. JP/L/351, undated, John to Herbert.
7. JP/L/349, undated, John to Herbert.
8. JP/L/353, 1.12.28, Hilda to Herbert.
9. Undated, uncatalogued letter, John to Herbert, BSA archive.
10. JP/L/350, 25.11.28, Hilda to her mother and sister.
11. ibid.
12. Undated, uncatalogued letter, BSA archive.
13. JP/L/358, 28.12.28, Hilda to Dickie and Herbert.
14. JP/L/359, 31.12.28, Hilda to her mother.
15. JP/L/358, 28.12.28, Hilda to Dickie and Herbert.
16. JP/L/359, 31.12.28.

17. JP/L/360, 2.1.29, Hilda to Dickie.
18. Undated, uncatalogued letter, John to Herbert, BSA archive.
19. JP/L/360, 2.1.29, Hilda to Dickie.
20. Undated, uncatalogued letter, John to Herbert, BSA archive.
21. ibid.
22. ibid.
23. JP/L/360, 2.1.29, Hilda to Dickie.
24. ibid.
25. *The Daily Telegraph*, 3-4 January 1929.
26. JP/L/366, 23.1.29, Hilda to her mother.
27. ibid.
28. EES archive, 27.1.29, Frankfort to Glanville.
29. JP/L/368, 24.1.29, Hilda to Dickie.
30. Uncatalogued and undated letter from John to Herbert. BSA archive.
31. JP/L/369, undated, John to Herbert.
32. JP/L/368.
33. JP/L/369.
34. Lloyd 1986, 18.
35. JP/L/369.
36. BSA archive, 23.12.28, Woodward to Macmillan.
37. EES archive, 1.2.29, Frankfort to Glanville.
38. JP/L/375, 12.2.29, Hilda to her mother and sister.

Chapter 6 February–April 1929
1. This and following, Pendlebury 1935, 1-32.
2. JP/L/376, 12.2.29, Hilda to her mother and sister.
3. JP/L/378, 18.2.29, Hilda to her mother and sister.
4. Letter from John to Sir Flinders Petrie, 8.6.30, Petrie Museum of Egyptian Archaeology at University College London. Quoted in Janssen 1996, 59. Petrie 1894.
5. Papers of Darren Baillieu. Letter from Darren Baillieu to Hilda Pendlebury, 1951. Courtesy of David Baillieu.
6. Lloyd 1986, 20.
7. Hilda 1929. BSA archive.
8. EES archive, 7.2.29, Frankfort to Glanville.
9. Lloyd 1986, 20.
10. Pendlebury 1935, 106-7.
11. Uncatalogued letter, 13.2.29, John to Herbert, BSA archive.
12. Lloyd 1986, 20.
13. Pendlebury 1935, 109-10.
14. Pendlebury 1935, 110-11.
15. Uncatalogued letter, 13.2.29, John to Herbert, BSA archive.
16. JP/L/380, 26.2.29, Hilda to Dickie.
17. Uncatalogued letter, 13.2.29, John to Herbert, BSA archive.
18. EES archive, 7.2.29, Frankfort to Glanville.
19. Chubb 1954, 16.
20. ibid.
21. JP/L/384, 12.3.29, Hilda to Dickie.
22. EES archive, 28.2.29, Frankfort to Glanville.
23. Undated, uncatalogued letter, John to Herbert, BSA archive.
24. EES archive, 28.2.29, Frankfort to Glanville.
25. Lloyd 1986, 21.
26. EES archive, 28.2.29, Frankfort to Glanville.
27. JP/L/384, 12.3.29, Hilda to Dickie.
28. Undated, uncatalogued letter, John to Herbert, BSA archive.

29. BSA archive, 8.3.29, Le Fanu to Woodward
30. ibid.
31. Uncatalogued letter, 28.3.29, John to Herbert, BSA archive.
32. EES archive, 27.3.29, Frankfort to Glanville.
33. Uncatalogued letter, 28.3.29, John to Herbert, BSA archive.

Chapter 7   April–December 1929
1. Undated, uncatalogued document, BSA archive.
2. JP/L/390, 4.4.29, Hilda to Dickie and Herbert.
3. JP/L/392, 14.4.29, John to Herbert.
4. JP/L/398, 28.4.29, Hilda to her mother and sister.
5. JP/L/397, 28.4.29, Hilda to Dickie and Herbert.
6. JP/L/401, undated, John to Herbert.
7. JP/L/400, 11.5.29, Hilda to her mother and sister.
8. JP/L/401, undated, John to Herbert.
9. *The Times*, 20-21.5.29.
10. JP/L/403, 22.5.29, Hilda to her mother and sister.
11. JP/L/405, undated, John to Herbert.
12. BSA archive, 15.7.28, Woodward to Macmillan.
13. Evans 1935, i.
14. BSA archive, 16.8.28, Woodward to Macmillan.
15. Uncatalogued letter, 21.6.29, FP David to Herbert, BSA archive.
16. EES archive, undated, uncatalogued letter, John to Glanville.
17. EES archive, 24.9.29, uncatalogued letter, Mary Jonas to John.
18. JP/L/407, undated letter, John to Herbert.

Chapter 8   January–November 1930
1. Undated letter, 1930, John to Payne, BSA archive.
2. Pendlebury, JEA XVI, 1930.
3. Wainwright 1913.
4. Pendlebury, JEA XVI, 1930; Henry Hall of the British Museum had tackled it briefly in a festschrift for Evans in 1927. Hall, HR, *Keftiu, Essays in Aegean Archaeology: Presented to Sir Arthur Evans in honour of his 75th birthday*, (Ed. Stanley Casson) Oxford University Press (OUP) 1927.
5. Pendlebury, op. cit.
6. ibid.
7. ibid.
8. JP/L/416, 22.2.30, John to Herbert; Hilda Lorimer, one of the first students at the British School at Athens, wrote on armour in Homer amongst other things.
9. Pendlebury, op. cit.
10. JP/L/417, 24.2.30, John to Herbert.
11. JP/L/418, 1.3.30, John to Herbert.
12. JP/L/420, 8.3.30, John to Herbert.
13. ibid.
14. JP/L/422, 23.3.30, John to Herbert.
15. JP/L/418, 1.3.30, John to Herbert.
16. JP/L/436, 29.6.30, John to Herbert.
17. JP/L/437, 6.7.30, John to Herbert.
18. ibid.
19. JP/L/415, 20.2.30, John to Herbert.
20. Nicholas Hammond speaking at the British School at Athens centenary conference, Athens 1986.
21. JP/L/415, 20.2.30, John to Herbert.
22. JP/L/421, 16.3.30, John to Herbert.
23. Peet 1930, 33-4.
24. Wainwright, review of *Ægyptiaca*, *JEA*, 1931.

25. JP/L/422, 23.3.30, John to Herbert.
26. BSA archive, uncatalogued letter, 23.3.30, John to Payne.
27. ibid.
28. ibid.
29. BSA archive, uncatalogued letter, 26.3.30, John to Payne.
30. JP/L/423, 31.3.30, John to Herbert.
31. ibid.
32. JP/L/428, 4.5.30, John to Herbert.
33. JP/L/429, 11.5.30, John to Herbert.
34. Travelling with Venizelos were Lord and Lady Crosfield. The latter, born in Asia Minor, was the sister of MN Elliadi, the British Vice-Consul in Heraklion. Elliadi dedicated his book on Crete to Lady Crosfield: 'Born on the classical shore of Ionia, she reminds one of a living caryatid of the Smyrna pantheon.' Elliadi 1933.
35. BSA archive, uncatalogued letter, 30, John to Payne.
36. JP/L/436, 29.6.30 , John to Herbert.
37. Two Protopalatial Houses at Knossos, BSA XXX, 1928-29, 1929-30; Evans, *Palace of Minos*, Vol IV Part 1, 48ff.
38. JP/L/433, 8.6.30, John to Herbert.
39. JP/L/435, 22.6.30, John to Herbert.
40. Preface, Pendlebury 1933, 7.
41. JP/L/434, 15.6.30, John to Herbert.
42. JP/L/433, 8.6.30, John to Herbert.

Chapter 9   November 1930–February 1931
1. Chubb 1954, 36.
2. ibid.
3. EES archive, uncatalogued letter, 12.11.30, John to Glanville.
4. Pendlebury 1931.
5. EES archive, uncatalogued letter, 20.11.30, John to Glanville.
6. EES archive, uncatalogued summary report on the excavations accompanying letter to Stephen Glanville, 4.12.30.
7. EES archive, uncatalogued letter, 20.11.30, John to Glanville.
8. JP/L/440, 28.11.30, John to Herbert.
9. EES archive, uncatalogued letter, 22.1.31, John to Glanville.
10. JP/L/441, 4.12.30, John to Herbert.
11. EES archive, uncatalogued letter, 4.12.30, John to Glanville.
12. DT 18.12.30
13. ibid.
14. ibid.
15. ILN 27.12.30, 1171
16. Frankfort and Pendlebury 1933, 61.
17. EES archive, uncatalogued letter, 25.4.31, Mary Chubb to Mrs Helen Hubbard.
18. JP/L/440, 28.11.30, John to Herbert.
19. EES archive, uncatalogued letter, 12.12.30, Phillips to Glanville.
20. EES archive, uncatalogued letter, 31.12.30, John to Glanville.
21. Interval, 35. Letter from John to Lloyd, 12.1.31.
22. ibid.
23. Pendlebury 1931.
24. EES archive, uncatalogued letter, 17.1.31, John to Glanville.
25. EES archive, uncatalogued letter, 22.1.31, John to Glanville.
26. JP/L/450, 5.2.31, John to Herbert.
27. EES archive, uncatalogued letter, 17.1.31, John to Glanville.
28. JP/L/450, 5.2.31, John to Herbert.

Chapter 10 February 1931–February 1932

1. Chubb 1957, 3.
2. ibid., 7.
3. ibid., 10.
4. Powell (1972) 1985, 84.
5. ibid., 85.
6. ibid., 86.
7. JP/L/458, 19.4.31, John to Herbert.
8. Pendlebury 1933: *A Handbook to the Palace of Minos at Knossos*.
9. JP/L/458, 19.4.31, John to Herbert.
10. JP/L/465, 6.6.31, John to Herbert.
11. Pendlebury 1933: *A Handbook to the Palace of Minos at Knossos*.
12. JP/L/457, 12.4.31, John to Herbert.
13. JP/L/477, 10.12.31, John to Herbert.
14. JP/L/460, 1.5.31, John to Herbert.
15. JP/L/467, 20.6.31, John to Herbert.
16. JP/L/465, 6.6.31, John to Herbert.
17. JP/L/462, 17.5.31, John to Herbert.
18. JP/L/464, 31.5.31, John to Herbert.
19. Papers of Hilary Waddington, undated. Courtesy of the Bodleian Library.
20. JP/L/470, 13.9.31, John to Herbert.
21. EES archive, uncatalogued letter, 18.10.31, Herbert to Mary Jonas.
22. EES archive, 28.10.31, 1931-2 Dig Diary.
23. EES archive, 31.10.31, 1931-2 Dig Diary.
24. Pers. Comm. Mary Chubb.
25. Papers of Mary Chubb. Courtesy of Mary Chubb.
26. BSA archive, undated, uncatalogued document.
27. JP/L/477, 10.12.31, John to Herbert.
28. ILN 19.3.32, 427.
29. EES archive, Dig Report.
30. EES archive, 10.12.31, 1931-2 Dig Diary; Meketaten was the second of the six daughters of Akhenaten and Nefertiti, who died young.
31. Pendlebury 1932: Greece and Rome.
32. Pers. Comm., Mary Chubb.
33. JP/L/477, 10.12.31, John to Herbert.
34. JP/L/478, 14.12.31, John to Herbert.
35. ibid.
36. Pers. Comm., Mary Chubb.
37. Papers of Mary Chubb. Courtesy of Mary Chubb. Hilary was called Walary after John's beloved Winnie the Pooh. He befriended a dog at Amarna which he called Leonard, 'because it was Woolley' – after the archaeologist Leonard Woolley, who had previously dug at Amarna.
38. ibid.
39. EES archive, 14.12.31, 1931-2 Dig Diary.
40. JP/L/479, 7.1.32, John to Herbert.
41. ibid.
42. Pendlebury 1935, 62.
43. ibid.
44. JP/L/480, 15.1.32, John to Herbert.
45. Pendlebury 1932: Greece and Rome.
46. Pendlebury 1935, xii.
47. ibid., xiii. There is an excellent website on Tell el-Amarna compiled by the EES team currently working there under the direction of Barry Kemp. It displays a wonderful interactive model reconstruction of the Central City of Akhetaten and can be found at www.amarnaproject.com.

Chapter 11 February 1932–March 1933
1. JP/L/482, 28.2.32, John to Herbert.
2. JP/L/483, 3.3.32, John to Herbert.
3. JP/L/484, 6.3.32, John to Herbert.
4. JP/L/487, 20.3.32, John to Herbert.
5. JP/L/494, 18.5.32, John to Herbert.
6. JP/L/496, 1.6.32, John to Herbert.
7. JP/L/498, 10.6.32, John to Herbert.
8. JP/L/499, 19.6.32, John to Herbert.
9. JP/L/502, 1.7.32, John to Herbert.
10. ibid.
11. JP/L/512, 12.9.32, John to Herbert.
12. EES archive, uncatalogued letter, 10.11.32, Mary Jonas to Mrs Hubbard.
13. EES archive, uncatalogued letter, 9.9.32, John to Mary Jonas.
14. JP/L/510, 2.9.32, John to Herbert.
15. JP/L/518, 8.11.32, John to Herbert.
16. JP/L519, 29.11.32, John to Herbert.
17. Brasch 1980, 193.
18. ibid., 195.
19. ibid., 196-7.
20. Pendlebury 1935, 72.
21. ibid.
22. JP/L/520, 8.12.32, John to Herbert.
23. Pendlebury, JEA XIX, 1933.
24. Davies 1903-8; 1921.
25. JP/L/521, 15.12.32, John to Herbert.
26. JP/L/522, 20.12.32, John to Herbert.
27. JP/L/523, 11.1.33, John to Herbert.
28. Petrie 1894; Kemp 1993, 88; the house was known as O.47.21 or Petrie No. 8.
29. BSA archive, uncatalogued, undated document.
30. JP/L/523, 11.1.33, John to Herbert. It must have worked, as David grew up to have six children from two marriages. The future of his grandchildren has yet to be decided.
31. JP/L/526, 30.1.33, John to Herbert.
32. EES archive, 6.2.33, John to Keen, the EES Treasurer.
33. JP/L/528, 22.2.33, John to Herbert. John would not be the last archaeologist working in Iraq to fall for the coats used by the shepherds almost as a tent in bad weather and as bedding.
34. ibid.
35. Lloyd 1986, 32.
36. JP/L/528, 22.2.33, John to Herbert.
37. Pers. Comm., Mary Chubb.
38. JP/L/530, 6.3.33, John to Herbert.
39. JP/L/531, undated, John to Herbert.

Chapter 12 March 1933–March 1934
1. Pendlebury 1933, 5.
2. JP/L/535, dated later by Hilda as 10.4.33, John to Herbert.
3. JP/L/536, dated later by Hilda as 21.4.33, John to Herbert.
4. Lloyd 1986, 43.
5. ibid.
6. Pers. Comm., Mary Chubb.
7. Lloyd, op. cit, 44.
8. JP/L/557, 17.9.33, John to Herbert.
9. JP/L/550, dated later by Hilda to 15.7.33, John to Herbert.

342

Notes

10. BSA archive, undated, uncatalogued letter, John to Herbert.
11. JP/L/561, dated later by Hilda to 26.9.33, John to Herbert.
12. EES archive, 26.4.33, John to the Honorary Secretary of the EES, Hugh Last.
13. EES archive, uncatalogued letter, 21.11.33, Hugh Last to John.
14. EES archive, uncatalogued, undated letter but receipt stamped 27.12.33, John to Mary Jonas.
15. Pendlebury 1935, 75-6.
16. ibid., 77.
17. JP/L/572, 14.12.33, John to Herbert.
18. JP/L/574, 28.12.33, John to Herbert.
19. JP/L/579, 1.2.34, John to Herbert.
20. JP/L/580, 8.2.34, John to Herbert.
21. JP/L/576, 10.1.34, John to Herbert.
22. Capart 1943, 272-3 (translated from the French by the author).
23. EES archive, Dig Diary 1934-4, 22.12.33.
24. JP/L/576, 11.1.34, John to Herbert.
25. *The City of Akhenaten II*, which John had co-written with Frankfort on the North Suburb and Desert Altars, was now published and had been well received. John, though, was already looking forward to the next volume, covering the Central City. 'C of A III will be the real show – some wonderful plans and objects.'
26. EES archive, uncatalogued, undated letter, but receipt stamped 5.3.34 , John to Miss Jonas.

Chapter 13 March 1934–April 1935
 1. JP/L/586, undated, John to Herbert.
 2. JP/L/587, 1.4.34, John to Herbert.
 3. JP/L/586.1, 24.3.34, John to Herbert.
 4. Emmanuel Akoumianos.
 5. JP/L/589, 13.4.34, John to Herbert.
 6. Pendlebury, Money-Coutts and Eccles 1934.
 7. ibid., 95.
 8. ibid., 96.
 9. Eremopolis is the classical Itanos.
10. JP/L/591, undated, John to Herbert.
11. Pendlebury, Money-Coutts and Eccles, op. cit., 99-100.
12. JP/L/592, undated, but dated later by Hilda to 5.5.34, John to Herbert.
13. ibid.
14. ibid.
15. JP/L/593, 10.3.34, John to Herbert.
16. JP/L/596, undated, but dated later by Hilda to 23.5.34, John to Herbert.
17. JP/L/601, undated, John to Herbert.
18. The British School in Egypt was founded and run by Sir William Flinders Petrie.
19. JP/L/603, 4.7.34, John to Herbert.
20. JP/L/614, 8.10.34, John to Herbert.
21. pers. comm. Mary Chubb.
22. JP/L/617, 4.11.34, John to Herbert.
23. EES archive, uncatalogued letter, 11.12.34, John to Hugh Last.
24. EES archive, uncatalogued, undated letter, John to Mary Jonas.
25. EES archive, uncatalogued letter, 11.12.34, John to Hugh Last.
26. JP/L/627, 21.12.34, John to Herbert.
27. JP/L/628, 27.12.34, John to Herbert.
28. JP/L/630, 6.1.35, John to Herbert.
29. EES archive, uncatalogued letter, 9.2.35, John to Mary Jonas.
30. JP/L/631, 12.1.35, John to Herbert.
31. JP/L/636, 14.2.35, John to Herbert.
32. JP/L/633, 25.1.35, John to Herbert.

33. JP/L/634, 31.1.35, John to Herbert.
34. EES archive, uncatalogued letter, 29.1.35, Mary Jonas to John.
35. EES archive, uncatalogued letter, 27.3.35, Mary Jonas to John.
36. EES archive, uncatalogued letter, 9.2.35, John to Mary Jonas.
37. JP/L/637, 18.2.35, John to Herbert.
38. JP/L/638, 28.2.35, John to Herbert.
39. JP/L/639, John to Herbert.
40. Shorter 1935.
41. Blackman 1935.
42. Wace 1943.
43. Pendlebury, *Greece and Rome*, 1932.

Chapter 14 March 1935–April 1936
1. ILN 9-16.3.35.
2. JP/L/640, 14.3.35, John to Herbert.
3. JP/L/641, 20.3.35, John to Herbert.
4. JP/L/664, undated, John to Herbert.
5. JP/L/643, 5.4.35, John to Herbert.
6. JP/L/645, 20.4.35, John to Herbert.
7. JP/L/646, 23.4.35, John to Herbert.
8. Pendlebury 1939, 8-9. Where John could not use his own personal experience, he used Kalemenopoulos 1894.
9. JP/L/650, 27.5.35, John to Herbert.
10. JP/L/652
11. Dunbabin in Dixon et al. 1948.
12. JP/L/647, 29.4.35, John to Herbert.
13. ibid.
14. JP/L/648, undated, John to Herbert.
15. Pendlebury 1939, 3.
16. JP/L/648, undated, John to Herbert.
17. ibid.
18. JP/L/651, John to Herbert, undated but later dated by Hilda to 3.6.35.
19. Evans archive, Ashmolean Museum, 4.6.35, John to Arthur Evans.
20. JP/L/651, John to Herbert, undated by dated later by Hilda to 5.6.35.
21. JP/L/652, John to Herbert, 10.6.35.
22. ibid.
23. JP/L/653, John to Herbert, undated.
24. EES archive, uncatalogued letter, 23.6.35, Hilda to Mary Jonas.
25. EES archive, uncatalogued, undated letter but receipt stamped 1.7.35, John to Mary Jonas.
26. EES archive, memorandum circulated by Stephen Glanville, as Honorary Secretary, prior to a meeting of the EES Executive Committee on 24.9.35.
27. ibid.
28. ibid.
29. JP/L/665, 19.11.35, John to Herbert.
30. JP/L/664, 11.11.35, John to Herbert.
31. EES archive, uncatalogued letter, 25.11.35, John to Mary Jonas.
32. Pers. Comm. Günter Rudnitzky.
33. ibid.
34. EES archive, uncatalogued letters, 25.11.35 and 12.12.35, John to Mary Jonas.
35. Janssen 1996.
36. EES archive, uncatalogued letter, 12.12.35, John to Mary Jonas.
37. EES archive, uncatalogued letter, 12.12.35, Mary Jonas to John.
38. EES archive, uncatalogued report from John to the EES committee, date of receipt 16.12.35.
39. EES archive, uncatalogued, undated report from John to the EES committee.

40. ibid.
41. JP/L/669, 29.12.35, John to Herbert.
42. JP/L/670, undated, John to Herbert.
43. JP/L/671, undated, John to Herbert.
44. JP/L/672, 26.1.36, John to Herbert.
45. JP/L/673, 30.1.36, John to Herbert.
46. EES archive, uncatalogued report from John to the EES committee, 12.2.36.
47. Pendlebury 1936.
48. JP/L/674, 14.2.36, John to Herbert.
49. JP/L/674, 14.2.36, John to Herbert.

Chapter 15   May 1936–August 1939
1. JP/L/682, 3.5.36, John to Herbert.
2. JP/L/684, undated, John to Herbert.
3. JP/L/685, undated, John to Herbert.
4. JP/L/684, undated, John to Herbert.
5. Pers. Comm. Shan and Roxanni Sedgwick.
6. JP/L/685, undated, John to Herbert.
7. JP/L/686, undated but dated later by Hilda to 27.5.36, John to Herbert.
8. This tradition still survives in Lasithi among the shepherds from Tzermiado. The author and a friend, after a dawn ascent to Karphi one spring, visited a shepherd's hut on Nesimos Plain above the village, where the shepherds were cheese-making and sheep-shearing with traditional hand shears. We were welcomed into the dry-stone mandra with spontaneous *mantinades* about our arrival woven together with a traditional story about Lasithi in Turkish times. This to the accompaniment of warm *misithra* cheese straight from the cauldron and a glass of local wine.
9. JP/L/685 undated, John to Herbert.
10. BSA archive, uncatalogued account of the trip written later by Hilda.
11. ibid.
12. ibid.
13. ibid.
14. ibid.
15. ibid.
16. JP/L/688, 4.6.36, John to Herbert.
17. JP/L/691, c.4.7.36, John to Herbert.
18. EES archive, uncatalogued, undated letter but received 8.7.36, John to Mary Jonas.
19. JP/L/693, 14.7.36, John to Herbert.
20. JP/L/695, 24.7.36, John to Herbert.
21. JP/L/694, undated but dated later by Hilda to 20.7.36, John to Herbert.
22. JP/L/702, 8.10.36, John to Herbert.
23. EES archive, uncatalogued letter, 9.10.36, Dows Dunham to Mary Jonas.
24. JP/L/703, 23.10.36, John to Herbert.
25. EES archive, uncatalogued, undated letter.
26. BSA archive, uncatalogued, undated letter, but c. 12-19.11.36, John to Herbert.
27. JP/L/707, 30.11.36, John to Herbert.
28. EES archive, uncatalogued letter, 1.12.36, Mary Jonas to John.
29. EES archive, uncatalogued letter, 8.12.36, John to Mrs Hopkins Morris.
30. EES archive, uncatalogued letter, 10.12.36, John to Mary Jonas.
31. JP/L/709, 16.12.36, John to Herbert.
32. BSA archive, uncatalogued, undated letter, John to Herbert.
33. JP/L/721, 22.4.37, John to Herbert.
34. JP/L/723, 10.5.37, John to Herbert.
35. EES archive, uncatalogued letter, 7.6.37, John to Mary Jonas.
36. JP/L/724, 15.5.37, John to Herbert.
37. JP/L/727, 3.6.37, John to Herbert.

38. JP/L/728, 9.6.37, John to Herbert.
39. JP/L/729, 19.6.37, John to Herbert.
40. JP/L/730, 23 or 28.6.37, John to Herbert.
41. JP/L/731, undated, John to Herbert.
42. JP/L/733, 12.7.37, John to Herbert.
43. JP/L/731, undated, John to Herbert.
44. JP/L/729, 19.6.37, John to Herbert.
45. JP/L/734, 24.7.37, John to Herbert.
46. JP/L/731, undated, John to Herbert.
47. JP/L/732, 5.7.37, John to Herbert.
48. JP/L/734, 24.7.37, John to Herbert.
49. JP/L/732, 5.7.37, John to Herbert.
50. JP/L/737, 24.8.37, John to Herbert.
51. JP/L/742, 12.10.37, John to Herbert.
52. JP/L/745, undated but dated later by Hilda to 5.11.37, John to Herbert.
53. EES archive, uncatalogued, undated letter, but received 3.1.38, John to Mary Jonas.
54. JP/L/757, 25.2.38, John to Herbert.
55. ibid.
56. JP/L/760, 31.3.38, John to Herbert.
57. JP/L/762, 20.4.38, John to Herbert.
58. An ancient embassy between two peoples. JP/L/765, 14.5.38, John to Herbert.
59. JP/L/766, 23.5.38, John to Herbert.
60. JP/L/770, 19.6.38, John to Herbert.
61. Frank Thompson was a member of SOE in Bulgaria. A committed communist, he was shot by the Gestapo in Sofia in June 1944. Thompson, EP 1947 and West 1993.
62. JP/L/766, 23.5.38, John to Herbert.
63. JP/L/767, undated but dated later by Hilda to 31.5.38, John to Herbert.
64. JP/L/771, 20 or 26.6.38, John to Herbert.
65. JP/L/770, 19.6.38, John to Herbert.
66. JP/L/765, 24.5.38, John to Herbert.
67. JP/L/766, 22.5.38, John to Herbert.
68. ibid.
69. JP/L/769, 12.6.38, John to Herbert. A cithara is an ancient harp-like instrument.
70. ibid.
71. Martin Hammond, unpublished memoirs. Courtesy of Robin Hammond.
72. Pers. Comm. Mercy Seiradaki.
73. BSA Pendlebury photographic archive.
74. JP/L/772, 11.7.38, John to Herbert. It was on this trip that the photograph of Molly, Martin and Hilda was taken.
75. JP/L/779, 25.9.38, John to Herbert.
76. JP/L/780, 30.9.38, John to Herbert.
77. JP/L/781, 6.10.38, John to Herbert.
78. JP/L/783, 18.10.38, John to Herbert.
79. JP/L/785, 1.11.38, John to Herbert.
80. JP/L/784, 24.10.38, John to Herbert.
81. BSA archive, uncatalogued and undated.
82. JP/L/798, 28.1.39, Forsdyke to John.
83. JP/L/801, 4.2.39, Cook to John.
84. JP/L/803, 5.2.39, Last to John.
85. JP/L/806, 6.2.39, Rendall to John.
86. ibid.
87. JP/L/812, 9.2.39, Dawkins to John.
88. JP/L/815, 13.2.39, Evans to John.
89. JP/L/832, 30.3.39, John to Herbert. The three-year hiatus in the Open Meetings was due to the

death in close succession of Humfry Payne and Alan Blakeway.
90. JP/L/835, 9.4.39, John to Herbert.
91. JP/L/838, 27.4.39, John to Herbert.
92. JP/L/835, 9.4.39, John to Herbert. David Iliffe was the Director of the Jerusalem Museum who had visited John at Amarna.
93. JP/L/837, 21.4.39, John to Herbert. Marte volente means 'war allowing'.
94. JP/L/838, 27.4.39, John to Herbert.
95. ibid.
96. JP/L/839, 6.5.39, John to Herbert.
97. JP/L/839, 6.5.39, John to Herbert.
98. JP/L/840, 14.5.39, John to Herbert.
99. JP/L/843, 3.6.39, John to Herbert.
100. ibid.
101. JP/L/846, 12.6.39, John to Herbert.
102. Pendlebury 1936–7.
103. ibid.
104. ibid.
105. ibid.
106. JP/L/846, 12.6.39, John to Herbert.
107. ibid.
108. JP/L/847, 25.6.39, John to Herbert.
109. ibid.
110. Pers. Comm. Mercy Seiradaki.
111. JP/L/848, 30.6.39, John to Herbert.
112. JP/L/849, 18.7.39, John to Herbert.
113. JP/L/851, 27.8.39, John to Herbert.

Chapter 16 3 September 1939–6 June 1940
1. David Pendlebury to the author, 22.5.86.
2. JP/L/852, 6.9.39, John to Herbert.
3. Foreign and Commonwealth Office, SOE archive, 14.9.39, Courtesy of Gervase Cowell, SOE Adviser.
4. JP/L/853, 12.9.39, John to Herbert.
5. ibid.
6. ibid.
7. FCO, SOE archive, 14.9.39.
8. ibid.
9. JP/L/854, 17.9.39, John to Herbert.
10. JP/L/852, 6.9.39, John to Herbert.
11. JP/L/856, 2.10.39, John to Herbert.
12. JP/L/ 862, 6.11.39, John to Herbert. The venereal disease unit of the old Addenbrokes Hospital on Trumpington Road, Cambridge, is now occupied by the restaurant 'Browns'.
13. JP/L/857, 7.10.39, John to Herbert.
14. JP/L/858, undated, but dated later by Hilda to 14.10.39, John to Herbert.
15. JP/L/860, 24.10.39, John to Herbert.
16. JP/L/867, 11.12.39, John to Herbert.
17. ibid.
18. FCO, SOE archive, 17.12.39, JCP Brunyate to John.
19. JP/L/871, 2.1.40, John to Herbert.
20. JP/L/872, 10.1.40, John to Herbert.
21. JP/L/873, 17.1.40, John to Herbert.
22. BSA archive, uncatalogued letter, 21.1.40, John to Hilda.
23. ibid.
24. JP/L/874, undated but 21.1.40, John to Herbert.
25. BSA archive, uncatalogued letter, 21.1.40, John to Hilda.

26. JP/L/875, 3.2.40, John to Herbert.
27. JP/L/876, 8.2.40, John to Herbert.
28. Ironically, both men alone are commemorated on a memorial inscription at the British School at Athens. Stanley Casson also examined Patrick Leigh Fermor in Greek.
29. JP/L/877, undated but 15.2.40, John to Herbert.
30. JP/L/878, undated but 20.2.40, John to Herbert.
31. JP/L/881, undated but probably 15.3.40, John to Herbert.
32. FCO, SOE archive, 21.5.40, MIR to MI L(b). JP/L/884, undated but probably 19.5.40, John to Herbert.
33. JP/L/884, undated but probably 19.5.40, John to Herbert.
34. Hammond in Dixon et al. 1948.
35. JP/L/885, undated but around 20.5.40, John to Herbert.
36. ibid. A klepht was a thief from the mountains in Greece, bands of whom would carry out raids in hard times on the more fertile lowlands or coastal regions.
37. JP/L/887, 2.6.40, John to Herbert.
38. Powell 1972. Hilda told Dilys Powell that John flew over northern France at about this time, though Nick Hammond does not mention it. What John saw sickened him, but the reason for the flight is not mentioned. It could perhaps have been the flight that both men were soon to take.
39. JP/L/888a, 4.6.40, John to Herbert.
40. JP/L/887, 2.6.40, John to Herbert. David eventually joined his mother and sister at Abersoch in Wales.
41. ibid.
42. JP/L/888b, undated, John to Herbert.
43. Pers. Comm. Mary Chubb.

Chapter 17 6 June 1940–October 1940
1. JP/L/889, undated but probably 9.6.40, John to Hilda.
2. Hammond in Dixon et al. 1948.
3. ibid.
4. ibid.
5. JP/L/889, undated but probably 9.6.40, John to Herbert.
6. Mackenzie 1931, 196–7.
7. JP/L/889, postscript undated but 11 or 12.6.40, John to Herbert.
8. TNA: PRO HS7/150 Pirie's report on D Section in Greece
9. ibid.
10. Ποτε θα καμει ξαστερια;
    ε ποτε θα φλεβαρισει
    Να παρω το ντουφεκι μου
    και την ομορφη την πατρονα
    να κατεβω στον Ομαλο
    και στη στρατα του Μουσουρο
    να καμω μανες διχω γιους
    και γυναικες διχως αντρες
    να καμω και μωρα παιδια
    ε να κλαιν διχως μαναδες
    να κλαιν τη νυχτα για νερο
    ε και την αυγη για γαλα
    και τ απο ξημερωματα
    ε για τη γλυκια τους μανα
    ποτε θα καμει ξαστερια;
    'When will there be a starlit night? And when will February come so that I can take my rifle and my beautiful mistress and descend to Omalos and the army of Mousouros; so that I can deprive mothers of their sons and women of their husbands and even make babies weep for the lack of their mothers and at night for water and at dawn for milk and from daybreak for the sweetness of their mother. When will there be a starlit night?' Roughly translated by the author.
11. BSA archive, uncatalogued letter, 20.6.40, John to Hilda.

NOTES

12. Pendlebury 1938, 61.
13. BSA archive, uncatalogued letter, 20.6.40, John to Hilda.
14. JP/L/895, 24.9.40, John to Herbert.
15. Pers. Comm. Maxwell Tasker-Brown.
16. BSA archive, uncatalogued letter, 16.9.40, John to Hilda.
17. Sphinx's real name was Papadoconstantinakis
18. TNA: PRO HS7/150 Pirie's report on D Section in Greece
19. BSA archive, uncatalogued letter, 16.9.40, John to Hilda.
20. JP/L/895, 24.9.40, John to Herbert.
21. ibid.
22. Hünger and Strassl 1942, . Translation by John Grundon.
23. JP/L/895, 24.9.40, John to Herbert.
24. JP/L/895, 24.9.40, John to Herbert.
25. ibid.
26. JP/L/898, 12.10.40, John to Herbert.
27. ibid.
28. ibid.

Chapter 18   28 October–31 December 1940
1. JP/L/901, telegram, 31.10.40, John to Hilda.
2. TNA: PRO WO169/20, 4.11.40, Simpson to Barbrook; 6.11.40, Barbrook to Simpson.
3. ibid., 6.11.40, Barbrook to Simpson.
4. ibid., 22.11.40, GHQME to Creforce, 50 ME Commando and Barbrook.
5. TNA: PRO HS7/150.
6. ibid.
7. Messenger 1988. Pers. Comm. Stephen Rose.
8. Pers. Comm. Stephen Rose.
9. The Dixon Papers, 13.3.44, HRF Burr to Pierson (Bob) Dixon.
10. Pers. Comm. Maxwell Tasker-Brown.
11. ibid.
12. ibid.
13. ibid.
14. ibid.
15. ibid.
16. ibid.
17. ibid.
18. Pers. Comm. Stephen Rose.
19. Unpublished MS memoir of Patrick Savage.
20. Pers. Comm. Maxwell Tasker-Brown.
21. Pers. Comm. Stephen Rose.
22. ibid.
23. Hünger and Strassl 1942
24. ibid.
25. TNA: PRO HS7/150.
26. ibid.
27. Giannadakis 1987.
28. Extract of Bandouvas Memoirs, courtesy of Patrick Leigh Fermor.
29. ibid.
30. TNA: PRO WO 169/1334a.
31. ibid., 2.12.40.
32. Hünger and Strassl 1942.
33. Giannadakis 1987.
34. Hamson was writing in secret on whatever scraps of paper he could salvage in the camp. His erratic writing style reflects the anger and frustration he felt at what he had witnessed.

35. Hamson 1989.
36. Pers. Comm. Stephen Rose.
37. ibid.
38. TNA: PRO WO169/923, 1.1.41.
39. Unpublished MS memoir of Patrick Savage.
40. BSA archive, uncatalogued, undated letter, c. 17.12.41, Round robin letter from John to Hilda but addressed 'To whom it may concern'.
41. Pers. Comm. Maxwell Tasker-Brown.
42. BSA archive, uncatalogued, undated letter, c. 17.12.41, Round robin letter from John to Hilda but addressed 'To whom it may concern'.
43. ibid.
44. Pers. Comm. Stephen Rose.
45. BSA archive, uncatalogued, undated letter, c. 17.12.41, Round robin letter from John to Hilda but addressed 'To whom it may concern'.
46. ibid.
47. TNA: PRO HS7/150 Pirie's report on D Section in Greece.
48. TNA: PRO WO169/923, 1.1.41.
49. TNA: PRO HS7/150 Pirie's report on D Section in Greece.

Chapter 19 1 January–early March 1941
1. TNA: PRO WO169/20, Conference held at D HQ in Cairo, 6.11.40. Attended by Brig. IN Clayton, Lieut. Col. AFS Simpson CMG, Major GG Green, Mr G Pollock and Mr RG Searight.
2. TNA: PRO WO/169, 12.1.41, GHQME to OC British Forces in Crete.
3. TNA: PRO WO/169
4. TNA: PRO WO/169, 15.2.41, CREFORCE to CINC ME, Admiral Cunningham.
5. Hamson 1989.
6. ibid.
7. ibid.
8. ibid.
9. ibid.
10. ibid.
11. Messenger 1988, 39.
12. Dixon 1968.
13. Messenger 1988, 39.
14. Pers. Comm. Maxwell Tasker-Brown.
15. ibid.

Chapter 20 7 March–5 April 1941
1. BSA archive, uncatalogued letter, 7.3.41, John to Hilda.
2. ibid.
3. Pers. Comm. Ralph Stockbridge.
4. BSA archive, uncatalogued letter, 7.3.41, John to Hilda.
5. ibid.
6. Casson 1941.
7. Dixon 1968.
8. Hamson 1989.
9. Pers. Comm.
10. Hamson 1989.
11. BSA archive, uncatalogued letter, 7.3.41, John to Hilda.
12. Dixon 1968.
13. BSA archive, uncatalogued letter, 7.3.41, John to Hilda.
14. Hamson, op. cit.
15. Bundesarchiv-Militärarchiv, Freiburg, RW 2/v.143. John's notebook captured after Battle of Crete.
16. ibid.

17. ibid.
18. ibid.
19. TNA: PRO WO 106/3224, Military Attaché to War Office, 25.5.40.
20. RW2/v.143.
21. ibid.
22. ibid.
23. ibid.
24. Hamson op. cit., 114-8.
25. Hammond in Dixon et al. 1948.
26. ibid.
27. Hünger and Strassl.

Chapter 21 6 April–c. 17/18 May 1941
1. Hammond in Dixon et al. 1948.
2. Pers. Comm. Ralph Stockbridge.
3. TNA: PRO HS7/150 Pirie's report on D Section in Greece.
4. Unpublished manuscript, courtesy of Theocharis Saridakis.
5. Hammond op. cit.
6. ibid. Arete, or αρετη, in ancient Greek means a virtue, an excellence or prowess in something.
7. ibid.
8. BSA archive, uncatalogued, undated letter, Mike Cumberlege to Herbert.
9. BSA archive, uncatalogued, undated letter, Mike Cumberlege to Herbert.
10. ibid.
11. Hammond op. cit.
12. ibid.
13. Politisches Archiv, Auswärtiges Amt, Bonn, R27543. Memorandum on possibility of using the Nida Plain as emergency landing ground, 19.5.41, signed by Captains Mitford and Hamson. Document found by the Sonderkommando von Künsberg, probably in John's office in Heraklion, 4.6.41.
14. Hamson, op. cit., 114.
15. St. John 1942, 299–300.
16. Hammond op. cit.
17. ibid.
18. ibid. This store, though, had already been dispersed.

Chapter 22 20–22 May 1941
1. Pers. comm., Patrick Leigh Fermor.
2. Limonakis, unpublished memoir.
3. RW2/v.143. The receipts were taken along with John's notebook.
4. Limonakis, op. cit.
5. Pallud, 1985.
6. ibid.
7. BSA archive, uncatalogued, undated letter, Mike Cumberlege to Herbert.
8. ibid.
9. Hammond in Dixon et al. 1948.
10. BSA archive, uncatalogued, undated letter, Mike Cumberlege to Herbert.
11. Hamson 1989, 114–8.
12. BSA archive, witness statements.
13. TNA: PRO HS7/150 Pirie's report on D Section in Greece.
14. BSA archive, witness statements.
15. TNA: PRO HS7/150 Pirie's report on D Section in Greece.
16. The son of one of these youths, Rethymniotakis, told the author that the experience had scarred his father for life. Source courtesy of Professor Peter Warren.
17. BSA archive, witness statements.
18. ibid.

19. ibid.
20. Powell 1972, 143.

Chapter 23 May 24 1941 onwards
1. Powell 1972, 156.
2. In the summer of 1993, the author, then working on the excavations at Knossos, went to visit the grave with Miki Akoumianakis, Manolaki's son, and two young Cretan τεχνιτες – skilled workmen – from the Knossos excavations. The younger men, Nikos and Giannis, composed the following mantinades in honour of Manolaki, the Old Wolf, whom they had never known, except by reputation. We took raki up to pour as a libation at the grave.
Αψε στον ταφο του το κερι για να μη νιωθει μονος
Και ποτισε τονερακι για να του φυγει ο πονος
Βαλε στον ταφο του σταυρο και ενα πουληνα κερι
Εδω ναι ταφος μερακλη κι οποιος περνα θα κλαιει
Light a candle at his tomb so he should not feel lonely
And so his pain should go away water the grave with raki
Set on his tomb a cross and a candle bought to keep
Here is the tomb of an enthusiast and whoso passes shall weep
(Translated by the author.)
3. There is a very good description of the evacuation in Evelyn Waugh's *Sword of Honour* trilogy, as Waugh – a member of one of the Middle East Commandos sent back into Crete to fight a rearguard action – was himself involved in the retreat.
4. Unpublished memoir of Martin Hammond. Courtesy of Robin Hammond.
5. Hünger and Strassl 1942.
6. BSA archive, uncatalogued, undated letter, Mike Cumberlege to Herbert.
7. BSA archive, uncatalogued document.
8. ibid.
9. Hünger and Strassl 1942.
10. The Dixon Papers, 9.3.44 and 16.3.44, Harry Burr to Bob Dixon.
11. Hünger and Strassl 1942.
12. The Dixon Papers, 9.3.44 and 16.3.44, Harry Burr to Bob Dixon.
13. Hünger and Strassl 1942.
14. The Dixon papers, 9.3.44 and 16.3.44, Harry Burr to Bob Dixon.
15. RW 5/v.26, 10.10.41. Bundesarchiv-Militärarchiv, Freiburg. Translated by John Grundon.
16. ibid.
17. ibid.
18. Hünger and Strassl 1942.
19. ibid.
20. ibid.
21. BSA archive, uncatalogued, undated letter, Mike Cumberlege to Herbert.
22. BSA archive, uncatalogued letter, Nick Hammond to Hilda.
23. Dunbabin in Dixon et al. 1948.
24. A full investigation of Bletchley Park has recently been undertaken by the Architectural Investigation team of English Heritage in Cambridge, resulting in a four-volume report by Imogen Grundon, Dr Linda Monckton, Kathryn Morrison and Andrew Williams. *Bletchley Park Report*, English Heritage, 2004.
25. Pers. Comm. Edith Clay. Another of John's friends working at Bletchley Park was Hugh Last, former Honorary Secretary of the Egypt Exploration Society, but by then a professor at Brasenose College, Oxford. He was working in the Air Section at Bletchley, based in the 19th-century mansion.
26. Many thanks to Gerry Dicker, John's contemporary at Winchester College, who found the origin of this quote.
27. The Dixon Papers.
28. Wace et al 1943.
29. See above.

BIBLIOGRAPHY

PRIMARY SOURCES
The archives of the British School at Athens, Athens
  The Pendlebury Letters:
  1913: JP/L/1
  1915: JP/L/2-16
  1916: JP/L/17-52
  1917: JP/L/53-85
  1918: JP/L/86-147
  1919-26: JP/L/148-261
  1927: JP/L/262-282
  1928: JP/L/283-359
  1929: JP/L/360-411
  1930: JP/L/412-444
  1931: JP/L/445-478
  1932: JP/L/479-522
  1933: JP/L/523-574
  1934: JP/L/575-629
  1935: JP/L/630-669
  1936: JP/L/670-709
  1937: JP/L/710-752
  1938: JP/L/753-793
  1939: JP/L/794-870
  1940: JP/L/871-904
  1941: JP/L/904.1-908
  Many of the Pendlebury's letters are undated and only those with a known sequence were catalogued. Undated and uncatalogued letters have been used where a date was discernible from the content.
  The British School at Athens also houses a considerable photographic archive, including both Pendlebury's and Mercy Money-Coutts' albums and negatives. A programme of conservation of this archive is currently being undertaken.
The archives of the Egypt Exploration Society, London
  This written archive is uncatalogued, so no reference numbers are given. Similarly, Pendlebury rarely put a date on his letters, so the stamped date of receipt at the EES is given where known. The EES archive also holds the photographs of Pendlebury's Amarna years. These too are as yet uncatalogued.
The archives of Pembroke College, Cambridge
The National Archive: Public Record Office, Kew, London
  TNA: PRO WO 106/3224: General Correspondence Greece: 4.40-12.40
  TNA: PRO WO 106/3239: Crete Garrison 3.11.40-5.41
  TNA: PRO WO 169/20: G(R) War Diary (Raiding) Oct-Dec 1940
  TNA: PRO WO 169/923: G(R) War Diary Jan-Mar 1941
  TNA: PRO WO 169/1334a: CREFORCE War Diary Nov 1940 – May 1941
  TNA: PRO WO 193/625
  TNA: PRO WO 201/8: Athens: Disposal of Secret Documents from HM Embassy, May–Dec 1940
  TNA: PRO WO 201/31: CRETE: GHQ Plans and Meetings

TNA: PRO WO 201/99: Report by the Inter-Services Committee on Crete
TNA: PRO WO 201/2660: Report on Operations Heraklion Sector, May 1-28 1941
TNA: PRO PREM/109
TNA: PRO HS7/150
The Imperial War Museum
The Foreign Office Archive
Bundesarchiv - Militärarchiv, Freiburg, Germany
    RH 28-5/36
    RH 28-5/3a
    RH 28-5/3b
    RL 33/32
    RL 33/33
    RL 33/34
    RW 3/v.134
    RW 2/v.135
    RW 2/v.138
    RW 2/v.139
    RW 2/v.140
    RW 2/v.142
    RW 2/v.143
    RW 5/v.26
Politisches Archiv des Auswärtiges Amt, Bonn, Germany
    213746
    R27356
    R27542
    R27543
    R27544
    R27545
Bundesarchiv, Coblenz, Germany
Wigan Library, Wigan, Lancashire
Cambridge University Athletics Club, courtesy of Dr Christopher Thorne, Cambridge

Personal Papers:
Darren Baillieu, courtesy of David Baillieu, Sydney, Australia
Sylvia Benton, courtesy of Lady Helen Waterhouse, Oxford
Rose Mary Braithwaite
Mary Chubb
Sir Pierson Dixon, courtesy of Piers Dixon, London
Sir Arthur Evans, courtesy of The Ashmolean, Oxford
Martin Hammond, courtesy of Robin Hammond
Limonakis, courtesy of Kostas Giannadakis
Stephen Rose
Theocharis Saridakis
Patrick Savage
Alan Wace, courtesy of Elizabeth French, Cambridge
Hilary Waddington, courtesy of Hilary and Olive Waddington and the Bodleian Library, Oxford

SECONDARY SOURCES

Bandouvas, Manolis, *Memoirs*, Heraklion, 1988

Beevor, Antony, *Crete, The Battle and the Resistance*, John Murray, 1991

Blackman, AM, Reviews of *Tell el Amarna* and *City of Akhenaten II*, University of Liverpool Annals of Archaeology and Anthropology XXII, 1935.

Brasch, Charles O, *Indirections: A Memoir 1909–1947*, Oxford University Press, 1980

Brown, A, *Arthur Evans and the Palace of Minos*, Ashmolean Museum Oxford, 1986

Buckley, C, *Greece and Crete*, Efstathiadis Group 1984

Butcher, K, and Gill, DWJ, The Director, the Dealer, the Goddess, and Her Champions: The Acquisition of the Fitzwilliam Goddess, *American Journal of Archaeology*, Vol 97 No. 3, July 1993

Capart, Jean, *Chronique d'Égypte*, 18, 1943

Casson, Stanley, *Greece Against the Axis*, 1941

Chubb, Mary A, *Nefertiti Lived Here*, Geoffrey Bles, 1954 (reissued by Libri, 1998)

Chubb, Mary A, *City in the Sand*, Geoffrey Bles, 1957 (reissued by Libri, 1999)

Cooper, Artemis, *Cairo in the War*, Hamish Hamilton, 1989

Davies, Norman de Garis, *The Rock Tombs of El Amarna*, I-IV, 1903-8

Davies, Norman de Garis, Mural paintings in the city of Akhetaten, *Journal of Egyptian Archaeology* VII, 1921

Dawson, WR and Uphill, E, *Who was Who in Egyptology*, The Egypt Exploration Society, 1972

Dixon, Pierson, et al., *John Pendlebury in Crete*, Cambridge University Press 1948

Dixon, Pierson, *Double Diploma*, 1968

Drower, Margaret S, *Flinders Petrie: A Life in Archaeology*, Victor Gollancz Ltd. 1985

Elliadi, MN, *Crete, Past and Present*, 1933

Evans, AJ, *The Palace of Minos*, Volume I, 1921

Evans, AJ, *The Palace of Minos*, Volume II, 1928

Evans, AJ, *The Palace of Minos*, Volume III,

Evans, AJ, *The Palace of Minos*, Volume IV, 1935

Evans, Joan, *Time and Chance: The Story of Arthur Evans*, Longmans, Green and Co., 1943

Flecker, James Elroy, *Hassan*, 1922

Forster, Edward S, *A Short History of Modern Greece 1821–1956*, Methuen 1958

Frankfort, H, Preliminary Report on the Excavations at El-Amarnah, 1928-9, *Journal of Egyptian Archaeology*, XV, 1929

Frankfort, H, *The Mural Paintings of El-'Amarneh*, 1929

Frankfort, H, and Pendlebury, JDS, *The City of Akhenaten II: The North Suburb and The Desert Altars: The Excavations at Tell el-Amarna during the seasons 1926-1932*, Egypt Exploration Society, 1933

Giannadakis, Charalambos, Απομνημονευματα, Heraklion, 1987

Glanville, SRK, JDS Pendlebury, *Journal of Egyptian Archaeology*, Vol. 28 1942

Hall, HR, *Keftiu, Essays in Aegean Archaeology: Presented to Sir Arthur Evans in honour of his 75th birthday*, (Ed. Stanley Casson) Oxford University Press (OUP) 1927

Hamson, CJ, *Liber in Vinculis*, Trinity College Cambridge, 1989

Hewlett, Maurice, *The Life and Death of Richard Yea-and-Nay*, Macmillan, 1900

Holton, David (Ed.), *The Battle of Crete 1941: A Symposium to mark the 50th anniversary*, University of Cambridge, 1991

Horwitz, Sylvia L, *The Find of a Lifetime: Sir Arthur Evans & the Discovery of Knossos*, George Weidenfeld and Nicolson Ltd, 1981

Hünger, Heinz, and Strassl, Ernst Erich, *Kampf und Intrige um Griechenland*, NSDAP (Nazi party), 1942

James, TGH (Ed.), *Excavating in Egypt: The Egypt Exploration Society 1882–1982*, British Museum Publications, 1982

Janssen, Rosalind, Recollections of 'a golden boy': John Pendlebury at el-Amarna, *Discussions in Egyptology*, 36, 1996

Kalemenopoulos, N, Κρητικα, 1894

Kemp, Barry J, and Garfi, Salvatore, *A Survey of the city of El-Amarna*, Egypt Exploration Society, 1993

Lawson, JC, *Tales of Aegean Intrigue*, Chatto & Windus, 1920

Lloyd, Seton, *The Interval: A Life in Near Eastern Archaeology*, Lloyd Collon, 1986

MacGillivray, JA, *Minotaur: Sir Arthur Evans and the Archaeology of the Minoan Myth*, Jonathan Cape, 2000

Mackenzie, Compton, *First Athenian Memories*, Cassel 1931

Marshall, AGG, *The Marshall Story: A century of wheels and wings*, Patrick Stephens Limited, 1994

Messenger, Charles, *The Middle East Commandos*, William Kimber 1988

Montserrat, Dominic, *Akhenaten: history, fantasy and ancient Egypt,* Routledge, 2000

Morgan, Estelle, Wykehamical Notions, *Archiv für das Studium der neueren Sprachen und Literaturen*, 1970

Naval Intelligence Division, *Dodecanese*, BR 500 Geographical Handbook Series, 1941

Pallud, Jean Paul, Operation Merkur: The German Invasion of Crete, *After the Battle* 47, 1985

Peet, TE, and Woolley, CL, *The City of Akhenaten* I, London 1923

Peet, TE, Reviews: Ægyptiaca, *University of Liverpool Annals of Archaeology and Anthropology* XVII, 1930

Pendlebury, JDS, *Ægyptiaca: A Catalogue of Egyptian Objects in the Aegean Area*, Cambridge University Press 1930

Pendlebury, JDS, Egypt and the Aegean in the Late Bronze Age, *Journal of Egyptian Archaeology* XVI, 1930

Pendlebury, HW and JDS, Two Protopalatial Houses at Knossos, *The Annual of the British School at Athens*, XXX, 1928–29, 1929–30

Pendlebury, JDS, Preliminary Report of Excavations at Tell el-Amarnah 1930–1, *Journal of Egyptian Archaeology,* XVII, 1931

Pendlebury, JDS, *Guide to the Stratigraphical Museum*, British School at Athens, 1932

Pendlebury, JDS, Preliminary Report of Excavations at Tell el-Amarnah 1931–2, *Journal of Egyptian Archaeology*, XVIII, 1932

Pendlebury, JDS, Archaeologica Quaedam, *Greece and Rome* Vol.II No.4, 1932

Pendlebury, JDS, Preliminary Report of Excavations at Tell el-Amarnah 1932–3, *Journal of Egyptian Archaeology*, XIX, 1933

Pendlebury, JDS, A Handbook to the Palace of Minos at Knossos, Macmillan, 1933

Pendlebury, JDS, and Frankfort, H, *City of Akhenaten* II, Egypt Exploration Society, OUP 1933

Pendlebury, JDS, Architecture of Akhetaten, *The Architectural Association Journal*, August 1933

Pendlebury, JDS, Discoveries in Crete, *The Architectural Association Journal*, November 1934

Pendlebury, JDS, Preliminary Report of Excavations at Tell el-Amarnah 1933-4, *Journal of Egyptian Archaeology,* XX, 1934

Pendlebury, JDS, Money-Coutts, MB and Eccles, E, Journeys in Crete 1934, *The Annual of the British School at Athens*, XXXIII, 1934

Pendlebury, JDS, Preliminary Report of Excavations at Tell el-Amarnah 1934-5, *Journal of*

Egyptian Archaeology, XXI, 1935

Pendlebury, JDS, *Tell el-Amarna*, Lovat Dickson & Thompson Limited, 1935

Pendlebury, JDS and HW, and Money-Coutts, MB, Excavations in the Plain of Lasithi I: The Cave of Trapeza, *The Annual of the British School at Athens*, XXXVI, 1935–6

Pendlebury, JDS, Preliminary Report of Excavations at Tell el-Amarnah 1935–6, *Journal of Egyptian Archaeology*, XXII, 1936

Pendlebury, JDS, Lasithi in Ancient Times, *The Annual of the British School at Athens*, XXXVII, 1936–7

Pendlebury, JDS and HW, and Money-Coutts, MB, Excavations in the Plain of Lasithi II, *The Annual of the British School at Athens*, XXXVIII, 1937–8

Pendlebury, JDS, Excavations in the Plain of Lasithi III, *The Annual of the British School at Athens*, XXXVIII, 1937–8

Pendlebury, JDS, *The Archaeology of Crete: An Archaeological Handbook*, Methuen, 1939

Pendlebury, JDS, Excavations at Karphi, 1937–8, *The Annual of the British School at Athens*, XXXIX, 1943

Pendlebury, JDS, Excavations at Karphi, 1938–9, *The Annual of the British School at Athens*, XXXIX, 1943

Pendlebury, JDS, *City of Akhenaten III*, London, 1951

Pendlebury, HW, A Journey in Crete, *Archaeology*, 11 September 1964

Petrie, WMF, *Tell el Amarna*, Methuen, 1894

Powell, Dilys, *The Villa Ariadne*, Hodder and Stoughton, 1973 (reprint, Michael Haag, 1985, used here). Reprinted by Libri, 2007

Rackham, Oliver and Moody, Jennifer, *The Making of the Cretan Landscape*, 1995

Rossiter, Stuart (Ed.), *Blue Guide, Crete*, 3rd Edition 1980

Shorter, Alan W, Review of Tell el-Amarna, *Journal of Egyptian Archaeology*, XXI, 1935

Smith-Hughes, J, *General Survey of Crete*, 1940-45, 1945

St. John, Robert, *From the Land of Silent People*, Garden City Publishing Company, New York, 1942

Stubbings, Frank, *Bedders, Bulldogs & Bedells: A Cambridge Glossary*, CUP 1991

Thompson, Edward P, *There is a Spirit in Europe..: A Memoir of Frank Thompson*, Gollancz 1947

Wace, Alan JB et al., John Devitt Stringfellow Pendlebury, 1938-9, *The Annual of the British School at Athens*, XXXIX, 1943

Wace, Alan JB, *Greece Untrodden*, 1964

Wainwright, GA, The Keftiu-people of the Egyptian Monuments, *Liverpool Annals of Archaeology and Anthropology* vi, 1913

Wainwright, GA, Notices of Recent Publications: Ægyptiaca, *Journal of Egyptian Archaeology* XVII, 1931

Wainwright, GA, Keftiu, *Journal of Egyptian Archaeology*, XVII, 1931

Wainwright, GA, Keftiu: Crete or Cilicia?, *Journal of Hellenic Studies*, LI, 1931

Waterhouse, Helen, *The British School at Athens: The First Hundred Years*, Thames and Hudson, 1986

West, Nigel, *Secret War*, Coronet Books (Hodder and Stoughton), 1993

Woodhouse, CM, *Something Ventured*, Granada, 1982

GENERAL REFERENCE

Who's Who, 1911

Annual Meeting of Subscribers, *The Annual of the British School at Athens*, XXIX, 1927–8

War Service of Students of the School, 1939-45, *The Annual of the British School at Athens,* XLII, 1947

NEWSPAPERS AND MAGAZINES

The Bystander
31 March 1926 – Varsity sports at Queen's Club
26 May 1926 – The General Strike
7 March 1927 – Inter-College Sports at Cambridge
6 April 1927 – Varsity sports at Queen's Club
20 June 1928 – AAA v. Cambridge Past & Present at Fenner's

The Daily Telegraph
11 December 1928 – Frankfort on Armant Excavations
14 December 1928 – Frankfort on Armant Excavations
3-4 January 1929 – Frankfort on Armant Excavations
18 December 1930 – Pendlebury on Tell el-Amarna Excavations

The Times
20-1 May 1929 – Italian Royal visit to Rhodes

Illustrated London News (ILN)
13 July 1929 – Frankfort on Armant Excavations
10 August 1929 – Frankfort on Tell el-Amarna Excavations
13 September 1930 – Evans on Knossos Excavations
27 December 1930 – Pendlebury on Tell el-Amarna Excavations
5 September 1931 – Pendlebury on Tell el-Amarna Excavations
19 March 1932 – Pendlebury on Tell el-Amarna Excavations
6 May 1933 – Pendlebury on Tell el-Amarna Excavations
15 September 1934 – Pendlebury on Tell el-Amarna Excavations
9 March 1935 – Cretan revolt
16 March 1935 – Cretan revolt
29 June 1935 – Evans on Knossos Excavations
5 October 1935 – Pendlebury on Tell el-Amarna Excavations

A note on transliteration: Transliteration has followed convention as far as possible, except for some Latinised names, and in quotations, where spelling and transliteration have been left as in the original sources.

Dramatis Personae

Akoumianakis, Manolis. Known as Manolaki. Foreman of Evans' excavations at Knossos and frequent companion on Pendlebury's expeditions. He became one of Pendlebury's right-hand men in the resistance. He was killed on the last day of the Battle of Crete.

Akoumianakis, Michaelis (Miki). Eldest son of Manolaki. On his return from the Albanian Front, he joined the resistance, eventually becoming head of the SOE Intelligence network for Eastern Crete. Given his connections with the Villa Ariadne, he was key, later in the war, to the success of the kidnap of the German General Kreipe.

Baillieu, Darren. An Australian friend of Pendlebury's and fellow athlete at Pembroke College, Cambridge, and a member of the Joyouse Companie.

Benton, Sylvia. Abandoned teaching to become an archaeologist, enrolling at the British School at Athens in 1927. Eventually she ran the excavations on the Ionian island of Ithaka.

Blakeway, Alan. Director of the British School at Athens, 1936. Died in 1936 of blood poisoning.

Blegen, Carl. American archaeologist at Troy, Korakou, Prosymna and Pylos.

Bosanquet, Robert Carr. Director of British School at Athens, 1900–06. Excavated at Palaikastro in Eastern Crete.

Brasch, Charles. New Zealander poet who joined the Amarna team in 1933.

Breasted, James Henry. Professor at Chicago, USA. Founder of the Chicago Institute of Oriental Studies.

Capart, Jean. Belgian Egyptologist and founder of la Fondation Egyptologique Reine Elisabeth aux Musées Royaux d'Art et d'Histoire, Brussels. Also associated with the Brooklyn Museum, New York.

Carter, Howard. Egyptologist who discovered the tomb of Tutankhamen.

Casson, Stanley. Assistant Director of the British School, 1920–23 before becoming a lecturer at Oxford. Lieut. Col. Intelligence Corps. Instructor at Intelligence Training centre, where he judged the standard of Greek of Intelligence Officers, including John Pendlebury and Patrick Leigh Fermor, 1939–40 and 1941–44. Greece 1940–41, working with SOE in Athens. Died in 1944 en route to take up a senior appointment at GHQME to deal with Greek affairs.

Chubb, Mary AC. Assistant Secretary of the Egypt Exploration Society, 1928–30. Expedition secretary at Tell el-Amarna, 1930–2. Member of the Tell Asmar expedition with the Chicago Oriental Institute, 1932–9. Author of *Nefertiti Lived Here*.

Clay, Edith. London Secretary of the British School at Athens, 1937–62.

Cook, Arthur B. Professor of Archaeology at Cambridge University.

Cullen, James. Classics Master at Winchester and later Director of Education in Cyprus (1930).

Cumberlege, Cle. Major in the Royal Artillery. With his cousin, Mike Cumberlege, crew member of *HMS Dolphin*, on which he manned the two-pounder and machine-guns. Cle and Saunders, another member of the crew, were killed not long after the Battle of Crete in an air attack on the *Dolphin* by a Messerschmitt 109.

Cumberlege, Mike. Lieutenant-Commander, DSO. Skipper of *HMS Dolphin*, 'a natural buccaneer of superlative courage, whose single earring was as famous as John's swordstick' (Hammond in Wace et al, 1948). Wounded in the attack that killed his cousin, he returned to England long enough to let Hilda know as much as he was allowed to tell about John's last days. He was one of the skippers who maintained a link for SOE between Mersa Matruh in Egypt and the south coast of occupied Crete. He was captured while trying to blockade the Corinth Canal and was killed in Flossenburg two days before the German surrender

(West 1992).

Davies, Oliver. Student at the British School at Athens from 1926. Later became Lecturer in Archaeology and Ancient History, Queen's University, Belfast.

Dawkins, Prof. Richard M. Director of the British School at Athens, 1906–13. Excavated at Palaikastro and in Lasithi. He was planning a book on Crete with Pendlebury when war intervened.

Dikaios, Porphyrios. A visiting member of the Lasithi team. He went on to become head of the Cyprus Department of Antiquities.

Dixon, Pierson (Bob) later Sir. Contemporary and friend of Pendlebury's at Pembroke College, Cambridge. They travelled to Greece together in 1927 as students of the British School at Athens. Fellow of Pembroke College. Joined the Foreign Office and became eventually British Ambassador to the United Nations.

Dunbabin, Tom J. Fellow of All Souls College, Oxford. Assistant Director of the British School at Athens, 1936–46. During the war, as a member of D Section, he commanded part of occupied Crete for SOE, becoming a Lieutenant-Colonel. This Tasmanian was 'a shy man yet possessed of a very determined character. He was large, and could be ferocious when necessary'. (Beevor 1991)

Dunham, Dr. Dows. Curator, Department of Egyptian Art, Museum of Fine Arts Boston, Massachusetts, USA.

Eccles, Edith. Started career on exploration walks with John Pendlebury and Mercy Money-Coutts, 1934. Her area of study was the seal stones and gems of the Late Minoan period. After studying sub-Minoan material at Knossos, she went on to run her own excavation on the island of Chios. Immediately after the war she worked with Mercy Money-Coutts once again, advising the Greek government on refugee affairs.

Emery, Walter Bryan. Member of the team Tell el-Amarna in 1928. Later became Director of Archaeological Survey of Nubia. During the war he was a colonel in Military Intelligence.

Engelbach, Rex. Egyptologist and friend of Pendlebury's. From a French Alsatian family, but brought up in England, he went to Egypt in 1909. He studied Ancient Egyptian, Coptic and modern Arabic, and was Chief Keeper at the Egyptian Museum when Pendlebury was working at Amarna. He excavated at Heliopolis, al-Lahun with Flinders Petrie and Abu Ghurab. He wrote the first catalogue of the Egyptian Museum, Cairo.

Evans, Sir Arthur J. Archaeologist, Honorary Fellow of Brasenose College, Oxford and Keeper of the Ashmolean Museum, Oxford. Evans had a passion for the Balkans and was the Balkans correspondent of *The Manchester Guardian*. He first went to Crete in 1894, when the island was still under Ottoman rule, and spent the following years exploring and discovering new sites. By 1899, he had bought enough land at Knossos to get permission to excavate. He was directly involved with the Knossos dig from 1900 to 1935. He built his Cretan home, the Villa Ariadne, at Knossos in 1906, and gave it to the British School in 1926 along with the palace and estate. He died in 1941 at his Oxford home of Youlbury.

Fairman, HW. Egyptologist. Crossed professional swords with Pendlebury on some Amarna matters and ended up running the expedition to Nubia that replaced the Amarna excavations. He later became Professor of Egyptology at Liverpool University. He brought to final publication Pendlebury's *City of Akhenaten III*, which Pendlebury had completed in 1939 but owing to the war could not see through to publication.

Fisher, Vronwy. Vronwy Hankey, member of the Lasithi team, and worked in Crete and on Aegean pottery from Amarna.

Forsdyke, Sir John. Excavated Minoan tombs at Mavrospelio, east of Knossos, and later became Keeper of Greek and Roman Antiquities at the British Museum.

Dramatis Personae

Frankfort, Henri (Hans). Dutch archaeologist who ran the excavations at Armant and Tell el-Amarna for the Egypt Exploration Society up to 1929, handing over the latter to John Pendlebury in 1929/30. He then ran the excavations of Tell Asmar and Khorsabad in Iraq for the Oriental Institute of Chicago, at which institution he then taught from 1932 to 1949. He also taught at the Warburg Institute at the University of London, taking over the directorship in 1949. He became an American citizen in 1944. Born in 1897 he died in 1954.

Gardiner, Sir Alan H. Egyptologist and later Professor at Chicago. He wrote the seminal work on Ancient Egyptian grammar.

Gayer-Anderson, Robert G. Administrator in the Egyptian Civil Service and collector. Restored two post-Medieval houses in Cairo which now form the Gayer-Anderson Museum. His collection is kept at the Ashmolean Museum in Oxford.

Glanville, Stephen RK. Glanville worked for the Egyptian Government Service in 1922 before joining the Egypt Exploration Society team at Tell el-Amarna in 1923. In 1924, he became Assistant Keeper in the Department of Egyptian and Assyrian Antiquities at the British Museum. Excavated at Armant and Tell el-Amarna under Hans Frankfort and became Honorary Secretary of the Egypt Exploration Society in 1928. When Sir Flinders Petrie retired in 1935, Glanville became Edwards Professor of Egyptian Archaeology and Philology at University College London. After serving with the RAF during the war, he moved in 1946 to Cambridge as Professor of Egyptology until his death in 1956. He married Ethel Chubb, sister to Mary, Tony and Philip Chubb, in 1925.

Gunn, Battiscombe. Egyptologist who excavated at Tell el-Amarna, Harageh and Saqqara. He was Assistant Curator at the Egyptian Museum, Cairo in 1928–31, then Curator of Egyptian Antiquities at the University Museum, Philadelphia, 1931–4 and finally Professor of Egyptology, Oxford from 1934 until his death in 1950. He was also the editor of the EES's *Journal of Egyptian Archaeology*, 1934–40.

Hall, Sir Henry. Henry Hall, Keeper of Egyptian and Assyrian Antiquities at the British Museum. Excavated at Abydos and Deir el-Bahari as well as in Mesopotamia.

Hammond, Nicholas GL. Nick Hammond was, like his friend Pendlebury, a former student of the British School at Athens. He was a Fellow of Clare College, Cambridge when he began to explore the topography of northern Greece and southern Albania. During the war, he changed from classical historian to instructor in sabotage techniques. After the exploits described in this book, when he was a crew member of *HMS Dolphin*, Hammond returned to occupied Greece and, among other operations, took part in the operation that blew up the Gorgopotamos railway viaduct in 1942. He was then parachuted into northern Greece as a British Liaison Officer with the partisans. After the war, he returned to classics as headmaster of Clifton College, Bristol, specialising in ancient battle sites, and became Professor of Greek at Bristol University in 1962. He died in 2001, aged 93.

Harding, Rowe. Rowe Harding was a friend of Pendlebury's at Pembroke College, Cambridge. As a Welsh Rugby International he captained Wales before going to university. He was very musical and used to lead the Joyouse Companie in their choruses. He became a lawyer and eventually a judge in Cardiff.

Heurtley, William A. Assistant Director of the British School at Athens, 1923–33. Became Librarian of the new British School in Jerusalem in 1933.

Hubbard, Mrs Helen. American collector and benefactress of the Amarna excavations

Hutchinson, Richard W. 'The Squire' worked with John and Hilda Pendlebury on the finds from the Chalkidiki dig in 1928 and took over the Curatorship at Knossos from Pendlebury, from 1934–47.

Iliffe, JH (David). Emmanuel College, Cambridge. Student of the British School at Athens from 1924–5. Director of the Jerusalem Museum and later lecturer at Toronto University.

Jonas, Mary. Secretary of the Egypt Exploration Society.

de Jong, Piet. Architect of the British School at Athens.

von Künsberg, Baron Eberhard. SS officer in charge of Sonderkommando of the Auswärtiges Amt. Investigated John Pendlebury after the Battle of Crete. Killed on the Russian Front.

Lacau, Pierre. Director of the Egyptian Museum, Cairo, he worked with Engelbach on the catalogue of the Egyptian Museum.

Lamb, Winifred. Archaeologist and Honorary Keeper of Greek and Roman Antiquities at the Fitzwilliam Museum, University of Cambridge. Ran the excavations at Thermi on the island of Lesbos.

Last, Hugh. Camden Professor of Ancient History, University of Oxford. Worked at Bletchley Park during the Second World War.

Lazarus, Julia. Member of the team at Tell el-Amarna. Under her married name, Julia Samson, she continued in Egyptology, publishing much of her own work, mainly dealing with Tell el-Amarna.

Le Fanu, WR. London Secretary of the British School at Athens, 1927–30, 1931–4.

Leigh Fermor, Patrick. Famously walked from the Hook of Holland to Constantinople from 1933–5. He lived in Greece for a while between then and the outbreak of war, and became a fluent Greek speaker. He enlisted and was commissioned into the Intelligence Corps, serving as British Liaison Officer to the Greek army fighting up on the Albanian Front. When the Germans swept down through Greece, he became interpreter to Brigadier Chappel in Heraklion and was evacuated to Egypt when Crete fell to the Germans. He returned to occupied Crete as an SOE officer, coordinating the resistance units on the island. His kidnap of the German General Kreipe led to his being awarded the DSO.

Livingstone-Learmonth, Tom. Fellow Pembroke student and member of the Joyouse Companie. Another Blue (hurdler), he joined the Colonial Service and was stationed in Khartoum, where he died of meningitis in 1931.

Mackenzie, Duncan. Archaeologist who worked on the island of Milos and in Palestine before agreeing to run the Knossos excavations under Sir Arthur Evans in 1900. When the Palace and estate were handed over by Evans to the British School at Athens, Mackenzie became the first Curator of Knossos, 1926–29.

Macmillan, George A. Chairman of the British School at Athens, 1903–33.

Mond, Robert Ludwig. Financier who supported excavations by the Egypt Exploration Society and other organisations in Egypt and Mesopotamia.

Myers, Oliver H. Member of the Armant excavation team in 1928.

Myres, John Linton. Chairman of the British School at Athens, 1933–47. Wykeham Professor of Ancient History, New College, Oxford. Worked for Naval Intelligence in the First World War, becoming known as 'Blackbeard of the Aegean'.

Newberry, Percy Edward. Professor of Egyptology at Liverpool. Excavated at Beni Hasan, al-Bersha and Thebes.

Payne, Humfry GG. Director of the British School at Athens, 1929–36, excavated at Eleutherna, 1929, Crete and Perachora, 1930–36. Died in 1936 of blood-poisoning.

Peet, Thomas E. Professor of Egyptology at Liverpool. Excavated at Abydos.

Petrie, Sir William Flinders. Edwards Professor of Egyptology at University College London. Initiated the practice of systematic excavation in Egypt.

Pirie, Ian. Head of MI(R) and D Section in Athens. Withdrew to Crete ahead of the German advance and then on to Cairo. Wrote the official war history of the SOE Greek Section, now in the Public Record Office.

Powell, Villiers (Pip). A New Zealander athlete at Caius College, Cambridge, and a good friend of Pendlebury's. Also a member of the Joyouse Companie.

Roberts, SC. Secretary of the Syndicate, Cambridge University Press, 1922–48. Master of Pembroke College, 1948.

Seltman, Charles. University Lecturer in Classics at Cambridge.

Shackleton, Pat. Cambridge friend and best-man at John's wedding.

Sherman, Stephen R. Member of the Amarna team 1934–7. Previously in the RAF.

Shorter, Alan. Assistant Keeper of Egyptian and Assyrian Antiquities at the British Museum. Excavated at Armant and Tell el-Amarna 1928.

Skeat, Theodore C. Editor of the *British School Annual*, 1934–9. Keeper of Manuscripts at the British Museum.

Thompson, Frank. Member of the Lasithi team in 1938, a poet and fervent Communist. Joined the Balkan Section of SOE. He was captured in Sofia and shot by the Gestapo in 1944.

Wace, AJB (Alan). Archaeologist and Director of the British School at Athens, 1914–23. Excavated at Mycenae from 1921. Keeper of Textiles at the Victoria and Albert Museum.

Wainwright, Gerald Avery. Egyptologist who excavated at Abydos and as-Sawama.

Woodward, Arthur M. Director of the British School at Athens, 1923–29. Excavated at Sparta.

Young, George Mackworth. Retired from the Indian Civil Service to become Director of the British School at Athens, 1936–46. Worked for the Legation on propaganda in Athens, 1939–41.

Guide Chronology

DATES BC	EGYPT		CRETE	GREECE
3100		Predynastic Period		
	3100/3000-2700	Early Dynastic Period	Early Minoan I	Early Helladic I
3000			I-II Dynasty	
2900				
2800				EH II
2700	2700-c.2136	Old Kingdom	III-VIII Dyn.	EM IIA
2600				
2500				
2400				EM IIB
2300				
2200				EM III	EH III
	c.2136-2023	First Intermediate Period	IX-X Dyn.	
	2116-1795	Middle Kingdom	XI-XII Dyn.	
2100				Middle Minoan IA	Middle Helladic
2000				
	1973-1795		XII Dyn.	
1900	c.1930-			MM IB
1800				
	1795-1638	Second Intermediate Period	XIII-XVII Dyn.	
1700	-1700			MMII
	17th century		Hyksos XV Dyn.	MM III
1600	about 1600-1530				Late Helladic I
	c. 1600/1580-			Late Minoan IA	
	1520/1510				
		New Kingdom	XVIII Dyn.		
	1540-1515		Aahmes (Ahmose)		
	1530-1470/1460				LH IIA
	c.1510-c.1440/1430			LM IB	
	1515-1494		Amenhotep (Amenophis) I		
1500					
	1494-1482		Thothmes (Tuthmosis) I		
	1482-1479		Thothmes (Tuthmosis) II		
	1479-1425		Thothmes (Tuthmosis) III		
	1470/1460-1400				LH IIB
	1479-1457		Hatshepsut		
	c.1440/1430-1400			LM II	
	1427-1401		Amenhotep (Amenophis) II		
	1400-			LM IIIA1	LH IIIA1
1400	1401-1391		Thothmes (Tuthmosis) IV		
	1391-1353		Amenhotep (Amenophis) III		
	c.1370-			LM IIIA2	LH IIIA2
	1353-1337		Amenhotep IV - Akhenaten		
	1338-1336		Smenkhara		
	1336-1327		Tutankhamen		
	1327-1323		Ay		
	1323-1295		Horemheb		
	c.1310-			LM IIIB	LH IIIB
1300					
	1295-1186		XIX Dyn.		
	1295-1294		Ramesses I		

	DATES BC	EGYPT	CRETE	GREECE
	1294-1279	Sethos I		
	1279-1213	Rameses II (The Great)		
	1213-1204	Merneptah		
1200			LM IIIC	LH IIIC
	1204-1198	Sethos II		
	1198-1193	Siptah		
	1198-1186	Twosre		
	1186-1070	XX Dyn.		
1100				
	1070-525	Third Intermediate Period XXI-XXVI Dyn.	Geometric and	
1000			Orientalizing period	
900				
800				
700				
	644-525	Saite Period XXVI Dyn.		
600			Archaic	
	525-332	Late Period (including 1st & XXVII-XXXI Dyn.	Classical	
		2nd Persian domination)		
500				
400				
	332-304	Macedonian kings		
	323-30	The Ptolemies	Hellenistic	
300				
200				
100				
			Roman	
0				

This guide chronology has been compiled in accordance with current theory on chronology, which is still subject to much debate. The Aegean dates are approximate and are based on the work of Peter Warren and Vronwy Hankey in *Aegean Bronze Age Chronology* (1989).

Index

AAA, *see* Amateur Athletic Association
Abd el Megelli, 172
Åberg, 226
Abrahams, Adolphe, 27
Abrahams, Harold, 20, 27, 29–30
Abu Bakr, Abdellatif, cook, 132
Abu Bakr, Hussein, 210–12
Abydos, 139, 210
Abyssinia, invasion by Italy, 194, 198
Achaean(s), 56, 117, 229, 230
Achilles, 17, 18, 41
Achilles Club, 21, 25, 33, 46
Acroceraunian Mountains, 244
Acropolis, of Keramai, 107
Adana, 277
Admiralty, 236–7
Adonais, 332
Aegean, 34, 37, 56, 83, 97, 109, 115, 156, 239
Aegina, 45, 47
Ægyptiaca, 37, 60, 64, 68, 75, 101, 103, 115, 117–18, 120, 126, 143, 255, 307
Aeschylus, Agamemnon, 9, 116–17
Africa, North, 56, 88, 97, 173, 249: *see also* Cairo; Egypt
Agamemnon, 9, 13, 116–17
Agia Photia, 285
Agia Triada, 116
Agios Barlaam, monastery, Meteora, 41
Agios Georgios, Lasithi, 205
Agios Georgios (Holy George), 269, 285
Agios Ioannis, monastery, 107
Agios Mama, near Olynthos, 62
Agios Myron, 165
Agios Nikolaos, 53, 285, 286
Agios Stephanos, monastery, Meteora, 41
Ahmose, 87
Air Raid Protection (ARP), 235, 246, 250–51
airfields, 250, 262, 273, 294, 299–300, 304, 308–9
Akhenaten, 18, 74, 86–9, 94, 97–8, 104, 116, 130–31, 134–5, 145–6: burial, 149, 152, 158; plaster mask, 169, 184; statues, 197
Akhetaten, 131, 169
Akhladies, 207
Akoumianakis, Michaelis ('Mikis'), 319
Akoumianakis, Phyllia, 319
Akoumianos, Manolis ('Manolaki'), 122, 166–7, 174, 193, 201, 213, 232, 312, 319
Akrotiri, 105
Albania(n), 240, 243–4, 247, 250, 258, 270, 272, 227–8: front, xv, 255, 260–61, 268–9, 277, 293, 313

Aldred, Cyril, 145
Alexander the Great, 75, stela of, 76
Alexandria, 71–2, 80, 105, 164, 179, 194, 209, 250, 255, 272, 278, 293, 297, 302
Alexena saddle, 207
Aliakmon Line, 277, 281, 290
Allies, 241, 255, 276, 290, 292: forces, 272, 287, 296, 305, 320,319–20
Almyro, 126
Al-Qataï, Cairo, 72
Amarna, *see* Tell el-Amarna
Amarna Letters, discovery, 91, 96, 104
Amateur Athletic Association (AAA) Championship, 21, 67
Amen, 74, 88
Amenhotep I, 87
Amenhotep III, 87, 116, 151–2
Amenhotep IV, 87–8
American School of Archaeology, 35, 124
Amira, 155
Amnisos, 188
Ampelos, 176
Analipsis, Chapel of, 300
Andros, 141
Angas, Rosaleen, 151, 166
Anglo-Egyptian Treaty, 158
Ankh-sen-pa-aten, 17, 18, 96, 103–4, 134
Annual of the British School at Athens, 125, 155, 175
Ano Phanari, 46
Anogia, 189, 247, 300
Antiquities Department of Cyprus, 11
Antiquities Service, Egypt, 150, 180
Anzacs, 323
Aphendis Kavousi, 223
Aphendis Sarakinos, 204
Apostles, The (codename), 246, 250
Apostolakis, N, 231
Aptera, 189
Arabic language, 130, 139, 159, 199, 239–40
Arachova, 12
Arcadia, 47
The Archaeology of Crete, 165, 174, 177, 189, 220, 224–5, 229
Archanes, 142, 317
Archbishop of Athens, 45
Argive Plain, 43, 44
Argo, the, 41
Argolid, 9, 44–7, 139
Argos, 48, 70, 293
Arkadi, Moni, monastery, 107
Armant, 67–8, 71, 74–5, 77, 80–82, 91, 94–5,

366

INDEX

103–4, 130, 145, 158, 240; Roman emperors named: Macrinus, Maximian, Valerian, 76
armed forces: Australian, 290, 294, 301, 306, 307; British, 241, 254–7, 259–62, 265–6, 287, 294, 307, 322; German, 226, 228, 241, 272–4, 277–9, 282–3, 305–6, 308–9, 312–15, 322, 326; Greek, 254, 256, 270, 290, 293, 294, 301, 306, 311, 320, 323; Italian, 228, 253; Tell el-Amarna, 173
ar-Rashid, Haroun, 18
Arvasami, spring of, 205
Arvi, 285, 329
Ashmolean Museum, 148, 195
Asia Minor Campaign, xv
Asine, 44
Asmar, Tell, 162–3
Asomaton, Moni, monastery, 107
Assault Regiment, 305
Asterousia Mountains, 155
Astros, 47
Aswan, 84–6
Atchley, Ismene, 48, 68
Atchley, Shirley, 48
Aten, 91, 103, 135, 160
Athens, 35: Cathedral, 63, 69; hospital, 35, 203; intelligence organisation, 246; John and, 11–12, 60, 109, 112, 114, 120, 163, 226, 247, 249, 252, 268; Military College, 186; Ministry of Archaeology, 124; National Museum, 11, 60; Payne in, 106, 123; revolt, 250; police, 50; war meeting, 277
Atherton (journalist), 301–2
athletics, 8, 21, 26–7, 29–30, 67: *see also* names of individual sports
Athlit, Castle of, 158, 164
Atlantis myth, 116
Atreus, 116
Attic Mountains, 47
Attica, 46, 277
Attwater, Aubrey, 16
Aulis, 40
Auswärtiges Amt, xix, 330
Averoff, commandeered, 186
Avgo, 175
Axis, the, 246, 248, 277, 283
Ayia Galene, 299
Ba'her'khat, Bucchis bull, 76
Baalbek, 163
Bab Zuwayla, gateway, 72
Babali, 307
Babylon, 87, 153, 162
Bacchanalian Procession, 256, 269, 324
Baghdad, 101, 161–3
Baillieu, Darren, 19, 26, 27, 31, 33

Bakirdzis, Colonel (wartime codename 'Odysseus'), 261–2
Baldwin, Stanley, 27
Balkan(s), 70, 243, 250, 281, 301: war xv, 10, 34, 41, 51
Balli, Captain Max, 313
Bandouvas, Manolis, 248: memoirs, 262, 264–5; unreliability, 248, 264, 266
Barbrook, Bill, 245–6, 250, 254–5, 262, 268
Bardakis, Kronis, 166, 249, 257, 269
Basitakis, Ali, foreman at Knossos, 111
Battle of Heraklion, 307–10
Bayfield, Rosalind, 25
Bayfield, Vera, 36
BBC, 134, 234
Beamish, Wing Commander, 294
Bearer of the Fan *see* May, Royal Chancellor
Beaudesert Park, school, 5, 6
Bedawi tribe, 89
Bedouin, 74
beehive tombs *see* Tholos tombs
Beirut, 163
Belgium, 156, 241
Belgrade, 10, 33, 34
Belle Hélène, Mycenae, 13, 43–4, 140, 227
Beni Amran, the, 89
Bennet, John, 129, 131–2, 135, 139, 163, 169
Benton, Sylvia, 38, 46, 47, 61: and John, 42–45
Berchtesgaden, 223, 234
Berlin, 33, 322, 324, 327: University, 195
Bes, figure of, 103
Bevan, Miss, nanny, 193
Bey, Djavid, 48
Bickersteth, Ashley,
Black Sea, 116
Black Watch, The, xv, 294, 298, 307
Blackman, Aylward M, 184
Blakeway, Alan, 207–8, 280
Blegen, Carl, 102, 144, 227
Bletchley Park, 299, 330
Boar's Hill, 114
Boeotia, 12, 215
Borchardt, Ludwig, 91, 113
Borwick, Lieut. Michael, 276
Bosanquet, Reginald Carr, 56
Boston Museum of Fine Arts, 209
Botsika, 69
Bowe, Sergeant David, 258, 280
Bowman, 251
Boyd, Harriet, 54
Braithwaite, Rose Mary, 17, 18
Brasch, Charles, 158, 160, 173, 182, 330
Braüer, Colonel, 308–10, 319
Breasted, James Henry, 100, 101

367

Britain/British, 234, 277, 280, 323: army, *see* armies, British; Consul, 265, 268; Empire, 73, 327; food shortage 1917, 4–5; General Strike, 27; Great Powers (with France and Russia), 51; India Line, 218; Military Mission, 15, 256, 293, 307; Minister, 251, 277, 295; navy, *see* navy, British; political crisis, 27

British Museum (BM), 29, 31, 71, 80–81, 83, 85, 101–2, 111, 117, 119, 134, 156, 225

British School in Egypt, 179

British School of Archaeology at Athens, 13–14, 28, 140, 164, 168, 244, 251: Annual, *see Annual of the British School at Athens;* Directorship, 84; 101, 114, 207–8; exhibition, 203; Finlay Library, 35, 38, 64, 226; and Knossos, 52, 60, 110, 144, 178; Open Meeting, 119, 226; Penrose Library, 35–6, 38, 245; students, 30, 35–7, 174, 213, 219, 239: hostel; 35

British School of Archaeology in Jerusalem, 139

British Vice-Consul, Piraeus, 114

Broadstairs, 5, 204: St George's school, 1–3, 5

Bronze Age: Aegean archaeology, 117; Cyprus, 231; fortifications, 38, 141; towns, 44

Brooklyn Museum, 156, 161, 168, 171–3, 183, 209

Brooks, Marshall J., 29

Bruce-Mitford, Terence *see* Mitford, Terence Bruce

Brunyate, Captain, 237

brutality: German, 323; Italian, 252

BSA, *see* British School of Archaeology at Athens

BSA see British School Annual

BSAJ *see* British School of Archaeology in Jerusalem

Bucchis bull(s), *see* bull(s)

Budapest, 33

Budge Fellowship, 208

Bulgaria(n), xv, 10, 34, 251, 280, 283

bull(s), 75: Bucchis, 75–6, 79, 94–5; head rhytons, 222; Hermonthis, 75; rings, 116

Burghley, Lord, 20–21, 24–5, 29

Burr, Captain Harry, 256, 320, 324–6

Butler, Richard Austin ('Rab'), 21, 30, 235

Butler, Sir Montague, 235

Byblos, 115

Byron, Lord, 35, 331

The Bystander, 30

Byzantine, 50: church, 205; city, 13; Eleutherna, 107

Cable and Wireless Company, 249, 291

Caccia, Harold, 277

Café Doré, Candia, 51

caïque(s), 48, 57, 255, 262, 265, 269, 272, 297, 321

Cairo, 71, 211: Continental Savoy Hotel, 128; General Research Headquarters, 245–6; Hammonds and, 210, 213, 320; Heliopolis, 88; Hilda and, 68, 109, 199; institute, 179; John and, 151, 157, 161, 186, 318, 322, 330; Middle East HQ, 255, 265, 272, 274, 281, 292; police, 194; Sharia Khayyammiya, 72; Sharia Nubar Pasha, 128; Sharia Seray el Gezira, 212; Shepheard's Hotel, 101, 103, 128, 282; Victoria Hotel, 128, 145; wartime, 253, 260, 277, 282, 291

The Cairo Museum, 76, 82, 137, 161, 182: division of artefacts, 137, 161, 173, 187, 199

Caldy, 68, 155, 167, 192, 213, 217

Caliph of Baghdad, 161

Calverley, Miss, 180

Cambridge, Mrs, 183

Cambridge, 144, 157, 167–8, 192–3, 208, 216–17, 223, 233–4, 239, 241: Abbey House, 15; Addenbrookes Hospital, 236; Barton Road, 157; Civil Commissioner, 27; Hershel Road, 168; Joint Recruiting Board, 236–7; Madingley Road, 157

Cambridge Review, 22, 24, 26

Cambridge University 33, 165, 195, 229, 244, 294: athletics clubs, 16, 19–21, 23; Christ's College, 208, 238–40; Clare College, 22; Classics, 17, 83, 102, 240; Emmanuel College, 26, 28; entrance exam, 9; Fenner's Sports Ground, 20–22, 24; Fitzwilliam Museum, 28, 36; Girton College, 44; Gonville and Caius College, 22; Jesus College, 15, 22; Magdalene College, 20; Newnham College, 36; Pembroke College, 2, 9, 13–16, 21, 26–9, 31, 155, 234–5, 331; Press, 24, 103; Queens' College, 28; undergraduates, 236; in war, 236

camps: Armant, 79; prisoner-of-war, 274

Candia, 50–51, 59, 111, 123, 187, 221, 226, 262, 265–6: Museum, 60, 123–4, 203, 215–16; *see also* Heraklion

Canellopoulos, Professor Panayiotis, 261

Capart, Jean, 156, 171–2, 179, 184, 195, 197

Cape Drepani, 285

Cape Goudouras, 285

Cape Malea, 47

Cape Sidero, 56, 175, 285, 310

Caprice, the, 60

carnelian, ring bezel, 131

Carter, Howard, 9, 76, 97

Cassandra, Gulf of, 61

Casson, Stanley, 239

Castellorizo, 109, 264, 276–8

Castor and Bollocks, *see* Tasker-Brown, Maxwell and Stockbridge, Ralph

INDEX

catalogues, 155: *see also Aegyptiaca*
cavalry, 237–40, 257
cave(s), 189, 240, 307: Diktaean, *see* Diktaean Cave; Matala, 299; Skaphidia, 214; Trapeza, *see* Trapeza Cave
censorship, 227
Chaironea, 141
Chalkidiki, 38, 42, 60–62, 70, 75
Chalkis, 38, 40
Chamber of Shipping, 2
Chamberlain, Neville, 223, 234
Chania, 188, 190, 254, 256, 259, 268, 284, 294, 314, 321
Chania Gate, 307–8, 310, 312–13, 322, 332
Chappel, Brigadier, xv, 294, 307–9, 312
Charlies, The, east of Heraklion, 307
Chelmos, Count, 47, 70
Chersonesos, 51
Cheshire, 144
Chicago, Oriental Institute, 112, 129, 135, 157, 161
Chicago House, 81, 99, 207
children, of John and Hilda, *see* Pendlebury, David and Pendlebury, Joan
Chios, 105
Chiron, 41
Christakopoulos, 287
Christos peak, 206
Chronakis, Kostis, 218, 122
Chubb, Ethel, 99
Chubb, Mary, 99, 129, 134, 140–41, 179, 330: argument over brother, 163; *City in the Sand*, 163; in Greece, 139, 166; and John, 242; let go by EES, 156; *Nefertiti Lived Here*, 129; poetry, 146; at Tell Asmar, 162–3; at Tell el-Amarna, 129, 136–7, 145, 151
Chubb, Philip, 159, 161, 163, 169, 173, 242
Chubb, Tony, 81, 99
Chums, children's magazine, 1–2
City in the Sand, 163
City of Akhenaten II, 144, 156, 181, 184
City of Akhenaten III, 217
Claridge's, 22, 69
Clay, Edith, 330
clothes, Cretan, 96, 249, 253, 318–20, 328
Clytaemnestra, 9, 13, 44
code(s), 268, 295–6, 300
codenames, 246, 250, 254, 261, 273
Comber, Henry, 15–16, 18, 155
Comber, Mrs, John's nanny, 3, 7
Commander Pool, 325
Constantine, Byzantine Emperor, 13
Constantinople, 13, 33, 34, 46, 50, 59
Cook, Arthur, 30, 165, 225

Copaïs, Lake, 141, 296
Copenhagen Museum, 168
Corbridge, 216
Corfu, 14, 243–4
Corinth, 14, 46, 288; bombing, 297; earthquake, 64
Corsica, 243
Corunna, 241
Coventry, bombing, 269
cover (disguise), 244–6, 248, 250, 253, 262
Craven Fund, 31, 33
Creforce, 254–5, 259, 265–7, 274
Crete/Cretan(s): Assembly, 51; autonomy, 51; clans, 248, 265; clothes, 171, 249, 253, 257–8, 279, 318–20, 328: collapse of (Minoan), 116; defence, 253, 255, 262, 282, 287, 294, 322, 324; dialect, 189, 204, 241, 329; Division, xv, 255, 258, 260, 268, 298, 307–8; Eleutherna, 106; Evans, Sir Arthur in, 125, 188; German invasion, 245, 256, 259, 262, 285, 288, 293, 296, 299, 304, 311; Greek army, 293, 307; Italians in, 252, 254, 258; and John, 50, 117, 233, 235, 245, 291, 307; Keftiu, 115; military intelligence, 250, 254, 265; occupation, 292, 320, 323–4; Operation Abstention, 278; origin of Egyptian finds, 74; Phaistos, 184; rebellion, 261; Republican, 186; resistance, xv–xvi, 240, 245, 247, 249, 256, 258–9, 295, 301, 305; rivalry, 287, 292; Roman colony, 187; storytelling, 262, 264, 294–5, 313, 323; strategic importance, 253; union with Greece, 51; vendettas, 247–9, 329; veterans, 248, 288, 298; wartime, xv–xvi, 280–81, 285–6, 297
Cromer, Norfolk, 207–8
Croydon Airport, 193
Cruiser, *Helle*, 251–2
Crusader castle, 164
Cullen, James, 10–12, 40, 64
Cumberlege, Cle, 297
Cumberlege, Mike, 297–9, 303, 310–11, 313, 315–16, 321–2, 329, 331
Cunningham, Admiral Sir Andrew, 273, 274, 276
Curzon, Lord, 41
Customs Force, 284
Cyclades, 47, 220, 226
Cyclopean walls, 44
Cyprus, 153, 179, 207, 225, 231, 278
Cyprus Museum, 231
D Section, 246, 250, 254–6, 261, 267–8, 272, 282, 284, 291, 293, 296, 303, 315, 324
D'Albiac, Air Vice-Marshal, 294
Daily Mail, The, 301
Daily Telegraph, The, 18, 76, 81–2, 133–4, 168, 324
Damala, 47
Damascus Museum, 163

369

Danube, 33, 34, 280
Danzig, 227
Daphnes, 317
Dardanelles, 34
Darius I, 75: stela of, 76
Dartmoor, agricultural camps, 7
Dassis, Spiros, 13, 43, 65, 69, 140, 203
Dassis family, 13, 43
Daulis, 12
David, F. P., housemaster, 5–8, 10, 111
Davies, Captain T. E. H. (Tom), 271–2, 274
Davies, Oliver, 36
Dawkins, Richard, 28, 33, 56, 191, 221, 226
De Jong, Piet, 66, 106, 110, 126, 144
Deauville of the Orient, 71
Decoy, see HMS Decoy
Deir el-Bahari, 74
Deir el Medina, tombs, 96
Deir Mowas station, 128
Delium, 12
Delougaz, Pierre, 162
Delphi, 12, 141
Derby, see HMS Derby
Desborough, Vincent, 219
Devitt, Sir Thomas Lane, 2, 22
Dickie, *see* Dickinson, Mabel
Dickinson, Mabel, 69, 81, 154, 192, 208, 213, 217, 238: marriage, 25
Dickinson, Robin, 25
Dikaios, Porphyrios, 225, 231
Diktaean Cave, Psychro, 57, 59, 175, 191, 201, 203, 228
Dikte Mountains, 155, 205, 215, 229, 247
Diktynnaion promontory, 190
Dilke, Oswald, 226
Dill, General Sir John, 277
Dimini, 41
Dinos, 105
Dionysiades Islands, 58, 175
Dixon, Pierson ('Bob'), 16–17, 21, 23, 27–8, 30, 33–4, 36, 38, 277, 281, 283, 327: in the Argolid, 42, 44–5; and Ismene Atchley, 48, 68
Diyala, Iraq, 157, 162
Dodecanese, 109, 249, 250, 252, 255, 262, 263, 273, 284, 288, 297, 328: Kasos, 186; operations, 267, 272–9, 280, 282; patriotic societies, 272; raid on, 262, 264–5
Dog's River, 163
Dolphin, see HMS Dolphin
Doorn, Else, 222
Dorians, 30, 220, 230
Doris, 40
Dover, 10
Downs, the, Kent, 4

Drepani, 285
Dromos, of Treasury of Atreus, 43
Drossoulaki, Asristea, 315–18, 321
Drossoulakis, George, 315–18, 321, 328
Dunbabin, Tom, 189, 216, 329
Dunham, Dows, 209
Dunkirk, 240–41, 320
Duo Aorakia ('The Charlies'), 307
Early Minoan: EMI, 191, 203
E-boats, 278
Eccles, Edith, 174, 190
École Française d'Athènes, 52
Eden, Sir Anthony, 277, 281
Edmonds, 291
EES, *see* Egypt Exploration Society
Egerton's, Mr, school, 3
Egypt(ian), 56, 81, 116, 140, 168, 208, 218, 244: anti-British sentiment, 158, 194; architecture, 184, 197, art, 74, 91, British presence, 194; Civil Service, 211; Empire, 116; funerary practice, 152; furniture, 96; Greek community, 187; jewellery, 96, 98–100; John's interest in, 9–10, 67, 126; political situation, 198; wartime, 249, 250, 253–4, 279, 294, 320–21, 329; *see also* Cairo; Tell el-Amarna
Egypt Exploration Society (EES), 217: Committee, 9, 152, 167, 194, 199; exhibitions, 135, 145, 156, 161, 167, 178; funding issues, 82, 145, 149, 161, 168–9, 211; and *New York Times*, 134; publications, 144; reports to, 99, 137; and Tell el-Amarna, 67, 78, 80, 91, 112, 172, 179, 210, 240: enquiry into dissent at, 193–4
Egyptologists, 71, 74, 118, 156, 182, 238
Egyptology, 7, 74–5, 117–18, 129, 157, 194
Eichmann, Sturmbannführer Adolf, 70
El Aksa Mosque, 164
el-Amariya, 92
Elasa Island, 175
Electra, 9
Eleutherna, 106–7
el-Haj Qandil, 92
el-Hawata, 92
Ellenika, Ta, 230
Elliadi, Mr M. N., 51, 124, 250, 252
Elounta, 166, 167
Embaros, 218
Emery, Brian and Molly, 80, 83, 94
Emmett, Mrs, 105
Engelbach, Rex, 76, 137–9, 150, 152, 184
Enigma enciphering machines, 299
Eos, 284
Epidauros, 46
Epirus, 240–41, 244, 293, 298
Epstein, Jacob, 167

INDEX

Eremopolis, 176
Eretria, 38
Erganos, 218
Erotokritos, 204
Eshnunna, 101, 162
et-Till, 89, 92
Euboea, 38, 40
Euphrates, 87
Europe, political situation, 223
Evangelismos Hospital, 35, 203
Evans, Sir Arthur, 28, 55, 83, 106, 124, 125, 156, 167, 177, 191, 215, 312: bust, 187; diaries, 175; and John, 110, 114, 120, 126, 144, 155, 165, 189, 226; at Knossos, 9, 52, 91, 142–3, 145: reconstruction, 66, 312; leaves Crete, 188; 'Little Arthur', 280; and Mackenzie, 60, 111; and Manolaki, 193, 201; *Palace of Minos*, 19, 65, 174; *Travels in Crete*, 207
exhibitions: BSA 50th Anniversary, 203; EES, *see* Egypt Exploration Society; London the Treasure House, 156; Treasure of Tutankhamen, 103–4
Fairman, Herbert, 145, 158–9, 180, 182–3, 193–5, 199
fantasia, 150, 151, 155, 180, 211
Fascist, 251, 270, 277, 286
Fell, Peter, 238
felucca, 86, 103, 159
Fermor, Patrick Leigh, 295, 307
Field Security Unit, 256, 258, 280, 313, 320, 324
Finlay, George, 35
Finlay Library *see* British School of Archaeology at Athens
Fiona, 255
First World War, *see* Great War
fish: amulets, 131; bones, 148
Fisher, Vronwy, 229, 244
fishermen, 269, 275, 302
Flecker, James Elroy, 18, 146, 161
Fleurent, Jules and Henri, 128
Flossenburg concentration camp, 331
Forbes, Arthur Viscount, 244
Foreign office, 284
Forest Lovers, The, 18
Forsdyke, John, 111, 225
forts, 38, 44, 141: Hellenic, 206; Minoan, 223; Venetian, 50, 228, 254
France, 238, 243: fall of, 248, 253
Frankfort, Henri (Hans), 84–5, 101, 113, 119, 130, 143, 168: at Armant, 71, 81–2, 91, 94, 97; and John, 67, 75, 79, 83, 102, 104, 118; and Mary Chubb, 156; at Tell Asmar, 112, 132, 157, 161–2, 179; reports, 99, 129
Frankfort, Jettie, 68, 79, 84, 101, 163
Freunde, Major, 324–5

Freyberg, General, 294, 300
Fuad, King, 158
Fyfe, Theodore, 111
Gabail (Byblos),115
Gambier-Parry, Major General, 267
Gardiner, Alan, 119
Gardner, Ernest, 125
Gardner-Brown, Reverend GEM, 331
Gauthier, Henri, 76
Gayer Anderson, collector, 211
Gaza, 161
Gazi, 216
Gdokia, 285
Gem Aten, *see* Tell el-Amarna
General (Research) Headquarters (G(R) HQ), 245–6, 254, 272
Geographi Graeci Minores, 189
George I of the Hellenes, 51
George II of Greece, 226, 293–5
Gergeri, 155, 317
German(s)/Germany, 71, 105, 219, 233, 234, 247, 249, 252, 258, 266, 271, 289: and Athens, 226, 296; army, *see* armies, German; base hospital, 324–5; Club, Cairo, 222; camp, 331; destroyers, 4, 5; excavations, 92, 160; Foreign Office, xix, 330; gliders, 304–5; government, 252, 324; and Greece, 281; Intelligence Service, 222, 324; invasions, 302: Crete, xv–xvi, 290, 293, 296, 299, 304, 320; Greece, 283, 292, 294; and John, 322, 326–9; propaganda, 277, 305, 322, 327; School, 244; spies, 251; SS, xvi, xvii, xix, 14; tourists, 174; Tripartite Pact, 283
Gestapo, 323, 325
Gezira Island, 73, 212
Gezira Sporting Club, 73
Ghaffirs, 172, 209, 258
GHQ ME, 254–5
Giannadakis, Haralambos, 264, 266
Gill, Eric, 224, 231
Gilliéron, Emile, 106
Giophyro, 295, 306, 314
Giza, 73, 218
Gkiona pass, 141
Gla, 141
Glanville, Stephen, 83, 94, 98, 103, 114, 119, 133, 137, 194–5: and Amarna, 72, 134–5, 179, 182; and Bennett, 129, 169; and BM, 156; description of, 71, 80, 99; on Egyptology, 118; and Frankfort, 85, 100; funding issues, 211; and *JEA*, 117; and John, 139, 242; and Philip Chubb, 158, 163; on Tell el-Amarna, 184
glass eye, 237, 307, 317, 322, 325
Glendi, 207, 231
gold, 133, 137, 139: Mycenae, 44; masks, 131;

371

ring, 142
Golden Fleece, 41, 116
Gonia Monastery, 190
Goniais, 314
Goura, 70
Gourneh, 83
Gournes, 308
Gournia, 54, 55
G(R) HQ, *see* General (Research) Headquarters
Gramvousa, 51, 228
Great Malvern, 25, 36, 68, 144, 178, 192, 213, 223, 233
Great Powers, The (Britain, France and Russia), 51
Great War, xv, 1, 10, 14–15, 21, 34, 91, 109, 221, 266, 239,
Greece/Greek, 61, 84, 101, 103, 112, 139, 155, 213, 234–5, 247, 254, 261, 283, 290, 293: Argolid, *see* Argolid; army, *see* armies, Greek; community, in Egypt, 187; Consul, 186; and Crete, 51; defence, 281; dialects, 221; German invasion, 283; Government, 246, 253, 261, 266, 328; islands, 105; and Italians, 260; and John, 10–14, 37, 122; language, 224, 234, 239; Minister of War, 323; neutrality, 243, 252, 253; Order of the Redeemer, 15; Prime Minister, 125; Republic, 186; resistance, 261, 272; Secret Police, 266
Griffith, Francis Llewellyn, 83, 91, 134, 146
Grigorakis, Antonis ('Satanas'), xv, 165, 248, 264, 266, 292, 302, 307–8, 311–12, 325, 328–9
Grymani, 214
guerrilla(s), xv–xvi, 272, 289, 303, 307, 322, 324, 328–9
Guftis, 129
Guide to the Palace of Knossos, *see* Handbook to the Palace of Minos
Gunn, Battiscombe, 76, 137–9
Hadley, W. H., 47
Hadrian's Wall, 216
Hague regulations, 323
Haifa, 164, 297
Haliartos, 12
Hall, Sir Henry, 101, 117, 119, 134
Hammond Martin, 210–12, 218, 221–3, 272, 320, 329
Hammond, Molly, 209–11, 218, 221–3, 320: and John, 213, 223
Hammond, Nicholas ('Nick'), 120, 243–4, 247, 255, 288–9, 291, 296–9, 302–3, 311: and John, 240
Hammurabi, 162
Hampstead, 151, 155, 213
Hamson, Jack, 254–7, 272, 281–4, 288, 291, 296, 300–301, 313, 315, 317, 320, 322, 324: and John, 313; Operation Blunt, 274–6
Handbook to the Palace of Minos, 143–4, 155–6, 165
Hapshetsut, Queen, 87, 149
Harding, Rowe, 18, 22–3, 27, 31
Hare Prize, 103
Hargreaves, Kathleen, 72–3, 77
Hargreaves, Lionel, 73, 210
Haroun al-Rashid, 161
Hartley, Dorothy, 123
Hartmann, 325
Harvati (Mycenae), 43
Hassan, 18, 146, 161
Hat Aten, 148
Hatiay, 135, 146
Hattusas, 104
Hawes, 54
Hawkes, Christopher, 8
Hawks Club, 27
Helicon, 47
Heliopolis, 88
Helle, 186, 251
Hellenes, 293
Hellenic: fortress, 206; scholarship, 245; pottery, 191
Henley-in-Arden, Warwickshire, 5
Heraklion, 50: airfield, 304, 308; ammunition store, 284, 303; communication in, 306; defence of, 262, 290, 295, 307–10, 312, 314–15, 319; evacuation from, 320, 324; Hotel Minos, 106; and John, 317; mapping, 269; Mayor of, 311; Museum, 331; Officers' Club, 302; Prefect of, 261, 266; tobacco factory, 255; Venetian fort, 310; Vice-Consulate, xix, 328; *see also* Candia
Hereward, *see* HMS *Hereward*
Hermione, 45, 47
Hermonthis *see* Armant
Hero, *see* HMS *Hero*
Heurtley, William, 42, 46–7, 60–62, 64, 79, 84, 101–3, 112, 120, 141, 164, 187
Hewlett, Maurice, 18, 26
Hieratic, 101, 129
hieroglyphs, 71, 81, 129, 149, 157, 182: mock, 7–8
High Desert, Egypt, 94, 97
high jump, 8, 19, 20, 24, 65: Queen's Club, 29–30
High Priest, 136, 160
Hillier, Tristram, 175, 177
hillmen, Pendlebury's, 258, 259, 265, 331
Himmler, Heinrich, 13, 294
Himmler of Greece, 251
hippopotamus, clay, 131
Hitler, Adolf, xvi, 219, 223, 227, 234, 243, 253, 280–81, 283, 313, 323, 325
Hittite Empire, 12, 30, 87, 97, 104, 133, 153

INDEX

HMS Decoy, 277–8
HMS Derby, 273–5
HMS Dolphin, 221, 255, 297–9, 302–3, 310, 321
HMS Hereward, 277–8
HMS Hero, 278
HMS York, 302
hockey, 46, 73, 229
Hogarth, David George, 12, 57
Holy George, *see* Agios Georgios
Holy Luke, *see* Osios Luokas, monastery
Home Guards, 287, 323
Home Security, 251
Home Service, BBC, 234
Homer, 13, 40, 166: bust of, 226
Homeric: epic, 296; epithet, 268
Hopkins Morris, Mrs, 211
horses, 78, 162: riding, 157, 159–60, 162–3, 239–40
Hospital, Evangelismos, *see* Evangelismos Hospital
Housesteads (Borcovicius), 216
Howland, Robert 'Bonzo', 29
Hubbard, Mrs, 134, 157, 183, 195, 197, 211
Hunstanton, 217
Hunt, David, 244
Hurricanes, (aircraft, Second World War), 293
Hussein, head servant at Armant, 77
Hutchinson, R. W. ('the Squire'), 70, 178, 186–7, 191–2, 216, 226, 228, 247, 249, 251–2, 270, 291, 301: mother of, 249, 252, 270
Hybrias the Cretan, 28
Hydra, 47
Hyksos kings, 87
ibex, 197–8
Ida range, 189, 229, 247, 292, 313
Idaean Cave, 59, 155
identity cards, 236, 284, 315–16
Idomeneus, 222, 230
Ierapetra, 55, 122, 177, 206, 222, 285, 302
The Iliad, 18
Iliffe, David, 164, 171
illnesses: blood poisoning, 203, 280; heat stroke, 306; staphylococcus, 203; streptococcal poisoning, 209–10; at Tell el-Amarna, 173
Illustrated London News, 18, 134, 148, 255
Imperia, 155
Imperial Airways, 155, 166
In the Library, play, 28
intelligence, military, 236, 240, 246, 253–4, 288–9, 308, 322, 324, 327
interpreters, 260, 325
interrogation, 219
Inter-Services Liaison Department (ISLD), 320
Iolcos, 41
Iraq, 87, 101, 112, 129, 132, 157, 163, 179

Ireland, 33
Irene, the, 296
Iron Age, 62, 247
Isle of Wight, 233–4
Ismail Pasha, 212
Issus, Gulf of, 115
Italian/Italy, 120: ambassador, 253; archaeologists, 110; government, 252; invasions: Abyssinia, 194, 198; Albania, 227, 243; Crete, 254–5; language, 189; people, 184, 252, 258, 281; Tripartite Pact, 283; war, 109, 186, 243, 245, 253: on Greece, 249, 253, 260, 268, 270–71
Itea, 13
Ithaca, 14
Iuktas, Mount, 174, 312
Jacobsen, Rigmor, 162–3
Jacobsen, Thorkild, 162–3
Jason and the Argonauts, 41, 116–17
JEA, see Journal of Egyptian Archaeology
Jebel esh-Sharqui, 163
Jekyll, 155
Jenkins, Romilly, 141
Jerusalem, 159, 164, 166, 171, 187
jewellery, 57, 96, 145
Jews, Balkan, 70, 153
JHS, see Journal of Hellenic Studies
Jonas, Mary, 112, 145, 157, 169, 181, 183–4, 193, 195, 207, 209–12, 217
Jones, Edwards, 29
Journal of Egyptian Archaeology (JEA), 115, 117, 120, 143–4, 184
Journal of Hellenic Studies (JHS), 117
Junker 52s, 305, 309
Kalabaka, 41
Kalamauka, 155, 214
Kalamata, 13, 64
Kalami, 284–5
Kalauria, 47
kalderimi, 59
Kalergi, 174
Kaloi Limenes, 155, 285
Kalymnos, 252
Kamares Cave, 155
Kamaris Ware, 125
Kaminia, 314
Kandilioro, 230
Kapetans (Kapetanoi), 165, 247–8, 262, 287, 322, 327–8
kapheneion, 56, 110
Kapodistrias, Madame, 48
Karnak, 74, 77
Karo, Georg, 28, 120
Karpathos, 56, 250
Karphi, 214–15, 219–20, 224, 229–31, 232,

373

247, 292: publication, 235–6
Karyotakis, M, 231
Kasapis, Doctor, 59, 216, 325
Kasarmi, Hellenic fortress, 46
Kasos, 56, 186, 254, 262, 273, 275–6, 298, 307: raid, 302; Straits, 56, 250, 254, 273, 310
Kassabanos River, 307
Kastelli Kissamou, 59, 190, 228, 298
Kastellos, Psarokorphe, 214
Kastri, near Stavrokhori, 230
Katharos, 58, 206, 223
Kathimerini, 281
Kato Phanari, 46
Kavousi, 55, 175, 230, 285
Keats, John, 332
Keftiu, 74, 115–16, 119
Kent, 1–5, 241
Kenya, 25, 217–18
Keramai, 107–8, 110
Khafaje, 162
Khartoum, 218
Khedivial Mail, The (shipping line), 71
Kia Ora, Ruiri, 217
Kimolos, 226
King Edward VI School, Louth, 37
Kingsley, Charles, 41
Kish, 162
Kitten's Cistern, 207
Klephts, 240
Knossos, 50, 52, 59, 65, 168, 186, 198, 230, 233, 280, 301, 312, 322: architects, 91, 111; bull-rings, 116; Egyptian finds, 60; estate, 122, 178; Evans at, 126, 187; fall of, 172; hostel, 66; John at, 110, 120, 123, 142, 167, 192, 216, 221, 332; king of, 56; Mackenzie at, 60, 114; Malevizi region, 175; Minoan town, 142; mosaics, 187; Muslim graveyards, 51; Palace of, 125; pottery, 167; publication, 18; reconstruction, 66; Roman remains, 188; sack of, 222; Stratigraphic Museum, 144; style, 9; Taverna, 106, 165, 177; Temple tomb, 142–3; Villa Dionysos, 187; wartime, 251; *see also* Villa Ariadne
Kokkinos Pyrgos, 107, 285, 299
Kolonna, 220, 222
Kommos, 66, 68, 106–7, 122, 155
Koprana, 215, 228
Koryzis, Alexander, 277, 293
koulouras (lined pits), 125
Kouphonisi, 285, 288
Kourtais, 230
kouskouras, 52
Krasanakis, Georgios, 205
Krasi, 166

Kritsa, 58, 206, 285, 286
Kronos, god, 203
Krousonas, 155, 165, 192, 292, 300–301, 307 8, 311–12, 315, 317, 321
Krousoniots, 301
Künsberg, Baron Eberhard von, xix, 328
Kurvelesh, 244
Kythira, 254
Lacau, Pierre, 137–8, 150, 180, 183
Ladybird, 277–8
Lakanida, 206
Lakkoi, 188
Lamb, Winifred, 36, 38, 43, 68
Lamia, 141
Langada Pass, 13, 64, 65
Larissa, 38, 42
Lasithi, 52, 57, 191, 201, 203–5, 207, 213–14, 216, 218–27, 231, 240, 247, 287, 325, 332
Lasithiotes, 230
Last, Hugh, 169, 179–80, 193–4, 225
Lato, 155
Lausanne, 10
Lavers, Ralph, 145, 150–51, 156–8, 173–4, 182–4, 194, 199, 201, 209
Lawrence, A. W., 192–3
Lawrence, T. E., 192
Lawson, Jock, 15, 27, 108, 234–5
Le Fanu, W. R., 102
Lear, Edward, 52
Lebanon, Mount, 163
Legation, the British, 227, 244–5, 250–51
Leicestershire Regiment, 294, 307
Leonidhi, 47
lepida, 230
Lesbos, 68, 105
Levant, 97, 115, 187
Levy, Rachel, 162
Libya(n), 249; Sea, 66; War, 109
The Life and Death of Richard Yea and Nay, 18, 23, 26, 67
Ligourio, 46
Lilibulero, 141
Limnarkaros Plain, 205, 215, 218
Limonakis, nephew of Satanas, 308
Lindsay, Lord, 20
Little-go, Cambridge entrance exam, 9
Livadia, 141
Liverpool Annals, 115, 120, 184
Liverpool University, *see* University of Liverpool
Livingstone-Learmonth, Tom, 21–3, 27
Lloyd Triestino (shipping line), 14
Lloyd, Joan, 166, 175–7
Lloyd, Seton, 84, 94, 100–101, 105, 129, 132, 135–6, 162–3, 166–7, 175–7, 188, 207, 219

INDEX

LMI, *see* Late Minoan I
LMII, *see* Late Minoan II
Locris, 40
London, 98, 144, 167, 178, 216, 239–40, 242, 273: Brook Street practice, 3, 25; General Hospital, 2; Great War, 1; World War II, 235 7
Longmore, Air Marshal Sir Arthur, 277
Lorimer, Miss, 117
lotus flower, decoration, 98
Loubier's, 140
Loukadakis, Konstantinos, 317
Loukas's kapheneion, 110
Louvain, devastation of, 2
Lowe, Douglas, 18, 20, 24–5
Lower Gypsades, 142
Luftwaffe, 293, 302, 320
Luke (wartime codename), 246
Lutyens, Sir Edwin, 84
Luxor, 71, 74, 76–7, 82, 84, 92, 115, 135
Lykabettos, 63
Lyttos, 59
Macedonia, 10, 41, 61, 78, 280
MacGougan, Malcolm, 23
MacGregor, William, 23
Mackenzie, Compton, 244
Mackenzie, Duncan, 14, 66–7, 106, 110, 114, 124, 126, 167, 177
Mackworth Young, George, 208–9, 216, 244, 251
Macmillan, George, 84, 102, 111, 143–4, 165
Macmillan studentship, 102–4, 111–12, 106
Maketaten, 152
Makrygialo, 176
Malda, 217
Maleme, 304, 310, 319
Malevizi region, 175
Malis, 40
Mallawi, 86, 103, 132, 158, 210
Mallia, 52, 166, 205
Malta, 225, 243
Malvern College, 25
Mamur of Mallawi, 169
Manolaki, *see* Akoumianos, Manolis
The Manchester Guardian, 172
Mandibles (codename), *see* Dodecanese
Mandra, 205–6
Mandras, 300
Maniadakis, 251, 261, 294
Manoussakis, Theonymphe, 317–18
Mantakas, General, 250
Mantinades, 204
Mantola, 217
Marathos, 107
Margate, German attack on, 5
Marinatos, Spyridon, 105, 123–4, 201, 203, 213, 216
Mark, codename, *see* Sinclair
Markatatos, Polybios, 314–15
Markogiannakis, George, 204–5, 228
Markogiannakis, Ourania, 204–5
Marmara, Sea of, 34
Martlets Society, 21
Maru-aten, 92
Masrur, 17, 18
Matala, 155, 285, 299
Matilda tanks, (British, 2nd World War), 294
Matthew, codename, 246
Mauser, 311
May, J. M. F., 244
May, Royal Chancellor, 137
Mazoi, 98
McFie, Lieutenant, 273, 275–6
Meade, Geoffrey, 268, 284
Meceberna, 61
medieval: castles, 109; houses, 72
Medinet Habu, 74, 81, 99
Medjay, *see* 'Mazoi'
Megaspelaion, 70
Megaw, Peter, 207, 225
Megiddo, 164
Meliarakes, Ioannes, 201
Melidoni, 189
Mena House Hotel, 218
Menelaion, Sparta, 65
Menkheperrasenb, tomb of, 74
Meritaten, 149
Meryre, High Priest of the Aten, 160
Mesogia, 191
Mesopotamia, 91, 97, 156
Messara, 174, 299
Messenian Gulf, 65
Messerschmitt (German aircraft, 2nd World War), 109, 321
Metaxas, General, 250–51, 253, 261, 265, 270, 277, 290, 294, 320
Meteora monasteries, 41–2
Methana, 46, 47
Methuen, 165, 177, 224
Metropolis Cathedral, 63
Metropolitan Museum of Art, 207, 209–10
MI, *see* military, intelligence
MI (R), *see* Military Intelligence Research
MI6, 246
Miamou, 155
Middle East, 254, 307: forces, 255, 281; Headquarters, 265, 268, 272, 274, 280–83
Middle Minoan, 57: I (MMI), 191; Ia (MMIa), 125; II (MMII), 125, 143, 191; III (MMIII), 214
Midea, 44

375

Milan, 10, 14
Milatos, 166, 213
military: incompetence, 276, 278, 292, 309–10, 313, 319; intelligence, 237, 245, 240, 250, 256, 268, 288–9, 308, 324; training, 237–41, 249, 274, 289
Military Intelligence Research (MI (R)), 235, 243, 245–6, 250–51, 254–6, 262, 267, 282–3, 288
Mille, Collette (wartime evacuee), 235
Milos, 310
Ministry of Information (MOI), 236
Minoan civilisation, 18, 55, 74, 96, 115, 116, 125, 172, 153, 176, 188, 229, 230: collapse, 115; refugees, 230; script, 172, 227, 229; settlement, 122, 188; villa, 189
Minos, King, 28, 116, 143, 230
Minya, Egypt, 132
Minyan ware, Greece 62
Mirabello, 53, 55, 58, 166, 166, 262, 292
Mistra, 13
Mitanni, The, 87, 97
Mitchell, Violet, 18
Mitford, Terence Bruce, 254–6, 267, 272, 281-4, 291, 296, 300-1, 315, 317
MNBDO (Mobile Naval Base Defence Organisation), 304
MO9, 273
Mochlos, 55, 57
Modena, 114
MOI, see Ministry of Information
Molyvopyrgos, 61
Mombasa, 218
monarchy, Greek, 186–7, 216, 226
monasteries, 41–2, 70, 176, 190; see also under names of individual monasteries
Mond, Robert Sir, 78, 80, 151
Money-Coutts, Mercy, 168, 174, 191–2, 201, 213, 216, 218, 227–80: and John, 215, 223, 232, 330–31
Mons, 241
Montreal, 67
Morosini, 280, 291
mosaics, Roman, 187
mosque of Ibn Tulun, 72, 211
Mount Bergadi, 59
Mount Cyllene, 47-8, 69
Mount Dikte, 58, 155, 205, 221, 291
Mount Hymettos, 11
Mount Ida (Psiloriti), 106–7, 155, 165, 189, 192, 216, 291, 300
Mount Iuktas, 50, 65–6, 174
Mount Lebanon, 163
Mount Lykabettos, 35
Mount Olympos, 10, 42

Mount Ossa, 42
Mount Prophitis Elias, 44
Mount Taygetos, 43, 65
Mount Thriphte, 175
Mount Zara, 44
mudbrick, 89, 133, 153, 160
Mudir (Director), 200
Munich, 33
The Mural Paintings of El-'Amarneh, 75
Murchison Falls, 218
Murray, Gilbert, 125
Murray, Margaret, 67, 179
Musées Royaux du Cinquantaire, 171
museums, 156, 168, 212, 215: see also under names of individual museums
music hall songs, 141
Muslim: Crete, 50; foreman, 111; graveyards, 51
Mussolini, 198, 204, 223, 243, 252, 269
Mycenae(an), 43, 69, 116, 140, 203, 227: 'Belle Hélène', 13, 43–4, 140, 227; citadel, 44; finds, 9, 11, 137; and Harvati, 43; ivory, 43; and John, 13, 48; palace, Pylos, 227; shaft graves, 120, 131; Tell el-Amarna, 139;
Myers, 169
Mykonos, 105
Myres, Sir John, 28, 177, 220, 240, 280
Myros, driver, 123
Myrtos, 285
myth(s), 41, 116–17, 201: John's, 321; Cretan, 264, 295
Nahas Pasha, 158
Napoleon, 163: wars, 238
National Crisis, the, 145
National Museum, Athens, 11, 60
Natural History Museum, 155
Natural History Society, Winchester College, 6
Nauplion, 46
navy/naval, 186, 273: base, Souda, 253; British, xv, 15, 235, 250, 253, 277, 310; intelligence, 15, 223; Italian, 249, 310
Naval Intelligence Department (NID), 234, 237, 245
Naxakes, 228
Naxos, 226
Neapolis, 53, 191
Near East, 109, 177, 223, 237
Neb maat Ra, 152
necklaces, 98–100
Nefertiti Lived Here, 129
Nefertiti, 18, 48, 86, 88, 91, 96, 98, 104, 134–5, 146, 148, 152–3, 160, 212
Nelson, Alec, 20
Neolaia (Metaxist Youth Movement), 270, 286
Neolithic, 155, 188

INDEX

Nesimos Plain, 214
Nestor, 227
New Phaleron, 114
New York Times, 134
New Zealand, 158, 330: forces, 290, 322
Newberry, Percy, 184, 179, 195
Newton, Francis, 71, 91, 146
Nicholl, Commander ('Nick the NOIC'), 273, 275–6
'Nick the NOIC', *see* Nicholl, Commander
NID, *see* Naval Intelligence Department
Nida Plain, 155, 247, 300, 315
Nile, 73–4, 77, 86, 91, 94, 128, 130, 158
North Foreland, Kent, 1–3
Northampton(shire), 237, 239
Norwegian Campaign, 241
Nubia, 88, 97, 173
OBE, *see* Order of the British Empire
observation posts, 285, 290
OCTU, *see* Officer Cadet Training Unit
Odos Speusippou (now Souedias), 35
Odysseus (Homeric), 14: wartime agent, 296
The Odyssey, 166
Officer Cadet Training Unit (OCTU), 237
Officer Training Corps (OTC), 6
Officers' Club, Heraklion, 302
Old Krone, *see* Bardakis, Kronis
Old Man Comber, 154
Olympia, 13
Olympic Games, 13, 20–21, 67
Olynthos, 61, 63
Omalos Plain, 191, 247
Omda (head of village), 132, 151
Operation Abstention, 276–9
Operation Blunt, 273–6
Operation Dynamo, 241
Orchomenos, 11, 141
Oreino, 223, 230
Orestes, 140
Orient Express, 67, 69, 120, 144, 156, 240
Orient Line, 2, 168, 209: SS *Oronsay*, 179
Oriental Institute, Chicago, 112, 129, 135, 157, 161
Orion sector, 308–10, 319
Osios Loukas, monastery, 12
Ottoman Turks, 50, 72, 228
Overseer of the King's Works *see* Hatiay
Overseer of the Soldiery *see* May, Royal Chancellor
Oxford University, 28, 33, 84, 195, 216, 219, 244: Ashmolean Museum, 148; Brasenose College, 225; Craven Fund, 36, 225; New College, 219; Press, 225; races against, 20
Oxford and Cambridge University Club, 240–42
Pachyammos, 55, 57, 167, 175, 214, 221–3

Pagasae, 40, 41
Palace of Minos, Knossos, 65–6, 126, 144, 301, 312
Palace of Minos, 18, 65, 125–6, 143, 174
Palaikastro, 55–6, 116, 118, 176, 285
Palairet, Sir Michael, 251, 277, 295
Paleocastro Fort, Castellorizo, 277
Palestine, 120, 139, 145, 157–8, 179, 187
Panathenaikos football ground, 46
Panehsy, Priest, 136
Papadakis, Colonel, 286–7, 320
Papaeliakis, Elias, 317
Papagos, General, 277, 290
Papastergiou, General, 260, 298
paratroopers, 228, 305–6, 308–9, 312–15, 322, 326
Paris, 10, 20, 21, 249
Parker, Captain R. N., 235
Parnassos, 47
Parnon, 47
Paros, 105, 227
Parthenon, 31
Pascoe, Marion, 213, 215, 219, 229, 232, 280
Paterakis, Nikos, 204
Pathé News, 234
Patras, 297
Paul, Prince Regent, Yugoslavia, 281, 283
Pawson, 296
Payne, Humfry, 84–5, 101, 107, 110, 114, 118–19, 123, 141–2, 155, 280: death of, 203, 207, 227; and John, 106
PCAC, *see* Cambridge, University, athletic clubs
Pearson, old Wykehamist, 238
Pedersen, M. O., 259
Pediada district, 174
Peet, Thomas, 91, 113, 118–20, 134, 157
Pelion, Mount, 41
Peloponnese, 13, 60, 64, 140, 175, 293, 328
The Pem, 15, 26
Pendlebury, David, 156–7, 163–5, 167–8, 173, 181, 184, 191–4, 207–8, 213, 217, 223, 233–4, 241: birth, 154, 178; jaundice, 224–5; and John, 179, 330
Pendlebury, Dickie, *see* Dickinson, Mabel
Pendlebury, Herbert, 3, 76, 192, 220, 250, 255, 330, 331: birth of grandchildren, 154, 178; education, 2, 15–16; and John, 68, 108, 241–2, 326; and Kenya, 217; letters to, 14, 36, 53, 61, 77, 95, 100, 106 (on BSA), 111, 117, 118 (on Egyptology), 126, 132, 139 (on BM), 171, 172 (on vandalism), 199 (on Cairo unrest), 213, 223, 233; marriage to Mabel, 25
Pendlebury, Hilda *see* White, Hilda
Pendlebury, Joan, 181, 191–4, 207–8, 213, 217,

377

223, 233, 241: birth, 177–8; and John, 178–9, 330

Pendlebury, John Devitt Stringfellow: academics, 225–6, 239; *Ægyptiaca*, 120; affairs, rumoured, 213, 223, 231–2; and archaeology, 183–4, 225–6, 229–30; *Archaeology of Crete*, 225; in Argolid, 42, 44–5; and authority, 268, 327; birth of children, 154–5, 178; and BSA, 36, 207–9; capture, 315; *City of Akhenaten II*, 181; Cretan dress, 127, 159, 171–2, 253; and Cretan resistance, 256; on Crete, 51–2, 245–6, 249–50; Cycladic book, 220, 227; death, 315, 317, 322–3, 326–7, 329, 331–2; description of, 129, 141–2, 206, 256, 257, 291, 307; and Evans, 143, 188; as a father, 208, 217, 225, 330; funding issues, 208–9; in German reports, 261; at Hadrian's Wall, 216–17; *Handbook*, 143–4, 165; at Heraklion, 307–10; and Heurtley, 42; and Hilda, 69, 242; holiday, 207, 223; in Iraq, 161–3; *JEA* article, 115; in Kenya, 217–18; meets King of Greece at Knossos, 294; at Knossos, 111–12, 177; at Lasithi, 214; linguistic abilities, 130, 199, 237, 239, 256, 259; Mackenzie, 114; Macmillan studentship, 104, 111; and Marinatos, 123–4, 213; and Mercy Money-Coutts, 231–2; and Molly Hammond, 222–3; Operation Blunt, 274–6; and Payne, 203; at Tell el-Amarna, 88, 95, 104, 112–13, 129, 153, 193–4, 212; Tell el-Amarna, 184; at Tzermiado, 232–3; at Vitsilovrysi fountain, 224; wartime service, 234–7, 244, 268–9, 280, 283–7; wounded, 313–14, 316

Pendlebury, John, senior, 2
Pendlebury, Lily, 2–3, 8, 10
Pendlebury's Thugs, 249
Peneus, River, 42
Pheneos, Plain of, 70
Peoples of the Sea, 115–17
Perachora, 141, 203
Per-hai, 171
Perkins, John Ward, 225
Perrins, Dyson, 81
Persia(n), 75: army, 40; War, 11
Peter, Prince of the Hellenes, 293
Petraki, Moni, monastery, 35–6
Petrakogiorgos, 248
Petrie, Sir William Flinders, 10, 18, 37, 67, 81, 91–2, 97, 113, 148, 159–60, 172, 179, 181–2, 197
Petrie Medal, 143
Petrou, Assistant Director of Candia Museum, 215
Phaistos, 122, 184
Phalasarna, 190–91, 228
Phaleron, 105, 243–4

Philae, ancient temples of, 85
Phillips, Gilbert, 134–5, 163, 169
Phocis, 40
Phokas, Nikephoros, 50
Phrati, 218
Pindar, 328
Pindus Mountains, 41, 141–2, 328
Piraeus, 34, 50, 63, 105, 114, 255, 290, 293
Pirie, Ian, 246, 250–51, 255, 261–2, 268, 270–71, 293, 296, 315
Plastiras, General, 186
Platanos Mesogeion, 228
Plateia Koraka, 308
Platon, Nicolas, 331
Pliny, 176
poet(ry), 146, 158, 204, 219, 224, 325
Poikilassos, 191
Poland, 227, 238
police, 222, 228, 250, 266, 285
Pompeii, 209
Pool, Commander, 166, 320–21, 326, 331
Poole harbour, 243
Poros, 45, 47
Port Said, 77, 150, 217
Porto Raphti, 63
Poseidon, 47, 50, 57
pottery, 109, 153, 155: Chalkidiki, 70; dating, 167; Hellenic, 191; Iron Age, 62; Knossos, 144, 167, 174; Kolonna, 220; Lasithi, 203; Minoan, 191, 175, 215; Mycenaean, 18; polychrome, 125
Powell, Dilys, 84, 141, 318, 332
Powell, Villiers ('Pip'), 22–3, 29
Polyrrhenia, 228
Praisos, 175
pranks, 204, 226, 236, 267–8, 301
Prefect of Heraklion, 261, 265–6
Preston, 2, 217
Priansos, 188
Prinias, 155
prisoner-of-war (camp), 267, 274, 314, 316, 318, 320–21, 324
Prometheus (wartime codename), *see* Bakirdzis, Colonel
Prometheus group, 296
Prometheus II (wartime codename), 262
propaganda, 246, 251, 246, 251, 261, 277, 305, 322, 326–7
Prophitis Elias, 312, 319
Proto-Geometric, 123, 220, 222
Psammetichus I, 37
Psarokorphe, 214
Pseira, 57
Psiloriti, 247, 300, 325, 329
Psychro, 57–9, 175, 201, 203–4, 215–16

INDEX

Ptolemies, the, 75
Pylos, Mycenaean palace, 227
Pyramids of Giza, 71–3, 218
Pyrgos, 155
Q movements, 267
Queen's Club, London, 21, 26–7, 29–30
quftis, 83, 92, 150
Quseir, 82
RAF, *see* Royal Air Force
Ramesses II, 163
Raphael, Mr, 195
rebellion, 186, 190, 248, 261: Venizelist
Red Cross, 233, 325–6
Red Sea, 82, 98
Regginakis', 280
Rekhmara, tomb of, 74
Rendall, Monty, 225
Resistance: Cretan, xv–xvi, 240, 245, 258–9, 295, 301, 305; Greek, 261, 272
Restoration, of monarchy, 187, 216
Rethymnon, 106, 189, 262, 304, 306, 319
Rhaukos, 165
Rhodes, 18, 101, 109, 131, 278
Rhokka, 228
Richard I, Coeur de Lion, 17, 18, 26, 58
'Ring of Minos', 142
Rinkel, John, 22
riots, Cairo, 194, 199
RNVR, *see* Royal Navy Volunteer Reserve
Roberts, Lane, 154, 213
Roberts, S. C., 24
Robertson, D, 231, 224
Robinson, David ('the Bince'), 9
Robinson, David (Olynthos), 61
Rockefeller, J. D., 100, 207
Rodger, Margaret, 38, 40, 41, 51
Rolston, 249, 252, 291
Rome/Roman(s), 52, 75, 188: cisterns, 190; colony, 187; emperors at Armant, 75; Knossos, 188; Makrygialo, 176
Rose, Stephen, 256, 259, 270, 282
Roukkaka, 175
Royal Air Force, 236, 250, 294, 319, 304–5
Royal Army Medical Corps, 2
Royal Artillery, 294
Royal Egyptian Airforce, 173
Royal Engineers, 241, 262
Royal Flying Corps, 1
Royal Marines, 304
Royal Navy, *see* navy, British
Royal Naval Volunteer Reserve (RNVR), 15
Royal Society, 156
Royal Tomb, *see* Tell el-Amarna
Royal Wadi, *see* Tell el-Amarna

Royal Welch Fusiliers, 16
Rudnitzky, Günther, 194–5, 199
Rumania, 34, 251, 280
Russell Pasha, Sir Thomas, 194, 198 : family, 197
sabotage, 246, 251, 254, 261, 267, 272, 284, 290, 296
Saida Zeinab, 72
St Bride's School, Helensburgh, 37
St George's Medical School, 1, 2, 3, 5, 204
St Gregory of Nazianzus, head of, 42
St John, Robert, 301
St Pol, Jehane, 23, 48
St Pol, Marie de, de Valence, 23
Salamis, 186
Salmon, Miss, 76–7
Salonika, 61, 70, 292, 296
Samaria Gorge, 191
Samarites, Myron, 312–3
Samos, 105
Santi Quaranta, 244
Saqqara, 73–4
Saracens, 78
sarcophagi, 75, 157, 199
Saridakis, Nikolaos, 55
Saridakis, Theocharis, 295, 325
Saronic Gulf, 35
Satanas, *see* Grigorakis, Antonis ('Satanas')
Saunders, Seaman, 297–8, 321
Savage, Patrick, 253, 259
Savoia, (Italian aircraft, 2nd World War), 81
Savoy Hotel, Luxor, 74, 81, 82
Sawag, Hussein, 129
Scarab, the, 81
Scarpanto, 250, 262, 273, 285
Schirmer, Captain Gerhard, 309–12, 319
Schliemann, Heinrich, 13, 17
Schulz, Major Karl-Lothar, 308–10, 312–13, 319
sculptors, 161, 167, 197
Seager, Richard, 55, 57: house, 167, 175, 221
Secret Intelligence Service (SIS), 237
Selassie, Emperor Haile, 198
Seltman, Charles, 28, 30–31, 83, 105, 244
Seltman, Isabel, 105, 244
Senmut, tomb of, 74
Sennacherib, 163
Serbia, 10, 34
Sessebi, 159
Seth Smith, Dr, 84
Sgouroprinos, 206
Shackleton, Pat, 69
shaft graves, Mycenae, 120, 131
Shelley, Percy Bysshe, 332
Sherman, Stephen, 151, 155–9, 168, 172–3
Sherraif, Ali, 129

379

Sherreif, Hassan, guide, 82–3
Sherwood Foresters, 278
Shorter, Alan, 79, 100–101, 184
Sicily, 120, 249
Sidon, 163
Siege of Corinth, 331
Simpson, Adrian, 245, 254–5, 268, 271
Sinclair, Adrian, 246, 250
SIS, *see* Secret Intelligence Service
Sitia, 55, 175, 252, 285
Skalani, 312
Skaphidia Cave, 214
Skeat, Theodore 'the Horse', 120
Skinokapsala, 223
Skopje, 10
Skoteino, 166, 175
Smenkhara, 97, 149, 179
Smith-Hughes, Jack, 320–21, 325, 328
SO2, *see* Special Operations 2
Society of Antiquaries, 167
SOE, *see* Special Operations Executive
Sofia, 33, 34
Solakakis, 321, 329
Sonderkommado von Künsberg, xix, 328
songs: Cretan, 221, 247; Victorian, 141
Soper, John, 26
Sophocles, Electra, 9
Souda Bay, 51, 189–90, 253–4, 297, 302–4
Souda Island, 254, 261–2, 272, 274, 283–4, 291, 296–7, 315
Souia, 188
Soviet Union, 236
Sparta, 13, 40, 64–5
Special Operations 2 (SO2), 267, 296, 303
Special Operations Executive (SOE), 303
Special Service, 240
Spetses, 47
Sphakia, 56, 240, 299, 320, 324
Sphakianakis, Mr, 214–15
Sphakianakis, Governor General, 265
Sphinx, the, 73, 159
Sphinx, codename, 250
spies, 228, 250–51, 261
Spilia, 312
Spina Longa, 51, 155, 166, 213
Spiro, *see* Dassis, Spiro
Sporting Life, 20
spring, Vitsilovrysi, Karphi, 280, 291
Squire, *see* Hutchinson, R. W.
SS Clan Fraser, 290
SS Mantola, 218
Stamford Bridge, 21, 33, 67
Standish, 2
Stavrochori, 230, 285

Stavromenos, 325
Steele, Jumbo, 298, 321
stelae, 75, 97, 148
Stiris, 12
Stockbridge, Lance Corporal Ralph, 258–9, 280, 291–2, 320–21, 325, 328
storytelling, Cretan, 221, 252, 262, 264, 294, 313, 323, 329
Stratigraphical Museum *see* Knossos
Stravodoxari, 223
Streatfeild, Granville, 23
Strumitsa Pass, 290
Stubbings, Frank, 226, 244
Stukas, (German aircraft, 2nd World War), 314, 315
Stymphalian Plain, 69
Stymphalos, Lake of, 69–70
Styx, 70
Sub-Minoan, 220, 222
Sudan expedition, 210
Sudan, 217
Suez Canal, 246
Sultanate of Ottoman Turks, 50
Sunderland flying boat, 243
Suppiluliumas, King, 104
swordstick, 240, 253, 255–6, 307, 313, 315
Symons, Lt Col. Peter, 256, 266–7, 272, 274, 287
Syria, 58, 87, 120, 164, 179, 226
Tanagra, 12
Tanganyika, 218
Tapis, 58
Tasker-Brown, Corporal Maxwell, 257–9, 260, 269, 278–80, 285, 320
Tatoi, 277
Taubes, (German aircraft, Great War), 1
tavernas, 106, 111, 124, 155, 165, 177, 227, 230, 245
Taxiarchis, caïque, 255
Taygetus range, 64
Tell Asmar, Iraq, 112, 162–3
Tell el-Amarna, 71, 83, 85, 103, 118, 128–9, 140, 162: Akhetaten, 74; animal stalls, 131; Amarna period, 87, 184; Amarna Plain, 159, architectural details, 160; avenue of sphinxes, 159; bakehouse, 131; boat to, 86; Broad Hall, 197; Central City, 148, 160, 170, 173, 182, 196; concession, 179, 209, 210; Corn merchant's quarter, 130; dawn at, 147; East and West Roads, 94, 130; estates, 136; film footage, 156; Fishermen's Quarter, 131; funding, 156, 168, 183, 195, 198, 207, 209, 211–12; German excavation, 160; Great Aten Temple, 169, 171; Great Palace, 137; Great Temple, 136, 159; Greek Street, 130, 131, 133; High Priest's resi-

dence, 136; 'House of Crock of Gold', 133; House of Hatiay, 135; houses, 136, 146; and John, 18, 67, 112–14, 200, 212, 231; King's House, 197; lectures on, 145; May, Royal Chancellor, 137; monumental sculpture, 183; Mycenaean merchant, 131, 139; North City, 136, *138*; North Dig House, 89, 92, 132, 136, 146, 168, 209, 210; North Palace, 92; North Riverside Palace, 137; North Suburb, 91–2, 94, 130, 134, 144, 156; official quarters, 199; painted pavement, 182; Palace, 134, 149, 179: excavation 181, 197, 198; Harem Quarter, 182; Panehsy, 136; publication of, 153, 225; Records office, 172; Royal estate, 148–9; Royal Road, 179; Royal Tomb, 149–50, 157, 172, 180–82, 199: excavation, 151–2; Royal Wadi, 182–3, 186; sanctuary, 171; sculptor's workshop, 161; silver, 133, 139; Small Aten Temple, 148, 159, 171; South City, 170; stables, 173; storage magazines, 131; Straight Street, 130, 131; tomb paintings, 169; wall painting, 136; walled garden, 136; Weben Aten, 197; Window of Appearances, 137; wine jar sealings, 146
terracotta figurines, Karphi, 216
Territorial Army, 2
Thacker, T. W., 194, 199
Theatral Area, Palace of Knossos, 125
Thebes, Greece, 12, 120, 240
Thebes (modern Luxor), 74, 88, 96, 103, 135
Thermopylae, 40, 141
Thermopylae Line, 293
Theseus, 47, 117
Thessalian plain, 42
Thessaloniki, 42
Thessaly, 41
Third Reich, 219
Thirlmere, 217
Tholos tombs, 41, 44, 226, 228: *see also* Treasury of Atreus
Thompson, Frank, 219
Thorikos, Mycenaean site, 11
Thothmes I (also Tuthmosis), 87
Thothmes II (also Tuthmosis), 87
Thothmes III (also Tuthmosis), 58, 87, 164
Thothmes IV (also Tuthmosis), 87, 88
Thrace, 280
Thriphte, Mount, 175
Throne Room, Palace of Knossos, 125
Tidbury, Brigadier Oliver, 254, 265, 267, 288
The Times, 109, 111, 168, 323
The Times Sporting News, 22
Tinos, 47, 105, 251
Tiryns, 11, 44
tomb(s): near Candia, 123; Egyptian, 73–4, 115, 135, 152; Knossos, 142–3; Koprana, 214–15; Meryre, 160; paintings, 169; Tsouli, 59; *see also* Tell el-Amarna, Royal Tomb
Toplou, Moni, monastery, 176
Toumba, Agios Mama, 61–3
Trades Union Congress, 27
Trapeza Cave, 191, 201, 203–4, 214
Travels in Crete, 207
Treasury of Atreus, 43, 44
Treaty of Lausanne, 109
Tripartite Pact, 283
Troizen, 47
Trojan War, 9, 13, 18, 40, 44, 117
Troy, 116–7
Tsaldaris, Greek Prime Minister, 187
Tsalikaki Metochi, 314, 316, 321
Tsouderos, 294
Tsountas, Christos, 13
Tsousis, 265–6
Tsoutsouros, 188, 285
Tunis, 243
Turf Club, Cairo, 199
Turkey/Turkish, 41, 276–8, 87: language, 189; messarlik, 65; occupation of Crete, xv, 50–51, 285, 329; pasha, 59, 60
Tut *see* Tutankhamen
Tutankhamen, 104, 134, 149, 153, 158: curse, 182; exhibition, 103–4; tomb of, 9, 71, 84, 96; wife, 17, 18
Tutankhaten *see* Tutankhamen
Tuyu, 88
Ty, Queen, 87–8, 116, 149
Tylissos, 189
Tyre, 163
Tzermiado, 168, 191, 201, 204–5, 207, 214–15, 218–19, 221, 224, 228, 332
Tzon Mpetlempouri Road, 331
Umbarak, Abderrahman, 129
Umbarak, Mahmoud, 129
United States, 4, 242
University College London, 67
University of Cambridge, *see* Cambridge University
University of Liverpool, 91, 118, 157
University of Berlin, 195
Ur of the Chaldees, 91
Useramun, tomb of, 74
Vale of Tempe, 11, 42
Valley of the Rocks, 7
van Geyzel, Carl, 20, 22, 24
vases: alabaster, 149; pilgrim, 131; proto-Geometric, 123–4
Vasiliki, 55
Vassits, Miloje, 34

Vathianos, 308
vendettas, 247–9, 329
Venice/Venetian(s), 10, 50, 58, 204, 329: forts, 51, 65, 166 (Spina Longa), 189 (Rethymnon), 228 (Gramvousa), 254, 284 (Souda), 308, 310, 311 (Heraklion); fountain, 280
Venizelist: politicians, 261; rebellion, 248
Venizelos, Eleutherios, 51, 58, 125, 186–7, 190, 294
Vianos, 155, 192, 230, 288
Vice Consul, 245, 252, 257, 284, 301, 324, 328
Victoria and Albert Museum, 28, 156
Victoria Hotel, 128, 145
Victoria Station, 243
Vienna, 33, 283, 324–5
Villa Ariadne, 65, 106, 155, 165, 228, 249, 252, 302, 312: and Evans, 187; garden, 107, 245, and John, 66–7, 110, 120, 122, 124; King of Greece stays, 294, 295
The Villa Ariadne, 332
Villa Dionysos, 187
Villa Mousa, 76
Vinca, 34
Vitsilovrysi spring, 231
Vlachos, George, 281
Volos, 40, 41
votive offerings, Diktaean Cave, 57
Vrokastro, 230
vultures, Egyptian (Vitsila), 224
Wace, Alan, 12–14, 28, 33, 37, 41, 43–4, 102, 111, 167, 184
Waddington, Hilary, 129–30, 139–40, 145, 151, 156, 158, 164
Waddington, Ruth, 160, 164
Wadi Halfa, 218
Wafd party, 158
Wainwright, Gerald, 74, 115, 119, 120
Wales, 241, 250
Walker, David, 36
Wallace, David, 251
War House, 240
War Office, 235–6, 239, 241–3, 268, 286
Wavell, General Sir Archibald, 255, 281, 294
Wavendon Manor, 330
Webb, Mabel, *see* Dickinson, Mabel
Webb, Will, 25, 217–18
Weben Aten, *see* Tell el-Amarna
Weedon, Northants, 237, 238, 240, 259,
Weightman-Smith, George C., 24, 29
Wellcome Historical Medical Museum, 144–5
West Kirby, Cheshire, 69, 157, 217
West Wadi, Tell el-Amarna, 307

Weston, General, 294
White Mountains, 190, 247, 284
White Nile, 218
White, Dora, 193
White, Hilda: academic, 38, 76, 81, 157; at 'Belle Hélène', 43; birth of children, 154–5, 178; on Chicago House, 81; on Crete, 51; description, 36–7, 167, 179, 223, 232; drawings, 103, 119; and Hammond, 329; illness, 213; and John, 49, 67, 69, 206, 242, 318, 330–31; Kenya, 217–18; at Lasithi, 205, 325; letters from John, 250–51, 269–70, 280, 283–4, 326, 328; on Lloyd, 94; at Mytilene, 68; pregnancy, 144, 149–50, 168; publications, 144; on Rhodes, 109
Whiteley, Brigadier, 254
Whitfield, Vivien, 51
Wigan, 2
Wigmore Hotel, 156
Wigmore Street, 145
William of Wykeham, 6
Williams, Fusilier George, 270
Willis, Arthur, 18, 21–2, 26
Wilson, General, 294
Winchester, 219, 225: Cathedral, 7; College, 4, 5–9, 16, 255
Window of Appearances, 137, 149
wine, 200, 208, 247, 256, 270: jars, 96, 146; sellers, 51–2
Winstanley, 25, 178
Woodhead, Professor of Greek, 67
Woodward, Director of BSA, 43, 65, 84–5, 105, 110
Woolley, Sir Leonard, 91, 103, 113, 134
World War I, *see* Great War
World War II, 109, 234–331
Wyndham, Captain G. R. (Dick), 175, 177
Xanthoudides, Stephanos, 123–4
Xerokampos, 176, 306
Xerxes, 40
Ye Joyouse Companie of Seynt Pol, 23–4
Ye Ordre of Ye Sevene Gai Tippelers, 24
York, see HMS York
York and Lancaster Regiment, 253, 294, 307
Youlbury, 114
Yugoslavia, 10, 34, 243, 281, 283, 290, 292, 296
Yuia, 88
Zaghloul, leader of Wafd party, 158
Zakros, 176, 285
Zamalek, 73, 212
Zeppelins, 1
Zeus, 59, 191, 203
Zeus, cult of at Palaikastro, 56

Also published by Libri

The Villa Ariadne, by Dilys Powell
With a new introduction by Isabel Quigly
1901965074. Paperback, £9.95
Dilys Powell's classic account of the Villa Ariadne at Knossos and its inhabitants – Arthur Evans, John Pendlebury and General Kreipe. Powell, who knew Crete and the Villa Ariadne for over 40 years, weaves her own memories of Evans and Pendlebury together with recollections of the Cretan people in a work that is at once a chapter of autobiography and a portrait of a mythical island that captured her heart.

Nefertiti Lived Here, by Mary Chubb
With a new introduction by Peter Lacovara
1901965015. Paperback, £9.95
Mary Chubb's delightful account of excavating at Tell el-Amarna with John Pendlebury and his team in 1930.
'A wonderful, enchanting book, full of humour, excitement and joy... a complete gem.' *The Mail on Sunday*
'Written with elegance and enthusiasm... Charming'. *The Evening Standard*
'As fast-moving and funny and as full of human interest as a novel... a book to cherish, a rare treat.' *The Tablet*

City in the Sand, by Mary Chubb
With a new introduction by Isabel Quigly
1901965023. Paperback, £12.95
It is 1932, and Mary Chubb's story continues in Iraq, ancient Mesopotamia, where she joins a team uncovering ancient Eshnunna, a vassal city of Ur.
'Delightful and beautifully written'. *The British Museum Magazine*
'Her perceptive and kindly eye brings alive life on a remote dig in the early 1930s. It is a world that is almost magical.' *Minerva*

Henry Salt: Artist, Traveller, Diplomat, Egyptologist, by D. Manley & P. Rée
1901965031 (HB); 190196504x (PB). Hardback, £29.95, paperback £18.50
The first biography of a key figure in early 19th-century travel, Egyptology and diplomacy.
'Fills in a great chunk of lost history, and is a readable blend of both scope and scholarship'. *The Spectator*
'Lyrical writing'. *The Mail on Sunday*

② CRETE

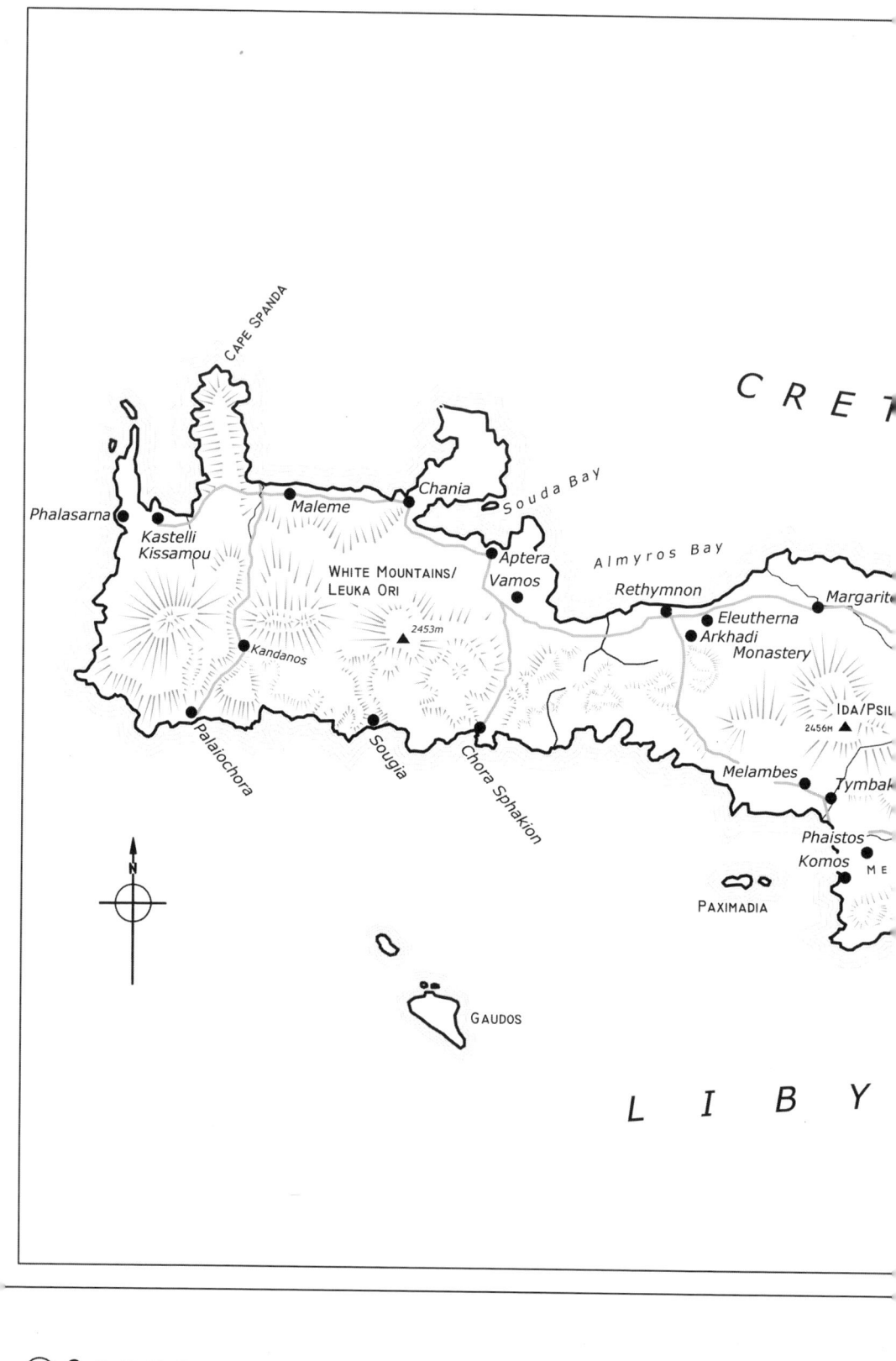